THE
FRENCH
REVOLUTION

ALBERT MATHIEZ

PROFESSOR OF MODERN HISTORY AT THE FACULTY OF LETTERS
OF THE UNIVERSITY OF DIJON; LECTURER ON THE HISTORY OF THE
FRENCH REVOLUTION AT THE UNIVERSITY OF PARIS

THE FRENCH REVOLUTION

TRANSLATED FROM THE FRENCH BY
CATHERINE ALISON PHILLIPS

NEW YORK

RUSSELL & RUSSELL · INC

1962

TRANSLATOR'S NOTE

❖◇❖◇❖

The translator would like to express her gratitude to Mr. Henry Higgs, C.B., Professor of Economics at the University of Bangor, for kindly reading the chapters on finance and giving her the benefit of his advice; also to her husband, W. Alison Phillips, Lecky Professor of Modern History at the University of Dublin, for his advice and assistance throughout.

PREFACE

❖❖❖❖

Since this book is intended for the cultivated general public, all learned apparatus has been omitted. This does not mean, however, that no attempt has been made to bring it up to date in respect of the latest scientific discoveries. Indeed, specialists will see—at least we hope so— that it is based upon an extensive use of authorities, some of them unpublished, interpreted by an independent critical method.

But erudition is one thing; history is another. Erudition seeks out and collects the evidence of the past, studies it piece by piece and by confronting these pieces of evidence with one another, brings the truth into the full light of day. History reconstructs and expounds. The former is analysis; the latter is synthesis.

In this book we have attempted to perform the function of a historian; that is to say, we have tried to draw a picture, as accurate, clear, and living as possible, of the different aspects of the French Revolution. We have made it our especial aim to set forth the concatenation of events by explaining them in the light of the ideas of the time and the play of interests and forces involved; nor have we neglected individual factors, in those cases where we have been able to trace their action.

The limits imposed upon us have made it impossible to say everything. We have been obliged to make a selection among the events, but we hope we have omitted nothing essential.

DIJON, OCTOBER 5, 1921

CONTENTS

❖❖❖❖

BOOK ONE

The Fall of the Monarchy

1787–1792

CHAPTER I

The Break-down of the *Ancien Régime*

R EVOLUTIONS properly so called—that is, those which go beyond a mere change in political forms and those who govern, transforming institutions and transferring property from one class to another—work underground for a long time before they break out openly as a result of fortuitous circumstances. The French Revolution, the overwhelming suddenness of which surprised those who provoked and profited by it as much as those who fell victims to it, had been slowly coming to a head for a century or more. It arose from the ever-increasing divorce between reality and law, between institutions and men's way of living, between the letter and the spirit.

The producing class, upon whom the life of society was based, were increasing their power every day, though work, according to the code, remained a stigma. A man's nobility was in proportion to his uselessness. Birth and leisure brought with them privileges which were growing more and more intolerable to those who created wealth and held it in their hands.

The monarch, as God's representative on earth, was theoretically absolute. His will was law. *Lex Rex.* In reality he could no longer command the obedience even of those of his officials with whom he was in immediate contact. He acted with so little energy that he seemed to doubt his own rights. Above him loomed a new and nameless power, that of opinion, which was undermining men's respect for the established order.

The old feudal system was based essentially upon landed property. The feudal lord combined in his person the rights of a landowner and the functions of an administrator, judge, and military leader. But long before the Revolution he had lost all of his public functions, which had passed into the hands of the king's agents. Serfdom had almost everywhere disappeared. The only serfs attached to the soil (*mainmortables*) were in certain ecclesiastical domains in the Jura, the Nivernais, and Burgundy. The land had been freed from almost all of its burdens, and was now attached to the landlord only by the somewhat lax bond of the feudal

3

dues, the survival of which was no longer justified by the services which he rendered.

The feudal dues, a sort of perpetual rents, levied sometimes in kind (*champart*), sometimes in money (*cens*), yielded the feudal lords barely a hundred million livres [1] a year—rather a poor sum in view of the steady decline in the value of money. Centuries before, when serfdom was abolished, they had been fixed once for all at an unvarying rate, whereas the prices of things had steadily increased. The feudal lords followed no profession and so had come to draw the greater part of their resources from the estates which they had kept as their own private property and which they managed themselves or through their intendants.

The patrimony of the heir was protected by the right of primogeniture; but the younger sons, if unable to enter the army or the Church, had to put up with a slender portion, which soon became insufficient to live on. In the first generation they shared a third of their father's property; in the second, a third of this third, and so on. Reduced to straitened circumstances, they sold their rights of justice, their rents in money and in kind, and their land, in order to live; but they did not dream of working, for they did not want to lose caste (*déroger*). A whole class of impoverished nobles sprang up, very numerous in certain provinces, such as Brittany, Poitou, and the Boulonnais, where they vegetated gloomily in their modest manor-houses. Detesting the higher nobility, who monopolized court appointments, and despising and envying the middle classes in the towns, who were growing rich by trade and industry, they stubbornly defended their last rights of immunity from taxation against the encroachments of the king's agents; and their arrogance increased in proportion to their poverty and impotence.

Excluded from all political and administrative power since the absolute monarchy had definitely taken root under Richelieu and Louis XIV, the country squires were often hated by their peasants, for they were obliged, in order to live, to be exacting about the payment of their rents. Their seigniorial courts, the last shred of their former power which they still retained, became hated instruments of extortion in the hands of their underpaid judges. They used them in particular as a means of gaining

---

[1] The livre at this period was a coin representing rather less than five grammes' weight of silver, and slightly less in value than the metric franc when first established. (Littré.) The sou was the twenty-fifth part of the livre parisis, and the denier the two hundred and fortieth part of the livre. The silver écu at this date was equivalent to three livres, and the louis d'or (first struck by Louis XIII) to about twenty-four francs.

possession of the common lands, a third of which they claimed on the pretext of the right of *triage*. The poor man's goat, deprived of its common rights, could no longer pick up even a scanty subsistence, and the complaints of the poor became more and more acrimonious. In spite of their share of the common lands the small nobles felt that they were being victimized, and were ready to show their discontent on the first opportunity. They were to prove a source of unrest.

The great nobles, and above all the four thousand families "presented" at court, who took part in its pageantry, hunted with the king, and rode in his carriages, had no apparent reason to complain of their lot. They shared among them the 33,000,000 livres annually expended on the households of the king and the princes, the 28,000,000 of pensions entered in serried rows in the Red Book, the 46,000,000 of pay of the 12,000 officers in the army, who alone absorbed more than half the military budget, and, lastly, all of the millions spent on the numerous sinecures, such as the officers of the provincial governors. They thus diverted to their own use almost a quarter of the budget. The great abbeys also fell to the share of the court nobles and were distributed by the king among their younger sons, who often received the tonsure at the age of twelve. In 1789 there was not one of the 143 bishops who was not a nobleman. These bishops of noble birth lived at court, far from their dioceses, which they hardly knew except from the income which they brought in. The property of the clergy produced about 120,000,000 livres a year, and the tithes, levied on the peasants' crops, brought in about the same amount, forming an addition of some 240,000,000 to the other endowments of the great nobles. The small fry of the clergy, who carried on divine service, merely picked up the crumbs from the rich man's table. Just before the Revolution their pittance had been raised to 700 livres for parish priests and 350 livres for curates. But what had these commoners to complain of?

The great nobles, then, were very expensive. As owners of broad estates, the value of which amounted to more than 3,000,000,000 livres when they were sold during the Terror, they commanded abundant resources, which should surely have enabled them to live in splendid state. A courtier with no more than 100,000 livres was a poor man. The Polignacs drew from the Treasury first 500,000 and later 700,000 livres a year in pensions and grants. But the courtier spent his time in living up to his position. Life at Versailles was a bottomless pit in which the greatest fortunes were swallowed up. Following Marie Antoinette's example, the courtiers gambled recklessly. Enormous sums were required for their sump-

5

tuous garments, woven with gold and silver, their carriages, liveries, hunting, and entertainments, for show and pleasures. The great nobles ran deeply into debt and ruined themselves in style. They left the administration of their revenues to their stewards, who robbed them, and sometimes they were even ignorant of their amount. Biron, Duc de Lauzun, the notorious Don Juan, had squandered 100,000 écus by the age of twenty-one, besides contracting debts of 2,000,000. The Comte de Clermont, a prince of the blood, Abbot of Saint-Germain-des-Prés, who had an income of 360,000 livres, managed to ruin himself twice over. The Duke of Orleans, the greatest landowner in France, contracted debts amounting to 74,000,-000. The Prince de Rohan-Guémenée went bankrupt for some thirty millions, the greater part of which was paid by a grant from Louis XVI. The King's brothers, the Counts of Provence and Artois, owed some ten millions by the time they reached the age of twenty-five. The rest of the courtiers followed suit, and mortagages accumulated on their estates. The less scrupulous of them took to speculating in order to retrieve their position. The Comte de Guines, the ambassador in London, was involved in a shady affair which ended in the courts. Cardinal Rohan, Bishop of Strasbourg, speculated upon the sale of the precincts of the Temple in Paris, a piece of Church property which he disposed of for building. There were some, like the Marquis de Sillery, the husband of Mme de Genlis, whose drawing-rooms were turned into gambling-dens. All of them violated the traditions of their caste by mixing with actors and actresses. Bishops like Dillon of Narbonne and Jarente of Orleans lived openly with mistresses, who received their guests.

Curiously enough, these court nobles, who owed everything to the King, were far from docile. Many of them were bored with their gilded idleness. The better and more ambitious of them dreamt of a more active life; they wanted to play a part in the State, like the English nobility, and to be something more than ciphers. They adopted the new ideas, adapting them to their own desires. Many of them, and not the least prominent either, such as Lafayette, Custine, the two Vioménils, the four Lameths, the three Dillons, who had fought in the cause of American liberty, came out as opponents to the existing régime on their return to France. The rest were divided into factions grouped round the princes of the blood, intriguing and conspiring against the Queen's favourites. When the hour of peril came, the great nobles were far from unanimous in defending the throne.

The nobility consisted, in fact, of distinct and rival castes, the most powerful of which were not those who could point to the longest pedigrees.

Side by side with the old hereditary or military nobility, there had sprung up in the course of the last two centuries a nobility "of the long robe" (*noblesse de robe*); that is to say, an official nobility which monopolized administrative and judicial offices. This new caste, which was as proud as the old nobility, and perhaps richer, was headed by the members of the parlements, or courts of appeal.[2] As owners of their offices, which they had bought at a high price and handed on from father to son, they were *de facto* irremovable. The administration of justice enabled them to take toll of innumerable litigants. They amassed wealth from their fees (*épices*) and bought large estates. The judges of the Bordeaux Parlement owned the finest vineyards in the neighbourhood. Those of Paris, whose wealth sometimes equalled that of the great lords, suffered because they could not be presented at court, for lack of sufficient quarterings. They entrenched themselves in the haughty arrogance of parvenus and set up a claim to control the State. Since no act, edict, or ordinance of the Crown, nor even any diplomatic treaty, could come into force until its text had been entered upon their registers, these magistrates seized this right of registration as a pretext for keeping an eye on the royal administration and presenting remonstrances. The country having been reduced to silence, they alone had the right of criticism, and they availed themselves of it to court popularity by protesting against new taxation, while denouncing the luxury of the court, and waste and abuses of every sort. They sometimes went so far as to issue summonses even against the highest officials, whom they submitted to the ignominy of a judicial inquiry, as they did to the Duc d'Aiguillon, commandant of Brittany, and to the minister Calonne, on the morrow of his disgrace. Under the pretext that in long past ages the court of justice, the Parliament properly so called, had been merely a section of the general assembly of the vassals of the Crown, which the kings were at that time bound to consult before imposing any fresh taxation; and on the further pretext that at certain solemn audiences, *lits de justice*,[3] the princes of the blood, dukes, and peers came and joined their

---

[2] It is not usual to translate "*parlement*" by "parliament," for the French parlements were courts of justice rather than legislative bodies. But they never forgot that they traced their origin to the "*cour-le-roi*," which exercised legislative, judicial, and financial functions, later distributed between the Council, parlements, and financial departments of State respectively; and in virtue of their right of examining, registering, and framing remonstrances against the laws, the parlements claimed to be the organ of the public will, and hence to rival, if not to surpass the authority of the Council.

[3] The *lit de justice* (i. e., bed of justice) was a solemn session at which the King was present, enthroned upon a pile of cushions beneath a canopy.

7

sessions, they affirmed that in the absence of the States General they represented the vassals, thus appealing to feudal law, the ancient constitution of the monarchy, to act as a check upon the Government and the King. Their resistance even took the form of a strike and mass resignations. The different parlements in the kingdom banded themselves together, and claimed to form but one body divided into classes; the other supreme courts, the Chambre des Comptes[4] and the Cour des Aides,[5] backed up their factious intrigues. Louis XV, who for all his indolence was a king, at last grew weary of their perpetual opposition. Acting on the advice of Chancellor Maupeou, he abolished the Parlement of Paris at the end of his reign and replaced it by courts (*conseils supérieurs*) exercising judicial functions alone. But the feeble Louis XVI, yielding to the exigencies of what he supposed to be public opinion, restored the Parlement on his accession, and thus helped to bring about the loss of his crown. If the frivolous pamphlets of the *philosophes*[6] contributed towards discrediting the old régime, it is certain that the impressive remonstrances of the judicial authorities did even more to implant in the people disrespect and hatred for the established order.

The king saw those of his "officers" who administered justice in his name turning against him; but could he even count upon the obedience and devotion of the other "officers" who formed his councils or administered the provinces for him? The time had passed when the king's agents were the natural enemies of the ancient feudal authorities which they had superseded. They had been ennobled by office. The commoners of yesterday had become a privileged class. Even under Louis XIV the ministers began to be called "Monseigneur." Their sons were created counts or marquises. Under Louis XV and Louis XVI they came more and more to be chosen from the nobility, and not only the "nobility of the robe," but the old "nobility of the sword." Of the thirty-six persons who held portfolios between 1774 and 1789, there was only one who was not noble: Necker, the citizen of Geneva, who was none the less glad that his daughter should

---

[4] The Chambre des Comptes had as its chief functions to manage the finances of the kingdom, to audit the public accounts, and to administer the domains of the Crown. It had also jurisdiction, both civil and criminal, in all matters concerning the administration of the finances.

[5] The Cours des Aides were tribunals having jurisdiction over all cases concerning taxation, and hearing appeals from the local courts dealing with these matters.

[6] The writers who propagated the doctrines of "enlightenment" and combated those of revealed religion; more especially the group associated with the *Encyclopédie* of Diderot and d'Alembert.

become a baroness. Contrary to what is often alleged, even the intendants, who were responsible for the administration of the provinces, were no longer chosen among men of low birth. All those who held office under Louis XVI belonged to noble or recently ennobled families, sometimes of some generations' standing. For instance, Trémond, intendant of Montauban, or Fournier de la Chapelle, intendant of Auch, could trace their descent back to the thirteenth century. There were dynasties of intendants just as there were judicial dynasties. It is true that the intendants did not hold their position by virtue of their office, and were therefore removable, like the *maîtres des requêtes* [7] of the Royal Council, from whom they were recruited; but their wealth and the judicial offices which they held concurrently with their administrative functions assured them of a real independence. Many of them tried to make themselves popular in their *généralité*. [8] They were no longer the docile instruments that their predecessors of the age of Louis XIV had been. The King was obeyed less and less. The parlements would not have dared to carry on such lengthy struggles with the ministers if the latter had been able to count upon the unfailing support of all members of the administration who were subordinate to them. But the different classes of nobility were becoming increasingly conscious of their common interests. When occasion arose, they were able to sink their rivalries and present a united front to the people, or to the King, should he happen to be in a reforming mood.

The *pays d'États*—that is to say, the provinces attached to the kingdom at a recent date, which had preserved a shadowy survival of feudal representation, showed signs of particularist tendencies under Louis XVI. It was the resistance of the Estates of Provence which in 1782 forced the King to withdraw an octroi (local duty) which had been imposed upon oil. In 1786 the Estates of Béarn and of Foix refused to vote a fresh tax. As early as the time of Louis XV the Estates of Brittany, in league with the Parlement of Rennes, succeeded in checkmating the intendant in the matter of the corvée (forced labour). They even assumed the control of public works. Thus the centralized administration began to lose ground.

Confusion and chaos reigned everywhere. There were two distinct

---

[7] The *maîtres des requêtes* had jurisdiction over certain cases referred to them by the Conseil du Roi; it was also their duty, among many others, to prepare and submit the reports upon which the Council deliberated.

[8] *Généralités*: the name given to the financial areas administered by the intendants and so called because they were originally administered by officials known as "generals of Finance."

central organs: the Council, divided into a number of sections, and the six ministers, who were each independent of the others, mere clerks, who did not deliberate in common and all of whom had not access to the Council. The various public services overlapped between one department and another, according to personal convenience. The controller-general of finances admitted that it was impossible for him to draw up a regular budget owing to the absence of a clearly defined financial year, the vast number of different accounts, and the absence of any regular system of accountancy. Everybody kept pulling in a different direction. When Sartine was Minister of Marine, he spent millions without the knowledge of the controller-general. There was no uniformity in the measures adopted. One minister would protect the *philosophes* while another was persecuting them. Jealousies and intrigues were rife. Their chief aim was not so much to administrate as to retain the favour of their master or of those about his person. The interests of the public were no longer protected. The divine right of absolutism served as an excuse for every kind of waste, arbitrary procedure, and abuse. And so the ministers and intendants were generally detested, and, far from strengthening the monarchy, the imperfect centralization which they represented turned public opinion against it.

The administrative divisions reflected the history of the growth of the kingdom. They no longer answered to the necessities of modern life. Frontiers were vague, even those bordering on foreign countries. Nobody knew exactly where the king's authority ended and where it began. There were towns and villages belonging half to France and half to the Empire. The commune of Rarécourt, near Vitry-le-François in the heart of Champagne, paid 2 sous 6 deniers three times over for each head of a family to its three suzerains, the king of France, the Emperor, and the prince of Condé. Provence, Dauphiné, Béarn, Brittany, Alsace, Franche-Comté, etc., appealed to the old "capitulations" by which they had been united to France, and were apt to consider that within their territories the king had no more position than that of a lord, count, or duke. At the beginning of the *cahier des doléances* (memorial of grievances) drawn up by the commune of Morlaas in Béarn in 1789, the mayor put the following question: "How far is it fitting that we should cease to be Béarnais and become more or less Frenchmen?" Navarre continued to be a distinct kingdom, which refused to be represented in the States General. As Mirabeau put it, France was still no more than an "unorganized aggregation of disunited peoples."

The old judicial divisions, known as *bailliages* in the north and as

10

sénéchaussées in the south, had remained superimposed upon the old feudal fiefs in the most motley and amazing fashion. The departments at Versailles had no precise knowledge of the number of seats of justice, still less of the extent of their jurisdiction. In 1789 curious mistakes were made in sending out the letters summoning the States General. The military divisions, or *gouvernements*, dating from the sixteenth century, may be said hardly to have varied; the financial divisions, administered by the intendants, and known as *généralités*, dating from the century after, were no better adapted to new needs. The ecclesiastical divisions, or provinces, had remained almost unchanged since the Roman Empire. In places they overlapped the political frontiers. There were French parish priests subject to the jurisdiction of German prelates, and vice versa.

When the social order began to totter, the old composite administrative machine, rusty and creaking, was incapable of offering any serious resistance.

Over against the privileged classes and "officers" who were in possession of the State, new forces were gradually arising: those of trade and industry. On the one hand stood feudal and real property, on the other the personal wealth of the middle classes.

In spite of the fetters imposed by the system of corporations—though this was less oppressive than has been supposed—in spite of the internal duties and tolls (*péages*), in spite of the diversity of weights and measures, trade and industry had increased for a whole century past. The foreign trade of France was second only to that of England. Colonial produce was the monopoly of the mother country. Her possession of Santo Domingo alone provided her with one-half of the sugar consumed in the world. Her silk industry, which employed sixty-five thousand workmen at Lyons, was unrivalled. Her brandies, wines, stuffs, fashions, and furniture were sold in all parts of Europe. Even the metal industries, the development of which had been but recent, were progressing. Le Creusot, then known as Montcenis, was already a model workshop, equipped with the latest improvements, and Dietrich, the king of ironmasters at the time, employed hundreds of workmen in his blast-furnaces and forges in Lower Alsace, fitted out in the English style. In 1791 Bonaffé, a Bordeaux shipowner, had a fleet of thirty ships and a fortune of sixteen million livres. Nor was this millionaire an exception. Far from it. There were very great fortunes at Lyons, Marseilles, Nantes, Havre, and Rouen.

Economic development was so intense that the number of banks increased greatly under Louis XVI. The Caisse d'Escompte (Bank of Discount) of Paris already issued notes similar to those of the modern

11

Bank of France. Capital began to come together and form joint-stock companies: the India Company (*Compagnie des Indes*), fire- and life-insurance companies, the Paris water-supply company. The metal works of Montcenis were turned into a joint-stock company. The shares, quoted on the Bourse alongside of the *rentes sur l'Hôtel de Ville*,[9] gave rise to active speculation. Dealings in futures were already a usual practice.

In 1789 the service of the public debt absorbed three hundred million livres a year; that is to say, more than half the total revenue of the State. The Company of the Farmers-General, which collected on behalf of the Crown the proceeds of the indirect taxes, *aides*,[10] gabelle (salt-tax), tobacco-duty, stamp-duties, had at its head financiers of the first rank, who vied in magnificence with the most splendid nobles. A great stir of business was making itself felt among the middle classes. The price of a place on the Stock Exchange doubled within a single year. Necker writes that France possessed nearly half the available cash in Europe. Merchants were buying the estates of noblemen with debts, and building fine mansions decorated by the best artists. Farmers-general had their *folies* (pleasure-houses) in the suburbs of Paris, like the great lords. The towns were being rebuilt and beautified.

An infallible sign that the wealth of the country was increasing was that the population was growing rapidly and the prices of commodities, land, and houses were steadily rising France already contained twenty-five million inhabitants, twice as many as England or Prussia. Comfort was gradually spreading downwards, from the upper·to the lower middle class and that of artisans and small shopkeepers. People dressed better and had better food than in former days. Above all, education was spreading. The daughters of commoners, who were now called "demoiselle" if they wore dresses with panniers, were buying pianos. The increased revenue from taxes on food-stuffs was evidence of the progress in comfort.

And so the Revolution was not to break out in an exhausted country, but, on the contrary, in a flourishing land on a rising tide of progress. Poverty may sometimes lead to riots, but it cannot bring about great social upheavals. These always arise from a disturbance of the balance between the classes.

The middle classes certainly possessed the greater part of the fortune of France. They were advancing steadily, whereas the privileged orders

---

[9] Loans issued by the State and secured upon the revenues of the City of Paris.

[10] This word had come to be used of taxes on consumption, especially upon liquor, snuff, etc.

were ruining themselves. Their very rise made them more acutely sensitive to the inferior legal status to which they were still condemned. Barnave became a revolutionary the day that his mother was turned out of the box which she was occupying in the theatre at Grenoble by a nobleman. Mme Roland complains that when she was asked to stay to dinner at the Château of Fontenay with her mother, it was served to them in the servants' quarters. How many enemies of the old régime were made by wounded self-esteem!

The middle classes, who owned the money, had also acquired moral power. The men of letters, who had come from their ranks, gradually emancipated themselves from the position of clients of the nobility. They now wrote for the great public, which read their works, whose tastes they flattered, and whose claims they defended. Their satirical pens never ceased scoffing at all the ideas upon which the old order of things was based, especially the religious idea. Their task was made very much easier by the theological quarrels which brought discredit upon those maintaining the traditional view. "Philosophy" found a way in through the breach between Jansenism and ultramontanism. The suppression of the Jesuits in 1763 overthrew the last barrier against the new spirit that was at all serious. The religious life had no longer any attractions. The convents were emptying, and pious donations sank to an insignificant figure. The innovators had by now won the day. The higher clergy scarcely put up a defence. The court prelates would have thought themselves dishonored if they had had a reputation for piety, and made it their pose to spread "enlightenment." In their dioceses they were only willing to act as auxiliaries of the administration. Their zeal was devoted to the pursuit no longer of celestial, but of earthly bliss. A utilitarian ideal was uniformly adopted by all speakers and writers. The traditional faith was left to the common people, as a necessary accompaniment of ignorance and humble birth. The very priests read the *Encyclopédie,* and became steeped in Mably, Raynal and Jean-Jacques.

None of the great noblemen who applauded the audacity and impertinences of the *philosophes* took into consideration that the religious idea was the corner-stone of the existing order. Once free criticism was turned loose, how could it be expected to confine itself to mocking at superstition? It attacked the most venerable institutions. It spread doubt and satire everywhere. Yet the privileged orders did not seem to understand. The Comte de Vaudreuil, the intimate friend of Mme de Polignac, had the *Mariage de Figaro* acted at his château of Gennevilliers, though it was the most stinging and audacious satire on the noble caste. Marie

13

Antoinette used her influence to have this play, which had hitherto been banned, acted at the Théâtre Français. The Revolution had been accomplished in the minds of men long before it was translated into fact, and those who were its first victims must in all justice be counted among those responsible for it.

The Revolution could come only from above. The working-classes, whose narrow horizon embraced nothing beyond their calling, were incapable of initiating it, still less of taking the control into their own hands. Industry on a large scale was in its first beginnings. Nowhere did the workmen form coherent groups. Those who were on the books of the *corporations*, and subordinate to them, were split up into rival workmen's associations (*compagnonnages*), more interested in petty squabbling than in presenting a united front to their employers. They hoped, moreover, to become employers in their turn and had a chance of doing so, since craftsmanship on a small scale was still the normal form of industrial production. As for the rest, those who were beginning to be employed in the "manufactories," many of them were peasants who regarded what they earned in industrial employment as a supplement to their agricultural earnings. Most of them were docile and respectful to the employers who provided them with work, so much so that in 1789 they looked upon them as their natural representatives. It is true that the workmen complained of their modest wages, which, to quote the testimony of Roland when he was a factory-inspector, had not increased at the same rate as the price of commodities. There was sometimes agitation among them, but they did not as yet feel themselves to be a distinct class of the third estate.

The peasants were the beasts of burden of this society. Tithes, rents in money and in kind, forced labour, royal taxes, service in the militia, all these burdens fell upon them. Their lords' pigeons and game ravaged their crops with impunity. They lived in houses of mud, often covered with thatch, and sometimes with no chimneys. They tasted meat only on feast-days, and sugar only in case of illness. Compared with our peasants of today, they were wretched; and yet they were less miserable than their fathers had been, or than the peasants of Italy, Spain, Germany, Ireland, or Poland at the same period. By dint of toil and saving, some of them had succeeded in buying a piece of a field or pasturage. The rise in the value of agricultural produce had favoured the beginnings of emancipation. Those who had not succeeded in acquiring a little land were the most to be pitied. They were angry at having to share the common lands with their lords, at the abolition of the rights of common pasture and

14

gleaning, which deprived them of the few resources which they had enjoyed under the system of primitive communism. There were also a number of day-labourers, who were often out of work, and were obliged to go from farm to farm in search of employment. It is hard to draw the line between them and the numerous class of vagabonds and beggars. It was from their ranks that was recruited the army of smugglers and dealers in contraband salt (*faux-sauniers*) who were perpetually at war with the excisemen (*gabelous*).

The workmen and peasants were capable of a brief movement of revolt when the yoke became too heavy, but could not see their way towards changing the social order. They were only just beginning to learn to read. But they had among them the priest and the local lawyer (*praticien*) to enlighten them: the priest, to whom they confided their sorrows, and the lawyer, who defended their interests in the courts. But the priests had read the literature of the day; they knew the scandalous existence led by their superiors in their sumptuous palaces, while they themselves subsisted meagrely on their pittance; and instead of preaching resignation to their flock, as in the past, they infected their minds with a little of the indignation and bitterness with which they were themselves filled. The country lawyer, for his part, obliged as he was by the exigencies of his profession to search among the old feudal deeds, could not fail to arrive at a just estimate of the archaic titles which formed the basis of wealth and oppression. It was in the exercise of his profession of feudal expert that Babeuf learnt his contempt for property. He pitied the peasants from whom the greed of their lord—who employed him to set his muniments in order—set to work to extort fresh dues which had become obsolete.

Thus criticism was working underground which long preceded and prepared for the explosion. The opportunity had only to arise, and all this accumulated and stifled rage would lend force to the attacks of these poor wretches, stirred up and directed by a host of malcontents.

CHAPTER II

The Revolt of the Nobility

W HAT was wanted at the head of the monarchy, to dominate the crisis which threatened, was a king. But there was nobody but Louis XVI. This fat man, with his common manners, was happy only at table, out hunting, or in Gamain the locksmith's workshop. Intellectual exertion fatigued him. He would go to sleep at the Council. He was soon the butt of the frivolous and thoughtless courtiers. His person was criticized in his very antechamber. He allowed the Duc de Coigny to make a scene in his presence about a reduction of his allowance. His marriage offered a rich opening for cruel jests. The daughter of Maria Theresa whom he had married was pretty, imprudent, and a coquette, and threw herself into pleasures with heedless ardour. She was seen at the public balls at the Opéra, where she took a pleasure in the most audacious familiarities, while her cold husband stayed at Versailles. She received the addresses of courtiers of the worst reputation, such as Lauzun or Eszterházy. The handsome Fersen, colonel of the Royal Swedish regiment, was said with some probability to be her lover. It was known that Louis XVI had been unable to consummate his marriage till seven years after it had taken place, and then only thanks to a surgical operation. Calumny found a vent in offensive songs, especially after the tardy birth of a dauphin. The epigrams spread from aristocratic circles to the middle and lower classes, and the Queen's reputation was ruined long before the Revolution. The Comtesse de Lamothe, an adventuress descended from an illegitimate son of Charles IX, was able to persuade the Cardinal Rohan that she could find a way to win him the good graces of Marie Antoinette if he would only help the latter to buy a magnificent necklace which her parsimonious husband had refused her. The Cardinal had moonlight interviews in the gardens at Versailles with a woman whom he took to be the Queen. When the intrigue was discovered, owing to the complaint of the jeweller Bœhmer, who had not been paid for his necklace, Louis XVI was imprudent enough to appeal to the Parlement to avenge his outraged honour. The Comtesse de Lamothe was sentenced, but the Cardinal was acquitted amid universal applause.

16

The verdict signified that it was no crime to consider that the Queen of France was easy to seduce. By the advice of the police Marie Antoinette henceforward abstained from visiting Paris, for fear of demonstrations. About the same time, in 1786, the Strasbourg mint struck a certain number of louis d'or upon which the King's effigy was surmounted with a horn of infamy.

This situation gave the princes of the blood some hope of succeeding to the throne. The King's brothers, the Count of Artois and the Count of Provence, and his cousin, the Duke of Orleans, intrigued in secret in order to profit by the discontent aroused among the courtiers as a whole by the exclusive preference of the Queen for certain families, upon which she showered favours. Théodore de Lameth relates that one day Madame de Balbi, the Count of Provence's mistress, addressed him as follows: "You know what they say about the King when they want change in a tavern? They throw down an écu on the table saying: 'Change that drunkard for me.'" This was only meant to sound Lameth as to the expediency of a change of kings. Lameth had no doubt that certain of the princes cherished the project of having Louis XVI declared incapable of ruling.

Yet the King was deaf and blind to everything. He allowed himself to be swayed by petticoat government, and hesitated between the reforming parties and the partisans of abuses, following the chance suggestion of those about him, and especially the desires of the Queen, who obtained a growing empire over his mind. Thus his vacillating policy added considerable fuel to the general discontent. Vaublanc's epigram is literally true in this connexion: "In France it is always the head of the State and his ministers who overthrow the Government."

The sharpest criticism of the abuses which were ruining the existing order was to be found in the preambles of the edicts of ministers· such as Turgot, Malesherbes, Calonne, Brienne, and Necker. These edicts were read out by the parish priests from the pulpit. Their echoes reached even the humblest. The necessity for reform was thus placed under the King's ægis. But when the promised reforms melted into thin air or were only partially carried into effect, the bitterness caused by the abuses was increased by the thwarting of all hopes of remedy. The corvée seemed more burdensome to the peasants since Turgot had in vain issued an edict for its suppression. It actually happened on this occasion that the peasants of Maine appealed to the minister's word as a pretext for refusing to pay their rents to the Marquis de Vibraye, whom they besieged in his country-house and forced to take to flight. The suppres-

17

sion of serfdom on the domains of the Crown, effected by Necker, made its maintenance on the estates of the nobility and the clergy more exasperating to those concerned. The abolition by Malesherbes of the "preparatory question" (that is, torture) in criminal investigations made the retention of the "preliminary question" appear more inequitable. The creation by Necker in 1778 of provincial assemblies in the two *généralités* of Berri and Haute Guyenne seemed to condemn the despotism of the intendants; but it merely exasperated that desire for representative institutions of which these two new assemblies were in reality no more than a caricature, since they were nominated and not elected. It discouraged the intendants by weakening their authority, without any benefit to the royal power. The same was true of all the other tentative reforms. They merely justified and lent strength to the discontent.

It could hardly be otherwise when these liberal edicts were followed by reactionary measures inspired by a purely feudal spirit, especially since the latter were carried into effect. The famous regulation of 1781 demanding that in future officers should prove four quarterings of nobility before being admitted into the military schools certainly had something to do with the future defection of the army. The more the nobility were threatened in their privileges, the more they contrived measures to consolidate them. They excluded commoners not only from the higher ranks in the army, but also from judicial offices and the higher ecclesiastical dignities. While applauding Figaro, they strengthened their own monopoly.

Could any other king than Louis XVI have found a remedy for this fantastic situation? Perhaps so, but it is by no means certain. After depriving the feudal nobles of their political powers the Bourbons had been pleased to console them by showering benefits upon them. Louis XIV and Louis XV had considered the nobility necessary to their own glory. Its privileges were bound up with their throne. Louis XVI did no more than follow an established tradition. He could have effected any serious reforms only by waging war to the knife on the privileged classes. But he took fright at the first brush with them.

Besides, the financial problem dominated all others. If reforms were to be effected, money was necessary. Amid the general prosperity the Treasury was growing emptier. It could be filled only at the expense of the privileged orders, and with the sanction of the parlements, which showed themselves but ill-disposed to sacrifice the private interests of their members on the altar of the public weal. The longer they evaded the point, the deeper the bottomless pit of the deficit became, and the more stubborn the resistance grew.

In the last years of his reign Louis XV had already been on the point of bankruptcy. The vigorous action of the Abbé Terray had prevented a catastrophe and prolonged the duration of the existing order for twenty years. After Terray's fall the squandering of millions began once more. One Minister of Finance followed hard upon another, and there was not a single financier among them all, not even Necker, who was a mere accountant. They made a few trifling economies in the king's household, which annoyed the courtiers without any real benefit to the Treasury. The royal bounties increased in number: 100,000 livres for the daughter of the Duc de Guines on her marriage, 400,000 livres to the Comtesse de Polignac to pay her debts, 800,000 for her daughter's marriage portion, 23,000,000 for the Count of Artois's debts, 10,000,000 to buy the Château of Rambouillet for the King, 6,000,000 to buy the Château of St. Cloud for the Queen, etc. But these were trifling sums compared with those involved by the participation of France in the War of American Independence, which have been estimated at 2,000,000,000! In order to meet this expenditure Necker borrowed wherever and however he could, paying even as high as ten and twelve per cent for his loans. He deceived the nation by his famous *Compte rendu*, in which he showed an imaginary surplus. All he wanted was to inspire confidence in those with money to lend, but in so doing he placed a weapon in the hands of the members of the parlements, by enabling them to pretend that a thorough-going financial reform was unnecessary.

When the war was over, the sprightly Calonne managed to increase the debt by 653,000,000 in three years. It became an accepted maxim that the Most Christian King did not base his expenditure on his receipts, but his receipts on his expenditure. In 1789 the debt rose to 4,500,000,000. It had increased threefold during the fifteen years of the reign of Louis XVI. At the death of Louis XV the service of the debt required 93,000,000; in 1790 it required about 300,000,000, out of a budget which scarcely exceeded 500,000,000. But all things have an end. Calonne was obliged to confess to the King that he did not know which way to turn. His last loan had been subscribed with difficulty. He had put up still more offices for sale, proceeded to remint the coinage, increased the caution money deposited by officials, sold some Crown lands, surrounded Paris with a wall of tolls, extorted 255,000,000 from the farmers-general in "anticipations" (that is, advances upon future taxa-

19

tion); he was preparing to borrow a further 70,000,000 from the Caisse d'Escompte under pretext of increasing the deposit of caution money, but all these expedients could not prevent a deficit of 101,000,000. What was more, war was threatening with Prussia over Holland. The Minister for War was demanding credits for the defence of the patriotic citizens of this little country, to whom the King had promised support against the Prussians.

Calonne was driven into a corner. He no longer felt it possible again to add to the existing taxes, which had increased by 140,000,000 in less than ten years. He was at open odds with the Parlement of Paris, which had presented a remonstrance with regard to the reminting of the coinage, with the Parlement of Bordeaux about the ownership of the reclaimed coastal areas of the Gironde, with the Parlement of Rennes on the question of snuff, with the Parlements of Besançon and Grenoble on the question of the provisional substitution of a cash levy for the corvée. It was certain that the parlements would refuse to register any loan or fresh taxation.

Calonne took his courage in both hands. He sought an audience of Louis XVI on August 20, 1786, and said: "Piecemeal measures are of no use for the salvation of the State; if ruin is to be staved off, it is indispensable to start reconstructing the whole edifice. . . . It is impossible to increase taxation, and ruinous to be always borrowing; it is not enough to confine ourselves to economic reforms. The only thing to be done, the sole means by which the finances may at last be reduced to order, must consist in infusing life into the whole State by recasting all the vicious elements in its constitution."

The existing taxes were vexatious and produced but little because they were badly distributed. The nobles were subject in principle to the *vingtièmes*[1] and the capitation (poll-tax), from which the clergy were exempt. The peasants alone paid the *taille*,[2] which varied according as they belonged to the *pays d'États* or the *pays d'élections*,[3] and was sometimes a tax on real estate, analogous to the modern French *impôt foncier*, sometimes a personal tax, analogous to the modern French *cote mobilière*,

---

[1] A tax of a twentieth, levied, in theory, on the whole income, but in practice only on certain kinds of income.

[2] The *taille*, one of the principal sources of the national revenue, was originally levied for military purposes; hence the nobility, whose profession was that of arms, was exempt, as well as the clergy.

[3] i.e., collection or levy. The *élu* levied the taxes under the direction of the intendant.

calculated on the basis of rental. There were free towns, towns which had compounded for their share of the tax, districts which had bought themselves off for good—in fact, the complications were endless. The price of salt varied according to the person and the place. The clergy, privileged classes, and officials paid cost price for it, in virtue of the right of *franc-salé* (free or cheap salt). But the farther one went from the salt-marshes or mines, the heavier and more inquisitorial the salt-tax became.

Calonne proposed to mitigate the severity of the gabelle and the *taille*, to suppress internal tolls, and to find the necessary resources for balancing the budget in a fresh tax, the territorial subsidy (*subvention territoriale*), which was to take the place of the *vingtièmes*. But whereas the *vingtièmes* were levied in cash, the territorial subsidy was to be levied in kind, on the produce of all land alike, whether owned by the clergy, nobles, or commoners. Thus equality of taxation would be established. The Caisse d'Escompte was to be transformed into a State bank. Provincial assemblies were to be created in those provinces which as yet had none, "so that the distribution of the public burdens should cease to be unequal and arbitrary."

Since the parlements could not be counted upon to register such a far-reaching reform, the matter was to be submitted for approval to an assembly of notables. There was no case on record in which the notables chosen by the king had resisted his will. But during the last century men's minds had undergone a complete change.

The notables, consisting of 7 princes of the blood, 36 dukes and peers or marshals, 33 presidents or procurators-general of the parlements, 11 prelates, 12 councillors of State, 12 deputies from the *pays d'États*, 25 mayors or councillors of the chief cities, etc., 144 persons in all, distinguished by their services or their functions, met on February 22, 1787. Calonne delivered in their presence an excellent indictment of the whole financial system: "One cannot take a step in this vast kingdom without coming upon different laws, contradictory customs, privileges, exemptions, immunities from taxation, and every variety of rights and claims; and this general lack of harmony complicates administration, disturbs its course, impedes its machinery, and increases expense and disorganization on all sides." He made a dead set against the gabelle, "a tax assessed so inequitably that one province is made to pay twenty times more than another, and levied with such severity that its very name inspires terror . . . a tax, in fact, of which a fifth of the proceeds are swallowed up by the cost of collection, and which, by the strong in-

21

centive which it offers to smuggling, annually condemns five hundred fathers of families to prison or the galleys and gives rise to four thousand arrests." This criticism of abuses was followed by an account of the proposed reforms.

The notables belonged to the privileged classes. Mockery and epigrams were showered upon them in pamphlets inspired by the members of the Parlement, which prophesied their capitulation. In order to prove their independence they stiffened their necks. They took care not to proclaim their unwillingness to pay the tax, but expressed their indignation at the amount of the deficit, which dumbfounded them. They recalled how, in his celebrated *Compte rendu,* which had appeared four years previously, Necker had shown an excess of receipts over expenditure. They demanded that the accounts upon which the budget was based should be submitted to them. They required that a monthly statement of the position of the royal treasury should be drawn up, and that a general account of receipts and expenditure should be printed annually and submitted for audit to the Cour des Comptes. They protested against the abuse of pensions. In order to defend himself Calonne had to expose the errors in Necker's *Compte rendu.* Necker replied, and was banished from Paris. The whole aristocracy, both of the sword and of the robe, took fire. Calonne was vilified in scurrilous pamphlets. Mirabeau joined in the hue and cry with his *Dénonciation contre l'agiotage (Denunciation of Speculation),* in which he accused Calonne of speculating on the Bourse with the funds of the State. Calonne was in a vulnerable position. He had debts and mistresses, and was surrounded by shady characters. The scandal of the Abbé d'Espagnac's attempt to speculate in the shares of the India Company had just come to light, and Calonne was implicated in it. The privileged orders had no difficulty in ridding themselves of the reforming minister. In vain did he take the offensive. He had an *Avertissement* drawn up by the barrister Gerbier, which was a sharp attack upon the selfishness of the nobles and an appeal to public opinion. This *Avertissement* was distributed broadcast throughout the realm, which increased the fury of Calonne's enemies. But there was no such revulsion of opinion as he had hoped for. The propertied classes maintained a cautious attitude. The middle classes did not seem to take the projected reforms seriously, though they had been framed to please them. The people remained indifferent to disputes which were beyond their comprehension. They required time to digest the truths which had been revealed to them and had filled them with astonishment. The excitement in Paris was intense, but it was at first confined to the upper classes. The bishops sitting among the notables demanded the dismissal of Calonne. Louis XVI yielded, and, in spite of his repugnance, ended by summoning as his successor Loménie de Brienne, the Archbishop of Toulouse, who was suggested to him by the Queen. The privileged orders could breathe again, but they had had a scare. They turned upon Calonne. On the proposal of Adrien Duport, the Parlement of Paris gave orders for an inquiry into his defalcations. The only course open to him was flight to England.

Brienne took advantage of a momentary lull to obtain from the notables and the Parlement a loan of sixty-seven millions in the form of annuities, which temporarily staved off bankruptcy. It was a mere truce. Brienne was forced by the nature of the case to adopt the projects of the man whom he had supplanted. Being more logical than Calonne, he tried to break the coalition between the privileged orders and the middle classes. He established provincial assemblies in which the third estate had a representation equal to that of both the privileged orders together. He restored civil rights to Protestants, to the fury of the clergy. He commuted the corvée for a money payment. Finally he stated his intention of making the clergy and nobles liable to the tax on real estate. The notables at once resisted. Only one out of the seven *bureaux* (committees) into which they were divided adopted the new project of a land-tax. The others declared that they had no power to grant it. This was tantamount to an appeal to the States General. Lafayette went further. He called for a National Assembly on the model of the American Congress, and a great charter which should secure the periodical meeting of this body. If Brienne's courage had been equal to his intelligence, he would have acceded to the desire formulated by the notables. The voluntary summoning of the States General at this date (May 1787), when the royal prestige was as yet unimpaired, would undoubtedly have consolidated the power of Louis XVI. The privileged orders would have been caught in their own trap. The middle classes would have realized that the promises of reform were sincere. But Louis XVI and the Court dreaded the States General. They remembered Étienne Marcel [4] and the

---

[4] Étienne Marcel, provost of the merchants of Paris, played a leading part in the States General of 1355 and 1357 and intrigued with Charles the Bad of Navarre against the Dauphin Charles, afterwards Charles V.

League.[5] Brienne preferred to dismiss the notables, thus letting slip the last chance of preventing revolution.

Henceforward there was no further check upon the revolt of the nobility, led by the judicial aristocracy. The Parlements of Bordeaux, Grenoble, Besançon, etc., lodged protests against the edicts restoring civil rights to heretics and instituting the provincial assemblies, whose competition they dreaded. They adroitly made the most of the point that these assemblies nominated from above were merely ministerial commissions, possessing no independence, and began to call for a revival of the ancient feudal Estates, which had ceased to be summoned.

The Parlement of Paris, followed by the Cour des Aides and the Cour des Comptes, won popularity by refusing to register an edict of Brienne's making petitions, receipts, announcements, newspapers, posters, etc., liable to stamp-duty. At the same time, on July 16, it demanded the summoning of the States General, which, it said, were alone competent to sanction fresh taxation. Further, it rejected the edict on the territorial subsidy, denounced the extravagance of the Court, and insisted upon economy. On August 6 the King overrode this opposition by a *lit de justice,* but on the following day the Parlement annulled the previous day's registration as illegal. This act of rebellion was punished by the exile of the Parlement to Troyes, but the agitation spread to all the provincial courts and infected the middle classes. The magistrates appeared to be defending the rights of the nation. They were treated as popular heroes and carried in triumph. Lawyers mingled with the artisans and began to cause breaches of the peace in the streets. Petitions in favour of the recall of the Parlement to Paris poured in at Versailles from all quarters.

The magistrates enjoyed their popularity, but they were uneasy at heart. By calling for the States General they had intended, by a bold move, to prevent the legal, military, and ecclesiastical nobility from bearing the cost of financial reform. They were not particularly anxious for the States General, which might escape from their control. If the Estates were summoned periodically, as Lafayette demanded, their own political role would disappear. Negotiations were carried on behind the scenes. Brienne was prepared to give up the stamp-duty and the territorial subsidy. In recompense for this they would grant him a prolongation of the two *vingtièmes,* which were to be levied "without any dis-

---

[5] The allusion is to the Holy League of the Catholic party, formed in 1576, during the Wars of Religion, and used by the ambitious Guise family in the attempt to overthrow Henri III and seize the throne.

tinction or exception whatsoever." The Parlement reciprocated this by granting its registration on September 19 and returned to Paris, where it was welcomed with fireworks.

Unfortunately the two *vingtièmes*, the collection of which took time, did not suffice to meet the urgent needs of the Treasury. Although Brienne had disregarded the royal promise and abandoned the Dutch patriots, bankruptcy was threatening. It was again necessary to turn to the Parlement to ask its authorization for a loan of 420,000,000 livres, accompanied by the promise that the States General should be summoned in five years' time; that is to say, in 1792. The struggle again broke out, more violently than ever. When, on November 19, the King ordered that the loan should be registered, the Duke of Orleans dared to say that this was illegal. On the following day the Duke was exiled to Villers-Cotterets, and two counsellors who were friends of his, Sabatier and Fréteau, were confined in the Château of Doullens. The Parlement demanded the liberation of the exiles and on January 4, 1788, on the motion of Adrien Duport, voted an address which was an arraignment of *lettres de cachet*,[6] repeating this shortly afterwards in spite of the royal prohibition. A little later, in April, it pushed its audacity to the point of arousing the uneasiness of subscribers to the last loan, and encouraging taxpayers to refuse to pay the new *vingtièmes*. This time Louis XVI was annoyed. He had the two councillors Goislard and Duval d'Esprémesnil arrested in the very law-courts, where they had taken refuge, and sanctioned the edicts presented to him by Lamoignon, the Keeper of the Seals, which were intended to break the resistance of the magistrates as well as to reform the judicial system. A plenary court, composed of high officials, was substituted for the parlements for the registration of all acts of the Crown. The parlements lost a considerable number of the civil and criminal cases which had previously been tried by them. These cases were in future to be decided by forty-seven *grands bailliages*, which should make justice more accessible to litigants. A number of special tribunals, such as the *greniers à sel* (salt-stores) [7] the *élections*, and the *bureaux de finances* [8]

---

[6] A *lettre de cachet* was a sealed letter from the king, countersigned by a secretary of State, and containing an order concerning some individual person—most frequently an order of imprisonment.

[7] The salt-stores were also the seat of courts which tried all cases concerning the salt-tax.

[8] The *bureaux de finances* had had jurisdiction over cases concerning the royal domain, certain branches of taxation, and public works; but by 1789 many of their functions were obsolete, and posts connected with them were regarded as sinecures.

were suppressed. The criminal law was reformed and made more humane, the preliminary question and the ignominious cross-examination on the *sellette* (prisoner's stool) were abolished. This was an even more thorough-going reform than that attempted by the Chancellor Maupeou in 1770. Perhaps it might have been a success if it had only been effected nine months sooner, before the exile of the Parlement to Troyes. The resistance to the establishment of the *grands bailliages* was not unanimous. Louis XVI's words denouncing the judicial and administrative aristocracy, which desired to usurp his authority, seemed to arouse an echo in the country. But since the *lit de justice* on November 19, and the measures taken against the Duke of Orleans, the struggle was no longer merely between the ministry and the parlements. All other forms of discontent had come out into the light and joined forces around this initial conflict.

A party known as the Americans, the Anglomaniacs, or the Patriots had appeared upon the scene, which drew its recruits not only from the higher nobility and upper middle classes, but also from among certain members of the Parlement, such as Duport and Fréteau. Its leaders met in the house of Duport or Lafayette. At these meetings were to be seen the Abbé Sieys, the President, Lepelletier de Saint-Fargeau, the Advocate-General Hérault de Séchelles, Huguet de Sémonville, a counsellor of the Parlement, the Abbé Louis, the Duc d'Aiguillon, the brothers Lameth, the Marquis de Condorcet, the Comte de Mirabeau, the bankers Clavière and Panchaud, etc. For them the States General were merely a first step towards an end. France was to be transformed into a constitutional and representative monarchy. Ministerial despotism was to be abolished. American ideas were gaining ground in the clubs and literary societies, of which there were already a number, and the cafés, which, as Counsellor Sallier said, were becoming "public schools of democracy and insurrection." The unrest which had affected the nobility was spreading to the middle classes. The Breton patriotic society at Rennes chose as its leaders great ladies who thought it an honour to assume the title of *citoyenne*. It gave lectures in a hall adorned with civic inscriptions which it pompously styled the Temple de la Patrie, in emulation of antiquity.

But the judicial aristocracy still took the lead. It sent out the same instructions to all its correspondents in the provinces: to prevent the setting up of the new courts of appeal or *grands bailliages,* to boycott the courts of law, to stir up disorders if necessary, and to demand the summoning of the States General and the old provincial Estates. This program was followed out point by point. The provincial parlements organized the resistance with the aid of their numerous following of lawyers.

They issued remonstrances and fulminated decrees, and by this means stirred up trouble. Demonstration followed demonstration. The nobility of the sword *en masse* made common cause with the parlements, and they were imitated by the ecclesiastical nobility. The assembly of the clergy reduced the subsidy demanded of it by more than three-quarters. It protested against the plenary court, "a tribunal whose subservience the nation would always have cause to dread" (June 15). Riots broke out at Dijon and Toulouse. In the frontier towns which had been united with the Crown late in the day, the agitation assumed the proportions of an insurrection. In Béarn the Parlement of Pau, where the court-house had been closed by the military, denounced the violation of the old local capitulations. The country people, stirred up by the nobles, assembled in the Estates, besieged the intendant in his official residence, and restored the magistrates to their benches by force (June 19).

In Brittany the agitation was left to develop freely, owing to the weakness or complicity of Thiard, the military commandant, and in particular of the intendant, Bertrand de Moleville. The Breton nobles forced duels upon the officers of the army who had remained faithful to the King. During the months of May and June there were frequent clashes between those taking part in demonstrations and the troops.

In Dauphiné, which Roland states to have been the most industrial province in France. the third estate played the chief part, but they were at one with the privileged orders. The Parlement, expelled from its court-house, declared that if the edicts were enforced, "Dauphiné would regard itself as entirely released from the duty of fidelity towards its sovereign"; thereupon the city of Grenoble rose on June 7, drove back the troops by pelting them from the roofs with tiles, and escorted the Parlement back to its court-house amid the ringing of bells. After this "day of the tiles" the Estates of the province met spontaneously, on July 21, at the Château of Vizille, belonging to the Périers, a family of big manufacturers. The military commandant did not dare to dissolve the assembly, which by the advice of the lawyers Mounier and Barnave, decided that in future the third estate should have double representation and that the voting in the Estates should be in common, by counting heads (*par tête*) and not by each order separately (*par ordre*). Lastly, it called upon the other provinces to unite, and swore to pay no taxes until the States General were summoned. All men vied with one another in singing the praises of the Vizille resolutions, and they at once became the ideal of every patriot.

Brienne could have triumphed over the growing rebellion only if he had succeeded in destroying the harmony between the third estate and the privileged orders. He did his best to do so by opposing the pens of Linguet, Rivarol, and the Abbé Morellet to those of Brissot and Mirabeau. On July 5 he announced that the States General would shortly be summoned, and on August 8 he fixed the day for May 1, 1789. But it was too late. The provincial assemblies themselves, which were his handiwork, and which he had set up in accordance with his own ideas, showed little docility. Many refused the increased taxation for which he had asked. The assembly of Lower Auvergne, inspired by Lafayette, drew up such a sharp protest that it brought down upon itself a severe reprimand from the King, and Lafayette's commission in the army was withdrawn.

The insurrection in Béarn, Brittany, and Dauphiné could be suppressed only if the troops could be relied upon. But they were led by nobles hostile to the ministry and its reforms, and fought only halfheartedly, or even fired into the air, as at Rennes. Some officers even resigned their commissions.

But the chief thing which paralysed Brienne was lack of money. The remonstrances of the parlements and the disturbances in the country had stopped the collection of taxes. After exhausting every expedient, including the seizure of the funds of the Invalides and the subscriptions for the hospitals and the victims of the recent hail-storms, after decreeing that the notes of the Caisse d'Escompte should be accepted as legal tender, Brienne had to announce that the Treasury had suspended payment. This was his ruin. The propertied classes, who had hitherto maintained an attitude of reserve—for they knew they were hated by the lawyers—now joined in the outcry raised by the nobles and the Patriots. Louis XVI sacrificed Brienne as he had sacrificed Calonne, and swallowed the humiliation of recalling Necker, whom he had previously dismissed (August 25, 1788). The Crown was no longer capable of choosing its ministers freely.

The Genevan banker felt himself to be indispensable, and made his own terms: Lamoignon's judicial reform, which had occasioned the revolt, was to be annulled, the parlements were to be recalled, and the States General were to be summoned on the date fixed by Brienne. The King had to accept everything. The revolt of the nobility had checkmated the Crown, but it had paved the way for the Revolution.

Brienne and Lamoignon were burnt in effigy in the Place Dauphine at Paris amid a delirium of joy. The demonstrations lasted several days, and degenerated into riots, in which there were some killed and wounded.

Instead of supporting the authorities, the Parlement upon its recall censured their repressive measures, cited the commandant of the watch before it, and deprived him of his post. Thus the judicial authorities encouraged disorder and disarmed the agents of the Crown. They were not aware that they would soon be the victims of the popular forces which had been unchained.

CHAPTER III

The States General

THE nobles and the Patriots had entered into a union, uneasy but without any visible discord, to oppose the measures of ministerial despotism, but as soon as Brienne fell, divisions arose between the two wings. The former, who soon came to be known as the "Aristocrats," could not imagine a reform of the kingdom except in the form of a return to feudal practices. Their idea was to guarantee the privileges, both honorary and practical, of the two higher orders, and, further, to restore to them the political power of which Richelieu, Mazarin, and Louis XIV had deprived them in the previous century. The utmost they would consent to—and that with a very bad grace—was to pay their share of the taxes in future. They were still living in the days of the Fronde and of Cardinal Retz. The "National" party or "patriots," on the other hand, desired a radical abolition of all the survivals of an accursed past. They had not fought against despotism merely to replace it by an aristocratic oligarchy. They had their eyes fixed on England and America. Civil, judicial, and fiscal equality, essential liberties, and representative government were the invariable substance of their demands, the tone of which was growing threatening.

Necker, a former clerk in Thelusson's bank, who had made a fortune by a lucky speculation in English consolidated stock on the eve of the treaty of 1763, was no more than a vain and insignificant parvenu, inclined to flatter all parties, and especially the bishops, whom the fact that he was a heretic made him anxious to conciliate. Satisfied at having secured some funds for the Treasury by borrowing from the notaries of Paris and the Caisse d'Escompte, he allowed the moment for imposing his mediation to go by. He shrank from a struggle. He had promised the States General, but had not ventured to issue regulations on the spot for the procedure to be adopted in summoning them. The privileged orders of course insisted on the ancient forms. As in 1614, the date when they had last met, every *bailliage*—that is, every electoral area—was to send only one deputy representing each order, whatever its population and importance. The nobles and clergy were to deliberate separately. No resolution was to be valid except by the unanimous consent of the three orders. The patriots indignantly denounced this archaic system, which would lead, in practice, to the indefinite adjournment of reforms, the failure of the States General, and the perpetuation of abuses. But the official classes clung to it. In 1614 the towns had been represented by the delegates of their municipal oligarchies, the *pays d'États* by deputies elected by the Estates themselves, without reference to the people. The peasants had not been consulted. If the old form were maintained, the representation of the third estate would consist for the most part of lawyers and nobles of recent creation. Necker considered the matter with some perplexity.

The Parlement of Paris profited by his hesitations to take a step forward. On September 25 it passed a resolution by the terms of which the States General were to be "regularly summoned and constituted according to the forms observed in 1614." The patriots denounced this resolution as a betrayal and began to attack the judicial aristocracy. "It is the despotism of the nobles," said Volney in the *Sentinelle du peuple*, "embodied in the person of its superior magistrates, which regulates the fate of the citizens at its good pleasure, by modifying and interpreting the contents of the laws; which creates itself rights on its own authority and sets up to be the maker of laws, whereas it is only their servant." From this time onwards the pens of the third estate set to work to denounce the sale and inheritance of judicial offices and the abuse of fees, and to deny this body of functionaries the right to examine or modify the laws. They declared roundly that, after the meeting of the States General, these functionaries would have no option but to submit, for the nation would make itself obeyed better than the King. Marie-Joseph Chénier proclaimed that the inquisition of the law-courts was more to be feared than that of the bishops. The Parlement of Paris was alarmed, and on December 5 beat a retreat by passing a fresh resolution reversing its own decision. It now accepted the doubling of the third estate, which was already the rule in the provincial assemblies created by Necker and Brienne. Its surrender was useless and, moreover, incomplete. The resolution said nothing about the question of the orders voting in common. The Parlement, but recently so popular, was now execrated.

Necker had thought he might get out of the difficulty by submitting the question to the assembly of notables, whom he now summoned afresh. As he might have foreseen, the notables pronounced in favour of the ancient forms, and on December 12, when they dispersed, five princes of the blood, the Count of Artois, the Princes of Condé and Conti, the

Dukes of Bourbon and Enghien, declared to the King in a public manifesto that there would be an immediate revolution if he were to weaken on the question of maintaining the traditional rules: "The rights of the throne," they said, "have been called in question; opinions are divided as to the rights of the two orders of the State; soon the rights of property will be attacked; inequality of fortune will be singled out as an object for reform. . . ." The princes overshot the mark, for at this date the third estate was redoubling its demonstrations of loyalty in order to win the King over to its side, and feudal rights were the only form of property as yet menaced.

Necker's dilatory tactics had ended by merely increasing the difficulties and rallying the feudal faction round the princes. On the other hand, the resistance of the privileged orders had given such impetus to the "patriotic" movement that in the end the minister was strong enough to obtain from the King a decision against the notables and princes. But here again he was satisfied with half-measures. He granted the third estate a number of deputies equal to that of the two privileged orders together, made the number of deputies proportionate to the importance of the electoral areas, and allowed parish priests to sit in person in the electoral assemblies of the clergy, a measure which was bound to have the most disastrous consequences to the ecclesiastical nobility. But having made these concessions to public opinion, he did not dare to settle the all-important question as to whether the orders were to sit and vote separately or together in the States General. The matter was left open, and so became the sport of unbridled passions.

The aristocracy made a desperate resistance, especially in the provinces which had preserved or recovered their ancient Estates. In Provence, Béarn, Burgundy, Artois, and Franche-Comté the privileged orders, backed up by the local parlements, profited by the period during which the Estates were in session to indulge in violent demonstrations against the innovations of Necker and the subversive and troublesome demands of the third estate. The Breton nobility took up such a threatening attitude that Necker had to suspend the provincial Estates. The nobles stirred up their servants and hangers-on against the students at the University, who were in favour of the third estate, and they came to blows, which resulted in some casualties. The young men of the middle classes hurried up from all the towns of Brittany, from Angers, Saint-Malo, and Nantes, to defend the students of Rennes, led by Moreau, the future general. The noblemen were attacked and pursued in the streets and besieged in the hall of the Estates, and had to leave the city full of wrath and return to their country-houses (January 1789). They vowed in dudgeon that they would not send representatives to the States General.

At Besançon, where the Parlement had taken the side of the privileged orders, who had voted a violent protest against Necker's regulation, the crowd got out of hand and sacked the houses of several counsellors, while the troops stood by without defending them. The military commandant, the Marquis de Langeron, a liberal nobleman, declared that the army was intended for marching against the enemies of the State, and not against its citizens (March 1789).

Mallet du Pan, that keen observer, was right when he wrote, as early as January 1789: "The public controversy has undergone a transformation. It is now only secondarily concerned with the King, despotism and the Constitution; it is a war between the third estate and the other two orders."

The privileged orders were bound to be beaten. This was not only because they could no longer reckon upon the whole-hearted co-operation of the agents of the Crown, whose patience they had exhausted by their previous revolt; nor was it merely because, when faced with a general rising of the whole nation, they were no more than an insignificant minority of parasites; but also, and above all, because they were divided among themselves. In Franche-Comté twenty-two noblemen had protested against the resolutions of their order and declared that they accepted the double representation of the third estate, equality of taxation, equality before the law, etc. The city of Besançon inscribed their names on its register of middle-class citizens. In Artois, where only those feudal lords were represented in the Estates who had seven quarterings and owned a fief à clocher (containing a church) the "non-entrant" nobles (that is, unrepresented in the États), supported by the barrister Robespierre, protested against their exclusion. The small gentry of Languedoc raised similar complaints against the great nobles of the province. Almost everywhere the noblesse de cloche, composed of commoners who had bought municipal offices which carried with them the rank of nobles, took the side of the third estate; but they did not meet with much gratitude.

The agitation began to strike deeper. The summoning of the States General, announced and commented upon from the pulpit by the parish priests, had awakened unlimited hopes. All who had a grievance—and they were legion—listened to these controversies and began to prepare for the great day. Both the middle classes and the peasants had begun for the last two years to serve their apprenticeship to public business in the provincial assemblies, the departmental assemblies, and the new

33

rural municipalities created by Brienne. These assemblies had assessed taxation, administered poor-relief and the funds allotted to public works, and controlled the expenditure of the local moneys. The rural municipalities, elected by those paying the heaviest taxation, had acquired a taste for their task. Formerly the syndic (mayor) had been nominated by the intendant. He was now elected by the farmers, and was no more than a passive agent. Village opinion crystallized around the council, whose opinion he consulted. Common interests were discussed and claims were formulated. In Alsace, as soon as the new municipalities were formed, their first care was to bring actions against their feudal lords, and the latter complained bitterly of the "innumerable abuses" which the establishment of the municipalities had occasioned.

The electoral campaign coincided with a grave economic crisis. The commercial treaty with England, signed in 1786, had reduced the customs dues, thus allowing English goods to enter the country. Textile manufacturers were forced to limit production. At Abbeville there were 12,000 workmen unemployed, at Lyons 20,000, and the numbers at other places were in proportion. At the beginning of the winter, which was a very hard one, it was necessary in the large cities to organize workshops supported by charity, especially as the price of bread was constantly rising. The harvest of 1788 had been much below the normal. The shortage of forage had been so great that the farmers had been forced to sacrifice part of their cattle and to leave some of their land uncultivated, or else sow it without previous manuring. The markets were short of supplies. Not only was bread very dear, but there was a risk that it would run short. It was in vain that Necker forbade the export of cereals and proceeded to purchase some abroad; the crisis remained as severe as ever and even got worse. The wretched people cast covetous glances upon the well-filled barns in which their lay and ecclesiastical lords stored up the proceeds of their tithes and their rents in kind (*terrages* and *champarts*). Innumerable voices were raised in denunciation of the aristocracy of the privileged orders. As soon as electioneering began, in March, there was an explosion of "popular emotion." Crowds gathered round the granaries and tithe-barns and demanded that they should be thrown open. They stopped the movement of grain, stole it, and fixed the price on their own authority. In Provence the insurgent workmen and peasants not only demanded that the price of corn should be fixed and the price of food-stuffs reduced, but also insisted upon the abolition of the flour-tax (*piquet*). In some places they soon began to force the feudal lords and priests to abolish tithes and manorial dues. There were risings and pillaging by bands at Aix, Marseilles, Toulon, Brignoles, Manosque, Aubagne, etc. (end of March). Similar disturbances, though of a less serious nature, took place in Brittany, Languedoc, Alsace, Franche-Comté, Guyenne, Burgundy, and the Île-de-France. In Paris, on April 27, Réveillon's great wall-paper factory was sacked in the course of a bloody riot. The rising was directed not only against those who were speculating in foodstuffs, against the old system of taxation, against internal tolls, and against feudalism, but against all those who exploit the populace and live upon its substance. It was closely connected with the political agitation. At Nantes the crowd besieged the Hôtel de Ville with cries of *"Vive la Liberté!"* At Agde it claimed the right of nominating the consuls. In many cases the agitation began simultaneously with the opening of electioneering, and this is understandable. These poor people had been disregarded by the authorities for centuries past, and only summoned before them to pay their taxes and furnish their corvée; now, suddenly, their advice was asked upon matters of State, and they were told they might address their complaints freely to the King. "His Majesty," said the royal regulation read from the pulpit, "desires every man to be assured that his desires and claims will reach His Majesty from the utmost bounds of his kingdom and its obscurest dwellings." The phrase was remembered and taken literally. The wretched people believed that in very truth all public authority was no longer turned against them, but that they had now found support at the very head of the social order, and that injustices would at last disappear. This was what made them so bold. Strong in the firmness of their will and in their stubborn endurance of suffering, they strove impetuously towards the object of their desires and complaints. By putting an end to injustice they were carrying out the royal intention, or at least they thought they were doing so. Later on, when they saw their mistake, they fell away from the King. But it took time to undeceive them.

It was amid this atmosphere of ferment that the national deliberations took place. For the last six months past, in spite of the censorship and the severe regulations controlling printing, liberty of the press had existed to all intents and purposes. Lawyers, parish priests, and publicists of every kind, who but yesterday had trembled in obscurity, now boldly criticized the whole social system in thousands of pamphlets, which were eagerly devoured in boudoir and cottage alike. Volney started his *Sentinelle du Peuple* at Rennes; Thouret his *Avis aux bons Normands* at Rouen; Mirabeau his *Appel à la Nation provençale* at Aix; Robespierre his *Appel à la Nation artésienne* at Arras; the Abbé Sieys his *Essai sur les privilèges* and afterwards his famous *Qu'est-ce que le Tiers État?*

(*What is the Third Estate?*); Camille Desmoulins his *Philosophie au peuple français;* Target his *Lettre aux États généraux,* etc. There was not a single abuse to which attention was not drawn, not a single reform which was not examined and demanded. "Politics," says Madame de Staël, "were a fresh sphere for the imagination of the French; everybody flattered himself that he would play a part in them, everybody saw an object for himself in the many chances which offered themselves on all sides."

The members of the third estate consulted together, promoted unofficial meetings of corporations and communities, and kept up a correspondence between town and town or province and province. They drew up petitions and manifestoes, collected signatures, and sent round forms, as models for the *cahiers de doléances* (memorials of grievances) which they distributed even in the country districts. The Duke of Orleans, who was supposed to be the secret patron of the Patriot party, had instructions drawn up by Laclos which he sent to his representatives in the electoral areas in which his estates were situated, and had a model drawn up by Sieys for the procedure to be followed by the electoral assemblies. Necker had enjoined upon the agents of the Crown to observe strict neutrality; but certain intendants—for instance, Amelot, the intendant of Dijon—were accused by the privileged orders of favouring the popular side. The parlements tried to burn a few pamphlets in order to overawe the publicists. The Parlement of Paris cited Dr. Guillotin before it for his *Pétition des citoyens domiciliés à Paris.* Guillotin made his appearance surrounded by a huge cheering crowd, and the Parlement did not dare to arrest him.

The electoral machinery set up by the royal regulation was rather complicated, but extremely liberal. The members of the two higher orders went straight to the chief town of their electoral area and formed the electoral assemblies of the clergy and the nobility respectively. All nobles whose rank was established and transmissible had the right to be present in person. Even noblewomen might be represented by proxy if they owned a fief.

Every parish priest had his seat in the assembly of the clergy, whereas canons, who were all nobles, had only one delegate to each group of ten, and the regulars, or monks, one delegate to each convent. Thus the parish priests were sure of a majority.

In the cities the inhabitants who had reached the age of twenty-five and whose names were on the list of taxpayers met at first according to their corporations. The corporations of arts and crafts had only one delegate to every hundred members, whereas the corporations of liberal arts, merchants, and ship-builders had two; which was giving an advantage to wealth and talent. Inhabitants not belonging to a corporation —and in certain towns, where there were no corporations, this meant all the inhabitants—held separate meetings for each district (or quarter) and likewise elected two delegates for every hundred members. All the delegates (or electors) so nominated next assembled at the Hôtel de Ville to form the electoral assembly of the third estate of the town, draw up the common memorial of grievances, and appoint their representatives to the assembly of the third estate of the electoral area (*bailliage*), whose duty it was to elect the deputies to the States General. The peasants in the parishes were represented in this assembly in the ratio of two to every hundred households. Every parish, corporation, or urban district provided its delegates with a special memorial (*cahier*), and all these memorials were subsequently combined to form the general memorial for that electoral area. When the principal *bailliage* included secondary ones, the electoral assembly of the secondary area nominated a quarter of its members to represent it in that of the principal area. In the latter case, which was fairly frequent, the electoral process had four stages: first, the parish, corporation, or urban district; second, the town assembly; third, the assembly of the secondary *bailliage;* fourth, that of the principal *bailliage.*

In the assemblies of the privileged orders there was a sharp conflict between the liberal minority and the reactionary majority, between the court nobles and the small country gentry, between the upper and the lower clergy. There was a split among the nobility of the *bailliage* of Amont (Vesoul) in Franche-Comté, which nominated two deputations to the States General. In Artois and Brittany the nobles who had been members of the old Estates absented themselves, as a protest against the royal regulation which compelled them to share their political power with the lesser nobility. The assemblies of the clergy were in general very stormy. The parish priests imposed their will and kept most of the bishops out of the deputations, except about forty chosen among the more liberal of them.

The assemblies of the third estate were calmer. Clashes took place only in certain towns, such as Arras, where the delegates of the corporations had a dispute with the *échevins* (municipal councillors) who claimed a seat in the electoral assembly, though they had acquired the status of nobles, and in certain *bailliages,* such as Commercy, where the country people complained that the townspeople had left their own special claims out of the memorial. Almost everywhere the third estate chose its deputies from among its own ranks, thus proving the strength of the class feeling with which it was inspired. The only exceptions were the few popular nobles like Mirabeau, who had been excluded from the assembly of his own order and was elected by the third estate of Aix and Marseilles, or a few ecclesiastics like Sieys, who had been rejected by the clergy of Chartres and elected by the third estate of Paris. Nearly half the deputation of the third estate was composed of lawyers, who had exercised a preponderating influence in the electoral campaign or in drawing up the memorials. The other half was made up of all the professions, but the peasants were still to a large extent illiterate and had no representatives. More than one publicist who had been prominent for his attacks on the aristocrats obtained a mandate: Volney, Robespierre, Thouret, Target, etc.

An examination of the *cahiers* shows that absolutism was unanimously condemned. Priests, nobles, and commoners concurred in demanding a constitution limiting the rights of the king and his agents and establishing a national representative body, to meet periodically, which should alone be competent to vote taxation and make laws. Nearly all the deputies had received a strict mandate to grant no subsidies until the Constitution had been accepted and secured. "The deficit," as Mirabeau wittily said, "became the national treasury." All the demands put forward were inspired by a love of liberty and a hatred of despotism.

Even the clergy protested in many of their *cahiers* against absolutism in the Church as well as in the State. They claimed for the parish priests the right of forming assemblies and taking part in the government of the Church by the restoration of diocesan synods and provincial councils.

Nobles and commoners were equally fervent in their condemnation of *lettres de cachet* and interference with the secrecy of the post, and in demanding trial by jury and liberty of speech, opinion, and the press.

The privileged orders accepted equality of taxation, but for the most part rejected equality of rights and the throwing open of all professions to all Frenchmen. Above all, they stubbornly defended the separate vote of the orders, which they regarded as a guarantee of their tithes and feudal rights. But the nobility and the third estate were perfectly ready to dispose of the property of the clergy in order to pay the debt. They nevertheless agreed with the clergy in condemning the existing financial system root and branch. All direct and indirect taxes were to be replaced by a more equitable tax, to be assessed by elected assemblies, and not, as before, by the agents of the king.

The third estate was united in opposition to the aristocrats, but its own demands varied, according as they came from the middle classes or the peasants, the merchants or the artisans. Every shade of interest and opinion among the various classes was reflected in it. The grievances against the feudal regime in the *cahiers* of the parishes were naturally more bitter than those in the *cahiers* of the *bailliages,* drawn up by the townspeople. Condemnation of the corporations was far from unanimous. The protests against the suppression of common pasturage and gleaning and the dividing up of common lands came only from a minority. It is evident that the middle classes, who already owned part of the land, would in case of need make common cause with the feudal property interest against the poor peasants. There are no instances of the claims of "labour" in the modern sense of the word. It was the "masters" who wielded the pen. The urban proletariate had as yet no voice in affairs. On the other hand, the wishes of the industrial and commercial interests, their protests against the pernicious effects of the commercial treaty with England, and the statement of the needs of the various branches of production form the subject of a most remarkable detailed examination. The class which was about to take the lead in the Revolution was fully conscious of its strength and its rights. It is not true that it allowed itself to be led astray by an empty ideology; it had a thorough knowledge of realities and possessed the means of adapting its interests to their exigencies.

CHAPTER IV

The Revolt of Paris

THE elections had asserted with startling clearness the firm resolution of the country. The Crown, having remained neutral, had its hands free. But it could only accede to the desires of the third estate at the cost of its own abdication. Louis XVI would continue to reign, but only like a king of England, accepting a national representative body at his side as a permanent check. The consort of Marie Antoinette did not for a moment contemplate such a renunciation. He was full of pride in his sacred office, and did not want it to be impaired. There was only one way of defending it still open to him, and this way was urged upon him by the princes: a close understanding with the privileged orders, and resistance.

It appears that, a fortnight before the meeting of the States General, Necker had advised him to make the necessary sacrifices, in order still to control the course of events. The King was to command the three orders to deliberate together and vote individually upon all questions concerning taxation. At the same time he was to combine the nobility and the higher clergy in an upper house, as in England, and form a lower house by combining the third estate with the lower clergy. It is doubtful whether the third estate would have been satisfied with this system, which would have given it control only of taxation. But it is certain that an unmistakable sign of royal goodwill would have softened dissensions and saved the Crown.

Necker would have liked the Estates to meet in Paris, doubtless in order to inspire confidence in the financial world. But the King decided in favour of Versailles, "because of the hunting." This was his first blunder, for the members of the third estate would have always before their eyes the sumptuous palaces and ruinous Court, which were draining the resources of the nation. Besides, Paris was not so far from Versailles as to be unable to make its influence felt upon the assembly.

From the first the Court did all it could to maintain a strict separation between the orders, even in the slightest details. While the King received the deputies of the clergy and nobility ceremoniously in his study, the deputies of the third estate were hurried through his bedroom in batches. The third estate had an official costume all in black prescribed for it, contrasting by its severity with the gold-laced decorations of the deputies of the two higher orders. It narrowly escaped being ordered to listen kneeling to the King's opening speech, as in 1614. All that happened was that the deputies of the third estate were introduced into the hall of session (Salle des États) by a little back door, while the grand entrance was thrown wide open for the first two orders. The parish priests had already been hurt because the prelates had not mingled with them acording to their respective *bailliages* at the procession on the previous day, but had been placed in a group apart, separated from them by a considerable space, which was occupied by the royal band.

The opening session, on May 5, increased the bad impression caused by these blunders. In a tone of snivelling sentimentality Louis XVI warned the deputies against the spirit of innovation and called upon them to turn their attention in the first place to the means of filling the treasury. Barentin, the Keeper of the Seals, was the next speaker. He was barely audible, and did little more than eulogize the monarch's virtues and favours. Finally, in a long statement, lasting three hours and bristling with figures, Necker dealt exclusively with the financial situation. According to him the deficit, of which he minimized the importance, could easily be reduced by a few measures dealing with details, reducing or suppressing certain items of expenditure, etc. It was like listening to the report of the chairman of a limited company. The deputies wondered why they had been brought there from their distant provinces. Necker made no statement on the highly important question whether the orders were to vote together or not, and made no mention of political reforms. The third estate manifested its disappointment by its silence. In order to triumph over the privileged orders, it could only rely upon its own efforts.

It soon made up its mind how to act. Its members held meetings that very evening, province by province; the Bretons, who had the greatest animus against the nobles, grouped themselves round Chapelier and Lanjuinais, the deputies for Franche-Comté round the barrister Blanc, those for Artois round Robespierre, those for Dauphiné round Mounier and Barnave. All these committees arrived at the same determination: that the third estate, or rather the Commons—by which new title they signified their intention of exercising the same rights as the English Commons—was to invite the other two orders to join it in examining jointly the mandates of all the deputies, regardless of their order, and until this joint examination (*vérification des pouvoirs*) had been carried out, the Commons were to refuse to constitute a separate chamber. They would have no secretariate and no minutes, nothing but a chairman (*doyen*) to keep order in the assembly. And so things actually happened. On the very first day the Commons passed an act asserting their determination to comply with the expressed wishes of France in regarding the old separation of the orders as non-existent.

A month passed by in fruitless negotiations between the three Chambers, which held their sessions separately. Under pressure from the parish priests, the clergy, who had already suspended the examination of their mandates, offered to act as intermediary. Commissaries were nominated by all three bodies to seek a basis of agreement, which was in fact impossible. The King intervened in turn and desired the Keeper of the Seals to preside in person over the conferences which were searching for a compromise. The third estate adroitly took advantage of the reservations made by the nobility to throw the responsibility for failure upon them. Then, having made it evident to the country that the privileged orders refused a compromise, it abandoned its waiting attitude. It sent the two higher orders a final invitation to join it and on June 12 proceeded to examine by itself the mandates of the deputies of the three orders by a roll-call of all the *bailliages* which had been called upon to send deputies. On the following day three parish priests of Poitou—Lecesve, Ballard, and Jallet—answered the roll-call; and during the next few days sixteen more followed their example. After the roll-call the Commons decided by 490 votes to 90 to form themselves into a National Assembly. By so doing they asserted that they alone were sufficient to represent the nation. They next took another step forward by simultaneously deciding that on the day when they should be forced to disperse, for any reason whatsoever, the taxes should cease to be collected. Having thus levelled against the Court the threat of a strike against taxation, they reassured the creditors of the State by placing them under the protection of the honour of France, and finally, by an act bolder, perhaps, than all the rest, they denied the king the right to veto the resolutions which they had just passed and all those which they might pass in future. Two days later, on June 19, after violent debates, the order of the clergy in turn decided by a small majority (149 to 137) to join the third estate. Unless the King intervened with the utmost haste to prevent this meeting, the privileged orders had lost the game.

Princes, great nobles, archbishops, judges, and high officials, all pressed Louis XVI to act. D'Esprémesnil offered to have the agitators in the third estate, and even Necker himself, tried by the Parlement of Paris on a

42

charge of *lèse-majesté*. On the evening of the 19th the King decided to quash the resolutions of the third estate at a solemn session, to be held like a *lit de justice*. Meanwhile, in order to make the prospective union of the clergy and the Commons impossible, he ordered that the Salle des Etats should be closed at once, on the pretext of the preparations going on in it. What petty measures to deal with such circumstances!

On the morning of June 20 the deputies of the third estate, on trying to assemble in the hall, found the doors shut and surrounded by soldiers. They assembled a few steps away, in the tennis-court used for the recreation of the courtiers. A few of them proposed to adjourn to Paris and deliberate in safety. But Mounier rallied all votes by asking them to pledge themselves each and all, by their oath and signature, "never to separate, and to meet wherever circumstances might demand, until the Constitution should be established and firmly based upon solid foundations." All of them, with a single exception—Martin Dauch, the deputy for Carcassonne—took this oath of imperishable memory amid great enthusiasm.

The royal session had been fixed for June 22. It was put off for a day in order to remove the public galleries, holding three thousand spectators, for fear of demonstrations. This postponement was a mistake, for it enabled the majority of the clergy to carry out their resolution of the 19th. On June 22 they joined the third estate in the Church of St. Louis. Five prelates, led by the Archbishop of Vienne (Dauphiné), and a hundred and forty-four parish priests accordingly swelled the ranks of the National Assembly. Two noblemen of Dauphiné, the Marquis de Blacons and the Comte d'Agoult, also joined its sessions. The result of the royal session was by now gravely imperilled.

The Court heaped blunder upon blunder. Whereas the privileged deputies were admitted directly into the Salle de Etats, the third estate had to wait outside the little door in the rain. The display of troops, far from overawing them, increased their annoyance. The King's speech made them indignant. It was a sharp reprimand, followed by a series of harsh and dictatorial declarations. The monarch ordered the maintenance of the three orders, which were to deliberate in separate rooms. He quashed the resolutions of the third estate. Though consenting to equality of taxation, he took care to state explicitly that all forms of property were to be maintained absolutely, "and by property His Majesty expressly means the tithes, rents in cash, feudal and manorial rents and dues, and in general all rights and prerogatives, whether real or honorary, attached to the estates and fiefs belonging to individuals." Of what use was it for him to go on to promise vaguely that he would consult the States General on financial matters in future? The prospect of political and social reform was fading away.

Louis XVI spoke again, and closed the *lit de justice* with the following threats: "If, by a fatality which I am far from anticipating, you were to abandon me in such a great enterprise, I alone would provide for the welfare of my people, I alone should regard myself as their true representative. . . . Consider, gentlemen, that none of your projects, none of your measures, can have the force of law without my special approbation. . . . I order you, gentlemen, to disperse at once, and to appear tomorrow morning each in the room set apart for his order, there to resume your sessions. I accordingly order the Grand Master of the Ceremonies to have these apartments made ready."

In obedience to the watchword received from the Breton deputies assembled at their club on the previous evening, the Commons remained motionless upon their benches, while the nobles and part of the clergy withdrew. The workmen sent to remove the royal dais stopped work for fear of interrupting the assembly, which continued in session. De Brézé, the Master of the Ceremonies, came and reminded Bailly, who was in the chair, of the King's order. Bailly answered shortly that the assembled nation could not receive an order, and Mirabeau thundered in his great voice the famous words: "Go and tell those who sent you that we are here by the will of the people, and will leave our places only if compelled by armed force." Camus, supported by Barnave and Sieys, obtained the passage of a motion to the effect that the National Assembly upheld its resolutions. This was a fresh act of disobedience. Mirabeau, foreseeing that *lettres de cachet* would be issued against the ringleaders of the third estate, further proposed to enact that the members of the Assembly were inviolable, and that whoever should infringe their inviolability would commit a capital offence. But such was the coldblooded determination which filled all hearts, and so great was their distrust of Mirabeau, whose immorality made all his motives open to suspicion, that several deputies wanted to reject the motion as cowardly. It was, however, passed.

These were memorable resolutions, braver, indeed, than those of June 20; for on June 20 the third estate was supposed to be in ignorance of the King's will, which had not yet been made manifest. On June 23 it reaffirmed its rebellion in an aggravated form, in the very hall which had echoed to the royal words.

La Révellière, who sat in the Assembly as deputy for Anjou, relates that on receiving the Marquis de Brézé's report Louis XVI gave orders to the Gardes du Corps to enter the hall and disperse the deputies by force. As the guards advanced, several deputies belonging to the minority among the nobles, the two Crillons, d'André, Lafayette, the Dukes of La Rochefoucault and of Liancourt, and others, drew their swords and barred the way. When Louis XVI heard of this, he gave way. He would willingly have had the rabble of the third estate cut down, but shrank from the necessity of subjecting part of his nobles to the same treatment.

As Necker had not appeared at the *lit de justice*, a report went round that he had resigned or been dismissed. A huge crowd made a demonstration before his house and in the courtyards of the palace. The King and Queen sent for him and begged him to remain at his post. They were dissimulating so as the better to prepare for vengeance.

A violent ferment reigned both in Paris and at Versailles, as well as in the provinces, for the latter were kept regularly informed by the letters of their representatives, which were read out in public. Since the beginning of June the funds had fallen steadily. When the *lit de justice* was announced, all the Paris banks had closed their doors. The Caisse d'Escompte sent its directors to Versailles to explain the dangers with which it was threatened. The Court had the whole financial world against it.

In these circumstances the King's orders could not be carried into effect. Even the humble public criers refused to announce them in the streets. On June 24 the majority of the clergy in turn disobeyed the King and joined the sessions of the third estate. On the following day forty-seven members of the nobility did the same, led by the Duke of Orleans.

Louis XVI swallowed the affront, but that very evening he secretly decided to send for twenty thousand troops, for preference foreign regiments, which he considered more trustworthy. The order went out on the 26th. On the following day, in order to lull suspicion, he requested the presidents of the nobility and of the clergy to join the National Assembly in turn, and in order to induce them to do so he sent word to them by the Count of Artois that it was necessary for the protection of his life, which was in danger.

No rising was being prepared against the King, but since the royal session the Patriots had been on the alert. On June 25 the four hundred electors of Paris who had elected the deputies to the States General met of their own accord in the Paris Musée, from whence they afterwards betook themselves to the Hôtel de Ville, in order to watch over the doings of the aristocrats and keep in close touch with the National Assembly. As early as June 29 they laid down the bases of a project for a bourgeois

45

guard which was to include the principal inhabitants of every part of the city. The Palais Royal, which belonged to the Duke of Orleans, had become an open-air club, which was never empty, day or night. The plans of the Court were known and discussed there as soon as they were made.

The Patriots were already tampering with the troops. The Gardes Françaises, the premier regiment of France, were soon won over. They were dissatisfied with their colonel, who subjected them to a rigid discipline, and numbered among their officers men like Hulin, Lefebvre, and Lazare Hoche, who would never win their epaulettes so long as the regulation of 1781 remained in force. On June 30 four thousand habitués of the Palais Royal released ten Gardes Françaises who had been imprisoned in the Abbaye for insubordination, and escorted them in triumph. The hussars and dragoons sent to restore order shouted *"Vive la nation!"* and refused to charge the crowd. Even the Gardes du Corps at Versailles had shown signs of relaxed discipline. Would the foreign regiments be more obedient?

If Louis XVI had mounted his horse and taken command of his troops in person, as Henri IV would have done, he might perhaps have succeeded in keeping them true to their duty and ensured the success of his forcible measures. But Louis XVI was a bourgeois.

The arrival of the regiments, which camped at Saint-Denis, Saint-Cloud, and Sèvres, and even on the Champ de Mars, was hailed with sharp protests. All these new mouths to feed would increase the famine! There could be no further doubt; the intention was to disperse the National Assembly by force! On July 2 a proposal to dethrone Louis XVI and set the Duke of Orleans in his place was mooted at the Palais Royal. The electors of Paris went to the Assembly and asked that the troops be sent away. On July 8, after a terrible speech, in which he denounced the evil counsellors who were undermining the throne, Mirabeau obtained the passage of their motion. Louis XVI's reply to this proceeding of the Assembly was that he had summoned the regiments to protect its liberty, but that if it feared for its safety, he was ready to transfer it to Nyon or Soissons. This was adding mockery to his threats. On the evening after they heard this reply a hundred deputies met at the Breton Club, in the avenue de Saint-Cloud, to concert resistance.

Louis XVI forced the situation. On July 11 he dismissed Necker, with the utmost secrecy, and reorganized the ministry under the Baron de Breteuil, an avowed counter-revolutionary. On the following day a report went round that national bankruptcy was about to be declared. A meeting of stock-brokers at once took place, which decided to close the Bourse as a protest against the dismissal of Necker. Money was distributed to win over the soldiers. Bankers like Étienne Delessert, Prévoteau, Coindre, and Boscary enlisted with their staffs in the bourgeois guard which was being formed. The busts of Necker and the Duke of Orleans were carried in procession through Paris. The theatres were closed. At the suggestion of Camille Desmoulins, who announced at the Palais Royal that a massacre of patriots was impending, a green cockade was worn, that being the colour of Necker's liveries. Finally, on hearing that the Royal Allemand regiment, led by the Prince de Lambesc, was charging the crowd in the Tuileries Gardens, the tocsin was rung and the populace assembled in the churches to enlist and arm themselves with weapons taken from the armourers' shops. Disreputable characters were carefully eliminated. Arming went on during the next day, July 13, twenty-eight thousand muskets and some cannon having been seized at the Invalides. The Assembly, for its part, passed a resolution to the effect that Necker bore with him the regrets and esteem of the nation. It remained in permanent session and declared the new ministers responsible for what had happened.

The strange thing is that the Court was paralysed and did nothing. Bezenval, who was in command of the regiments concentrated on the Champ de Mars, pending orders, did not dare to enter Paris.

On July 14 the electors, who had formed a permanent committee at the Hôtel de Ville, in concert with the old municipality, sent several requests to the Governor of the Bastille that he should give out arms to the militia and remove the cannon from the towers of the fortress. A final deputation having been received with musket-fire, in spite of the fact that it carried the white flag, the siege began. The artisans of the faubourg Saint-Antoine were strengthened by the Gardes Françaises, led by Hulin and Élie, who brought up cannon and trained them on the drawbridge, so as to break in the gates. After a sharp action, in which the besiegers lost some hundred killed, the pensioners, who, with a few Swiss, formed the garrison and had had no food, for victuals were short, forced the Governor, De Launay, to capitulate. The crowd indulged in terrible reprisals. De Launay, who was believed to have given the order to fire on the envoys with the white flags, and Flesselles, the "provost of the merchants" (chief municipal official of Paris), who had tried to mislead the electors as to the existence of stores of arms, were massacred on the Place de Grève, and their heads stuck on the end of pikes. A few days later Foullon, a member of the Council of State, whose duty it was to supply food for the armies round Paris, and his son-in-law, the intendant Berthier, were hanged on the lamp-bracket of the Hôtel de Ville. Babeuf, who looked on at their execution with a heavy heart, remarked in a letter to his wife: "Our

47

punishments of every kind, quartering, torture, the wheel, the stake, and the gibbet, and the multiplicity of executioners on all sides, have had such a bad effect upon our morals! Our masters, instead of policing us, have made us barbarous, because they are barbarous themselves. They are reaping and will reap what they have sown."

Paris could have been subdued only by street-fighting, and even the foreign troops could not be relied upon. Louis XVI, at the prompting of the Duc de Liancourt, who had returned from Paris, went down to the Assembly on July 15 and announced that the troops were to be sent away. The Assembly insisted upon the recall of Necker. But the King had not yet made up his mind to capitulate entirely. While a deputation from the Assembly visited Paris, and the victorious Parisians appointed Bailly, the hero of the Tennis-court, mayor of the city, and Lafayette, the friend of Washington, commandant of the National Guard—while the Archbishop of Paris had a Te Deum sung at Notre-Dame in honour of the capture of the Bastille, and the pickaxes of the destroyers were furiously attacking the old political prison, the princes were endeavouring to persuade the weak monarch to flee to Metz, from whence he was to return at the head of an army. But Marshall de Broglie, the commandant of the troops, and the Count of Provence opposed his departure. Was Louis XVI afraid that in his absence the Assembly would proclaim the Duke of Orleans king? It is by no means impossible. He stayed behind and had to drain the cup to the dregs. He dismissed Breteuil and recalled Necker, and on the following day, July 18, having given these guarantees, he went to Paris, sanctioning the results of the insurrection by his presence at the Hôtel de Ville, and emphasizing his own loss of authority by accepting the new tricolour cockade from Bailly, the mayor.

Indignant at the poor spirit displayed by the King, the Count of Artois and the princes, Breteuil and the leaders of the party of resistance fled abroad, thus taking the lead in the movement of emigration.

Louis XVI, though humiliated, kept his crown, but he had been forced to recognize a new sovereign, superior to himself: the French people, of which the Assembly was the organ. Nobody in Europe failed to grasp the importance of what had happened. "From this moment," wrote the Duke of Dorset, the British ambassador, to his Government, "we may regard France as a free country, the king as a monarch whose powers are limited, and the nobility as reduced to the level of the nation." The middle classes of all Europe realized that their hour had come, and thrilled with joy and hope.

CHAPTER V

The Revolt of the Provinces

THE provinces had been kept regularly informed of the course of events by their deputies, whose letters—for instance, those of the Bretons—were often printed as soon as they arrived. They had followed the developments of the struggle between the third estate and the privileged orders as anxiously as the capital. They hailed the capture of the Bastille with the same shout of triumph.

Certain towns had not even waited for the glorious news before rising against the hated regime. At the beginning of July the unemployed artisans of Lyons burnt the toll-gates and tollhouses in order to reduce the cost of living. The aristocratic municipality, the "Consulate," of which Imbert-Colomès was president, was obliged to jettison some of its privileges. On July 16 it consented to share the administration of the city with a permanent committee consisting of representatives of the three orders. A few days later the permanent committee organized a National Guard on the Parisian model, from which the proletariate was excluded.

It was the same in all the towns, small or great, with a few variations. Sometimes, as at Bordeaux, it was the electors who had chosen the deputies to the States General who constituted the nucleus of the permanent committee; that is to say, the revolutionary municipality. Sometimes, as at Dijon, Montpellier, and Besançon, the new committee was elected by the general assembly of the citizens. Sometimes, as at Nîmes, Valence, Tours, and Évreux, the permanent committee arose out of the collaboration of the old municipality with the electors nominated by the corporations. It sometimes happened—for instance, at Évreux—that several permanent committees followed one another in rapid succession, based on varying forms of election. When the old authorities showed signs of resistance, as at Strasbourg, Amiens and Vernon, a rising of the populace soon brought them to their senses.

The first care of the permanent committees everywhere was to set up a National Guard to maintain order. It was hardly formed before it insisted upon taking over from the commandants the fortresses and citadels

49

which formed the local Bastilles, and for the most part they yielded with a good grace. At Bordeaux the National Guard took possession of the Château Trompette, at Caen of the Citadel and the Tour-Lévi, in which salt-smugglers had been imprisoned, etc. By this means they obtained possession of arms and secured themselves against a counter-attack by the agents of despotism, while at the same time wiping out old grudges.

As a rule the military commandants and the intendants offered no resistance. At Montpellier the permanent committee passed a vote of thanks to the intendant. The permanent committees and the general staffs of the National Guard counted among their members the notables of the districts, together with the élite of the third estate. They very often had agents of the king at their head. At Évreux the lieutenant-general of the *bailliage*, the counsellor presiding over the salt-store, and the procurator-royal rubbed shoulders with barristers, tanners, grocers, or doctors. What chance had the king's agents of resisting? The troops could no more be relied upon in the provinces than in Paris. At Strasbourg they had looked on unmoved at the sack of the Hôtel de Ville. The old order was disappearing without an effort, like the sudden collapse of a ruined, crumbling building.

While the middle classes were arming on all sides and boldly taking the local administration into their own hands, how could the peasants remain inactive? They had calmed down a little after the great ferment of the elections. The bourgeois whom they had sent as delegates to Versailles had told them to be patient, and the demands formulated in the *cahiers* would be satisfied. They had been waiting for three months, with famine drawing nearer. The revolt of Paris and the other cities put arms into their hands too. They took down their sporting-guns, their scythes, pitchforks, and flails, and, prompted by a sure instinct, collected in mobs round their masters' country-houses at the sound of the tocsin. They demanded that the title-deeds in virtue of which the innumerable seigniorial dues had been levied should be given up to them, and burnt the accursed parchments in the courtyards. Sometimes, when the landowner was unpopular, when he refused to open his muniment-room and prepared to defend himself by the aid of his household, the rustics burnt the house and wreaked their vengeance on its owner. A M. de Montesson was shot near Le Mans by one of his old soldiers as a punishment for his severity; a M. de Barras was killed in Languedoc; a Chevalier d'Ambly was dragged on to a dunghill, etc. The privileged orders paid dearly for their fault of exploiting the peasants for centuries and leaving them in a state of barbarism.

The peasant revolt started in the Île de France as early as July 20, and spread rapidly from place to place till it reached the farthest limits of the kingdom. As was natural, the excesses of the rioters were exaggerated by rumour. It was said that brigands were cutting down the growing crops, marching on the towns, and showing no respect for property. The panic thus spread abroad gave a strong impetus to the formation of the permanent committees and National Guards. The Great Fear and the peasant rising formed part of one simultaneous movement.

The brigands whose imminent irruption haunted men's imaginations could not as a rule be distinguished from the artisans who burnt the toll-gates and fixed the price of wheat in the market, or the peasants who forced their lords to give up their title-deeds. But that the crowds of poor wretches in the country and the working-class districts of the towns saw in the growing anarchy a chance to revenge themselves upon the social order is too natural to be called in question. The rising was directed not only against the feudal system, but against monopolies of commodities, taxes, bad judges, all those who exploited the people and lived upon its work. In Upper Alsace the peasants attacked the Jewish merchants at the same time as the country-houses and convents. At the end of July the Jews of Alsace were obliged to take refuge in Basel by hundreds.

The property-owning middle classes were suddenly faced with the grim figure of the fourth estate. They could not allow the nobles to be expropriated without being anxious for themselves, for they owned a considerable part of the estates of the nobility, and in virtue of so doing levied seigniorial dues upon their peasants. Their permanent committees and National Guards at once set to work to restore order. Circulars were sent round to the parish priests requesting them to recommend calm. "Let us be chary," said the appeal of the Dijon committee, dated July 24, "of setting an example of licence to which we may all fall victims." But force was brought to bear without delay. In the Mâconnais and Beaujolais, where seventy-two country-houses had been burnt, repression was swift and vigorous. On July 29 a band of peasants was defeated near the Château of Cormatin and lost twenty killed and sixty prisoners. Another band was defeated near Cluny and lost a hundred killed and a hundred and seventy prisoners. The permanent committee of Mâcon turned itself into a court of justice and condemned twenty rioters to death. In this province of Dauphiné, where the union of the three orders had been preserved intact, the disturbances had definitely assumed the character of a class war. Peasants and workmen made common cause against the middle classes and their allies the nobles. The National Guard of Lyons lent its support to the

51

National Guards of Dauphiné against the insurgents, with whom the workmen of Lyons were in sympathy.

The Assembly looked on in alarm at the terrible outburst which it had been unable to foresee. At first its only thought was to organize repression, and it was not the privileged orders, but the deputies of the third estate who were most ready to urge severity. The Abbé Barbotin, one of those democratic priests who detested the bishops, wrote anxious and threatening letters from Versailles at the end of July to the Capuchin who succeeded him in his cure in Hainaut: "Impress upon them strongly that no society can subsist without obedience." According to him, it was the aristocrats who were stirring up the people: "None of this started until our enemies at court were scattered." It was obviously the *émigrés*, the friends of the Count of Artois and the Queen, who were revenging themselves for their discomfiture by letting loose these poor wretches against property! How many deputies of the third estate shared the opinion of this obscure priest? On August 3 Salomon, the secretary of the committee appointed to propose what measures were to be taken, could do nothing but violently denounce those responsible for the disorder and propose indiscriminate repression, without a word of pity for the sufferings of the wretched poor or the slightest promise for the future. If the Assembly had followed the advice of this hard-hearted landowner, it would have created a dangerous situation. The King would have had to take in hand a policy of ruthless general repression. This would have restored to him the means of checking the Revolution. And, on the other hand, it would have placed an impassable gulf between the middle classes and the peasantry. Under cover of the civil war, which would go on for a long time, the old regime would have been able to establish itself permanently.

The liberal nobles, both more politic and more generous than the middle classes, realized that a way had to be found out of this quandary. One of them, the Vicomte de Noailles, Lafayette's brother-in-law, proposed on the evening of August 4 that, in order to induce the peasants to lay down their arms, the following measures should be taken:

1. A proclamation should be issued stating that henceforward "taxes shall be paid by every individual in the kingdom in proportion to his income." This involved the suppression of all fiscal exemptions.

2. "All feudal dues shall be redeemable by the communities" (that is, by the communes) "for a money payment or commuted at a fair valuation." This involved the suppression of seigniorial dues in return for an indemnity.

3. "Seigniorial corvées, serfdom, and other forms of personal servitude shall be abolished without compensation."

Thus Noailles divided the feudal system into two parts. All personal burdens were to be abolished outright. All burdens on property were to be redeemable. Men would be set free, but the land retained its burdens.

The Duc d'Aiguillon, one of the greatest names and richest landowners in the kingdom, warmly seconded Noailles's propositions: "The people is at last trying to cast off a yoke which has weighed upon it for so many centuries past; and we must confess that, though this insurrection must be condemned, like all violent acts of aggression, an excuse can be found for it in the vexations of which the people has been the victim." This noble language aroused deep emotion, but at this pathetic moment a deputy of the third estate, an economist who had been the collaborator and friend of Turgot, Dupont of Nemours, once more called for severe measures. The nobles were accessible to pity; this bourgeois censured the inaction of the authorities, and spoke of sending orders to the local tribunals to act with severity.

But the impetus had been given. An obscure Breton deputy, Leguen de Kerangal, who had lived in country fashion in the little town where he was a linen-draper, rose and related the sorrows of the country people with an eloquence touching in its simplicity: "Let us be just, gentlemen; let them bring to us here those title-deeds which are an outrage, not only to our sense of shame, but to our very humanity. Let them bring us those title-deeds which humiliate the human race by demanding that men should be harnessed to the plough like beasts of burden. Let them bring us the title-deeds which oblige men to spend the night beating ponds to prevent the frogs from disturbing the sleep of their pleasure-loving lords. Which of us, gentlemen, in this enlightened century, would not make an expiatory pyre of these infamous parchments and set fire to it in order to sacrifice them upon the altar of the fatherland? You will not restore calm to a distracted France, gentlemen, until you have promised the people that you will commute for a money payment, redeemable at will, all feudal dues whatsoever, the slightest traces of which give the people just cause for complaint and will be abolished by the laws you are about to promulgate." It was certainly a bold act to justify the burning of the records before an assembly of landowners, but the conclusion was moderate, since on the whole the Breton orator accepted the redemption of those dues of which he proclaimed the injustice.

This redemption was reassuring to the deputies. The sacrifice demanded of them was more apparent than real. They would continue to collect their rents, or their equivalent. They would lose nothing, or hardly anything, by the operation, and would gain by the recovery of their popularity with the mass of the peasants. Then, having grasped the clever manœuvre of the minority of the nobles, they gave themselves up to enthusiasm. The deputies of the provinces and towns, the priests, and the nobles came in turn to sacrifice their ancient privileges "on the altar of the nation." The clergy renounced their tithes, the nobles their rights over hunting and fishing, warrens and dovecots, and their courts of justice; the middle classes renounced their special exemptions. This imposing renunciation of the past lasted all night. Before dawn a new France had come into being under the urgent pressure of the poorest classes.

Territorial and political unity had at last been achieved. In future there would be no more *pays d'États* or *pays d'élections*, no more provinces "reputed foreign," no more internal dues and tolls, no more regions governed by customary law and regions governed by Roman law. There would no longer be Provençals and Dauphinois, a Breton people and a people of Béarn. In the France of the future there would be nothing but Frenchmen, subject to the same law, with all professions open to them, and paying the same taxes. The Constituent Assembly was soon to abolish nobiliary titles and coats of arms, even the decorations of the ancient royal orders of the Saint-Esprit and of St. Louis. A nation which had been confined for centuries within narrow castes was suddenly levelled to a state of equality.

The provinces and towns eagerly sanctioned the sacrifice of their ancient franchises, which were often, moreover, no more than high-sounding and empty words. Nobody, or hardly anybody, regretted the old local particularism. On the contrary! At the height of the Great Fear, in order to defend themselves at once against the "brigands" and the aristocrats, the towns of one and the same province had promised one another mutual help and support. From November 1789 onwards these federations sprang up one after another, in Franche-Comté, Dauphiné, and Rouergue. Next came federations between province and province, splendid celebrations, partly of a military and partly of a civil character, at which the delegates of the National Guards, together with representatives of the regular army, solemnly swore to renounce their ancient privileges, to uphold the new order of things, to repress disorder, to see that the laws were carried out—to form, in fact, for the future one great family of brothers. Such was the federation between the Bretons and the Angevins at Pontivy, from January 15 to 19, that of Franche-Comté, Burgundy, Alsace, and

Champagne at Dôle on February 12, carried out amid a patriotic exalta-
tion which assumed a religious character. Next all these local federations
were fused in the great National Federation which took place in Paris on
the Champ de Mars on July 14, 1790, the anniversary of the capture of
the Bastille.

More than five hundred spectators found places in a huge amphitheatre of earth and turf, erected by the voluntary labour of Parisians of
all classes, from monks and actors to butchers and coalmen, and they
applauded ecstatically the delegates of the National Guards of the eighty-
three departments and the troops of the line. Talleyrand, Bishop of Autun,
surrounded by the sixty almoners of the districts of Paris, in tricolour
albs, said mass at the altar of the nation; after which Lafayette, in the
name of all, took an oath not only to maintain the Constitution, but "to
protect the safety of persons and property, the free circulation of corn
and food-stuffs, and the collection of the public taxes in whatever form
they may exist." The whole company repeated: "I swear to do so!" The
King in turn swore to respect the Constitution and see that the laws were
carried out. The crowd dispersed through the rain, happy, though soaked
to the skin, singing "*Ça ira!*"

These good souls thought that the Revolution had ended in a state of
brotherhood. But it was a fallacious illusion. The festival was that of the
National Guards, not of the whole people. The very form of the oath which
they had sworn showed that order was not secure, that there were malcontents of both parties on the horizon: on the one hand the expropriated
aristocrats, and on the other hand the mass of the peasants.

The latter had at first rejoiced at the abolition of tithes and feudal
servitude. After the resolutions of August 4 they had stopped burning
country-houses. They took at its face value the opening phrase of the
decree: "The National Assembly totally abolishes the feudal regime,"
without noticing the provisions by which the collection of rents continued
indefinitely until such time as they should be redeemed. As the arrival of
officers with distress-warrants brought it home to them that they were
bound as before to pay their rents in kind (*champarts* and *terrages*),
rents in cash, transfer dues, and even lay tithes, they were disagreeably
surprised. They could not understand why, when they were dispensed from
the obligation of redeeming the ecclesiastical tithes, they should still be
obliged to compensate their lay lords. In some places they banded themselves together and refused all further payments, accusing the middle
classes, many of whom owned fiefs, of having deceived and betrayed them.
The accusation was to a certain extent justified. The sacrifices accepted in

55

the contagious enthusiasm of the memorable session of August 4 had left regrets in the hearts of many deputies. "I have drunk my fill of vexation since August 4," wrote Barbotin, the priest, naively, for he regretted his tithes, and realized, not without painful anxiety, that he was in future to become a creditor of the State—a State on the verge of bankruptcy. There were many Barbotins, even among the third estate, whose inner voice began to tell them that they had been foolish. A reactionary spirit could be detected in the laws implementing the resolutions, which had as their object to regulate the procedure for the redemption of feudal dues. The Assembly was obviously endeavouring to modify in practice the scope of the great measure which it had been forced to vote in a hurry in the sinister glare of the burning châteaux. It assumed that feudal dues, as a whole, were the result of a supposed bargain in the past between the tenants and their lords, involving the cession of the land. It admitted without proof that the landowner had originally owned the holdings of his peasants. Better still, it exempted the landowners from producing proof that these agreements between them and their peasants had really existed. Forty years' possession sufficed to legalize ownership. It was for those from whom payment was due to show proof that they owed nothing. But such proof was impossible. Moreover, the procedure for redemption was so arranged that, even had the peasants been willing, they would not, as a matter of fact, have been able to carry it into effect. All the peasants of a fief were declared jointly responsible for the debt due to the feudal lord. "No debtor having joint obligations can discharge these unless all his co-debtors do so with him, or unless he pays for them all." What is more, the law laid down that no fixed charge or obligation should be redeemed unless the casual dues were redeemed at the same time; that is to say, the dues which would have accrued in case of transfer by sale or otherwise. Not only did the obligation of redemption keep all the peasants under the feudal yoke indefinitely, unless they were in easy circumstances, but the conditions attached to redemption were impracticable even for those who had a little cash in hand. Finally, the law did not compel the landowners to accept redemption, nor, on the other hand, could they compel the peasant to carry it into effect. We can understand why one historian, M. Doniol, has even asked himself whether the Constituent Assembly sincerely desired the abolition of the feudal system. "The feudal forms disappeared," he says, "but the effects of feudalism would take a long time to die out, and would continue to exist owing to the difficulty of escaping from them; and thus the interests of the landowners would be maintained without any apparent breach of the pledges of August 4."

It is possible that the Constituent Assembly reckoned upon this, but events were to upset their calculations. The peasants again began to form themselves into bands. They sent violent petitions to Paris against the resolutions, and in more than one canton they stopped paying the dues still legally in force till such time as their claims should be met. Their sporadic resistance lasted three years. The disturbances to which it led enabled M. Taine to represent France at that period as given over to anarchy. If there was anarchy, the Assembly was largely responsible for it, for it did nothing to satisfy the legitimate claims of the peasants. It maintained its class legislation up to the very last day of its sessions. Thanks to the National Guards in the towns, who were for the most part middle class, thanks, too, to the lack of agreement among the peasants, it managed to prevent the disorders from degenerating into such a widespread insurrection as that of July 1789; but it could never restore peace entirely. The municipalities of the country districts and country towns were sometimes openly reluctant to lend their support to the king's agents. Certain of them ceased levying the feudal dues owing from the peasants on the ecclesiastical domains confiscated by the nation. "And thus," says Jaurès, "they created a terrible precedent, a sort of legal system of complete abolition, which the peasants next applied to the dues owed by them to their lay lords." It is true that in those regions where the upper middle class was supreme, as in Cher and Indre, the feudal rents continued to be exacted and collected. It seems, indeed, that such was most frequently the case. The department for administering the national domains proved very severe in collecting the seigniorial dues belonging to the nation.

The total abolition of the last feudal rents was only gradually effected, by the votes of the Legislative Assembly, after war had been declared on Austria and after the fall of royalty; and by the votes of the Convention after the fall of the Gironde.

CHAPTER VI

Lafayette as Mayor of the Palace

RANK based upon birth and custom is more permanent than that based upon law. The very bourgeois who had brought about the Revolution in order to make themselves equal to the nobles continued for a long time to choose nobles as their guides and leaders. The Marquis de Lafayette was their idol throughout almost the whole duration of the Constituent Assembly.

Possessing a splendid fortune, which he used generously, passionately fond of popularity, young and attractive, Lafayette thought himself pre-destined to play the same part in the French Revolution as his friend Washington had played in the American Revolution. He had been the first to demand the States General in the assembly of notables summoned by Calonne. His house had been the centre of resistance to the Court at the time when the parlements and the Patriot party were struggling hand in hand against the edicts of Brienne and Lamoignon. Louis XVI had relieved him of his military command as a punishment for having insti-gated the protest of the provincial assembly of Auvergne. Immediately af-ter the other orders had joined the third estate, he hastened to lay on the table of the Constituent Assembly a draft declaration of rights in imitation of the American Declaration. On July 8 he joined Mirabeau in demanding that the troops be sent away from Paris. On July 13 the Assembly elected him as its vice-president. Two days later the permanent committee in Paris, on the motion of the district of the Filles Saint-Thomas, inspired by Brissot, appointed him commandant of the newly-formed National Guard. He now had force in his hands, the only force that counts in time of revolu-tion: namely, revolutionary force. In order to increase its power he was careful to associate the middle-class companies with the paid troops in barracks, among whom were included the old Gardes Françaises. Order depended upon him, and, in consequence, so did the fate of the Assembly and the monarchy. For the moment his ambition did not go beyond mak-ing himself felt to be indispensable as mediator and intermediary between the King, the Assembly, and the people.

58

Louis XVI was afraid of him, and treated him with respect. He certainly thought he was pleasing him when on August 4 he included in the ministry three staunch friends of his: the two Archbishops of Bordeaux and of Vienne, Champion de Cicé and Lefranc de Pompignan, and the Comte de Saint-Priest, who was especially intimate with Lafayette, whom he kept informed of what went on at the Council. "The fact that I actually choose them from among your assembly," wrote Louis XVI to the deputies, "shows you my desire to maintain the most confident and friendly harmony with it." It looked as if an experiment in parliamentary government was beginning, as Lafayette desired. The whole problem now consisted in getting together a solid and trustworthy majority in the Assembly. Lafayette worked at this with a will. But he was no orator, and his official position often kept him in Paris. He could only pull wires in the background, through the agency of his friends, the most intimate of whom were Lally-Tollendal and Latour-Maubourg, both of them second-rate men.

Signs of a split in the Patriot party were already apparent during the discussion on the Declaration of Rights. Moderates like Malouet, formerly intendant of the fleet, and La Luzerne, Bishop of Langres, were alarmed at the disorders and considered the Declaration useless, if not dangerous. Others, like the Jansenist Camus, formerly an ecclesiastical lawyer, and the Abbé Grégoire, formerly parish priest at Embermesnil in Lorraine, would at least have liked to supplement it by a declaration of duties. They were overridden by a majority of only 140, influenced by the eloquence of Barnave.

The Declaration not only condemned the ancient abuses by implication, but formed a sort of catechism stating the philosophic basis of the new order of things.

Born in the heat of conflict, it sanctioned "resistance to oppression"— in other words, it justified the revolt which had just triumphed, heedless of the fact that it justified other revolts in advance. It proclaimed the natural and imprescriptible rights of liberty, equality, property, the vote, control of taxation and laws, the jury, etc. It omitted the right of association, out of hatred for the orders and corporations. It substituted the majesty of the people for the majesty of the King, and the authority of the law for arbitrary power.

It was the work of the middle classes, and bore their imprint. It proclaimed equality, but it was a limited equality, subordinated to "social utility." The only equality which it expressly recognized was equality as regards taxation and before the law, and the throwing open of professions to all, with ability as the sole test. It forgot that ability is itself conditioned by wealth, which is in turn conditioned by birth, owing to the right of inheritance.

Property was proclaimed as an imprescriptible right, regardless of those who possess none, or of feudal and ecclesiastical property, part of which had just been confiscated or abolished.

Finally, the Declaration belongs to an age when religion still appeared indispensable to society. It placed itself under the auspices of the Supreme Being. To other forms of worship it granted mere toleration within the limits of public order as established by law. Mirabeau's paper, the *Courrier de Provence*, protested indignantly in the following terms: "We cannot disguise how pained we are at the fact that the National Assembly, instead of eradicating the germ of intolerance, has, so to speak, placed it in reserve in a declaration of the rights of man. Instead of proclaiming religious liberty unequivocally, it has declared that the *manifestation* of opinions of this kind can be interfered with; that this liberty may be checked by a *public order;* that it may be restricted by *law;* all of which are false, dangerous, and intolerant principles, by which a Dominic or a Torquemada supported his blood-thirsty doctrines." In fact, Catholicism preserved its character as the predominant religion. It was the only one which was a charge on the budget, and whose ceremonies were conducted in public. Protestants and Jews had to content themselves with worshipping in private and concealment. The Jews of the east were regarded as foreigners and were not placed on the same footing as Frenchmen till September 27, 1791, when the Assembly was about to disperse.

Not only did the Declaration of Rights fail to grant complete and unreserved religious liberty, but it granted the liberty of the press only within certain limitations. It made it subject to the caprice of the legislator. Such as it was, however, it was a magnificent page of public law, the source of all the political progress which was to be achieved in the world in the following century. It should not be judged with reference to the future, but in comparison with the past.

The discussion of the Constitution began immediately after the voting of the Declaration, which served as its preamble. The divisions now became sharper and more irremediable. Mounier and Lally-Tollendal, who were responsible for the report of the Constitutional Committee, proposed to create an upper chamber side by side with the popular one, and to provide the king with an absolute veto on the deliberations of the two Chambers. They were inspired by ideas of social conservatism. Mounier had expressed a fear lest the abolition of feudal property might strike a serious blow at all forms of property. For putting down peasant risings and defending order he wanted to restore the necessary force to the executive—that is, to the king. This was also the opinion of Necker and of Champion de Cicé, the Keeper of the Seals. They advised the King to postpone his acceptance of the resolutions of August 4 and the following days and prompted him to sign a message in which these resolutions were criticized minutely and at length. This was tantamount to calling in question the whole work of pacification which had been attempted since the Great Fear. It involved a risk that the conflagration, which had been quenched with difficulty, might blaze up again. It held out a hope of revenge to the feudal order. The absolute veto was, to use Sieys's phrase, a *lettre de cachet* directed against the general will, and would place the Revolution at the mercy of the Court. As for the Senate, it would be the refuge and stronghold of aristocracy, especially if the king were allowed to choose its members as he desired.

The Breton deputies' club, which had gradually been swelled by the most active representatives of the other provinces, decided to oppose the plan of the moderates at all costs. Chapelier organized the resistance of Brittany. A threatening address opposing the veto was sent up from Rennes. Mirabeau, who kept a whole staff of publicists in his service, stirred up the districts of Paris. The Palais Royal fulminated against it. On August 30 and 31 Saint-Huruge and Camille Desmoulins tried to lead the Parisians to Versailles to demand that immediate sanction be given to the decrees of August 4, to protest against the veto and the second chamber, and to bring the King and the Assembly back to Paris, so as to remove them from the influence of the Aristocrats. The National Guard quelled the tumult only with great difficulty.

Lafayette, whose arbitration was requested by both sides, tried to find a modus vivendi, for he had friends in both camps. He brought together the leading men, either at his own house or at that of Jefferson, the American ambassador: on the one hand, Mounier, Lally, and Bergasse, and on the other, Adrien Duport, Alexandre and Charles Lameth, and Barnave. He proposed that for the absolute veto of the king should be substituted a suspensive veto, valid for the duration of two legislatures, that the initiative in legislation should be reserved to the popularly elected chamber, and finally that the duration of the upper chamber's veto on the deliberations of the lower chamber should be limited to a year. It was impossible to come to an agreement. Mounier wanted a hereditary upper chamber, or at any rate one with life members. Lafayette proposed that it should be elected by the provincial assemblies for a term of six years. As for the "triumvirate," Lameth, Duport, and Barnave, they did not want a second chamber at all; they refused to divide the legislative power for fear of weakening it and were afraid of restoring the higher nobility under another name. They knew that in England the Lords were at the mercy of the king. The meeting broke up in an atmosphere of bad feeling. Barnave broke with Mounier, whose lieutenant he had hitherto been. "I have failed to please either party," wrote Lafayette to Maubourg, "and am left with vain regrets and racking anxieties." He imagined that the Lameth brothers, who were soldiers and noblemen like himself, were jealous of him and were trying to supplant him in the command of the National Guard. He believed that the disorders in Paris were surreptitiously fomented by the Duke of Orleans, of whom the *factieux* (factionists, sectaries), as the Breton deputies were now called in private, were supposed to be merely the instruments.

The second chamber was rejected by the Assembly on September 10 by the huge majority of 849 to 89, with 122 abstentions. The provincial nobles had voted on the side of the third estate and lower clergy, out of distrust of the higher nobility. But on the following day the suspensive veto was granted to the king, by a majority of 673 to 325, for the duration of two legislatures; that is, for at least four years. Barnave and Mirabeau had influenced the voting; the former by negotiating with Necker, who promised that the measures of August 4 should be sanctioned, and the latter because he did not wish the way leading to the ministry to be closed to him. Robespierre, Pétion, Buzot and Prieur, deputy for Marne, maintained an uncompromising resistance to the end. Having obtained the vote, Necker was unable to keep the promise he had made to Barnave. The King still evaded giving his sanction to the measures of August 4 and the Declaration of Rights under a variety of pretexts. The Bretons considered that they had been tricked, and the agitation began again more violently than ever.

In spite of the sensational defeat which it had sustained in the matter of the second chamber, Mounier's party gained strength daily. By the end of August it had formed a coalition with a large section of the right. A directing committee of thirty-two members had been formed to continue the work of resistance, on which Maury, Cazalès d'Esprémesnil, and Montlosier sat beside Mounier, Bergasse, Malouet, Bonnal, Virieu, and Clermont-Tonnerre. This committee resolved to ask the King to transfer the government and Assembly to Soissons or Compiègne in order to protect it against the schemes of the Palais Royal. Montmorin and Necker supported the request. But the King, who possessed a certain passive courage, felt a sort of shame at leaving Versailles. The only concession he would make to the "monarchists" (*monarchiens*) was to send for cavalry and infantry detachments towards the end of September, among them the Flanders regiment. The summoning of the troops was construed by the left as a challenge. Even Lafayette remonstrated. He was astonished at not having been consulted before a step was taken which would revive the agitation in Paris.

The capital was so short of bread that people were fighting for it at the doors of the bakeries. The artisans were beginning to suffer from the departure of the nobles for foreign parts. Hairdressers', bootmakers', and tailors' assistants who were out of work gathered to demand work or an increase of wages. Deputation after deputation was received by the Commune. Marat, who had just started his *Ami du peuple,* and Loustalot, who was editing the *Révolutions de Paris,* fanned the flames. The district assemblies and the Commune supported Lafayette in demanding that the troops be sent away. The "Breton" deputies, Chapelier, Barnave, Alexandre, Lameth, and Duport renewed this petition to Saint-Priest, the Minister of the Interior. The old Gardes Françaises were already talking of reporting at Versailles and again taking up their posts in the King's guard. Lafayette kept sending in alarming reports.

But the ministers and monarchists thought themselves masters of the situation, because the Assembly had just voted Mounier into the presidential chair, as if parliamentary power were of any use in times of revolution, unless backed up by popular force. Public opinion, however, was rebellious, and Lafayette, who had bayonets at his command, was in the sulks. In order to appease Lafayette and win him over once more, Montmorin, the Minister for Foreign Affairs, offered him the constable's sword, and even the title of lieutenant-general. He disdainfully refused, adding: "If the King is afraid of a riot, let him come to Paris; there he will be in safety, surrounded by the National Guard."

A final imprudence hastened the explosion. On October 1 the Gardes du Corps gave a banquet in the opera-house of the palace to welcome the Flanders regiment. The King and the Queen, the latter with the Dauphin in her arms, came to greet the guests, while the band struck up Grétry's air, "*Ô Richard; ô mon roi! l'univers t'abandonne!*" Inflamed by music and wine, the guests burst into a storm of applause, and, trampling the national cockade underfoot, assumed the white cockade or the black (the Queen's colours). They deliberately omitted to drink the health of the nation.

When these events were reported in Paris, on October 3, by Gorsas's

63

Courrier, the Palais Royal was indignant. On Sunday, October 4, the *Chronique de Paris* and the *Ami du peuple* denounced the royalist plot, the obvious aim of which was to overthrow the Constitution before it was completed. The King's repeated refusal to give his sanction to the measures of August 4 and to the articles of the Constitution already voted were even better evidence of the plot than the banquet at which the nation had been flouted. Marat called upon the districts to arm and exhorted them to fetch their cannon from the Hôtel de Ville and march on Versailles. The districts held meetings and sent deputations to the Commune. On the motion of Danton, the district of the Cordeliers called upon the Commune to give Lafayette strict orders to wait upon the National Assembly and the King on the following day, Monday, and demand that the troops be sent back.

On October 5 a crowd of women of all classes broke into the Hôtel de Ville, for it was feebly defended by the National Guards, who were in sympathy with the rising. Maillard, the beadle, one of those who had taken part in the victorious attack on the Bastille, placed himself at their head and led them to Versailles, where they arrived during the afternoon. The National Guard moved off in turn a few hours later. The grenadiers urged Lafayette to start for Versailles and threatened him with hanging, till he obtained the sanction of the Commune for yielding to the popular wish. He started, he said, because he was afraid that if the rising took place without him, it would be turned to the profit of the Duke of Orleans. He arrived at Versailles during the night.

Neither the Court nor the ministers had been prepared for this irruption. The King was out hunting, but the left wing of the Assembly was presumably aware of what was going to happen. On that very morning, October 5, a lively debate had taken place in the Assembly with regard to the King's fresh refusal to accede to their request that he sanction the decrees. Robespierre and Barnave had asserted that the King had no right to oppose the Constitution, for the constituent power was superior to the king. He had, as it were, been recalled to existence by the Constitution, and could use his right of veto only in regard to the ordinary laws; but the constitutional laws were by definition beyond his province and ought not to be sanctioned by him, but accepted purely and simply. The Assembly adopted this theory, which traced its origin straight back to Rousseau's *Social Contract,* and decided, on the motion of Mirabeau and Prieur of Marne, that Mounier, the president, should at once make fresh representations to the King and demand his immediate acceptance. Such was the position of affairs when, during the afternoon, a deputation of women from Paris appeared at the bar. Their spokesman, the beadle Maillard, complained of the price of food and the machinations of speculators and then of the insult offered to the national cockade. Robespierre supported Maillard, and the Assembly decided to send a delegation to the King to inform him of the complaints of the people of Paris.

Brawling had already broken out in front of the palace between the National Guard of Versailles and the Gardes du Corps. The Flanders regiment, which was drawn up in battle array on the parade ground, showed by its attitude that it did not intend to fire upon the demonstrators and began to fraternize with them.

The King, who had at last returned from the hunt, held a council. Saint-Priest, the spokesman of the monarchists, considered that the King ought to retire to Rouen rather than give his sanction to the decrees under pressure of violence. Orders were given to begin the preparations for departure. But Necker and Montmorin persuaded him to reconsider the decision at which he had arrived. They pointed out that the Treasury was empty and that the shortage of food made it impossible for them to feed a body of troops of any size. Finally they added that the King's departure would leave the way clear for the Duke of Orleans. Louis XVI yielded to their arguments. With despair in his heart he gave his sanction to the decrees. Lafayette arrived about midnight with the National Guard of Paris. He waited upon the King and offered him his services and regrets, which were more or less sincere. The sentries outside the palace were chosen from the Paris National Guard, those inside being still chosen from the Gardes du Corps.

At dawn on the morning of the 6th, while Lafayette was having a little rest, a troop of those who had come from Paris made their way into the palace by a badly guarded door. A Garde du Corps tried to drive them back and fired. A man fell in the Cour de Marbre. Upon this the crowd rushed the Gardes du Corps, who were forced back into their guard-room. The mob invaded the courtyards and staircases. The Queen had to take refuge hurriedly in the King's apartments, only partly dressed. Several of the Gardes du Corps were killed and their heads stuck on the ends of pikes.

In order to put an end to the massacre, the King, accompanied by the Queen and the Dauphin, had to consent to appear with Lafayette on the balcony overlooking the Cour de Marbre. He was greeted with a shout of "The King to Paris!" He promised to go to the capital and that very night slept at the Tuileries. The Assembly passed a decree stating itself to be inseparable from the king, and a few days later went to take up its quarters in Paris.

This transfer was even more important than the capture of the Bastille. From that time onwards the King and the Assembly were in the hands of Lafayette and the people of Paris. The Revolution was securely established. The Constitution had been "accepted," not sanctioned, and no longer depended upon the King's absolute power. The monarchists, who had organized the resistance since the night of August 4, had lost the day. Their leader, Mounier, resigned the presidency of the Assembly and retired to Dauphiné, which he tried to excite to revolt. But, meeting with nothing but coldness and hostility, he became discouraged and soon went abroad. His friends, like Lally-Tollendal and Bergasse, met with no greater success in rousing the provinces against this fresh act of violence on the part of Paris. A second batch of *émigrés*, this time composed of men who had started by working for the Revolution, went to join the first, though without mingling with them.

Lafayette manœuvred very skilfully so as to reap the benefit of a day in which, to all appearances at least, he had only taken part under compulsion. At his instigation the Commune and districts made repeated protestations of loyalty to the monarch in their addresses. The scenes of horror which had taken place on the morning of October 6 were repudiated, and an investiagtion of the conduct of those responsible for them was opened. The Court of the Châtelet, before which it was held, spun it out for a very long time and tried to turn it against the Duke of Orleans and Mirabeau; that is to say, against Lafayette's rivals. On October 7 the Patriot Gonchon, an agent of Lafayette's, organized a demonstration of marketwomen, who marched to the Tuileries to cheer the King and Queen and ask them to take up their permanent abode in Paris. Marie Antoinette had become so unaccustomed to hearing shouts of *"Vive la Reine!"* that she was moved to tears and that very evening gave artless expression to her joy in a letter to her confidant and mentor, Mercy-Argenteau, the Austrian ambassador. Word was sent .round to the newspapers to repeat that the King was staying in Paris voluntarily, of his own free will. Measures were taken against "pamphleteers" (*libellistes*); that is to say, independent publicists. A writ of seizure—that is to say, a warrant for his arrest—was issued against Marat on October 8. After the death of the baker, François, who was massacred by the crowd for refusing bread to a woman, the Assembly voted that martial law should be proclaimed in view of the riots (October 21).

Lafayette waited assiduously upon the King and Queen. He assured them that the rising had been stirred up in spite of his efforts and aimed at him by certain of the *factieux*, whom he named. He implicated their leader, the Duke of Orleans, in the charge. He overawed the Duke, and on October 7, at an interview which he had with him at the house of the Marquise de Coigny, he obtained from the weak prince a promise that he would leave France, on the pretext of a diplomatic mission to England. After some hesitation the Duke started for London about the middle of October. This flight discredited him, and he was no longer taken seriously even by his former friends. "They allege that I belong to his party," said Mirabeau, who had tried to prevent him from leaving; "I would not have him for my valet."

Having thus got rid of his most dangerous rival, Lafayette handed the King a memorandum in which he tried to prove to him that he had everything to gain from frankly reconciling himself to the Revolution and severing all connexion with the *émigrés* and partisans of the old regime. A royal democracy, he said, far from placing restrictions upon his power, would increase it. He would no longer have to struggle against the parlements and provincial particularism. In future he would hold his authority by the free consent of his subjects. The suppression of orders and corporations would be to his advantage. Nothing would now come between his person and the French people. Lafayette added that he would defend royalty against the *factieux*. He would be answerable for order, but in return for this he asked for full confidence.

Louis XVI had not conceded anything. In order to gain time he resorted to artifice. He accepted Lafayette's offer, while at the same time sending a secret agent, the Abbé de Fonbrune, to Madrid to interest His Catholic Majesty, his cousin, in his cause; the Abbé handed the King of Spain a declaration stating in advance that all Louis XVI might do and sign under pressure from the revolutionaries would be null and void. Louis pledged himself to accept and follow Lafayette's advice, and, as a mark of confidence, invested him on October 10 with the command of the regular troops within a radius of fifteen miles of the capital. On October 7 the Comte d'Estaing assured the Queen that Lafayette had vowed to him that the atrocities of the previous day had made him a royalist, and added that Lafayette had begged him to persuade the King to have entire confidence in him.

Lafayette had a grudge against certain of the ministers for not following his advice before the rising. Towards the middle of October he tried to get rid of them. He had an interview with Mirabeau at the house of the Comtesse d'Aragon. The leaders of the left—Dupont, Alexandre Lameth, Barnave, and Laborde—were present. The matter under discussion was the formation of a new ministry, in which should be included friends of Lafayette's, such as Talon, the *lieutenant criminel* (that is, head of the criminal court) at the Châtelet, and Sémonville, a counsellor of the Parlement. Champion de Cicé, the Keeper of the Seals, conducted the intrigue. Lafayette offered Mirabeau fifty thousand livres, to help him pay his debts, and an embassy. Mirabeau accepted the money, but refused the embassy. He wanted to be a minister. The public got wind of these negotiations. The Assembly, which despised Mirabeau as much as it feared him, cut them short by passing a decree on November 7 forbidding the king in future to choose his ministers from among its members. "If," said Lanjuinais, "an eloquent man of genius can carry the Assembly away when he is merely on an equality with all its members, what would happen if he combined with his eloquence the authority of a minister?"

Mirabeau in his annoyance embarked upon a fresh intrigue with Monsieur, the Count of Provence, the King's brother. This time the idea was to get Louis XVI to leave Paris, his escape being covered by a corps of royalist volunteers, the recruiting of which was entrusted to the Marquis de Favras. But Favras was denounced by two of his agents, who told Lafayette that there was a plan to kill him and Bailly. When Favras was arrested, a letter compromising Monsieur was found on him. Lafayette chivalrously returned it to its writer and did not divulge its existence. Monsieur came down to the Commune and read a speech composed by Mirabeau disowning Favras, who allowed himself to be sentenced to death without breaking silence with regard to his exalted accomplices. Marie Antoinette granted a pension to his widow.

This abortive plot still further increased Lafayette's importance. The "mayor of the palace" as Mirabeau called him, represented to the King that he ought to put an end to the hopes of the aristocrats by a decisive step. Louis XVI docilely went down to the Assembly on February 4, 1790, and read a speech composed by Necker under Lafayette's inspiration. He declared that he and the Queen had accepted the new order of things without any mental reservations, and called upon all Frenchmen to do likewise. The deputies, full of enthusiasm, took the oath of fidelity to the nation, the law, and the king; and all the dignitaries of state, including ecclesiastics, had to repeat the same oath.

The *émigrés* were indignant at being disowned by the King. The Count of Artois, who had taken refuge at Turin with his father-in-law, the King of Sardinia, had correspondents in the provinces through whose agency he attempted to stir up insurrection. He was not very religious and did not at first realize what a valuable support religious sentiment might be to his cause if properly exploited. But his friend the Comte de Vaudreuil, who was staying in Rome, undertook to open his eyes. "Eastertide," he wrote on March 20, 1790, "is a period which bishops and priests can use to great advantage in bringing back those who have erred to religion and fidelity to the King. I hope that they will be sufficiently alive to their own interest and that of the public weal not to neglect this occasion, and if the steps they take are well concerted, success seems to me certain." This advice was carried out. Preparations were made for a widespread insurrection in the south. The presence of a small nucleus of Protestants at the foot of the Cévennes and in the country regions of Quercy made it possible to represent the revolutionaries as the allies or prisoners of heretics. The nomination of the pastor Rabaut de Saint-Étienne as president of the Constituent Assembly on March 16 and, above all, the refusal of the Assembly on April 13 to recognize Catholicism as the State religion were made the most of. Copies of a vehement protest by the right wing of the Assembly were distributed. Froment, an agent of the Count of Artois, set the confraternities of penitents to work. At Montauban the vicars-general ordered forty hours' prayer in view of the perils which threatened religion. The royalist municipality of that town chose May 10, Rogation Sunday, for proceeding to take the inventories of the suppressed religious houses. The women formed a crowd before the Church of the Cordeliers. A struggle ensued in which the Protestants got the worse of it. Many of them were killed or wounded, and the rest disarmed and forced to beg for pardon kneeling on the blood-stained pavement of the churches. But the National Guards of Toulouse and Bordeaux hurried to the spot and restored order.

At Nîmes the disorders were even more serious. The royalist companies of the National Guard, called *Cébets*, or onion-eaters, sported the white cockade and afterwards a red favour. There was brawling on the first of May. On June 13, after a struggle, Froment occupied a tower on the ramparts and the Capuchin monastery. The Protestants and Patriots summoned to their aid the peasants of the Cévennes. The royalists were overwhelmed by superior numbers, beaten, and massacred. There were some three hundred deaths in three days.

About the same time Avignon, which had shaken off the yoke of the Pope and, forming a revolutionary municipality, demanded reunion with France, was the scene of bloody events. Some aristocrats, who had been accused of making fun of the new municipal authorities, were acquitted by the court, but the patriots would not allow them to be released. On June 10 the companies of the National Guard who had papal sympathies revolted and seized a convent and the Hôtel de Ville. But the patriots, reinforced by peasants, made their way into the Palace of the Popes, drove out their opponents from the Hôtel de Ville, and indulged in terrible reprisals.

The King, who had disapproved of the attempt at counter-revolution in the south, saw in its failure still further reason for adopting the plan of action laid down for him by Lafayette in a fresh memorandum, which he handed him on April 16. He wrote with his own hand on this document: "I promise M. de Lafayette my entire confidence in all matters which may concern the establishment of the Constitution, my legitimate authority, as specified in the memorandum, and the return of public tranquillity." Lafayette had pledged himself to use all his influence to strengthen what remained of the royal authority. At the same time Mirabeau, through the agency of the Comte de La Marck, offered his services towards the same end. The King took him into his pay on May 10, allowing him 200,000 livres to pay his debts, 6000 livres a month, and promising him a million, to be paid at the close of the National Assembly. He tried to form a combination of Lafayette and Mirabeau, and to a certain extent succeeded.

Mirabeau was undoubtedly jealous of Lafayette and despised him. He pelted him with epigrams, calling him "Gilles César" or "Cromwell Grandison." He tried to detract from him and destroy his favour with the King in order to get rid of him, but at the same time flattered him and gave him constant promises of collaboration: "Be a Richelieu, dominating the Court in the interest of the nation," he wrote on June 1, 1790, "and you will reconstitute the monarchy, while increasing and consolidating public liberty. But Richelieu had his Capuchin Joseph; do you, then, also have your *Éminence grise* [1] or you will be ruined by making no attempt to save yourself. Your great qualities have need of my driving force; my driving force has need of your great qualities." Yet on that very day, in the first note which he composed for the Court, this cynical adventurer indicated what course of action it ought to follow so as to ruin the popularity of the man to whom he had no intention of acting as "*Émi-*

---

[1] *Éminence grise.* "His grey Eminency" was the nickname bestowed by his contemporaries upon the Capuchin friar Father Joseph (François Leclerc du Tremblay), who from 1612 to his death, in 1638, was the all-powerful confidant and agent of Richelieu.

nence grise." But Lafayette was under no illusions as to Mirabeau's morality.

They acted in concert to defend the royal prerogative when in May 1790, on the occasion of the imminent rupture between England and Spain, the Assembly was faced with the question of the right of deciding peace or war. Spain protested against the seizure by England of Nootka Sound on the Pacific coast, in what is now British Columbia. She called upon France for help in virtue of the Family Compact. The left was unwilling to see any more in this conflict than a counter-revolutionary intrigue, intended to draw France into a foreign war which would provide the King with a means of regaining his power. Barnave, the two Lameths, Robespierre, Volney, and Pétion denounced dynastic wars and secret diplomacy, demanded the revision of all the old alliances, and claimed that the representatives of the nation should have the sole right of declaring war, controlling diplomacy and concluding treaties. But Mirabeau, Lafayette, and all their partisans, Clermont-Tonnerre, Chapelier, Custine, the Duc du Châtelet, Dupont of Nemours, the Comte de Sérent, Virieu, and Cazalès, harped upon the patriotic string, denounced the ambition of England, and concluded in favour of allowing diplomacy to remain the king's especial province. They stressed the point that assemblies were composed of too many persons, and were too impressionable to exercise such a dangerous right as that of declaring war. In support of their opinion they cited the Swedish Senate and the Polish Diet, which had been corrupted by foreign gold; they insisted upon the necessity for secrecy and uttered warnings against the danger of isolating the king from the nation and turning him into a mere puppet with no prestige. They further pointed out that, according to the Constitution, no act of legislative body could be fully put into execution except by the king's sanction. The orators of the left rejoined that if the right of peace and war continued to be exercised by the king alone, "the whims of a mistress, the ambition of a minister, would decide the fate of the nation," as they had done before (d'Aiguillon); that they would always be having dynastic wars, that the king was merely the officer of the nation, whose duty it was to execute its will, and that the representatives of the country "would always have a direct and even a personal interest in preventing war." They made fun of diplomatic secrecy, denied that there was any analogy whatsoever between an assembly elected on a very broad franchise, such as that of France, and feudal assemblies such as the Polish Diet or the Swedish Senate. Many of them violently attacked the Family Compact and the Austrian Alliance

71

and recalled the dismal results of the Seven Years' War. They all denounced the snare in which the Anglo-Spanish conflict might involve the Revolution. "They want to prevent the assignats from meeting with favour, and the sale of the Church lands; that is the real cause of this war" (Charles Lameth).

During this great debate Paris was given over to violent agitation. A pamphlet inspired by the Lameth brothers, entitled: *The Comte de Mirabeau's Great Betrayal*, was being sold in the streets. Lafayette surrounded the assembly hall with an imposing array of troops. On the last day, Mirabeau seized the pretext of this ferment to make his famous retort to Barnave: "A few days ago they wanted to carry me, too, in triumph; and now they are crying *The Comte de Mirabeau's Great Betrayal* in the streets. I did not need this lesson to teach me that it is not far from the Capitol to the Tarpeian rock, but the man who is fighting for reason and country does not easily admit that he is beaten. Let those who for the last week have been forecasting my opinion without knowing what it was, who are at this moment misrepresenting my speech without having understood it, accuse me of burning incense to impotent idols at the moment of their overthrow, or of being the vile hireling of those whom I have never ceased to combat; let them denounce as an enemy of the Revolution one who has not perhaps been useless to it and who can find safety in it alone, however little it may conduce to his glory; let them abandon to the fury of the deluded populace one who for twenty years past has fought oppression of every sort, and who was talking to Frenchmen of liberty, the Constitution, and resistance when these vile slanderers were making a living out of all the prejudices which then prevailed. What matter? These attempts to strike at me from below will not check me in my career; I will say to them: 'Answer me if you can, and then slander me as much as you like.'" This superb audacity triumphed. That day Mirabeau earned the money of the Court. The Assembly was subjugated by his genius as an orator and would not let Barnave reply. It voted that the draft decree presented by Mirabeau should be given priority, and greeted with applause a short statement by Lafayette. But when the time came to vote upon the separate articles, the left once more regained the majority. It managed to carry amendments changing the sense of the decree. The king alone had the right to propose peace or war, after which the Assembly would give its decision. In case of imminent hostilities, the king would be bound to make known their causes and motives without delay. If the legislature were on vacation, it was to meet immediately and remain in permanent session. Treaties of peace, alliance, and commerce would be valid only after ratification by the legislature. Existing treaties were to remain in force provisionally, but a committee of the Assembly, known as the Diplomatic Committee, was appointed to revise them, bring them into harmony with the Constitution, and keep in touch with foreign affairs. Lastly, by a special article, the Assembly announced to the world that "the French nation renounced entering upon any war with a view to conquest, and would never use its forces against the liberty of any people."

The patriots hailed the passing of the decree as a triumph. "We shall not have war," wrote Thomas Lindet on leaving the session. Lindet was right. By the decree which had just been passed the exclusive control of foreign policy was taken out of the king's hands. In future he was obliged to share it with the representatives of the nation. But he owed it to Lafayette and Mirabeau that his prerogative had not been still more seriously impaired.

The great Feast of the Federation, presided over by Lafayette, was a striking demonstration of the immense popularity which he enjoyed; the members of the deputations kissed his hands, his coat, his boots, his horse's harness, and his very horse itself, and medals were struck bearing his effigy.

It was a splendid opportunity for Mirabeau to excite the King's jealousy of "this peerless man, the pet of the provinces." But Louis XVI and Marie Antoinette had also received the applause of the provincials. The democratic press noted with annoyance that the shouts of *"Vive le Roi!"* had drowned those of *"Vive l'Assemblée!"* and *"Vive la Nation!"* Louis XVI wrote to Mme de Polignac: "Believe me, Madame, all is not lost." The Duke of Orleans, who had come back from London specially to be present at the ceremony, had passed unnoticed.

If the Duke of Orleans was no longer to be feared, and if "all was not lost," this was to a large extent due to Lafayette. No doubt the King still had a grudge against him for his past rebellion and his present attachment to a constitutional regime, and had great hopes that a day would come when he would be able to dispense with Lafayette's services. Meanwhile he was all the more ready to avail himself of them, since Fonbrune, his secret agent, whom he had sent to Vienna to sound his brother-in-law the Emperor, informed him, about the middle of July, that for the moment he could not count upon the assistance of foreign powers.

Besides, Lafayette was still indispensable, for, in the disturbed state of the kingdom, he alone was able to maintain order. The incorrigible Count of Artois made another attempt to stir up revolt in the south after the

Feast of the Federation. His agents, priests like Canon de la Bastide de la Mollette, and the parish priest Claude Allier, or nobles like the mayor of Berrias, Malbosc, summoned the National Guards belonging to their party to the Château of Jalès, near the frontiers of the three departments of Gard, Ardèche, and Lozère, for August 17, 1790. Twenty thousand royalist National Guards appeared at the meeting-place bearing the cross as their standard. Before separating, the leaders who had organized the threatening demonstration formed a central committee whose task it was to co-ordinate their efforts. They next published a manifesto in which they declared "that they would not lay down their arms till they had reinstated the King in all his glory, the clergy in their property, the nobles in their honours, and the parlements in their ancient functions." The camp at Jalès remained in being for several months. It was not till February 1791 that it was dissolved by force. The Assembly sent three commissaries to pacify the district.

More serious, perhaps, than the plots of the aristocrats were the military mutinies. The officers, who were all nobles and nearly all aristocrats, could not bear their soldiers to frequent the clubs and fraternize with the National Guards, whom they despised. They showered punishments and ill-treatment upon soldiers of the Patriot party. They dismissed them from their corps with "yellow cartridges"; that is to say, in disgrace, so that they had difficulty in re-enlisting. At the same time, dressed up as soldiers in the uniform of the National Guards, they took a delight in slighting and offering provocation to the middle classes. The soldiers belonging to the Patriot party felt that popular sympathy was with them and soon got tired of being bullied by their leaders. They took the offensive in turn. They demanded their share of the funds of their corps, over which the officers had unlimited control. These funds were very often not in good order. The clerks drew upon them for their own personal needs. The request for an audit was met with punishment, and mutinies broke out everywhere.

At Toulon Admiral d'Albert prevented the workmen of the port from enlisting in the National Guard and wearing its cockade inside the arsenal. In November 30, 1789 he dismissed two foremen for this offense alone. On the following day the sailors and workmen rose in revolt, besieged his house with the aid of the National Guard, and finally took him off to prison, on the pretext that he had given the regular troops the order to fire. He was released only by a special decree of the Assembly. He was given an appointment at Brest, but a few months later the crews there also revolted.

Similar incidents took place in all the garrison towns, at Lille, Besançon, Strasbourg, Hesdin, Perpignan, Gray, Marseilles, etc. But the bloodiest mutiny was the one which took place at Nancy in August 1790. The soldiers of the garrison, and especially the Swiss of Châteauvieux's Vaudois regiment, demanded from their officers their share of the regimental fund to which they contributed, which had been in arrears for several months. Instead of acceding to their soldiers' just demands, the officers punished them for a breach of discipline. Two of them were made to run the gauntlet and ignominiously flogged. Feeling ran high in the town, where Châteauvieux was beloved, because he had refused to fire on the people at the time of the capture of the Bastille. The Patriots and National Guard of Nancy fetched the two victims, led them through the streets, and forced the officers who were to blame to pay each of them an indemnity of a hundred louis. The soldiers examined into the regimental funds and, finding the cash-box half empty, complained that they had been robbed. The other regiments at Nancy likewise demanded a statement of their accounts and sent delegations to the National Assembly to lay their complaints before it.

In the previous mutinies Lafayette had taken the part of the officers against the soldiers. He had sent urgent letters to the deputies of his party to ensure that the Comte d'Albert, who was responsible for the mutiny at Toulon, should not only be exonerated from blame, but loaded with compliments.

This time he determined to "strike a great blow," to use his own words. He had the eight soldiers sent by the royal regiment as delegates to Paris arrested, at the same time inducing the Assembly, on August 16, to pass a decree organizing drastic repression. He wrote two days later to his cousin General Bouillé, who was in command at Metz, that he was to take vigorous measures against the mutineers. Finally, he appointed M. de Malseigne, an officer of Besançon, who was considered "the best brain in the army," to examine the accounts of the garrison at Nancy. Though the soldiers had shown signs of repentence on the arrival of the decree, Malseigne treated them as criminals. His provocative action revived the disturbances. At the barracks occupied by the Swiss he drew his sword and wounded several men, and then took refuge at Lunéville, saying that his life had been threatened. Bouillé now assembled the garrison of Metz and some National Guards and marched on Nancy. He refused to parley with the deputations sent to meet him at the town gates. A fierce struggle at the Porte de Stainville took place on August 31, in which the Swiss were in the end defeated. Some twenty of them were hanged, and forty-one, tried by a council of war, were summarily condemned to the galleys. Bouillé closed the club at Nancy, and a perfect reign of terror prevailed throughout the whole region.

This massacre at Nancy, which was openly approved by Lafayette and the Assembly, had the most serious consequences. It revived the courage of the counter-revolutionaries, who began raising their heads again on every side. The King congratulated Bouillé, and on September 4, 1790, gave him the following advice: "Nurse your popularity, it may be useful to me and the kingdom. I regard it as a sheet-anchor, and consider that it may one day serve to restore order." The Parisian National Guard held a memorial celebration on the Champ de Mars in honour of those of Bouillé's army who had been killed. Similar ceremonies took place in most cities.

But the democrats, whose hearts were instinctively on the side of the soldiers, protested from the very first against the cruelty of this deliberate repression. There were tumultuous demonstrations in Paris on September 2 and 3 in favour of Châteauvieux's Swiss. The young journalist Loustalot, who had defended them, died suddenly. He was said to have been overcome by the grief caused him by the massacre, which he had stigmatized in his last article in the *Révolutions de Paris*. From this moment Lafayette's popularity, which had previously been as great among the people as among the middle classes, declined steadily.

For more than a year the "hero of two worlds" had been the most important man in France, because he had given the middle classes confidence against the double peril which threatened them, on the right from the plots of the "aristocrats," and on the left from the confused aspirations of the proletariate. This was the secret of his strength. The middle classes placed themselves under this soldier's protection because he guaranteed them what they had won in consequence of the Revolution. They had no objection to a strong power, provided that this power was exercised for their benefit.

The authority exercised by Lafayette was essentially a moral authority, based upon free consent. The King was ready to abandon his sceptre to him, and the middle classes were likewise ready to obey him. He sheltered himself behind the throne. Patronage was in his hands, both that to which the people appointed and that which was in the King's gift, for his recommendation was supreme in the eyes of the electors. By this means he gained a court, or, rather, a following.

He was not lacking in political sense. He had learnt in America to know the power of the clubs and newspapers. He kept on good terms with them and made use of them.

After the October days, the club of the Breton deputies had moved to Paris with the Assembly. It now sat in the library of the Jacobin convent in the rue Saint-Honoré, a few steps from the riding-school where the Assembly held its sessions. It adopted the name of Society of the Friends of the Constitution. It was open not only to deputies, but to bourgeois in easy circumstances, whom it co-opted as members. In it were to be found men of letters and publicists, bankers and merchants, nobles and priests. The Duke of Chartres, son of the Duke of Orléans, obtained admission to it in the summer of 1790. The entrance fee was twelve livres, and the annual subscription twenty-four livres, payable in four instalments. By the end of 1790 there were more than a thousand members. It kept up a correspondence with the clubs which had been founded in the principal towns and even in small country towns. It gave them letters of affiliation, distributed its publications among them, sent them word how to act, and infected them with its own spirit. It thus rallied round it the whole of the militant and enlightened element in the revolutionary bourgeoisie. Camille Desmoulins, who was a member, defined its function and activities rather well when he wrote: "Not only is it the grand inquisitor which strikes terror in the aristocrats; it is also the great accuser, redressing all abuses and coming to the aid of all citizens. It is, indeed, as though the club exercised the functions of public prosecutor to the National Assembly. In its bosom are poured out the grievances of the oppressed, which come to it from every side before being taken before the august assembly. Deputations keep crowding to the hall of the Jacobins, whether to congratulate them, to ask for affiliation, to arouse their vigilance, or to redress wrongs" (February 14, 1791). The club had as yet no official organ, but an echo of its discussions was to be heard in a number of newspapers, such as Gorsas's *Courrier*, Carra's *Annales patriotiques*, Brissot's *Patriote français*, Prudhomme's *Révolutions de Paris*, edited by Loustalot, Silvain Maréchal, Fabre d'Eglantine, and Chaumette, Camille Desmoulins's *Révolutions de France et de Brabant*, Audouin's *Journal universel*, etc. The Jacobins were becoming a power.

Lafayette was careful not to neglect them. He had himself enrolled as a member. But he was no orator and felt that the club was slipping away from him. His rivals the Lameth brothers, who were great noblemen like himself and far better speakers, had won a following in it. They had on their side the subtle Adrien Duport, who was well versed in the law and at the same time a clever parliamentarian, and the young Barnave, with his vigorous eloquence, wide knowledge, and ready wit and repartee. The inflexible Robespierre was listened to with increasing readiness, because he was the champion of the people and because his eloquence, instinct with sincerity, was capable of lifting the debate to a higher plane and unmasking trickery. The philanthropic Abbé Grégoire, the ardent Buzot, the vain and solemn Pétion, the brave Dubois-Crancé, the energetic Prieur of Marne, tended more to the left than the "triumvirs," but kept company with them for a long time.

Lafayette did not break with the Jacobins; on the contrary, he never ceased to lavish praise on them in public; but shortly afterwards, with the aid of his friends the Marquis de Condorcet and the Abbé Sieys, he founded the Society of 1789, which was a political debating-society and a social assembly rather than a club. It did not admit the public to its sessions, which after May 21, 1790 took place in sumptuous apartments at the Palais Royal. The subscription, which was higher than that of the Jacobins, kept out people of small means. Moreover, the number of members was limited to six hundred. It was here that the moderate revolutionaries, who were equally attached to the King and the Constitution, gathered together round Lafayette and Bailly at great formal banquets. Among them were to be seen Chapelier, the harsh and dour Breton lawyer, who had been one of the most determined opponents of the Court in the previous year, but had become very much more moderate, thanks to his fondness for gambling and good food; Mirabeau himself; the publicist Brissot, who was under particular obligations to Lafayette and had been introduced into these prosperous circles by Mirabeau's agent, Claviere, the Genevan banker; d'André, a former counsellor at the Parlement of Aix, who had had experience in public affairs and possessed a real authority over the centre of the Assembly; and other deputies, such as the Duc de La Rochefoucauld and his cousin the Duc de Liancourt, the lawyers Thouret and Target, who were to play a great part in carrying through the Constitution, the Comtes de Custine and de Castellane, Démeunier, Rœderer, Dupont of Nemours; financiers, like Boscary, Dufresne Saint-Léon, Huber, Lavoisier; men of letters, such as the two Chéniers, Suard, De Pange, Lacretelle; and bishops, like Talleyrand. The set was numerous and not lacking in talent. The club ran a periodical, the *Journal de la société de 1789*, edited by Condorcet, which was more like a review than a newspaper. Apart from this, it controlled a considerable number of the leading papers: the *Moniteur*, published by Panckoucke, the fullest and best-informed newspaper of the period; the *Journal de Paris*, an old paper dating from the beginning of Louis XVI's reign and read in the best intellectual circles; Millin and François Noël's *Chronique de Paris;* the *Ami des Patriotes,* edited by the two friends Adrien Duquesnoy and Regnaud de Saint-Jean-d'Angély, both of them deputies on the civil list. A little later, Lafayette and Bailly controlled various ephemeral papers of a violent character, which carried on a guerrilla warfare against the papers belonging to the extreme left; among them were the *Ami de la Révolution, ou les Philippiques,* which, as the subtitle indicates, was particularly devoted to polemics against the Duke of Orleans; Parisau's *Feuille du jour,* the *Babillard,* the *Chant du coq,* etc.

To the right of Lafayette's party the old monarchist party continued its existence under another name. Stanislas de Clermont-Tonnerre, who had been its leader since Mounier's departure, founded in November 1790 the club of the *Amis de la Constitution monarchique,* which published a paper with Fontanes as its first editor. Its headquarters were also near the Palais Royal, in the rue de Chartres, in a building known as the Panthéon. Almost all the deputies of the right met there, with the exception of the eloquent Abbé Maury and the cynical Vicomte de Mirabeau, who flaunted his aristocratic opinions. Clermont-Tonnerre's friends Malouet, Cazalès, the Abbé de Montesquiou, and Virieu, who lacked neither talent nor ability, denied, indeed, that they were reactionaries. They adopted the name of the Impartials. They tried to gain a footing in the working-class quarters by distributing bread-tickets to the poor at a reduced price; but this plan was at once denounced as a means of corruption and had to be given up, and, having become the object of hostile demonstrations, the monarchist club was obliged to suspend its meetings in the spring of 1791.

As for the out-and-out Aristocrats, the irreconcilable party who shared the opinions of the Abbé Maury, they at first met in the Capuchin monastery and afterwards at the Salon Français, where they indulged in dreams of a violent counter-revolution.

The whole gamut of royalist opinion was represented by the numerous papers subsidized by the civil list: the Abbé Royou's *Ami du Roi,* the tone of which was usually weighty, in contrast with the violent language of Gauthier's *Journal général de la cour et de la ville, or* Durozoy's *Gazette de Paris,* and with the sometimes witty lampoons of the *Actes des Apôtres,* to which Champcenetz and Rivarol contributed.

Up to the great debate of May 1790 on the right of peace and war the relations between the Club of '89 and the Jacobins—that is to say, between the Fayettists and Lamethists (followers of Lafayette and the Lameths

respectively)—preserved a surface cordiality; and even afterwards they
were still characterized by a well-bred restraint. Men like Brissot and
Rœderer had a foot in each camp. Even in July Lafayette was taking
pains to win over certain agitators whom he knew to be amenable to
the influence of money, such as Danton. Mirabeau and Talon negotiated
the business for him, and Danton became more peaceable. But though the
great leaders on both sides observed restraint, the hangers-on of the two
parties were already sparring with one another. Marat, whose political
foresight was seldom at fault, was the first to attack the "divine Mottier"
and the "infamous Riquetti," whom he denounced as in the pay of the
Court as early as August 10, 1790. Little good came of it, for his paper was
confiscated by the police, and writs of seizure were issued against him,
which he managed to evade, thanks to the protection offered him by the
district of the Cordeliers. After Marat, Loustalot and Fréron continued
the opposition to the Fayettists, the latter in the *Orateur du Peuple*.
Camille Desmoulins did not make up his mind till a little later, when he
disclosed to his readers that he had been promised a post worth two thousand écus, in the name of Bailly and Lafayette, as the price of his silence.
All of them got into trouble with the Hôtel de Ville or the Châtelet. At
first their campaigns only aroused an echo among the lower middle classes
and artisans, the class which was beginning to be known by the nickname of sansculottes, because they wore trousers instead of knee-breeches
(*culottes*). Robespierre was almost the only one at the Jacobin Club and
in the Assembly to protest against the persecution of these journalists
and by means of his speeches to fight some of their battles in the Assembly.

The fact is that, at any rate at the beginning, there were no fundamental differences based upon political doctrines between the Jacobins and
the Club of '89; it was rather a matter of personal rivalries. Lafayette
wanted to strengthen the executive power, but that was because the executive power was vested in himself. The triumvirs, Lameth, Duport, and
Barnave, accused him of sacrificing the rights of the nation, but that was
because they had as yet no share in ministerial favours. When the Court
appealed to them for advice a year later, they hastened to adapt Lafayette's opinions to their own purposes and follow out his policy. For the
time being the majority in the Assembly belonged to their rivals, from
whose ranks its presidents had been almost exclusively drawn for the last
year.[2] The '89 Club and the Jacobins were in fact only separated by the

2 List of presidents of the Assembly since the October days: Camus, October 28,
1789; Thouret, November 12; Boisgelin, November 23; Montesquiou, January 4,

fact that the former had the power in their hands. The former were the ministerial party, while the latter desired to be. There was a change in the autumn of 1790, when the King altered his opinion and withdrew his confidence from Lafayette. Lameth's party then gained the advantage. They had Barnave nominated as president of the Assembly on October 25, 1790. The journalists of the extreme left congratulated themselves upon this election as a victory for democracy. Marat was the only one who did not share their illusion. He wisely wrote: "In our eyes Riquetti was never more than a formidable instrument of despotism. As for Barnave and Lameth, I have but little faith in their *civisme* (devotion to the common weal)." Marat was right. The democratic idea never had a majority in the Constituent Assembly. It was a middle-class assembly to the very end and reconstructed France upon a bourgeois plan.

1790; Target, January 18; Bureau de Puzy, February 3; Talleyrand, February 18; Montesquiou, March 2; Rabaut, March 16; De Bonnai, April 13; Virieu, April 27; Thouret, May 10; Beaumetz, May 27; Sieys, June 8; Saint-Fargeau, June 27; De Bonnai, July 5; Treilhard, July 20; D'André, August 2; Dupont of Nemours, August 16; De Gessé, August 30; Bureau de Puzy, September 13; Emmery, September 27; Merlin of Douai, October 11; Barnave, October 25.

CHAPTER VII

The Reconstruction of France

N o assembly, perhaps, has been more respected than that known as the Constituent Assembly, which had, in fact, the honour of "constituting" modern France. Its deliberations were not disturbed by riots. The galleries of the Riding-school, where it had sat since its removal to Paris in November 1789, were filled with a fashionable crowd in which high society predominated. The ladies of the liberal aristocracy showed off their dresses there, and their applause did not go beyond the bounds of discretion. Among those to be seen were the Princesse d'Hénin, the Marquise de Chastenois, the Comtesse de Chalabre (a fervent admirer of Robespierre), Mmes de Coigny and de Piennes, with their patriotic enthusiasm, the Maréchale de Beauvau, the Princesse de Poix, the Marquise de Gontaud, Mmes de Simiane and de Castellane, the beautiful Madame de Gouvernet, Madame de Broglie, with her fine complexion, the piquante Madame d'Astorg, the charming Madame de Beaumont, Montmorin's daughter, who was afterwards loved by Chateaubriand—in short, a considerable portion of the faubourg Saint-Germain. They all went to the Assembly as if it had been a show. Politics had for them the attraction of novelty, of forbidden fruit. It was not till the end of the sessions, when first the religious struggle and afterwards the flight to Varennes had stirred the people to their depths, that the public in the galleries underwent a change, and artisans attempted to make their way into them. But even then Lafayette and Bailly prudently managed to station sixty secret agents in good places to support the cause of order by their hired applause. Voting in the Constituent Assembly was absolutely free.

Its work of political and administrative reconstruction was inspired by a single idea, arising out of the situation: that it was necessary to prevent a return to despotism and feudalism, and secure the peaceful domination of the victorious middle classes.

The Constitution preserved a hereditary king as head of the nation. But this king was, as it were, recreated by the Constitution. He was subordinate to it and took the oath to it. Formerly he had been "Louis, by the

82

grace of God, King of France and Navarre"; now, since October 10, 1789, he was "Louis, by the grace of God and the Constitution of the State, King of the French." The delegate of Providence had become the delegate of the nation. The sacerdotal monarchy had been laicized. France was no longer the property of the king, transmitted by inheritance. The new title, King of the French, implied a leader, not a master.

Precautions were taken to prevent the constitutional king from transforming himself into a despot. He was a functionary appointed by the Constitution, and could no longer draw freely upon the State Treasury. Like the king of England, he would have to be content in future with a civil list voted at the beginning of each reign, and fixed by the Constituent Assembly at twenty-five million livres. Further, he was obliged to entrust the administration of this civil list to a special official, whose private fortune would if necessary be held answerable for his management. This was in order to prevent the monarch from contracting debts for which the nation would be held responsible.

The king would be deposed by the Assembly in case of high treason or if he left the kingdom without its permission. If he were a minor and had no male relative who had taken the civic oath, the regent of the kingdom was to be nominated by the people. Every district was to elect an elector, and these electors were to meet in the capital and choose the regent, with no obligation to choose him from the royal family. This was an important corrective to the hereditary principle. A regent of this nature would be no more than a president of a republic chosen for a term of years.

The king retained the right of choosing his ministers, but in order to prevent him from corrupting the deputies he was forbidden to choose them from among the members of the Assembly, and, on the same principle, the deputies were forbidden, on relinquishing their functions, to accept any office in the gift of the executive power. It was necessary to guard the representatives of the nation against the temptation of honours and office and to confine them strictly to their role of independent and disinterested supervisors.

The ministers were held strictly responsible for their administration, and this responsibility was enforced by legal safeguards. Not only could the Assembly arraign them before a High Court, but it insisted upon a monthly statement as to the disposal of the funds allotted to their departments; this monthly statement was first examined by the Treasury Committee, and even then could be put in force only after being formally approved by the Assembly. It was thus rendered impossible to divert funds to unauthorized uses or exceed the credits voted. Further, the ministers were bound, when called upon, to render an account to the Assembly "both of their conduct and of the state of expenditure and business," and were bound to produce their accounts, administrative reports, and diplomatic dispatches. The ministers would no longer be viziers. A little later those giving up office were called upon to render an account of their steward-ship, both moral and financial. Until their accounts were approved, the ministers under examination could not leave the capital. Danton, as Minister of Justice under the Convention, had great difficulty in obtaining a vote approving his financial statement, which was severely criticized by the upright Cambon. When Roland resigned the Ministry of the Interior after the death of the King, he never succeeded in getting his accounts formally passed, so that he might leave Paris.

The king could do nothing without the signature of his ministers, and this obligation deprived him of all power of personal decision and placed him in constant dependence upon his Council, which was itself dependent upon the Assembly. In order that the responsibility of each of the ministers might be defined easily, it was laid down that all the de-liberations of the Council should be reported in a special minute-book, kept by an official appointed for the purpose, but Louis XVI evaded this provision, which came into effect only after his fall.

The six ministers had sole charge of the whole central administration. The old councils had disappeared, together with the Minister of the King's Household, who was replaced by the intendant of the civil list. The gen-eral control of finance was now divided between two ministerial depart-ments, those of the *Contributions publiques* and of the Interior. The Ministry of the Interior alone was in touch with the local authorities. Public works, navigation, hospitals, poor-relief, agriculture, commerce, factories and workshops, and education, all fell within its province. For the first time the whole of the provincial administration was connected with a single centre.

The king appointed the higher officials, ambassadors, marshals, and admirals, two-thirds of the rear-admirals, and half of the lieutenant-generals, brigadier-generals, naval captains, and colonels of *gendarmerie,* a third of the colonels and lieutenant-colonels, a sixth of the naval lieu-tenants, always in accordance with the laws controlling promotion and subject to the countersignature of his ministers. He continued to direct diplomacy, but we have seen that he could no longer declare war, or sign treaties of any sort, without the previous consent of the National Assembly, the Diplomatic Committee of which worked in close collaboration with the Ministry for Foreign Affairs.

In theory the king remained the supreme head of the civil administration of the kingdom, but it was taken out of his hands *de facto*, for the administrators, and even the judges, were elected by the new sovereign, the people.

In theory, again, the king retained a share of the legislative power, thanks to his right of suspensive veto. But this veto did not apply either to constitutional or fiscal laws, or to debates concerning ministerial responsibility, and the Assembly had the further resource of addressing the people directly by proclamations, which were not subject to the veto. This was the procedure adopted on July 11, 1792 for declaring that the country was in danger, and this proclamation, which mobilized all the National Guards in the kingdom and caused all the administrative bodies to function night and day, was the indirect means by which the Legislative Assembly broke through the veto which Louis XVI had previously applied to some of its decrees.

In order to render it impossible for the King to repeat his attempt of July 1789, the Constituent Assembly stipulated that no troops should be allowed to be stationed within less than thirty miles of the place where the Assembly was sitting unless the Assembly authorized it. The Assembly had the right to maintain order during its sessions and to use for its protection the troops of the garrison in the place where its sessions were held. The king retained a guard, but it was not to exceed 1200 infantry and 600 cavalry, who were bound to take the civic oath.

The legislative functions of the old councils, which were suppressed, had been transferred to a single assembly, elected by the nation. This assembly, the legislative body, was appointed for two years only. It met by its own right, without any royal summons, on the first Monday in May. It fixed the place and duration of its sessions itself, and the king was unable to cut them short, still less to dissolve the Assembly. The person of the deputies was inviolable. Any proceedings against one of them had first to be authorized by the Assembly, which gave its decision only after seeing the documents relating to the case, and appointed the tribunal to try the case. When the Châtelet petitioned for the suspension of the privilege of parliament enjoyed by Mirabeau and the Duke of Orleans, whom the court wanted to bring within the scope of the proceedings started against those responsible for the events of October 6, 1789, the Constituent Assembly refused the request.

Thanks to its right of supervising the administration of ministers, its financial prerogatives, its control of diplomacy, the immunities of its members before the law, etc., the legislative body was the supreme power in the State. Under the guise of a monarchy, France had in fact become a republic, but it was a bourgeois republic.

The Constitution abolished privileges arising out of birth, but it respected and strengthened those based upon wealth. In spite of the article in the Declaration of Rights proclaiming: "The law is the expression of the general will. All citizens have the right to co-operate in its formation, whether personally or by their representatives," it divided Frenchmen into two classes in respect of electoral rights: namely, passive and active citizens. The former were excluded from electoral rights because they were excluded from possessing property. They were, to use the term invented by Sieys, "machines for work." It was feared that they might be docile instruments in the hands of the aristocrats. Moreover, since they were for the most part illiterate, they were believed to be incapable of taking even the smallest part in public affairs.

The active citizens, on the other hand, were, to quote Sieys, "the real shareholders in the great social concern." They paid in direct taxation an amount at least equal in value to three days' work at the local rate. They alone took an active part in public life.

Like the labouring classes, hired servants were included among the passive citizens, because it was assumed that they did not enjoy liberty.

In 1791 the active citizens numbered 4,298,360, out of a total population of twenty-six millions. Three million poor remained excluded from the rights of citizenship. As compared with the electoral methods which had prevailed in the election of the deputies of the third estates to the States General, this was a retrograde movement, for at that time no condition had been insisted upon save that the elector's name should be included in the list of taxpayers. Robespierre, Duport, and Grégoire protested in vain. The only echoes they aroused were outside the Assembly, in the ardently democratic newspapers published in Paris. It is significant that, as early as August 29, 1789, four hundred Parisian workmen came to the Commune and demanded "the status of citizens, the power to become members of the assemblies of the various districts, and the honour of forming part of the National Guard." The protests of the labouring classes were faint as yet, but became more and more marked as events developed.

The Constitution established fresh grades even among the mass of active citizens. The primary assemblies, which in the country districts met at the chief town in each canton—with the object of eliminating those who were less well off on account of the cost of the journey—could choose as electors of the second degree, in the proportion of one to a hundred members, only such of the active citizens as paid taxes amounting to the value of ten days' work. These "electors," who next assembled at the capital of the department (like French senatorial delegates nowadays), formed the electoral assembly, which chose the deputies, judges, members of the departmental and district assemblies, bishops, etc. But the deputies might be selected only from among those electors who paid taxes at least equal in value to a silver mark (about fifty francs), besides possessing some real estate. Thus an aristocracy of the eligible was created among the aristocracy of the electors. The electors were not many in number, from three to eight hundred to a department. Those eligible as deputies were even fewer. The aristocracy of birth had been replaced by an aristocracy of wealth.

The active citizens alone composed the National Guard—that is to say, bore arms—whereas the passive citizens were unarmed.

Robespierre carried on an impassioned campaign against the "silver mark"—that is, against the tax qualification for eligibility. Marat denounced the aristocracy of wealth. Camille Desmoulins pointed out that J.-J. Rousseau, Corneille, and Mably would have been ineligible. Loustalot recalled the fact that the Revolution had been made "by a few patriots who had not the honour of sitting in the National Assembly." The campaign produced its effect. Twenty-seven districts of Paris sent in protests as early as February 1790.

But the Assembly trusted to its strength and took no notice of these complaints. It was not till after the flight of the King to Varennes, on August 27, 1791, that it became reconciled to the suppression of the silver-mark qualification for eligibility as a deputy; but, by way of compensation, it raised the qualification necessary for the electors chosen by the active citizens. In future they had to own or enjoy the use of property of a taxable value equal to the local value of two hundred days' work, in towns with more than six thousand inhabitants, or of a hundred and fifty in towns with less than six thousand inhabitants and in country districts; or else they had to rent premises of the same value, or to be *métayer* or farmer on a property estimated at a value of four hundred days' work. It is true that this decree was passed at the end of the session and remained a dead letter. The elections of the Legislative Assembly were over, and had taken place while the silver-mark qualification was still in force.

The Constitution swept away the whole intricate and chaotic old system of administrative divisions which had become superimposed upon one another in the course of ages: *bailliages, généralités, governments,* etc. It substituted for them a single division, the department, subdivided into districts, cantons, and communes.

It is sometimes said that by creating the departments the Constituent Assembly intended to wipe out the memory of the ancient provinces, to break the particularist spirit for ever, and, as it were, to perpetuate the spirit of the Federations. This is possible, but it should be remarked that as far as possible the delimitation of the departments followed the ancient lines. Thus Franche-Comté was divided into three departments, Normandy and Brittany into five each, etc. The fact is that the chief thing borne in mind was the conditions requisite for good administration. The original idea had been to form administrative areas of such a size that all the inhabitants could reach the chief town in a single day. The desire was to bring the administration as near to the public as possible. There were eighty-three departments, the boundaries of which were fixed by an amicable agreement between the representatives of the various provinces. They were given names taken from rivers and mountains.

Whereas the old *généralités* had been administered by intendants appointed by the king, with absolute powers, the new departments had at their head a council of thirty-six members elected on the group system (*scrutin de liste*) by the electoral assembly of the department, and bound to be chosen from among citizens paying at least the equivalent of ten days' work in direct taxation. This council, whose functions were deliberative, met once a year for a month. Since the members were unpaid, only rich citizens or those in comfortable circumstances could accept a position in it. The council was nominated for two years, half the members being renewable every year. From among its members it chose a directory of eight, which held permanent sessions and received salaries. This directory was the executive committee of the council. It allotted the districts their share of direct taxation, supervised its collection, controlled expenditure, administered poor-relief, prisons, schools, agriculture, industry, and public works, saw that the laws were executed, etc.; in short, it inherited what had formerly been the powers of the intendants. To each directory was attached a *procureur général syndic,* elected by the electoral assembly of the department for four years, whose duty it was to initiate prosecutions. He sat on the directory, but had no voice in its deliberations. He had the right to call for all the documents bearing upon any affair, and no resolution could be arrived at before he had been allowed to state his views. In short, he was the organ of the law and of public interest, and was in direct communication with the ministers.

The department, then, was a little republic administering its own affairs freely. The central authority was not represented in it by any direct agent. The application of the laws was entrusted to magistrates who all held their powers by election. The king no doubt possessed the right of suspending the departmental administrators and annulling their ordinances, but it was open to them to appeal to the Assembly, whose decision was final. There was a sudden transition from the stifling bureaucratic centralization of the old regime to decentralization of a most extensive kind, on the American plan.

The districts were organized on the same system as the department, with an elected council, directory, and *procureur syndic*. Later on, their special duty was to be the sale of national property and the distribution of taxation among the communes.

The cantons were the simplest electoral unit, and were also the seat of the courts of justices of the peace.

But it was above all the intense activity of its municipal life which gave revolutionary France its resemblance to free America.

The old oligarchical municipality of the towns, consisting of mayors and councillors (*échevins*), who purchased their offices, had in practice already disappeared almost everywhere before its place was legally taken by elected bodies. But whereas the departmental and district administrations were the outcome of an indirect franchise based on a property qualification, the new municipalities were elected on a direct franchise. The mayor and municipal officers—the number of the latter varying in proportion to the population—were elected for two years by all the active citizens, but were bound to be chosen among those with a property qualification equivalent to ten days' work. Each urban district formed an electoral section. The number of municipal officers corresponded to the number of sections, and these officers, whose function was to co-operate with the mayor in the task of administration, were more like the modern French *adjoints* (deputy mayors) than like municipal councillors. The functions of the latter were discharged by elected notables, twice as many in number as the municipal officers. A meeting of the notables was summoned for all important business, when they formed, with the municipal officers, the general council of the commune. Side by side with the mayor there was a procurator (*procureur*) of the commune, with deputies in the important towns, whose duty it was to defend the interests of the community. He represented the taxpayers and was *ex officio* their legal representative. Finally, he acted as public prosecutor to the police court formed by the officers of the municipal council for trying petty offences.

The communes possessed extensive powers. It was through their agency that the department and the districts executed the laws and that the taxes were assessed and collected. They had the right to call out the National Guard and the troops. They enjoyed a wide autonomy under the inspection and supervision of administrative bodies which sanctioned their financial enactments and audited their accounts. The mayor and *procureurs syndics* might be suspended, but the municipal assembly could not be dissolved.

Half the members of the communes came up for re-election annually on the Sunday after St. Martin's day (November 11), so that they were in constant touch with the people, whose sentiments they faithfully reflected. In towns with more than twenty-five thousand inhabitants the sections, like the cantons in the country districts, had permanent officers and committees, and could hold meetings which controlled the action of the central municipality. At the outset the mayors and municipal officers were chosen from the rich middle classes, but they were far more exposed to the constant pressure of the people than the departmental and district directories, so that in 1792, and especially after the declaration of war, a certain lack of harmony was apparent between the communes, which were rather more democratic in character, and the administrative bodies, which were more conservative. This discord became more marked later on, after August 10, when the new municipalities became impregnated with popular elements. This was the cause of the Girondist, or federalist, insurrection. In the country and in the country towns it was the lower middle classes and even the artisans who took the power into their hands. It was no rare occurrence for the parish priest to find himself elected mayor.

The organization of justice was reformed on the same system as that of the administration. All the old jurisdictions, whether feudal or exceptional, were abolished, and in their place there was set up a new and graduated system of tribunals for all alike, based on the sovereignty of the people.

The lower grade consisted of the *juges de paix* (justices of the peace), elected for a term of two years from among those with a property qualification equivalent to ten days' work, and assisted by four or six good men and true as assistants (*prud'hommes assesseurs*), forming the *bureau de paix*. Their function was not so much to pronounce judgment as to reconcile litigants. They formed a tribunal, from which there was no appeal, for judging petty cases in which the sums involved did not exceed fifty livres, and a court of the first instance for sums up to a hundred livres. This expeditious and inexpensive procedure was of the greatest service and rapidly became popular.

The district tribunals, composed of five judges, who were elected for a term of six years, but were bound to have practised for at least five years, gave judgment without appeal in cases involving sums of less than a thousand livres.

As regards criminal cases, petty offences were tried by the municipalities, misdemeanours by the *juges de paix,* and felonies by a special tribunal which sat at the capital of the department and was composed of a president and three judges chosen from the district tribunals. There was a public prosecutor, elected like the judges, who initiated prosecutions. The accused had the advantage of two juries. The grand jury (*juré d'accusation*), composed of eight members, with a district judge as president, decided whether there were sufficient grounds for proceedings. The petty jury (*juré de jugement*), composed of twelve citizens, decided on the matter of fact concerned in the accusation, and the judges then gave judgment as to the penalty. A minority of three votes out of twelve sufficed for acquittal. The members of both juries were drawn by lot from a list of two hundred names drawn up by the *procureur général syndic* of the department from the active citizens eligible as deputies—that is to say, paying the equivalent of ten days' work in direct taxation. Thus the jury was composed of none but rich or well-to-do citizens, and, as before, the criminal tribunals were class tribunals. Robespierre and Duport would have liked to introduce the jury even in civil cases, but Thouret obtained the rejection of their proposal.

Penalties were henceforward made proportionate to the crime and were no longer at the discretion of the judges. "The law," said the Declaration of Rights, "must only lay down penalties which· are strictly and obviously necessary." Torture, the pillory, branding, and public confession were abolished, but the iron collar (*carcan*) and the chain (that is, irons), were maintained for punishments to which ignominy attached. Robespierre did not succeed in abolishing the death penalty.

There were no courts of appeal. The Assembly, which had had to deal vigorously with certain rebellious parlements, was afraid of reviving them under another name. The district tribunals acted reciprocally as courts of appeal, according to an ingenious system which allowed the parties to the suit to reject three tribunals out of the seven offered to them. The exclusive right of barristers to plead was abolished, on the motion of Robespierre. Every litigant might defend his case himself, or choose an unofficial defender. But the former *procureurs* were retained with the new name of *avoués*.

There were commercial tribunals, formed of five judges, elected among themselves by those paying the *patente*, or commercial tax.

There was a court of cassation, elected in the ratio of one judge to each department, which might reverse the judgment of the other tribunals, but only for flaws in procedure. It could not interpret the law; this power the Assembly reserved to itself. Disputed cases concerned with administrative matters were not under the jurisdiction of any special tribunal, but were settled by the departmental directories, with the exception of those concerning taxation, which were referred to the district tribunals. There was no Council of State, its place being taken by the council of ministers, and in certain cases by the Assembly itself.

Finally there was a High Court, formed of judges of the court of cassation and members of a special jury (*hauts jurés*) chosen by lot out of a list of 166 members, elected in the proportion of two to a department, which tried offences committed by ministers and high officials, and crimes affecting the safety of the State. The legislature decided what cases were to be tried by it, and chose from among its own members two Grand Procurators (*Grands Procurateurs*) whose business it was to initiate prosecutions.

The striking point about this judicial organization is that it was independent of the king and ministers. The High Court was, as it were, a weapon in the hand of the Assembly directed against the executive power, for the Assembly alone possessed the right of accusation. The king was represented in the courts by commissaries appointed by him and irremovable. These commissaries had a right to be heard in cases concerning wards and minors. It was their duty to defend the property and rights of the nation and to see that the courts exercised their functions with proper discipline and regularity. But they had no power in themselves; they could only set in motion those who had the right to act. Justice was always administered in the king's name, but it had in fact become the concern of the nation.

All judges elected were bound to be graduates in law. The works of Douarche and Seligman permit us to conclude that the choice of the electors was in general a very happy one. The frequent complaints of their "aristocratic" verdicts made by the Jacobins at the time of the Convention suffice to bear witness to their independence. They had to be purged under the Terror.

If the members of the Constituent Assembly established what was *de facto* a republic—though a bourgeois republic—this was because they had only too much reason to distrust Louis XVI, whose acceptance of the new regime did not seem to them very sincere. They had not forgotten that he had only sanctioned the resolutions of August 4 under pressure of mob violence. They justly suspected that he would seize any opportunity of ruining their work. Hence the precautions which they took to deprive him of all real authority.

If they entrusted the political, administrative, and judicial power to the middle classes, this was owing not only to class interest, but to the fact that they believed the people, the mass of whom were still illiterate, to be incapable of directing the State. They had still to be educated.

The new institutions were liberal in character. Power was everywhere in the hands of elected bodies. But if these bodies failed, if they fell into the hands of secret or avowed opponents of the new order of things, the whole system was imperilled. The laws would not be executed, or would be badly executed. The taxes would not be collected; the recruiting of soldiers would become impossible; in fact, anarchy would reign. It is a law of democracy that it cannot work normally unless it is freely accepted.

In the United States similar institutions produced excellent results, because they were worked in accordance with the spirit of liberty by a people long since accustomed to self-government. France was an old monarchical country, accustomed for centuries to look to the central authority for everything, and now entirely recast in a fresh mould. In America democracy was unchallenged. Its people deserved to be trusted and to have the care of their own destiny placed in their hands. In France a considerable part of the population did not in the least understand the new institutions, or else would not. The only use it made of the liberties granted to it was to frustrate them. It wanted to be given back its chains. And so the decentralization inaugurated by the Constituent Assembly, far from consolidating the new order of things, unsettled and almost overthrew it. The revolutionary middle classes thought they were protecting themselves against a restoration of feudalism behind the sovereignty of the people, which they had organized for their own benefit; but the sovereignty of the people threatened to make this restoration easier by everywhere weakening the authority of the law.

Two years later, in order to defend the work of the Revolution under the strain of war at home and abroad, the Jacobins had to revert to centralization; but for the moment nobody foresaw this necessity. Marat alone, who possessed a political sense, had apprehended from the very first day that it would be necessary to organize the revolutionary power in the form of a dictatorship, in order to oppose a despotism of liberty to the despotism of kings.

CHAPTER VIII

The Financial Question

THE outbreak of the Revolution, far from strengthening the credit of the State, completed its ruin. The former taxes were abolished. Those which had been set up in their place—the *contribution foncière*, which fell upon real estate; the *contribution mobilière*, levied upon income calculated upon the basis of rent; the *patente*, levied upon the profits of trade and industry—came in slowly for a variety of reasons. Registers had to be drawn up and new officials trained to their work. The municipal bodies whose duty it was to collect the taxes had no previous experience in their task. Beside, the taxpayers, and especially the aristocrats, were in no hurry to pay. The Assembly had not wanted to raise revenue by taxes on consumption, which it considered inequitable, because they fell with equal weight upon unequal fortunes. But fresh expenditure had been added to that already existing. Owing to the scarcity, a great deal of wheat had to be bought abroad. The reforms which were being carried out plunged the country into still deeper financial abysses. The old debt, which amounted to about 3,119,000,000, half of it in credits payable on demand, was increased by more than 1,000,000,000 proceeding from the liquidation of the old regime: 149,000,000 to redeem the debt of the clergy, 450,000,000 for the redemption of the judicial offices which had been abolished, 150,000,000 for that of financial offices, 203,000,00 for repayment of caution money held on deposit, 100,000,000 for the redemption of lay tithes, etc. The total amount of the old and the new debt thus reached 4,262,000,000, involving an annual payment of about 262,000,000. Moreover, the maintenance of public worship, which had fallen upon the State since the abolition of tithes, cost as much as 70,000,000, and the pensions due to the regular clergy as much as 50,000,000, while the expense of the various ministerial departments was estimated at no more than 240,000,000.

So long as the Court had maintained a threatening attitude, the Assembly's tactics had been to refuse all fresh taxation. It was financial embarrassments as much as insurrections which had forced Louis XVI to capitulate. But while cutting off the king's credit in every way, the Assembly inspired confidence in the propertied classes by solemnly disclaiming all intention of bankruptcy.

In order to meet current expenditure Necker was forced to resort to all kinds of shifts. He begged the already overburdened Caisse d'Escompte for fresh advances. He prolonged the term for which its notes were to be legal tender. In August 1789 he issued two loans, at 4½ and 5 per cent, but they were not fully subscribed. He persuaded the Assembly to vote a "patriotic contribution," which came in slowly and yielded only an insufficient amount. The King sent his plate to the Mint, and private individuals were requested to do the same. Patriotic women offered their jewels, and men their silver buckles. But these were mere petty devices. The time had arrived when no more could be obtained from the Caisse d'Escompte. On November 21, 1789 Lavoisier, in the name of the directors, handed in to the Assembly a statement of the bank's position.

The Caisse d'Escompte had notes in circulation to an amount of 114,000,000, but behind them were only securities and a bullion reserve amounting together to 86,790,000 livres. There remained an unsecured balance of 27,510,000 livres. But the Caisse could reckon among its assets the 70,000,000 which it had deposited at the Treasury as caution money, and 85,000,000 representing advances which it had made to the State. Of the 114,000,000 of notes in circulation, 89,000,000 had been placed at the disposal of the Treasury and only 25,000,000 kept for the requirements of trade. By July 1789 the metallic reserve had fallen below the statutory twenty-five per cent.

The mere statement of the bank's accounts showed that its solvency depended upon that of the State, since that part of its note issue which was not covered by its own reserve was secured only upon what the Government owed it. The State was using the Caisse to put into circulation paper money which it had not itself been able to induce the public to accept. Necker was obliged to admit that "the foundations of the Caisse were tottering, and that it was on the point of falling" (November 14, 1789). He realized that it could not provide the Treasury with further sums without increasing its capital. In order to facilitate this operation, he proposed to transform it into a national bank. The note issue was to be increased to 240,000,000, and the new notes were to bear the words "National guarantee."

The Constituent Assembly rejected his project on both financial and political grounds. It did not believe that the Caisse would be able to get another fifty millions' worth of shares taken up. Talleyrand said that the notes issued had already no security but the State credits, while the new ones, having no other security, would have no better chance of maintaining their value than if they were issued directly by the State. The Caisse charged a high interest on the sums it advanced to the Treasury. It was better to save this interest by means of a direct issue, since it was no longer possible to avoid paper money. Besides, the Assembly was afraid of the idea of a national bank. Mirabeau made the most of the argument that it would be a formidable weapon in the hands of the executive. The control of financial affairs would be taken out of the Assembly's hands. "What, then, must be done now that we have no credit whatsoever, now that we are neither willing nor able to go on mortgaging our revenues, but want, on the contrary, to free them from encumbrance?" said Lecoulteux of Canteleu on December 17, 1789. "We must do what honest owners of property do in similar conditions: we must sell our patrimony."

This patrimony consisted of the Church property, which recently, on November 2, the Assembly had "placed at the disposal of the nation." This solution had been in the air for a long time past. Calonne had advocated it, and a number of the *cahiers* had recommended it. Under Louis XV the commission on the religious orders had already suppressed nine of them and used their property for purposes of general utility. It was Talleyrand, a bishop, who formally proposed that the property of the Church should be used for the payment of the debt (October 10, 1789). This property, he said, had not been given to the clergy, but to the Church—that is to say, to the whole body of the faithful—in other words, the nation. It had been intended by the donors for charitable foundations or works of general utility. In resuming possession of it the assembly of the faithful—the nation—would assume responsibility for fulfilling the purposes of the foundations, for education, poor-relief, and the maintenance of public worship. Treilhard and Thouret added that the clergy could own property only by virtue of the sanction of the State. The State had the right to withdraw its sanction. It had destroyed corporations. The order of the clergy no longer existed. Its property reverted to the community.

In vain did Camus, the Abbé Maury, and Archbishop Boisgelin reply that the property had not been given to the clergy as a body, but to certain definite ecclesiastical establishments, which it would be an act of injustice to despoil. In vain did Maury attempt a diversion by pointing out that there was a band of Jews and speculators who coveted the Church property; in vain did Boisgelin offer, in the name of his brother bishops, to advance a sum of 400,000,000, raised on the security of the church property; the Constituent Assembly had already taken up its position.

97

The question, Talleyrand said, had already been prejudged by the abolition of tithes. While making no definite statement on the question of the clergy's rights to their property, the Assembly resolved, by 508 votes to 346, to use the vast ecclesiastical estates, valued at 3,000,000,000, as security for the State debts.

Once this great step was taken, everything became easy. On December 19, 1789 the Assembly resolved to create a financial department solely dependent upon itself, and gave it the name of Extraordinary Exchequer (Caisse de l'Extraordinaire). Into the new Caisse were to be paid the proceeds of exceptional taxation, such as the patriotic contribution, but its main resource would be the proceeds of the sale of the property of the Church. Four hundred millions' worth would be offered for sale as a beginning, and would be represented by assignats for that amount, with which, in the first instance, would be repaid the advances made by the Caisse d'Escompte, amounting to 170,000,000. Thus this first issue of assignats was no more than a Treasury device. The assignat was as yet no more than a Treasury bond. The notes of the Caisse d'Escompte still formed the paper currency. The very word "assignat" is significant. They were assignments, bills of exchange drawn on the Extraordinary Exchequer, bonds secured upon certain specified sources of revenue.

A security, a certificate, carrying with it the privilege of purchasing national lands is not, as yet, a currency. The assignats created on December 19, 1789 bore interest at five per cent, for they represented a debt of the State which itself bore interest: namely, the debt owing to the Caisse d'Escompte. It was a Treasury bond redeemable in land instead of in cash. As the property of the Church was gradually disposed of, the assignats would return to the bank, whereupon they would be cancelled and burnt, thus wiping out the State debt.

If the operation had succeeded, if the Caisse d'Escompte had been able to increase its capital, negotiate and place the 170,000,000 of assignats which had been delivered to it, it is to be presumed that the Assembly would not have had recourse to a paper currency, for which it had a distrust, due to the fact that the "system" of Law and the more recent example of the American Revolution were still in men's minds. Satisfied at having maintained the value of the assignat and provided for the most pressing expenditure, while getting rid of the trammels of the Treasury, it would no doubt have pursued a different financial policy.

But the Caisse d'Escompte did not succeed in disposing of the assignats. Investors hesitated to accept them, for at this period, in the early months of 1790, the clergy, though dispossessed in theory, in reality still kept in their hands the administration of the Church property, which was, moreover, encumbered with private debts, not to mention the fact that the question of clerical stipends and of the expenditure for which their establishments had hitherto been responsible had not yet been settled. The public felt no confidence in bonds that were merely problematical promises to sell property the acquisition of which was not free of all mortgages and might give rise to inextricable complications. "The assignats," said Bailly, on March 10, 1790, "have not met with the popularity which was hoped for and the circulation which was necessary, for confidence can be based only upon a secure and visible foundation." Shares in the Caisse d'Escompte fell and its notes depreciated by more than six per cent. The louis d'or was already at a premium of thirty sous.

The Assembly realized that in order to inspire confidence in the assignats it must deprive the clergy of the administration of their property which was still in their hands, and must clear off all mortgages or encumbrances of any kind, by making the State take over the debt of the clergy and all the expenses of public worship (decrees of March 17 and April 17, 1790). Having done this, it imagined that it had done enough towards strengthening the position of the assignats and facilitating their acceptance to make it possible in the future to dispense with paper money. So far the assignats had been merely cover for the paper currency. Paper money had depreciated because this cover was insecure. But the assignats had now been freed from all suspicion and encumbrance, because the church property had been liquidated. It was certain that the former owner would not disturb the new purchaser. It was certain that the Treasury bond payable in land would be met when it fell due. Now that the assignats were secured and freed from encumbrance, they might take the place of paper money with advantage. The Caisse de l'Extraordinaire would itself induce the public to accept the assignats which the Caisse d'Escompte had been unable to put into circulation. The first batch of assignats which had not been taken up would be cancelled, and a fresh issue would be made on different conditions. As an additional precaution it was decided, on March 17, 1790, on the motion of Bailly, that the lands to be sold should be disposed of through the agency of the municipalities. "How many people," said Thouret, "will negotiate with a greater feeling of security when the ecclesiastical property reaches them through these channels, after undergoing a change which will purge them of their former character!"

There were some who would have liked the new issue of assignats to have been free assignats, which anyone might accept or refuse—in short, still having the character of Treasury bonds. But the Assembly allowed itself to be persuaded by those who advocated making them legal tender. "It would be unjust," said Martineau, on April 10, "to force the creditors of the State to accept them unless they can also force their own creditors to do so." The decree of April 17 stipulated that the assignats "should be legal tender among all persons throughout the whole extent of the realm and should be accepted like metal currency for all payments, both public and private." Private individuals were, however, allowed to exclude them from contracts for future payment, so that they had not really been made legal tender. The Assembly had omitted to allow for the fact that the metal currency was bound to compete with the paper currency, and that the latter was bound to be beaten in the struggle. Bad money drives out good. The Assembly did not dare to withdraw gold and silver from circulation. It did not even contemplate doing so. The earlier issues of assignats were only for large denominations, of a thousand livres. Gold and silver were necessary to pay the balance of accounts and for small purchases. Far from forbidding the exchange of cash for assignats, the Assembly encouraged it. It required écus and small change for the pay of the troops. The Treasury itself bought metallic currency in exchange for assignats, and was content to do so at a steadily increasing loss. Thus the exchange of paper money for metallic currency became a legal transaction. The decree of May 17, 1791 lent official sanction and encouragement to this. The louis d'or and the assignat were quoted on the Bourse. Metallic money was regarded as something to be bought and sold at a variable rate. Thus the Assembly itself legalized the depreciation of paper money compared with specie. This constituted a rift in its financial system which was to grow wider and wider.

The first batch of assignats, issued on December 19, 1789, bore interest at five per cent. On those issued on April 17, 1790 to replace them the rate was reduced to three per cent. The interest was reckoned by the day. An assignat of the value of a thousand livres bore interest at the rate of 1 sou 8 deniers a day, one of the value of three hundred livres at six deniers. The last holder drew the total interest at a public pay office at the end of the year. Those who had held it in the interim were paid the share due to them by their debtors, who were always bound to offer the exact sum (an obsolete condition which still holds good in France in the case of payments to the State).

By reducing the rate of interest the Constituent Assembly had intended to prevent investors from keeping their assignats instead of exchanging them for land. The deputy Prugnon had demanded the abolition of all interest on the ground that the assignats were becoming a form of currency.

Écus bore no interest. "Either the assignats are good money," he said, "or they are not. If they are, of which I have no doubt, they do not require interest; if they are not, interest will not make them good; it will prove that they are bad and that, at the very moment of their issue, the Government feels no confidence in them." The Assembly did not dare to follow this reasoning to its logical conclusion all at once.

The issue of the assignats, which had originally been no more than a Treasury operation, was a temptation to the Assembly to enlarge its scope. The Caisse de l'Extraordinaire now performed the same services as the Caisse d'Escompte had done before. Assignats took the place of bank-notes. The Assembly was creating money. By the first issue it had succeeded in wiping out the most pressing debts; what was to prevent it from conceiving the idea of wiping out the whole of the debt by the same means, in order to liquidate the arrears of the old regime at one stroke?

On August 27, 1790 the Marquis de Montesquiou-Frezenac, in the name of the Finance Committee, laid before the Assembly a choice between two systems: either to create *quittances de finances*, bearing interest at five per cent, which should be accepted as payment for the national lands and with which the offices that had been suppressed and the debts that had fallen due should be redeemed; or else to have recourse to fresh issues of assignats, by means of which the debt would be liquidated by the rapid sale of Church property.

After a long and impassioned debate which lasted more than a month, the Constituent Assembly chose the second alternative. On September 29, 1790 it decreed the repayment "in non-interest-bearing assignats" of the debt of the State and clergy, and at the same time raised the limit of issue of assignats, which had so far been fixed at 400,000,000, to 1,200,000,000.

The Constituent Assembly did not make up its mind in ignorance or without mature consideration. "This," said Montesquiou, "is the greatest political question that can be submitted to statesmen."

They rejected the *quittances de finances* for weighty reasons. These "quittances," which would only be accepted in payment for national property, had the disadvantage that they did not improve the financial situation until the sale of the property had been effected. Since they bore interest, they did not reduce expenditure. "The debt would not cease to exist" (Beaumetz). "The *quittances* would enable capitalists to speculate in the lands for sale and to dictate to the country districts" (Mirabeau). Their holders, in fact, would control the market, since there could be no purchase except with their paper. The investing classes lived in the towns;

they were not interested in land. They would be in no hurry to get rid of the *quittances* placed in their hands, for they bore interest. This being the case, the question arose whether the sales, which were the most important matter, would be facilitated or hampered. Everybody on the committee was agreed that "the salvation of the State depended upon the sale of the national property, and this sale would not be rapid as long as citizens had not in their hands the right securities for acquiring it" (Montesquiou).

The assignats seemed preferable to the *quittances*, because, bearing no interest, they would circulate freely, instead of being hoarded; because they would effect a perceptible saving, estimated by Montesquiou at 120,000,000 a year, the sum which would no longer have to be met by taxation; but, above all, because without them the national property would not sell: "for more than twenty years past there have been ten thousand estates for sale which have found no purchasers; therefore the only way to ensure and expedite their sale is to make an issue in order to sell" (Montesquiou).

Those opposed to the assignats insisted that the repayment of the debt in paper money would be tantamount to a partial bankruptcy. It was an illusion, said Dupont of Nemours, to believe that the debt could be paid with assignats. They were advances secured on the national property. Payment would not really be effected till the property represented by the assignat had been sold, and in the mean time the assignat would have undergone an inevitable depreciation; for the paper money would certainly lose on exchange for metallic currency. Talleyrand pointed out that its bankruptcy would be felt even in private transactions. "All creditors paid in notes lose the difference (between the current rate of notes and that of metallic currency), all debtors who have received loans in metallic currency are the gainers by it; this will lead to a subversion of the idea of property, and a universal dishonesty in the making of payments, a dishonesty all the more hateful for being legal." Lavoisier and Condorcet proved that if a fresh mass of fiduciary paper was suddenly put into circulation, prices would immediately rise. "If you double the tokens representing exchange while the things to be exchanged still remain the same in number, it is obvious that twice the amount of the tokens is required to purchase the same amount of a commodity" (Pérès).

The high price of commodities would reduce consumption and consequently production. French manufacturers would be out-distanced by the competition of foreigners, the more so since the exchange would become adverse to France. She would have to pay for her purchases abroad in precious metals. Her gold and silver reserves would disappear. This would lead to an appalling economic and social crisis.

While not entirely denying that such a risk existed, the advocates of the assignats replied that no solution but theirs was possible. Metallic currency having already disappeared, it was necessary to replace it by paper money in order to ensure the sale of the Church property. "They say that paper drives out coin. Very well. Only give us coin and we will not ask you for paper" (Mirabeau). Law's system was not to the point. "Is the Mississippi to be set up against the abbeys of Cîteaux and Cluny?" (Montesquiou). Besides, if the worst came to the worst, if the assignats became depreciated, their holders would only be all the more eager to exchange them for land; and this was the essential thing. The assignats were necessary for the sale of the national lands. "We must dispossess those now enjoying the use of them, we must destroy their illusory hopes" (Beaumetz). In other words, the question was not merely a financial one. It was pre-eminently political. "Are we discussing the Constitution? The issue of assignats cannot be impugned; it is the one infallible means of establishing the Constitution. Are we discussing finance? We must not argue as if this were a normal situation; we cannot meet our engagements; we can bear trifling losses, but we cannot suffer the Constitution to be based upon any but solid and stable foundations" (Chapelier). "What we have to do," said Montesquiou, even more explicitly, "is to consolidate the Constitution, deprive its enemies of all hope, and bind them to the new order of things by their own interest."

Thus the assignats were at the same time a political weapon and a financial expedient. As a political weapon they proved their efficacy, since they hastened the sale of the property of the clergy and made it irrevocable and since they enabled the Revolution to vanquish its enemies at home and abroad. As a financial measure they did not escape the dangers foreseen by their opponents. But these dangers were for the most part the outcome of political causes, which developed and aggravated them beyond all remedy.

The higher denominations of assignats were exchanged for specie at a loss from the very moment of their appearance. They could be exchanged for écus only at a premium of 6 or 7 per cent at first, and later of 10, 15, or 20 per cent. Those for amounts of fifty livres, which appeared in the spring of 1791, were in their turn at a premium as compared with the higher denominations, and finally, when the assignats of five livres, known as *corsets*, were created, the distribution of which started in July 1791, they in turn were at a premium as compared with the assignats of fifty livres. For important reasons the Assembly hesitated for a long time before creating these small denominations. Workmen were paid in écus and copper coinage. At first it was their employers who bore the loss on the exchange of assignats for metallic currency. If assignats of five livres were created, it was to be feared that écus would disappear and that the workmen, who would henceforward be paid in paper, would have to bear the loss which had so far fallen upon their masters. For there were already two prices for every article or commodity, the price in coin and the price in assignats. To pay workmen in paper amounted to reducing their wages. In vain was it attempted to stave off the crisis by melting down the bells of the churches which had been closed and coining a vast quantity of copper money. Silver coins disappeared because it was to people's interest to melt them down. The lack of small change was at first a serious embarrassment to those engaged in industry and trade and to the labouring classes. In many towns payment in money was replaced by payment in kind. Corn or cloth was distributed as wages. In March and April 1792 the scarcity of small change and the depreciation of paper money led to disorders at Besançon. The workmen employed on the fortifications struck and demanded payment in coin. They threatened to pillage the bakers' shops. The same thing happened in many places. The people would not tolerate any differentiation between the price in coin and that in assignats. They were angry with the shopkeepers and ill-treated them.

The Monnerons, a big firm of Paris merchants, struck token sous of their own. Their example was followed by others. The copper money issued by private persons was known as fiduciary tokens (*médailles de confiance*). The banks in turn had the idea of adopting the plan of putting small notes into circulation under their own name, fiduciary notes, which they exchanged for assignats. This seems to have started at Bordeaux. From the beginning of 1791 issues of these notes became frequent. Departmental administrations, municipalities, and sections of Paris had recourse to them. There were sixty-three different kinds of these notes simultaneously in circulation in Paris.

The issuing banks gained on the transaction in two respects. In the first place, they sometimes demanded payment of brokerage or a premium for exchanging assignats for their notes. Moreover, instead of withdrawing from circulation the assignats which they received in exchange, they took advantage of the absence of any system of checking to make use of them in commercial or financial speculation. They speculated in sugar, coffee, rum, cotton, wool, and corn. The danger was that if the speculation failed, the fiduciary notes would lose their cover and could no longer be met by payment. Speculation had caused the security to disappear. The purchase of commodities on a large scale carried out by the issuing banks which wanted to invest their assignats led to a rise in prices and a devaluation of the currency. Certain issuing banks, such as the Caisse de Secours in Paris, stopped payment of their notes, and this failure, for sums amounting to several millions, and others like it, led to a panic among the public. The depreciation of the fiduciary notes, which had at last to be withdrawn from circulation, reacted upon the assignats. And, finally, we should not forget that clever forgers flooded the market with quantities of counterfeit assignats, and that Calonne, who was with the army of the *émigrés*, directed a special manufacture of them.

Yet further causes contributed towards the depreciation of the assignats and, as an inevitable consequence, to a rise in the cost of living. The assignats were to have been burnt as they returned to the Treasury, in payment either for the national domains or of taxes. Elementary prudence should have expedited these payments, in order rapidly to decrease the mass of paper in circulation. But the Constituent Assembly made the mistake of allowing purchasers a very long time to make their payments. They were allowed to meet their obligations in twelve annual instalments.

Another mistake was the acceptance in payment for national property, not only of assignats, but also of warrants (*quittances*) for compensation for the abolished offices, certificates of ownership of lay tithes, and, in general, all the forms of paper by means of which the State paid its debts (decrees of October 30 and November 7, 1790). This created fresh competition for the assignats, and there was also the risk of increasing the fiduciary currency.

Lastly, the Assembly wished the sale of national property to proceed concurrently with the paying off of the debt. It was thus led constantly to add to the mass of assignats, thereby increasing their depreciation proportionately. The original issue of 1,200,000,000, voted on September 25, 1790, was increased by successive issues of 600,000,000 on May 18, 1791; 300,000,000 on December 17, 1791; and 300,000,000 on April 30, 1792; making 2,500,000,000 in eighteen months. It is true that part of the assignats returned to the Treasury and were burnt (370,000,000 on March 12, 1792). It was none the less true that the quantity of assignats in circulation had been swelled with disquieting regularity (980,000,000 on May 17, 1791, 1,700,000,000 on April 30, 1792). And all this was before war had been declared.

As early as January 30, 1792, if we are to believe the correspondence of the papal internuncio, the assignats had depreciated by 44 per cent in Paris. The louis d'or was worth thirty-six livres in assignats. If the testimony of the "aristocrat" Salamon is considered suspect, that of the official lists of the depreciation of paper money cannot be. They show us that at the same date, more than two months before the declaration of war, 100 livres in assignats were worth in Paris no more than 63 livres 5 sous. In the department of Doubs, at the end of the same month (January 1792), the loss was 21 per cent, in Meurthe 28 per cent, in Gironde and Bouches-du-Rhône 33 per cent, and in Nord 29 per cent. We can see from this that if the price of commodities had risen everywhere in proportion to the depreciation of paper money, the cost of living must have increased by a third or a quarter.

By the spring of 1792 the assignats had depreciated on the average from 25 to 35 per cent in France, but in Geneva, Hamburg, Amsterdam, and London from 50 to 60 per cent. When the exchange is against a country, the reason generally is that the country is not producing and selling much for export, but is buying largely. In order to make its purchases it is obliged to buy foreign currency, and the more it needs, the dearer it has to pay. In 1792 France was selling largely to foreign countries, and the only thing she was buying in large quantities was wheat. The fall of her exchange could not be explained, then, by the discrepancy between her purchases and sales. It had other causes. The old regime, now nearing its end, had borrowed heavily in Holland, Switzerland, and Germany, especially during the American War. When the time came to repay these debts, at the beginning of the Revolution, large amounts of specie, assignats, and other securities had to be exported. These sudden repayments flooded the foreign money-markets with French paper, which became depreciated. The purchases of metallic currency by the Ministry for War for the payment of the troops increased this tendency.

Such were the purely economic causes of the fall in the value of assignats and of the exchange, which had as their result a rise in the price of commodities at home. But there were other causes, of a political nature.

The flight of Louis XVI to Varennes, and the threat of war which followed, aroused doubts in many people, both in France and abroad, as to the success of the Revolution. If it was necessary to issue fiduciary notes to make up for the lack of assignats of small dominations, this was because the old metallic currency, louis d'or, écus, silver coins, and even small copper coins, disappeared from circulation. The *émigrés* had carried a certain amount with them over the frontier, but a great deal had re-

mained in the country. If the metallic currency was no longer in circulation, this was because those in whose hands it was had no confidence in the
Revolutionary currency and feared or hoped for a restoration of the monarchy. They jealously hoarded and concealed the king's money. Later on,
royal assignats were to be at a premium as compared with republican
ones. France was torn by deep-rooted divisions, which was one of the
underlying reasons for the financial crisis and the economic crisis alike.

Certain historians, in order to prove that the mass of Frenchmen
had an unshakable confidence in the new regime, are wont to appeal to
the undeniable success of the sale of the national property. Sales were
rapid and purchasers were found sometimes at a higher price than had
been estimated. The success of this great revolutionary operation was
due to various causes, one of the chief of which seems to me to have been
the very keen desire felt by many purchasers of finding an investment
for their assignats and getting rid of them as quickly as possible, by exchanging this paper for solid property, for land. Since the assignats were
accepted at their face value in payment for the national lands, the purchaser was the gainer by the whole difference between the nominal value
of the Revolutionary paper money and its real value. It is a well-
ascertained fact that some who were well known to·be "aristocrats" purchased Church property, non-juring priests, nobles like d'Elbée and Bonchamp, who took part in the insurrection in the Vendée. In the department
of Vienne could be counted 134 purchasers who were ecclesiatics and 55
who were nobles.

Speaking generally, it was the middle classes in the towns who bought
most of the lots put up to auction. The peasants, for lack of money, only
picked up a scanty portion of this rich booty, but there were many small
purchasers among them, and this was enough to attach them to the Revolution.

It is also said that the assignats revived industry at first, and, indeed,
for a few months factories enjoyed an artificial prosperity. The holders of
assignats had hastened to get rid of them, not only by buying national
property, but also by bartering them for manufactured goods. The astute
observers who foresaw war laid in stocks of goods of every kind. Their
repeated purchases stimulated manufactures, but also as their inevitable
result increased the price of goods and so enhanced the cost of living.

Whenever and wherever an economic crisis arose, the revolutionaries
denounced the manœuvres of the Aristocrats. They maintained that the
latter had come to an understanding and banded themselves together to discredit the Revolutionary currency, to monopolize commodities and metallic

currency so as to hinder circulation, thus creating an artificial scarcity and an increase of prices. It is certain that such manœuvres did take place. The Jacobin Club at Tulle on February 2, 1792 denounced the district president of that town, one Parjadis, for advising taxpayers not to pay their taxes and foretelling that the *émigrés* would soon return in triumph. On March 18, 1792 the directory of the department of Finistère represented to the King that it would have found it impossible to levy the taxes if it had not adopted the course of interning the non-juring priests at Quimper. About the same time a man of position and ancient family, Séguier, an official of the Parlement, published a provocative pamphlet, *La Constitution renversée (The Constitution Overthrown)*, with the object of alarming Frenchmen about their property. "How could they be sure of their property," he said, "in such an acute crisis, amid this infernal speculation, with an unlimited issue of assignats and paper of every kind, when the Colonies were ablaze and France was threatened with the same disaster, when movable property was confiscated, and subjected to tedious and alarming formalities by a host of decrees," etc. Séguier did not scruple to threaten the purchasers of national property, by telling them that the former creditors of the State and the clergy had a lien on the property they had acquired, and would one day make good their claim.

The struggle between these two different tendencies in France went on in every sphere. Each political crisis was accompanied by an economic and social one. We must not forget this when we want to form an equitable judgment of men and things at this period.

The high cost of living caused by the assignats was soon to contribute towards the fall of the rich bourgeoisie which had governed during the Constituent Assembly, all the more so since the political and economic disturbances were commingled with a religious agitation of growing intensity.

CHAPTER IX

The Religious Question

T HE reorganization of the State necessarily involved that of the Church.
Their provinces had encroached upon each other to such an extent
in the course of centuries that they could not be separated by a stroke
of the pen. Nobody, with the possible exception of the eccentric Anarchar-
sis Cloots, wanted this separation, which would not have been understood by public opinion, but would rather have been interpreted as a
declaration of war on the religion which was still practised with fervour
by the masses. But financial reform, upon which the salvation of the State
depended, would have been a failure if all ecclesiastical foundations had
been preserved (and at that time schools, universities, and hospitals all
fell within the sphere of the Church), for, as before, these would have
swallowed up the revenues accruing from the sale of the property of the
clergy. In order to effect the necessary saving it was therefore necessary
to abolish a large number of the existing establishments. Hence it became
necessary for the Constituent Assembly to decide which were to be preserved and which abolished; in other words, to reorganize the Church
in France.

Quite as much as a measure of economy as out of contempt for the
monastic life, monks belonging to the mendicant or contemplative orders
were given permission to leave the cloister, and a number of them hastened
to avail themselves of it. It was thus possible to abolish a number of
convents, but the charitable and teaching orders were respected. It was
useless to recruit members for the religious orders now that the religious
houses were being closed. The taking of perpetual vows was henceforth
forbidden.

As a further measure of economy, as much as out of concern for good
administration, the number of dioceses was reduced to eighty-three, one
for each department. The number of parishes was reduced in like manner.
The bishops, formerly elected by the king, were henceforth, like the other
officials, to be elected by the new sovereign, the people. Were they not the
"officers of morality"? Was not the nation indistinguishable from the as-

sembly of the faithful? No doubt Catholicism had not been proclaimed as the State religion, but it was the only form of worship receiving a State grant. Its processions were the only ones allowed in the streets, which it was obligatory upon all the residents to decorate. The dissidents, who were not numerous, had to conduct their worship in private, under various disguises, and on sufferance. The parish priests were elected by the "electors" of their district, as the bishops were by the electors of the department. What did it matter if a few Protestants slipped in among the electors? Had not Protestant lords of manors formerly made appointments to benefices in virtue of their right of patronage? Besides, election would be a sort of "presentation." Those newly elected to livings were bound to be chosen from among the priests, and they would have to be instituted by their ecclesiastical superiors. The bishops would be instituted by their metropolitans, as in the early days of the Church. They would no longer go to Rome to purchase the pallium. The Assembly had abolished annates —that is to say, the first year's income from vacant benefices paid by the new incumbent to Rome. The new bishops were simply to write the Pope a respectful letter to say that they were in communion with him. Thus the Church of France would become a national Church and would no longer be governed despotically. Those privileged bodies the chapters would disappear, their place being taken by episcopal councils, which would have a share in the administration of the diocese.

In future Church and State would be drawn closer together and intermingled, inspired by one and the same spirit, a spirit of liberty and progress. The parish priests received the mission of announcing the decrees of the Assembly from the pulpit and explaining them to the faithful.

The Assembly was full of confidence. It did not think it had exceeded its rights in giving a *civil* Constitution to the clergy. It had not touched spiritual matters. By denouncing the Concordat and suppressing the annates it had no doubt done grave damage to the interest of the Pope, but it did not imagine that he would take the responsibility of provoking a schism. In 1790 the Pope had as yet no right to define and interpret dogmas on his own sole authority, still less to interfere arbitrarily in matters of discipline or matters falling under both secular and spiritual jurisdiction, such as were now in question. His infallibility was not proclaimed till the Vatican Council of 1871.

The French bishops, then, were for the most part Gallican—that is to say, hostile to the absolutism of Rome. In the great speech which he made in their name on June 29, 1790, during the debates on the decrees concerning the clergy, Boisgelin, Archbishop of Aix, had only recognized the *primacy* of the Pope over the Church, not his *jurisdiction,* and all his efforts had been confined to asking the Assembly to allow the summoning of a national council which should take the canonical measures essential for giving effect to the reforms. Since the Constituent Assembly would not sanction this council, which would have been an infringement of its own sovereignty, Boisgelin and the liberal bishops turned to the Pope to obtain the canonical sanctions without which they did not believe they could in conscience put in force the rearrangement of the dioceses and the reform of the episcopal councils. They entrusted Boisgelin with the drawing up of proposals for an agreement, which were transmitted to Rome through the agency of the King. The Constituent Assembly was aware of this negotiation and approved of it. Like the bishops in the Assembly, and the King himself, who had had no hesitation in accepting the decrees, it believed that the Pope would not refuse to grant them his sanction, to "baptize" them, to use the expression of the Jesuit Barruel in his *Journal ecclésiastique.* "We think we may foresee," said Barruel, "that the interests of peace, and considerations of the greatest weight, will inevitably induce the Holy Father to forward this desire." Far from discouraging the bishops who favoured conciliation, the Nuncio reassured them. "They implored His Holiness," he wrote in his dispatch of June 21, 1790, "to come to the aid of this Church, like an affectionate Father, and make every possible sacrifice in order to preserve the union which is essential. I felt it my duty in this connexion to assure them that His Holiness is aware of the deplorable condition through which the interests of religion are passing in this country and will do all he possibly can on his side to preserve it." The Nuncio added that the bishops had already taken the necessary measures for modifying the ecceliastical divisions in accordance with the decree, and that the bishops whose sees were abolished would hand in their resignations of their own accord. "The majority of the bishops has entrusted Monseigneur d'Aix with the task of delimiting the dioceses. The clergy would like the King to beg His Holiness to depute sixteen Apostolic commissaries from among the French clergy, in accordance with the liberties of the Gallican Church, who should be divided into four committees and turn their attention to defining the limits of the new dioceses" (dispatch of June 21).

There was a recent precedent which justified the bishops and members of the Constituent Assembly in indulging in hopes. When Catherine II, Empress of Russia, annexed her share of Poland, she revised the boundaries of the Catholic dioceses in that country on her own authority. In 1774 she created the episcopal see of Mohilev, giving it jurisdiction over

111

all the Roman Catholics in her Empire. On her own authority, too, she nominated to this see the Bishop *in partibus* of Mallo, who was regarded with suspicion at Rome, and forbade the Polish Bishop of Livonia to interfere for the future with that part of his former diocese which had been annexed to Russia. Pius VI had not dared to provoke a conflict with the schismatic sovereign, whose encroachments in the spiritual sphere were essentially of the same nature as those upon which the members of the French Assembly were venturing. He had regularized after the event the reforms carried out by the civil power, and in doing so had used exactly the same procedure as that to which the French bishops advised him to have recourse in order to "baptize" the Civil Constitution of the clergy.

But the Pope was driven into resistance by a number of reasons, the most decisive of which were perhaps not of a religious order. From the very first day he had condemned the Declaration of the Rights of Man in secret consistory as impious, although the Keeper of the Seals, Archbishop Champion de Cicé, had had a hand in it. The sovereignty of the people seemed to him a menace to every throne. His subjects in Avignon and Venaissin were in open revolt. They had driven out his legate, adopted the French Constitution, and asked to be united with France. In response to the proposals for an agreement which Louis XVI had conveyed to him with a view to putting the Civil Constitution of the clergy in force, he requested that French troops should help him to put down his insurgent subjects. The members of the Constituent Assembly took no action save to postpone the annexation to France demanded by the inhabitants.[1] The Pope then decided to issue a formal condemnation of the Civil Constitution. But several months dragged on in tedious negotiations. It must be added that he was encouraged in his resistance, not only by the *émigrés*, but also by the Catholic powers, and particularly by Spain, which had a grudge against France for having abandoned her at the time of her conflict with England. And lastly we must not overlook the activity of the French ambassador in Rome, the Cardinal de Bernis, an ardent Aristocrat, who used every possible means to bring about the failure of the negotiations which had been confided to his care.

By declaring to the Pope that, in default of a national council, he alone possessed the canonical powers necessary for putting the Civil Constitution into execution, the French bishops had put themselves in the power of the Roman Curia. When the Constituent Assembly, tired of waiting, imposed the oath on them, it was too late to draw back. They re-

---

[1] The annexation of Avignon, justified by the right of peoples to self-determination, was not voted till September 14, 1791.

fused to take the oath, and then at last the Pope took advantage of their refusal, which had been provoked by his dilatory tactics, to launch against them a condemnation which surprised and affronted them.

Up to the last moment Boisgelin, Archbishop of Aix, who was the spokesman of the majority of the bishops, had hoped that the Pope would hesitate to plunge France into schism and civil war. On December 25, 1790, the eve of the imposition of the oath, he wrote to Louis XVI: "The principle upon which the Roman Curia ought to act should be to do all that it ought to do, and to postpone only such matters as may be less pressing and less difficult; when only canonical forms are lacking, the Pope can supply them; he can do so and he ought; and such is the nature of the articles which Your Majesty had proposed to him." Even after they had refused to take the oath, the bishops still hoped for conciliation and the papal briefs filled them with consternation. For more than a month they kept secret the first of these briefs, dated March 10, 1791, and sent the Pope a courteous but tart reply in which they took up the defence of liberalism and offered their resignation in a body as a means of restoring peace.

The Pope refused to accept their resignation, and the schism became irretrievable. All but seven of the bishops refused to take the oath. About half the priests followed their example. In many regions, such as Haute-Saône, Doubs, Var, Indre, Hautes-Pyrénées, etc., the number who took the oath was very considerable, but in others, such as Flanders, Artois, Alsace, Morbihan, the Vendée, and Mayenne, there were very few. Throughout a large portion of the land religious reform could be imposed only by force. France was severed into two parties.

This unexpected result took the Constituent Assembly unawares and surprised even the Aristocrats. Up till then the great mass of the lower clergy had made common cause with the Revolution, which had almost doubled the stipends of the parish priests and curates (raising those of the former from seven hundred to twelve hundred livres). But the sale of the property of the Church, and the closing of the convents after the suppression of tithes, had already made uneasy more than one priest who was attached to tradition.

Moreover, scruples due to considerations of Church order had done their work. A future constitutional bishop like Gobel had expressed a doubt as to whether the civil authority alone had the right to modify the boundaries of the dioceses and interfere with the jurisdiction of the bishops. The Church alone, he said, "can bestow upon the new bishop, within the limits of his new territory, that spiritual jurisdiction which is necessary for the exercise of the power which he derives from God." So far as he himself was concerned, Gobel had made light of this objection and taken the oath, but many conscientious priests had been deterred by it.

The Constituent Assembly had desired to create a national Church and to use the ministers of this Church to consolidate the new order; but it had merely created a party Church, the Church of the party in power, in violent conflict with the ancient Church, which had become the Church of the party defeated for the time being. The religious struggle was embittered from the very outset by the whole fury of political passion. What a joy, what good luck for the Aristocrats: Monarchical sentiment had so far been powerless to provide them with a means of retaliation, and now Heaven had come to their assistance! Religious sentiment was the great lever which they used to set in motion the Counter-revolution. As early as January 11, 1791 Mirabeau was advising the Court, in his forty-third note, to fan the flames and aggravate the situation by provoking the Assembly to adopt extreme measures.

The Assembly saw the trap and tried to avoid it. The decree of November 27, 1790 on the oath forbade non-juring priests to take part in any public ceremony. Now, at that time baptisms, marriages, funerals, administering the communion, confession, and preaching were public ceremonies. If the decree were construed literally, the refractory priests—that is to say, nearly all the priests in certain departments—would have to cease abruptly to perform their functions. The Assembly feared that there might be a suspension of all public worship and requested the refractory priests to continue to carry on their functions until they were replaced. There were some who were not replaced till August 10, 1792. It granted the parish priests who were deprived of their positions a pension of five hundred livres. The first constitutional bishops were obliged to employ lawyers and judges in order to obtain their canonical institution by the former bishops. One of these alone, Talleyrand, consented to consecrate them. The lack of priests made it necessary to shorten the stages through which candidates for the priesthood had to pass. Since there were not enough secular clergy, they had recourse to the former regular clergy.

It was in vain that the revolutionaries refused at first to recognize the schism. They were gradually forced to admit what was only too evident. Religious war had broken out. Devout believers were indignant that their priest or bishop should be changed. The new, elected priests were regarded as intruders by those whom they had supplanted. They could enter upon their functions only with the support of the National Guard and the clubs. Timid consciences shrank from their ministrations.

They preferred to have their children baptized in secret by the "good priests," even thought this deprived them of their civil status, for none but the official priests were in possession of the registers of births, marriages, and deaths. The "good priests" were treated as suspects by the revolutionaries, and consequently as martyrs by their partisans. Families were divided against themselves. The women in general went to the mass said by the refractory priest, the men to that of the constitutional priest. Brawling broke out even in the very sanctuary. A constitutional parish priest would forbid a refractory priest who desired to say mass in the church to enter the sacristy or have access to the vestments. In Paris all the female communities refused to receive Gobel, the new bishop. The refractory priests took refuge in the chapels of convents and hospitals. The Patriot party demanded that these should be closed. As Easter approached, pious women on their way to the Roman mass had their skirts turned up and were whipped before the eyes of the jeering National Guards. This diversion was repeated several weeks running in Paris and other towns.

The persecuted refractory priests appealed to the Declaration of the Rights of Man to obtain the recognition of their religious rights. La Luzerne, Bishop of Langres, as early as March 1791, advised them to make a formal request that they might share in the benefits of the edict of 1787, which had allowed Protestants to have their civil status registered before the judges in their place of residence, an edict which the assembly of the clergy had condemned at the time. What a lesson could be drawn from this coincidence! The heirs of those who a century before had revoked the edict of Nantes, destroyed Port-Royal, and burnt the works of the *philosophes*, were now placing themselves under the protection of those ideas of toleration and freedom of conscience which they had previously been unable to condemn strongly enough!

Pushing the logic of events to its extreme conclusion Bishop La Luzerne demanded that civil status should be made a matter for the civil authorities, in order to rid his fathful flock of the vexatious monopoly of the priests who had taken the oath to the Constitution. The Patriot party were well aware that if they took the custody of the registers away from the constitutional priests they would deal the official Church a blow which would have a reaction upon the Revolution itself. They refused to go so far all at once. They maintained in the teeth of the facts that the dissidents did not form a separate Church. But the growing disorders forced them to make concessions, which were wrung from them by Lafayette and his party.

Lafayette's wife was a very religious woman, who took the part of the refractory priests and refused to receive Gobel; so he had been obliged to admit toleration at home. His friends in the Club of 1789 thought they could put an end to the religious war by proposing to grant the refractory priests freedom to have their own special places of worship. The directory of the department of Paris, of which the Duc de La Rochefoucauld was president and the Abbé Sieys and Bishop Talleyrand members, issued an ordinance on April 11, 1791 organizing the ministrations of the refractory priests, but only as a tolerated cult. Roman Catholics might enter into possession of the churches which had been closed, and hold meetings in them in perfect freedom. They at once availed themselves of this permission and rented the Theatine church, but they could not settle down there undisturbed. A few weeks later, after an excited debate, the Constituent Assembly extended to the whole of France, by its decree of May 7, 1791, the toleration granted to the dissidents of Paris.

It was easier to enter toleration on the statute-book than to obtain its acceptance in practice. The constitutional priests were indignant. They had drawn down upon themselves the thunders of the Vatican, they had made common cause with the Revolution, they had braved prejudice and danger, and in return for all this they were threatened with being left to their own devices at the first sign of difficulty! How were they to struggle against their rivals in that half of France which was already slipping from them if, after they had compromised themselves, the public authority now declared itself neutral? If a Roman priest's right to open a rival church without opposition was recognized, what was to become of the constitutional priest in his deserted official church? How long would he be able to retain his privileged character if, in half the departments, this privilege was no longer justified by the services he rendered? A form of worship once abandoned would become useless. The clergy who had taken the oath feared lest this policy of freedom might prove their death-warrant. They combated it fiercely in the name of the principles of traditional Catholicism. They gradually fell away from Lafayette and his party and grouped themselves round the Jacobin clubs, which became their strongholds.

Under the often well-founded pretext that the carrying on of worship under the auspices of the refractory priests was causing disorders, the authorities who favoured the constitutional priests refused to put in force the decree of May 7 on liberty of worship. As early as April 22, 1791 the department of Finistère, at the instance of the constitutional Bishop Expilly, issued an ordinance commanding the refractory priests to withdraw to a distance of four leagues from their former parishes. In the department of Doubs the directory, under the presidency of Bishop Séguin, passed an ordinance that, in cases where the presence of refractory priests gave rise to any disorder or division, the municipalities might expel them from the commune. There were a great many ordinances of this kind. The preambles of all of them assert that the Civil Constitution of the clergy—in fact the Constitution itself—could not be maintained unless the refractory priests were placed outside the protection of the law.

It is certain that in many cases the refractory priests lent a handle to the accusations of their opponents. The Pope did much to incite them to revolt. He forbade them to give the intruding priests a statement of the baptisms and marriages which they had celebrated. He forbade them to officiate in the same churches, although the use of them by both parties had at first been the practice almost everywhere, with the approbation of most of the former bishops. The Abbé Maury complained of the decree of May 7, which granted the refractory priests no more than the right to worship in private—that is to say, a lower status. He demanded complete equality with the priests who had taken the oath. The Bishop of Luçon, M. de Merci, denounced as a snare the liberty left to dissidents of saying mass in the national churches. It is a well-established fact that in the parishes where the refractory priests had the upper hand, their rivals were not secure. How many constitutional priests were not molested, insulted, beaten, and sometimes put to death! All accounts agree in accusing the refractory priests of pressing the confessional into the service of counter-revolution. "The confessionals are schools in which rebellion is taught and commanded," wrote the directory of Morbihan to the Minister of the Interior on June 9, 1791. Reubell, a deputy for Alsace, exclaimed during the session of July 17, 1791 that there was not a single refractory priest in the departments of Haut- and Bas-Rhin who would not be convicted of being in insurrection.

The result of the religious struggle was not only to double the strength of the "aristocratic" party; it also brought about the formation of an anticlerical party which had not previously existed. In order to uphold the constitutional priests and also to put the people on their guard against the suggestions of the refractory priests the Jacobins violently attacked Roman Catholicism. The shafts which they launched against "superstition" and "fanaticism" ended by falling upon religion itself. "We have been reproached," said the *Feuille villageoise*, which was devoted to this campaign, "with having ourselves displayed some little intolerance for popery. We have been reproached with not having always spared the immortal tree of faith. But if one looks closely at this inviolable tree,

117

one will see that fanaticism is so closely entwined with all its branches that one cannot strike at one without appearing to strike at the other." The anticlerical writers became bolder and bolder and gave up any hypocritical attempts to deal tenderly with Catholicism or even with Christianity. They soon attacked the Civil Constitution of the clergy, and proposed to imitate the Americans who had had the sense to abolish State grants to religion and to separate Church and State. Little by little these ideas began to make progress.

As early as 1791 some of the Jacobins, combined with some of Lafayette's party and with those who were afterwards to be known as the Girondins—Condorcet, Rabaut de Saint-Etienne, Manuel, Lanthenas—had the idea, first of completing, and afterwards of replacing the Civil Constitution of the clergy by a whole system of national festivals and civic ceremonies on the model of the Federations, using them, as it were, as a school of *civisme*.[2] And there was, in fact, a whole series of festivals in commemoration of the great events of the Revolution: June 20, August 4, July 14, festivals commemorating the martyrs of liberty, commemorating Desilles, who was killed during the affray at Nancy, commemorating the removal of Voltaire's ashes to Paris, commemorating the liberation of the Swiss of Châteauvieux from the hulks at Brest, commemorating Simoneau, mayor of Etampes, killed in a food riot, etc. Thus there was gradually evolved a sort of national religion, a patriotic religion still mingled with the official religion, upon which, moreover, it modelled its ceremonies, but which emancipated minds were afterwards to attempt to separate from it and endow with an independent life. They did not as yet believe that the people could dispense with worship, but they held that the Revolution was a religion in itself, which it was possible to raise above the old mystic cults by providing it with a ritual. Though they desired to separate the new State from the dogmatic and traditional churches, they did not intend that this State should be left unprotected against them. They desired, on the contrary, to endow it with all the prestige, all the æsthetic pomp tending to morality, and all the forces of attraction exercised by religious ceremonies upon men's souls. Thus there gradually came into being that religion of patriotism which was to find its final expression under the Terror, and which, like the separation of Church and State, arose out of the failure of the religious policy of the Constituent Assembly, which was becoming more and more irreparable.

---

[2] The qualities of a good citizen. To the supporters of the Revolution the term came to signify devotion to the revolutionary government.

CHAPTER X

The Flight of the King

Louis XVI had never been sincere in renouncing the heritage of his an-
cestors. If he had consented to follow Lafayette's directions after the
October days, it was because the latter had promised to maintain and
strengthen what power was left to the King. But by October 1790 the
Constitution had begun to come into force, the departmental and district
assemblies and the courts of justice were taking shape, convents and chapters were closing down, and the national property was about to be put
up for sale. Louis XVI realized that a definitive system was becoming
established. At the same time he noted that Lafayette's power was waning
daily. The forty-eight sections which were substituted in June 1790 for
the sixty former districts of the capital were so many turbulent little
municipalities within the larger one. They very soon adopted an attitude
of opposition to the Hôtel de Ville. In September and October 1790 they
passed votes of censure on the ministers, whom they accused of incapacity
and of conniving with the aristocrats. Their mouthpiece, Danton, the
lawyer orator, no doubt at the prompting of the Lameths, came to the
bar of the Assembly and demanded in their name the dismissal of the
ministers. The vote of censure which they moved was defeated on October
20, but by such a small majority that the ministers at whom it had been
aimed resigned. Montmorin alone was spared by Danton and remained
in office. The King was enraged at submitting to such coercion, and re-
luctantly accepted the ministers who were forced upon him at the behest
of Lafayette: Duportail as Minister for War, Duport-Dutertre as Minister of Justice, Delessart of the Interior, etc. He felt it to be a violation
of the Constitution, which had given him the right to choose his ministers
freely. He could not forgive Lafayette for his equivocal attitude during
the crisis and definitely went over to the policy of counter-revolution.

On October 20, the very day on which the debate about the ministers
had taken place at the Assembly, he gave audience to one of the earliest
émigrés, Bishop d'Agout of Pamiers, who had returned from Switzerland
on purpose to rouse him to action. He gave d'Agout and the Baron de

Breteuil full powers to negotiate in his name with foreign courts, with a view to obtaining their intervention in the favour of the restoration of his legitimate authority.

His plan was a simple one. It was to lull the suspicions of the revolutionaries by an apparent resignation to their will, while doing nothing to facilitate putting the Constitution in force. On the contrary, when the aristocrat bishops protested violently against the decrees concerning the clergy, he would give not a word, not a sign, to repudiate them and recall them to a sense of their duty. He would give a personal example of hostility to the decrees which he had accepted by choosing as his chaplains none but non-juring priests. He had already taken measures to ensure that his tardy acceptance of the decree concerning the oath, which he granted on December 26, 1790, should appear to have been extorted by force. He waited till the Constituent Assembly had sent him repeated demands, and his minister Saint-Priest had offered his resignation; and when he did at last sign the decree, he exclaimed in the presence of his family: "I had rather be King of Metz than remain King of France under such conditions, but this will not last long."

He did not, however, encourage local insurrections, which he considered premature and doomed to certain failure, and he censured the Count of Artois and the *émigrés* who continued to foment them against his advice (the Lyons plot of December 1790). The only thing in which he believed was collective intervention by the sovereigns, back up by military demonstrations, and all the efforts of his secret minister Breteuil were directed towards this end. He was delighted at the *rapprochement* which took place between Prussia and Austria at Reichenbach at the end of July 1790 through the mediation of England. This *rapprochement* enabled his brother-in-law the Emperor to reconquer Belgium, which at the end of 1788 had risen in revolt against his reforms. On November 22, indeed, Austrian troops re-entered the Netherlands, and by December 2 the whole country was pacified. When the moment arrived, Louis XVI was to escape secretly by the Montmédy route and join Bouillé's army. The Austrian army would be close at hand to lend its support.

The Emperor found a pretext ready to hand for setting his troops in motion. The interests of the German princes possessing fiefs in Alsace and Lorraine had been injured by the ordinances of August 4 suppressing their seigniorial courts and the personal servitude to which their peasants were subject. The Constituent Assembly had resolved to offer them compensation, but in order to foment discord it was important that it should be refused. Louis XVI sent Augeard, the farmer-general, to Germany to obtain a secret promise that they would submit their claims to the Diet of the Empire. As soon as the conquest of the Netherlands was complete, the Emperor took the matter in hand. On December 14, 1790 he sent Montmorin an official note protesting on the strength of the treaties of Westphalia against the application of the August resolutions to the German princes owning property in Alsace and Lorraine.

The Emperor's support was the decisive factor upon which the King and Queen counted to ensure success. But Breteuil tried to enrol in the monarchist Holy League not only the Pope, but Spain, Russia, Sweden, Sardinia, Denmark, and the Swiss cantons. They did not anticipate any assistance from Prussia or England, but tried to obtain at least their neutrality. Bouillé advised them to cede an island to England, and Champcenetz was actually sent to London at the beginning of 1791 to offer territorial compensation in India or the Antilles. Spain was winding up her colonial struggle with England and bringing pressure to bear upon the Pope to stir up a religious war in France. King Gustavus III of Sweden, the champion of divine right, made peace with Russia and established himself at Spa, from whence he sent encouraging communications to Louis XVI. The Pope sent sharp notes of protest at the loss of his territories of Avignon and the Venaissin. But everything depended upon the Emperor, and the prudent Leopold, who was more concerned with the affairs of Turkey, Poland, and Belgium than with those of France, displayed some scepticism with regard to his brother-in-law's proposed escape, raised endless objections, resorted to every form of evasion, sheltered himself behind the idea of obtaining a preliminary agreement between the powers, and would only promise his conditional assistance for a limited period. Eight months were lost in fruitless negotiations with Vienna, and the secret leaked out. As early as December 1790 the democratic papers, Marat's *Ami du peuple* and Prudhomme's *Révolutions de Paris*, alluded to the King's impending flight, and Dubois-Crancé disclosed the plan at the Jacobins on January 30, 1791.

A campaign inspired by the republicans was already taking shape in the press of the extreme left, in Robert's *Mercure national*, in Rutledge's *Creuset*, in Bonneville's *Bouche de fer*, and in the *Révolutions de Paris*. Voltaire's *Brutus* was acted at the Théâtre Français in November 1790 and met with a "delirious" reception. Lavicomterie brought out his republican pamphlet *Du peuple et des rois*. In February 1791 the Abbé Fauchet wound up one of his speeches before the Friends of Liberty with some words which roused an echo far and wide: "The tyrants are ripe for their fate!"

The progress of the democratic party became more marked. In October 1790 the freemason Nicolas de Bonneville, editor of the *Bouche de fer*, assembled the Friends of Truth once a week in the amphitheatre of the Palais Royal, where the Abbé Fauchet expounded Rousseau's *Social Contract*. The Friends of Truth held cosmopolitan views, and dreamt of putting an end to hatred between nations and classes. Even to the Jacobins their social theories seemed very bold.

Side by side with the great clubs, local clubs were beginning to appear. In the summer of 1790 Dufourny, the engineer, Saintex, the doctor, and Momoro, the printer, founded in what had formerly been the section of the Cordeliers, but was now the section of the Théâtre Français, the Society of the Friends of the Rights of Man and the Citizen, also known by the shorter name of the Club of the Cordeliers, because it first held its sessions in the convent of the Cordeliers, until it was driven out by Bailly and moved to the Musée in the rue Dauphine. The Friends of the Rights of Man were not a political debating-society, but a fighting group. "Their main object," says their foundation charter, "is to denounce before the tribunal of public opinion the abuses of the various authorities, and every sort of infringement of the rights of man." They announced it as their mission to protect the oppressed and redress abuses. Their objects were to exercise vigilance, examine into the actions of others, and act. Their official papers were adorned with a "vigilant eye (*œil de la surveillance*)," wide open to all the failings of elected representatives and officials. They visited persecuted patriots in prison, undertook inquiries, opened subscriptions, and got up petitions and demonstrations, and, when necessary, riots. Thanks to the very low subscription of two sous a month, they recruited their members among the lower middle classes and even among the "passive" citizens, those not possessing the property qualification of electors. It was this that gave them their strength. In case of need they were able to stir and rouse the masses.

The Cordeliers were soon backed up by the clubs of other districts, numbers of which came into existence during the winter of 1790 and 1791 under the name of fraternal or popular societies. The earliest of them, founded by a poor schoolmaster, Claude Dansard, held its sessions in one of the halls of the Jacobin convent, where the Friends of the Constitution already held their sessions. By the light of a tallow candle, which he brought in his pocket, Dansard held meetings of the artisans, greengrocers, and manual labourers of the neighbourhood, reading and expounding to them the decrees of the Constituent Assembly. Marat, with his usual clearness of vision, realized how useful these clubs for humble people might be to the democrats. He did all he could to encourage their formation. There was soon one in every part of Paris. It was through them that the political education of the masses was carried on and the big popular battalions raised and organized. Their founders, Tallien, Méhée Latouche, Lebois, Sergent, Concedieu, the Abbé Danjou, were all Cordeliers. They played an important part during the Terror. For the time being they supported with all their might the democratic campaign against Lafayette, the refractory priests, and the Court. Their ideal, borrowed from Jean-Jacques Rousseau, was that of direct government. They held that the Constitution and even the laws should be subject to the ratification of the people, and they were not slow to express their distrust of the oligarchy of politicians which had replaced the oligarchy of nobles and priests. They blamed the Constituent Assembly for not submitting the new Constitution to the people and for opposing so many obstacles to its revision.

In May 1791 the Cordeliers and fraternal societies came together and formed a federation. A central committee, presided over by the republican journalist Robert, served as a link between them. The economic crisis caused by the depreciation of the assignat was already beginning to make itself felt. Robert and his friends realized to what advantage they could turn this and did their best to win the hearts of the Paris workmen, who were clamouring for increased wages. A number of strikes broke out: strikes of carpenters, printers, hatters, blacksmiths, etc. Bailly desired to prohibit meetings of corporate bodies. On June 14, 1791 the Constituent Assembly passed Chapelier's motion for the strict repression of all combinations for imposing a uniform wage on employers, which became an offence against the law. Robert protested in the *Mercure national* against the ill will shown towards workmen by the public authorities. He skilfully blended the claims of democracy with those of the corporations and, supported by Robespierre, reopened the campaign against the property qualification for electors. The agitation spread to the provincial towns and openly assumed the character of a class struggle. The Fayettist newspapers unanimously denounced the democrats as anarchists inspired by an animus against property.

If Louis XVI and Marie Antoinette had paid attention to these symptoms, they would have realized that the growing strength of the republican movement was gradually diminishing the chances of a counter-revolution, even supported by foreign bayonets. But they shut their eyes or else let themselves be lulled into security by Mirabeau, who represented to them that the divisions among the revolutionaries were working in their favour. Indeed, the antagonism between the Fayettist and the Lamethist

123

parties was becoming more and more pronounced. The former no longer set foot inside the Jacobins. The latter were daily losing their influence over the club, where they had to look on at the rise of Robespierre, who reproached them with their treachery in the matter of giving the vote to the coloured races. Ever since Barnave, in order to please the Lameths, who owned large estates in Santo Domingo, had become the mouthpiece of the white colonists against the enfranchised blacks, he had become unpopular. Mirabeau did his best to foment these internecine conflicts. He had obtained a rich grant from the civil list for organizing, by the aid of Talon and Sémonville, an agency for propaganda and corruption, which distributed royalist pamphlets and newspapers and bribed the more venal members of the clubs. The Court had its agents even on the committee of the Jacobins (Villars, Bonnecarrère, Desfieux, etc.) and among the Cordeliers (Danton), which gave it a false sense of security. Imprudences were committed, one of the most serious being the departure of Mesdames, the daughters of Louis XV, who left France for Rome in February 1791. Their departure caused intense agitation throughout the whole of France. "The safety of the common weal," wrote Gorsas in his *Courrier,* "forbids that Mesdames should betake themselves with their millions to the Pope or elsewhere. Their persons ought to be guarded with the greatest care, for they help to provide us with a pledge against the hostile intentions of their nephew M. d'Artois and their cousin Bourbon-Condé." "We are at war with the enemies of the Revolution," added Marat. "We must keep these pious sisters (*béguines*) as hostages and surround the rest of the family with a triple guard." This idea that the royal family was a hostage to protect them against the vengeance of the *émigrés* and sovereigns took deep root in the minds of the revolutionaries. Mesdames were twice stopped on their way, at Moret and at Arnay-le-Duc, and a special order from the Assembly was necessary before they could continue their journey. Disturbances broke out in Paris. The marketwomen from the Halles waited upon Monsieur, the King's brother, and asked him to pledge his word that he would stay in Paris. The Tuileries were besieged on February 24, and Lafayette relieved the palace only with difficulty.

Mirabeau would have preferred the King to escape in the direction of Normandy rather than in that of Lorraine. On February 28 workmen from the faubourg Saint-Antoine went to raze the keep of the Château of Vincennes. While Lafayette and the National Guard were on their way to Vincennes to stop the disturbance, four hundred noblemen, armed with daggers, met by appointment at the Tuileries, but Lafayette was warned in time and succeeded in returning to the palace to disarm "the knights of the dagger" (*chevaliers du poignard*). It was suspected that the disorders at Vincennes had been fomented out of the court funds, and that the knights of the dagger had assembled to cover the King's escape while the National Guard was kept busy outside of Paris.

Hostile though the Assembly was to the *factieux* (agitators, sectaries) —that is to say, the left wing of the opposition—it could not fail to be uneasy at the manœuvres of the aristocrats. Both the Lamethists and the Fayettists were at that time in agreement with Robespierre and the extreme left in repudiating any intervention of the sovereigns in the internal affairs of France. Since the Congress of Reichenbach their eyes had been turned towards the frontier. At the end of July 1790, when the Austrian Government asked leave for part of the troops sent to put down the Belgian revolt to pass through French territory, they had already obtained the passage of a decree (July 28) expressly refusing them permission to do so; and another decree of the same date called upon the King to provide for the manufacture of cannon, guns, and bayonets. When reports of the King's impending escape began to spread abroad, the Assembly decided, on January 28, 1791, that the regiments on the frontier should be reinforced. On February 21, the day after the departure of Mesdames, it began debating a law directed against the *émigrés*, to the great indignation of Mirabeau, who in opposing the project appealed to the Declaration of the Rights of Man. On March 7 the Committee of Inquiries of the Assembly discussed a compromising letter from the Queen to the Austrian ambassador, Mercy-Argenteau, and at once proceeded to consider the proposed law providing for a regency. On this occasion Alexandre Lameth exclaimed that the nation had the right "to repudiate a king who should desert the position assigned to him by the Constitution," and added, among interuptions from the right: "The committee rightly regards a possible desertion on the part of a king as an abdication." A decree was passed excluding women from the regency, which was aimed straight at Marie Antoinette. When, at the end of March, the Austrian troops occupied the district of Porrentruy, the Alsatian deputy Reubell, supported by Robespierre, protested vigorously against this menace and violently denounced the mustering of *émigrés* on the French frontier.

Mirabeau died suddenly on April 2, 1791, as the result of a night of orgy. The democrats were well-informed and knew that he had been in the pay of the Court for a long time past. The Cordeliers Club rang with curses upon his memory, but the popularity of the Machiavellian

125

champion of the people was still so great that the Assembly was forced to vote him a state funeral in the Church of Sainte Geneviève, now transformed into the Panthéon.

The Court was not left long without advisers. The Lameths and Talleyrand offered to take Mirabeau's place, and their services were accepted. Alexandre Lameth was placed in charge of the distribution of the civil list. With the money provided by the Court his brother Charles, with Adrien Duport, immediately founded the *Logographe*, a great newspaper which was intended to supplant Lafayette's organ, the *Moniteur*. Talleyrand promised to obtain the grant of freedom of worship to those adhering to the refractory priests, and, as we have seen, kept his promise. But though Louis XVI made use of these men, he despised them and did not trust them with his secret counsels.

He was growing impatient at the procrastination of Leopold, of whom he had in vain requested an advance of fifteen millions, and now resolved to act promptly. On April 17 he received the communion from Cardinal de Montmorency, to the great indignation of the National Guards present, who protested and murmured audibly in the chapel. On the following day, April 18, he was to have gone to spend the Easter holidays at Saint-Cloud, as he had done the year before. A report had gone round that the journey to Saint-Cloud was merely the prelude to a longer one. Crowds gathered before the Tuileries, and when the King tried to drive out, the National Guards not only refused to clear the way for the carriages, but prevented his departure. Lafayette suspected that this had all been arranged in advance, so as to enable the King to prove to the Emperor and the European sovereigns that he was a prisoner in his palace. The riot was supposed to have been got up for this purpose by Danton. As the Queen returned to the palace, she remarked to those about her: "Now at least you will admit that we are not free."

Henceforward Louis XVI had no further scruples about deceiving the revolutionaries. On the following day he went to the Assembly and declared that he was free and that it was of his own free will that he had given up his visit to Saint-Cloud. "I have accepted the Constitution," he said, "of which the Civil Constitution of the clergy is a part. I will maintain it with all my power." He attended the mass said by the constitutional priest of the parish of Saint-Germain l'Auxerrois; he sent a circular letter to the sovereigns through diplomatic channels declaring that he had espoused the revolutionary cause without reserve and with no intention of going back upon his word; but at the same time he sent warning to the sovereigns through Breteuil that they were not to attach

126

any importance to his public utterances. Marie Antoinette begged her brother the Emperor to move fifteen thousand men to Arlon and Virton in order to lend their support to Bouillé. On May 18 the Emperor informed the Comte de Durfort, who had been sent to him at Mantua, that he would send the troops, but could not intervene till the King and Queen had left Paris and repudiated the Constitution by a manifesto. He refused the fifteen millions.

Louis XVI raised money by borrowing from bankers. He left about midnight on June 20, disguised as a valet, in a great berline specially made for the occasion. The Count of Provence left at the same time, by another route, and reached Belgium without difficulty. But Louis XVI was recognized at Sainte-Menehould by Drouet, the postmaster, and stopped at Varennes. Bouillé's army arrived too late to save him, and the hussars stationed at Varennes went over to the people As the royal family re-entered Paris, their route was lined by National Guards who had hurried up from the most distant villages to prevent this precious hostage from passing into the enemy's hands. The only result of the manifesto published by Louis XVI on his departure, condemning the work of the Constitution and calling upon his faithful adherents for assistance, was to rouse the whole of revolutionary France. Aristocrats and refractory priests were placed under observation, disarmed, and interned. The more ardent of them emigrated and this fresh emigration still further weakened the forces in the country upon which the Crown might have relied. In certain regiments all the officers deserted.

The whole of France believed that the flight of the King was the prelude to a foreign war. The first act of the Assembly on the morning of June 21 was to give orders to close the frontiers and to forbid the removal of specie, arms, and munitions from the country. It mobilized the National Guards in the north-eastern region and gave orders to raise a hundred thousand volunteers, recruited from among the National Guards and paid at the rate of fifteen sous a day. It dispatched a number of its members into the departments as delegates, invested with almost unlimited powers, to make the troops of the line take the oath and to inspect the fortresses, arsenals, and magazines. The eastern towns had already placed themselves in a state of defence without waiting for the arrival of these commissaries.

The fear of a foreign war was by no means groundless. Diplomatic relations with the Pope had already been broken off. The King of Sweden ordered all Swedish subjects to leave France. The Empress Catherine II of Russia cut off all intercourse with Genêt, the French chargé d'affaires.

Spain expelled French subjects by thousands and gave orders for troops to be moved into Catalonia and Navarre. As for the Emperor, on July 6 he issued from Padua a circular letter to all the sovereigns calling upon them to join him "in deliberation, in joint action, and in measures for demanding liberty and honourable treatment of the Most Christian King and his family and for setting bounds to the dangerous excesses of the French Revolution." On his return to Vienna he intimated to the French ambassador, the Marquis de Noailles, that he was not to appear at Court so long as the suspension of Louis XVI lasted. On July 25 his chancellor, old Kaunitz, signed the preliminaries of a treaty of offensive and defensive alliance with Prussia; he also contemplated summoning a European congress at Spa or Aix-la-Chapelle specially for dealing with French affairs.

War was averted, however, chiefly because Louis XVI himself requested his brother-in-law to postpone it, and also because the leaders in the Constituent Assembly were so afraid of the democratic party that they durst not dethrone the perjured and renegade monarch, and ultimately preferred to restore the crown to him.

The return from Varennes, the sight of the armed and seething crowds, the impressive silence of the people of Paris, who stood with their hats on as the royal berline passed by, the sight of the democratic papers, full of insults and cries of hatred, all gave the King and Queen serious food for thought. They realized the full extent of their unpopularity and said to themselves that a foreign war would increase the ferment and threaten their own personal safety. They were afraid.

Monsieur was already thinking of proclaiming himself regent during his brother's captivity. Louis XVI, whose confidence in his brothers was strictly limited, did not want to abdicate in their favour, and tried to restrain the Emperor. "The King," wrote Marie Antoinette to Fersen on July 8, "thinks that the open exertion of force, even after a preliminary manifesto, would prove an incalculable danger, not only to him and his family, but to all Frenchmen in the realm whose opinion is not in favour of the Revolution."

Now, it so happened that the leaders in the Constituent Assembly also wanted to maintain peace, for a variety of weighty reasons. They had been alarmed by the explosion of democratic and republican sentiment in Paris and throughout the whole of France which had greeted the news of the King's flight. In Paris, Santerre the brewer had armed two thousand sansculottes, "passive" citizens of the faubourg Saint-Antoine. Statues of kings had been overthrown almost everywhere, and the word "royal" had been effaced from nearly all shop-fronts and even from the street signs. Numbers of violent petitions had come in from Montpellier, Clermont-Ferrand, Bayeux, Lons-le-Saunier, etc., demanding the punishment of the perjured King, his immediate supersession, and even a republic. The conservatives in the Assembly banded themselves together to check the democratic movement. As early as June 21 Bailly made use of the word "abduction (*enlèvement*)." The Assembly adopted the word, intending by this means to exculpate Louis XVI personally, in order to keep him upon the throne in certain conditions. The Marquis de Bouillé, who had fled to Luxemburg, indirectly aided this manœuvre by the insolent manifesto in which he declared that he alone was responsible for what had happened. The members of the Assembly took him at his word.

Among the conservatives of the Patriot party it was only the little group of Lafayette's friends, La Rouchefoucauld, Dupont of Nemours, Condorcet, Achille Duchâtelet, Brissot, Dietrich, mayor of Strasbourg—all members of the Club of 1789—who inclined for a moment towards a republic, no doubt with the secret intention of placing at the head of it "the hero of two worlds." But Lafayette did not dare to declare himself. He required the support of the Lameths in order to meet the attacks of the democrats, who accused him, through the mouth of Danton, of complicity in the King's flight; and he went over to the opinion of the majority.

When they heard that Louis XVI had been stopped, the Constituent Assembly breathed once more. They said to themselves that it would be possible to avoid war. The person of Louis XVI, their hostage, would serve as their safeguard. Their calculations are clearly to be seen in the semi-official paper, *La Correspondance nationale*, of June 25. "We must avoid affording the foreign powers hostile to our Constitution any pretext for attacking us. If we dethrone Louis XVI, they will arm all Europe against us on the pretext of avenging outraged royalty. Let us respect Louis XVI, guilty though he be of an act of infamous treason to the French nation, let us respect Louis XVI, let us respect his family, not for his sake, but for our own." All the worthy people who wanted peace understood this language and applauded it. Moreover, the Lameths had good reasons to deal gently with the King, for they were already drawing on the civil list for their paper, *Le Logographe*.

In order to keep Louis XVI on the throne, they made the most of the point that if he were dethroned, it would be necessary to establish a regency. Who would be the regent? The Duke of Orleans. But would the duke be recognized without opposition? The King's brothers still had partisans, although they had emigrated. They would be supported by the foreign powers. Besides, the Duke of Orleans was surrounded by adventurers. He was accused of subsidizing popular agitators, especially Danton, who, with Réal, was actually demanding the deposition of Louis XVI and the substitution for him of a protector, who could be none other than the Duke, or his son, the Duke of Chartres, afterwards Louis Philippe, whose candidature was definitely advocated in the press. If the regency was rejected, would they go as far as a republic? But the republic demanded by the Cordeliers meant not only foreign but civil war, for the people did not seem prepared for such a novel form of government.

The Constituent Assembly accordingly preferred to maintain Louis XVI, subject to certain precautions. They would not reinstate him in his functions till they had revised the Constitution and he had once more accepted it and taken the oath to it. Louis XVI was no doubt bound to be a discredited king, with no prestige. The Lameths and Barnave easily consoled themselves for this. They said to themselves that a puppet, who would owe the preservation of his crown to them, would no longer be able to govern without them and the class of society which they represented. As early as the return from Varennes they offered the Queen their services, which were eagerly accepted. The alliance was not sincere on either side. The Lameths and Barnave thought they would be able to exercise the real power in the King's name. The King and Queen reserved the right of throwing away these instruments as soon as the danger was past.

The King was therefore not put on trial by the Assembly, in spite of Robespierre's vigorous efforts. The only persons tried were those responsible for his "abduction"—Bouillé, who had fled, and a few lay figures. On July 15 Barnave carried the Assembly with him by a great speech in which he took pains to identify the republic with anarchy: "I now come to the real question. Are we going to put an end to the Revolution, or are we going to reopen it? You have made all men equal before the law, you have established civil and political equality, you have recovered for the State all that had been taken away from the sovereignty of the people; any further step would be a fatal and criminal act, another step in the direction of liberty would mean the destruction of royalty, another step in the direction of equality would mean the *destruction of property*."

This appeal to conservatism found an echo among the middle classes. But the populace of Paris, stirred up by the Cordeliers and fraternal

130

societies, was harder to convince. Threatening petitions and demonstrations followed one upon the other. For a moment the Jacobins allowed themselves to be carried away into demanding the deposition of the King and "his replacement by constitutional means"—that is to say, by a regency. But the Cordeliers repudiated this Orleanist petition, drawn up by Brissot and Danton. On July 17 they assembled on the Champ de Mars to sign a frankly republican petition, drawn up by Robert, on the altar of the nation. The Assembly took fright. Seizing the pretext of a disturbance which had occurred that morning at Le Gros-Caillou, but was totally unconnected with this movement, it gave orders to the mayor of Paris to disperse the gathering on the Champ de Mars. At seven o'clock in the evening the peaceful crowd was fired upon without previous warning by Lafayette's National Guards as they entered the enclosure at the double. There were a number of casualties.

The massacre was followed by repression. A special decree was passed, a regular law of general security, which suspended the threat of repressive measures over the leaders of the popular societies, who were arrested and put on trial by hundreds. Their papers were suppressed or ceased to appear. The idea was to strike down the heads of the democratic and republican party just as the elections to the Legislative Assembly were about to begin. The conservative wing of the Jacobins had already seceded on July 16 and had founded a new club in the convent of the Feuillants (Cistercian monks of the stricter observance). Robespierre, Anthoine, Pétion, and Coroller were almost the only deputies who remained at the Jacobins, but they still had the good fortune to carry in their wake most of the clubs in the departments.

From this time onwards there was violent opposition between the Feuillants—that is to say, the united followers of Lafayette and the Lameths—and the Jacobins, now purged of their right wing. For the time being, the former kept the power in their hands. Adrien Duport, Alexandre Lameth, and Barnave, through the agency of the Abbé Louis, whom they sent to Brussels, negotiated secretly with the Emperor to preserve peace. Leopold concluded from their advances that the revolutionaries had been awed by his threats from Padua and were less dangerous than he had supposed; and as they promised to save the monarchy, he gave up the idea of the congress and of war, all the more easily since he gathered from the very cold response made by the powers to his circular letter that a European concert directed against France could not possibly be achieved. In order to mask his retreat he agreed to sign a joint declaration with the King of Prussia, in which the threat to the revolutionaries would be

131

only a conditional one. But this Declaration of Pillnitz, dated August 25, 1791, was turned to their own ends by the princes, who affected to see in it a promise of assistance. On September 10 they issued a violent manifesto adjuring Louis XVI to refuse his signature to the Constitution.

It no doubt cost the triumvirate considerable efforts to induce the King to give his signature, for he had put it off from September 3 to 14. The triumvirs represented to him that the Constitution had been improved by the revision to which they had submitted it after his return. They particularly emphasized the point that in future the Civil Constitution of the clergy would not be a constitutional law, but an ordinary law, and could consequently be modified by the legislature. Considerable restrictions had been imposed upon the liberty of the clubs. Though the property qualification (the silver mark) for candidates for election as deputy had been abolished, that required from electors had, on the other hand, been made heavier. They added that they would endeavour in future to put in force the two-chamber system, which they had opposed so vigorously in September 1789, and they again pledged themselves to defend the absolute veto and the king's right to appoint judges. The King submitted, adroitly asking the Assembly for a general amnesty, which was passed with enthusiasm. Both aristocrats and republicans were released from prison. Celebrations were everywhere organized in honour of the completion of the Constitution. The middle classes believed that the Revolution was over. They were overjoyed, for the danger of civil and foreign war seemed to have been removed. It remained to be seen whether the Feuillants, by whom they were represented, would be able to keep control at once of the Court and the new Assembly which was about to meet. But by appealing to the disinterestedness of his colleagues Robespierre had obtained the passage of a decree making them all ineligible for the Legislative Assembly. The direction of political affairs was about to pass into fresh hands. Moreover, it remained to be seen whether the democratic party would forgive the conservative middle classes for the severe repression which the former had recently had to endure, or consent for long to support the domination of those enjoying the privileges of wealth after overthrowing those enjoying the privileges of birth.

CHAPTER XI

The War

To judge from appearances only, the Legislative Assembly, which met on October 1, 1791, seemed likely to carry on the traditions of the Constituent. Only 136 of its members joined the Jacobins, whereas 264 entered themselves on the books of the Feuillants. But the centre, the 345 independent members who formed the majority, were sincere adherents of the Revolution. Though they were afraid of playing into the hands of the factions, they were quite determined not to be duped by the Court, which they did not trust.

The Feuillants were divided into two groups with different tendencies, or rather into two cliques. Some, such as Mathieu Dumas, Vaublanc, Dumolard, Jaucourt, and Théodore Lameth (the brother of Alexandre and Charles), took their orders from the triumvirate. The others, such as Ramond, Beugnot, Pastoret, Gouvion, Daverhoult, and Girardin (the former marquis, Jean-Jacques Rousseau's patron), drew their inspiration from Lafayette.

Lafayette was detested by the Queen, and the fact that he was not admitted to the secret negotiations between the triumvirs and the Court wounded his vanity. Whereas the triumvirs went very far in the direction of reaction, even accepting the principle of two chambers, the absolute veto, and the appointment of judges by the king, Lafayette clung to the Constitution and was loath to sacrifice the principles of the Declaration of the Rights of Man, which he regarded as his own work. Since the Court had begun to hold him at arm's length, he had not the same personal interest in the restoration of the royal power as the Lameths.

It was the internal divisions of the Feuillants that led to the election in November 1791 of a mayor of Paris from outside their ranks. On the retirement of Bailly, Lafayette, who had resigned his position as commandant of the National Guard, had his own name put forward as candidate for Bailly's place. The court newspapers opposed his candidature and brought about its failure. The Jacobin Petion was elected on November 16 by 6728 votes, whereas the general on the white horse received only 3126. The number of abstentions from voting was enormous (there were 80,000 active citizens in Paris). The King and Queen congratulated themselves upon the result. They were convinced that the revolutionaries would be ruined by their own excesses. "The very excess of evil," wrote Marie Antoinette to Fersen on November 25, "will enable us to profit by all this sooner than anyone thinks, but great prudence is necessary." Their policy was to make things worse in the hope of profiting by them.

Shortly afterwards Lafayette was given the command of an army on the frontier. Before leaving he avenged his reverse at the elections by obtaining the appointment of Rœderer, a friend of Brissot's, to the important post of *procureur général syndic* of the department of Paris in competition with Dandré, a former member of the Constituent Assembly, whose candidature was promoted by the Lameths.

While the Feuillants were weakening themselves by their dissensions, the Jacobins were boldly taking the initiative in a policy of national action against all the enemies of the Revolution, both at home and abroad. Elected by the business people who were buying national property and made a living by trade, they were particularly interested in raising the value of the assignat, which was already becoming depreciated, and in restoring the exchange, the rise of which was ruining France for the benefit of foreign countries. For them the economic and political problems were closely bound together. If the revolutionary currency was becoming depreciated, the reason was that the threats of the *émigrés* and kings, and the disorders instigated by aristocrats and priests, were destroying confidence. It was necessary to take vigorous measures to put an end to the hopes and intrigues of the counter-revolutionaries and to obtain the recognition of the Constitution by the monarchist governments of Europe. By this means alone would it be possible to check the serious economic and social crisis, which was going from bad to worse.

In the autumn, disorders again broke out in the towns and country districts, which grew worse as winter advanced and lasted for several months. In the towns they were caused in the first place by the excessive rise in the price of colonial produce, sugar, coffee, and rum, a scarcity of which had been produced by the race war which had broken out in Santo Domingo. At the end of January 1792 there were riots in Paris round the warehouses and shops of the grocers, who were forced by the crowd to lower the price of their goods under the threat of having their shops sacked. The sections in the working-class districts began to denounce "monopolists," and certain of these, such as Dandré and Boscary, ran a certain risk. In order to check the rise of prices and strike a blow at speculators the Jacobins took an oath to go without sugar.

In the country districts the riots had their origin in the high price of corn, but they were also a protest against the maintenance of the feudal system and a violent rejoinder to the threats of the *émigrés*, who were heralding invasion from beyond the frontier. Perhaps on the whole the agitation was less widespread and more superficial than that of 1789, but it resembled it in its causes and characteristics. In the first place, like the former, it was spontaneous: it is impossible to find any trace of concerted action. This direct action had not taken place on the advice of the Jacobins, who were alarmed at it and tried first to prevent the disorders and afterwards to set bounds to them. The insurgent mobs relied upon the authorities to lower the cost of living, and demanded regulations and fixed prices. They pillaged the estates of the *émigrés* and wanted to place the aristocrats and refractory priests in such a position that they would be harmless. Thus they were groping their way towards a program of revolutionary defence which was afterwards gradually carried into effect.

From November onwards disorderly crowds were beginning to collect round grain-carts, and markets were being pillaged on every side. At Dunkirk, in February, the houses of several merchants were sacked and there was a bloody engagement which left 14 killed and 60 wounded lying on the quays of the harbour. About the same time at Noyon thirty thousand peasants, armed with pitchforks, halberds, muskets, and pikes and led by their mayors, stopped the grain-boats on the Oise and divided the corn among themselves. At the end of the month the woodmen and nail-makers of the forests of Conches and Breteuil, with drums beating and flags flying, led the mob into the markets of Beauce and forced the municipalities to fix prices not only for cereals, but for eggs, butter, iron, wood, coal, etc. At Étampes the mayor, Simoneau, a rich tanner employing sixty workmen, attempted to oppose the fixing of prices, but was killed by two musket-shots. The Feuillants and even the Jacobins celebrated his memory as a martyr to the law and voted him a public funeral. Next it was the turn of the woodmen of the Morvan, who stopped the floating of lumber down the river and disarmed the National Guard of Clamecy. The disturbances were perhaps even more serious in the centre and south. In March the National Guards in the villages of Cantal, Lot, Dordogne, Corrèze, Gard, etc., attacked the country-houses of the *émigrés* and burnt or sacked them. As they marched along, they forced the rich "aristo-crats" to pay a contribution for the benefit of the volunteers leaving for the army. They demanded the entire abolition of the feudal system, and in the mean time they pulled down weathercocks and pigeon-houses.[1]

It is true that in royalist districts, like Lozère, it was the Patriots who were not safe. On February 26, 1792 and the following days the peasants in the neighbourhood of Mende, stirred up by their priests, marched on the town, forced the troops of the line to evacuate it and withdraw to Marvejols, and levied contributions on the Patriots as compensation for the working-days that they had lost. Ten members of the Patriot party were imprisoned, the constitutional bishop held as a hostage, the club closed, and several houses sacked. It may be noted, moreover, that these royalist disturbances in Lozère happened before the revolutionary disturbances in Cantal and Gard, which came as a rejoinder to them.

If we consider that during that winter of 1791–2 the sale of the property of the Church was already far advanced—for by November 1, 1791, 1,526,000,000 livres' worth had been sold—we may understand the powerful motives which prompted the peasants. War was threatening and they had interests of vast importance at stake. If the Revolution were overthrown, the gabelle, *aides, tailles,* tithes, and feudal dues which it had abolished would be re-established, the property which had been sold would be restored to the Church, the *émigrés* would return thirsting for vengeance. Woe to the peasants if they did! They trembled at the very thought.

In 1789 the urban middle classes had armed themselves with one accord to put down the risings of peasants and workmen with the utmost rigour. This time the middle classes were divided. Since the flight to Varennes the richer of them had been alarmed, and would have been glad of a reconciliation with the monarchy. They formed the bulk of the party of the Feuillants, which was becoming more and more fused with the old monarchist and aristocratic party, and they dreaded a republic and the prospect of war. But the rest of the middle classes were less timorous and not so rich, and had lost all confidence in the King since Varennes. They thought of nothing but their own self-protection, and realized that this could be secured only by keeping in touch with the mass of the workers. Their leaders therefore endeavoured to avert a split between the lower and the middle classes. In a letter to Buzot, of February 6, 1792, Petion complains that the middle classes are drawing away from the

---

[1] Since none but the feudal lords had the right to have weathercocks on their houses, these had become a symbol of feudalism; pigeon-houses too were a privilege of the nobles, and the peasants complained bitterly of the damage done to their crops by hosts of pigeons.

masses: "They are setting themselves above them," he said; "they consider themselves on an equality with the nobility, who despise them and are only waiting for a favourable moment to humiliate them. . . . They have been told so often that it was a war between the 'haves' and the 'have-nots' (*ceux qui avaient et ceux qui n'avaient pas*) that they cannot get rid of the idea. The masses, on their side, are angry with the middle classes and indignant at their ingratitude; they remember what services they have done them, and how they were all brothers in the palmy days of liberty. The privileged classes are covertly fomenting this war which is leading us by imperceptible degrees to our ruin. The middle classes and the masses together made the Revolution; nothing but union between them can preserve it." In order to stop pillaging and burning throughout the country the Legislative Assembly on February 9, 1792 hastily enacted that the property of the *émigrés* should be handed over to the nation. Goupilleau, who drew up the report on this measure which was submitted to the Assembly, justified it by saying that the *émigrés* had caused enormous damage to France, for which they owed compensation. By taking up arms against their country they had forced her to arm herself in turn. "Their property is the natural security for the loss and expenditure of every sort which they have caused." Gohier added that if they were allowed to retain the enjoyment of their revenues, they would use them against their country. War had not yet been declared, but it was already looming close upon the horizon.

On February 29, 1792, in the midst of the disorders in central France, Robespierre's friend Couthon, the paralytic, who was deputy for Cantal, asserted from the tribune of the Assembly that in order to vanquish the coalition which was being formed, "it was necessary to secure the moral support of the people, more powerful than that of armies," and that there was only one means of doing so—to bind them to the Government by just laws. He proposed to suppress without compensation all such feudal dues as were not justified by a genuine transference of land to those liable for these dues. Only such rights would be maintained as the feudal lords could prove, by producing their original title-deeds, fulfilled this condition. When we consider that it had hitherto been incumbent upon the peasants to prove that payment was not due from them, whereas now, on the contrary, the lord had to prove that payment was due to him, and when we consider, moreover, that the only proof admissible was to be the production of a contract which had perhaps never existed, or had been mislaid or lost in course of time, we may understand the full significance of Couthon's proposal. The Feuillants tried to obtain its re-

137

jection by persistent obstruction. On June 18, 1792 the Assembly voted merely for the abolition, without compensation, of all casual dues—that is, those payable to the feudal lord on every transfer of property held by payment of a money rent and known as *lods et ventes*. Moreover, all of these casual dues which could be proved valid by the production of the original title-deeds were maintained in force. The opposition of the Feuillants had to be crushed by the Revolution of August 10 before the rest of Couthon's motion passed into law. It was the war which completed the liberation of the peasants.

War was desired at once by the left wing of the Assembly, the Fayettists and the Court. It was only the Lameths on the one hand and the little groups of democrats gathered round Robespierre at the Jacobins on the other who made any attempt to preserve peace. The advocates of both war and peace were, moreover, inspired by different and even conflicting views.

The left had as its leaders two Parisian deputies, Brissot and Condorcet, and a group of brilliant orators sent to the Assembly by the department of the Gironde, Vergniaud, Gensonné, and Guadet. Other prominent members were the declamatory orator Isnard, the Protestant pastor Lasource, Fauchet, the constitutional bishop of Calvados, a grandiloquent and rhetorical speaker who had come out in favour of a republic after Varennes. Finally, on the extreme left, there was the Cordelier trio, consisting of three deputies, Basire, Merlin of Thionville, and Chabot, who were intimate friends and lived for pleasure and money. They did not exert a great influence in the Assembly, but their effect upon the clubs and popular societies was considerable.

Brissot directed the foreign policy of the left. He had lived for a long time in England, where he had founded a newspaper and reading-room which had not been a success, and the winding up of which had involved him in a scandalous lawsuit. He had been in trouble at one time with Louis XVI's police and had even been imprisoned in the Bastille as the author or distributor of lampoons on Marie Antoinette. A little later he had been associated with the Genevese banker Clavière in speculating in the United States debt and in this connexion had paid a short visit to the United States, which had furnished him with material for a hastily written book. His enemies alleged that, being pressed for money, he had been in the pay of the police before 1789. He was certainly an active man, full of imagination and resource and not very scrupulous in the choice of his methods. He subsequently passed into the service of the Duke of Orleans, afterwards becoming a follower of Lafayette. He detested the

Lameths, whose reactionary colonial policy he attacked at the Society of Friends of the Negro, which he had founded. The Lameths accused him of having caused the revolt of the islands and the pillage of the plantations by his anti-slavery campaigns. During the crisis after Varennes he at first advocated a republic, together with Lafayette's friend Achille du Châtelet, but afterwards suddenly went over without any transition to the Orleanist solution. His election to the Legislative Assembly met with much opposition and was made possible—as, indeed, was Condorcet's—only by the aid of the Fayettist vote. In short, a dubious character and a schemer was about to become the most prominent leader in the new Assembly and its leading statesman.

The former Marquis de Condorcet was an important figure in the academic world; he had been the friend of d'Alembert and was the best-known survivor of the school of the Encyclopædists. But, like Brissot, he had an unstable and versatile character. In 1789 he had defended the privileged orders in the assembly of the nobility at Mantes, and he had afterwards opposed the Declaration of the Rights of Man. In 1790 he had written against the clubs and in favour of the monarchy and protested against the abolition of titles of nobility, the confiscation of the property of the clergy, and the assignats. With Sieys he had been one of the founders of the Club of 1789, with its Fayettist sympathies, but this had not prevented him from ostentatiously going over to the republic after Varennes.

It is understandable that Brissot and Condorcet should easily have come to an understanding with the deputies of the Gironde, who represented the interests of the Bordeaux merchants. The commercial interest was suffering from the economic crisis and demanded that vigorous measures should be taken to cope with it. Condorcet, who was Master of the Mint and had written a great deal on the subject of the assignats, was regarded as an authority on finance.

Brissotins and Girondins were convinced that the disturbances obstructing business were in the main caused by the uneasiness resulting from the supposed measures of the foreign powers and by the threats of the émigrés. There was only one remedy: to force the sovereigns to recognize the Revolution; to persuade them by a manifesto, and, if need be, by war, to disperse the gatherings of émigrés; and simultaneously to strike a blow at all their accomplices at home—above all, at the refractory priests. Brissot pointed out that the kings were disunited and their peoples ready to rise in imitation of the French; should it be necessary to fight, he prophesied an easy victory.

The Fayettists joined in the chorus. Most of them were former nobles, and military to the core. War would provide them with commands, and victory would restore their influence and power. With the support of their soldiers they would be strong enough to cow the Jacobins and impose their will on both the King and the Assembly. The Comte de Narbonne, whom they shortly afterwards caused to be appointed Minister for War, endeavoured to carry their policy into effect. Brissot, Clavière, and Isnard met Condorcet, Talleyrand, and Narbonne in Madame de Staël's drawing-room.

In these circumstances it was easy to carry the Assembly with them. The only long debates were those on the measures to be taken against the refractory priests, for the Fayettists, who were in favour of the widest religious toleration, were loath to abandon the policy of which they had obtained the triumph by the decree of May 7, 1791. At last, by a decree of October 31, 1791, the Count of Provence was given two months to return to France on pain of being deprived of his right to the throne; by a decree of November 9 the *émigrés* were given till January 1 to do the same, on pain of being regarded as under suspicion of conspiracy, and having the revenue from their estates sequestrated and collected on behalf of the nation; a decree of November 29 deprived the refractory priests of their pensions unless they took a fresh oath of a purely civic nature; it also gave the local administrative bodies the right to deport them from their residences in case of disorder and to impose various disabilities upon them. Finally, another decree of the same date requested the King to "call upon the Electors of Treves and Mainz and other princes of the Empire who are harbouring French refugees to put an end to these assemblies and the enlistment of troops which they are tolerating upon the frontier." The King was further requested to conclude as soon as possible the negotiations long since entered into with the Emperor and the Empire for compensating the German lords owning property in France who had been injured by the decrees of August 4.

Louis XVI and Marie Antoinette welcomed the warlike measures of the Brissotins with secret joy. Their request to Leopold to postpone his intervention after their arrest at Varennes had been made solely with a view to averting the imminent danger which threatened their lives. But as soon as Louis XVI had regained his crown, they urged Leopold in the most pressing terms to put into execution the measures which he had threatened from Padua and Pillnitz by summoning as soon as possible the congress of sovereigns which was to bring the revolutionaries to their senses. "It is armed force that has destroyed everything; armed force alone can make everything good," wrote Marie Antoinette to her brother as early as September 8, 1791. She was simple enough to imagine that France would tremble as soon as ever the monarchical governments of Europe raised their voices and brandished their arms. She little knew Europe and France, and her mistake no doubt arose from the pleasant surprise which she had experienced when she saw the very men who had brought about the Revolution—Barnave, Duport, and the Lameths—transformed into courtiers, destroying what they had formerly venerated, and stooping to play the part of suppliants and counsellors. She thought that the Feuillants represented the nation and that fear alone had made them so reasonable, and she tried to impart her conviction to Leopold. At first he proved very recalcitrant. His sister Maria Christina, regent of the Netherlands, pointed out to him the danger of a fresh revolt in Belgium if war broke out with France. Marie Antoinette had almost despaired of overcoming the Emperor's inertia when the Assembly provided her with the means of reviving the diplomatic conflict. On December 3 Louis XVI immediately wrote a personal letter to Frederick William, King of Prussia, asking him to come to his aid. "I have just written," he said, "to the Emperor, the Empress of Russia, and the Kings of Spain and Sweden, to lay before them the idea of a congress of the chief European powers, supported by an armed force, as the best means of putting a check on factious persons here, providing a means of re-establishing a more desirable order of things, and preventing the evil which is harassing us from spreading to the other European states." When the King of Prussia demanded an indemnity for the expenses which would be caused by his intervention, Louis XVI promised him compensation in money.

He naturally concealed these secret negotiations from the Lameths; he asked their advice, however, about giving his sanction to the decrees of the Assembly. The Lameths were thoroughly annoyed with the Assembly for being so insubordinate to their leadership. The attacks of the Brissotins on the ministers belonging to their party had aroused their indignation. They found themselves thrown more and more into the arms of the Court and of Austria in order to find support against the Jacobins. They advised the King to divide the decrees into two categories. He was to accept the one depriving Monsieur of the regency in certain circumstances, and the one calling upon him to send an ultimatum to the Electors of Treves and Mainz and to negotiate with the Emperor; but he was to veto the measures aimed at the *émigrés* and priests. By protecting the *émigrés* and priests the Lameths had no doubt desired to pave the way towards rallying all the conservative elements round their party. They also desired to inspire confidence in the Emperor, by proving to him that the

141

Constitution left the king real power. For their whole policy was based upon a whole-hearted and loyal understanding with Leopold. They hoped that, since he had remained pacific, he would use his good offices with the Electors threatened by the decree and persuade them to submit amicably. By this means war would be avoided, but the warlike attitude which they advised Louis XVI to adopt would have the advantage of restoring his popularity. It would merely be a move in their internal policy.

If the Lameths could have read the secret correspondence of Marie Antoinette, they would have realized the full gravity of the imprudence which they were committing. "The fools!" she wrote to Mercy on December 9. "They do not see that if they do such a thing [that is, threaten the Electors], it is a service to us, for if we begin, it will be necessary in the the end for all the powers to intervene and defend the rights of each and all." In other words, the Queen hoped that the incident might lead to the armed intervention which she was in vain demanding from her brother.

Louis XVI followed the advice of the Lameths in every point. He vetoed the decrees on the priests and *émigrés* and on December 14 went down to the Assembly and solemnly declared that "as the representative of the people he had felt the insult offered to it," and that consequently he had notified the Elector of Treves that "if before January 15 he had not put an end to all assemblies and hostile intentions within his territories on the part of the Frenchmen who had taken refuge there, he would henceforward regard him as nothing but an enemy of France." The applause which had greeted this vainglorious declaration had hardly died away when, on his return to the palace, he desired Breteuil to inform the Emperor and the sovereigns that he ardently desired the Elector of Treves not to yield to his ultimatum. "The party of the Revolution would be too puffed up with arrogance, and this success would keep the machinery running for a time." He requested the powers to take the affair in hand. "Instead of a civil war it will be a political war, and things will be all the better for it. . . . The physical and moral state of France is such that it is impossible for her to carry on [this war] for half a campaign, but it is necessary that I should appear to enter upon it whole-heartedly, as I should have done in former times. . . . It is necessary that my course of action should be such that the nation may find its only resource in its troubles in throwing itself into my arms." Always the same naïve duplicity and the same illusions with regard to the forces of the Revolution. Louis XVI was hurrying France into war in the hope that it would turn out badly and that as a result of defeat he would regain his absolute power.

He tried to bring about this defeat by tampering with the national defences as much as he could. He stopped the manufacture of munitions, and his Minister of Marine, Bertrand de Moleville, encouraged officers to emigrate by obtaining them leave and passports.

The war was further delayed for a time by the resistance of Robespierre, supported by a party in the Jacobins, and of the Lameths, supported by Leopold and a majority of the ministers.

Since the massacre of republicans on the Champ de Mars, Robespierre had distrusted Brissot and Condorcet, whose political vacillations and whose attachment to the party of Lafayette were disturbing to his clear-sighted intelligence. In his eyes, Girondins of the type of Vergniaud, Guadet, and Isnard, with their exaggerated language and empty assertions, were dangerous rhetoricians. He was aware of their aristocratic tastes and close connexion with the commercial world and remained upon his guard. Since he had attacked the distinction between active and passive citizens, the property qualifications for electors and those eligible for election, the restrictions of the right of holding meetings, of presenting petitions, and of forming associations, and the exclusive privilege of the middle classes of bearing arms; since he had outspokenly pronounced against reinstating the perjured King in his functions and had demanded the summoning of a convention to give France a new constitution, since he was almost the only member of the Constituent Assembly who had remained at the Jacobins, and had prevented their dissolution by a brave resistance to the repression of the Feuillants, he had become the unchallenged leader of the democratic party. His rigorous probity and repugnance for anything resembling intrigue were well known and his ascendancy over the populace and the lower middle classes was unlimited.

Robespierre's suspicions at once warned him that the Court was not sincere in proposing war, for by vetoing the decrees on the priests and *émigrés* and thus indirectly encouraging the continuance of disorder it was depriving the Revolution of the means of bringing this war to a victorious issue. As early as December 10, in an address to the affiliated societies which he drew up in the name of the Jacobins, he denounced to the country the manœuvre of the Lameths and the Court, who desired to prolong a state of anarchy with a view to the restoration of despotism. He soon asked himself whether in working for war, as desired by the Court, Brissot and his friends might not be indulging in an adroitly calculated attempt to outbid all rivals and direct the Revolution into dangerous paths. "To whom," he asked at the Jacobins on December 12, "would you entrust the conduct of this war? To the agents of the executive power?

If so, you will be abandoning the safety of the empire to those who want to ruin you. This leads us to conclude that war is the very thing which we ought most to fear." And, as though he had read the thoughts of Marie Antoinette, he added: "They want to drag you into a compromise by which the Court will gain a wider extension of its power. They want to embark upon a sham war, which may lead to a capitulation."

In vain did Brissot attempt in his speech of December 16 to remove Robespierre's prejudices and prove that war was necessary to purge liberty of the vices of despotism and consolidate it. "If," said Brissot, "you want to destroy the aristocracy, the refractory priests, and the malcontents at a single blow, destroy Coblenz. The head of the nation will be forced to reign in accordance with the Constitution, to see salvation nowhere save in fidelity to the Constitution, and to direct his course of action by it alone." In vain did Brissot attempt to strike the chord of national honour and appeal to interest: "Can we hesitate to attack them [the German princes]? Our honour, our public credit, the necessity for consolidating our Revolution and giving it a moral basis—all make this course of action obligatory."

On January 2, 1792 Robespierre subjected Brissot's ideas to a criticism full of wit and acumen. He noted that war was acceptable to the *émigrés*, the Court, and the Fayettists. His rejoinder to Brissot's remark that they must banish all mistrust was a palpable hit: "It was left for you to defend liberty without arousing distrust, without displeasing its enemies, without incurring the opposition of either the Court, the Ministers, or the moderates. How easy and smiling you have found the paths of patriotism!" Brissot had said that the centre of evil was at Coblenz. "So it is not in Paris?" inquired Robespierre. "So there is no connexion between Coblenz and another place not far from where we are?" Before setting out to attack the handful of aristocrats abroad, Robespierre wanted to crush those at home; and before carrying revolution to other nations, he wanted first to establish it firmly in France. He laughed at their illusions and propaganda and refused to believe that foreign nations were ready to rise against their tyrants at a word from France. "Armed missionaries," he said, "are loved by nobody." He feared lest the war might end badly. He pointed to the army without officers or officered by aristocrats, the regiments below strength, the National Guards without arms or equipment, the fortresses without munitions. He foresaw that, in the event of a successful war, there was a risk that liberty would succumb beneath the blows of ambitious generals; and he foretold a Cæsar.

For three months Robespierre and Brissot carried on a violent controversy from the tribune at the Jacobins and in the press, which led to an irrevocable split in the revolutionary party. All the deputies composing what was afterwards known as the Mountain rallied to Robespierre's side: Billaud-Varenne, Camille Desmoulins, Marat, Panis, Santerre, Anthoine. Danton played a double game, as was his habit. He first followed Robespierre, but ultimately took his place at Brissot's side when he saw that the majority of the club and the affiliated societies were decidedly in favour of war.

The opposition between Robespierre and Brissot was fundamental. Robespierre believed that no reconciliation was possible between the perjured King and the Revolution. He sought salvation in an internal crisis which should overthrow the treacherous monarchy, and desired to use the Constitution itself as a legal weapon to provoke this crisis. He advised the Assembly to abolish the royal veto on the ground that it was applicable only to the ordinary laws and not to exceptional measures. The abolition of the veto would have been the signal for the hoped-for crisis. Brissot, on the other hand, was unwilling to enter upon a life and death struggle with the Court. He merely proposed to win it over to his views by a policy of intimidation, and was revolutionary only in appearance. Like the Girondins, he dreaded mob rule and an attack on property, and did not want a social crisis. Robespierre, on the other hand, while professing a great respect for the Constitution, was trying to find in its own provisions the means of reforming it and overcoming the King's opposition.

The Lameths and Delessart, Minister for Foreign Affairs, flattered themselves, however, that by the aid of Leopold, with whom they were secretly in correspondence, they would avoid war. The Emperor did indeed bring pressure to bear upon the Elector of Treves to disperse the bands of *émigrés*, and the Elector complied with his request. Leopold advised France of this in a note of December 21, which arrived in Paris at the beginning of January. All pretext for war was disappearing. But in the same note the Emperor justified his attitude at the time of Varennes, refused to repudiate the Declaration of Pillnitz, and added that if the Elector of Trier were attacked, he would come to his assistance. Brissot took advantage of this closing passage in the Austrian note to demand fresh explanations. Narbonne, the Minister for War, who had just returned from inspecting the fortresses in the east, alleged that everything was in readiness. On January 25, 1792 the Assembly called upon the King to ask the Emperor "whether he renounced all treaties and conventions directed against the sovereignty, independence, and security of the nation"—in

145

other words, to demand a formal repudiation of the Declaration of Pill-nitz. Austria at once entered into a closer alliance with Prussia, and on February 20 Prussia notified France that she would regard the entrance of the French into Germany as a *casus belli*. Brissot's crusade in favour of taking the offensive and suddenly attacking became all the more active. His ally Narbonne, supported by the generals of the army, requested Louis XVI to dismiss his colleague Bertrand de Moleville, whom he accused of failing in his duty, and further requested that the King would remove the aristocrats still in his palace. Incensed at his audacity, Louis XVI deprived him of his portfolio.

The wrath of the Gironde at once blazed up. The Assembly had no power under the Constitution to force the King to change his ministers, but it had the right to arraign them before the High Court for high trea-son. On March 10 Brissot delivered a violent attack upon Delessart, the Minister for Foreign Affairs, who was in favour of peace. He accused him of having concealed important diplomatic documents from the Assembly, of failing to carry out its decisions, and of displaying during the negotia-tions with Austria "a cowardice and weakness unworthy of the greatness of a free people." Vergniaud supported Brissot in a fiery oration, in which he covertly threatened the Queen. The decree citing Delessart before the High Court was passed by a large majority. Narbonne was avenged and war had become inevitable.

The Lameths advised the King to resist. They pointed out the risk that he might share the fate of Charles I, who had abandoned his min-ister Strafford in similar circumstances. They advised him to dissolve the Assembly and maintain Delessart in office. But the Brissotins remained masters of the situation. They set on foot a rumour that they were about to denounce the Queen, dethrone the King, and proclaim the Dauphin king in his place. This was merely an adroit manœuvre for getting power into their hands; for they were simultaneously negotiating with the Court through the agency of Laporte, intendant of the civil list.

Louis XVI resigned himself to dismissing his Feuillant ministers and choosing in their stead Jacobins, almost all of whom were either friends of Brissot or Girondins: Clavière as Minister of Finance, Roland of the Interior, Duranthon of Justice, Lacoste of the Marine, de Grave for War, Dumouriez for Foreign Affairs. Dumouriez, formerly a secret agent of Louis XV, a venal and discredited adventurer, was the strong man of the Cabinet. He had promised the King to defend him against the *factieux* by bribing or paralysing their leaders. His first care was to attend the Jacobins, wearing the red cap, in order to set their suspicions at rest. He adroitly obtained a following among them by a timely distribution of posts. Bonnecarrère, formerly a president of the correspondence committee of the club, became an assistant secretary (*directeur des services*) in his ministry, the journalist Lebrun, a friend of Brissot's, and the journalist Noël, a friend of Danton's, became senior clerks (*chefs de bureau*). There was a cessation of the attacks on the Court in the Girondin press. Louis XVI and Marie Antoinette regained their confidence. Besides, Dumouriez wanted war, and in this he was meeting their wishes half-way.

Leopold died suddenly on March 1. His successor, the young Francis II, was martial to the core and resolved to bring the affair to a speedy conclusion. He answered the latest French notes by a sharp and peremptory refusal, but took good care not to declare war, for, as Kaunitz advised him, by keeping the law on his side he reserved the right to make conquests under the pretext of indemnities.

On April 20 Louis XVI attended the Assembly and proposed, in a perfectly unmoved tone, to declare war upon the King of Bohemia and Hungary. Becquey, a follower of the Lameths, alone made a valiant attempt to strive for peace. He pointed to the divisions and disorders in France, and the bad state of the finances. Cambon interrupted him with the remark: "We have money enough and to spare!" Becquey went on to describe the disorganized condition of the army and navy. He alleged that Prussia, to which Dumouriez had made no allusion in his statement, would support Austria, and that if France entered Brabant, Holland and England would join the coalition. He was listened to impatiently and amid frequent interruptions. Mailhe, Daverhoult, and Guadet demanded that the voting should be immediate and unanimous. Only ten voted against it.

But this war, which was desired by all parties except the Mountain and the Lamethists as a move in their internal policy, was to falsify all the calculations of those who brought it about.

CHAPTER XII

The Overthrow of the Throne

B Y provoking a war Brissot and his friends had succeeded in getting the power into their hands. They could keep it only on one condition —a prompt and decisive victory over the enemy.

Dumouriez ordered the three armies already concentrated on the frontier to take the offensive. The Austrians had only 35,000 soldiers in Belgium and 6000 in the Breisgau to oppose to the 100,000 French troops. The Prussians were only beginning their preparations. A sudden attack would enable France to occupy the whole of Belgium, which would rise in revolt at the sight of the tricolour.

But though the French generals, Lafayette, Rochambeau, and Luckner, had applauded Narbonne's boastful speeches, they now suddenly turned very prudent. They complained that their armies were not yet provided with their full equipment, and Rochambeau in particular did not trust the volunteer battalions, which he considered undisciplined. It was most unwillingly that he carried out his orders to take the offensive. The left column, starting from Dunkirk, arrived before Furnes, where there was no garrison, but retired without venturing to enter the town. The centre column, which set out from Lille to take Tournai, beat a hasty retreat, without joining battle, at the sight of a few uhlans. Two cavalry regiments, which had gone on ahead, disbanded amid cries of treachery. They streamed back as far as Lille, murdering their general, Théobald Dillon, and four persons suspected of being spies. The second battalion of volunteers from Paris was the only one to give a good account of itself, by protecting the retreat and bringing back one cannon which it had taken from the enemy. Finally, on April 28, the main column, under the command of Biron, took Quiévrain, over against Mons, but on the following day beat a disorderly retreat, on the pretext that the Belgians had not rallied to its appeal. Lafayette was to have supported Biron's advance on Brussels from Givet, but checked his march on hearing of this retreat. Custine alone reached his objective, with a column formed at Belfort. He occupied Porrentruy and the gorges of the Jura, commanding the approach to Franche-Comté.

148

On the very day when war was declared, Robespierre had called upon the Girondins to appoint generals belonging to the Patriot party and dismiss Lafayette. On May 1 he stated at the Jacobins that these reverses confirmed his anticipations: "No! I do not trust the generals, and, with a few honourable exceptions, I assert that almost all of them regret the old order of things and the favours at the disposal of the Court; I rely upon the people, and the people alone." Marat and the Cordeliers raised the cry of treachery; and, as a matter of fact, Marie Antoinette had communicated the plan of campaign to the enemy.

The generals openly threw the whole blame on the undisciplined condition of the troops. Rochambeau abruptly offered his resignation, and a number of officers deserted. Three cavalry regiments went over to the enemy, the Saxon Hussars and Bercheny's Hussars on May 12 and the Royal Allemand on May 6. De Grave, the Minister for War, took the side of the generals and would no longer hear of an offensive. Failing to convince his colleagues, he resigned on May 8 and was replaced by Servan, who was more subservient to Dumouriez's control.

In vain did the Brissotins endeavour to reassure and calm the generals. They started a vigorous attack upon Robespierre and his partisans in the press and the Assembly, making them out to be anarchists. On May 3 Lasource and Guadet joined Beugnot and Viennot-Vaublanc in citing Marat before the High Court. By way of compensation the Abbé Royou, editor of the *Ami du Roi*, shared Marat's fate. A law was passed increasing the severity of military discipline, and Théobald Dillon's murderers were caught and punished severely. But Lafayette, who had from the outset claimed to treat with the ministers on a footing of equality, rejected all the advances of the Brissotins. He had not been consulted about the substitution of Servan for de Grave, and this had embittered him against Dumouriez. He drew definitely nearer to the Lameths in order to cope with the threats of the democrats. He took Charles and Alexandre Lameth into his army and gave them commands; about May 12 he had an interview with Adrien Duport and Beaumetz at Givet and at last resolved upon a step which on the part of the commander of an army in the field was an act of treason. He sent an emissary, the ex-Jesuit Lambinet, to the Austrian ambassador, Mercy-Argenteau, at Brussels, to tell him that Lafayette was prepared, in concert with the other generals, to march on Paris with his troops, to disperse the Jacobins, recall the princes and *émigrés*, abolish the National Guard, and establish a second chamber. Before doing so he asked for a suspension of hostilities, and a declaration of neutrality on the part of the Emperor. Mercy-Argenteau, who shared

149

the Queen's prejudice against the general, thought his proposals concealed a trap, and referred him to the Court of Vienna.

The three generals next held a conference at Valenciennes on May 18 and actually decided to cease hostilities. They sent the ministers a memorandum to the effect that an offensive was quite impossible. Lafayette's aides-de-camp, La Colombe and Berthier, assured Roland that the soldiers were cowards. Roland indignantly reported their alarmist reports to Lafayette himself, who shielded his aides-de-camp and answered Roland in the most contemptuous terms. About this time the general wrote to Jaucourt that he aspired to a dictatorship and felt himself worthy of it. These events made a breach between Lafayette and the Brissotins inevitable. Roland durst not or could not persuade his colleagues and the King to dismiss Lafayette. But from this time onwards the Girondins considered that the generals had the support of the Court and that it was therefore necessary to make a demonstration against the palace in order to intimidate them. They began denouncing the "Austrian Committee" working under the Queen's direction for the victory of the enemy. On May 27 they obtained the passage of a new decree against the priests who were causing disturbances, in place of the one which Louis XVI had vetoed in December. Two days later the Assembly announced that the King's guard, formed of aristocrats who rejoiced at the reverses of the French armies, was disbanded. Their commanding officer, the Duc de Cossé-Brissac, was cited before the High Court. Finally, on June 4, Servan proposed to form a camp of twenty thousand Fédérés, outside Paris, to protect the capital in case of an advance of the enemy, and further—though he did not say this—in case of need to resist a *coup d'état* on the part of the generals. His motion was passed on June 8.

By these vigorous attacks the Girondins hoped to force the Court to capitulate and the generals to obey. Servan once more sent explicit orders to Luckner and Lafayette to advance boldly into the Netherlands.

Louis XVI had given way in March because the generals had confirmed Narbonne's opinion. But this time the generals were opposed to the ministers and were trying to regain his favour. With the aid of the ex-minister Bertrand de Moleville he had just reorganized his agency for espionage and corruption. Bertrand and a *juge de paix* named Buob had founded the National Club, frequented by seven hundred workmen, who were paid at the rate of from two to five livres a day out of the civil list and chiefly recruited from Périer's great metal-works. Bertrand had ventured to start proceedings against the journalist Carra, who had accused him of belonging to the "Austrian Committee," and found a *juge de paix*

150

full of zeal for the royalist cause who took up the case and issued warrants for the arrest of the deputies Basíre, Chabot, and Merlin of Thionville, from whom Carra obtained his information. The Assembly did, it is true, repudiate Larivière, the *juge de paix*, and cite him before the High Court for venturing to infringe the inviolability of members of the Assembly. But the Court could count as a success the celebration in honour of Simoneau, the martyr to the law, which the Feuillants had organized as a rejoinder to the celebration in honour of Châteauvieux's Swiss. The success of this celebration even induced Adrien Duport to advise Louis XVI to veto the decrees recently passed by the Assembly.

The King made up his mind to do so, but if his veto was to be valid, it would have to be countersigned by the ministers. All the ministers refused to countersign the letter which he had drafted to give notice of his veto on the decree disbanding his guard. With rage in his heart he was forced to sanction this decree. If the ministers had remained firmly united, Louis XVI might perhaps have sanctioned the other decrees as well. But Dumouriez, who had been the real Minister of War behind Servan, complained that the latter had proposed the camp of twenty thousand men to the Assembly without troubling to consult him. There was a violent scene between the two ministers in the presence of the whole council. They exchanged threats and almost drew their swords before the King's very eyes. These divisions enabled Louis XVI to evade giving his sanction. On June 10 Roland pointed out to him with scant politeness, in a long and peremptory remonstrance, that his veto would provoke a terrible explosion, for it would make the French people think that the King was at heart on the side of the *émigrés* and the enemy. Louis XVI remained firm. Adrien Duport had told him that the camp near Paris would be a weapon in the hands of the Jacobins, whose intention it was, in case of a reverse, to seize his person and take him with them as a hostage to the departments of the south. The Fayettist National Guards sent in a petition against the camp, which they regarded as an insult to their patriotism. After thinking it over for two days, the King sent for Dumouriez, on whom he believed he could rely, for he had given him his appointment on the recommendation of Laporte. He requested him to remain in office, with Lacoste and Duranthon, but to get rid of Roland, Servan, and Clavière. Dumouriez accepted. He advised Louis XVI to replace Roland by Mourgues, an engineer whom he had known at Cherbourg, and himself took the portfolio of the Ministry for War. The dismissal of Roland, Clavière, and Servan was a counterblast to the proceedings against Delessart, and at once brought on a decisive struggle.

151

The Girondins obtained the passage by the Assembly of a motion to the effect that the three ministers who had been dismissed took with them the regrets of the nation, and when Dumouriez appeared at the same session, on June 13, to read a long and pessimistic report on the military situation, he was shouted down. The Assembly then and there nominated a commission of twelve to inquire into the administration of the successive Ministers for War, and in particular to examine Dumouriez's allegations. The latter might well fear that this inquiry was merely the prelude to proceedings against himself before the High Court. He hastened to put pressure upon the King to sanction the two decrees which remained in abeyance. He wrote to him that in the event of a refusal he would run the risk of assassination.

But Louis XVI had not allowed himself to be overawed by Roland and did not intend to capitulate to Dumouriez, who was acting in the same way. On the morning of June 15 he informed Dumouriez that he refused his sanction, upon which Dumouriez offered his resignation. The King took him at his word and sent him to command a division of the army in the north.

It was Duport and the Lameths who recommended the new ministers to the King, from among their own partisans and those of Lafayette: Lajard as Minister for War, Chambonas for Foreign Affairs, Terrier de Monciel of the Interior, Beaulieu of Finance. Lacoste remained at the Ministry of Marine and Duranthon at that of Justice.

The dismissal of Dumouriez, following upon that of Roland, and the refusal of the King's sanction, accompanied by the formation of a purely Feuillant ministry, showed that the Court, with the support of the generals, was going to try and carry out Duport and Lafayette's program; that is, to break the power of the Jacobins, dismiss, if necessary, the Assembly, revise the Constitution, recall the *émigrés*, and stop the war by coming to terms with the enemy. As early as June 16 a report went round that the new ministry was about to suspend hostilities, and a few days later the detail was added that the King was going to take advantage of the Feast of the Federation of July 14 to demand a full and complete amnesty for the benefit of the *émigrés*. In his newspaper *L'Indicateur*, subsidized out of the civil list, Duport advised the King to dissolve the Assembly and seize the dictatorship. As early as June 16 Lafayette, from his camp at Maubeuge, sent the King and the Assembly a violent diatribe against the clubs, the ministers who had been dismissed, and Dumouriez. He even ventured to cite the sentiments of his soldiers in support of his denunciations. His letter was read in the Assembly on June 18. Vergniaud declared it to be unconstitutional, and Guadet compared the general to Cromwell. But the Girondins, who had had Delessart prosecuted at Orleans for a far less serious offence, did not dare to resort to the same procedure against the factious general who had been their accomplice. Their rejoinder took the form of the popular demonstration of June 20, the anniversary of the oath of the Tennis-court and the flight to Varennes.

Processions from the working-class districts, led by Santerre and Alexandre, marched first to the Assembly and then to the palace to protest against the dismissal of the Patriot ministers, the inaction of the army, and the refusal of the King to sanction the decrees. Petion, mayor of Paris, and Manuel, the *procureur syndic* of the Commune, did nothing to prevent the demonstration. They did not appear at the Tuileries till very late, after the King had already withstood the onrush of the demonstrators for two hours with calm courage. Hemmed in in a window embrasure, he donned the red cap and drank the health of the nation, but he refused categorically to give his sanction or to recall the ministers, who no longer possessed his confidence. By Robespierre's advice the deputies of the Mountain took no part in the demonstration. They did not trust the Girondins and did not want to take part in a mere demonstration, but only in some action which was likely to be decisive.

The failure of the Girondin demonstration turned out to the advantage of the royal cause. The departmental assembly of Paris, which was completely Feuillant, suspended Petion and Manuel. Petitions threatening the Jacobins and protestations of loyalty to the King poured in from every province. One of them, deposited at the office of a Parisian notary named Guillaume, obtained twenty thousand signatures. Many departmental assemblies censured the demonstration of June 20. The royalist leader Du Saillant besieged the Château of Jalès, in Ardèche, with two thousand royalists and assumed the title of lieutenant-general of the army of the princes. Another royalist insurrection broke out in Finistère about the same date, at the beginning of July.

Lafayette left his army in the field and on June 28 appeared at the bar of the Assembly, demanding that it should dissolve the Jacobin clubs without delay and visit with an exemplary punishment those responsible for the acts of violence committed at the Tuileries on June 20. The royalist reaction was so strong that Lafayette was greeted with cheers. A vote of censure on him proposed by Guadet was rejected by 339 votes to 234, and the general's petition was simply referred to the Commission of Twelve which was already playing the part afterwards enacted by the Committee of Public Safety. This time Lafayette did not mean to stop at threats. He reckoned upon carrying with him the National Guard of Paris, a division of which, under the command of his friend Acloque, was to be reviewed by the King on the following day. But Petion, warned by the Queen, who was even more afraid of Lafayette than of the Jacobins, put off the review. In vain did Lafayette attempt to rally his partisans and summon them to meet him that evening in the Champs-Elysées. Only a hundred of them appeared and he had to return to his army without attempting anything.

He failed because his ambitions clashed with national sentiment. The inaction in which he had kept the armies for more than two months past seemed inexplicable. It had given the Prussians time to finish their preparations and concentrate upon the Rhine undisturbed. After a sham offensive in Belgium, Luckner quite unnecessarily abandoned Courtrai and withdrew beneath the walls of Lille. The struggle was about to be carried into French territory. On July 6 Louis XVI informed the Assembly that the Prussian troops were advancing.

In the face of imminent peril the Jacobins forgot their divisions and thought of nothing but the safety of the Revolution and the country. At the club on June 28 Brissot and Robespierre both made an appeal for union, and both demanded a prompt punishment for Lafayette. In the Assembly the Girondins kept threatening the Feuillant ministers with impeachment, took the initiative in demanding fresh measures of national defence, and called the popular forces to arms. On July 1 they threw open the sessions of all administrative bodies to the people, which meant placing them under the vigilance of the populace. On July 2 they neutralized the veto which the King had placed on the decree concerning the camp of twenty thousand men, by obtaining the passage of another decree authorizing the National Guard of the departments to visit Paris and celebrate the Federation of July 14, allowing them their travelling-expenses and allotting them quarters.

On July 3 Vergniaud gave a wider scope to the debate by uttering a terrible threat against the King's person: "It is in the King's name that the French princes have tried to rouse all the courts of Europe against the nation, it is to avenge the dignity of the King that the treaty of Pillnitz was concluded and the monstrous alliance formed between the Courts of Vienna and Berlin; it is to defend the King that we have seen what were formerly companies of the Gardes du Corps hurrying to join the standard of rebellion in Germany; it is to come to the assistance of the King that the *émigrés* are soliciting and obtaining employment in the

Austrian armies and preparing to stab their fatherland to the heart . . . it is in the name of the King that liberty is being attacked . . . yet I read in the Constitution, chapter II, section i, article 6: '*If the king place himself at the head of an army and turn its forces against the nation, or if he do not explicitly manifest his opposition to any such enterprise carried out in his name, he shall be considered to have abdicated his royal office.*' " Vergniaud recalled the royal veto, the disorders which it had caused in the provinces, and the deliberate inaction of the generals who had opened the way to invasion; and he put it to the Assembly—though by implication rather than directly—that Louis XVI came within the scope of this article of the Constitution. By this means he put the idea of deposing the King into the minds of the public. His speech, which made an enormous impression, was circulated by the Assembly through all the departments.

On July 11 the Assembly issued a proclamation that the country was in danger. All the administrative bodies and municipalities were to remain in permanent session. All the National Guards were called to arms. Fresh battalions of volunteers were enrolled. Fifteen thousand Parisians enlisted within a few days.

Threatening addresses came in from the large towns, Marseilles, Angers, Dijon, Montpellier, etc., demanding the deposition of the King. On July 13 the Assembly annulled the suspension of Petion and restored him to office. At the Feast of the Federation on the following day no shouts of "*Vive le Roi!*" were to be heard; the spectators had the words "*Vive Petion!*" chalked upon their hats!

It was clear that the great crisis was imminent. In order to avert it the Feuillant party ought to have formed a solid body and made sure of the explicit and unconditional support of the Tuileries. But there were misunderstandings among them. Bertrand did not trust Duport. In order to anticipate the proclamation stating the country to be in danger, the ministers had advised the King to put himself at their head, go down to the Assembly, and denounce the peril which the *factieux* were causing France by openly conspiring for the overthrow of the monarchy. By the advice of Duport, who could see salvation only in the intervention of Lafayette, Louis XVI refused. The ministers thereupon resigned in a body on July 10 on the very day before the Assembly proclaimed that the nation was in danger.

Lafayette, who had come to an understanding with Luckner, proposed to the King that he should enable the latter to leave Paris and reach Compiègne, where troops would be in readiness to receive him. The departure, first fixed for July 12, was postponed to the 15th. But Louis XVI ultimately refused Lafayette's offer, for he was afraid of becoming a mere hostage in the general's hands. He remembered how during the Wars of Religion the different factions had struggled for the possession of the king's person. He trusted nothing but foreign bayonets, and Marie Antoinette insisted to Mercy that the coalition of sovereigns ought as soon as possible to publish a manifesto calculated to overawe the Jacobins and even to strike terror to their hearts. Far from saving the Court, this manifesto, at the foot of which appeared the signature of the Duke of Brunswick, generalissimo of the allied troops, was to be the cause of their ruin. It threatened to shoot all National Guards who should attempt to defend themselves, and to raze and set fire to Paris if Louis XVI and his family were not immediately set at liberty.

The resignation of the Feuillant ministers, however, caused further divisions in the Patriot party. The Girondins imagined it to be an excellent opportunity to overawe the King in his helpless state and regain their power. They entered into secret negotiations with the Court. Vergniaud, Guadet, and Gensonné sent a letter to the King between July 16 and 18, by the agency of Boze, the painter, and the valet Thierry. Guadet had a meeting with the King, Queen and Dauphin.

At the same time the Girondins adopted a more moderate attitude in the Assembly. They began to repudiate the agitation for a republic and to threaten the *factieux*.

The Paris section of Monconseil had passed a resolution declaring that it no longer recognized Louis XVI as King of the French, but Vergniaud had this resolution quashed on August 4. As early as July 25 Brissot was fulminating anathemas against the republican party. "If," he said, "there are any persons inclined to set up a republic now on the ruins of the Constitution, the sword of the law ought to strike them just as much as the active partisans of two-chamber government· and the counter-revolutionaries of Coblenz." And on the same day Lasource tried to convince the Jacobins that it was necessary to remove the Fédérés from Paris by sending them to the camp at Soissons or to the frontiers. It was becoming clear that the Girondins were not in favour either of an insurrection or of deposing the King.

But the movement had been given a start, and now nothing could stop it. The Paris sections sat day and night. They formed a central committee between them. Several of them allowed passive citizens to take part in their deliberations, gave them permission to enter the National Guard, and armed them with pikes. The popular movement was directed by Robespierre and Anthoine at the Jacobins and the Cordelier trio at the Assembly, Robespierre in particular playing an important part. As early as July 11 he harangued the Fédérés at the Jacobins and inflamed their wrath with such words as these: "Citizens, have you hastened here for a mere ceremony, the renewal of the Federation of July 14?" He described the treachery of the generals and pointed out that Lafayette remained unpunished. "Does the National Assembly still exist? It has been outraged and degraded, but has not avenged itself!" Since the Assembly was evading the issue, it was the Fédérés who must save the State. He advised them not to take the oath to the king. The provocation was so flagrant that the Minister of Justice reported this speech to the public prosecutor and requested that proceedings should be taken against Robespierre. But the latter would not be overawed and drew up petitions more and more threatening in tone, which the Fédérés presented to the Assembly one after another. The one presented on July 17 demanded the deposition of the King. At Robespierre's instigation the Fédérés appointed a secret directory, of which his friend Anthoine was a member, and which sometimes met at the house of Duplay, the carpenter, where he and Anthoine had their lodgings.

When he saw that the Girondins were again temporizing with the Court, Robespierre once more took up the struggle against them. Speaking at the Jacobins as early as July 25 he declared, in answer to Lasource, that great evils called for great remedies. The deposition of the King did not seem to him a strong enough measure. "A suspension which left the title and rights of the executive power still vested in the king's person would evidently be no more than a manœuvre concerted between the Court and the schemers in the Legislative Assembly with a view to restoring it to him the moment the suspension should cease. Abdication or unconditional deposition would be less open to suspicion; but if unaccompanied by other precautions, would still leave an opening for the drawbacks on which we have enlarged." Robespierre feared, then, that "the schemers in the Legislative Assembly"—in other words, the Brissotins—might play the same game with Louis XVI as the Feuillants had already played on a previous occasion after Varennes. He refused to be duped by this manœuvre and demanded the immediate dismissal of the Legislative Assembly and the substitution for it of a convention for reforming the Constitution. He involved the Assembly and the King in the same condemnation. He wanted the Convention to be elected by all citizens indiscriminately, whether active or passive. In other words, he appealed to the masses against the middle classes. By so doing he cut short the last manœuvres of the

Girondins for regaining power in the King's name. The plan which he proposed was carried into execution.

Brissot endeavoured in vain to answer Robespierre in a great speech before the Assembly on July 26. He denounced the agitation of the *factieux* who demanded the abdication of the King. He condemned the plan of summoning the primary assemblies to nominate a new Assembly. He insinuated that to do so would be playing into the hands of the aristocrats. The struggle between Robespierre and the Girondins became more and more embittered. Isnard denounced Anthoine and Robespierre as conspirators and pledged his word at the Club de la Réunion, where the deputies of the left concerted their measures, to cite them before the High Court. Petion did his best to prevent an insurrection. As late as August 7 he visited Robespierre and requested him to calm the people. During this time Danton was taking a rest at Arcis-sur-Aube, from whence he returned only on the evening before the great day.

On August 4 Robespierre, who was very well-informed, denounced a plot on the part of the aristocrats for conniving at the King's escape, and, as a matter of fact, Lafayette did make a fresh attempt at it. At the end of July he had sent an agent, Masson de Saint-Amand, to Brussels to beg Austria for a suspension of hostilities and the mediation of Spain with a view to negotiating a peace. At the same time he dispatched cavalry to the neighbourhood of Compiègne to assist the King's escape. But all his efforts were in vain. Once more Louis XVI refused to leave. The secret negotiations of the Girondins had made him sanguine. Besides, he had distributed large sums of money among the popular agitators. Duport had received the mission of corrupting Petion, Santerre, and Delacroix (of Eure-et-Loir). Bertrand de Moleville says that a million had been placed at his disposal. Lafayette alleges that Danton received 50,000 écus. Terrier de Monciel, Minister of the Interior, alone distributed 547,000 livres at the end of July and 449,000 livres at the beginning of August. Westermann, an old Alsatian soldier and a member of the directory of the Fédérés, stated in April 1793, before a commission of inquiry held under the Convention, that he was offered three millions and that he informed Danton of this. Fabre d'Églantine, a disreputable poet, attempted to obtain considerable sums from Dubouchage, the Minister of Marine. The King and Queen were convinced that they had nothing serious to fear from men whose only desire was to make money. They did not consider that these very men, having no scruple, were capable of taking money and still betraying them afterwards. The garrison of the palace was strength-

158

ened. The commandant of the National Guard, Mandat de Grancey, was a zealous royalist.

Lafayette having received his definitive absolution from the Assembly on August 8, the secret committee for organizing the insurrection allotted their parts to the chief agents. During the night of August 9–10 Carra and Chaumette went to the barracks of the Marseilles Fédérés in the section of the Cordeliers, while Santerre roused the faubourg Saint-Antoine, and Alexandre the faubourg Saint-Marceau, and the tocsin was rung. The sections sent commissaries to the Hôtel de Ville, who installed themselves there as a revolutionary municipality in place of the legal municipality. Petion was speedily confined to his house under guard of a detachment. Mandat was summoned to the Hôtel de Ville and convicted of having given the order to attack the Fédérés in the rear. The Revolutionary Commune ordered his arrest, and as he was being led off to prison, a pistol shot stretched him stone-dead on the Place de Grève. Mandat having been disposed of, the defence of the Tuileries was paralysed.

Louis XVI was irresolute. As the demonstration approached, he allowed himself to be persuaded by Rœderer, *procureur général syndic* to the department of Paris, that he ought to leave the palace with his family and take refuge with the Assembly, which was sitting quite near by, in the Riding-school. As soon as he had left the Tuileries, the greater part of the National Guards of the royalist sections (those of the Filles-Saint-Thomas and the Petits-Pères), with the whole of the gunners, went over to the insurrection. The Swiss and the gentlemen of the Court alone put up a good defence. They swept the courtyard of the palace with a devastating fire. The insurgents had to bring up cannon and take the palace by storm. The Swiss were overpowered and numbers of them massacred. There were five hundred killed and wounded on the side of the populace.

The Assembly looked on anxiously at the vicissitudes of the struggle. So long as the issue was doubtful, Louis XVI was treated like a king. When he appeared and asked for protection, Vergniaud, as president, declared to him that the Assembly knew its duty and had sworn to uphold "the constituted authorities." Guadet shortly afterwards proposed to appoint a tutor for the "prince royal." But as soon as the insurrection was definitely victorious, the Assembly announced the suspension of the King, and voted that the Convention demanded by Robespierre, to the great annoyance of Brissot, should be summoned. The King was now placed under a strong guard. The Assembly would have liked to assign him the Palace of the Luxembourg, but the insurgent Commune demanded that he should

159

be taken to the Temple, a smaller prison, which would be easier to guard.

The throne had been overturned, but with it also fell its last defenders, that minority of the nobility who had brought about the Revolution, flattering themselves that they would be able to moderate and direct it; who had even for a time had the illusion that they were governing, first under Lafayette, and then under the Lameths.

Lafayette attempted to incite his army to revolt against Paris. He succeeded at first in carrying with him the department of the Ardennes and a few municipalities; but he was deserted by the majority of his troops and soon afterwards, on August 19, had to escape to Belgium, followed by Alexandre Lameth and Latour-Maubourg. The Austrians gave him a bad reception and imprisoned him in the castle of Olmütz. His friend Baron Dietrich, the famous mayor of Strasbourg, in whose apartments Rouget de Lisle had recited the marching-song of the Army of the Rhine, which afterwards became the "Marseillaise," met with no more success in rousing Alsace. He was deprived of his position by the Assembly and also fled over the frontier.

But it was not only the Feuillant party—that is to say, the upper middle classes and liberal nobility—who were crushed by the cannon of August 10, at the same time as the Crown; the Girondin party, which had come to terms with the Court *in extremis* and had endeavoured to prevent the insurrection, also came out of this victory with diminished prestige, for the insurrection had not been its work, but had been forced upon it.

The passive citizens—that is to say, the proletariate—mobilized by Robespierre and the Mountain, had amply revenged themselves for the massacre of the Champ de Mars in the previous year. The fall of the throne amounted to a new revolution. The dawn of democracy was visible on the horizon.

BOOK TWO
The Gironde and the Mountain

PART I

The Last Days of the Legislative Assembly
(August 10–September 20, 1792)

CHAPTER I

The Commune and the Assembly

THE six weeks which elapsed between August 10 and September 21, 1792—that is to say, from the capture of the Tuileries and the imprisonment of Louis XVI in the Temple to the meeting of the Convention—are of capital importance in the history of the Revolution.

Up to this time the regularly elected delegates of the nation had not had their powers called in question. Even during the crisis of July 1789, which ended in the capture of the Bastille, the Parisian rioters had submitted docilely to the direction of the Constituent Assembly. All they had wanted was to second its action and secure it against the coercive forces of absolutism. Two years later, after Varennes, when the republicans tried to insist that the country should be consulted as to whether Louis XVI should be maintained upon the throne, the Constituent Assembly had easily overcome their resistance. The bloody repression which had taken place on the Champ de Mars had sealed its victory, which was that of legality and parliamentary government.

But the insurrection of August 10 was quite unlike those which had preceded it; it was not directed merely against the throne. It was an act of defiance and a threat to the very Assembly itself, which had just exonerated the "factious" general Lafayette and formally repudiated the petitions for the deposition of the King. A new situation had been created: the legal power was face to face with a revolutionary power. The struggle between these two powers occupied the six weeks which preceded the meeting of the Convention.

The struggle was continued after September 20 in the form of opposition between the two parties struggling for the majority in the new

Assembly. The party of the Mountain was in all essentials the party previously represented by the Revolutionary Commune, while the Girondin party consisted of the deputies who had formed the left wing of the Legislative Assembly and were now to become the right wing of the Convention.

It may at once be observed—though we shall return to this point in greater detail—that the two parties were separated by radically divergent views upon all essential problems. The Girondins were the party of legality, with a repugnance for those exceptional "revolutionary" measures of which the Commune had set the example and which the Mountain received as a part of its inheritance. These measures were as follows: in the economic and social sphere, regulations, drawing up returns of the available supplies of commodities, requisitioning, the enforced acceptance of the assignats as legal tender—in short, restrictions upon commercial liberty; and in the political sphere the proclamation as suspects of all opponents of the existing Government, the suspension of individual liberty, the creation of exception jurisdictions, the concentration of power by a strict subordination of the local authorities—in short, the policy of "public safety." This program was not fully carried into effect till a year later, under the Terror, but it was mapped out and defined by the Commune of August 10.

The opposition between the two programs was the expression of a fundamental opposition of interests—almost of a class struggle. The Commune and the Mountain, which was derived from it, represented the lower classes (artisans, labourers, and consumers), who were suffering from the war and its consequences: namely, the enhanced cost of living, lack of work, and the unsettlement of earned incomes. The Assembly and its offspring the Gironde represented the trading and property-owning middle classes, who were determined to defend their possessions against the restrictions, impediments, and confiscations with which they felt themselves to be threatened. The struggle was a dramatic one and assumed every sort of form; and it must be studied in detail if we are to grasp its full complexity.

The throne was no sooner overturned than the difficulties of the victorious party began. It had to induce France and the army to accept the *fait accompli,* it had to forestall or crush all possible resistance, to repel the invading forces which were already encroaching upon the frontiers, and finally to set up a national government on the ruins of royalty— arduous problems which were not to be solved without terrible upheavals!

The commissaries of the Parisian sections, which had formed themselves into a Revolutionary Commune at the Hôtel de Ville on the night of August 9–10, derived their powers from the direct choice of the people. As opposed to the Assembly, which was based upon an indirect franchise with a property qualification and discredited by its repudiation of the republicans and the threats which it had fulminated against them, as well as by the secret parleying between its leaders and the Court, the Commune represented a new type of legality. Strong in the prestige of its bloody victory over the defenders of the Tuileries, conscious of the immense service which it had rendered to the Revolution and to France by crushing royal treachery, it had no intention of confining its action within the narrow scope of its municipal functions. It regarded itself as the incarnation of the public interest and as having acted in the name of revolutionary France as a whole, and the presence of the Fédérés [1] from the departments side by side with the Parisian revolutionaries during the attack on the Tuileries had set a seal upon the fraternal alliance between the capital and the nation.

On the very evening of August 10 Robespierre, speaking at the Jacobins, advised the Commune boldly to assume its responsibilities. According to him there was only one way in which they could enjoy the full advantage of their victory: to recommend the people "to make it absolutely impossible for its mandataries to harm the cause of liberty"—in other words, to tie the hands of the Assembly, if not to abolish it. He showed "how imprudent it would be for the people to lay down their arms until they had made liberty secure." The Commune, he added, must "take the important measure of sending commissaries into the eighty-three departments to explain our situation to them." By this proposal he not only expressed an insuperable distrust of the Assembly, but advised the Commune to seize the dictatorship by getting into direct touch with the departments.

The Commune had not waited for Robespierre's exhortations before asserting its right to exercise a dictatorship. Having once asserted the right, however, it did not dare to put it fully into practice. Just as at the height of the struggle it had not removed the mayor, Petion, who was justly suspected of lukewarmness, so now it did not venture to announce the dissolution of the Assembly, which it knew to be hostile to its plans. The fact is that these simple people, for the most part artisans, publicists, lawyers, and schoolmasters, who had not been afraid to risk their lives in the insurrection, were, none the less, still impressed by the parliamentary prestige of the brilliant Girondin orators. They themselves were

---

[1] See page 159.

unknown outside their own neighbourhood; their obscure names meant nothing to France. In turning out the Assembly was there not a risk that they might imperil the cause which they desired to serve? They resigned themselves to a compromise. They allowed the Assembly to survive on condition that it should consent to disappear before long and shortly summon the citizens to elect a Convention: that is to say, a fresh Constituent Assembly, which should revise the monarchical Constitution, now superseded, on democratic lines.

At eleven o'clock on August 10, when the cannon had ceased thundering against the conquered Tuileries, a delegation from the Commune, led by Huguenin, a former customs-house clerk, appeared at the bar of the Legislative Assembly. "The people, by whom we are sent," said Huguenin, "has instructed us to declare that it has once more invested you with its confidence; but at the same time it has instructed us to declare that the French people, your sovereign and ours, as met together in its primary assemblies, is the sole judge which it could recognize as competent to decide upon the extraordinary measures to which it has been led by necessity and resistance to oppression."

The Assembly made a wry face at this imperious language. The conditional and short-lived confidence thus offered made it dependent upon the irregular power which had arisen from the insurrection.

It was, however, bound to consent to recognize the rightfulness of the insurrection and give pledges to it. It confirmed the Revolutionary Commune, but affected to regard it as a provisional and transitory power, which was bound to disappear with the circumstances which had given rise to it. It consented to summon a Convention, which was to be elected by universal suffrage, with no distinction between active and passive citizens, but still by an indirect franchise. It provisionally suspended the King until this new Constituent Assembly should meet, but it refused to pronounce his deposition pure and simple, as the insurgents had demanded. It was evident that the Gironde was seeking to save as much as possible of the monarchical Constitution. The suspension maintained the crown by implication. Two days later, on the motion of Vergniaud, the Assembly even resolved by a fresh vote to appoint a tutor for the "royal prince."

The King had been suspended, but the Constitution remained in force. As had happened after Varennes, the executive power was placed in the hands of six ministers, chosen outside the Assembly out of deference to the principle of the "separation of powers," but appointed by an oral and public vote out of a desire to calm mistrust. Roland, Clavière, and Servan once more obtained the Ministries of the Interior, Finance, and War respectively, of which the King had deprived them on June 13. They were each given an assistant elected by an oral vote: the equivocal Danton, upon whom Brissot and Condorcet relied to hold the mob in check, was attached to the Ministry of Justice; the mathematician Monge, the nominee of Condorcet, to the Ministry of Marine; and the journalist Lebrun, a friend of Brissot's, to whom Dumouriez had given a senior clerkship, to the Ministry for Foreign Affairs.

Power was thus divided between three distinct authorities: the Commune, the Assembly, and the Ministry, which formed the Executive Council; and these three authorities kept encroaching upon one another's provinces. The circumstances, the double peril at home and abroad, called for a dictatorship, but this dictatorship did not succeed in assuming a definite form or identifying itself with any one institution, man, party, or class. It had neither definite organs nor precise functions, nor were there any written laws formulated for its exercise. It was an impersonal dictatorship exercised in turn by rival authorities, as events might prescribe, a dictatorship as chaotic and fluctuating as the opinion from which it drew its strength.

"The French people has conquered Austria and Prussia in Paris," as the wife of Julien of Drôme, a future member of the Convention, wrote to her husband on the very day of August 10. Three days before this, on hearing that the King of Sardinia was about to join the coalition, she had written: "I am no more afraid of the Savoyards than of the Prussians and Austrians. I am only afraid of traitors!" This was the general feeling among the revolutionaries. They feared lest the generals might be tempted to imitate Lafayette, who had roused the municipality of Sedan and the department of the Ardennes against the Assembly and was trying to lead his army on Paris. They foresaw resistance in the regions loyal to the refractory priests. They knew that a great number of the departmental administrations had protested against the events of June 20. They did not trust the courts of justices, or the High Court at Orleans, which was suspiciously dilatory in trying those accused of crimes against the security of the State. The Assembly shared these fears. On the very day of August 10 it sent twelve of its members as delegates to the four armies, three to each, "with power provisionally to suspend not only the generals, but all other officers and public functionaries, both civil and military, and even to have them placed under arrest should circumstances require it, likewise providing temporary substitutes to take their place." This amounted to conferring upon the deputies chosen as commissaries a considerable share in the executive power, and these commissaries of the Legislative Assembly already foreshadow the proconsuls of the Convention.

The Assembly next ordered all State officials and pensioners, even including priests, to take the oath to uphold liberty and equality or die at their posts. As early as August 11, on the motion of Thuriot, it entrusted the municipalities with the mission of searching out crimes against the security of the State and authorized them to take steps to place suspicious persons provisionally under arrest. On August 15, on hearing the news that foreign troops had surrounded Thionville, it gave orders that the parents, wives, and children of *émigrés* were not to leave their communes, in order that they might act as hostages. It ordered that the papers of the ex-ministers, for whose arrest the Commune had already issued warrants, should be sealed up, and cited them all in turn before the High Court. The Executive Council, in its turn, suspended the administrative bodies of the departments of Rhône-et-Loire, Moselle, and Somme. On the other hand, the officials who had been dismissed or suspended for excess of zeal in the revolutionary cause—for example, Anthoine, mayor of Metz, or Chalier, a municipal officer of Lyons—were reinstated in their posts.

It was not long before the documents found at the house of Laporte, intendant of the civil list, were made public. These documents proved that the King had never ceased to carry on secret dealings with the *émigrés* and, in particular, had continued to pay those of his former bodyguard who had crossed the frontier to Coblenz, while most of the aristocrat newspapers and pamphlets had been subsidized out of his privy purse.

But owing to the exasperated state of opinion even these measures, most of which had been extorted from the Assembly under pressure from the Commune, seemed inadequate. On August 13 Thomas Lindet expressed his astonishment that Lafayette had not forthwith been deprived of his command. But in spite of the general's open rebellion the Girondins hesitated to attack him; they negotiated with him in secret and did not decide to take proceedings against him till after he had crossed the frontier, on August 19. This unaccountable indulgence had the effect of increasing suspicion. The period of conflict between the Commune and the Legislative Assembly was close at hand.

The Commune had renounced the task of governing France, but was bent at least upon exercising the entire sovereignty in the administration of Paris. It refused to tolerate any intermediate authority between itself and the Assembly. It sent Robespierre to the Assembly to demand in its name that the elections which had already begun for the renewal of the administrative assembly of the department of Paris should be stopped. "In order to secure public safety and liberty," said Robespierre, "the general council of the Commune requires the preservation of the full power with which it was invested by the people during the night of August 9–10. To nominate members for a new departmental assembly in present circumstances would tend to set up an authority in rivalry with that of the people itself. . . ." Thuriot supported Robespierre, but Delacroix obtained the passage of a decree which merely provided that the new departmental assembly should in future exercise no control over the operations of the Commune except as regards taxation and the national property. The Commune acquiesced, but on August 22 Robespierre, as its spokesman, introduced to the Assembly the members of the new departmental assembly and expressed in their name the desire to bear no title save that of Commission for Taxation (*commission des contributions*). Thereupon Delacroix, who had veered completely round since August 12, protested violently that it was not the Commune's business to deprive the departmental assembly of its administrative functions. "It would mean overthrowing all the departmental assemblies in the kingdom at once." But these were petty conflicts compared with the graver ones which were also proceeding.

The victory of August 10 had been a bloody one. The sections and the Fédérés had lost a thousand killed or wounded before the Tuileries, and they wanted vengeance. The Swiss Guard had been the first to fire, at the very moment when the National Guards were trying to fraternize with them. After the fighting large numbers of the Swiss had been massacred. Those who escaped took refuge with the Assembly, but it could save them only by promising to have them brought to trial. Not only were the Swiss Guard accused of disloyalty, but it was alleged that the insurgents slain by their bullets had received horrible wounds caused by broken glass, buttons, and crushed lead. On August 11 Santerre declared before the Assembly that he could not be responsible for order unless a court martial was at once set up to try the Swiss. In order to satisfy him a motion to this effect was adopted in principle. But the mob murmured and demanded an immediate trial. Danton had to place himself at the head of the Swiss in order that they might be conducted to the prison of the Abbaye. His first attempt to force a way through the crowd of demonstrators was not a success. The Swiss had to turn back and take refuge in the building where the Assembly held its sessions. Next Petion intervened. In order to calm the populace he demanded that an extraordinary tribunal should be set up for the summary punishment, not only of the

Swiss, but of all enemies of the Revolution. On that same evening the police commissioners at the Hôtel de Ville wrote Santerre the following note: "We are informed, sir, that a plan is being formed for going round the prisons of Paris and carrying off all the prisoners, in order to execute *summary justice* upon them (*une prompte justice*); we beg you to extend your supervision without delay to those at the Châtelet, the Conciergerie, and La Force." This is the exact plan of the massacre which was carried out three weeks later. Marat had not yet written on the subject. He merely adopted an idea which was already in the air.

The Assembly could have avoided a catastrophe only by making the mob feel that it was sincere in voting for the establishment of an extraordinary tribunal for counter-revolutionary crimes. In order to do so it would have had to organize this tribunal without delay. It resorted to artifice and so lost time. The decree which it voted on August 14 was inadequate in the eyes of the Commune, which sent Robespierre to the bar of the Assembly on the following day as its delegate, to complain of the faults of omission contained in the decree. It applied only to the crimes committed in Paris during the 10th, and ought, he said, to be extended to crimes of a similar nature committed in the whole of France; it was necessary that they should have legal powers to deal with Lafayette! And Robespierre asked that the tribunal should be formed of commissaries nominated by the sections and that its judgments should be final and without appeal. The Assembly decreed that the verdicts on the crimes of August 10 should not be subject to appeal, but upheld its decree of the previous day, by which it had referred the preliminary examination and trial of these crimes to the ordinary tribunals. The Commune was exasperated, for it regarded these tribunals as suspect, and was asking for their renovation. On August 17 it again demanded a special tribunal, in which both judges and jury should be elected by the people assembled in their sections. One of its members, Vincent Ollivault, addressed the Assembly in threatening language: "As a citizen and a representative of the people, I have come to announce to you that tonight at midnight the tocsin will be rung and the drums will beat to arms. The people is weary of being balked of its revenge. Beware lest it take the law into its own hands. I propose that, here and now, you decree that a citizen be nominated by each section as a member of a criminal tribunal. I propose that this tribunal be set up in the palace of the Tuileries. I propose that Louis XVI and Marie Antoinette, greedy for the blood of the people, shall glut their eyes upon that of their infamous satellites." The Assembly was recalcitrant. On the very day of August 10 Vergniaud had exclaimed: "Paris is but a section of the Empire!" This time it was Choudieu, who usually sat with the Mountain and had taken an active part in the insurrection, who protested against the violence which they were trying to do to the representatives of the nation: "All those who come and bawl here are not friends of the people. I want it to be en-lightened, not flattered. They want to establish an inquisitorial tribunal. I shall oppose it with all my might." Another member of the Mountain, Thuriot, joined his protests to those of Choudieu, but in the end the Assembly yielded, though with a bad grace. By its delays and resistance it had lost the moral advantage of its concessions and had only aggra-vated its unpopularity.

The extraordinary tribunal was formed of judges and a jury elected by the Parisian sections. Robespierre refused the position of president, in a letter stating that, since most of the political prisoners were his per-sonal enemies, he could not be both judge and a party in the case. Per-haps there were also other reasons for his refusal which he did not men-tion. The Gironde had already started violently attacking this man, whom they mistrusted and regarded as the real leader of the Commune. In a poster headed "The Dangers of Victory," probably inspired by Roland, which was pasted up all over Paris, he was represented as a "violently jealous man," who wished to "make Petion unpopular, put himself in his place, and proceed amid ruins to the tribunate, which was the con-stant object of his insensate desires." By refusing the presidency of the tribunal set up on August 17 Robespierre pointed the contrast between his disinterestedness and the accusation, fabricated by the Girondins, of aiming at a dictatorship.

It was not long before the sections in which the commercial middle classes predominated came into opposition with the Commune. That of the Lombards, stirred up by Louvet, protested as early as August 25 against its encroachments, the lack of confidence which it displayed towards Petion, and the restrictions on the powers of the departmental assembly. It recalled its representatives from the Hôtel de Ville, in which action it was imitated by four other sections (those of the Maison Com-mune and Ponceau on August 27 and those of the Marché des Innocents and the Halle au Blé on the 29th). The movement against the Commune spread to the provinces and assumed the form of an anti-Parisian cam-paign. On August 27 Albitte, a deputy of the Mountain, drew the at-tention of the Assembly to a circular issued by the departmental assembly of Côtes-du-Nord requesting the other departmental assemblies to concert measures for inducing the Convention to meet in some place other than in the capital. But the Assembly refused to endorse Albitte's indignant protest and merely voted that the matter should not be debated. The project for transferring the Convention to the provinces had some justification, for on August 20 the Montagnard Chabot had adjured the Fédérés to remain in Paris "in order to keep their eye on the National Convention" and prevent it from restoring the monarchy and leaving Paris.

The struggle had now reached an acute stage. The Commune had sealed up the papers of Amelot, the director of the Caisse de l'Extraordinaire, and a notorious aristocrat, and had had him put in prison. On August 21 Cambon angrily inquired "whether the Commune of Paris could order the arrest of administrators and officials directly subject to the supervision of the National Assembly, on the pretext of malversation." A motion was passed ordering the immediate removal of the seals.

On August 27, the day after news arrived of the capture of Longwy, the Commune had given orders that the residences of suspects should be searched and their arms confiscated. A Girondin journalist named Girey-Dupré, who edited Brissot's paper, announced that the Commune was preparing to search the houses of all citizens indiscriminately. The Commune summoned Girey-Dupré to its bar and asked for an explanation of his malicious mis-statement. The Gironde saw in·this incident a means of ridding itself of its rival.

Roland opened the attack at the session of August 30. He stated that, since the Commune had suppressed the Paris food-committee (*comité des subsistances*), which possessed his confidence, he could no longer be responsible for the food-supplies of the city. Choudieu pronounced a regular arraignment of this Commune which disorganized everything, besides being illegal. Cambon went still further. Roland made another speech describing how Restout, inspector of the State furniture-store (*Garde-meuble*), had complained that an agent of the Commune had carried off from his depository a little silver-mounted cannon (it had been taken to the committee of the section of Le Roule). Choudieu again mounted the tribune and denounced the summons issued by the Commune to Girey-Dupré two days previously, citing him before it. Grangeneuve requested that the former municipality should resume its functions, and finally Guadet wound up the debate by obtaining the passage, without previous discussion, of a decree ordering the immediate renewal of the whole Commune. Chabot and Fauchet, however, carried a decree that this "illegal" Commune, which "was disorganizing everything," had deserved well of the nation.

The Girondin offensive had taken place during the fever of patriot-

172

ism aroused by the advance of the invading forces. On August 19 the Prussian troops, led by Frederick William in person and under the command of the Duke of Brunswick, had crossed the frontier, followed by a little army of *émigrés*, which proceeded from the very first to carry out the threats of the famous manifesto. On August 23 Longwy surrendered after fifteen hours' bombardment. Lavergne, the commandant of the garrison, was left by the enemy in possession of his liberty and was justly suspected of not having done his whole duty. It was soon learnt that Verdun was about to be besieged, and hard upon this came the news that several thousand royalists in the district of Châtillon-sur-Sèvre, in the Vendée, had revolted on August 24 against the attempt to recruit them. Headed by Baudry d'Asson, they had seized Châtillon and marched on Bressuire. The patriots had driven them back only with difficulty, by bringing up cannon and joining battle with them three times, in the course of which they lost fifteen killed and twenty wounded, while the insurgents lost two hundred killed and eighty prisoners. It had just been discovered that a widespread royalist conspiracy was about to come to a head in Dauphiné, and it was known that there was an agitation among the nobles of Brittany. It was feared that the invasion might be the signal for an extensive rising led by the clergy and nobles.

Yet this tragic situation did not prevent the Gironde from making a stand against the Commune of August 10. While the latter was devoting itself entirely to national defense, by actively pressing on the entrenchment works outside the city in order to establish a camp there, by inviting all citizens to work in the trenches as they had done on the site of the Feast of the Federation, and by having thirty thousand pikes forged, and while, from August 27 onwards, it was proceeding to enlist fresh troops amid great enthusiasm and disarming suspects in order to obtain guns for those leaving for the front, the Assembly was thinking of nothing but revenge for its past humiliations and how to crush its political rivals, in order to gain control of the impending elections to the Convention. There were angry murmurs, which would have been angrier had the Commune known that the most prominent leaders of the Gironde, losing their heads, regarded the military situation as desperate and were thinking only of fleeing from Paris with the Government in order to escape from the Prussians and "anarchists" at the same time. Roland and Servan were preparing to withdraw all troops beyond the Loire, a plan which had been in their minds for a long time. On August 10 Roland had said to Barbaroux that it would no doubt be necessary to retire to the central plateau and set up a republic of the south. Others had advised opening negotiations with the Prussians. On July 25 the journalist Carra wrote in his *Annales patriotiques,* which were widely read, a strange article revealing terror and intrigue in every line. In it he praised Brunswick, the "greatest warrior," he said, "and the greatest statesman in Europe. . . . If he reaches Paris, I will go bail for it that his first move will be to come to the Jacobins and don the red cap of liberty." Carra had had dealings in the past with the King of Prussia, who had presented him with a gold snuff-box with his portrait on it. Previous to this, as early as January 4, 1792, he had thrown out the idea, at the Jacobins, of inviting an English prince to assume the crown of France. His praise of Brunswick could have but one meaning—that he believed the victory of the enemy armies inevitable and advised a friendly understanding with Prussia. He was not the only one in his party who held this opinion, for in May Condorcet too had sung Brunswick's praises in his paper, *La Chronique de Paris.* It is certain that, though they had light-heartedly embarked upon war, a state of mind prevailed among the Girondins which we should call "defeatist." After the capitulation of Longwy the ministers and a few influential deputies met in the garden of the Ministry for Foreign Affairs to listen to Kersaint, who had returned from Sedan, and foretold that Brunswick would be in Paris in a fortnight's time "as surely as a wedge is driven into a log when you hammer it." Roland, pale and trembling, declared that they must leave for Tours or Blois, taking the treasury and the King with them. Clavière and Servan supported him. But Danton exclaimed indignantly: "I have sent for my mother, who is seventy years of age. I have sent for my two children; they arrived yesterday. Before the Prussians enter Paris, I am prepared for my family to perish with me, I am prepared for twenty thousand torches to reduce Paris to a heap of ashes in an instant. Beware, Roland, of talking of flight. Be careful lest the people hear you!"

Danton's valour, it is true, was partly due to calculation and ulterior motives. It was in Paris that he was popular and made his influence felt upon the sections and clubs. At Blois or Tours he would no longer have been the man who could let loose or check the forces of insurrection by turns. Besides, he had yet another motive for opposing the flight of the Gironde. He had never lost touch with the royalists, of whom he had been the hired agent. He had just obtained for Talon, who had formerly dispensed the funds of the civil list, the passport which enabled him to elude the police of the Commune and escape to England. By the instrumentality of Chèvetel, a doctor who was his instrument, he kept in touch with the Marquis de la Rouarie, who was at that very moment organizing the rising in Brittany. In opposing the transfer of the Government to the provinces he was killing two birds with one stone. If the enemy was victorious and the war ended in the restoration of the monarchy, Danton would be in a position to remind the royalists of his dealings with La Rouarie through the agency of Chèvetel, and the protection which he extended to the Lameths, Adrien Duport, Talon, and many other royalists, and would claim his share in the triumph of order. If, on the other hand, the Prussians were beaten back, he would be able to boast to the revolutionaries that he had never despaired when the danger was at its height; he would be the saviour of the country.

But, great as was his ascendency, he would not have succeeded in preventing the evacuation of the capital had not men as influential as Petion, Vergniaud, and Condorcet joined their efforts with his. The Gironde therefore resolved to remain in Paris, but to take advantage of the patriotic emotion produced by the bad news brought by Kersaint to break the power of the Commune. Only they reckoned without Danton.

On the evening of August 28, at the close of the debate in which he had obtained the rejection of Roland's timid counsels, he sprang to the tribune. In a voice of thunder he announced that he was about to speak "as minister of the people, as a revolutionary minister." "The Assembly," he said, "must show itself worthy of the nation! It is by an upheaval that we have overthrown despotism; it is only by a great national upheaval that we shall make the despots retreat. So far we have only been waging Lafayette's sham war; we must wage a more terrible war. It is time to tell the people that it must hurl itself in a mass upon the enemy. When a ship is wrecked, the crew throws overboard everything which exposed them to mortal danger; just so everything capable of injuring the nation must be cast out of its bosom, and all that may be of use to it must be placed at the disposal of the municipalities, with due compensation to the owners." Having laid down this principle, he at once deduced its consequences: the Executive Council was to appoint commissaries "to go into the departments and exert the influence of opinion there," to assist in raising troops and commandeering supplies, to proceed to purge the authorities and keep them under supervision, and to throw overboard everything which might endanger the safety of the Revolution. Danton went on to praise the Commune of Paris, which had been right in closing the gates of the capital and arresting traitors. "Were there thirty thousand to arrest, they must be arrested tomorrow, and Paris must communicate tomorrow with the whole of France!" Lastly he asked them to pass a decree authorizing the search of all citizens' houses, and further proposed that the Assembly should nominate a few of its members to accompany the commissaries of the Executive Council on their mission of recruiting men and commandeering supplies.

The Assembly voted without discussion the decree for which he had asked authorizing domiciliary visits, but Cambon, supported by the Girondins, saw the disadvantages of mixing commissaries of the Assembly with those of the Commune and of the Executive Council and appealed to the principle of the separation of powers. Basire had to intervene before the Assembly would consent to send six of its members as delegates to help in recruiting.

On the following day, August 29, as though to draw his alliance with the Commune still closer, Danton went to the Hôtel de Ville and made a speech on "the vigorous measures to be taken in present circumstances." [2] Domiciliary visits started on August 30 at ten o'clock in the morning and went on for two days without stopping, each section employing thirty commissaries for the purpose. All houses were searched, one after the other, residents receiving orders not to go out till the commissaries had called. Three thousand suspects were taken off to prison.

These operations were in full swing when, on the evening of the 30th, news reached the Commune of the decree dissolving and reconstituting it. An obscure member named Darnauderie gave eloquent expression to the feelings of his fellow members, winding up with the conclusion that they must offer resistance to a decree so disastrous to the public weal, summon the people to the Place de Grève, and present themselves in force at the bar of the Assembly. Robespierre in turn extolled the work of the Commune of August 10 and spoke in scathing terms of its enemies, Brissot, Condorcet, and their like. But, unlike Darnauderie, his conclusion was that the Commune ought to appeal to the sections, hand over its power to them, and ask them for the means which should enable its members to remain at their posts or die.

On the following day Tallien defended the Commune at the bar of the Legislative Assembly: "All that we have done has been sanctioned by the people." And he proudly enumerated the services it had rendered: "If you strike at us, strike also at the people, who made the Revolution on July 14, consolidated it on August 10, and will uphold it." The president, Delacroix, replied that the Assembly would consider the petition. September I passed by without any attempt to execute the decree quash-

---

[2] See Barrière, *Histoire parlementaire de la Révolution française*, pp. 17, 18, and Buchez and Roux. This document was not known to Messieurs M. Tourneux and André Fribourg.

ing the Commune. That very evening Robespierre induced the Commune
to vote an address which was at once its own apologia and a vigorous indictment of the Gironde, but wound up with the conclusion that it must
obey the law and seek a fresh mandate from the people. For the first time
the Commune did not follow its usual guide. Manuel, its *procureur syndic*,
opposed a resignation *en masse*. He reminded the Council of the oath
which they had taken to die at their post and not abandon it till the country should be out of danger. The Commune decided not to relinquish its
functions; but its vigilance committee (*Comité de surveillance*), which had
just been strengthened by the addition of Marat, had already begun to
devise a terrible rejoinder to the Gironde.

CHAPTER II

September

O N the morning of September 2 news reached Paris that the siege of Verdun had begun. A volunteer of the Maine-et-Loire battalion brought the terms of the summons to surrender sent by Brunswick to Beaurepaire, commandant of the fortress, and added that Verdun, the last fortress between Paris and the frontier, could not hold out for more than two days. Another messenger announced that the uhlans had entered Clermont-en-Argonne on the way from Châlons. The Commune at once issued the following proclamation to the Parisians: "To arms, citizens, to arms! The enemy is at our gates. March out this instant with your flags. Let us meet on the Champ de Mars! Let an army of sixty thousand men be instantly formed!" By order of the Commune an alarm-gun was fired, the drums beat to arms, the tocsin was sounded, the town gates were closed, all horses fit for use were commandeered for the service of those starting for the frontier, and able-bodied men were summoned to the Champ de Mars and formed on the spot into marching battalions. The members of the Commune dispersed to their respective sections. "They are to describe to their fellow-citizens in vigorous terms," ran the minutes, "the imminent dangers of the country, the treachery with which we are surrounded or threatened, the invasion of French territory; they are to bring home to them that the aim of all our enemies' measures is to reimpose upon us the most ignominious slavery and that, rather than endure it, we ought to bury ourselves beneath the ruins of our country and refuse to surrender our cities till they are no more than a heap of ashes."

Once more the much-maligned Commune had forestalled the Assembly in carrying out a patriotic duty. When its deputation appeared at the bar of the Assembly about noon to give an account of the steps which it had taken, Vergniaud was forced to pay a solemn tribute to it. After an enthusiastic eulogy of the Parisians he poured contempt upon cowardly panic-mongers and enjoined upon all good citizens to betake themselves to the camp outside Paris and by their voluntary labour to complete the fortifications begun there, "for the time for speech-making has gone by; we must dig the grave of our enemies or every step in their advance will dig our own!" The Assembly gave a favourable reception to this appeal for union. On the motion of Thuriot it voted a decree maintaining the Commune in its functions, while at the same time empowering the sections to strengthen it by nominating new members. A letter was then read from Roland announcing the discovery of a royalist plot in Morbihan.

Next Danton presented himself at the tribune, accompanied by all the ministers. "All is stir and movement; every man is burning to fight. Part of the people is about to betake itself to the frontiers, part to dig trenches, and yet a third part, pike in hand, will defend the towns from within." Paris had deserved well of the whole of France. Danton requested the Assembly to choose twelve of its members as delegates to co-operate with the Executive Council in carrying out great measures of public safety. They must decree that whosoever refused to serve in person or to give up his arms should be punished by death. Finally Danton wound up his brief and glowing oration with the famous words which have kept his memory alive: "The tocsin which is about to be rung is no alarm-signal; it sounds the charge against the enemies of the country. If we are to conquer them, gentlemen, what we need is daring, yet more daring, and more daring again, and France is saved! (*de l'audace, encore de l'audace, toujours de l'audace et la France est sauvée!*)" He resumed his seat amid a redoubled outburst of applause, and all his proposals were adopted without debate.

Thanks to Vergniaud, Thuriot, and Danton, union seemed to have been restored between all the forces of revolution in the face of danger. But dark suspicions lingered at the back of men's minds. As they listened to the alarm-gun and the tocsin, the idea of treachery haunted them more and more and they imagined themselves to be surrounded with snares. A rumour spread like wildfire that the suspects with whom the prisons were crammed were plotting to revolt, with the aid of outside accomplices. The volunteers who were enlisting on the Champ de Mars had read the notices posted up on the walls by Marat a few days previously, advising them not to leave till they had been to the prisons and meted out justice to the enemies of the people. They had also read the placards, which were still fresh, in which, under the title of *Compte rendu au peuple souverain* ("Report to the Sovereign People"), Fabre d'Eglantine was publishing the chief documents containing the record of the crimes of the King and Court. Their nerves were still affected by the series of funerals by which all the sections, and finally the whole Commune, had celebrated the memory of those who on August 10 had fallen victims to the disloyalty of the Swiss Guard. The last funeral, which had been celebrated in the setting of the Tuileries, the very scene of the fighting, had taken place barely a week before and had been accompanied by violent speeches ending in a call for vengeance.

But the people of Paris saw no sign of this promised vengeance. The extraordinary tribunal, created after so much hesitation and ill will, worked very slowly. So far it had condemned only three agents of the Court to death: Collenot d'Angremont, the recruiting-officer, at whose house had been found lists of royalist stalwarts; Laporte, intendant of the civil list, the chief paymaster of the secret agents; de Rozoy, the journalist, who was exulting over the enemy's successes in his *Gazette de Paris*. But after August 25 the activity of the tribunal had slackened. On August 27 it acquitted Dossonville, the police agent, whose name had been on d'Angremont's list. On August 31 it further acquitted Montmorin, governor of the palace of Fontainebleau, a compromising note from whom had been discovered among the papers at the Tuileries. This last acquittal aroused a storm of protests. The crowd hooted the judges, and threatened with death the prisoner, who was saved only with great difficulty. Danton used his authority as Minister of Justice to quash the verdict, ordered the case to be reconsidered, and dismissed Botot-Dumesnil, the national commissary, whom he caused to be arrested in turn. "I have reason to expect," wrote Danton severely to Réal, the public prosecutor, "that the outraged people, whose indignation against those who have violated liberty is unabated and who reveal a character worthy at last of eternal liberty, will no longer be reduced to executing justice itself, but will obtain it at the hands of its representatives and magistrates." It seemed natural to Danton that the people should "itself execute justice" when judges and juries refused to strike down its enemies by the arm of the law.

The new vigilance committee of the Commune, upon which its former clerk Deforgues now had a seat, was already busy sorting out the prisoners, releasing those accused of petty offences, poor debtors, those imprisoned for brawling, etc. Inflamed by the harangues of their representatives on the Commune, the sections were organizing recruiting, and at the same time threatening conspirators with the vengeance of the nation. That of the faubourg Poissonnière passed a motion that all priests and suspicious persons detained in the prisons should be put to death before the departure of the volunteers for the army. This sinister resolution was approved by the sections of the Luxembourg, the Louvre, and the Fontaine-Montmorency.

Words were followed by action. On the afternoon of September 2 some refractory priests who were being taken to the Abbaye were massacred on the way by their guards, who were Fédérés from Marseilles and Brittany. Only one of them was saved, the Abbé Sicard, a teacher of deaf-mutes, who was recognized by a man in the crowd. A band of shop-keepers and artisans, mingled with Fédéres and National Guards, went to the Carmelites, where a number of refractory priests were imprisoned, and did them to death with the butts of their guns, their pikes, sabres, and cudgels. Next, when night fell, it was the turn of the prisoners in the Abbaye. Here the vigilance committee of the Commune intervened in the following terms: "Comrades, your orders are to try all prisoners in the Abbaye, without distinction, with the exception of the Abbé Lenfant, whom you will place in safe-keeping. [Signed:] Panis, Sergent." The Abbé Lenfant, formerly the King's confessor, had a brother who was a member of the vigilance committee. A sham tribunal was impro-vised, with Stanislas Maillard as its president. Maillard, with the prison register before him, examined the prisoners and consulted his assistants as to the penalty. "Release them!" was his formula in the case of those condemned; and the bodies of the victims formed a growing heap. Petion, who visited the prison of La Force on September 3, informs us that "those who gave judgment and executed the sentence were as confident as if the law had called upon them to discharge these functions." "They boasted to me," he says, "of their justice, their care in distinguishing the innocent from the guilty, and the services which they had rendered."

The butchery went on at the other prisons on the following days: at La Force at one o'clock in the morning, at the Conciergerie during the morning of the 3rd, at the Tour Saint-Bernard, then at the Châtelet, Saint-Firmin, and the Salpêtrière on September 4, and lastly at Bicêtre. The murderers became so intoxicated with slaughter that common-law and political prisoners, women and children, were slain indiscriminately. Some of the bodies—that of the Princesse de Lamballe, for instance—were horribly mutilated. There are different estimates of the numbers of the slain, varying from eleven hundred to fourteen hundred.

The populace looked on indifferently or with satisfaction at these scenes of horror. The wife of Julien of Drôme wrote to her husband on the very evening of September 2: "The people has arisen, the people, terrible in its rage, is avenging the crimes of three years of the basest

181

treachery! The martial fury which has seized all the people of Paris is prodigious. Fathers of families, bourgeois, soldiers, sansculottes, everybody is leaving for the front. The people has said: 'We are leaving our wives and children at home surrounded by our enemies; let us purge the land of liberty.' The Austrians and Prussians might be at the gates of Paris, but I should not take a step backwards. I should only cry the more confidently: 'Victory is ours!' " We may judge what were the sentiments of other classes from the elation of this excellent bourgeoise, a disciple of Jean-Jacques.

The fever of patriotism, the approach of the enemy, and the sound of the tocsin lulled men's consciences to sleep. While the murderers gave themselves up to their horrible task, the women spent the nights in the churches making garments for the volunteers and lint for the wounded. At the Commune and the sections there was an unceasing stream of citizens offering their arms or gifts to the country. Many took charge of the children of those leaving for the front. Gaming-establishments were closed by order of the Mairie. The lead out of coffins was melted down to make bullets. All wheel-wrights were busy making gun-carriages and ammunition-wagons. The enthusiasm was magnificent. The sublime and the vile were to be seen side by side.

The authorities had let matters take their course. When the Commune sent to him for help, Santerre, the commandant of the National Guard, replied that he could not count upon the obedience of his men. The Commune compensated the murderers for the working-days which they had lost. The deputations sent by the Assembly to the scene of the murders were powerless. On September 3 Roland, the Minister of the Interior, wrote it a letter in the following terms: "Yesterday was a day over the events of which a veil must be cast. I know that the people, terrible though its vengeance may be, yet displays in it a sort of justice!" The Girondin newspapers—which at that time constituted almost the whole of the press—even excused the massacres at the time or pleaded extenuating circumstances in their favour.

As for Danton, the Minister of Justice, he made not the slightest move to protect the prisons. According to Mme Roland's account, when Roland's clerk Grandpré requested him to act, he replied: "I don't care a damn for the prisoners; let them shift for themselves! (*Je me fous bien des prisonniers, qu'ils deviennent ce qu'ils pourront!*)" And a few days later, when Alquier, president of the criminal tribunal of Seine-et-Oise, called upon him to ask for his interest on behalf of the prisoners from the High Court at Orleans who were being brought to Versailles by

Fournier's band in order to be massacred, Danton replied with a shrug of his shoulders: "Don't interfere with those people. It might lead to a great deal of unpleasantness for you." His words to the Duke of Chartres, afterwards Louis Philippe, during the early days of the Convention are well known: "At a time when all the male portion of the population was rushing to the armies and leaving us defenceless in Paris, the prisons were overflowing with a crowd of conspirators and wretched creatures who were only awaiting the approach of the foreigner to massacre us. I did no more than forestall them. I intended that all the youth of Paris should arrive in Champagne covered with blood as a warrant of their fidelity. I intended to set a river of blood between them and the *émigrés*." Need we further recall that Danton's secretary, Fabre d'Eglantine, openly defended the massacres and held them up as an example to the rest of France?

Since August 28, when Roland and the Girondins had proposed to leave Paris, Danton had openly made common cause with the Commune, and made its animosities his own. To his mind the object of the massacres was not only to make the enemy's accomplices tremble, but to give the Girondins pause. The elections were beginning and it was a good opportunity for striking a blow at political rivals. Danton's calculations were shared by all his party.

On the very day of September 2, during the evening session of the Commune, Billaud-Varenne and Robespierre denounced "the conspiracy in favour of Brunswick, whom a powerful party desires to set upon the throne of the French." The allusion was not only to Carra's equivocal campaign, but also to that openly carried on by the Abbé Danjou at the Jacobins in favour of the Duke of York. They were no doubt thinking of the grave words said to have been uttered by Brissot himself in the commission of twelve, on July 17, as reported by Barère: "This evening," Brissot had said to one of his colleagues, "I will show you, from a correspondence carried on with the Cabinet of St. James's, that it only depends on ourselves to amalgamate our constitution with that of England by putting the Duke of York in the place of Louis XVI as constitutional king." The day after Robespierre's attack at the Commune, Brissot's house was searched by order of the vigilance committee, and on the next day warrants were signed for the arrest of Roland and eight deputies of the Gironde. This time Danton considered that they were going too far. He owed his office to Brissot and Condorcet. He went down to the Hôtel de Ville and after a sharp altercation with Marat had the warrants withdrawn. Danton had too much contempt for human life to be blood-thirsty. Once the blow had been struck and the object attained, his heart was accessible to pity. He facilitated the escape of Adrien Duport, Talleyrand, Charles Lameth, and many others.[1] He shrank from useless acts of cruelty. If he had allowed Roland and Brissot to be struck down, he would have made his position in the ministry impossible, and he did not want to break with the Assembly yet. He was content to frighten it and even found a grim satisfaction in playing the part of protector to it.

Revolutionary France did not repudiate the massacres at the time. The same spirit, the same fever, prevailed from end to end of her territory. As early as September 3, in a famous circular letter sent to the departments and countersigned by Danton, the vigilance committee of the Commune justified its work and held it up as an example: "The Commune of Paris hastens to inform its brethren in the departments that part of the ferocious conspirators detained in its prisons have been put to death by the people—acts of justice which seemed indispensable to it in order to restrain by terror the legions of traitors concealed within its walls at the moment when it was preparing to march upon the enemy; and after the long series of betrayals which have led it to the verge of the abyss, no doubt the whole nation will hasten to adopt this necessary measure of public safety. . . ."

The circular was superfluous. The provincials had no need for Paris to set them an example. They had sometimes forestalled it. Two priests had been massacred in the department of Orne on August 19, another in Aube on August 21, a bailiff (*huissier*) at Lisieux on August 23, etc. In all the places through which the volunteers passed on their way to the frontier, the aristocrats had to be on their best behaviour. At Reims on September 3, at Meaux on the 4th, in the department of Orne on the 3rd and 6th, at Lyons on the 9th, at Caen on the 7th, at Vitteaux on the 12th, officers, priests, and suspects of every kind met their death, even in the prisons. At the electoral assembly of Bouches-du-Rhône, presided over by Barbaroux, the news of the massacres in Paris was enthusiastically applauded. Like the ancient gods, the new god "patriotism" demanded human victims.

Those who were regarded as the most dangerous suspects, and furnished most of the victims, were everywhere the refractory priests. On one point alone, perhaps, had the three organs of power—the Commune, the Legislative Assembly, and the Executive Council—been entirely in agree-

---

[1] It is true that in Brissot's pamphlet against the Jacobins which appeared in October 1792, after his name was struck off the books of the club, he insinuates that Talleyrand paid five hundred louis for his passport.

ment—on the necessity of making it impossible for the refractory clergy to do any damage to the defence of the Revolution or the nation.

The Constituent Assembly had suppressed only part of the religious houses. A notable exception was those devoted to charity and education. On July 31 a deputy declared that these houses were "bastilles of monarchism, of which the refractory priests are the door-keepers," and on August 4 the Assembly decreed that the houses belonging to the religious orders which had already been suppressed should all be evacuated by November 1 and put up for sale. There remained the so-called secular congregations, which the Constituent Assembly had spared, and in which no solemn vows were taken, such as the Oratorians, who had a number of schools under their direction, the Lazarists, Sulpicians, and Eudists; the lay congregations, such as the Christian Brothers; or female congregations, such as the Daughters of Wisdom, of Providence, of the Cross, of the Good Shepherd, etc. All of these were suppressed on August 18 and their property liquidated. The nuns who worked in the hospitals, however, received individual permits to continue their service.

The refractory priests, many of whom had maintained their position in their former parishes, seemed even more dangerous than the religious orders. Before the cannon had ceased firing on August 10, the Assembly had decreed that all measures vetoed by the King should at once be put in force. The decree of May 27 concerning the internment and deportation of refractory priests who might cause disorder was now carried into effect. On the very evening of August 10 the Commune sent off to the sections the list of suspect bishops and priests. They were immediately imprisoned in the Abbaye, the Carmelites, and the seminary of Saint Magloire, to become the prey of the Septembriseurs, as those responsible for the massacres were called. But the decree of May 27 applied only to such priests as had been functionaries of the Constitutional Church, for these alone had been compelled by the Constituent Assembly to take the oath. In order to strike at the rest, who were very numerous, the Assembly on August 14 made it obligatory for them to take the oath of fidelity to liberty and equality. A certain number submitted, in order that they might continue to draw their stipends and celebrate religious services. But in the eyes of the revolutionaries the decree of May 27 had yet another defect. It affected only such priests as were denounced by twenty active citizens. In many regions, where the whole population was in league with the refractory priests, it was impossible to collect twenty signatures. On August 19 Cambon and Lanjuinais demanded a fresh law, which should enable them to take summary proceedings against all priests indiscriminately. On August 23 the Girondin Lariviere tried to infuse energy into the extraordinary commission whose task it was to prepare the new law. "If," he said, "you can no longer endure the sight of the emblems of tyranny, I cannot conceive how you have so long been able to endure the sight of the fanatical originators of our internal discords, or the sight of the evils and disasters to which they daily give rise. I propose that a report should instantly be made upon the means of deporting them, for every moment's delay is tantamount to a murder." (Enthusiastic applause.) The revolutionaries had a weighty reason for clearing up this matter. The elections to the Convention were impending: the primary assemblies were to meet on August 26 and the electoral assemblies on September 2. It was necessary to make haste and expel the refractory priests from France, so as to prevent them from exercising any influence upon the choice of the deputies. Marans, Delacroix, and Cambon expressed their fears in no measured terms. On August 24 Marans said: "Aristocrat priests, driven out at first by fear, are already venturing to return to their parishes and using their endeavours to give us bad electors. It is necessary that their deportation should be announced before the 28th." Delacroix's words were: "Let us expel the priests! Let us expel them, lest, by worming their way into the assemblies of the people, they make their pestilential presence felt in the election of deputies to the National Convention." Cambon, amid frantic applause from the public galleries, proposed their immediate deportation to Guiana, where, he said, agriculture was in need of labourers. Delaunay supported him, but when Lasource, a former Protestant pastor, backed up by Bishop Fauchet and Vergniaud, pointed out that to send them to Guiana would be sending them to certain death, the Assembly allowed the refractory priests to choose to what country they would go. The decree of August 26 gave them a fortnight in which to leave France, at the expiry of which period they were to be deported to Guiana. Priests over sixty or in bad health were, however, explicitly exempted from deportation, nor did the decree affect those ecclesiastics who had not been compelled to take the oath, who were only to be deported if they were denounced by six householders. Thousands of priests (perhaps twenty-five thousand) started out for foreign countries, where they did not always meet with a cordial or ready welcome. In Spain, particularly, they were treated almost as suspicious characters. It was in England that they met with the best reception.

In spite of the proportions assumed by this forced emigration, the

Church of Rome did not entirely disappear. There were still a number of priests who had not been compelled to take the oath and of refractory priests over sixty or in bad health. The Bishop of Sarlat continued to live at Sarlat, of which he was actually mayor till the Terror, when he was put in prison. The Bishop of Riez retired to his native town of Autun; de Belloy, Bishop of Marseilles, to a village in the neighbourhood of Paris, from which he still carried on the administration of his former diocese; the Bishop of Angers, Couet de Lorry, to a village in Normandy; Mailly de la Tour Landry, Bishop of Saint-Papoul, to Paris, where he ordained clergy; the Bishop of Senlis to Crépy-en-Valois, etc. It is true that most of these prelates and refractory priests who remained in France took the oath of liberty and equality, to the great indignation of their colleagues who had emigrated, who sometimes regarded them as semi-schismatic. But the Pope did not dare to condemn them.

The inevitable consequence of the deportation of the refractory priests was the secularization of the registers of births, marriages, and deaths, which was voted by the Assembly at its closing session, on September 20, 1792. There were a number of departments—for instance, Côtes-du-Nord—where the refractory priests had continued to officiate in their parishes up to August 10, because there were not enough constitutional priests; and they had the custody of the registers in these parishes. When they had gone, there was nobody to replace them in either their civil or their religious functions, which had hitherto been united, and the registers had perforce to be entrusted to the municipalities. This measure had been demanded for a long time past by the Feuillants, or constitutional monarchists, who laid stress upon the aversion felt by those faithful to the Roman priests from applying to the official priests, whom they regarded as schismatic, for baptism, burial, and marriage. Many families preferred to deprive their new-born children of the status of citizens rather than have recourse to the intruders. For a long time the revolutionaries had stood out against the pressure of the refractory priests and Feuillants, for fear of weakening the position of the constitutional clergy by depriving them of the right to register births, marriages, and deaths.

But now that the refractory priests had been deported *en masse*, the revolutionaries had no further cause to fear that by passing the desired measure they would be swelling the numbers of those in favour of counter-revolution. They therefore handed over the registers to the lay authorities, now that they were sure they could do so without danger. In many places it was actually the constitutional parish priests who were made registrars. It is none the less true that this dissociation of the civil registers from the sacraments was an important innovation, pregnant with consequences for the future. The State was steadily losing its religious character. The same law which handed over the registers to the secular authorities authorized divorce, which was forbidden by the Church.

The constitutional priests had no doubt rejoiced at being rid of their rivals, but those of them who were capable of reflection felt a certain apprehension. As early as August 11 Thomas Lindet, Bishop of Eure, wrote to his brother: "Soon you will want no more kings or priests." How indeed could the fall of the earthly monarch fail to shake the position of the King of heaven? The same Thomas Lindet expressed himself as follows on August 30: "The Parisians will end like the English, by shouting: 'Down with the bishops!' Theism and Protestantism have more in common with republicanism. Catholicism has always been attached to the monarchy, and at the present moment it has the drawback of being very expensive." A few weeks later Lafont de Savine, Bishop of Ardèche, wrote in a similar strain to Roland: "I think it my duty to point out that the Civil Constitution of the clergy is nearing its end. It is obvious that, as a necessary consequence of its principles, the State is about to become entirely divorced from all religious matters, that the stipend allotted to the ministers of the Catholic religion will be regarded merely as a retiring allowance and as compensation for the property which they formerly enjoyed; that laws establishing universal toleration are incompatible with granting to one form of worship the exclusive privilege of being supported out of the public funds, and likewise with a hierarchical system defined by law. . . ." The views of both bishops were sound. The days of the constitutional clergy were indeed numbered. The logical development of its principles, together with the pressure of events, involved the Revolution in bold measures before which it would have recoiled in alarm two years earlier.

The constitutional Church was treated more and more cavalierly. It was not enough that it was obliged to place its spiritual influence, its sermons, and its blessings at the service of the new State; it had further to sacrifice its superfluous resources in the same cause. As early as July 19 a decree based on a report of the Finance Committee was passed, by which the former episcopal palaces with their gardens were put up for sale. In future the bishops were to find accommodation at their own expense in furnished rooms, as best they could, a tenth of their salary being specially set aside for the purpose. One article in the preamble of the decree says that "the sumptuousness of the episcopal palaces is hardly suitable to the simplicity of the ecclesiastical state." The bishops were not only despoiled, but lectured.

These tendencies became still more marked after August 10. On August 14, on the motion of Delacroix and Thuriot, the Assembly decreed that all bronze objects and monuments reminiscent of feudalism existing in the churches were to be melted down to make cannon. The Commune of Paris, whose example was followed by others, put the widest interpretation upon this decree and took advantage of it to strip the holy places of most of their ornaments. On August 17, "anxious"—to quote its ordinance—"to serve the common weal by every means in its power," and "considering that great resources for the defence of the country are to be found in the mass of all those shams which owe their existence only to the knavery of priests and the barbarism of the people," it laid violent hands upon "all bronze crucifixes, reading-desks, angels, devils, seraphim, and cherubim," in order to melt them down for cannon, and all grilles for making pikes. On August 18 a deputation from the confraternity of Saint Sulpice offered the Assembly a silver statue of St. Roch, and its spokesman accompanied the offer by a speech which might almost have been delivered under the Terror: "The various confraternities formed within the realm the rings of that sacerdotal chain by which the people was enslaved; we have broken them and joined the great confraternity of free men. We invoked the aid of our St. Roch against the political pestilence which has wrought such havoc in France,[2] but he did not grant our prayers. We thought that his silence was due to his shape, and we bring him to you in order that he may be converted into coin. Under this new form he will no doubt lend his aid in destroying the pestilential race of our enemies." The Assembly followed suit. On September 10 it commandeered all the gold and silver vessels in the churches, with the exception of the monstrances, ciboria, and chalices, and ordered that they should be coined into money for paying the troops. Thus every day the public worship established by the Constitution was losing all the outward prestige which it exerted over the minds of the simple, and becoming gradually reduced to a state of apostolic poverty.

As early as August 12 the Commune had forbidden all priests to wear their canonical dress except during the exercise of their functions. Once more the Assembly followed the Commune. Six days later it renewed the

---

[2] St. Roch's great work was nursing those suffering from plague in the early years of the fourteenth century.

prohibition of ecclesiastical costume which had already been laid down by the decree of April 6.

The Commune was already laying down the rule that religion ought to remain a private matter. On August 16 it enjoined "upon all religious sects not to obstruct the public highway in the exercise of their functions"; in other words, it abolished processions and ceremonies taking place outside the churches. In so doing it was giving a bold extension to the decree by which, two days previously, the Assembly had revoked Louis XIII's edict on the procession of August 15. It excluded priests from the funeral celebration which it held in memory of those who had fallen on August 10.

With scant regard for logic, however, it none the less proposed to interfere in the internal administration of the constitutional form of worship. Immediately after the insurrection it suppressed the perquisites of the clergy, "in consequence of the complaints made by many citizens as to the exactions of the constitutional clergy," and, by the same decree, it abolished the different classes of funerals and did away with churchwardens and their special seats. In future all citizens were to be buried by two priests, with the same ceremonial, and there were to be no more funeral draperies at the church doors. On September 7 the Legislative Assembly in turn docilely decreed that ecclesiastics receiving a State salary who should accept any perquisites, upon any pretext whatsoever, should be condemned by the courts to lose their positions and salaries.

The marriage of priests was already viewed with favour by the Assembly and held up as an example to be followed. On August 14 the deputy Lejosne requested that Gratien, Bishop of Seine-Inférieure, who had reminded his clergy in a pastoral of the duty of continence, should be prosecuted before the courts, and that priests should be warned that they would lose their salaries if they published any writings contrary to the rights of man. Both proposals were referred to the Legislative Committee.

Here we may see the germ of the theory which was to meet with such success under the Convention. The constitutional clergy, for the sole reason that they are constitutional, ought to be incorporated, as it were, in the Constitution. The rights of man are incompatible with perpetual vows. Hence priests must be forbidden to teach that these vows are to be respected, and bishops must be forbidden not only to remove, dismiss, or molest such of their priests as might take a wife, but even to censure them publicly by word of mouth or in writing. The laws of the State are absolutely binding upon the constitutional clergy, even when they are opposed to the discipline or dogmas of Catholicism. In other words, the constitutional clergy were no longer to have their own special laws, but those of the State alone.

Under the Convention, penalties were added. By a proclamation of the Executive Council, dated January 22, 1793, all bishops were forbidden to order priests to keep registers of baptisms, marriages, and burials, to publish banns, "to impose conditions not ordered by the civil law, before pronouncing the nuptial benediction"—in other words, it was made obligatory for them to marry without question all those who might present themselves to receive the sacrament, even divorced persons, priests, and atheists. The verdict of the courts obliged priests to conduct the marriage service for their brother clergy. Some bishops were put in prison for having placed impediments in the way of these marriages. A decree of July 19, 1793 inflicted the penalty of deportation upon bishops who should commit this offence. It was on this occasion that Delacroix exclaimed: "The bishops are appointed by the electoral assemblies and paid by the nation; they ought to obey all the laws of the Republic." And Danton added: "We have continued to pay the bishops' stipends; let them imitate the founders of the Church. The latter rendered unto Cæsar that which was Cæsar's. Well! the nation is above all Cæsars." In other words, the nation was master even in the religious sphere; it was the source of all law, authority, and truth. Thomas Lindet had been right when on the morrow of August 10 he wrote that the fall of the King foreshadowed that of the priests.

CHAPTER III

The Elections to the Convention

THE Legislative Assembly and the Commune came to an understanding upon the religious question easily enough, but upon all other questions they were either covertly or openly in opposition.

The Commune regarded the fall of the throne as a definitive act implying the Republic. The Assembly shrank from a decision and adjourned the issue.

In order to prevent a revival of the monarchy the Commune did its best to keep from voting all those whom it suspected of regretting Louis XVI. On August 11 it decided to print a list of those Parisian electors who had met at the Club of the Sainte Chapelle the year before to prepare for the elections to the Legislative Assembly. On the following day it suppressed all royalist newspapers and distributed their presses among the patriot papers; nor did the Assembly venture to protest against this act of violence, which had grave consequences. Royalism was deprived of its organs and rendered incapable of making its voice heard in France at the very moment when the electoral campaign was about to open. From August 13 onwards the Commune dated its acts from "the year I of equality," thereby intending to signify that a new era was beginning.

The Assembly followed only by slow degrees. On August 11 one of its members, Sers, protested against the demolition of statues of kings, which were being overthrown in Paris and all the large towns. It is true that the only argument which he advanced in defence of the august effigies which were in danger was the fear of accidents; but another deputy, Marans, shed a tear over the statue of Henry IV. In vain; for Thuriot obtained the passage of a decree that all these bronzes should be converted into coin or cannon. Two days later Robespierre requested that a monument to those who had fallen on August 10 should be erected on the site of the statue of Louis XV.

The Commune proceeded on its course. On August 14 it sent a deputation to the Assembly requesting it to strike the king's name off the list of public functionaries, and on the following day Gensonné obtained the passage of a decree that the judgments of the courts should in future be pronounced and the laws promulgated in the name of the nation. Ducos had the "scandalous" effigy of Louis XVI, which still adorned the hall in which the Assembly met, covered with the Declaration of the Rights of Man.

The Commune resolved that the voting at the elections should take place orally and by roll-call (*par appel nominal*), and the Assembly raised no objection. Robespierre protested at the meeting of his section against the maintenance of the indirect franchise, and the Commune hastened to add a rider to the law by framing an ordinance, at his dictation, by which the names of those chosen by the electoral assembly were to be submitted for the ratification of the primary assemblies. On August 17 the Commune resolved to publish the lists of those who had signed the two royalist petitions after June 20, numbering eight thousand and twenty thousand respectively. On August 22 it called upon the ministers to substitute the word "Citoyen" for "Monsieur." The democrats of the Commune and the Jacobins demanded that the people should have the right to sanction the Constitution and the laws and to dismiss deputies: that is to say, they wanted to apply the precepts of the *Social Contract* literally, by instituting the referendum and the *mandat impératif*.[1]

The republican movement was spreading rapidly in the provinces. The volunteers in the Vosges, on hearing of the suspension of Louis XVI, shouted: *"Vive la Nation sans Roi!* (Long live the nation with no king!)" The judges at La Rochelle wound up their congratulations to the Assembly by expressing their desire for "the sovereign nation and nothing more!" The Jacobins of Strasbourg shouted: *"Vive l'Égalité et point de roi!* (Long live equality! Down with the king!)." The election address of the Parisian Jacobins openly advocated the Republic.

It was becoming evident that the maintenance of the forms of monarchy was opposed by a strong current of hostile opinion, against which the deputies were powerless to struggle. On August 22 Cambon declared: "The people no longer want a monarchy. Let us make its return impossible." On September 1, in order to show that he was no longer thinking of Brunswick, Carra advised his readers to demand from the future deputies "an oath that they would never propose a king or royalty, under pain of being buried alive in their departments on their return." Condorcet in turn proclaimed himself a republican, explaining that a change of dynasty would be folly. On the following day, September 4, moved by the "atrocious slander" which represented them as contemplat-

---

[1] i.e., practically what is now known as the "initiative."

ing the accession of the Duke of Brunswick or the Duke of York to the throne, the deputies took an oath to combat kings and royalty with all their might and addressed a republican proclamation to the nation, though they did so as individuals and not officially.

It is hard to tell how far these tardy demonstrations were sincere. Chabot, the very man who on September 3 referred to the alleged project for offering the crown to a foreign prince as an "atrocious calumny," had on August 20 advised the Fédérés, from the tribune at the Jacobins, to stay in Paris and watch over the Convention, to prevent it from restoring the monarchy and leaving Paris. And a few days later he voted at the electoral assembly of Paris for the Duke of Orleans, who was chosen as a deputy to the Convention at the bottom of the list, in spite of Robespierre's opposition. Danton and his friends voted with Chabot for the Duke of Orleans. Had the Duke any ambition beyond that of a vote in the legislature? His correspondence proves that he was trying to obtain the election to the Convention of his son, the Duke of Chartres, afterwards King Louis Philippe, although he had not yet reached the statutory age. But in the end the Duke of Chartres did not dare to come forward and his father offered himself as a candidate. Before soliciting the votes of the Parisian electors he sent a request to the Commune begging it to give him a new name, and the Commune, by a formal decree, bestowed upon him that of Égalité, which he accepted "with extreme gratitude" on September 14. It was believed at the time that Danton, who was not capable of much enthusiasm for political metaphysics, was secretly in the pay of the house of Orleans. Some manuscript notes of King Louis Philippe have recently been discovered in which he relates that, after Valmy, Danton offered him his support and advised him to make himself popular with the army: "That is essential for you and yours, it is essential even for us, and above all for your father." Danton closed the interview with the words: "You have a good chance of reigning." In his eyes, then, the Republic was only a provisional solution.

For the moment royalty stood condemned. The Girondins, feeling that Paris and certain large towns were slipping from them, endeavoured to secure the vote of the country districts. As early as August 14 one of them, François (of Neufchâteau), had persuaded the Assembly to pass a decree by which the property of the communes was divided among all the citizens, while that of the *émigrés* was split up into small lots, which were to be paid for in fifteen annual instalments, so that the poor could easily purchase them. On August 16 all proceedings for the recovery of former feudal dues were suspended. Finally, on August 25, the Assembly abolished without compensation all feudal dues to which the owners were unable to produce their title. The fall of the throne was accompanied by that of feudalism, so that the peasants should no longer regret the king.

The electoral assemblies, which met on September 2, sat for several days, and sometimes even for several weeks. In spite of the fact that the suffrage had been granted to passive citizens, there was very little eagerness to vote. The poor did not care to lose their day's wages in tiresome and unfamiliar operations. The royalists and Feuillants, the aristocrats and the timid abstained out of prudence or from constitutional scruples. Nobody was allowed to vote before taking the oath of fidelity to liberty and equality. In the department of Oise there were fewer voters at the primary assemblies of 1792 than at those of 1791 or 1790. In at least ten departments, Bouches-du-Rhône, Cantal, Charente, Corrèze, Drôme, Hérault, Lot, Gers, Oise, Hautes-Pyrénées, and Seine-et-Marne, the voting took place orally and by roll-call in imitation of Paris. The same thing happened at the primary assemblies of Le Mans. Often, too, the electoral assemblies purged themselves by expelling from their midst citizens suspected of "anti-civic" opinions (that is, those opposed to the prevailing regime). Almost everywhere the predominant influence of the middle and property-owning classes asserted itself unchallenged. Except in Paris and a few other towns the artisans and labourers either effaced themselves or docilely allowed themselves to be led to the poll. At Quingey, in the department of Doubs, an ironmaster named Louvot took possession of the premises of the primary assembly with his workmen, whom he had marched to the spot in a body, led by a man playing the clarinet. He expelled from the room in which polling was taking place all those who offered any resistance and had himself nominated as elector; and this case cannot have been an isolated one. The deputies to the Convention were elected by a determined minority. Most of them belonged to the middle classes, whose interests were bound up with those of the Revolution. It would be useful to ascertain what proportion of the electors were purchasers of national property. This point has never been the subject of research. Out of the 750 deputies, two alone were artisans, Noël Pointe, an armourer elected by Rhône-et-Loire, and Armonville, a wool-carder, elected by the department of Marne.

With the exception of Paris, where the party of the Commune, with Robespierre at its head, was the only one represented, the elections were not influenced, so to speak, by the antagonism between the Legislative Assembly and the Commune, the Gironde and the Mountain, which was hardly patent as yet. In the departments the revolutionaries, who felt themselves to be few in number, were bent upon union rather than upon division. Buzot, the future Girondin, was elected for Eure, together with the future Montagnards Robert and Thomas Lindet, and was at that time on perfectly good terms with them. The chief concern of the electors was to choose men capable of defending the Revolution against its enemies at home and abroad. The monarchy found no defenders. Since the Girondins were better known and had the press and the tribune of the Legislative Assembly on their side, besides which they were still in force at the Jacobins, a large number of them were elected. Brissot's paper on September 10 contained a pæan of victory. But the electors had not voted on party lines. They had given their deputies no mandate to avenge the wounds inflicted on their pride by the Commune on August 10.

Unfortunately the Girondins were incapable of laying aside their grudges. Petion's vanity had suffered cruelly from the reverse which he had sustained at the hands of the electoral assembly of Paris, which had preferred Robespierre to him. Madame Roland, who governed her elderly husband, suffered from the predominant position acquired by Danton on the Executive Council. Brissot, Carra, Louvet, Guadet, Gensonné, Condorcet, all the leaders of the party, detested Robespierre as the man who had obstructed their warlike policy, who had exposed their hesitations and manœuvres before and after the insurrection, who had credited them with the intention of coming to terms with the Court and the enemy, and who had been the instigator of the Commune's insolent usurpations; they were bent upon revenge.

Madame Roland's intimate letters reveal the full depths of her hatred and fear. She was convinced that the theft of the crown diamonds—really carried out by professional burglars—was due to Danton and Fabre d'Eglantine. She despised and hated Danton, though he had just obtained the withdrawal by the Commune of the warrant issued for her husband's arrest. In her eyes salvation was to be found only in the formation of a guard from the departments which should be stationed in Paris to protect the Assembly. "We are not yet safe," she wrote to Bancal, "and if the departments do not send a guard for the Assembly and the Council, you will lost them both. Set to work quickly, then, to send it to us, *under the pretext of foreign enemies,* whom all Parisians capable of defending their country are being sent to face, and to induce the whole of France to lend its aid for the preservation of the two powers which it possesses and holds dear." We may here see the beginnings of that fatal policy which, by setting the departments against Paris, was to lead a few months later to the federalist agitation and civil war.

Unfortunately Madame Roland was listened to, especially by those who had been alarmed at the capture of Longwy and projected transferring the seat of government to the departments of the centre and south. As early as September 4 Cambon, who was at that time in the ranks of the Gironde and never ceased to distrust the Commune, even after he had rallied to the Mountain, threatened Paris with the vengeance of the south: "If, through our blindness and our weakness, these contemptible slanderers were to become our cruel masters, believe me, gentlemen, the generous citizens of the south, who have sworn to uphold liberty and equality in their territory, would come to the aid of the oppressed capital. [Loud applause.] . . . If by some unhappy chance liberty were to be vanquished and .they were forced to withdraw without being able to visit their hatred and thirst for vengeance and death upon the new tryants, I do not doubt that they would throw open their inviolate homes as a sacred refuge for those unfortunates who might escape from the ax of these French Sullas." Thus Cambon's idea was that, if the help for which they appealed to the departments was insufficient, they would revive the project of a republic of the south which had already been secretly elaborated during the previous days in the private conclaves of Kersaint and the Rolands. And Cambon justified his threats by the rumours of a dictatorship which came to his ears. But these were dangerous accusations, and were to lead far!

This project of secession announced from the tribune in Cambon's vehement words had so much substance that it alarmed even Anacharsis Cloots, who did not hesitate to repudiate it, though he had at that time a horror of the Commune. "Frenchmen," he wrote in the *Annales patriotiques* of September 10, "let us not dream of the south; it would be to hasten our ruin and expose ourselves to the kicks of all the tyrants of Europe, especially the Sultan of Madrid. . . . Paris is the city of the French; the conquest of the capital would utterly disorganize the body politic." Such an article was bound to estrange Cloots from the Rolands and soon afterwards from the rest of the Girondins.

In order to obtain the departmental guard which would set their minds at rest, the Rolands used every conceivable means to produce a panic in the Assembly during its closing days. They stirred up its horror of the Commune, which they represented as a band of hired assassins and brigands. On September 17 Roland announced to the Assembly that

197

the robbery of the State furniture-store (*Garde-meuble*) was part of "a vast plot," and went on, with no transition, to denounce the electoral assembly of Paris, which, if he were to be believed, had on the previous day proposed an agrarian law—that is to say, the dividing up of the land among the people. He alleged that those responsible for the massacres were not satisfied and were about to resume their exploits. "The people are being advised by certain plotters to rise once more, if they have not lost their daggers; I know the authors of these placards, and by whom they are paid." This last insinuation was certainly aimed at Danton, who was still Roland's colleague in the ministry. And the whole arraignment, based upon false or distorted data, was intended to lead up to the following conclusion: "Gentlemen, it is necessary that you should summon a strong guard to your side; it ought to be at your disposal." In a tragic tone Roland declared that meanwhile he was braving death. On the following day he once more returned to the charge.

It was a great misfortune that the leaders of the Gironde let themselves be led by this arrogant, timorous, and narrow-minded old man. On September 17 Lasource carried his gloomy prophecies still further in an official report which he made to the Assembly, as spokesman of the commission of twelve. "A plan exists," he said, "for preventing the Convention from assembling. . . . I denounce this infamous project. . . . It is proposed in the last resort to burn or sack the city of Paris, so that it may be impossible for the camp to be formed"; and he represented the Parisian revolutionaries as allies or agents of Brunswick. Vergniaud, who usually had more sense, guaranteed the accuracy of Lasource's romancing. He denounced the vigilance committee of the Commune, threw down a challenge to the assassins, and obtained the passage of a decree by which the members of the Commune were to answer for the lives of the prisoners with their own! Next Petion in turn arraigned the fanatical and perfidious patriots, who, according to him, were preparing for fresh massacres. On the following day a fresh decree was voted, on Guadet's motion, which this time definitely suppressed the Revolutionary Commune, ordered its reconstitution, and reinstated the mayor Petion in the exercise of all the functions of which he had been deprived by the insurrection. In future, warrants for arrests were to be issued only by the mayor and the police commissioners. The tocsin and alarm-gun were in future to be used only by formal order of the legislature. Thus in the long struggle which had gone on for six weeks between the Commune and the Assembly, the latter had the last word.

Its ultimate victory is to be attributed not only to the result of the

198

elections to the Convention, which had delighted and given new life to (*ranimé*) Madame Roland, but above all to the revulsion of feeling which had taken place after the massacres, both in the populace of Paris and afterwards in the whole of France. The Girondins, who had kept silence during the massacres, and had, moveover, a few months before, proclaimed an amnesty for the atrocities at the ice-house of Avignon, eagerly encouraged and artfully exploited this reaction. As early as September 10 Brissot in his paper represented the massacres as the result of a Montagnard plot, the ultimate object of which was, according to him, an agrarian law—that is to say, the division of land and fortunes among the people. Following his lead and Roland's example, the publicists of the party, many of whom, such as Louvet, were subsidized out of the propaganda fund of the Ministry of the Interior, gave the signal to property-owners to rally against the Mountain. Henceforward the Gironde posed as the party of order and social stability. It had already taken under its wing those who had previously belonged to the Feuillant party. In Paris the section of the Lombards, of which Louvet was the moving spirit, followed by the sections of the Mail and the Marais, all three composed of rich tradespeople, came to the support of the eight thousand and the twenty thousand who had signed the royalist petitions, who had been treated as suspects by the Commune and excluded from the electoral assembly. On September 8 the section of the Lombards announced at the Assembly that it had taken the initiative in forming "a sacred and conservative confederation" of all good citizens in all sections for the protection of life and property. At the express request of the petitioners the Assembly decreed that the originals of the two petitions of the eight thousand and the twenty thousand should be destroyed. So strong was the reaction that on September 19 even the Commune swore to protect property.

Was property really in danger? Were the fears of the Girondins well founded? The time has now arrived to review briefly the economic and social problem as it then appeared.

The war had had a peculiar effect upon the position of artisans and manual labourers in general. Luxury trades were at a standstill. During August the assignats fell forty-one per cent in Paris and almost as much at Marseilles, Lille, Narbonne, and Bordeaux. Wages had not increased fast enough to make up for the rise in the price of commodities.

In spite of the fact that the year's harvest bade fair to be a good one and in general more abundant than that of 1791, the markets were but poorly supplied. Grain was hoarded, and bread was scarce and very dear. The revolutionaries put this down to the manœuvres of the aristocrats. Farmers preferred to keep their corn rather than exchange it for assignats. They knew that a strong Prussian army was advancing on Paris. The future seemed very precarious, and their attitude was one of mistrust and caution. It was easier for them to do so now than it had been formerly, for by ridding them of the tithes and salt-tax the revolution had enabled them to put by some savings. They were no longer bound to sell at any price in order to pay their taxes and rents. Moreover, the owners of their farms were not at all anxious to accept assignats in payment of their rent and begged them to wait and take their time. The enormous purchases made for the war and the fleet were a still further factor tending to produce a scarcity of commodities and a rise in prices. Army bread had previously been made of a mixture of wheat and rye. In order that the soldiers should share in the rejoicing at the fall of the throne, the Legislative Assembly had decreed on September 8 that their rations should consist of pure wheaten bread, which led to an increased consumption of wheat. The cost of living was increasing at the very moment when the course of the Revolution was opening up wider and more hopeful prospects to the people.

The Revolutionary Commune represented the interests of the humbler classes. As early as August 11 it resolved to petition the Assembly to pass severe laws against venders of silver coin. It demanded the abrogation of the Constituent Assembly's decree authorizing competition between the assignat and metallic currency. "The death penalty," we read in its minutes, "did not seem to be too severe for those who take advantage of public misfortunes to indulge in speculation." But the Assembly, in which the wealthy classes predominated, turned a deaf ear to them. A deputation of citizens which repeated the request of the Commune on August 13 met with no better fortune. But the Commune found a means of providing relief for the needy by using their labour to dig trenches for the camp outside Paris at a rate of forty-two sous a day. Artisans were employed in war-work, and the young men enlisted as volunteers.

The same resources were not always to be found in other towns. At Tours, where the silk-factories had closed down, many of the workmen had fallen into want. Early in September they agitated to have a fixed price established for bread. On September 8 and 9 they besieged the directory of the department and compelled it to fix the price of bread at two sous—that is, half the market price. The directory requested the electoral assembly to replace it by a fresh one, and protested against the fixing of prices, which was calculated, they said, to empty the markets of supplies.

At Lyons the disturbances were more serious, for thirty thousand silk-weavers were out of work. In order to relieve their indigence, a friend of Chalier, Dodieu, president of the section of the Juiverie, proposed towards the end of August to follow the example of Paris, as he said, and proceed "to conduct a search for hoards of corn and flour" and sell them at a compulsory rate, and, lastly, to appoint a special tribunal to punish food-speculators of every kind. His aim was "to crush sordid and interested aims and the greed of food-speculators, which was encouraged by the weakness or moral complicity of aristocratic judges." The central club, hearing that the Parisian Commune had set the guillotine at work night and day, called upon the authorities to do likewise in order to overawe the speculators and those bakers who were making bad bread or threatened to retire from their trade. The municipality at first refused the demands of the central club. But during the night of August 25–26 a mob took possession of the guillotine and set it up on the Place des Terreaux, opposite the Hôtel de Ville. It next broke into the prisons. Two prisoners were seriously wounded in the affray, one of them a forger of assignats and the other a baker accused of cheating. The idea was gradually taking shape that it was necessary to adopt terrorist measures against food-speculators, and use the guillotine · to solve economic difficulties. Meanwhile the Jacobins of Lyons had recourse to direct action. In September, Bussat, the police commissary, a Jacobin who afterwards became a judge on the district tribunal presided over by Chalier, drew up a tariff of commodities and articles of consumption, which included sixty articles. Threatening crowds of women collected, and the municipality ratified the tariff, which was put in force for three days.

The unrest in the country districts was almost as great as in the towns, for at that time there were a large number of manual labourers reduced to buying their own bread.

On August 11, 1792, large consignments of wheat intended to provision the departments of Gard and Hérault were stopped on the Canal du Midi near Carcassonne by a riotous crowd. The National Guards summoned to restore order by the departmental assembly made common cause with the rioters. The numbers increased during the following days, and six thousand men collected at the sound of the tocsin. On August 17, hearing a rumour that the authorities had sent for troops of the line, a column of rioters marched on Carcassonne, seized the cannon and muskets stored in the town, murdered Verdier, the *procureur général syndic,* and finally unloaded the grain which was stored at Carcassonne. It was necessary to send four thousand soldiers to restore order.

About the same time it was found necessary to station considerable bodies of troops along the Seine to prevent those dwelling on its banks from seizing the consignments of wheat sent up the river from Havre or Rouen to Paris.

The local authorities were overpowered and compelled almost every-where to issue regulations for the control of supplies analogous to those existing under the old regime. For instance, by an ordinance of August 14 the departmental assembly of Haute-Garonne enjoined upon the municipalities to keep a watch over corn-speculators, especially "those who have never been engaged in this trade before, but are now going about the country-side purchasing wheat." In other words, trade in wheat ceased to be free, and could henceforward be carried on only by the permission and under the supervision of the authorities. The ordinance of Haute-Garonne made it their duty to apprehend unauthorized purchasers and cite them before the courts, there "to be dealt with according to the rigour of the laws," though no such laws existed. They were also to arrest "ill-disposed persons who introduce themselves surreptitiously into the markets and secretly buy up grain, not to supply themselves, but to sell it again, thus causing a rise in the price of commodities." On September 14 this same departmental assembly of Haute-Garonne resolved to make fiduciary notes legal tender.

These examples will suffice to explain the misgivings with which the commercial and property-owning classes were filled when they saw the results of the revolution of August 10. They felt themselves surrounded by the lowering hatred of the labouring classes as by a rising tide. Besides, contributions were constantly being levied upon them. The volunteers would consent to enlist only on condition that they were handed a sort of bonus on departure, the expense of which was borne by the rich. Moreover, they demanded relief in money for their wives and children. The municipalities raised the necessary sums by more or less voluntary collections. It was regarded as natural that the rich, who did not go to the front, should be bound to compensate those who sacrificed themselves to defend their property. But the wealthy classes took their stand on the law and did not consider themselves bound to provide the repeated levies with which they were burdened. They were only waiting for a signal and a pretext to protest and turn recalcitrant.

On the night of September 2–3, during the sensation produced by the news of the capture of Verdun, and while the prison massacres were already beginning, the Revolutionary Commune had resolved to ask the Legislative Assembly for a decree compelling the farmers to thresh their corn, so that it could be commandeered in case of need to feed the army of volunteers which was being raised. Danton, as was his habit, adopted the idea put forward by the Commune, and on the following day, September 4, induced his colleagues on the Council, with the exception of Roland, to sign a proclamation giving orders for extraordinary measures to compel those in possession of corn to sell it to the army agents and provide them with the necessary transport by commandeering wagons. Prices were to be fixed by the administrative bodies. This involved not only compulsory sales but the fixing of prices.

Shortly afterwards the Legislative Assembly was obliged by its decrees of September 9 and 16 to extend the principles already laid down for the provisioning of the army to that of the civil population. The municipalities were given power to impress labourers to thresh corn and till the soil, and the administrative bodies were empowered to obtain provisions for the markets by commandeering them from private individuals. Orders were given to draw up returns of existing commodities. Persons refusing to comply with the requisition orders were to be liable to have their corn confiscated and to a penalty which might amount to a year's hard labour (gêne). But they did not venture to order that prices should be fixed for provisioning the civil population. These laws hardly did more than legalize a state of affairs which already existed, for many municipalities and administrative bodies had already, on their own authority, adopted the measures laid down in them. Thus, as early as September 3, the directory of the district of Chaumont had called upon all the communes within its jurisdiction to see that the new season's corn was threshed and brought to market.

The commissaries whom the Executive Council had resolved to send into the departments to hurry on enlistment, keep watch upon suspects, and give an impetus to national defence, started on September 5, taking with them the proclamation of the 4th, which gave orders for the requisitioning of food-stuffs. It was not long before their operations met with sharp criticism.

Most of them had been chosen by Danton from among the members of the Commune. The Executive Council granted them the most extensive powers. They were given the right "to requisition from the municipalities and the district and departmental councils whatsoever they

203

might judge necessary for the safety of the country," a very elastic formula, which was capable of many interpretations. In the department of Yonne, Chartrey and Michel considered it indispensable, "in view of the discontent with the administrators of the department of Yonne and its district directories displayed by the inhabitants of the districts of Sens, Villeneuve-sur-Yonne, and Joigny and those of Auxerre," to form a vigilance committee of fifteen members, whose business it was to take cognizance of all the actions of the administrators of the districts under their jurisdiction, to receive from the public complaints of every kind and appeals against the decisions of the courts, and to keep a record of them. This extra-legal vigilance committee, the members of which were chosen by the local club, was presided over by the merchant Villetard, and took up its quarters on September 10 in a room on the premises of the departmental administration. Its members took the oath administered by Chartrey and Michel, "to denounce, on their individual responsibility, all those who should place obstacles in the way of the public weal." They took their mission seriously and at the end of October were still carrying it out, apparently to the satisfaction even of the authorities. I am not aware whether similar measures were initiated by the commissaries in other departments. But some regions did not resign themselves with a good grace to these extraordinary measures, which they regarded as intolerable and vexatious encroachments.

The departmental directory of Haute-Saône refused to receive the commissaries Danjou and Martin and had them put under arrest and taken back to Paris by the national *gendarmerie*, passing them on from brigade to brigade. They had not, however, in any way overstepped their powers, for the Executive Council had them released on October 5 and ordered that an inquiry should be held into the action of the departmental assembly.

In the department of Eure the commissaries Momoro and Dufour distributed a declaration of rights which they had themselves drawn up in justification of their requisitions, which ran as follows: "(1) The nation recognizes industrial property, and assures its security and inviolability; (2) the nation likewise guarantees to citizens the security and inviolability of what is falsely called landed property, till such time as it has framed laws dealing with this subject." This threat of an agrarian law and interference with real property provoked a regular insurrection against the commissaries. The municipality of Bernay caused them to be arrested on September 8 and led before the electoral assembly of Eure, the president of which, Buzot, released them after recommending them to behave with circumspection and not to go beyond the object of their mission.

A few days later, in Calvados, the commissaries Goubeau and Cellier were arrested by the municipality of Lisieux, which censured them for alarming the populace and committing arbitrary acts.

Finally, the departmental directory of Finistère arrested Guermeur, who had been sent to Brest and Lorient by the Executive Council "to search the arsenals for arms for the equipment of the volunteers." Guermeur had made disparaging remarks about Roland, Guadet, and Vergniaud, sung the praises of Robespierre, and distributed pamphlets by Marat. He was deprived of his liberty for several months, and the Convention had to pass a special decree, on March 4, 1793, before the authorities of Finistère would release him.

The Gironde naturally made the most of these incidents in its campaign against the Commune and the Mountain. Roland seized the opportunity of striking at Danton through the unfortunate commissaries. On September 13 he wrote to the Assembly complaining of their abuse of power. They were, he said, disseminating uneasiness, they had carried out an arbitrary house-to-house search at Ancy-le-Franc to look for plate. They had presented themselves at the electoral assembly of Seine-et-Marne, which at their prompting had adopted the system of oral voting and the appointment of parish priests by the communes, and expressed the desire that a cannon should be cast with a calibre equal to the size of Louis XVI's head, so that in case of invasion the traitor's head could be fired at the enemy. The Assembly was alarmed at this, and on the following day Vergniaud obtained the passage of a decree limiting the powers of the commissaries to the work of recruiting only, and forbidding them to requisition goods or dismiss officials. Those whom they had already dismissed were reinstated and the local authorities were ordered to place them under arrest in case of disobedience. On September 22 all the commissaries were recalled by an ordinance of the Executive Council, and Roland sent out a circular letter censuring them as a body for having caused disorder and imperilled the security of life and property.

The whole of the Girondin press, with wonderful unanimity, denounced the partisans of the Commune and the Mountain as "anarchists" and advocates of the agrarian law. Brissot did so in his paper from September 17 onward, Carra on the 19th in the *Annales patriotiques*. "Everyone who talks of an agrarian law or dividing up the land," said the latter, "is an out-and-out aristocrat, a public enemy, a villain who ought to be exterminated." And Carra remarked that propaganda of this nature would scare property-owners and thus hinder the sale of the property of the *émigrés*. In the *Chronique* of the 22nd, Keralio violently denounced Momoro and his imitators, "who want to degrade mankind by reducing them to the level of brutes and making the land their common property." Cloots, the cosmopolitan banker, launched a telling reprimand against disturbers of the public peace: "Absurd or perfidious persons are taking a pleasure in striking terror to the hearts of property-owners. They would like to sow discord between Frenchmen living on the produce of their land and Frenchmen living on the produce of their industry. This scheme for the disturbance of the social order was hatched at Coblenz." Brissot said still more roundly that the enemies of order were the agents of the Prussians.

Whether the alarm of the Girondins was exaggerated, assumed, or sincere, it was none the less based upon certain definite facts. There is no proof that the commissaries of the Executive Council imitated Momoro and, following his example, drew a distinction between industrial and landed property in order to hold over the latter a threat which was any-way vague and remote. But it can hardly be questioned that there were revolutionaries here and there who wanted a further social revolution and, in order to put an end to the economic crisis, were proposing measures of a more or less communist nature, and more or less far-reaching restrictions on the right of property.

After the serious riots in the Beauce in the spring of 1792, Pierre Dolivier, parish priest of Mauchamp, had sent a petition to the Assembly demanding an amnesty for the peasants arrested on the occasion of the murder of Simoneau, mayor of Étampes, in which he ventured to contrast natural law with the law of property, primitive with legal justice. "With-out going back to the true principles according to which property can and ought to exist, it is certain that what are called property-owners are only such in virtue of the law. The nation alone is the true owner of its soil. Now, supposing that the nation could and ought to accept the exist-ing system of private property and its transmission, could it do so in such a way as to strip itself of its right of suzerainty over the products, and could it grant such extensive rights to landowners as to leave none to those who own no land, not even the imprescriptible rights of nature?" But he might have used a far more conclusive argument than this. To find a basis for such an argument it would be necessary to ask oneself what constitutes the real right of property, and this is not the place to do so. Rousseau has said somewhere that "whosoever eats a loaf of bread that he has not earned is stealing it." The language of the Jacobin parish priest will be found curiously bold, and people will say that it is socialism. But socialism of this kind does not take its rise in the philosophy of the extremists and "natural law" alone; in a certain sense it is very ancient. What more was Dolivier doing than regaining possession for the benefit of the nation of that "eminent right" which the kings had formerly exercised over all the territory of their realm? The nation was the heir of Louis XIV. Besides, Dolivier's socialism only aimed at justifying a return to the ancient system of fixed prices and food-regulations, abolished by the Constituent Assembly, and this only in case of a shortage of food. It is modern in tone, no doubt, but very ancient in its juridical form, in its evangelical spirit, in its end and its means alike.

It should be noted that all the demonstrations of a more or less socialist character which took place were inspired by anxiety to deal with the food crisis.

At Lyons a municipal officer named Lange, whom Michelet considers to have been, with Babeuf, one of the precursors of modern socialism, had published, as early as the summer of 1792, a pamphlet entitled: *Simple and Easy Means of Maintaining an Abundance of Bread at a Just Price*, in which he proposed a regular system of general nationalization of food-stuffs. Lange laid it down as a principle that the price of commodities ought to be settled, not in relation to the claims of the landowners, but according to the resources of the consumers. The State was to purchase the whole crop from the farmers at a fixed price, which would secure them against the fluctuations of the market. A joint-stock company with a capital of twelve hundred millions, under State control, managed by the owners of the crops and the consumers themselves, who would be given a certain number of shares, was to store the harvest in thirty thousand public granaries (*greniers d'abondance*) and fix an average price for bread, which was to be uniform for the whole of France. This was no theoretical conception, but a system closely worked out down to the smallest details. The company was at the same time to be an insurance company against hail, fire, and damage of every kind. In the previous year Lange had announced his adherence to socialist principles.

It was the priests who were the chief disseminators of subversive ideas. In Paris the Abbé Jacques Roux, curate of Saint-Nicolas-des-Champs, revealed his views, on May 17, 1792, in a violent speech on the means of saving France and liberty. "Ask," he said, "for the death penalty to be pronounced against those who speculate in food-stuffs, discredit our assignats by trafficking in silver and fabricating debased coinage, unduly raise the price of commodities, and are causing us to progress rapidly in the direction of counter-revolution." He called for severe regulations for the control of food-stuffs, and the establishment of public stores where the prices of goods would be competitive. In his case there was no communism, only the threat of terrorist measures against the abuse of property.

The country districts were already affected by this propaganda. In the department of Cher, Petitjean, parish priest of Épineuil, said to his parishioners after August 10: "Property is going to be owned in common; there will be only one cellar and one granary, from which every man will take what he requires." He advised that stores should be deposited in cellars and granaries upon which everyone should draw, so that there should be no further need of money. This was indeed a radical method of dealing with the monetary crisis! He further called upon his parishioners to "give their consent freely to the renunciation of all their property and a general sharing of all their goods." And lastly he exhorted them to pay no more rent. The result of this "incendiary" propaganda was that he was placed under arrest on September 23, 1792, and on December 18, 1792 condemned by default to six years' hard labour by the criminal tribunal of his department. On appeal the penalty was reduced to a year's imprisonment.

Nicolas de Bonneville, an obscure but voluminous writer, who was no doubt in touch with the German Illuminati, and had founded the newspaper *La Bouche de fer* in 1790, was at this time assembling the Friends of Truth at the Cercle Social to listen to the discourses of the Abbé Fauchet. After August 10 he brought out a new edition of a curious book entitled *On the Spirit of Religions (De l'esprit des religions)*, the first edition of which had appeared just after Varennes, but attracted no attention; this time, however, it found an atmosphere already prepared for it. In it a whole plan for a future commonwealth was set forth in passages of an oracular cast, but of unmistakable significance, in the middle of which was laid down the necessity for an agrarian law: "Jehovah! Jehovah! Upright men render Thee an eternal worship. *Thy law* [2] is an eternal worship. *Thy law* is the terror of the proud. Thy name is the rallying-cry and the Law of the Franks. . . . *Agrarian!*" Or again, in chapter xxxix, entitled "Of a means of execution for preparing for a universal sharing of the land," could be read the following words: "The only possible means of arriving at the great social *Communion* is to di-

---

[2] The italics occur as quoted in Bonneville's original text.

vide inherited lands into fixed or equal shares for the children of the deceased, and to call in all the remaining relatives to share in the rest. Fix the limits of inheritance, from today onwards, at five or six acres (*arpents*) for every child or grandchild, and let the other relatives make an equal division of the remainder of the inheritance. You will still be far removed from justice and from the admissions which you have made regarding the equal and imprescriptible rights of all men. . . ."

So the agrarian law which alarmed the Girondins was neither a myth nor a phantom. There were some obscure revolutionaries, for the most part priests, who did indeed dream of a new revolution, more thorough-going than the one which had been accomplished, to be achieved at the cost of the middle classes and owners of property. The counter-revolutionary party had alarmed the latter for a long time past by representing that the abolition of the privileges of wealth would be a logical and inevitable consequence of the abolition of the privileges of birth. Were they not already beginning to be justified by the facts? Such feudal dues as were not based on the original title-deeds had been abolished without compensation, and, in the course of the debate on June 14, 1792, a deputy named Chéron had bethought himself of a skilful manœuvre for obtaining the rejection of the measure which he dreaded. "There is no blinking the fact," he said, "that the possession of many landed estates is due to a usurpation. I propose that the principle laid down should be so extended that all real properties for which the original title-deeds cannot be produced may be declared to be national property." The argument told, and the Assembly did not come to a decision till after August 10. But, seeing that the rich were crushed by taxation and their rights of ownership restricted by requisitions and the fixing of prices, how could they fail to believe that the agrarian law was a serious danger, especially when the Girondins, who were themselves regarded as revolutionaries, kept anathematizing the communists? Many departments were indeed disturbed by the fear of an agrarian law. In the department of Lot the electoral assembly issued an appeal to the peasants to dissuade them from dividing up the estates of the *émigrés* among themselves.

The Legislative Assembly had insisted that all legal and administrative officials and electors should take the oath of fidelity to liberty and equality. The administrators of the department of Marne expressed a fear that, in taking the oath to equality, they might be giving their consent to an equal division of wealth—that, in a word, they might be taking the oath to what was called at the time *"de facto* equality (*l'égalité de fait*)."* Several electoral assemblies—for instance those of Eure, Cantal, and Indre—protested against the propaganda in favour of an agrarian law and demanded the maintenance of property. The Montagnard Thomas Lindet, Bishop of Eure, wrote on August 20, 1792 to his brother Robert: "The Revolution is leading us far. Beware of the agrarian law!"

We may grant, then, that the alarm of the Girondins was not altogether without foundation. But we have to ask ourselves whether they were justified in identifying the Mountain with the communists.

Now the communists did not form a party. They were isolated individuals, with no connexion between them. Lange of Lyons was almost unknown, even in his own city. Jacques Roux's notoriety had as yet hardly spread beyond the gloomy neighbourhood of Gravilliers, with its narrow alleys. When, after August 10, he tried to get himself elected to the Convention, he obtained exactly two votes and had to rest content with the scarf of a municipal officer. Dolivier and Petitjean were even more obscure. Momoro and Bonneville alone had some reputation. Momoro was one of the most influential members of the Cordeliers Club, and was soon to obtain a seat on the new directory of the department of Paris. He was afterwards one of the leaders of Hébertism. Bonneville ran a newspaper and printing-press. But though he was bold when he had a pen in his hand, he was very timid when it came to action. He was bound to the Girondins by every tie of friendship and association. He was entrusted with missions by Roland, joined the ranks of his partisans, and attacked the Montagnards in his *Bulletin des Amis de la Vérité*. Though a theoretical exponent of the agrarian law, he inspired nothing but confidence and friendship in the Girondins. Brissot called him his friend and had recommended him to the electors as a deputy to the Convention.

The Commune had sworn to respect both person and property. Nothing authorizes us to treat it as being one with the Mountain. As for the Montagnard leaders, however much their sympathies, as well as their interests, inclined them to satisfy their sansculotte adherents, however ready they may have been to adopt even the most radical measures for mitigating the food crisis and the high cost of living, there is no proof that they cherished any mental reservations of a communist order. They accepted requisitioning because the situation seemed to demand it, but for a long time they resisted the fixing of prices demanded by popular agitators. They wanted to take precautions against the abuse of the right of property and make it subordinate to the public interest; they had no idea of abolishing it.

As early as July 1792 Marat had denounced wealth and social inequality as the origin of the servitude of the labouring classes. "Before you think of being free," he said, "you must think how you are to live." He indignantly assailed the insolent plutocrats who devoured at one meal enough to feed a hundred families. In all his writings about the distress of the poor, with whom he was well acquainted, there is a ring of sincerity and compassion He reviles the food-speculators and threatens them with popular justice, but we should seek in vain for an exposition of any social system from his glowing pen.

Hébert, whose *Père Duchesne* was beginning to be widely read, kept telling the rich that had it not been for the sansculottes, the volunteers, and the Fédérés, they would already have succumbed under the blows of the Prussians. He held up their avarice to contempt, but at that time he was as devoid of any plan of economic reform as Marat.

For a long time past Robespierre had been the unchallenged leader of the Montagnard party. During the Constituent Assembly he had consistently espoused the cause of the weak and unfortunate. He was the first to protest with indefatigable fervour against the property qualification for the suffrage, and it had at last collapsed under his continued blows; he had protested against martial law and demanded the arming of the people; when the abolition of the right of primogeniture was under discussion, he exclaimed: "Legislators, you have done nothing for liberty unless your laws tend to reduce by gentle but efficacious measures the extreme inequalities of wealth"; he had wanted to impose restrictions on inheritance, and as convinced a communist as Babeuf based his hopes upon him, as may be seen in his letter to Coupé of Oise, dated September 10, 1791. It is significant that in his paper, the *Défenseur de la Constitution*, Robespierre printed in full the petition of the parish priest of Mauchamp against Simoneau, followed by sympathetic comments. He complained in this connexion that those who had benefited by the Revolution despised the poor, and he attacked the middle-class oligarchy with cold fury; but he expressly repudiated communism. He alluded to the agrarian law as an "absurd scarecrow set up for the stupid by the depraved . . . as if the defenders of liberty were madmen capable of conceiving a project as dangerous as it is unjust and impracticable." Robespierre never varied in this respect. He always regarded communism as an impossible and insensate dream. He desired to set limits to the rights of property and prevent its abuse, but he never dreamt of abolishing it.

As for Danton, at the first session of the Convention he sprang to the tribune and repudiated the commissaries of the Executive Council, such as Momoro and Dufour, who had caused a hue and cry among property-owners by their subversive doctrines. There was not a single avowed communist in the Convention.

But is this equal to saying, as we have lightly been assured, that there was no disagreement in principle between the Girondins and the Mountain, that the two parties were separated only by personal rivalries and by their conception of the part which ought to be played by the capital in the control of public affairs? Nothing could be more inaccurate The conflict between the Girondins and the Mountain was a deep-rooted one, almost amounting to a class conflict. The Girondins, as Daunou observed, included "a large number of property-owners and enlightened citizens"; they had a sense of social distinctions which they desired to maintain and strengthen, and felt an instinctive repugnance for the coarse and uncultivated populace. They regarded the rights of property as absolute and sacrosanct; they believed the people to be incapable of government, and reserved the monopoly of it to their own class. Anything of a nature to hamper the free action of the property-owning middle classes seemed to them an evil. Like Roland, they professed a thorough-going economic liberalism. In their eyes the most perfect State was that which put the least check upon the individual.

The Mountain, on the other hand, represented the humbler classes, those who were suffering from the crisis caused by the war, who had overthrown the monarchy and·risen to political power through insurrection. Less swayed by theories than the Girondins, and greater realists, because they lived closer to reality, they saw that the terrible crisis through which France was passing called for extraordinary measures. They were quick to plead the right to a livelihood as opposed to the right to property, and public as opposed to individual interest. They could not understand how anyone could balance class against country under the pretext of respect for principles. In case of need, they were prepared to have recourse to restrictions upon individual liberty and property, should the predominant interest of the masses demand it.

The Girondins detested Paris, not only as the city which had defied and repudiated them, but as the city which had first invented this policy of public safety and had formulated and put into execution those emergency measures of which the middle classes were bound to bear the cost. But it was not only fear which roused them against the Mountain, it was also the instinct of self-preservation.

This fundamental opposition between the two parties is strikingly apparent in the works published simultaneously during October by Brissot on the one hand and Robespierre on the other.

In his *Appeal to All the Republicans of France* Brissot wrote, with reference to his having been struck off the books of the Jacobins: "The fomenters of disorder (*désorganisateurs*) are those who desire to level everything, property, comfort, the price of commodities, the various services to be rendered to society, etc., who want the workmen in the trenches to receive the same pay as the legislator, who even desire to reduce talent, knowledge, and virtue to the same level, because they possess none of them!" And having thus extended his protection to all those who had anything to preserve, he mentioned, among the "fomenters of disorder," Marat, Chabot, Robespierre, and Collot d'Herbois; but not Danton.

Robespierre, for his part, developed a diametrically opposite program in the first number of his *Letters to his Constituents (Lettres à ses commettants)*. "Royalty is annihilated," he wrote; "the nobility and the clergy have disappeared; the reign of equality is beginning." And he at once proceeded to a sharp attack upon false patriots, "who wanted to set up the Republic for their own benefit alone . . . who had no idea of governing save in the interest of the rich and the public officials." With these false patriots he contrasted the true patriots, "who will seek to base the Republic upon the principles of equality and the general interest." "Observe," he said again, "this eternal tendency to connect the idea of sedition and brigandage with that of the people and poverty."

Nobody could mistake his meaning. The rivalry between the Gironde and the Mountain, which had arisen in connexion with the war and been embittered by the question of deposing the King, had become, since August 10, more than a purely political rivalry. The class struggle was already taking shape. But Baudot rightly saw that for many of the Montagnards, of whom he was one, the policy of *rapprochement* and collaboration with the masses was primarily a tactical move rendered necessary by the exigencies of the war. Most of the Montagnards, indeed, were, like the Girondins, of middle-class origin. The class policy which they inaugurated had not sprung directly from the people. It was a policy dictated by the situation, a plebeian method, as Karl Marx puts it, of making an end of kings, priests, nobles, and all enemies of the Revolution. This alone sufficed to place it in fundamental opposition to the policy of the Gironde.

CHAPTER IV

Valmy

THE fall of the monarchy, like the flight to Varennes in the previous year, was bound to increase the tension between revolutionary France and the monarchical powers still at peace with her.

England recalled her ambassador, Lord Gower, from Paris, and before his departure, on August 23, he handed the Executive Council a somewhat sharp note in which, while reaffirming his neutrality, King George expressed "his solicitude for the position of Their Most Christian Majesties and the royal family," in terms which, to the new masters of France, had an offensive and threatening ring. A few days later, on September 2, W. Lindsay, the English chargé d'affaires, in turn asked for his passports and left for London, while Grenville notified Chauvelin, the French ambassador, that he would no longer be received at court. Catherine of Russia expelled Genêt, the French chargé d'affaires.

News arrived that the troops of the two Hesses were joining those of Austria and Prussia, and it was daily expected that the Diet of the Empire would declare war on France.

The murder of the Swiss Guards responsible for the defence of the Tuileries had aroused deep indignation against France beyond the Jura. The patricians of Bern were raising regiments, and on the pretext that the neutrality of the free city of Geneva was threatened by the troops that Montesquiou was concentrating on the Isère, they sent a garrison into that city, regardless of the treaties regulating its relations with France. There was some fear that Bern and Zurich might carry the other cantons with them.

As early as August 11 Yriarte, the Spanish ambassador in Paris, asked for his passports, and his Government shortly afterwards informed Austria that it was moving troops along the line of the Pyrenees.

Even the smallest powers ventured to offer slights and actual provocation to France. The prince-bishop of Liége, a member of the Holy Roman Empire, refused to receive Pozzi d'Aubignan, who had been sent to his court as minister plenipotentiary by the French Government.

214

In his report of August 23 Lebrun, the Minister for Foreign Affairs, had to confine himself to stating that France maintained satisfactory relations only with Denmark and Sweden, and congratulated himself upon the fact that the Dutch ambassador was still in Paris; yet it was not long before he too was recalled. Thus the circle was drawn more and more closely round revolutionary France, now under the ban of monarchical Europe.

The Commune and the Mountain accepted this situation without a tremor. Manuel, the procureur of the Commune, announced to the Assembly on August 21 that the Venetian ambassador was about to leave Paris by night, accompanied by fourteen persons. "Ought the Assembly," he asked, "to allow the ambassadors of foreign powers to leave before it is sure that those of France will be respected at the various courts of Europe?" This was a hint to keep the ambassadors of the kings as hostages and adopt a preventive policy of reprisals. The Assembly did not dare to come to a decision. In practice it left the conduct of diplomacy to the Executive Council.

The Council at first inclined towards strong measures. On August 24, the day after Lord Gower's departure, it decided to recall Chauvelin, the French ambassador, from London. But on September 6 it changed its mind and instructed Chauvelin to remain at his post. The capture of Longwy and Verdun in the mean time had damped its ardour.

Even Danton, though he had opposed the evacuation of Paris proposed by Roland and Servan, actively supported and took part in a policy of concessions and negotiations with the monarchical powers. The former Abbé Noël, a friend of his who had turned journalist in 1789, and in the spring of 1792 had been found a post as senior clerk in the Ministry for Foreign Affairs by Dumouriez, he had sent to London on August 28 to negotiate secretly with Pitt. Noël took with him to London two relatives of Danton, his half-brother Recordain and a connexion named Mergez, and corresponded with him assiduously. His instructions laid down that he was to endeavour at all costs to keep Great Britain in a state of neutrality, to which end he was empowered to offer to cede her the island of Tobago, which had recently been restored to France by the treaty of Versailles. He was also to reassure her as to the intentions of the Executive Council with regard to Holland. Noël, who was shortly afterwards joined by Benoist, another secret agent, also in close connexion with Danton, had hardly arrived before he demanded a considerable sum of money to win over supporters. Lebrun advised him to spread abroad the idea among the English public that it was a favourable moment for

215

Great Britain to seize Louisiana and the Spanish colonies in America. France would offer no opposition and would even give her consent. But Pitt contemptuously refused to hold any communication with Noël.

Another sign, showing still more clearly how perplexed the ministers were, was a secret mission entrusted at the same time by Lebrun to another agent of Danton's, Félix Desportes, a young man poor in experience, though not in ambition, who had been sent to the court of the Duke of Zweibrücken (Deux-Ponts). On September 3 Desportes was requested to enter into secret *pourparlers* with Prussia with a view to detaching her from the coalition. "Your genius and patriotism," wrote the minister in all seriousness, "have been highly praised to me. You will be able to display both of them brilliantly and cover yourself with undying glory by bringing France's most redoubtable enemy to her feet." And Lebrun went on to assert in the same dispatch that the Duke of Brunswick, that "hero," as he called him in imitation of Carra and Condorcet, was making war upon France against his own inclination, and that by his influence peace might be obtained, not only with Prussia, but with Austria. It goes without saying that, in spite of his genius, Desportes met with no better fortune than Noël.

To avert the danger from abroad the Girondins relied more upon the action of revolutionary principles—which they believed to be all-powerful —beyond the frontiers of France than upon these tortuous intrigues. In vain did Robespierre warn them against this dangerous illusion, even before the declaration of war. They still imagined in their simplicity that foreign nations were only waiting for a signal in order to imitate the French and deliver themselves in turn from their nobles, priests, and "tyrants."

Since the French Revolution had been the work of the middle classes, nurtured in the writings of the *philosophes*, they considered that writers and thinkers would be the chief agents of the European revolution. On August 24 Marie-Joseph Chénier, accompanied by a number of men of letters, came to the Legislative Assembly and asked it to regard as "allies of the French people" such foreign publicists as had already sapped "the foundations of tyranny and prepared the way for liberty" by their writings. He proposed to declare them French citizens, in order that "these benefactors of humanity" might be elected deputies. "If the choice of the people were to bring these illustrious men into the National Convention, what an imposing and solemn spectacle would be offered by this assembly, which is about to determine such great destinies! The élite of mankind, brought together from every quarter of the globe—would it not seem to be a

216

congress of the whole world?" Two days later, in spite of the timid opposition of Lasource, Thuriot, and Basire, Chénier's proposal was reported upon by Guadet and passed into a decree, and rights of citizenship were granted to Priestley, the famous chemist, to Jeremy Bentham, the celebrated utilitarian philosopher, to Clarkson and Wilberforce, the eloquent defenders of the Negroes, to James Mackintosh and David Williams, who had answered Burke's pamphlets against the Revolution, among Englishmen; to Washington, Hamilton, and Thomas Paine among Americans; to Schiller, Klopstock, Campe, and Anacharsis Cloots among Germans; to the Swiss Pestalozzi; the Italian Gorani; the Pole Thaddeus Kosciuszko, and the Hollander Cornelis Pauw. Priestley, Cloots, and Thomas Paine were elected to the Convention, as M.-J. Chénier had desired; the first-named declined the nomination, but the other two took their seats.

For a long time past the revolutionaries had eagerly welcomed the foreign exiles who had come to France to take refuge from the vengeance of aristocrats. They had admitted them not only to the clubs, but also into the National Guards, public departments, elected bodies, and even the offices of the Ministry for Foreign Affairs. After war had been declared, these political refugees formed the nucleus of foreign legions, which were to carry freedom to their native countries, once victory had been gained. There was a Liége legion in the army of the centre, a Belgian legion in the army of the north. A Batavian legion was organized after August 10, then an Allobrogian legion formed of Savoyards, and also of inhabitants of Geneva, Neuchâtel, and Vaud; and lastly a Germanic legion, the commanding officer of which, Colonel Dambach, had served under Frederick the Great.

The Executive Council endeavoured to maintain a number of secret agents abroad to propagate revolutionary ideas. It subsidized newspapers in London and distributed a perfect flood of pamphlets in Switzerland, Belgium, Germany, Italy, and Spain. Exiles of every nation had their special clubs and committees, which published gazettes for the benefit of their nationals. Thus at Bayonne the Spaniard Marchena, a friend of Brissot's, edited a *Gazette de la liberté et de l'égalité* in French and Spanish.

The Girondins even flattered themselves that they would induce large bodies of the Austrian and Prussian troops to desert. On August 2 Guadet obtained the passage of a decree granting deserters from the enemy a pension of a hundred francs a year, with reversion to their wives, and a gratuity of fifty livres. The decree was scattered in profusion along the whole of the northern and eastern frontier and translated into several languages, and it was imagined that on entering France the armies of the enemy would disintegrate. A few dozen miserable wretches were picked up by the outposts, among them a number of spies, who found it convenient to ply their trade under the protection of the tricolour cockade and the red cap. This was all the easier because no measures had been taken against enemy subjects since the declaration of war. Whereas in Prussia and Austria French subjects had been expelled or interned, in France Austrian and Prussian subjects moved about freely and were favoured by special protection so long as they made a show of "civic" sentiments.

So great was the belief in the efficacy of propaganda that even Dumouriez—who had, however, the reputation of a practical man—sent Lebrun on August 24 a project for revolutionizing Switzerland by the aid of the exiles who had founded the Helvetic Club in Paris. The exiles from Savoy, led by a doctor named Doppet, who had founded the Allobrogian legion, led the Executive Council to believe that the conquest of Savoy would be no more than a military promenade. On September 8 Montesquiou's little army received secret orders to attack the King of Sardinia, with whom France was still at peace. This abrupt and preventive attack was justified after the event by Lebrun, who explained, on September 15, that the King of Sardinia had tolerated assemblages of *émigrés*, massed troops at Montmélian, allowed the Austrians to pass through his territory, and, lastly, refused to receive the French diplomatic agents. The Assembly greeted his speech with loud applause.

The Austrians and Prussians had profited by the three months' respite generously allowed them by the French generals while they dabbled in politics. While the latter disobeyed orders by remaining inactive and employed their leisure in plotting with the Court or the Feuillants, thus allowing the opportunity to slip by for invading Belgium, which was stripped of troops, the enemy were able to make up for their delay in mobilization and concentration.

The methodical Brunswick marched out from Coblenz on July 30 with the main army, consisting of 42,000 Prussians and 5,000 Hessians, and approached the frontier up the valley of the Moselle. He was flanked on the right by a corps of 5,000 *émigrés* and Clerfayt's Austrian corps, with a strength of 15,000 men. On the left another Austrian corps, of 14,000 men, under Hohenlohe-Kirchberg, was marching on Thionville and Metz. Lastly an Austrian army, 25,000 strong, with 4,000 *émigrés*, was concentrating in Belgium, opposite Lille, under the Duke of Saxe-Teschen.

It was generally believed outside France that Brunswick would be

218

in Paris by the beginning of October. Was not the French army disorganized by the emigration *en masse* of most of its officers? Was it not paralysed by the rivalry between the soldiers of the line, known as *culs blancs* (from their white breeches), and the volunteers, known from their blue uniforms as the *bleuets?* The latter were paid fifteen sous a day and elected their officers. How could civilians, appointed as officers with no preparation, have made themselves obeyed? Was election a substitute for competence and experience? Even the seniors among the *bleuets* had not yet been with the colours for a year. At the first contact with the enemy they scattered, shouting that they were betrayed, as they had done in the engagements at Tournai and Mons, at the beginning of the war. The *émigrés* openly proclaimed that they had sympathizers in every fortress. They kept repeating that the mass of their former vassals and subjects remained royalist to the core and would rise against the tyranny of the Jacobin minority as soon as they caught sight of the white cockade. It would be quite a short campaign, a mere pleasure outing.

The first successes of the Coalition came up to these hopes. The Prussians crossed the frontier on August 16 and laid seige to Longwy, of which the commandant, Lavergne, surrendered on August 23 after a mere pretense of resistance, and was allowed to retain his liberty. They next laid siege to Verdun, the district assembly of which had censured the proceedings of August 10. Beaurepaire, lieutenant-colonel of the battalion of Maine-et-Loire, who was in command of the garrison, was a patriot and wanted to join battle, but the royalists in the town murdered him, spreading a rumour that he had committed suicide. Verdun surrendered on September 1, and some of the ladies of the place visited the victors in their camp.

Hohenlohe-Kirchberg's Austrians invested Thionville on September 4, and the commandant of the garrison, Félix Wimpfen, who had been a member of the Constituent Assembly, entertained the Prince's proposals, which were laid before him by the Jew Godchaux; but the determined attitude of the people and troops prevented him from capitulating.

If Brunswick had been more confident after the capture of Verdun and marched straight on Châlons, he would have met with no serious obstacles on the way. But Brunswick despised his enemy and was in no hurry.

The Executive Council had lost a fortnight by its hesitation and vacillations. When Lafayette was deserted by his troops and forced to take flight, on August 19, it replaced him by Luckner, an old German veteran trooper, who was an object of legitimate suspicion to the patriots

219

owing to his intrigues with Lafayette. He was almost immediately raised to the rank of generalissimo, and transferred on August 21 to Châlons, where he was employed exclusively in organizing the new levy of volunteers who were pouring in from every quarter of France. Two agents of the Council, Laclos and Billaud-Varenne, were attached to him to keep him under observation, and at once they denounced him as incapable and ill-disposed. He was recalled to Paris on September 13.

Kellermann had been given the command of the army of the centre, Biron of that of the Rhine, Dumouriez of that of the north. These three armies, drawn up in a continuous line along the frontier, had not moved from their positions. Biron had about 25,000 men under his command behind the Lauter, Kellermann 28,000 in Lorraine, at Metz and Thionville. The army of the north was divided into two parts, the larger of which was stationed in the department of Nord, from Dunkirk to Maubeuge, the rest, 19,000 strong, round Sedan. In the rear a disorderly rabble of National Guards and volunteers was concentrating between Reims and Châlons to defend Paris.

Political considerations predominated over strategic ones. Fearing an insurrection in Paris, Servan and the Executive Council wanted to check Brunswick's advance at all costs. They instructed Dumouriez to come up with all possible speed to take command of the forces round Sedan, and to effect a junction with Kellermann in the Argonne. But Dumouriez dreamed of conquering Belgium. He raised objection after objection, did not arrive at Sedan until August 28, and even then again proposed to Servan to march up the Meuse and invade Belgium. It was not till September 1, the very day upon which Verdun was captured, that he at last decided to leave Sedan and occupy the defiles of the Argonne. Brunswick, who had less ground to cover, could have forestalled him, or at any rate seriously hampered his flanking march. But he did not move and Dumouriez reached Grandpré on September 3. Summoning reinforcements from Flanders, he barred the roads through the forest and waited for Kellermann to join him from Metz by way of Bar-le-Duc.

Brunswick did not attack the French line till September 12, when he broke through on the north at La Croix-aux-Bois. Instead of retreating towards Châlons as Servan wished, Dumouriez fell back towards the south on Sainte-Menehould. The road to Paris was open. But on September 9 Kellermann, with his army from Metz, at last effected a junction with Dumouriez, so that there were now 50,000 French against 34,-000 Prussians.

Brunswick had not followed up Dumouriez in his retreat from Grandpré towards Sainte-Menehould. Slow and methodical as usual, his idea was to dislodge the French from their position by a skilful enveloping movement in the direction of Vienne-le-Château and La Chalade. But the King of Prussia was growing impatient at all these delays and ordered Brunswick to start a frontal attack on the sansculotte army without more ado. Accordingly, towards noon on September 20, the Prussian infantry deployed as if on manœuvres before the Mont d'Yvron and the hill of Valmy, which was occupied by Kellermann's army. The King of Prussia expected the "Carmagnoles" [1] to flee in terror, but they acquitted themselves bravely. The explosion of three ammunition-wagons in their second line caused a certain confusion. But Kellermann, brandishing his hat on the end of his sword, shouted: *"Vive la Nation!"* and the cry was handed on from battalion to battalion. The Prussian infantry stopped dead and Brunswick did not dare to give the order to attack. The day ended in an artillery duel, in which the French gave proof of their superiority. Towards six o'clock in the evening a perfect deluge of rain began to fall. The two armies spent the night in the field. The losses on both sides had been slight, 200 on the Prussian side and 300 on the French.

Valmy was not a strategic victory, for the Prussian army remained intact and still lay between Paris and the French army; but it was a moral victory. The despised sansculottes had stood their ground under fire. The Prussians and Austrians lost the illusion that they would be able to defeat them without difficulty in the open country.

Nurtured in tradition, they had believed in their simplicity that outside the monarchical order there was room for nothing but anarchy and impotence. The Revolution now revealed itself to them for the first time in its organized and constructive aspect. They received a profound shock, which Goethe, who was present in the German camp, is said to have expressed in the famous words: "From this place and this day dates a new era in the world's history." The truth had suddenly manifested itself to the great philosopher poet. The old order, based upon dogma and authority, was giving place to a new one based upon liberty. Professional armies, trained in a passive discipline, were being succeeded by a new army, animated by a sentiment of human dignity and national independence. On the one hand stood the divine right of kings, on the other

---

[1] The Carmagnole was a short tunic worn by the Italian workmen from Carmagnola, who introduced it into France. It was adopted by the Marseilles Fédérés, who made it the fashion in Paris. Hence the word came to mean an advanced revolutionary or Jacobin. There were also a revolutionary song and dance known by this name.

the rights of men and nations. What Valmy signified was that, in the struggle which had been so rashly entered upon, the rights of man would not necessarily get the worst of it.

Brunswick had been reluctant to advance into Champagne and would rather have confined himself to conquering methodically all the frontier fortresses, in order to take up his winter quarters in them quietly. He was in no hurry to resume the attack. His soldiers were harassed by trying marches over soaking wet ground. The grapes of Champagne had caused an epidemic of dysentery among them. Besides, his supply-trains coming from Verdun were forced to make a long detour by way of Grandpré, and arrived only irregularly. Finally, the peasants of Lorraine and Champagne, far from welcoming the allies as benefactors, resisted their requisitioning, fled to the woods, and sniped their stragglers. It was clear that the masses detested the *émigrés* and would shudder at the restoration of feudalism. Brunswick pointed out to the King that his position was hazardous and that they could no longer dream of marching on Paris. Those of the King's advisers who were hostile to the Austrian alliance, such as Lucchesini and Manstein, added that the war with France would bring him nothing but expense and losses, and that he would be acting as a cat's-paw to the Emperor.

Dumouriez, for his part, wanted to resume the execution of his designs on Belgium as soon as possible. He had always believed that it was to the common interest of France and Prussia to form an alliance against Austria. He did nothing to transform his moral victory at Valmy into a strategic victory. What is more, on the pretext of exchanging Lombard, secretary of the King of Prussia, who had been taken prisoner on September 20, for Georges, the mayor of Varennes, who was being kept as a hostage by the enemy, he sent Westermann, an agent of the Executive Council, to the Prussian camp on September 22, to open secret negotiations, which lasted several days. Dumouriez flattered himself that he would detach Prussia from Austria. Brunswick and the King of Prussia hoped to win over Dumouriez, whom they knew to be ambitious and venal, and use him as the instrument, if not of a monarchical restoration, at any rate for obtaining the liberation of Louis XVI and his family. Manstein, Frederick William's aide-de-camp, dined with Dumouriez and Kellermann at their headquarters at Dampierre-sur-Auve on September 23, and handed them a note entitled: "Essential points for finding a means of amicably settling all misunderstandings between the two kingdoms of France and Prussia." "(1) The King of Prussia and his allies desire a representative of the French nation, in the person of its king, in order to be able to treat with him. There is no question of restoring things to their former footing, but, on the contrary, of giving France a government adapted to the good of the kingdom; (2) the King and his allies desire that all propaganda should cease; (3) it is desired that the King should be set entirely at liberty."

Manstein had hardly gone when Dumouriez and Kellermann heard that the Republic had been declared. Hence the bases underlying the negotiations which had been entered upon were no longer valid. A suspension of hostilities was, however, agreed upon, and Westermann was sent to Paris as the bearer of the Prussian proposals. The Executive Council, on which Danton was still sitting, examined them on September 25 and was of opinion that the negotiations should be continued. It requested Manuel, who was still *procureur* to the Commune, to make a collection of extracts from the decisions at which it had arrived, with a view to securing a decent existence for Louis XVI and his family in the Temple. But the Commune was surprised at Manuel's request and refused to accede to it without referring it to the Convention, which, after a slight debate, in the course of which Manuel thoughtlessly referred to Westermann as an agent of the King of Prussia, gave the Executive Council a free hand. Westermann went back to Dumouriez's camp bearing the minutes of the debates of the Commune, which were intended to reassure Frederick William as to the fate of Louis XVI, and a letter from Lebrun renewing the offer to the Prussians not only of a separate peace, but of an alliance with France, on the sole condition that they should recognize the Republic.

Meanwhile Dumouriez prolonged the armistice and exchanged courtesies and visits with the enemy generals. On September 27 he sent some sugar and coffee to Frederick William, who was short of them, accompanied by a friendly letter to the "virtuous Manstein." But Dumouriez at the same time assured him that it was necessary to treat with the Convention and recognize the Republic. Frederick William was not yet prepared to take this great decision. He sent an abrupt reply to Dumouriez, intimating that his presents were superfluous: "I venture to beg you not to give yourself so much trouble," and on September 28 he caused Brunswick to sign a violent manifesto in which he denounced to the universe "the scenes of horror" which had preceded the imprisonment of the King of France, the unspeakable outrages and audacity of the factions, and finally "the latest crime of the National Assembly"—namely, the proclamation of the Republic.

On receiving this manifesto it was Dumouriez's turn to be disappointed and annoyed. His answer to it was a proclamation to his troops, in which he said: "An end to the truce, my friends! Let us attack these tyrants and make them repent of having sullied a free nation!" But these were mere phrases intended for the gallery. Dumouriez did not attack the Prussians, but continued to hold frequent communication with them. Frederick William, who had only seventeen thousand able-bodied men left, profited by his friendly attitude to strike his camp on September 30 and carry out unhampered a retreat which might have turned into a disaster. Dumouriez followed him with polite deliberation, making no attempt to overwhelm him on his way through the valleys of the Argonne, and even ordering his lieutenants to carry out certain sham evolutions, in order to prevent them from pressing the enemy too closely.

During the early days of the Convention everything looked bright for the Girondins. The invasion had been repelled, and the French troops were soon to take the offensive on the other frontiers. Though the Girondins had despaired at the worst moments of peril, they would reap the benefit of the unexpected successes. But already their one idea was to use them as a weapon against their political opponents. Brissot said that these successes "were the torment and despair of the agitators." Thus victory, far from calming party conflicts, merely aggravated them.

PART II

The Girondin Government

CHAPTER I

The Three Days' Truce

THE Convention, in virtue of its functions as the new Constituent Assembly, was the titular depositary of all powers, and was alone quali-
fied to interpret the wishes of the nation. Consequently the Paris Commune could not do otherwise than efface itself before it. The period of
rivalry between the national representative body and an insurrectionary
municipality had now gone by, and a legal sovereignty had been re-
established.

It only depended on the Gironde to convert a sterile party struggle
into a rivalry between all revolutionary parties such as would have
brought forth fruit for the common weal. The Commune, aware that it was
discredited since the September massacres, had sobered down; it had repudiated its vigilance committee and formed a new one, set its accounts
in order preparatory to relinquishing its functions, and endeavoured, in
short, to prove to the provinces that it had been wronged by those who
represented it as a force tending to anarchy and disorder.

As early as September 22, in recording the defeat of the Mountain
at the elections, Marat announced in his paper that he was going to follow a "fresh course (*une nouvelle marche*)." He appealed for confidence
in the Convention and promised to moderate his suspicions and adapt his
line of action to that of the defenders of the people.

As he himself tells us, Marat was merely following the tactics of
his whole party. A few days before the Convention assembled, Danton had
called upon Brissot and attempted to effect a reconciliation and agreement with him. "He put a few questions to me," said Brissot, "with regard to my republican doctrine; like Robespierre, he said he was afraid
I might desire to establish a federal republic, and that this was the opinion

225

of the Gironde. I set his mind at rest on this point." [1] So the Montagnards made the first advances, and their actions show that they loyally endeavoured to keep their promises.

When the Convention assembled on September 21, 1792, the day after Valmy and two days after Montesquiou's triumphal entry into Savoy, Paris was calm, so calm that it surprised the new deputies, who had been accustomed, from the descriptions of Roland and his journalists, to regard the capital as a hotbed of murder and anarchy. "We must have peace at home," wrote Jeanbon Saint-André on September 23 to the municipality of Montauban, "and, above all, good citizens must not let themselves be led astray by the hypocrites of the patriot party (*les hypocrites du patriotisme*), as happened at Lyons, where the people were so blind as to venture to fix food prices which were ruinous for the sellers, so that they are perforce kept away from this unhappy city, abandoned by this cruel blunder to the horrors of famine." [2] It is impossible to suspect the good faith of Saint-André, who was to be one of the most determined of the Montagnards. Here we find him repudiating the extremists, the "hypocrites of the patriot party," the friends of Chalier who drew up the tariff of food prices at Lyons.

Nothing, then, would have been easier for the Girondins than to govern in an atmosphere of confidence and harmony. Their former opponents were stretching out their hands to them and giving them pledges.

But the Girondins were intoxicated by the victory of the French armies, which justified their foreign policy, and strong in their majority, which, according to Brissot, amounted to two-thirds of the seats in the new Assembly; and, not content with dominating the Executive Council, filling all the offices connected with the Assembly, and finding places for their partisans on all the great committees, they allowed themselves almost immediately to be carried away by their passionate feelings of resentment, and went in for a thorough-going policy of reprisals. The truce patched up between Danton and Brissot lasted for only three days, which were, moreover, occupied by memorable decisions.

As early as September 20, while the Legislative Assembly was still in session, the Convention had completed its organization, appointing Jérôme Petion as its president by 235 votes out of 253, and completing its official staff by choosing Condorcet, Brissot, Rabaut de Saint-Etienne, Vergniaud, and Camus as its secretaries. The choice was significant. It was Petion's revenge for the disdain of the Parisian electors, who had

---

[1] *Brissot à tous les Républicains de la France*, pamphlet dated October 24, 1792.
[2] Letters of Jeanbon Saint-André, published in *La Révolution française* (1895).

preferred Robespierre to him. All the secretaries were Girondin leaders, except Camus, who was regarded as a Feuillant. On October 24 Bentabole taxed him with having signed the royalist petition of the twenty thousand. In choosing Camus the Girondins were making an advance to the former royalists.

On the following day, September 21, the Convention held its first session. In welcoming it in the name of the outgoing Legislative Assembly, François of Neufchâteau made an appeal for union, using the words: "All motives of division must cease," and expressed his condemnation of the plans for a federal republic which had already caused misgivings to Danton and Robespierre. "Above all, you will maintain the unity of the Government of which you are the centre and the connecting link, between all parts of the empire."

Manuel next proposed to set aside a mansion for the residence of the president of the Assembly, whom he called the "president of France," and to surround him with marks of honour. Chabot at once protested, recalling the fact that the members of the Legislative Assembly had individually taken the oath to oppose kings and royalty. It was not only the name of king that France wanted to abolish, but all that might recall the royal power. His conclusion was that the first act of the Convention ought to be to declare to the people that it would submit its decrees to them for their approval. Chabot was supported by Tallien: "It is not without astonishment that I listen to a discussion upon ceremonial in this place."

Manuel's proposal was rejected unanimously; and this vote signified that the Convention was not going to imitate America, in appointing a president invested with the executive power in place of the king.

Couthon took up Chabot's idea and requested that the new Constitution which the Assembly had a mandate to draw up to replace the monarchical Constitution should be submitted to the people for their ratification. "I have listened with horror," he went on to say, "to talk about creating a triumvirate, a dictatorship, a protectorship. . . . These rumours are doubtless means devised by the enemies of the Revolution for causing disorder." He requested his colleagues to swear that they execrated equally royalty, dictatorship, and triumvirate, and he met with hearty applause.

Basire went still further and demanded a law fixing the death penalty for "whosoever should dare to propose the creation of an individual and hereditary power." Rouyer and Mathieu expressed their acquiescence, upon which, in order to exorcize "the vain phantoms of a dictatorship, the extravagant ideas of a triumvirate, all these absurdities invented to alarm the people," Danton in turn proposed a decree to the effect that the new

227

Constitution should be submitted to the primary assemblies for their acceptance. He dissociated himself from all extremes—in other words, repudiated Momoro—by going on to propose a decree confirming the maintenance in perpetuity of all rights of property, whether territorial, individual, or industrial, in order to reassure property-owners. The words "in perpetuity" struck Cambon, who had already begun to distrust Danton's demagogical tendencies, as a little strong. He proposed that they should not pass an irrevocable decree, and after a slight altercation the Convention adopted the wording proposed by Basire: "(1) There can be no constitution save that which is accepted by the people. (2) Life and property are under the safeguard of the nation."

The Assembly had been unanimous in rejecting simultaneously the dictatorship and the agrarian law; it was equally so in abolishing royalty.

This was proposed by Collot d'Herbois. He was supported by Bishop Grégoire, who exclaimed that "dynasties had never been anything but predatory races, devouring the blood of the nations." With one spontaneous impulse all the deputies rose and asseverated their hatred of royalty. Basire alone, while recalling that he had been the first to raise his voice against Louis XVI, and declaring that he would not be the last to vote for the abolition of royalty, tried to put the Assembly upon its guard against voting under the sway of emotion. He was interrupted by murmurs, and Grégoire rejoined vehemently: "Kings are in the moral order what monsters are in the physical. Courts are workshops of crime, hotbeds of corruption, and the lairs of tyrants. The history of kings is that of the martyrdom of nations." The abolition of royalty was decreed unanimously, amid transports of joy on the part of the deputies and the audience in the galleries.

At nightfall, by torchlight, the decree was forthwith read out with great pomp in Paris. Monge, accompanied by the other ministers, congratulated the Assembly upon having proclaimed the Republic by its decree, and pledged himself in their name to die, if necessary, for liberty and equality, like true republicans. On the same day Roland justified the great measure expected of them in a circular letter to the administrative bodies: "Pray, gentlemen, proclaim the Republic; that is to say, proclaim fraternity; it is one and the same thing." The Republic was solemnly proclaimed everywhere simultaneously with the abolition of royalty. The word "republic" did not occur in the decree; it was only inserted in it on the following day, by an amendment to the minutes of the previous day's proceedings; but there was no need to express the word in writing, for the thing was already in existence practically and in the hearts of men.

The enemy was retreating; the royalists were crushed and silent. The Republic was dawning with an aureole of glory as the saviour of the Revolution and the country.

On that very day, September 21, Roland made an appeal for fraternity. It seemed as though the party truce was going to last. On September 22 the session of the Convention opened amid perfect harmony. A deputation arrived from the sections of Orleans, complaining of the municipality of that city for favouring the rich, and censuring the events of June 20. The deputation added that the sections had suspended the municipality, but that the latter refused to relinquish its functions. Both Danton, a Montagnard, and Masuyer, a Girondin, thereupon came forward and proposed to send three members of the Assembly to Orleans to hold an inquiry into what was happening and take all measures which they might deem necessary. The Convention adopted their motion. Next Couthon gave the matter a wider extension by casting suspicion upon all administrative and municipal bodies and requesting that they should be replaced by new ones. Couthon was warmly supported by the Girondin Louvet, who proposed that even the judges should be renewed. A number of deputies spoke to the same purpose. But suddenly Billaud-Varenne proposed that the judges should be done away with and replaced by mere arbiters; whereupon Chasset, a deputy of moderate views, called out: "I request that the speaker be called to order. Does he want to disorganize everything and plunge us into anarchy?" The debate now assumed a more impassioned character, and latent discords were revealed. Montagnards and Girondins began to come out in opposition to each other. "If," said Lasource, "you destroy the administrative bodies and tribunals, you will surround yourselves with havoc and see nothing but ruins on every side." Léonard Bourdon replied that the most pressing necessity was to remove all royalists from the public department. The Convention passed a decree that all administrative, municipal, and judicial bodies should be entirely reconstituted, save those which had already been so treated as an exceptional measure since August 10. This was greeted with loud applause.

But the dispute cropped up again in connexion with a motion of Tallien's, expressing the wish that every citizen might be a judge without being obliged to have his name entered on the roll of lawyers. Lanjuinais and Goupilleau demanded an adjournment, but it was vigorously opposed by Danton. "All lawyers," said Danton, "are revoltingly aristocratic; if the people are forced to choose among these men, it will not know whom to trust. On the contrary, I think that if it is possible to set up a principle of exclusion in the elections, it ought to be directed against lawyers, who have hitherto arrogated to themselves an exclusive privilege, which is one of the great plagues of the human race. Let the people choose at its pleasure men of talent deserving of its confidence. . . . Those who have made it their profession to act as judges of men were like priests; both of them have everlastingly deceived the people. Justice ought to be dispensed in accordance with the simple laws of reason."

Once again Chasset raised the cry of anarchy and disorder: "Those who want to place on the tribunals men devoid of professional knowledge desire to set up the will of the judge in the place of that of the law. With this incessant toadying to the people, one would place one's fate at the mercy of a man who had usurped its confidence. I repeat, this is sycophancy." Stung by his criticism, Danton parried it by a personal attack upon the speaker: "You did not toady the people at the time of the revision, I suppose!"—for Chasset had been a member of the Constituent Assembly, and one of those who after Varennes had supported Barnave and the Lameths in obtaining the revision of the Constitution in a monarchical sense. Prolonged murmuring broke out against Danton, and Masuver proposed that he should be called to order. Petion, who was presiding, confined himself to censuring him, and the altercation continued with some asperity. In the end the Girondins were defeated and the decree proposed by Danton was passed.

Was it this defeat which alarmed the Girondins and caused them to break the truce? It is very probable, for on the following day, September 23, Brissot in his newspaper accused the Montagnards of desiring the destruction of all existing authorities, of tending to a general levelling, and of toadying the people. To choose the judges indiscriminately from among all citizens, he wrote, was a most grave menace in the eyes of the party of order. Those who dispense justice are responsible for property. Were not the Montagnards preparing to seize control of the tribunals? Brissot sounded the alarm; but this did not prevent him later on from accusing Robespierre, in the pamphlet quoted above, of having caused the failure of the pact of pacification and conciliation which he had concluded with Danton.

The fact that, on the very day upon which Brissot launched his attack, Roland once more entered upon the scene proves that Brissot was not acting solely on his own initiative. In a long report to the Convention Roland denounced the anarchists in the pay of Brunswick and made it his endeavour to convince the Assembly that it was unable to deliberate freely and would not be safe until it had surrounded itself with an imposing armed force: "I believe this force ought to be composed of men solely intended for military service, who should discharge their duties with assiduous regularity. Nothing but a professional armed force can achieve this aim." On the following day Roland again raised the alarm in connexion with an insignificant event, the arrest of a postal messenger on the road to Châlons. Thereupon the Girondin Kersaint, taking Roland's letter as his text, made an impassioned speech calling for emergency measures to put an end to excesses and acts of violence. "It is time," he said, "to set up scaffolds for those who commit murders and those who incite to them. . . . Appoint four commissaries to devise a law dealing with this matter; let them be charged to lay it before you tomorrow; for you can no longer delay avenging the rights of man, which are violated by all that is going on in France." A sharp altercation arose. The Montagnards Billaud-Varenne, Basire, and Tallien protested that Kersaint and Roland were exaggerating with regard to the condition of France. "We have laws," said Tallien; "the penal code has provisions dealing with murder; it is for the courts to apply them." But Vergniaud declared that to adjourn the vote on Kersaint's motion would be to "proclaim openly that it is permissible to commit murders, to proclaim openly that Prussian emissaries are able to carry on their work in the country, to arm fathers against their children!" Garran de Coulon was even more violent, maintaining that the laws contained no provisions against incitements to murder or against the agitators who were leading the people astray: "The walls are covered every day with inflammatory posters; incendiarism is advocated, proscription lists are to be read, the best citizens are slandered, and fresh victims are indicated." Collot d'Herbois expressed his astonishment that, only three days after the Assembly had met, offensive suspicions should be displayed and blood-thirsty laws proposed. Lanjuinais replied that the citizens of Paris were "in a state of stupefaction and alarm." But this allegation was in such contradiction with the facts that murmurs arose in the Assembly. Next Buzot ascended the tribune. He had sat beside Robespierre in the Constituent Assembly, and had the reputation of a democrat in the eyes of those who were as yet unaware that this vain and restless spirit had been fascinated by the beauty and persuasive arts of Madame Roland, whose salon he frequented. Buzot was the mouthpiece of all the malice of the Roland household.

He began by recalling the September massacres. "And if these scenes had been repeated in the heart of our provinces in all their horrible reality, perhaps, legislators, our electoral assemblies would have ordered us to sit elsewhere." Having uttered this threat, he took pains to justify Kersaint's proposal by eulogizing Roland and heaping insults upon the Mountain—"that rabble," as he called them, "of whose principles and aim I am ignorant." Not only was a law against incitements to murder needed, but it was necessary to surround the Convention with such a formidable guard that the provinces should be reassured of the safety of their deputies. Thus and thus only would they be able to vote with complete independence, without becoming the slaves of certain Parisian deputies.

Buzot was loudly applauded. Basire wanted to answer him, but was prevented from doing so by the close of the day's session. The Convention passed a decree that a commission should be appointed to review the situation of the Republic, and especially of the capital, to draft a law against incitements to murder and assassination, and, lastly, to propose the necessary measures for providing the Convention with a guard drawn from the eighty-three departments.

The die was cast: the Gironde had declared war on Paris.

The Mountain had received a challenge which it was bound to take up. At the meeting of the Jacobins on the previous day one of them, Chabot, had discussed Brissot's violent article which had appeared that morning. He asked that Brissot should be called upon to explain what he meant by the expression "party of disorder (*parti désorganisateur*)" which he had employed. But it was obvious that the club had as yet no desire to enter upon hostilities. At this same session it elected Petion as its president.

But after the session of the Convention on September 24, the Jacobins took up a different attitude. Chabot denounced the "sect of the Endormeurs" (those who lull others into a sense of false security) who, if he were to be believed, were cherishing the project of setting up a federal government. Fabre d'Eglantine next dealt with the charges levelled against Paris by Roland and Buzot. Petion, who was presiding over the Assembly, attempted to defend Buzot, upon which a tumult broke out. Fabre protested against the prejudice which was being displayed and the insults which were being showered upon the Parisian deputies. The departmental guard, he said, was an inquisitorial measure dictated by suspicion, and might provoke a civil war. Faithful, however, to the conciliatory ideas of his friend Danton, Fabre wound up by requesting all good citizens to lay aside their mutual hatreds, and Petion associated himself with these sentiments. But Billaud-Varennne, who spoke after Fabre, was not content to parry the attacks of the Girondins and incriminated them in turn. He recalled their mistakes and accused them of ulterior designs which they dared

232

not avow: "Now, when the enemy is advancing and our forces are inadequate to check him, blood-thirsty laws are proposed and men of the purest opinions are represented as being in collusion with the enemy—we, who have striven without respite against a war of aggression! And who are our accusers? Those who have led us into this war of aggression. No doubt they are ascribing their own treachery to us." Billaud was supported by Collot. The Girondin Grangeneuve attempted to reply, by defending Brissot against Chabot; whereupon the tumult broke out afresh, and the session closed with a threat uttered by Barbaroux: "Eight hundred men from Marseilles are on the march to Paris and may arrive any minute. This corps is composed of men of independent means; every man has received from his father and mother a pair of pistols, a sabre, a musket, and an assignat for a thousand livres." How wonderful are the effects of party spirit! Barbaroux, the very man who was now summoning the well-to-do sons of Marseilles to the aid of the Convention, had been president of the electoral assembly of Bouches-du-Rhône, and this assembly—as he himself tells us in his memoirs—had applauded the news of the massacres in Paris!

At the Jacobins, as in the Convention, the two parties were now ranged against each other, while between them floated the phantom of treachery to the nation.

At this time there were still a large number of Girondins among the Jacobins. Petion, the president of the club, was coming out more and more on their side, in spite of the pose of impartiality which he always affected. The Girondins might have attempted to wrest the club from their rivals, but on Brissot's advice they adopted tactics of contemptuous abstention. When called upon to give an explanation before the Jacobins with regard to the attack on the party of disorder which he had inserted in his paper, Brissot refused to answer the summons, and was struck off the books on October 10 by an almost unanimous vote. He rejoined with a violent pamphlet, in which he called upon the provincial clubs to break off their affiliation with the central club. A few of them—for example, those of Marseilles and Bordeaux—followed his advice; certain others —for instance, those of Châlons, Le Mans, Valognes, Nantes, Lorient, Bayonne, Perpignan, Angers, and Lisieux—threatened to do so; but that was the only result. The mass of the revolutionaries remained faithful to the Parisian Jacobins. Deserted by the Girondins,[3] the Montagnards now reigned unchallenged at the club, which served as a party organiza-

---

[3] On October 5 only 113 deputies still had their names on the books at the Jacobins. See Buchez and Roux, Vol. XIX, p. 234.

tion for them, where they concerted their measures freely and in broad daylight.

The Girondins were giving themselves out more and more as the party of order and good breeding, preferring private conversations, confabulations round a well-appointed table or in an elegant drawing-room, in a perfumed feminine atmosphere, to public meetings, which were too noisy and indiscreet for their taste. They might have gathered their partisans together in a new club, as the Feuillants had done after the massacre of republicans on the Champ de Mars. But the Feuillants had failed lamentably in their attempt, and though Brissot was endeavouring to attract the fragments of the Feuillant party, he repudiated the charge of "feuillantism" as an insult. The most prominent deputies in his party, Guadet, Gensonné, Vergniaud, Ducos, Condorcet, and Fauchet, gradually made it their habit to meet almost every day before the session of the Assembly in the drawing-room of Madame Dodun, the wife of a wealthy director of the Compagnie des Indes, who lived in the same house as Vergniaud, No. 5, Place Vendôme. These same deputies, with the addition of Buzot, Barbaroux, Grangeneuve, Bergoeing, Hardy, Salle, Deperret, Lidon, Lesage, and Mollevault, also met at the house of Dufriche-Valazé, No. 19 rue d'Orléans Saint-Honoré. They used also to dine at the houses of Clavière and Petion, at a restaurant in the Palais Royal, and at the house of Madame Roland. Madame Roland's dinners, which took place regularly twice a week at the Ministry of the Interior, were the meeting-place of the élite of the party, its protagonists; and it was there that its great coups were planned.

At that time, when all that savoured of intrigue and faction met with general disapprobation, the secret confabulations in which the Girondin leaders delighted could not fail to lower them in the public estimation. The Montagnards, who for their part conducted their deliberations openly at the club, found it easy to accuse their rivals of manœuvres and intrigue, and it was not long before Brissot had to defend himself and his friends against the charge of forming a party, a faction. "Guadet has too proud a spirit," he wrote in his pamphlet against the Jacobins, "Vergniaud is too deeply imbued with that carelessness which is the accompaniment of talent and makes it walk by itself, Ducos is too clever and upright, and Gensonné is too deep a thinker, ever to stoop to fight beneath the standard of any leader." Brissot was skilfully playing with words. It was no doubt true that the Girondins did not form a party in the sense of a modern parliamentary group; they had neither president nor leaders, and the only discipline which they obeyed was a moral one. But that was not the point. What they were taxed with was meeting among themselves before the sessions, confidentially assigning to each his line of action, and trying to impose a ready-made and premeditated plan upon the Assembly. This may seem a strange ground for reproach nowadays, but it was a serious charge at the time, for a representative of the people was then surrounded with quite a novel prestige and regarded as a sort of priest of social welfare. It was considered that he ought to follow nothing but the promptings of his own conscience, and that the best guarantee of the public weal lay in his absolute independence.

Not all the deputies took part in the secret conclaves of the Girondin leaders. Those who were excluded from them suffered from wounded vanity and soon noticed that the guests of Madame Roland or Madame Dodun not only monopolized the tribune, but kept all the important places, both on the committees and on the official staff of the Assembly, for themselves and their friends. On October 11 the Constitutional Committee was appointed, and at least seven out of its nine members were intimates of Madame Roland's: Thomas Paine, Brissot, Petion, Vergniaud, Gensonné, Barere, Condorcet. The eighth, Sieys, had the reputation of being a moderate, and an out-and-out adherent of the party. The ninth was Danton.

On the following day Couthon, a deputy who had hitherto affected a neutral attitude between the factions and shown some distrust of the Commune, ascended the tribune at the Jacobins and commented upon the results of the voting. "There are two parties in the Convention," he said. ". . . There is a party consisting of men of extremist principles, whose limited resources cause them to tend towards anarchy. There is another party, consisting of clever, subtle, scheming, and, above all, extremely ambitious men; they want the Republic; they want it because public opinion has pronounced in its favour; but they want an aristocracy, they want to perpetuate their own influential position, and dispose of appointments, offices, and, above all, the treasury of the Republic. . . . Look at the appointments; they are all filled from among this faction. Look at the composition of the Constitutional Committee; that is what did most to open my eyes. It is this faction, which wants liberty only for itself, that we must combat with all our might."

Thus Couthon turned a Montagnard, though he still disclaimed any weakness for extremists, and began to declare that all those who left the Jacobins were apostates deserving the anathema of the country. He added that he now saw quite well that the project of the departmental guard was intended to favour one faction alone: "The sovereignty of the people would be annulled and we should see the birth of an aristocracy of functionaries." More than one conversion may be attributed to the same motives as that of Couthon. The Girondins were not careful enough to spare the over-sensitive susceptibilities of those of their colleagues who were not admitted into their secret conclaves. They lent themselves too easily to the accusation of forming a sect—a "cave," as it would be called in modern political parlance. But this was the least important of their errors.

236

CHAPTER II

The Attack on the "Triumvirs"

THE first eight months of the Convention were occupied by the struggle between those who had provoked the events of August 10 and those who had been powerless to prevent them. It was conducted from the first with extreme violence. The Girondins took the offensive, and as early as September 25 endeavoured by a bold move to exclude from the Assembly Robespierre and Marat, the leaders of the Mountain, whom they feared above all things and pursued with the bitterest rancour. By so doing they intended to strike down the opposition, preparatory to reigning over a docile Assembly.

The pastor Lasource, who on the eve of August 10 had already attempted to have Robespierre cited before the High Court, opened the attack. "What I do not want," he said, "is that Paris, under the control of schemers, should become to the French Empire what Rome was to the Roman Empire. Paris must be confined to her eighty-third share of the total influence, like all the other departments." And Lasource vented his malice against "the men," as he put it, "who have never ceased to utter incitements to assassinate those members of the Legislative Assembly who have the most tenaciously defended the cause of liberty . . . the men who want to produce anarchy by the disorderly activities of the brigands sent by Brunswick, and by this anarchy to attain that domination for which they are thirsting." Lasource mentioned no names; but when Osselin defended the Parisian deputies, of whom he was one, and proposed that in order to dispel suspicion all the members of the Convention should be forced to pronounce an anathema on oligarchy and dictatorship, young Rebecqui, a deputy from Marseilles, interrupted him in the following terms: "The party which has been denounced to you, and whose intention it is to establish a dictatorship, is the party of Robespierre; so we have learnt from the common talk of Marseilles. I call my colleague M. Barbaroux to witness; it is to combat him that we have been sent here. I denounce him to you." Thus the plan of the Gironde was suddenly unveiled.

It was then that Danton, conscious of all the political dangers of a personal and retrospective debate which should range the leaders of the two parties against each other as irreconcilable enemies, and who had, moreover, himself reason to dread too thorough an inquiry into his actions and associates, made a most skilful attempt to create a diversion from these mutual recriminations by a simultaneous repudiation of the principles of dictatorship and federalism. In order to inspire confidence he opened his personal apologia by dissociating himself entirely from Marat, "a man whose opinions are to the republican party what those of Royou were to the aristocratic party." "I have been accused too much and for too long past of being the author of that man's writings . . . but let us not arraign the deputies of a whole city on account of a few individual extremists." And so, having thrown over the Friend of the People, Danton wound up with a double proposition calculated to satisfy the two opposing parties in the Assembly. He asked for the death penalty to be decreed against those who should demand a dictatorship or a triumvirate, and the same penalty for such as might desire to dismember France. He stepped down from the tribune after a patriotic appeal for union: "The Austrians will tremble as they learn of this holy concord; and then I swear to you that our enemies are dead men"—a sentiment which aroused hearty applause.

Buzot, who dreaded lest Danton's proposals might be voted at once, next boldly brought forward his own project of a departmental guard, representing it as inspired by the idea of union and unity; upon which Robespierre pronounced a long and haughty apologia, full of allusions to his past services. "I do not regard myself as a culprit," he said, "but as the defender of the patriotic cause. . . . Far from being ambitious, I have always combated the ambitious." He expressed his indignation at the slanders of the Girondins, who had represented him before August 10 as conferring with the Queen and the Princesse de Lamballe. He confessed that he had suspected his opponents "of wanting to turn the Republic into a mass of federated republics" when he had seen them rise up and accuse the heroes of August 10, falsely representing them as champions of the agrarian law. He defied his opponents to adduce any charge against him which had the slightest foundation, and concluded by demanding that Danton's two propositions should be voted.

Barbaroux wanted to take up Robespierre's challenge. As a proof that Robespierre had aspired to the dictatorship, he alluded to a conversation which he had had with Panis a few days before the insurrection: "Citizen Panis mentioned Robespierre to us by name as the virtuous man who was to be the dictator of France." This curious proof provoked the murmurs of the Assembly. Panis gave Barbaroux the lie. "On what grounds can he base such an accusation? Who are his witnesses?"—"I am one, sir," interrupted Rebecqui.—"You are his friend; I challenge you," replied Panis, and he added: "What! At a moment when the lives of patriots were in danger, when our sole care, our only thought, was to lay siege to the Tuileries, we are alleged to have dreamt of a dictatorship—at a moment when we were only too conscious of the inadequacy of our forces! . . . At a moment when I expected every instant to see a massacre in Paris, I am alleged to have dreamt of establishing a dictatorial power!"

Feeling that the accusation against Robespierre was hanging fire, other Girondins, such as Boileau and Cambon, created a diversion by indulging in a sharp retrospective attack upon the more tangible dictatorship of the Paris Commune. Brissot recalled the search-warrant which it had issued against him during the massacres. This gave Panis a chance of justifying the vigilance committee. "Consider our position," he said; "we were surrounded by citizens enraged at the treachery of the Court. . . . Many citizens came out and told us that Brissot was leaving for London with the written proofs of his machinations; no doubt I did not believe this accusation, but I could not answer for it personally and pledge my life that it was not true. I had to moderate the excitement of the best citizens, who were recognized as such by Brissot himself. I thought I could not do better than send commissaries to his house to ask him in a brotherly way to show them his papers, convinced that this would make his innocence obvious and dispel all suspicions—which was, in fact, what happened. . . ." This explanation bore the stamp of truth. The accusation of the Gironde, which was, moreover, entirely retrospective, fell to the ground.

Marat desired to speak, but the Girondins raised an outcry of "Sit down! (A bas de la tribune!)" Marat turned on them calmly and disdainfully with the words: "It seems I have a great number of personal enemies in this Assembly!"—"All of us! All of us," shouted the Girondins.—"If," he continued, unmoved, "I have a great number of enemies in this Assembly, I recall them to a sense of decency and appeal to them not to greet with vain clamour, hooting, and threats a man who has sacrificed himself for the country and for their own safety." This attitude imposed respect and he was allowed to speak. He at once took up the charge of dictatorship, to which he pleaded guilty, and, with an adroitness only equalled by his audacity, hastened to exonerate Robespierre and

Danton. "It is my duty," he said, "in justice to declare that my colleagues, and particularly Robespierre and Danton, as well as all the rest, have consistently disapproved of the idea of either a triumvirate or a dictatorship. If anyone is guilty of having disseminated these ideas among the public, it is I; I believe I am the first political writer, perhaps the only one in France since the Revolution, to propose a military tribune, a dictator, or a triumvirate as the sole means of crushing traitors and conspirators." He appealed in his defence to the liberty of the press, and without repudiating a jot of his opinions, without stooping to retract them, he once more expounded his theory of a dictator, "a wise, strong man, who would have no authority save to strike down the heads of the guilty, and would be attached to the country, as it were, by fetters." He most skilfully put the Assembly on its guard against those who wanted to sow discord in its midst and distract it from the weighty matters which ought to engage its attention.

The sincerity of Marat's language made a visible impression, and Vergniaud was greeted with murmurs when, on ascending the tribune after him, he affected to cast contemptuous aspersions upon him. "If there is one thing more unfortunate than another for a representative of the people, it is, to my mind, that of being obliged to follow on this tribune a man who has been cited before the courts and has raised his head above the laws—a man, in fact, reeking with calumny, malice, and blood." This melodramatic indignation struck a false note. Vergniaud was interrupted and Petion had to intervene in order to enable him to continue. Vergniaud read out the famous circular by which the vigilance committee of the Commune had advised the departments to make the massacres general. Now, at the very moment when this circular was drawn up, Robespierre was denouncing to the Commune the alleged plot formed by the Girondin leaders for handing France over to Brunswick. "It is false," interrupted Robespierre "I have the proofs," rejoined Lasource. Instead of insisting that the question should be cleared up on the spot, Vergniaud did not press the matter. "Since I speak without bitterness, I shall rejoice at a denial proving that Robespierre too may have been slandered." Vergniaud concluded his impassioned indictment of the Commune by demanding that the signers of the vigilance committee's circular —among them Panis, Sergent, and Marat—should meet with an exemplary punishment.

In order to crush Marat, the Girondin Boileau read out an article in which Marat had called for a fresh insurrection and advocated the setting up of a dictator. A number of deputies shouted that Marat must be sent to the Abbaye, and the decree indicting him was about to be voted when Marat admitted quite calmly that he was the author of the article denounced by Boileau, but added that the article had appeared a long time ago and had been written in a moment of indignation. Since then he had changed his mind and given his adhesion to the Convention, in proof of which he read out a recent article in which he laid down his new course of action ("*nouvelle marche*"). The effect produced was considerable. Marat ended by taking a pistol out of his pocket and pointing it at his brow. "I am bound to state that if my indictment had been decreed, I should have blown out my brains at the foot of the tribune. So this is the result of three years spent in dungeons, and the tortures I have endured to save the country! This is the result of my vigils, my toil, my poverty, my sufferings, and the dangers to which I have been exposed! Very well! I will remain among you and brave your fury!"

The Girondin coup had failed. Impotent to strike down Robespierre, they had increased Marat's prestige by giving him an opportunity to reveal his true nature before the Convention and France. Finally Couthon pointed the moral of the debate by proposing to pass a decree asserting the unity of the Republic. The only discussion was with regard to its wording, and they adopted the famous formula: "The French Republic is one and indivisible." This was a repudiation of federalism and of the project attributed to the Girondins of desiring to apply the Constitution of the United States to France. Couthon next proposed that the death penalty should be decreed against anyone who should propose a dictatorship. Marat demanded the addition of the words "and against any schemer who shall declare himself inviolable." "If you raise yourself above the people," he said, "the people will tear up your decrees." This rider had as its aim the suppression of parliamentary privilege. Cambon and Chabot in turn opposed Couthon's proposition in the name of liberty of opinion and the imprescriptible right to freedom of thought, and the Assembly allowed itself to be convinced by them. It was quite ready to condemn federalism, but refused to condemn dictatorship in principle.

At this great session of September 25 Danton had revealed himself as a remarkable tactician, a perfect master of the art of controlling assemblies by appealing to their passions as much as to their reason. It was he who had frustrated the plan of the Gironde, and they could not fail to owe him a grudge on this account. He had not at first been included in their attacks, but they now realized that they could not get the better of the Mountain without involving him.

Danton would have liked the Convention's first care to have been the appointment of a fresh ministry, consisting of new men, who had taken no part in past disputes. The law of the Constituent Assembly which established the principle of the incompatibility between the functions of a minister and those of a deputy was still in force. At the very first session he stated that he preferred to take his seat in the legislature, which made it incumbent upon Roland to do likewise. The position of minister was far better paid than that of deputy. Could Roland be less disinterested than the agitator upon whom the Girondins were so anxious to pour contempt? After some hesitation—for his election for the department of Somme was being opposed—Roland made the sacrifice in a sententious and commonplace speech, adorned with maxims such as the following: "It is easy to be great when one does not think of oneself, and a man who does not fear death is always powerful." After outlining the duties of his successor he commended to the Convention one of his former clerks, named Pache, whom he eulogized in pompous terms: "Like a modern Abdolonymus, he ought to be placed in a position where his wisdom may effect the greatest good." But Roland's resignation had only been a matter of form. His friends in the Assembly regarded it as a "public calamity" and endeavoured to obtain a vote inviting him to remain in office. During a lively discussion which sprang up on this subject, on September 27, Danton so far forgot himself as to say: "If you give him this invitation, give it to Madame Roland too, for everybody knows that Roland was not single-handed in his department. As for me, I was single-handed in mine, and what the nation needs is ministers who can act without being guided by their wives." Although the Assembly was well aware that Danton was saying no more than the truth, there was a prolonged outburst of murmuring. In the well-ordered eighteenth century an attack on a woman was an ill-bred action which was mercilessly castigated by the whole press, with scarcely an exception. But Danton made no pretence of being a gentleman, and the protests only made him more brutal. He struck another terrible blow at Roland by revealing a fact hitherto unknown—that the virtuous old man had wanted to evacuate Paris after the capture of Longwy. The minutes note that Danton's words caused a violent sensation. He concluded that Roland must be replaced by Pache without delay; but it was the opposite that happened. On the following day, in a long letter full of moral sentiments, but devoid of all modesty, the husband of Madame Roland declared that he would remain in office: "I am remaining because there is danger; I brave it because I fear nothing so long as it is a question of serving my country." And he embarked upon a vague and perfidious attack upon the Sullas and Rienzis of the day, asserting intrepidly that there had really been projects for a dictatorship or a triumvirate. His letter provoked four bursts of applause and was circulated among the departments.

Servan had left the Ministry for War to take command of the army which was in course of formation in the region of the Pyrenees, and was replaced by Pache; but Pache was a sincere revolutionary, a stranger to intrigue and still more to faction. He was to be a cruel disappointment to the Girondins and justify the eulogy which Danton had spontaneously pronounced upon his patriotism. As for Danton himself, on October 9 his place at the Ministry of Justice was definitively taken by Garat, a man of letters of unstable character, who was a close associate of the Girondin leaders.

But the latter were not content with having appointed to the Executive Council men whom they believed to be their devoted adherents. They had old scores to pay off and reprisals to carry out.

In the letter of September 30 which Roland had written to the Convention to withdraw his resignation, he had already inserted a highly suggestive phrase: "I am profoundly convinced that true patriotism cannot exist where there is no morality." Now morality was Danton's weak point, the chink in his armour.

On leaving office a minister had in those days to render an account of his stewardship, not only in the moral, but in the financial sphere. It was no mere formality. The minister's report was carefully examined and checked by comparison with the records on which it was based. When Danton's accounts came up for examination on October 10—the report being presented by Mallarmé—Cambon, who was always very hostile to the Commune, expressed himself in severe terms. "I note," he said, "that the system followed by the Minister of Justice is destructive of all orderly accountancy, for expenditure sanctioned by ministers ought to be paid as occasion arises, and by their order; consequently they ought never to have sums of money lying at their disposal." Cambon did not rest content with this censure; he drew the conclusion that ministers ought to render an account, not only of their extraordinary expenditure—as Danton had done—but also of their secret expenditure, which he had omitted to do. Thus called to account, Danton sheltered himself behind the Executive Council, to which, he said, he had accounted for his secret expenditure. Cambon had been greeted with hearty applause, but Danton stepped down from the tribune amidst chilly silence. The Convention passed a motion calling upon him to give a fresh explanation to the

243

Executive Council of how he had spent the 200.000 livres which had been placed at his disposal as secret-service money. Since he remained obdurate, Roland ostentatiously went down to the Assembly on October 18 and laid his own accounts before it, accompanied by comments aimed directly at his former colleague: "As I know no secrets, and desire that my administration should be as clear as the day, I beg the Assembly to have these accounts read out to it." Upon which Rebecqui added: "I propose that all the ministers should produce their accounts, like Roland." Danton had once more to ascend the tribune and justify himself. But he got confused between his admissions and denials and ended by acknowledging certain facts: ". . . When the enemy seized Verdun, when consternation was rife even among the best and bravest citizens, the Legislative Assembly said to us: 'Spare no means, lavish money, if necessary, to revive confidence and give a lead to the whole of France.' We did so: we were forced into extraordinary expenditure; and for most of this expenditure I admit that we have no absolutely legal receipts. Everything was done in a rush and a hurry. You wanted the ministers to take joint action; we did so, and there are our accounts." There was an outburst of murmuring. Cambon challenged Roland to say whether he had checked the accounts of Danton's secret-service fund. Roland replied "that he had looked for some trace of them in the minutes of the Council, but had not found them." The Assembly was stirred by strong emotion. Camus proposed that "ministers who have squandered State funds should be cited before the courts." Finally, on the motion of Larivière, a decree was passed ordering the Council to give an explanation within twenty-four hours "of the debate which it must have held with a view to drawing up an account of the sums placed at its disposal for the secret-service fund."

It was impossible for the Council to produce minutes of a debate which did not exist, so it decided to give no sign of life. But on October 25, when Danton attempted to speak, the Girondins shouted him down and demanded his accounts. On October 30 a new decree was voted, which left the ministers no option but to comply with it. On November 7 Monge, Clavière, and Lebrun resigned themselves and obeyed. They made a statement to the effect that on October 6 Danton and Servan had rendered them a detailed account of the disposal of their secret-service funds, but that they had not thought it their duty to put it on record. But neither Cambon nor Brissot was to be mollified. They renewed their criticisms, and the Convention refused to pass Danton's accounts. It is true that it also refused to censure him; but from this time onward the Girondins lost no opportunity of holding this affair of the accounts *in terrorem* over Danton. It was unfortunately an easy matter for them to impugn his honesty. Danton gave his protection to contractors of dubious reputation, such as the notorious Abbé d'Espagnac. He had taken as his secretary at the Ministry of Justice the broken-down poet Fabre d'Eglantine, who had suddenly turned army-contractor in order to retrieve his fortunes, and incurred the criticism of Pache for pocketing the sums advanced to him and then failing to carry out his contracts. Danton's fortune had unaccountably increased. He lived in style, bought national property in the department of Aube, and owned three residences in and near Paris. His position was vulnerable. The Girondin newspapers, Brissot's pamphlets, and Madame Roland's memoirs are full of transparent allusions to his venality. Roland engaged in his police force an adventurer named Roch Marcandier, a former secretary of Camille Desmoulins, and employed him to discredit Danton and his friends in a periodical pamphlet of great violence, but not entirely fabricated, entitled *L'Histoire des hommes de proie* (*History of Men of Prey*). Whether from weariness, contempt, or tactics—for fear of making his position worse—Danton made no reply to the savage attacks of which he was the object. He came out of the affair lowered in the esteem of many deputies in the Convention and was unable to do all the good which he had intended to effect by his policy of conciliation and union, which was beneficial not only to his own repose, but to the Republic. By depreciating Danton the Girondins contributed towards the elevation of Robespierre.

CHAPTER III

The Formation of the Third Party

B Y indulging in a policy of reprisals against the Mountain, the Girondins were bound in the nature of things to encourage the revival of conservative forces. In the political as in the social sphere their trend towards the right was very rapid. They first made a dead set against the organs of vigilance and repression created by the Revolution of August 10 to deal with royalists acting as accomplices or agents of the enemy.

After a violent arraignment by Vergniaud on September 25, the vigilance committee of the Commune appeared before the Assembly five days later in order to defend itself. Assuming the offensive in its turn, it produced some disquieting documents from its archives, including a letter from Laporte, intendant of the civil list, in which he demanded 1,500,000 livres from Septeuil, the king's treasurer, in order to win over supporters on the liquidation committee of the Legislative Assembly, and manage to have the pensions of the king's military household made a charge on the nation; besides receipts showing that considerable sums, amounting to 500,000 and 550,000 livres respectively, had been distributed on the very eve of August 10, and other documents proving that the *Logographe,* run by Duport and the Lameths, and other newspapers, had been subsidized out of the civil list. Robert Lindet and Tallien supported the vigilance committee, but the Girondins, backed up by certain deputies with financial interests, such as Reubell and Merlin of Thionville, obtained a decision that the vigilance committee's papers should be submitted to a commission of twenty-four members chosen from the Convention. In vain did Panis, Marat, and Billaud-Varenne attempt to prevent the appointment of this commission and the supersession of the vigilance committee. The commission of twenty-four was chosen then and there, almost exclusively from the right wing, and was further given the power of issuing warrants for arrests. The committee was no sooner formed than it chose Barbaroux as its president. He was in sympathy with its policy, which was to prove that the vigilance committee of the Commune had received unfounded denunciations, proceeded to arrest

246

the innocent, and molested peaceable persons The commission of twenty-four only followed up the interrogations and prosecutions already started by the now superseded vigilance committee as a matter of form. It issued a few warrants for arrests, but at once discharged the accused persons after a mere show of examining them. Thus it accepted at their face value the disclaimers of one Durand, who had been the agent of Mont-morin and the Court in their dealings with the Jacobins and Danton. It took no steps to verify his statements and did not confront him with any witnesses or call in any handwriting experts. It likewise shelved a complaint received on October 4 against an English banker named Boyd, who was strongly suspected of being Pitt's agent in France, and against whom grave charges were subsequently made. It did not seriously molest the members of the Liquidation Committee of the Legislative Assembly, which had been seriously compromised by Laporte's papers. It did nothing to clear up the affair of the *Logographe*, in which the chief Feuillant leaders were implicated, etc.

By attacking and paralysing the vigilance committee the Girondins had intended not only to avenge their own personal slights, but also to disarm the organs of revolutionary repression so as to inspire confidence in the Feuillants, their opponents of yesterday, by protecting them and giving them pledges. And so, by the middle of October, the aristocrats and the rich, who had fled from Paris in August, were flocking back again.

The extraordinary tribunal created on August 17 for the repression of royalist plots and crimes against the nation did its duty conscientiously. It had acquitted for lack of evidence certain well-recognized royalists, some of whom were in close connexion with the Court—for instance Gibé, the notary of the civil list. On the other hand, it had taken vigorous measures against the robbers of the Garde-Meuble, who had been handed over to it. But it failed to win the good graces of the Girondins, one of whom alluded to it at the session of October 26 as a "bloody assize (*tribunal de sang*)." The tribunal wanted to defend it-self, but on October 28 Lanjuinais persuaded the Assembly to refuse it permission to print its apologia. Next, on November 15, Garat, Minister of Justice, accused it of having exceeded its powers, which gave Buzot a pretext for demanding its suspension. "It is an instrument of revolution," he said; "now that the Revolution is effected, it must be broken." In vain did Tallien reply: "You cannot suspend a tribunal which has the clue to the conspiracies of August 10, a tribunal which ought to try the crimes of the wife of Louis XVI, a tribunal which has deserved so well of the nation." Barère obtained the passage of a decree that the judgments of the tribunal should in future be subject to appeal, and a fortnight later, as the result of the report of Garran de Coulon, its suppression was announced. This was a grave step, for it not only was a fresh repudiation of those responsible for August 10 and their policy, but resulted in increasing the the security of the enemies of the existing order, who agitated more than ever. The High Court having already been suppressed, no tribunal was now left for trying crimes against the safety of the State. But the foreign war was still going on and civil war was brewing.

The Girondins attempted to gain control of the Commune, which the Legislative Assembly, during its last moments, had ordered to be reconstituted. Perhaps they might have succeeded had they acted with more promptitude and resolution. On October 9 Petion was re-elected mayor without opposition by 13,899 votes out of an electorate of 15,474. But he declined office. The elections dragged on, because the electoral system was complicated, the mayor and municipal officials being nominated separately, before the general council, and because the Girondin candidates one after another declined to stand. On November 21 d'Ormesson, a Feuillant who had their support, was finally elected on the third ballot by 4,910 votes, against 4,896 cast for the Montagnard Lullier. He also declined. On November 30 Chambon, a doctor who enjoyed the protection of Brissot, was in turn elected by 8,358 votes, Lullier this time receiving only 3,906. He accepted office, but explained later, in 1814, that he had done so only in order to advance the royalist cause beneath a show of republicanism. Through Chambon the Girondins controlled the office of the mayor, but they failed to obtain a hold on the municipal officials and the general council. Though they had induced the Convention to pass a decree forbidding oral voting, the new Commune formed at the end of November was as revolutionary as the old one, from which, moreover, it was largely recruited. The municipal officials, who were next elected, at the beginning of December, were, if possible, still more Montagnard in tendency. Chaumette, who had been president of the Commune set up on August 10, was elected *procureur syndic,* with Réal and Hébert as his deputies. Lullier, the defeated candidate for the mayoralty, was elected *procureur général syndic* of the departmental assembly of Paris.

The great idea of the Girondins had been the departmental guard with which they wanted to surround the Convention; but they failed to carry it into effect. The report laid before the Assembly by Buzot on October 8 could not be debated. The majority was loath to pass an exceptional measure armed against Paris, the calm of which was in contrast with the furious attacks of the Roland group.

Buzot, who was even more supple and crafty than he was tenacious, did not persist in trying to obtain the passage of his measure, but preferred to overcome the opposition by ingenious means. As early as October 12 he announced to the Assembly that several departments, among them that of Eure, which was his own, were enrolling contingents of Fédérés, whom they were preparing to send to Paris to protect their representatives. Though it had not been voted, his law was already being put into execution.

As Buzot had announced, the Girondin departments were already sending Fédérés to Paris. Those of Bouches-du-Rhône, summoned by Barbaroux, arrived on October 19, and two days later their spokesman came to the bar of the Convention and threatened "agitators greedy for the tribunate and a dictatorship." On November 3 they pervaded the streets of Paris, singing a song of which the chorus ran as follows:

La tête de Marat, Robespierre et Danton
Et de tous ceux qui les défendront, ô gué!
Et de tous ceux qui les défendront!

(The heads of Marat, Robespierre, and Danton, and of all those who may defend them!)

The crowd, swelled by private persons, proceeded to the Palais Royal shouting: "Death to Marat and Robespierre!" mingled with cries of "No trial for Louis XVI!" A rumour went round that the Fédérés intended to carry off the King from the Temple with the help of a number of returned émigrés.

By the middle of November there were nearly sixteen thousand Fédérés in Paris, from Bouches-du-Rhône, Saône-et-Loire, Calvados, Hérault, Manche, Yonne, etc. They claimed the right of mounting guard over the Assembly jointly with the Parisians. If the latter had lost their heads and met the demonstrations of the Fédérés with counter-demonstrations, disorders would have broken out which would have provided the Girondins with the desired pretext for transferring the Assembly to another city. But in a great speech delivered at the Jacobins as early as October 29, Robespierre put them on their guard against "the snares of schemers," and advised them to be patient and keep cool; and Marat did likewise. On October 23 he boldly visited the barracks of the Marseilles

Fédérés, displayed solicitude for their comfort, and, finding that their quarters were uncomfortable, promised to have the deficiencies made good. Meanwhile he asked three men out of each company to dinner. The Parisian populace not only failed to respond to the provocations of the Fédérés but made overtures to them in order to dispel their prejudices.

Powerful support was given to the Commune and the sections by Pache, the Minister of War, who on November 1 declared in an open letter that he had not summoned any forces to Paris, and added: "I am not aware of any reason which renders their presence here necessary, and the first order which they receive from me will be for their departure." Pache did not hesitate next to castigate those who had sown the seeds of hatred and division between the Parisians and the volunteer Fédérés, and he made several attempts to send the latter to the front. Letourneur, who submitted the reports of the War Committee to the Assembly, adopted his views and on November 10 proposed a decree stopping the pay of all volunteers who should not leave the capital within a fortnight. But Buzot, supported by Barère, made an appeal for the maintenance of order and succeeded in obtaining permission from the Assembly for the Fédérés to stay in Paris. The calculations of the Gironde were none the less thwarted. As they came in contact with the Parisians, the volunteers from the provinces abandoned their prejudices and gradually went over to the party of the Mountain. Towards the end of December they grouped themselves into a society of Fédérés from the eighty-three departments, a sort of military club inspired by the Jacobins.

During the early days of confidence and illusions caused by the arrival of the Fédérés, the Gironde had attempted a last effort against the leaders of the Mountain. On October 29 Roland communicated to the Assembly a police report from Roch Marcandier in which Robespierre was once more indirectly accused of intriguing for the dictatorship. Robespierre contemptuously justified himself amid tumultuous interruptions from the right wing, encouraged by the attitude of the president Guadet. Afterwards Louvet, the novelist, read out from the tribune a lengthy and laboriously composed arraignment in which the absence of arguments was poorly compensated for by his rhetoric. "Robespierre, I accuse you of having for a long time past slandered the purest patriots . . . at a time when slanders were tantamount to a proscription . . . I accuse you of having constantly put yourself forward as an object of idolatry; I accuse you of having tyrannized over the electoral assembly of the department of Paris by every device of intrigue and terrorism; finally, I accuse you of having obviously worked for the supreme power. . . ."

250

But as though himself aware of the flimsiness of his proofs, Louvet merely wound up with the demand that Robespierre's behaviour should be examined into by a commission of inquiry. It is true that he made up for this by asking that Marat, whom he had hardly mentioned, should be cited before the courts. The Convention refused to pronounce an opinion until it had allowed Robespierre to answer his accuser, and a week later Louvet's feeble attempt at a Catilinian oration was torn to shreds. The Convention, at first hostile and prejudiced, was gradually won over by Robespierre's logic and sincerity, and shelved the matter by voting that they should pass to the order of the day.

Buzot had already met with a serious defeat. The draft of a law for muzzling the Montagnard press which he had laid before the Assembly, under the pretext of putting down incitements to murder and assassination, had come up for debate on October 30. An ill-advised friend of his, Bailleul, tried to make its provisions more severe by an amendment authorizing the immediate arrest of anyone guilty of an incitement to disobey the laws or offer resistance to public officials. Some murmuring was heard against this provision, which was regarded as arbitrary and vague. Even the Girondin Ducos exclaimed: "I propose that this article should be referred to the grand inquisitor." Bailleul had the imprudence to admit that it was a piece of "emergency legislation (*une loi de circonstance*)"; whereupon Lepelletier de Saint-Fargeau, a former member of the Constituent Assembly, made a cogent speech against the motion, which met with great applause. "The proposed law," he said, "is an infringement of the liberty of the press." "Liberty or death!" cried Danton. In vain did Barbaroux attempt to create a diversion by proposing that the Convention should pass a decree that it would leave Paris as soon as it judged that its safety there was no longer assured; his proposals were regarded even by Petion as excessive and unjustifiable. The Girondins failed to obtain the passage of the emergency measures which they had intended as a weapon against the Mountain.

Their influence over the Assembly was waning every day. Their perpetual denunciations and impassioned recriminations about the past seemed to conceal hidden designs alien to the public weal. The independent deputies, who had at first been full of prejudices against the Commune, began to wonder whether they had not been deceived.

Speaking at the Jacobins on October 24, Fabre d'Églantine noted the change which had taken place in the attitude of the Assembly. "During its early days," he said, "the whole Convention was united in opposition to the Parisian deputies, but we have arrived at a sort of balance, so that the issue of several trials of strength has already been doubtful." Fabre was not exaggerating. On October 18 the Girondins nearly lost the presidency of the Assembly. On the first ballot Guadet had obtained only 218 votes out of a possible 466, Danton, who had been put up against him by the Mountain, receiving 207. Guadet was elected on the second ballot by 326 votes.

Cloots had for a long time followed the Girondins and been a regular guest at Madame Roland's dinner-parties; but he now broke violently with his former friends in a pamphlet entitled *Ni Marat ni Roland* (*Neither Marat nor Roland*), which created a sensation. In it he attacked the Girondins alone. He revealed the fact that he had heard Buzot maintain, at Roland's table, "that a republic ought to extend no farther than the village forming it," and accused Roland of advocating federalism. These attacks told, for in September Cloots had come out as a determined enemy of the agrarian law.

By November 5, after Robespierre's reply to Louvet, a third party had definitely appeared between the Girondins and the Montagnards. The list of speakers who put down their names as intending to take part in the debate fell into three divisions. There were those who wanted to speak *in favour* of the motion under debate—that is, in favour of rejecting Louvet's accusation. There were those who wanted to speak *on* the motion—that is, who did not want to pronounce an opinion on the question at issue. And lastly there were those who wanted to speak *against* the motion—that is, in support of Louvet's accusation.

The Girondin press was not unanimous in its approval of Louvet's attacks. Condorcet repudiated them, and his paper, *La Chronique*, refused to believe in the reality of the hideous plots daily denounced by Roland.

In No. 25 of Camille Desmoulins's *Tribune des patriotes*, which appeared at the beginning of November, he, like Fabre d'Eglantine, commented upon the formation of a third party, which had split off from the Gironde: "I must here inform the reader that for some time past a third party has formed itself in the Convention, which it is worth while to characterize. . . . It might be called the party of the *phlegmatics*. Petion, Barère, Rabaud, Condorcet, and, I believe, even Lacroix and Vergniaud are those who, it seemed to me, form the nucleus of it . . . regular speculators who hold the balance between Brissot and Robespierre just as the Abbé d'Espagnac did between a rise and fall of prices on the Bourse. . . ."

This was an event of importance. The Gironde was no longer to be

252

sole master of the Convention. By November 15 it had lost the president-ship of the Assembly, which fell to Bishop Grégoire, an independent who had just made a vehement speech against the inviolability of the king's person. He was elected by 246 votes out of 352.

The Gironde would keep the Government in its hands only if it abandoned its policy of hatred and consented to give due weight to the considerations of public interest represented by those independent mem-bers whom Camille Desmoulins contemptuously alluded to as "the phleg-matics." But was it capable of a vigorous rally which would save its already precarious situation? The equivocal part which it played in con-nexion with the trial of the King put the finishing touch to the doubts which were felt as to its patriotism and republicanism.

253

CHAPTER IV

The Trial of the King

A MONG the papers of the treasurer of the civil list at the Tuileries had been found proof that Louis XVI had continued to pay his Gardes du Corps, who had been disbanded and had crossed the frontier to Coblenz; and, furthermore, that he had set up an agency for corruption and espionage in Paris and was subsidizing aristocrat newspapers. The extraordinary criminal tribunal of August 17 punished a few subordinate agents, Laporte, Collenot d'Angremont, Cazotte, and de Rozoy. But when the Gironde became master of the Assembly, after August 10, it took no steps to settle the preliminaries of the suspended monarch's trial. Nobody was instructed to collect fresh evidence, carry out domiciliary visits, or search the houses of the accomplices of those who had already been condemned. It allowed the moment to go by when an important mass of proofs might have been got together.

Nor did the Gironde display any greater assiduity after the Convention had met. When, on October 16, Bourbotte expressed his astonishment at their hesitation in approaching the great question of the King's responsibility, Barbaroux, the president of the commission of twenty-four, which had charge of the documents bearing on the case, replied that they were bound to proceed in a deliberate and well-considered fashion, and proposed that the consideration of the forms to be prescribed for this great trial should be referred to the Legislative Committee. Manuel was afraid that even this procedure might be too rapid. He proposed that the question of the abolition of royalty should first be submitted to the people in their primary assemblies. He was supported by Lehardy; and Danton was forced to point out that, since the abolition of royalty was a constitutional question, the people could be consulted on the subject only by submitting the Constitution itself to them. It is obvious that the Gironde's one idea was to gain time. The trial of the King filled it with alarm. It affected to fear that the people might repudiate its action. Instead of taking up a frank and definite attitude and openly explaining the reasons for which it considered the trial inopportune, it took refuge in artful tricks of procedure, thus laying itself open to the accusations of its opponents.

Yet the Revolution had every interest in acting quickly and trying the King while the impressions of August 10 and of the victory of Valmy were still fresh. "The world"—to quote a historian—"would have been, so to speak, surprised by the rapidity of events, and paralysed as by a thunderbolt." But the Gironde, which had tried to prevent the insurrection of August 10, seemed to doubt both the Revolution and itself, and floundered in a morass of contradictions. It wanted to strike down the Montagnards as implicated in the September massacres, and for that very reason was prevented from making an appeal for pity in favour of the King.

On October 16 the Legislative Committee examined at length the question of the procedure to be followed in the trial of Louis XVI. By the end of the month, however, it did at last chose Mailhe, who was said to be in favour of the Montagnards, to report to the Assembly. Feeling that the Legislative Committee was slipping away from it, the Gironde at once attempted to forestall Mailhe's report. On November 6 Valazé presented a hasty and ill-digested report on the King's crimes in the name of the commission of twenty-four, which only adduced a few familiar and comparatively insignificant facts against him, but dilated at length upon a commercial correspondence carried on by Septeuil, the treasurer of the civil list, with some foreign bankers and merchants for the purchase and sale of various commodities, corn, coffee, sugar, and rum. It claimed to deduce from these commercial operations proof that Louis XVI had not hesitated to profit by the rise in the cost of living, and had added to the list of his crimes against the nation the unexpected offence of food-speculation. Even Petion could not help regarding the report as inadequate, and the Assembly was of the same way of thinking.

Mailhe was obviously inspired by other ideas than those of Valazé. His report of November 7 was well reasoned and clear, and brought the trial a long step nearer. Setting aside the objection of those who appealed to the Constitution of 1791 to justify their refusal to try the King, he deprived the King, who had violated it, of the benefit of this Constitution, which had, moreover, lapsed on the assembly of the Convention. The Constitution, he argued, could not be set up against the nation, which had resumed possession of its rights. Since August 10 Louis XVI had become an ordinary citizen, amenable to the penal code like other citizens. It was impossible, however, to have him tried by the ordinary courts, for the inviolability conferred on him by the Constitution had ceased to exist

255

only in relation to the nation as a whole. The Convention alone represented the nation and could alone try the first functionary of the State. There could be no question of sending the case before a special tribunal. The dogma of the separation of powers did not apply in this case. The Convention, having a mandate to give France a new Constitution, united in itself the entire authority of the nation. To refer the trial to a special tribunal would be an infringement of the Convention's position as the depositary of all power, a denial that it was the Convention, and a cause of embarrassment and hindrance to it. To maintain that the deputies could not try the case because they were both accusers and judges could not be admitted as an argument, for in the trial of Louis XVI every Frenchman was both judge and party in the case. "Must we, then," exclaimed a member of the Convention, "send for judges to some other planet?" Mailhe's conclusion was that the Convention should appoint three commissaries to collect proofs of the crimes imputed to Louis and to draw up his indictment. This amounted to saying that, in the eyes of the Legislative Committee, Valazé's report was as good as non-existent.

The debate opened on November 13 and dragged on for several days with numerous interruptions. The leaders of the Gironde avoided joining issue on the question of the king's inviolability They allowed speakers of the second rank to take their place in the debate: Morisson, who maintained that in the absence of any positive law the trial was impossible; Fauchet, who pointed out that the execution of Louis XVI would recoil upon the Revolution by setting up a revulsion of feeling due to pity; Rouzet, who courageously reminded the Assembly that Louis XVI had abolished serfdom on the royal domains, chosen enlightened ministers, and summoned the States General. Saint-Just made a crushing reply. He admitted that in strict law the king could not be tried. This was not a question of holding a trial, but of accomplishing a political act. Louis XVI was not a defendant, but an enemy. There was only one law that could be applied to him, the law of nations—in other words, the law of war. "Louis has combated the people and has been defeated. He is a barbàrian, a foreign prisoner of war; you have seen his perfidious designs; you have seen his army; he is the murderer of the Bastille, of Nancy, of the Champ de Mars, of Tournay, of the Tuileries. What enemy, what foreigner, has done you more harm?"

Saint-Just's speech produced all the more impression for being delivered by a man hardly past his first youth and absolutely unknown till that day. The Assembly was about to vote in accordance with Mailhe's conclusions, and proclaim itself a court of justice, when Buzot, who had so far kept silence, intervened with a characteristic motion. He suddenly proposed that the Assembly should annul its decree of November 13, by which it had decided to settle first of all the question whether Louis XVI could be tried. "You are speaking," he said, "only of Louis XVI, and not of his family; now, for my part, I am a republican and will have nothing to do with the race of the Bourbons." In other words, Buzot's idea was to confuse the debate by introducing the question of the trial of Marie Antoinette, and also that of Philippe Égalité, who had a seat in the Mountain. It was an astute diversion, the only object of which can have been to confuse the issue, and, under the pretext of strict legality, to save Louis XVI by broadening the basis of the accusation.

It is a strange thing, and gives food for thought, that Danton supported Buzot's motion, which was carried. Henceforward the debate would no longer be confined to the question of inviolability, but would deal with the substance as well as the form of the trial.

Danton's attitude is explained by the revelations in Théodore Lameth's memoirs. Théodore Lameth had left London in the middle of October and, braving the terrible penalties of the law against the émigrés, had returned to Paris to have an interview with Danton, who was under obligations to him, with regard to the means of saving Louis XVI by his co-operation. Danton promised to do everything in his power to prevent the trial, for, as he said, "if he is tried, if the trial begins, he is a dead man."

But the calculations of Buzot and Danton were defeated by a dramatic event which reopened the whole question—the discovery on November 20 of the iron safe. This was a secret cupboard constructed by Gamain, the locksmith, in a wall of the Tuileries, by Louis XVI's orders. Following on information received from Gamain, who imagined that he had been poisoned by the royalists, Roland in his arrogance committed a terrible imprudence. He had the safe opened without any witnesses present, and himself brought to the Assembly the documents contained in it, thus exposing himself to the suspicion of having gone through them previously and destroyed those concerning his friends the Girondins. In the iron safe was discovered the King's correspondence with Mirabeau, with Talon, the chief of his secret police, with the Bishop of Clermont, his spiritual director, with Dumouriez, with Lafayette, with Talleyrand, and with others besides. The Jacobins smashed the bust of Mirabeau which adorned their hall, and the Convention had a veil thrown over his effigy. Talon, who was absent on a secret mission to Pitt, with which he had been entrusted by Danton, was cited before the courts, but he was out of reach. His agents and relatives, Dufresne Saint-Léon and Sainte-Foy, were arrested, but no hurry was made to try them, for their accomplices, and especially Dumouriez, would necessarily have been implicated. Brissot hastened to exonerate the latter in his newspaper, and Rühl shortly afterwards whitewashed him in the Assembly.

It was now becoming more and more impossible to avoid the trial of Louis XVI. On November 21 the Assembly set up a fresh commission of twelve to make an inventory of the documents in the iron safe. This commission was chosen by lot, and Girondin influence on it was weaker than in the previous commission of twenty-four. Besides, public opinion had been worked up to a high pitch of excitement by the mystery and was beginning to make itself felt. On December 2 delegates from the forty-eight Parisian sections came to the bar to protest against delaying the trial: "Do not let vain terror cause you to draw back. Now that our armies are marching from triumph to triumph, what do you fear? Are not the crimes of Louis the perjured manifest enough yet? Why give the factions time to recover?" The sections were followed by the Commune, which next presented to the Assembly a violent denunciation of Roland, who had had a chance to make away with part of the documents removed from the Tuileries—Roland, who, at the expense of the Republic, was circulating in the departments a number of libels slandering Paris. The Montagnards, who had hitherto had to remain on the defensive, now began to attack.

The Gironde could no longer hope to confuse the trial of the King with that of the Bourbons in general. On December 3 Barbaroux himself proposed that Louis XVI should at last be put on trial. Robespierre then took up Saint-Just's argument, amplifying it and supporting it by political considerations: "The King is not a defendant; you are not judges. You are not, you cannot be anything but statesmen and representatives of the nation. You have not to pronounce a verdict for or against a man, but to adopt a measure of public safety, to perform an act of national foresight. A dethroned king in a republic can only serve one of two purposes: to disturb the tranquillity of the State and upset liberty, or else to establish both of them firmly at the same time. . . . Now, what course of action does a sane policy dictate with a view to consolidating the infant Republic? It is to stamp indelibly upon our hearts a contempt for royalty and to paralyse all the partisans of the King. . . ." Robespierre next described the growing reaction, which he ascribed to the calculated delay in trying the King, and roundly accused the Gironde of ulterior motives of a royalist nature: "What other means could they employ if they desired to restore the monarchy?"

The attack was so direct that once again the Gironde yielded and re-sorted to stratagems. True to his demagogical tactics, the astute Buzot pro-posed on the following day that, in order to avert all suspicion, the Con-vention should decree that "whosoever shall propose to re-establish kings or royalty in France shall be punished by death. . . . I add: *'under what-soever guise this may be,'* and I demand an oral vote by roll-call." This was an insinuation that there were some in the Convention who desired to restore the monarchy, under some guise or another, and at the same time it was a justification of the dilatoriness of the Gironde. For what would have been the good, it was hinted, of hastening to behead the King if his death only played into the hands of those whose idea it was to revive the monarchy under the form of a dictatorship? On the pretext of respecting the sovereignty of the people, Merlin of Thionville was imprudent enough to propose to add the following reservation to Buzot's motion: "unless it be in the primary assemblies"; upon which Guadet seized the opportunity of defining Buzot's terrible insinuation still more clearly and emphasizing its gravity. He saw in Merlin's motion proof that a plan actually existed "for replacing one despotism by another; I mean to say, for setting up a despot under whose ægis those who had supported him in this usurpation would be sure to obtain not only impunity for their misdeeds, but the cer-tainty of being able to commit others." The whole of the Mountain was thus accused of veiled royalism, and it was represented that the most urgent question was not the trial of the dethroned King, but the sending to the scaffold of royalists disguised as revolutionaries. As Robespierre per-sisted in demanding the immediate trial of Louis XVI, Buzot replied that those who wanted to rush the trial through were no doubt interested in preventing the King from speaking. The object of this was nothing less than to represent Robespierre as a timid accomplice of Louis XVI. That day Buzot triumphed; his motion was carried.

But on December 6 the Montagnards had their revenge. It was de-cided that the commission of twelve, which had already been entrusted with the task of looking through the papers in the iron safe, should be strengthened by nine new members, chosen, three from the commission of twenty-four, three from the Legislative Committee, and three from that of General Security; and that this new commission of twenty-one should submit to the Convention as soon as possible the draft indictment of Louis XVI. The Convention further decreed that all voting in the course of the trial should take place orally and by roll-call. It was Marat, sup-ported by Quinette, who voiced this proposal, which was an enormous ad-vantage for the party in favour of death. The Convention would have to vote in the presence of the public in the galleries, and under its pressure! There was no debate, for not a single Girondin dared to admit that he was afraid of a public vote.

On December 9 Guadet attempted a fresh diversion. He proposed to summon the primary assemblies, "to make a pronouncement as to the recall of members who had betrayed the nation." But Prieur of Marne, supported by Barère, obtained the annulment of the motion, which had at first been carried by acclamation. Had it been carried, the Gironde would have had deputies voting with the Mountain at its mercy, for it could have suspended over them the threat of being recalled by the primary assemblies.

By December 10 Robert Lindet, as spokesman of the commission of twenty-one, laid before the Convention his report on the crimes of Louis XVI. It was a sort of historical review of the whole Revolution, in which prominence was given to the duplicity of the Crown at every critical moment. On the following day the King was examined by Barère. He confined himself to meeting the questions put to him by the plea of a lapse of memory, or else with a blank denial, when he did not shelter himself behind the responsibility of his ministers. Valazé next showed him the documents bearing his signature upon which the prosecution was to be based, but he refused to recognize them as genuine. He denied that he had caused the iron safe to be constructed. He would not identify the key which opened it, and which came from his valet Thierry. This obvious lack of good faith destroyed the favourable impression which had been produced at first by his good humour and evident self-possession.

But the more Louis XVI's peril increased, the more ingenious were the means devised by the Girondins for averting or adjourning it. On December 16 Buzot tried a fresh manœuvre: in order to prevent for ever the restoration of royalty he proposed to banish the Bourbons, and the Orleans branch in particular, which "for the very reason that it was more beloved is all the more disquieting to liberty."

This was a bold and deep move! If the Mountain rejected Buzot's motion, the accusation of Orleanism brought against it would gain credit. If it sacrificed Philippe Égalité, it proclaimed abroad that Louis XVI was not the only danger to the Republic and admitted that the Girondins had defended republican liberty better than they had themselves. Besides, what would be the use of Louis XVI's death if the royalist peril continued to exist in the person of Égalité?

The exasperated Montagnards rose in their wrath. Chabot found an apt argument: Philippe Égalité, he said, was a representative of the people. To banish him would be to violate the sovereignty of the people in his person, it would be to mutilate the Convention. Saint-Just unmasked the secret thoughts of the Gironde: "They are at present affecting to connect the fate of Orleans with that of the King; this is perhaps in order to save them all, or at least to soften the verdict on Louis Capet." The Jacobins and the Parisian sections openly took sides against Buzot's motion, in spite of Robespierre, who would have liked it to be carried in order to dissociate the Mountain from the Orleanist cause. The King's trial had to take its course. In trying to obstruct it the Girondins had by an insincere policy only succeeded in compromising themselves to no purpose.

On December 26 Louis XVI appeared before the Convention for the second time. His counsel, De Sèze, read out a well-reasoned, well-turned, conscientious, but not very brilliant pleading. In the first part of his speech he laid stress on proving that everything to do with the trial was exceptional and illegal—as he did without much difficulty. In the second part he examined the counts in the accusation, trying to screen the person of the monarch from responsibility. In a pathetic peroration he eulogized his virtues and recalled the benefits of the early years of his reign. Lanjuinais courageously attempted to take advantage of the emotion which he had aroused to obtain the rejection of the indictment. But he did so clumsily, alluding ironically to "the conspirators who have declared themselves to be the actors in the illustrious day of August 10." The Mountain taxed him with royalism and he withdrew his words.

The Girondin leaders no more ventured to oppose the death penalty directly than they had dared to compromise themselves by defining their position in the question of inviolability. They left to minor speakers with more courage than themselves the dangerous honour of proposing banishment or internment and took refuge in the subterfuge of an appeal to the people, which they endeavoured to justify by theoretical and practical arguments. Vergniaud appealed to the Constitution of 1791, which had made the king's person inviolable and maintained that the people alone could deprive him of this inviolability. But Vergniaud forgot that the people had not been consulted as to this Constitution. Salle pointed out that the death of the King would alienate foreign nations and rouse against France even the peoples who had been united to the Republic by her victories. "In our debates," said Brissot, "we do not keep Europe sufficiently in view." Brissot and Salle forgot that a few months earlier they had provoked the war and hailed the rapid progress of revolutionary ideas. But why did they adopt this subterfuge of an appeal to the people if they believed that the death of Louis XVI would rouse Europe against the Republic? Why did they not say clearly that the King's life was necessary for the defence of France? What a strange idea, to submit a European war to a plebiscite of the French people!

But the Gironde relied upon more than speeches and votes to save Louis XVI. Lebrun, the Minister for Foreign Affairs, who had Girondin sympathies, had assured the neutral powers that the Convention would display clemency and magnanimity. On December 28 he announced to the Assembly that he had succeeded in bringing to a happy issue the negotiations with Spain for the purpose of obtaining her neutrality and reciprocal disarmament on the frontier. He added that it was thanks to the fact that the King of Spain took a keen interest in the fate of his cousin, the ex-King of France, that he had arrived at this result. He next read to the Assembly a letter from Ocariz, the Spanish chargé d'affaires, beseeching the Convention to perform an act of generosity in order to maintain peace. It was a tactless letter, in which he lectured a touchy and proud Assembly, and it was referred without debate to the Diplomatic Committee.

On December 21 the English Liberals Lansdowne, Fox, and Sheridan, with whom the Girondins were in correspondence, requested Pitt in the House of Commons to intervene in favour of the King of France. And two days later, at the Jacobins, François Robert, a friend of Danton's, suggested that it would be good policy "to adjourn the condemnation of Louis Capet."

We now know from the memoirs of Théodore Lameth, the letters of Miles (an agent of Pitt), the testimony of Talon, and the memoirs of Godoy that vigorous efforts were made to obtain the assistance of the European governments on the one hand, and to buy votes in favour of Louis XVI on the other. In 1803 Talon made a deposition before a tribunal appointed by the Consulate, to the effect that "Danton had accepted the mission of securing the safety of the whole royal family by a decree of deportation." "But," he said, "the foreign powers, with the exception of Spain, refused to make the pecuniary sacrifices asked for by Danton."

The threats from foreign powers and the corrupt intrigues failed to carry away the majority in the Assembly. In a fine speech delivered on December 28 Robespierre set forth the dangers to which the country would be exposed by an appeal to the people. What! he argued, was this the moment to consult the primary assemblies, in the middle of the war, when the royalists were already recovering their position and plotting in the west? Who would attend these assemblies? Certainly not the workers, absorbed in their daily toil and incapable as yet of following long and complicated debates. And while Frenchmen were arguing and squabbling from one end of the country to the other, the enemy would be advancing. And, as though Robespierre had divined the attempts at corruption which were being secretly made, he denounced the manœuvres of scoundrels and uttered his famous phrase: "Virtue was always in a minority upon earth." As for the arguments based on the diplomatic situation, he replied that the more the Revolution seemed to be afraid, the more it would be threatened and attacked: "Victory will decide whether you are rebels or benefactors of humanity, and it is the greatness of your character which will determine the victory!"

The Mountain was not content merely to refute from the tribune the idea of an appeal to the people. In order to ruin the prestige of the Girondins in the eyes of the independent deputies it disclosed the fact that three of their leaders, Guadet, Gensonné, and Vergniaud, had compromised themselves with the Court on the very eve of August 10. This revelation was made from the tribune on January 3 by the deputy Gasparin, a friend of the painter Boze, who had acted as intermediary between the Girondins and Thierry, the King's valet. Boze was summoned to the bar of the Convention and confirmed Gasparin's account.

On the following day, Jaunary 4, Barère, perhaps out of a desire to remove the suspicions which had been aroused against him by the documents in the iron safe, dealt the death-blow to the idea of an appeal to the people by a criticism which was the more formidable in that it came from a man who denied that he was a Montagnard and expressed in his soft voice his regrets for agreeing with Marat for once. "A law," he said, "may be submitted for the ratification of the people, but the trial of the King is not a law. . . . The trial is in reality an act of public safety or a measure of general security, but an act of public safety is not submitted for the ratification of the people."

The voting began on January 14 and dragged on interminably, for it took place orally and by roll-call, and every deputy was given full latitude to expound the reasons for his vote. The vote on the question of the King's guilt was unanimous, save for a few abstentions. On the question of the appeal to the people the Girondins were beaten by 424 votes to 287. A number of dissentients of their own party—Carra, Boyer-Fonfrède, Condorcet, Daunou, Debry, Ducos, La Révellière, Mercier, and Paine—had voted with the Mountain. The partisans of the appeal to the people came chiefly from the departments of the west. In the decisive vote on the penalty, 361 deputies voted unconditionally for death, and 26 also voted for death, adding a query as to whether there was not a case for considering the question of granting a reprieve; there were 334 votes in favour of detention, imprisonment in chains, or death on certain conditions. The absolute majority numbered 361. The 26 deputies who had expressed a desire that the question of a reprieve should be considered were asked whether their vote was dependent upon the examination into the question of a reprieve. The deputy Mailhe, who had first thought of this reservation, repeated what he had said word for word. The others declared that their vote in favour of death was independent of their request for a reprieve. Thus the votes in favour of death were increased to 387.

It was suspected that Mailhe had accepted a sum of 30,000 francs from Ocariz, the Spanish minister, for his amendment, with the mental reservation that he would interpret his idea according to the turn taken by the voting. Of the Girondins, Vergniaud, Guadet, Buzot, and Petion voted with Mailhe; Ducos, Boyer-Fonfrède, Carra, Lasource, Debry, Isnard, and La Révellière voted for death pure and simple.

Buzot, Condorcet, Brissot, and Barbaroux proposed to postpone the execution of judgment in view of the external situation. Barère replied that this postponement would reopen the question of the appeal to the people, that it placed the Revolution in a position of weakness with regard to foreign countries, and that it prolonged internal dissensions: and the reprieve was rejected by 380 votes to 310.

On January 20 the infuriated Girondins, on the motion of Guadet, obtained a decree in favour of prosecuting the authors of the September massacres. But on the following day the decree was repealed under the influence of the emotion caused by the assassination of Le Pelletier de Saint-Fargeau, a member of the Convention, by Pâris, a former member of the King's Gardes du Corps.

The assassination of Le Pelletier took place on the day before the King's execution and calmed the obscure misgivings which the more timid regicides may have conceived. It was a tragic rejoinder to the slanders of the Girondins, who for three months past had been abusing the Montagnards as assassins. "It is these assassins who are being murdered," wrote Saint-André. An imposing funeral was given to the "martyr of liberty," and his bust soon adorned their assembly-halls and civic festivals.

Except for the assassination of Le Pelletier, an act of impotent despair, the royalists had taken no serious steps to save Louis XVI. Pamphlets, topical articles, attacks on trees of liberty, a mysterious plot by the Baron de Batz to save the King on the very day he was led to the scaffold, a more serious plot organized in Brittany during the last few months by the adventurous Marquis de la Rouarie, who died before carrying his projects into execution, and, finally, some vague intrigues on the part of Dumouriez, who stayed in Paris from January 1 to 24—this was all that happened.

The assassination of Le Pelletier and the execution of Louis XVI marked the beginning of a fresh period in the history of the Convention. "The reign of political scoundrels is at an end," wrote Le Bas to his father on the very day of the King's death. And on February 19 he added, by way of amplifying his idea: "For my part, I believe that this act (the execution of the King) has saved the Republic and is a guarantee to us of the energy of the Convention. . . ." All the representatives of the people who had voted for his death had now a personal interest in preventing at all costs a restoration that would cause them to expiate their vote dearly. They threw themselves into the struggle against monarchical Europe with redoubled energy. "It is now," said Le Bas on January 21, "that the representatives of the people are going to display their greatness; we must conquer or die; all patriots feel the necessity of this." He had also written on the day before: "We have now started on our way; the roads behind us have been torn up, we must go on whether we will or no, and now, above all, is the time when we may say: 'We must live in freedom or die.' "

In short, the death of Louis XVI was a blow at the traditional and mystic prestige of royalty itself. The Bourbons might return, but in the heart of the nation they would no longer be surrounded by the aureole of divine right.

CHAPTER V

Finance and the Rise in the Cost of Living

I T was the social policy of the Gironde, even more than its equivocal attitude towards the trial of the King, that ruined its popularity with the masses. Its policy had been purely negative, and consisted in the main in the defence of property, in the narrow and absolute sense of the word.

The victories upon which the Gironde had reckoned to solve the economic crisis had brought no solution whatsoever. The few contributions levied by Custine on the Rhine cities were a mere drop in the ocean of expenditure. On November 13 Cambon stated that for the month of November the estimated receipts were 28,000,000 and the expenditure 138,-000,000, leaving a deficit of 110,000,000. On the same day Jacob Dupont made a statement showing that out of the estimated revenue of 300,000,000 from the *contribution foncière* and the *contribution mobilière* for 1791, only 124,000,000 had come in. In December 1792 the sums paid into the Treasury amounted to 39,000,000, and the expenditure on the war alone amounted to 228,000,000. How were they to fill this abyss, which was constantly growing deeper?

Had the Gironde not been animated by a class policy, it would have occurred to it to apportion the cost of the war according to accumulated property; it would have proceeded to raise loans and have voted fresh taxation. It would have tried at all costs to check the issue of assignats, which had as its consequence a rapid rise in the cost of living. Marat, Saint-Just, Chabot, and Jacob Dupont advised this policy of healthy finance, but they were not listened to.

The leading financial expert in the Assembly, both then and for a long time after, was the merchant Cambon, who hated the Commune and anarchists and had recourse to the easiest solution, the printing of assignats. On November 13 he proposed, in opposition to Jacob Dupont, to decrease the existing taxes, abolish the *impôt mobilier* (tax calculated on the basis of rental) and the *patente* (commercial tax), and reduce the total of the *contribution foncière* (tax on real property) by forty millions! It is true that, as a set-off against this, he wanted to do away with the State pro-

266

vision for public worship, the whole burden of which would consequently fall upon the lower classes, for at that time the people could not dispense with priests.

Jacob Dupont and the Montagnards were in favour of withdrawing the assignats from circulation by shortening the long period allowed to buyers of national property for completing their purchase; of redeeming the debt by means of *quittances de finances,* which were to be used only for the purchase of the property of *émigrés;* of raising forced loans, graduated according to the capacity to pay; and of insisting that the *contribution foncière* should be paid in kind. But this policy of deflation was not even seriously considered.

Most of the property of the Church, estimated at a value of 2,500,000,000 livres, had already been sold. But there remained the property of the *émigrés,* estimated by some at a value of at least 2,000,000,000, the forests, valued at 1,200,000,000, and the property of the Order of Malta, valued at 400,000,000. This represented a reserve of more than 3,000,000,-000 livres. By October 5, 1792, assignats to the value of 2,589,000,000 had already been issued on the security of the property of the clergy; 617,000,000 had returned to the Treasury and been burnt; so by that time the assignats in circulation amounted to 1,972,000,000. On October 17 Cambon obtained a decree authorizing a fresh issue, thus raising the amount in circulation to 2,400,000,000. Fresh issues followed. At the moment of the declaration of war the Legislative Assembly had already been forced to suspend the redemption of the old pre-Revolutionary debt, with the exception of small amounts, of less than 10,000 livres, amounting to a total of not more than 6,000,000 monthly. The property-owning classes, who had taken such a leading part in bringing about the Revolution, were sacrificed to the exigencies of war. But they nearly all lived in Paris, and the Gironde did not trouble much about them, preferring to advance the interests of trade and agriculture.

The paper currency was doing its work, and wage-earners were suffering. The average wage was twenty sous a day in the country and forty in Paris. In some places—Montpellier, for instance—bread now cost eight sous a pound, and all other commodities had risen proportionately.

Not only was bread dear, but the inhabitants of the towns had difficulty in obtaining it. Yet there was no shortage of grain. The evidence is unanimous that there had been a good harvest. But the landowners and farmers were in no hurry to take their grain to market and exchange it for a paper currency which they distrusted. The great upheaval of August 10, the trial of the King, the threat of an agrarian revolution, exaggerated to excess by the Girondin press, and, lastly, the foreign war—all these abnormal events, following close upon one another, filled landowners with vague misgivings. They jealously hoarded their grain, which was a substantial form of wealth, far superior to all monetary tokens.

The movement of grain had ceased, and the large towns were short of bread. At the end of September Rouen had flour enough for only three days, and the municipality was forced to commandeer grain from the army storehouses. It asked the Convention for powers to raise a loan of a million livres to purchase grain abroad. The loan was authorized on October 8, and was to be raised from those of the inhabitants who paid a rent of at least five hundred livres. At Lyons thirty thousand silk weavers were unemployed, their looms standing idle owing to the falling off of the sale of silks, and in November the city had to be authorized to raise a loan of three millions. Even in the country districts the agricultural labourers had difficulty in obtaining bread, for the farmers preferred to keep their corn in the ear rather than thresh it. Since all movements of grain had stopped, the prices varied enormously from one department to another. At the beginning of October a *setier* (220 pounds) was sold for 25 livres in the department of Aube, 43 in that of Ain,.53 in Basses-Alpes and Aveyron, 26 in Eure, 58 in Hérault, 42 in Gers, 34 in Haute-Marne, 47 in Loir-et-Cher. Every region isolated itself from the rest, and clung jealously to its own produce. If Rouen went hungry, it was because Havre had intercepted the supplies intended for it.

The legislation arising out of the crisis which followed the capture of Verdun made it possible to override obstruction on the part of landowners by ordering returns of available supplies to be made, and giving the authorities power to commandeer them. But Roland, the minister whose duty it was to apply these laws, was an orthodox economist, who regarded any intervention on the part of the authorities as unsound and all regulations and requisitions as an infringement of the rights of property and a criminal concession to anarchy. Not only did he take no steps to put them into execution, but he discredited them by his vehement attacks and paralysed them, as a preliminary to obtaining their abrogation.

Anyway these laws were inadequate, for they had set up no central organ for distributing the available grain between the departments which produced it and those in which there was a shortage. The departments carried on their own administration like so many little republics and often closed their frontiers. Hence the rapid rise in prices.

The Girondins put forward no remedy for the sufferings of the lower classes. It was one of their tenets that free competition was a sovereign panacea. If prices rose, the workmen must obtain an increase of wages. But the workmen were not organized and could not bring sufficient pressure to bear upon their employers. They were reduced to begging for increased wages as a charity, and sent imploring appeals to the public authorities. They could not imagine that the new authorities elected by their votes would be more callous to their sufferings than the old ones, who had been in the habit of intervening in such circumstances.

The crisis was more acute in the towns than elsewhere. Where they were administered by working-class municipalities, these sought every means of devising palliatives. In Paris the entrenchment works ordered after August 10 were intended as much for charitable as for military purposes, but they were carried out at the expense of the Treasury. Under the pretext of economy the Girondins began, as early as September 25, by ordering that work for a daily wage should be replaced by piece-work. They next reduced wages; but the workmen protested, on the ground of the cost of living, and were supported by the Commune. Thereupon the Girondins, and Rouyer and Kersaint in particular, denounced the entrenchment gangs as "a hotbed of intrigues and cabals, the resort of perfidious agitators." On October 15 the Convention voted that work should be stopped and the workmen discharged.

At Lyons the crisis was much more serious than in Paris, and in November Nivière-Chol, *procureur* to the Commune, though a friend of Chalier and a Montagnard, used his influence with the manufacturers to make them reopen the factories. Failing in this, on November 21 he asked the Convention for an advance of three millions to restart a few looms for manufacturing stuffs on behalf of the nation. The three commissaries sent down by the Convention, Vitet, Alquier and Boissy d'Anglas, were quite willing to transmit his request, but declared that the sum demanded was excessive; and the Convention refused to make any grant.

The Gironde, which formed the Government, remained unmoved by the complaints of the workers. It justified its inaction, or hostility, by an argument which was repeated a thousand times from the tribune or in the press: the originators of the complaints were merely "anarchists," or deluded persons led astray by them. Brissot attributed the cost of grain "to the agitators alone," in which he was merely echoing Roland, the whole of whose social policy consisted in meeting starving mobs with bayonets.

But the workers could contrast their own destitution with the insolent and ostentatious luxury of the new rich. Now was the time when complaints against army-contractors were pouring in on every side, when the honest Pache denounced the scandalous contracts granted by his predecessor Servan to the notorious Abbé d'Espagnac, a protégé of Danton and Dumouriez, to the Jew Jacob Benjamin, to Lajard, Fabre d'Eglantine, Cerfbeer, etc. "The Revolution," cried Cambon on November 1, "has affected everybody except financiers and speculators. This rapacious tribe is even worse than under the old regime. We have food commissaries (*commissaires ordonnateurs*) and army commissaries whose brigandage is appalling. I shuddered with horror when I saw contracts for supplying the army of the south, in which bacon (*lard*) was thirty-four sous a pound." The Convention had a few of these traders arrested, but most of them, d'Espagnac in particular, were at once released. The sight of the impunity enjoyed by these new contractors was bound to aggravate the popular discontent.

From the early autumn onward there were serious disturbances both in the country districts and in the towns: at Lyons, where the three commissaries sent by the Assembly had to raise a company of paid *gendarmerie* and make some arrests; at Orleans, where at the end of September a porter was killed and seven houses sacked on the occasion of the departure of a load of grain for Nantes; in October at Versailles, Étampes, and Rambouillet, and in November throughout the whole region of the Beauce, gradually extending from province to province. On November 22 the wood-cutters of the forest of Vibraye, in the department of Sarthe, stirred up the workmen at the glass-works of Montmirail and went round the neighbouring market towns with them, fixing the prices of food-stuffs. During the following days bands headed by the local authorities extended these operations throughout the whole of Sarthe, Eure, Eure-et-Loir, Loir-et-Cher, Indre-et-Loire, and Loiret. On November 28 a band three thousand strong, led by a troop of horsemen, appeared at the market of Vendôme and proclaimed a tariff of fixed prices. On the same day the departmental administration and municipality of Le Mans set their signatures to a tariff. The same thing happened at Nogent-le-Rotrou, La Ferté-Bernard, Brou, Cloyes, Mer, Bonnétable, Saint-Calais, and Blois. At Blois the price of wheat was fixed at twenty sous a bushel of twelve pounds, rye at sixteen sous, barley at twelve sous, butter at ten sous a pound, and a dozen eggs at five sous. Those who drew up the tariff wore oak-leaves on their hats and danced round the trees of liberty to shouts of *"Vive la Nation!* The price of wheat is coming down!" At the beginning of December from ten to twelve thousand men marched on Tours, but dispersed on receiving a promise that the municipality and departmental assembly would support their claims.

On November 29 the three commissaries sent by the Convention to Eure-et-Loir—Birotteau, Maure, and Lecointe-Puyraveau were surrounded by six thousand armed men at the big market at Courville and threatened with being thrown into the river or hanged unless they sanctioned a tariff of prices not only for wheat and barley, but for candles, beef, cotton and linen stuffs, shoes, and iron. The commissaries yielded; but on their return the Girondins poured scorn upon them. Petion raised a scare of anarchy and the agrarian law, condemned all fixed prices as inevitably leading to a shortage, and called for prompt and vigorous measures of repression. In spite of Buzot and Robespierre, who wanted the repressive measures to be entrusted to civil commissaries, and gentle methods tried first, the Convention decided that the troops should be led by a general. It also censured the action of the three deputies in yielding to the rioters, and order was restored in the Beauce by measures of repression as vigorous as those of the preceding April.

How could the mass of labourers in the towns and country districts fail to bear the Gironde a grudge on account of its class policy? But it is significant that even the Mountain very nearly became suspect in the eyes of the obscure leaders who were the mouthpieces of the popular claims. When Goujon, the *procureur général syndic* of Seine-et-Oise, came to the Convention on November 19 and in the name of the electoral assembly of that department demanded not only a tariff of prices, but the setting up of a central food-control department, his petition met with but little support in the ranks of the Mountain. Fayau did indeed support the creation of a central food-control department, but the Montagnards were not at all anxious to provide their enemy Roland, the Minister of the Interior, with such a powerful weapon; and in voicing their desire for the rejection of the proposal, Thuriot reminded the Jacobins of the precedents of Terray and Necker.

Not a single deputy of the Mountain had demanded the fixing of prices, not even Fayau, in spite of his words on November 19: "If the rich, who are none too fond of the Revolution, could close their granaries for a week, France would be in bondage. . . . And then what sort of a republic would this be, where the lives of the poor were in the power of the rich?" Nor was Beffroy in favour of it, though on December 8 he delivered a vigorous refutation of the liberal theories of Turgot and Adam Smith; nor even Levasseur (of Sarthe), though he had said on December 2: "When a town is besieged, the authorities have certainly the right to force those inhabitants who have several guns to share them with their fellow-citizens, so as to contribute to their common defence; and yet when citizens are threat-

271

ened with starvation, the authorities cannot force the farmers to sell their surplus supplies!" Even Robespierre was against it, though on the same day he had laid down the following principles: "The food necessary to man is sacred as life itself. Everything that is necessary for preserving life is common property. Only the surplus belongs to the individual." The Montagnards had confined themselves to demanding the maintenance of the regulations of September, and they were defeated. The Convention had let itself be convinced by the Girondin speakers, Féraud, Serre, Creuzé-Latouche, who had denounced the manœuvres of anarchists and argued that the food-shortage had been caused by the census of supplies and the requisitions, which had alarmed the farmers. If the farmers were not protected against this inquisition, said Creuzé-Latouche, it would no longer be possible to sell the property of the *émigrés*, which was the only cover for the new assignats; and this argument decided the voting.

During the whole of this crisis the Jacobins had maintained a sort of prudent and cautious neutrality. When, on November 29, the Commune and sections of Paris demanded a fixed tariff of prices, they refused to express an opinion. And so it is not surprising that the popular agitators bore them a grudge. On December 1 the Abbé Jacques Roux, the mouthpiece of the small artisans of the Parisian section of Gravilliers, made a violent speech on the "trial of Louis the Last, the prosecution of speculators, monopolists, and traitors," in which he did not hesitate to attack the Convention as a whole and denounce what he called "senatorial despotism." "The despotism which is propagated under the government of the many, senatorial despotism, is as terrible as the sceptre of kings, for it tends to rivet chains upon the people without their knowledge, since they are degraded and subjugated by the very laws which they are themselves supposed to dictate." And Jacques Roux called upon the Convention to put down food-speculation and lower the cost of living. His speech had such a success that the section of the Observatory debated whether it should not have it read out twice a week for a month.

Nor was Jacques Roux an isolated case. A young post-office clerk, Jean Varlet, who was in comparatively easy circumstances and had had a good record at the Collège d'Harcourt, was also inflaming the passions of the crowd. As early as August 6, 1792 he had proposed laws against food-speculators and demanded that the revolutionary currency should be compulsorily accepted as legal tender. A little later he set up a movable platform a few steps from the meeting-place of the Assembly, on the terrace of the Feuillants, from which he harangued the crowd. The discourses of this "apostle of Liberty," as he called himself, soon became antiparliamentary in character. Like Jacques Roux, he accused the Convention, Montagnards and Girondins alike, of forming an oligarchy of politicians who were wresting the sovereignty of the people to their own exclusive profit. When, at the end of December, the Jacobins refused him a hearing, he left the club; he blamed them for failing to instruct the people and for not attending the fraternal societies formed by the artisans. He now called himself the "apostle of Equality." The rioters of the Beauce had already repeated the cry that the deputies in the Convention were all rich and that their wealth was obtained by robbing the national treasury.

The propaganda of Varlet and Jacques Roux—the *"Enragés"* (rabid fanatics), as they were called—made rapid progress in the Parisian sections, as is shown by their petitions, which became increasingly frequent and threatening, and by their pamphlets against Roland, whom they held responsible for the cost of living. One of these pamphlets spoke of Madame Roland as if she had been another Marie Antoinette: "To murder the good French people with the sword of famine is, I say, a pleasing idea in which she delights, and the honest National Convention, which shares her thirst for blood, grants this monster, this second Galigaï [1] twelve millions to buy grain abroad, while by all accounts France has an abundance of it."

The advocates of fixed prices, the Enragés, were no longer isolated, as they had been during the previous period. They communicated with one another between town and town and were obviously trying to arrange concerted action. Those of Lyons were in frequent contact with those of Paris. Dodieu, who as early as August had proposed to set up a special tribunal for punishing food-speculators, came to Paris in October and handed in a memorial, which the Convention rejected without more ado. In December another of them, Hidins, the national commissary attached to the district tribunal, submitted to the Commune of Lyons a draft ordinance, consisting of twenty-five articles, abolishing the grain-trade, creating a national department for food-control, nationalizing mills, and regulating bakeries. The Jacobins of Lyons adopted his views and in January sent several of their members as delegates to Paris to demand of the Convention that prices should be fixed for all commodities of prime necessity.

At Orleans one Taboureau, secretary to the section of the Hôpital, played the same part as Dodieu and Hidins at Lyons, or Varlet and Jacques Roux in Paris. After the disorders in the Beauce a warrant was issued for his arrest, but on the day when the *juge de paix* tried to arrest

---

[1] Léonora Galigaï, wife of the Italian adventurer Concini, a favorite of Marie de' Medici, notorious for her rapacity and intrigues. She was accused of witchcraft and burnt in 1617.

him, two hundred persons assembled to defend him and he succeeded in escaping.

It is true that the Enragés had as yet no newspapers at their command. Silvain Maréchal supported them only intermittently in the *Révolutions de Paris,* Marat was hostile to them, and Hébert maintained a cautious attitude and made advances to the Mountain. But the Enragés had the secret instinct of the mob on their side, and the continuation, or rather aggravation, of the economic crisis was working in their favour. In their struggle against the Gironde the Montagnards were obliged to make concessions to them and throw them an occasional sop. On January 6, 1793 one of them, the deputy Duroy, declared before the Convention that Roland's economic policy had been a complete failure: "The price of commodities has not decreased. On the other hand, it has unfortunately gone on increasing, and the decree which you voted [on December 8] has not had the expected effect. Wheat, which is extremely dear in my department [Eure], was worth only thirty livres before; it is now worth thirty-six." Even the Girondins themselves defended Roland only feebly. When he resigned on January 22, 1793, it was hardly to be anticipated that his policy of economic non-intervention would survive him. The Convention appointed as his successor the prudent Garat, who was always anxious to avoid compromising himself and ready to rally to the strongest side. The cost of living was to contribute largely towards the fall of the Gironde.

CHAPTER VI

The Conquest of the Natural Frontiers

THE Gironde had been kept in power by the successes of the armies. As soon as these were lacking and were succeeded by reverses, it was ruined. Valmy was followed by a series of victories which carried the French arms with unprecedented rapidity as far as the Alps and the Rhine.

Montesquiou entered Savoy during the night of September 21–2 with eighteen thousand men, largely volunteers, and without striking a blow took possession of the redoubts of Chapareillan, the castle of Les Marches, and the fortress of Montmélian. "The progress of my army," he reported to the Convention on September 25, "is a triumph. In both country and town the people troop out to meet us; the tricolour cockade is worn on all sides." He was not so much conquering the country as bringing it freedom.

The aristocrats of Geneva were alarmed, and appealed for help to the cantons of Zurich and Bern, which sent them reinforcements of 1,600 men. The Executive Council, prompted by Clavière, whom the Genevan aristocrats had banished ten years before, at once ordered Montesquiou to call upon the free city to send the men of Bern and Zurich back again. On the motion of Brissot and Guadet the Convention confirmed the order of the Executive Council, in spite of the opposition of Tallien, Barère, Danton, Garran de Coulon, and even Petion himself, after two doubtful attempts. But Montesquiou did not come up to the expectations of the Gironde. Instead of entering Geneva, he negotiated. The Genevan aristocrats promised to send back the Swiss reinforcements. This was not what Clavière wanted. The Convention refused to ratify the convention negotiated by Montesquiou, and on November he was cited before the courts and forced to emigrate. Geneva remained independent, but the revolution there was only postponed.

D'Anselme, with the army of Var, composed of nine battalions of the new levy and six thousand National Guards from Marseilles, had set out on the march a week after Montesquiou, his superior officer. Supported by

275

Admiral Truguet's fleet, he entered Nice on September 29 without a struggle and on the next day took possession of the fortress of Villefranche, where he found a good supply of artillery, plentiful provisions, a frigate, and a corvette.

The French took the offensive on the Rhine as well as on the Alps. Seeing that the Austrians and Prussians were engaged in the Argonne and that their magazines were left without any adequate guard, Custine, who was in command at Landau, marched out with 14,300 men, two-thirds of whom were volunteers, and took Spires on September 25 after a fairly sharp engagement, bringing back three thousand prisoners and considerable booty to Landau. Encouraged by this success, he marched out again a few days later, entered Worms on October 5, and appeared before Mainz on October 19, with 13,000 men and forty-five pieces of field-artillery, but no siege-artillery. The fortress was very strong, and was defended by a garrison of three thousand men, well provided with artillery and stores. But Custine had friends inside the city, the burgesses of which had ·refused, as early as October 5, to man the ramparts and had assumed the tricolour cockade. At the second summons Mainz capitulated, and Eckmeyer, the officer commanding the garrison engineers, at once entered the service of France. Two days later the revolutionary troops entered Frankfurt.

Had Custine been a good tactician, he would not have left the Rhine; but would have marched downstream and seized Coblenz, thus cutting off the retreat of the Prussion troops, who were at that very moment evacuating Longwy before the advance of Kellermann's army. But he let the opportunity go by, and then wrote in vain to Kellermann to follow up the Prussians vigorously in order to effect a junction with him. But Kellermann alleged the weariness of his troops as an excuse for not marching on Treves. The Executive Council sent him to the army of the Alps, replacing him by Beurnonville, who was slow in starting and, after being defeated by Hohenlohe before Trier between December 6 and 15, was finally thrown back in disorder on the Sarre. Meanwhile, on December 2, Custine had met with his first reverse, at Frankfurt. The Hessians had made a surprise attack on the city, and the inhabitants had risen against the French and opened their gates to the attacking forces. Custine spoke of evacuating Mainz; but the Executive Council sent him orders to stay there, accompanied by reinforcements drawn from the army commanded by Biron in Alsace.

Belgium was conquered at the same time as Savoy and the middle Rhine. After Valmy, Saxe-Teschen's Austrians had had to raise the siege of Lille, which they had vainly attempted to terrorize by an intensive bombardment, lasting from September 29 to October 5. After receiving the congratulations of the Convention on October 5, followed by those of the Jacobins, for whom Danton was the spokesman, Dumouriez entered Belgium on October 27 by way of Valenciennes and Mons, with the pick of the French army, chiefly composed of troops of the line. On November 6 he came up against Clerfayt and Saxe-Teschen's Austrians, who had strengthened their positions opposite Mons by hastily throwing up redoubts on the wooded hill-sides. The battle was stubbornly contested, especially in the centre, round the village of Jemappes. Towards evening the Austrians, whose numbers were only half those of the French, withdrew, leaving four thousand dead and thirteen cannon on the field of battle. Dumouriez did not venture to pursue them, so that their defeat was not turned into a disaster. The impression which it produced in France and Europe was none the less a profound one: "Valmy was a mere engagement of outposts; Jemappes was a general engagement, the first memorable battle fought by France for a long time past, and, as it were, the Rocroi of the Republic" (A Chuquet). Moreover, Jemappes had more important results than Valmy. In less than a month the Austrians were driven out of the whole of Belgium, losing Brussels on November 14, Liége on the 24th, Antwerp on the 30th, and lastly Namur on December 2. Instead of obeying the orders of the Executive Council and following up the Austrians, who were in retreat beyond the Roer, in such a way as to annihilate them and extricate Beurnonville and Custine, who were engaged with the Prussians, Dumouriez suddenly called a halt.

Dumouriez was already at open odds with Pache, the Minister for War, and with the national Treasury, which kept too close a watch on his financial operations. He was surrounded by a horde of speculators, with whom he made illegal contracts, among them the notorious Abbé d'Espagnac and the Brussels banker Simon. It was such a crying scandal that Cambon gave orders for the arrest of d'Espagnac and the paymaster-in-chief Malus. But Dumouriez took a high hand in defence of his agents and offered his resignation. The Gironde came to his assistance and sent commissaries to Belgium to appease him, among them being Delacroix and Danton. Malus and d'Espagnac were released and the scandals hushed up. The Gironde was no longer able to keep the generals under control, for it wanted in case of need to use their popularity as a support against the Mountain. It no longer dared to impose obedience upon them, because it had need of them.

Should they make peace? Should they keep what they had conquered?

For an instant the Girondins hesitated. Certain of them realized that if they were to retain the conquered territory, they would have to continue the war and make it a general one. On September 28, after listening to a letter from Montesquiou announcing that the people of Savoy had informed him of their desire to form an eighty-fourth department, several Girondins, Bancal, Louvet, and Lasource, supported, moreover, by Camille Desmoulins, declared themselves opposed to all conquests. "France is large enough," said Bancal. "Let us beware of behaving like kings by fettering Savoy to the Republic," added Camille Desmoulins. When Delacroix interrupted him with the practical query: "Who is to pay the costs of the war?" Louvet replied amid the enthusiastic applause of the Assembly: "The costs of the war? You will find an ample recompense for them in the enjoyment of your liberty, which will be secured for ever, and in the sight of the happiness of the peoples whom you have set free!" But this generosity was not to Danton's taste. "While it is our duty to give liberty to neighbouring peoples," he said, "I declare that we have the right to say to them: 'You shall have no more kings, for, so long as you are surrounded by tyrants, a coalition of them may imperil our own liberty.' . . . By sending us here as its deputies the French nation has created a great general committee of insurrection of the peoples against all the kings in the universe." The Assembly was unwilling to make a definite pronouncement on the subject of the debate, but was obviously inclined towards the creation of independent sister republics.

To the majority of the Diplomatic Committee, indeed, the democratization of the conquered countries seemed a hazardous policy, which they ought to renounce. On October 24 the Girondin Lasource, as spokesman of the committee, read a long report to the Convention, in which he forcibly combated the opinion of Danton and those who, like him, were unwilling to promise assistance and protection to the people of Savoy except in so far as they would first promise to abolish royalty and feudalism. "Is it not," he said, "an infringement of the liberty of a people to exclude any form of government from its choice?" Lasource blamed Anselme for having municipalized the countship of Nice by setting up fresh administrative bodies and courts of law there: "To give laws is to conquer!"

Lasource's opinion was that of the Government. On October 30 Lebrun wrote to Noël, the French agent in England: "France has renounced conquests, and this ought to reassure the English Government on the question of Dumouriez's entry into Belgium." And on November 11, after Jemappes, he again wrote: "We do not want to take it upon ourselves to give any people a particular form of government. The inhabitants of

Belgium will choose the one which suits them best; we shall not interfere in the matter."

In this respect Robespierre and a large number of the Jacobins were in agreement with the Diplomatic Committee and the Executive Council. On November 9 at the Jacobins Chabot explained the drawbacks of conquests, in opposition to Lullier and Dubois-Crancé, amid the applause of the majority. On December 12 Bentabole won the plaudits of the public in the galleries by a demand for peace: "Let us beware of continuing a war in which we shall play the part of dupes!" In his *Lettres à ses commettants*, Robespierre demanded that "a wise limit should be set to our military enterprises," and soon pointed out "the danger of starting all over again with the Belgians the painful and bloody struggle which we had to carry on with our own priests."

But there were two influential men on the Executive Council and the Diplomatic Committee, Clavière, a native of Geneva, and Anacharsis Cloots, a Prussian subject and a native of Cleves, who were close friends and for personal reasons in favour of a policy of conquest. Both of them were political refugees, who could return to their native country only if it were set free from the yoke of its former tyrants, who had persecuted them; and they could see no other means of protecting their country save that of uniting it with France. As early as 1785 Cloots had written in his *Vœux d'un gallophile* (*Desires of a Francophil*), which was printed in the following year: "An object of which the Court of Versailles ought not to lose sight is that of throwing back the frontiers of France as far as the estuary of the Rhine. This river is the natural boundary of Gaul, like the Alps, the Pyrenees, the Mediterranean, and the Atlantic." And as early as September 29 he had demanded the annexation of Savoy.

Now behind Cloots and Clavière there was a strong party formed of the numerous foreign exiles who had come to France in search of fortune and liberty: natives of Savoy, who had rallied round Doppet, a doctor who had founded the Allobrogian Club and legion, and the Abbé Philibert Simond, the deputy for the department of Bas-Rhin in the Convention; Genevans and Swiss, grouped round Clavière, Desonnaz, and Grenus; natives of Neuchâtel round Castella, J.-P. Marat, and Roullier, founder of the Helvetic Club; Dutchmen round the bankers de Kock, Van den Yver, and Abbema; natives of Liége round Fabry, Bassenge, Fyon, and Ransonnet; Belgians belonging to the Statist party, who had taken refuge at Douai, with the young Comte de Béthune-Charost as their centre; Belgians of the Vonckist party, who had taken refuge in Paris, with the bankers Proli and Walckiers as their centre; and lastly Germans from the Rhinelands, most of whom had taken refuge at Strasbourg, with the Capuchin monk Euloge Schneider, Cotta the bookseller, the merchant Bœhmer, the doctor Wedekind, etc., as their centre. Intelligent and active, these refugees were very numerous in the clubs, especially at the Cordeliers, where they formed the nucleus of the Hébertist party. Many of them had found employment in the public departments or the army. The rapid succession of victories in the autumn of 1792 seemed to a large extent their work.

There arrived a moment, after Jemappes, when the Girondins on the Diplomatic Committee and the Executive Council allowed themselves to be carried away, and adopted in their turn the annexationist policy of the refugees. This was a decisive turning-point. The war of defence was followed not only by a war of propaganda, but by a war of conquest. This came about imperceptibly for a number of reasons, partly of a diplomatic, partly of a military, and partly of an administrative and financial nature.

If the leading members of the Executive Council and the Diplomatic Committee had at first adopted a prudent and cautious attitude towards the policy of expansion, this was because they did not despair of obtaining a speedy peace by breaking up the Coalition. The failure of the negotiations entered upon with the Prussians after Valmy had not discouraged them. On October 26, 1792, by their orders, Valence and Kellermann had a meeting at Aubange with Brunswick, Lucchesini, Hohenlohe, and the Prince of Reuss. They offered the Prussians an alliance with France, in return for the recognition of the Republic; to the Austrians they proposed peace in return for the exchange of Bavaria for the Austrian Netherlands, and the dismantling of the fortresses in Luxemburg. But on November 1 Frederick William informed the French agent Mandrillon that, before entering into any negotiations, he demanded the evacuation by the French of the territory of the Empire, and guarantees with regard to the fate of Louis XVI and his family. As for Austria, on the advice of Kaunitz she decided to lay down as the preliminary conditions of peace the release of the royal family, who were to be escorted to the frontier, the assignment of apanages to the French princes, the restoration of the authority of the Pope at Avignon, and, lastly, compensation for the German princes whose rights had been infringed by the ordinances of August 4. All hope of a speedy peace vanished.

What was more, the entry of Spain into the war appeared probable. To meet this contingency Brissot and Lebrun were already thinking of stirring up a revolt of the Spanish colonies in South America through the agency of the Spanish American Miranda, who was serving in the army of Dumouriez. A war of propaganda, a revolutionary war, appeared in this case as a continuation of the defensive war.

The conquered countries differed greatly from one another in their social structure, language, and civilization. Was it possible to lay down uniform administrative regulations for them all?

Savoy, the language and civilization of which were French, was trammelled in its economic development by the customs barriers separating it from both France and Piedmont. The middle classes hated the police methods and military tyranny of the King of Sardinia. The peasants, compelled by the edicts of Victor Amadeus to redeem their feudal dues, envied the French peasants, who had freed themselves from the yoke of their lords without paying anything. On the arrival of the French, Savoy was soon covered with a network of clubs, which at once expressed their desire "to cast themselves upon the bosom of the French Republic, and in future to form with her but one nation of brothers." The Allobrogian National Assembly, formed of delegates from all the communes, which met at Chambéry on October 20, proclaimed the deposition of Victor Amadeus and his heirs, and proceeded to abolish nobility and the seigniorial regime, confiscate the property of the clergy, and finally, on October 22, expressed the desire of the country to be united with France. An almost unanimous people was offering itself, was giving itself, to France.

The old bishopric of Basel, which had been occupied as soon as war was declared, was in a somewhat similar position to that of Savoy. The greater number of the lordships and communities of which it was composed were occupied by French-speaking people who had been agitating for the abolition of the feudal system since 1789. The inhabitants of Porrentruy, the capital of the Prince-Bishop, who had fled, had planted a tree of liberty in October and founded a club. Délémont, Saint-Ursanne, and Seignelegier had done likewise. One party demanded union with France, while another was in favour of forming an independent republic.

At Nice, an Italian-speaking region, the friends of France were far less numerous than in Savoy. When Anselme's troops marched in, all the shops put up their shutters. The soldiers revenged themselves by sacking the town, and this pillaging, which Anselme winked at, still further swelled the number of those hostile to France. In order to form a club and provisional administrative bodies it was necessary to appeal to the colony of French residents from Marseilles, of whom there were a number in Nice. The request for union with France which was issued on October 21 certainly represented the will of no more than a small portion of the population.

The German-speaking Rhinelands contained no sincere friends of France—or rather of the Revolution—save in the cities, especially in Mainz, among university professors, lawyers, liberal clergy, and business men, who met mostly in the reading-rooms to read the newspapers from Paris. The open country, which was divided up into a number of lay and ecclesiastical lordships, not all of which were at war with France, was indifferent or hostile. Unlike Montesquiou, Dumouriez, and Anselme, who made no demands upon the inhabitants, Custine, upon entering Spires, had levied contributions upon the privileged classes. It was all very well for him to say that, in accordance with the catchword "Peace to the cottages, war on the châteaux," he had only aimed at the privileged classes; but at Frankfurt it was the bankers who were subjected to the levy, and it so happened that the authorities of Worms, who were also affected, were artisans of somewhat small means, so that Custine molested even part of the middle classes. Lebrun approved of this method of warfare, by which the army lived on the country. In a letter of October 30 he even recommended Custine to send the finest books in the libraries of the occupied towns to Paris, "notably Gutenberg's Bible." This already foreshadowed the policy of looting which afterwards prevailed under the Directory and Napoleon.

Custine was aware that his high-sounding proclamations, accompanied by the planting of trees of liberty, were not enough to win over public opinion to the French. He wanted to give the Germans some more solid satisfaction. He did not dare to suppress tithes,· corvées, seigniorial rights and privileges of every kind, on his own responsibility; so he asked the Convention itself to order their suppression, which he could not expect to take place on the spontaneous initiative of the Rhenish people themselves. "Regencies, *baillis*, provosts," [1] he wrote, "all the administrative bodies composed of the subordinate agents of the petty despots who hold this unhappy land in a state of oppression, have not lost a single moment in increasing their credit in the eyes of the people."

The behaviour of Dumouriez in Belgium formed a contrast with that of Custine on the Rhine. Dumouriez was well acquainted with the country, where he had been sent on a mission by Lafayette in 1790, when the revolt against Austria was still meeting with success. He knew that the Belgians, who numbered at that time two and a half millions, were divided into two parties; the Statists, or aristocratic party, who took their

---

[1] Various types of feudal tribunal.

stand upon their old feudal liberties and were supported by a very rich and fanatical clergy, which had great power over the indigent poor; and the Vonckists, or democratic party, who had been persecuted by the former because of their hostility to the clergy, and desired a thorough-going reform of the old institutions. He knew that the ecclesiastical principality of Liége, which belonged to the Holy Roman Empire and had a population of five hundred thousand souls, contained a number of democrats who were quite determined upon the overthrow of the seigniorial regime. Having consulted the Committee of United Belgians and Men of Liége, composed chiefly of Vonckists, he made it his object to fuse Belgium and the territory of Liége in a single independent republic, while respecting as far as possible the national susceptibilities of both the Belgians and the natives of Liége. The exiles who accompanied his army summoned meetings of the conquered peoples in the churches and caused them to appoint provisional administrators, who proclaimed the rupture of all ties with Austria. Clubs were set up everywhere. But when General La Bourdonnaye tried to imitate Custine and levy a contribution on the inhabitants of Tournai, Dumouriez censured him severely: "To turn the public contributions of Belgium to the uses of France is to sow mistrust of our operations and sully them with an appearance of baseness and venality! It is to set up a military tyranny on the ruins of Austrian despotism!" He had La Bourdonnaye recalled. Miranda replaced him.

Dumouriez was careful not to wound Belgian susceptibilities. He made his supply-trains pay the local tolls and did not meddle with the existing laws. Though he had sanctioned commandeering, he resorted to it unwillingly. He preferred to enter into contracts and to pay bills in metallic currency and not in assignats, raising the necessary money by loans from the ecclesiastical corporations. Thus with two millions which he borrowed from the clergy of Ghent, he endeavoured to raise a Belgian army to reinforce his own.

In all the conquered countries there was a larger or smaller body of the inhabitants who had compromised themselves with the French by putting their names on the books of the clubs or accepting positions in the new administrative bodies. These accomplices of the French dreaded the return of the princes who had been ousted. The French advised them to set up republics; but would these little republics be capable of surviving after the peace, when the revolutionary troops were no longer there? "Can we be free without being Frenchmen?" said the delegates from Nice to the Convention, on November 4. "No! Insurmountable obstacles stand in the way. Our position is such that we are bound to be either Frenchmen or slaves." They had given the treasures of their churches, the property of their religious houses. What would Europe think of the French people "if, after having drained the sources of our wealth by dangling before us the lure of liberty, it were afterwards to cast us out of its bosom, handing us over in our indigence to the mercy of implacable tyrants?" The Rhenish revolutionaries expressed the same fears.

By calling upon the peoples to revolt, republican France had entered into moral obligations towards them which she could not evade. Her propaganda logically involved the protection of those who had revolted; and was not annexation the best protection she could afford them?

Encouraged by the club at Landau, the inhabitants of the *bailliage* of Bergzabern in the duchy of Zweibrücken (Deux-Ponts), a neutral territory, had planted a tree of liberty, abolished feudal dues, and demanded union with France. The revolt had spread to the rest of the duchy and the Duke had had to send troops and arrest the agitators. Rühl informed the Convention of these facts and on November 19 asked whether it was going to abandon to the mercy of despots the patriots who were applying its principles. "I beg you to make a declaration to the effect that peoples desiring to fraternize with us shall be protected by the French nation." A number of speakers—Defermon, Legendre, Reubell, Mailhe, Birotteau, Carra, Dentzel, Treilhard, L. Bourdon, and Saint-André—supported Rühl. In vain did Brissot and Lasource attempt to gain time by postponing the decision till the Diplomatic Committee had presented the report which it had been charged to make on the action of the generals in enemy countries. The Convention adopted with acclamation a proposed decree submitted to it by La Révellière-Lepeaux: "The National Convention declares, in the name of the French nation, that it will grant fraternity and assistance to all peoples desirous of recovering their liberty, and charges the executive power to give the generals the necessary orders to bear aid to these peoples and defend citizens who have been or may be molested in the cause of liberty."

This was a memorable decree, for it proclaimed the solidarity of revolutionaries throughout the whole world, and consequently threatened all previously existing thrones and organs of government; it also risked provoking a universal war, which would no longer be a war between power and power, but a social war, supported and maintained by a nation already emancipated, which constituted itself the protector and guardian of all others which were still oppressed. The Revolution, which at the outset had repudiated conquests and militarism, was being driven by the force of events to appear before the world in the full panoply of war. It was to propagate its new gospel as the religions of old had propagated theirs, by the power of the sword.

The first annexation soon followed. On November 27 Bishop Grégoire proposed in a long report that the resolution of the people of Savoy should be ratified. He justified the measure not only by the imprescriptible right of a people to choose its nationality freely, but also by considerations of interest. The French frontier would thereby be shortened and consolidated, the number of customs officials would be reduced, the people of Savoy would be able to exploit their natural wealth by the aid of French capital, etc. Grégoire's answer to those timorous souls who objected that the annexation of Savoy would prolong the war indefinitely was full of proud defiance. "It in no way adds to the hatred of oppressors for the French Revolution," he said; "it adds to the resources by which we shall break their league. Moreover, the die is cast: we have started on our course; all the governments are our enemies, all the peoples are our friends." The annexation was voted unanimously, with the exception of the Girondin Penières, who tried in vain to protest during the session, and Marat, who protested afterwards in his newspaper. It is true that the ingenious Buzot managed to reserve his friends a loop-hole for escape by proposing that the decree should be declared to be an *article constitutionnel;* that is to say, that, like the Constitution itself, it should be submitted for the ratification of the people. He was interrupted by murmuring and at first withdrew his amendment, but it was taken up again by Danton, who said: "I say that such a contract will not become permanent till the French nation has accepted it." The amendment was supported by Barère and carried. The annexation of Savoy, then, was only provisional, which was an adroit way of satisfying the inhabitants, while reserving the possibility of negotiating with their former masters in view of the uncertainties of the future!

But for the moment the majority in the Convention allowed itself to be carried away by Grégoire's enthusiasm, and there was a sudden outburst of expansionist policy.

Brissot, who directed the activities of the Diplomatic Committee, wrote to Servan on November 26: "I hold that our liberty will never be undisturbed so long as there is a Bourbon left on his throne. No peace with the Bourbons; we must consequently think about a Spanish expedition. I never stop preaching this to the ministers." It was not only Spain and her colonies that he wished to incite to revolt, but Germany and the whole of Europe: "We cannot rest till Europe, and all Europe, is ablaze. . . . If we push back our frontiers as far as the Rhine, if in future the

Pyrenees divide none but free peoples, our liberty is firmly established."
Brissot was dressing up the old monarchist policy of the natural frontiers
in the red cap of revolution.

The expansionist policy of the Gironde was closely bound up with its
policy of social preservation. Clavière, says M. Chuquet, was afraid of
peace. On December 5 he wrote to Custine: "We must maintain a state of
war; the return of our soldiers would increase the disorder everywhere,
and ruin us." Such was also Roland's opinion. "It is necessary," he admitted one day, "to march the thousands of men whom we have under
arms as far away as their legs will carry them, or else they will come
back and cut our throats."

But this policy was a costly one. "The farther we advance into enemy
territory," complained Cambon on December 10, "the more ruinous the
war becomes, especially with our principles of philosophy and generosity.
Our position is such that we must make up our minds once and for all.
It is constantly being repeated that we are bringing liberty to our neigh-
bours. We are also bringing them our cash and provisions; but they do
not want our assignats!" Cambon was given the task of drafting a decree
on the course of action to be prescribed to the generals in the occupied
countries, and by December 15 it was ready. It laid down the principle
that the object of the revolutionary war was the annihilation of all
privileges: "All who are privileged, all who are tyrants, ought to be treated
as an enemy in the countries we enter." It was because this principle had
been forgotten, because of the delay in authorizing Custine to destroy the
seigniorial regime, that the Rhenish peoples, who had at first been enthusiastic, had grown cold, thus rendering possible the Sicilian Vespers
of Frankfurt. If the Belgian people remained passive or hostile, it was
because Dumouriez had not *put an end* to the oppression of which it was
the victim. No doubt it would be a fine thing if the populations of the
occupied countries were to imitate the example of the French and overthrow feudalism of their own accord. But since this was unfortunately impossible, the French must declare themselves a *revolutionary power*, and
destroy the old regime which held them in bondage. France should exercise a revolutionary dictatorship for their benefit, and she should exercise
it in the full light of day: "It would be fruitless to disguise our proceedings and principles: the tyrants are already aware of them. . . . When
we enter a country, it is for us to sound the tocsin." The French generals
were therefore at once to abolish tithes and feudal dues and every form
of servitude. They were to destroy all existing authorities and obtain the
election of provisional administrative bodies from which the enemies of

the Republic should be excluded; for only those citizens were to take part in the election who should take the oath to be faithful to liberty and equality and to renounce privileges. The former taxes were to be abolished, but the property belonging to the Treasury, the princes, the lay and ecclesiastical corporations, and all partisans of tyranny should be placed in reserve to guarantee the assignats, which were to be imposed as legal tender. If the new administrative bodies considered it their duty to levy taxes, these should not be borne by the labouring classes. "It is by these means that we shall make the people love liberty: it will have nothing to pay and will control everything." When, on October 20, Anacharsis Cloots had previously proposed similar measures, he had met with no success; but ideas had progressed during the last two months. This time Cambon was enthusiastically applauded and his decree was voted on the spot.

The foreign policy of the Gironde was summed up in the decrees of November 19 and December 15, which were complementary to each other. The former granted protection to the peoples, the latter laid down as a preliminary condition of this protection that the peoples should accept the revolutionary dictatorship of France.

If such a policy was to succeed, the Government which formulated it ought to have been strong enough to impose it upon the peoples who had not demanded it, upon the enemy powers whose territorial integrity it was infringing, and, lastly, upon the neutrals whom it was threatening in their vital interests. In other words, the French army ought to have been a docile instrument in the hand of the Gironde, and powerful enough to break the resistance of almost the whole of Europe.

The question may be asked whether the universal war of which the germ is contained in these two decrees was the inevitable consequence of the march of events. It is certain that at one moment the Gironde tried to obtain peace by negotiation with Prussia and Austria. But it could only have succeeded in its negotiations with the kings if it had taken up a clear and resolute position with regard to the trial of Louis XVI. If it had·from the very outset appealed to national interest for the purpose of pardoning the King, if it had openly declared that his trial would prevent the conclusion of peace, if it had bravely assumed the responsibility of proposing to escort the royal family to the frontier on the very day when the Republic was proclaimed, then perhaps it might have brought the negotiations upon which it had entered to a happy issue. Peace would have been possible on the basis of the status quo. Austria and Prussia asked nothing better than to extricate themselves honourably from the hornets' nest of France, in order to look after their interests in Poland, which were threatened by Russia. But the Gironde had not enough courage to pay the necessary price for peace. It would not only have been obliged to demand that Louis XVI should escape punishment; it would also have had to renounce the spirit of revolutionary propaganda which it had done so much to encourage. It did not dare to break with its past, and ended by allowing itself to be carried away by the intoxication of victory.

As for the Mountain, it had, it is true, supported Robespierre a year earlier in opposing the war; but now, though it tried to moderate the annexationist policy of the Gironde, though it uttered a few far-sighted warnings, though Marat protested in his newspaper against the annexation of Savoy, it none the less abstained from formulating any precise and concrete proposals in opposition to the policy of the Gironde. How, indeed, could it have done so, when it was grimly bent upon the trial of Louis XVI, and was welcoming to its bosom deserters from the Gironde such as Anacharsis Cloots, the advocate of the political exiles and the apostle of annexation?

It may therefore be said that party struggles contributed quite as much towards preventing peace and increasing the bitterness of the war as did the development of the external situation.

CHAPTER VII

The First Coalition

THE Convention had thought that by its decrees of November 19 and December 15 it was strengthening the position of France in the occupied countries by binding the oppressed masses to her cause. But events turned out contrary to its expectations. The peoples took fright at the "revolutionary power" imposed upon them. They saw in it merely a means of spoliation, an instrument of arbitrary power and domination, an intolerable blow at their independence.

In Belgium most of the provisional administrative bodies created at the time of the conquest were composed of former members of the Statist party, who wanted to wear the colours of Brabant in Brussels, and when they were forbidden to do so, replied by great demonstrations, one of which, on December 7, ended in a serious affray. When the decree of December 15 became known, a number of Vonckists joined their protests to those of the Statists. Those composing the administrative body of Hainaut declared to the Convention, in an address dated December 21, that the revolutionary power which had been proclaimed would in their eyes never be anything but "a usurped power, the power of force." The resistance was almost unanimous, for it was based upon interest. Nobody would accept the assignats as legal tender, and there were a large number of persons injured by the sequestration of the property of the Treasury or the Church.

Faced with this unexpected resistance, certain ministers, such as Lebrun and Roland, and certain deputies, such as Brissot, Gaudet, and Gensonné, inspired by Dumouriez, began to wonder whether it would not be better to draw back and repeal the decree of December 15. But the commissaries attached to the army in Belgium, and especially Camus, Danton, and Delacroix, supported by Cambon and Clavière, demanded the immediate application of the decree, if necessary by force. This lack of harmony among those in control of policy led to the waste of valuable time, and gave the opposition time to concert measures. The Diplomatic Committee, led by Brissot, managed to delay for more than a month the nomination of the agents whom the Executive Council was to send to Belgium to proceed with the elections and sequestration, and the latter did not leave Paris till after the middle of January. But Cambon overruled all resistance by appealing direct to the Convention, which adopted his views on January 31.

The decree of December 15 was now put into execution, but only by violence. Sham popular assemblies, under the threat of French bayonets, passed measures for the union of the cities and the country-side with France. They did not dare to summon a general assembly of the whole of Belgium, as had been done in Savoy. The decisions in favour of union were proclaimed one after the other, city by city, during the month of March, amid a threatening ferment which found expression at Bruges in attacks on French soldiers, and almost everywhere in seditious cries. As early as February 17 the commissaries in Belgium warned the Convention that if the French troops suffered any reverses, "the signal for the Sicilian Vespers would most certainly be sounded for the French throughout the whole of Belgium, and the Belgian patriots, trembling for their own fate, would be unable to be of any assistance to them."

The Rhineland was divided among more than twenty different States and lordships, all intermingled with one another, and had none of that local patriotism which was so tenacious in Belgium. But it was suffering from the hardships of war. The peasants complained of the fixed prices, requisitioning, and forced labour. Their priests frightened them with threats of hell-fire if they broke the oath binding them to their former princes, and foretold the return of the latter. Nobody would have anything to do with the assignats. They were all afraid that union with France would make them liable to military service, of which they had a horror. Soon the only people who remained faithful to France were those members of the city clubs who were most deeply compromised, and even they were divided, as, for instance, at Mainz.

The decree of December 15 could be applied only by force. The commissaries of the Convention, Reubell, Merlin of Thionville, and Haussmann, violated the neutrality of the duchy of Zweibrücken and caused it to be occupied on February 8 by General Landremont. The Duke fled, but his minister, von Esebeck, was thrown into the military prison of Metz and afterwards taken to Paris, where he was soon joined by the princes of Leiningen. The members of the clubs, supported by detachments of soldiers, were scattered about the country-side to control the elections. Abstentions from voting were very numerous. There were attempts at resistance here and there, which could be put down only by arrests and mass deportations to the other bank of the Rhine. Yet whole villages refused to take the oath, and as soon as it was heard that the French were falling back in Belgium, there were partial revolts. The Convention of the Rhine, nominated in these circumstances, met at Mainz on March 17, and after a speech by Förster, voted four days later for the union of the Rhineland with France.

The other conquered territories were united to France by means of similar procedure. Porrentruy, which had already become the Rauracian Republic in December, was transformed into the department of Mont-Terrible on March 23, in spite of the opposition of the German *bailliages* within its territory and even of several French villages.

Nice had been united to France by a decree of January 31, 1793. When Ducos expressed his misgivings, Lasource, now a convert to Cambon's policy, replied that the Alps were the frontier of the Republic, and that furthermore the harbour of Villefranche would be indispensable to France in case of a rupture with England. The inhabitants of Nice were becoming more and more hostile to the French, and in March the district of Sospello rose in revolt. The country districts were no longer safe, and French postal messengers were being assassinated. The conscripts formed themselves into bands, and these "Barbets," as they were called, terrorized the outlying districts of the towns. Even Savoy, which had been so unanimous in October, began to show signs of weariness and disaffection.

Such were the bitter fruits of imperialist policy in the occupied regions. Elsewhere, in the neutral countries, it alienated many sympathies from France, and, above all, gave the absolutist governments a pretext for increasingly strict measures of surveillance and repression over newspapers and books suspected of disseminating French principles. The more timid of the foreign writers who had at first applauded the Revolution broke with it ostentatiously: Klopstock, Wieland, Körner, Stolberg, and Schlosser in Germany, Arthur Young and Watson in England, Alfieri and Pindemonte in Italy. They found no lack of pretexts, but those most frequently appealed to were the September massacres and the execution of Louis XVI. Those who, in spite of everything, remained faithful to revolutionary principles, such as the Germans Fichte and Reichardt, and in England Wordsworth, Coleridge, Godwin, and Robert Burns, had either to take refuge in anonymity and silence, or resign themselves to persecution.

After the conquest of Belgium, which was in his eyes a threat to the independence of Holland, Pitt gradually began to depart from the policy of neutrality which he had hitherto imposed upon the Court and part of his colleagues in the Cabinet. As early as November 13 he sent word to the

Stadtholder that in case of an invasion of Dutch territory by the French, the English Government would fulfil all its duties as his ally. The invasion which he feared did not take place, but on November 16 the Executive Council proclaimed the opening of the Scheldt, and a French flotilla at once put this proclamation into force, sailed up the estuary, and appeared before Antwerp. This was an explicit violation of the treaty of Münster, which had been several times confirmed subsequently. Henceforward the war party in England had a definite cause of complaint against France; she had violated the neutrality of Holland guaranteed by the treaties. The decree of November 19 promising aid and relief to peoples in revolt furnished them with a second cause of complaint.

The English Liberals had rejoiced at the victories of France. Their political societies—the Society of the Revolution of 1688, the Society of the Friends of the People, the Society for Constitutional Reform—had sent deputations to the Convention bearing enthusiastic addresses with thousands of signatures, collected mostly in the manufacturing districts. Grégoire, the president of the Assembly, made an imprudent reply to the two deputations which appeared at the bar on November 28: "The shades of Pym, Hampden, and Sidney are hovering over your heads, and no doubt the moment is approaching when Frenchmen will carry their congratulations to the National Convention of Great Britain!" All Englishmen attached to the monarchy—and there were many—saw in these demonstrations a proof that France was fomenting agitation in their country and preparing for a revolution there.

Pitt summoned an extraordinary session of the Houses of Parliament for December 13, and the speech from the throne demanded that measures of defence should be voted against ill-disposed persons at home, and armaments for opposing the menace of French aggrandizement. It was in vain for Lebrun's secret agent, Maret, who was received by Pitt on December 2 and 14, to explain that the decree of November 19 had not the scope ascribed to it, but applied only to nations at war with France. Pitt remained distrustful; for Lebrun wanted to oblige him to continue the negotiations through the medium of Chauvelin, the French ambassador, whose official character the Court had ceased to recognize since August 10. Besides, Lebrun was tactless. In his statement of December 19 upon the relations between France and England he affected to draw a distinction between the English ministry and the English nation and threatened to appeal to the latter against the former. Pitt keenly resented the insult and threat, and on December 26 he easily obtained the passage of an emergency bill directed against foreign residents in England, the Aliens

Bill, which placed them under police surveillance, hampered their movements, and gave powers to expel them. Lebrun at once protested against this violation of the commercial treaty of 1786, which guaranteed to French residents in England the same rights as those enjoyed by English residents in France. Pitt ignored the protests and laid an embargo on shipments of wheat to France.

On hearing of the execution of Louis XVI the Court of St. James's went into mourning, and Chauvelin received orders to leave the country immediately. On January 13, after a report by Kersaint, the Convention had already passed a decree ordering the commissioning of thirty ships of war and twenty frigates. At the last minute, however, Lebrun and the Diplomatic Committee tried to maintain peace. Maret returned to London and tried to see Pitt. If we may believe Pitt's agent, Miles, he was empowered to promise that France would make restitution of all her conquests on the Rhine and be content with an independent Belgium, which should be turned into a republic. He might even hold out the possibility that France would try to find means of annulling the annexation of Savoy. But Pitt refused to receive Maret, though he was careful not to take the initiative in declaring war. On February 1 Brissot obtained a vote from the Convention in favour of war against both England and Holland.

This time it was impossible to ascribe the war to monarchist intrigues. Pitt and Grenville had not allowed themselves to be guided by their political preferences. The conflict which now presented itself was of quite another order. It belonged to the old category of wars of interest, wars for the maintenance of the balance of power in Europe. As in the time of Louis XIV and Louis XV, the City merchants, of whom Pitt was merely the mouthpiece, could not allow Antwerp to fall into the hands of France. And, on the other hand, the politicians of the Convention saw in the war with Holland chiefly a means of carrying out a financial operation by gaining control of the Bank of Amsterdam. Brissot had been in the right when he had warned his fellow-countrymen that they were entering upon a fight to the death. The struggle was now no longer a war against kings, nobles, and priests, as before, but between nation and nation. The kings were soon to come to terms with revolutionary France, but the English nation was the last to lay down its arms.

The breach with Spain was not of the same character as that with England. It was provoked by what was essentially a question of the monarch's personal and family honour. Charles IV and his worthless wife were in favour of peace because their Treasury was empty and war would disturb their tranquillity. Charles IV had tried unsuccessfully to save

293

his cousin Louis XVI by negotiating a simultaneous disarmament with France. After January 21 Bourgoing, the French chargé d'affaires, received notice from Godoy, the Prime Minister and the Queen's lover, to discontinue his visits. Bourgoing sent him a note from Lebrun demanding a definite answer on the subject of the armaments begun by Spain. He received his passports. On March 7 Barère read a report on the matter to the Convention, which voted by acclamation a decree in favour of war. "Another enemy for France," said Barère, "is only another triumph for liberty." The politicians of the Convention addressed the monarchs of Europe in language worthy of Roman senators.

The Bourbon Court of Naples had refused to recognize Mackau, the French diplomatic agent, and its representative at Constantinople had intrigued with the Sultan against Sémonville, the ambassador whom the Republic proposed to send there in the place of Choiseul-Gouffier, who had joined the emigration. The French fleet from Toulon at once appeared off Naples. Ferdinand IV, King of the Two Sicilies, was as degraded a character as his cousin the King of Spain. His wife, Maria Carolina, the sister of Marie Antoinette, flaunted her liaison with Acton, the Prime Minister. The King and Queen trembled when, on December 17, 1792, they saw the French fleet, and submitted to all the demands that were made of them. "Another Bourbon conquered! Kings are the order of the day!" exclaimed Treilhard, president of the Convention, when a grenadier named Belleville arrived with Mackau's triumphant dispatches.

The Pope had ordered the imprisonment of two French artists, students at the French School at Rome, named Chinard and Rater, under the pretext that they were freemasons and had used offensive language. Orders were given to the French fleet to cruise off the coasts of the Papal States on its way back from Naples, and the Pope hastened to set the artists free. But on January 13 Hugon de Bassville, Mackau's secretary, who had gone to Rome to reassure French subjects there, was massacred by the populace, who on the following day tried to burn the Ghetto, the inhabitants of which were regarded as in league with the French. The Convention adopted Bassville's child and gave orders that his assassination should be signally revenged. But the Toulon fleet had just met with a humiliating reverse off Sardinia, where it had tried to land troops at La Maddalena, and vengeance for Bassville's death had to be postponed till a later date.

Coming as it did a month after the Sicilian Vespers at Frankfurt, this incident was a clear enough sign that in the campaign which was about to open, revolutionary France could rely upon herself alone. The nations were not ripe for revolt. France was paying for the fact that she was intellectually in advance of other nations. When military operations began, she was left with no allies. She was only too fortunate to have retained the neutrality of the Swiss, the Scandinavian nations, and the Italian states. Alone against the greatest powers of Europe, never, even in the time of Louis XIV, had she had to carry on such a gigantic struggle; for in the days of Louis XIV she had Spain, at least, on her side at the most critical moment. But under Louis XIV she was fighting to vindicate the pride of a royal house. This time it was not only her independence that was at stake, but her national dignity, her right to govern herself, and, above all, the enormous advantages which she had obtained from her Revolution.

CHAPTER VIII

The Treason of Dumouriez

T HE natural frontiers won in the autumn of 1792 were lost in the spring of 1793 in the course of a few weeks. The whole of Belgium was evacuated at the end of March, after the defeat at Neerwinden, and a few days later the left bank of the Rhine met with the same fate. At the beginning of April all that France held beyond her north-eastern frontier was the citadel of Mainz, in which she was being besieged. How are these rapid reverses to be explained after the prodigious successes which had preceded them?

Thanks to the error of Dumouriez, who had refused to let his soldiers advance as far as the Rhine, Custine's army was separated from the army in Belgium by a whole zone of territory occupied by the Austrians and Prussians. The latter were interposed like a wedge between the two main French armies all along the Moselle, from Coblenz to Luxemburg, and thus had a very strong central position, which enabled them to manœuvre on inside lines.

Besides, the Coalition had profited by the respite which Dumouriez had allowed them, to reinforce their effectives and draw their alliance closer. Frederick William was bent upon revenging the reverse at Valmy and had given orders to his generals to co-operate more closely with the Austrians.

During the previous phase, the French armies had obtained the victory only thanks to their numerical superiority and the complicity of part of the population of Belgium and the Rhineland. They now lacked both these advantages. Badly fed and clothed, as a result of the embezzlement of contractors shielded by Dumouriez, many volunteers used their legal right of returning home. French territory having been delivered, they thought their mission was at an end. The French armies were no longer superior to those of their adversaries in morale, and now they no longer possessed superiority in numbers.

On December 1 they had numbered about 400,000; but by February 1, 1793 they were no more than 228,000. The army in Belgium had perhaps been more sorely tried than the others. "There are some battalions of volunteers," said Dubois-Crancé on February 7, "which have not a hundred men left." There were companies consisting of five men. Those who remained were either poverty-stricken wretches, or professional soldiers who indulged in pillage and looting and were not distinguished by their discipline, though they still bore themselves bravely in the field.

If only the Government and the higher command had at least remained united! But never had the divisions and rivalries among those controlling the State been more acute. The Committee of General Defence set up on January 1, 1793 was too numerous (it had twenty-four members), its debates took place in public, and it was a perfect court of misrule. The Exeutive Council, which was now subordinate to it, could not succeed in settling anything. Business was carried on in a dilatory fashion, and the generals, confident in their past victories, became more and more disobedient. Custine was respectful for a long time, but he now imitated Dumouriez and in his letters to Lebrun denounced the alleged incapacity of Pache. Lebrun allowed him to continue, without recalling him to obedience and a sense of propriety. Dumouriez made a long stay in Paris during the King's trial, from January 1 to 26, during which he indulged in dubious intrigues. He tried without success to entangle Cambon, but Danton, Cloots, and the Girondin leaders lent him their most cordial support. On January 21 Danton did not hesitate to take sides against Pache, though with a hypocritical parade of scrupulousness. Pache was dismissed on February 4 on the pretext that the Ministry for War was too heavy a burden for one man, and replaced by Beurnonville, the friend and instrument of Dumouriez, who was provided with six assistants in charge of the various branches of the service. Thus on the eve of the reopening of hostilities the reorganization of the war department was in full swing; there was a complete muddle. The generals, having got rid of Pache, were hardly inclined to be more docile towards his successor, and Custine did not like Beurnonville.

One of the great weaknesses of the French army was that it was composed partly of regiments of the line and partly of battalions of volunteers, and these two categories of troops had each its own distinct status and were jealous of each other. The volunteers elected their own officers and had a higher rate of pay, but were subject to a less severe discipline. On February 7, in order to put an end to this dual system of recruiting and regulations, which was doing such harm, Dubois Crancé proposed a thorough-going reform: amalgamation, which consisted in fusing two battalions of volunteers and one of the line in a single corps, known as a

THE FRENCH REVOLUTION

demi-brigade; and granting the troops of the line the same advantages and rights as the volunteers, besides allowing these to compete with them for vacant posts. A third of these posts were to be reserved and appointments were to be made to the two remaining thirds by an ingenious system of co-optation. As soon as a post fell vacant, the men of the rank next below it were to nominate three candidates, from whom the officers or non-commissioned officers of the rank to be filled up were to make their choice. By this means the army would be "nationalized," inspired by a uniform spirit, provided with equal rights, and subject to uniform laws. The troops of the line would become imbued with the civic spirit of the volunteers, and the volunteers would be disciplined by contact with the old soldiers. All the generals, except Valence, displayed hostility to this reform. Most of the Girondins, including Barère himself, spoke against it from the tribune. It was, however, voted, thanks to the Montagnards and especially Saint-Just; but it was too late for it to be carried into effect before the reopening of the campaign. It was not put into execution till the winter of 1793–4, when it produced the very best results. In the mean time the line regiments and the battalions of volunteers remained separate.

In spite of the evident inferiority of the French armies, the Committee of General Defence and the Executive Council adopted the plan for an offensive advocated by Dumouriez, but it was a counsel of despair. On February 3 Dumouriez wrote from Antwerp: "If the army of Belgium does not forestall the enemy, it is lost." He added: "If we are given assistance, and above all if the Belgians are treated in a wise and fraternal spirit, I dare to promise victory yet; if not, I shall know how to die like a soldier." He had no desire to die, but he wanted the Belgians to be treated with consideration, for fear they might rise in revolt in the rear of his troops. His plan was for Miranda's corps to remain on his right, in order to besiege Maestricht and guard the fords of the Roer, while another corps, under Valence, took up its position on the central Meuse, ready to meet either the Austrians from Luxemburg or those from the Roer; and he himself, with a third army, known as the army of Holland, or of the north, would fall upon Holland from Antwerp by way of the lower Meuse, striking straight at Dordrecht and Amsterdam. The other armies— those of the Rhine, the Moselle, the Alps, Italy, and the Pyrenees—were to remain upon the defensive. Dumouriez explains in his memoirs that, had he been victorious, he would have united Belgium and Holland in a single state, of which he would have proclaimed the independence, and would then have marched on Paris, dissolved the Convention, and annihilated Jacobinism. He says that he confided his project to only four persons, among

298

whom, according to Miranda, were Danton, Delacroix, and Westermann.

Dumouriez's plan had this defect: it scattered the already feeble forces of the Republic instead of concentrating them upon a single point. If Miranda gave way under Austrian pressure, Dumouriez's communications would be threatened and his Dutch expedition brought to a dead stop.

At first all went well. On February 16 he entered Holland with twenty thousand men and rapidly made himself master of the three fortresses of Breda, Gertruydenberg, and Klundert, which capitulated almost without resistance. But on March 1 Coburg's army fell upon the army of Belgium, which was scattered along the Roer in cantonments and caught almost without leaders. The disaster was appalling, and the troops evacuated Aix-la-Chapelle in disorder, without joining battle. Miranda hastily raised the siege of Maestricht, and Liége was evacuated in turn amid indescribable disorder. Valence, who had hurried to the spot, had great difficulty in rallying the broken remnant of the armies.

After this disaster, of which they had been witnesses, Danton and Delacroix returned to Paris, not so much to reassure the population as to sound the alarm. On March 8 Delacroix gave the lie downright to Beurnonville's optimism and painted the military situation in the darkest colours. Danton went even further than Delacroix. They persuaded the Convention to vote for the immediate dispatch of commissaries chosen from among its members to the Paris sections and the departments, in order to hasten on the levy of three hundred thousand men for which orders had been issued. On that same evening the Paris sections assembled, amid a fever of patriotism like that which had seized them at the end of August, at the moment of the capture of Longwy. Many of them, for instance the section of the Louvre, at the instigation of Desfieux, a friend of Danton, demanded the establishment of a revolutionary tribunal to punish enemy agents within the country, and on the following day, March 9, Carrier proposed a motion to this effect. Danton supported it strongly, and the motion was voted, in spite of the violent opposition of the Girondins. That same evening the agitation in Paris grew more intense. The Society of the Defenders of the Republic, the section of the Quatre Nations, and the Cordeliers Club issued a threatening manifesto against Dumouriez and the Girondins, whom they held responsible for the defeats. An insurrectionary committee was formed, and tried unsuccessfully to win over the Jacobins and the Commune. The presses of the *Chronique de Paris* and the *Patriote français* were sacked by mobs.

On the following day, March 10, Danton again ascended the tribune and made an attack on the ministry, proposing that it should be replaced by a new one, formed of members of the Convention. The Girondins accused him of aspiring to a dictatorship, and his proposal was rejected. But disturbances broke out again that evening, and an attempt was made to rouse the sections by agitators notoriously in connexion with Danton. The rioters were dispersed by the rain, by the refusal of Santerre and Pache to support the insurrection, and by the firm attitude of the Fédérés from Finistère.

It was believed at the time that the disturbances on March 9 and 10 were organized by Danton in league with Dumouriez. While Danton was attacking the ministers in the Convention, de Maulde, an agent of Dumouriez, was attacking them at the Jacobins. Danton, however, praised Dumouriez warmly, whereas the rioters demanded his dismissal and the expulsion of the "appellants." [1] The contradiction was only too apparent and it was intentional. The rioters were led by men such as Desfieux and Proli, who had recently been Dumouriez's accredited instruments and were shortly to be involved with him in dubious intrigues on the eve of his impending treason. Nobody believed in their sincerity when they were heard vituperating the general whom only lately they had extolled to the skies and with whom they were on good terms immediately afterwards. Their doubtful past was well known and it was believed that these unprincipled men were playing the part allotted them by Danton, in whose pay they were.

The arrogant attitude adopted by Dumouriez at the very moment of these disturbances added substance to these suspicions. On March 2 Valence had summoned him distractedly to his aid in the following terms: "Come here. We must change the plan of campaign. Every minute is a century." At first he had refused to take any notice and maintained that the best way to defend Belgium was to continue his march on Rotterdam. When at last, on March 10, he set out to join Miranda, by the express instructions of the Executive Council, he started alone, leaving his army in Holland, though it was indispensable if the disaster was to be made good. Thus while Danton was setting the minds of the Convention at rest on his account, he was behaving like a dictator and setting himself above the law. By a series of proclamations, issued one close after the other on March 11, he ordered the restoration of all the plate taken from the Belgian churches, the closing of all the clubs, some of which he had visited, and the arrest of several commissaries of the Executive Council—for instance,

---

[1] The *appelants* were those who had voted for the appeal to the people at the trial of Louis XVI.

Chépy. In short, he swept away by a stroke of the pen all the work of revolution accomplished since the decree of December 15. When the commissaries of the Convention, Camus and Treilhard, joined him at Louvain and censured his proceedings, he wrote the Convention a most insolent letter, on March 12, holding the war department responsible for the defeat, declaring that the union of Belgium with France had been carried out at the point of the sword, and going so far as to recall memories of the Duke of Alva. His letter was read to the Committee of General Defence on March 15, together with a dispatch from Treilhard and Camus drawing attention to the general's actions and threats, which they characterized as "grave events." Barère forthwith proposed to the Committee that Dumouriez should be cited before the courts. But Danton opposed this essential measure, which would have saved the army. He said that Dumouriez possessed the confidence of the soldiers and that his dismissal would be disastrous. The committee allowed itself to be convinced. Danton and Delacroix once more started for Belgium. "We will cure him or garrotte him!" they said; but these were empty words.

Dumouriez reorganized the armies of Valence and Miranda and on March 16 started by driving the imperial troops out of Tirlemont, but two days later he sustained a serious defeat at Neerwinden on the Geete. His demoralized troops were retreating on Brussels when Danton and Delacroix joined him at Louvain during the night of March 20–1. They asked him to retract his letter of March 12 to the Convention, but Dumouriez endeavoured to turn them against the Girondins and refused to retract. All the commissaries could obtain of him was a curt note in which he begged the Assembly not to come to any hasty conclusion as a result of his letter of March 12, before hearing the result of his conferences with the commissaries, and they had to be satisfied with this. While Delacroix remained at the army headquarters, Danton returned to Paris to report to the committee. A curious mystery attaches to his return. He ought to have made haste to get back as soon as possible, in order to give an account of the disaster at Neerwinden and Dumouriez's rebellion. But he did not appear before the committee till the evening of March 26, whereas he had left Brussels early on the morning of the 21st, and it took only two days at the outside to cover this distance. For five whole days he disappeared and could not be found; and Dumouriez took advantage of this respite to throw off the mask and convert his rebellion into treason. On March 23 he opened communications with Coburg through the agency of his aide-de-camp Montjoye. He described his project of dissolving the Convention by force and restoring the monarchy and undertook to evacuate the whole of Belgium and hand over to the enemy the three fortresses of Antwerp, Breda, and Gertruydenberg, which was done at once. On March 26 Dumouriez had a meeting at Tournai with three Jacobins of very dubious character, secret agents employed by Lebrun, named Dubuisson, Pereira, and Proli, who had figured in the disturbances in Paris on March 9 and 10 and had probably conferred with Danton before seeing Dumouriez. According to the latter's account, these three men had come to propose to him that he should arrive at an understanding with the Jacobins, with a view to dissolving the Convention. According to their version, it was Dumouriez himself who made this proposal, which they rejected. The question of obtaining the Queen's liberation was touched upon during the interview

Now, while Dumouriez was conferring at Tournai with these three dubious emissaries, Danton persisted in defending him before the Committee of General Defence, in opposition to Robespierre, who demanded in vain that he should immediately be dismissed, on that very day, March 26. It was not till the evening of March 29 that the committee at last decided to adopt the measure which Danton had delayed for a fortnight. It decided to send four fresh commissaries to the army, Camus, Quinette, Lamarque, and Bancal, with Beurnonville, the Minister for War, to deprive Dumouriez of his command and place him under arrest. But it was the commissaries and the minister who were arrested. Dumouriez handed them over to the enemy on the evening of April 1, and for two years they remained in captivity.

Dumouriez made an attempt to lead his army against Paris in order to restore the monarchy. But not all the commissaries of the Convention had been arrested. Those who had remained at Lille proclaimed him an outlaw and forbade his lieutenants to obey him. Le Veneur, the officer in command of the camp at Maulde, hurriedly dispatched his aide-de-camp, Lazare Hoche, to warn the Convention of the orders given by Dumouriez, and on April 4 Davout, who was in command of the third battalion of volunteers from the department of Yonne, ordered his men to fire on Dumouriez. In order to escape their bullets Dumouriez was forced to gallop at full speed to the Austrian lines, and when he returned to the camp of Maulde on April 5, escorted by the imperial dragoons, his flagrant treason roused the army against him and it marched off toward Valenciennes of its own accord. Dumouriez took refuge with the Austrians, together with the Duke of Chartres, Valence, and a thousand men.

The committees believed that Dumouriez had accomplices even in Paris and in the very Convention. The Committes of General Defence and of General Security held a joint session on the night of March 31–April 1 and gave orders for the arrest of Philippe Égalité and his friend the Marquis de Sillery, who was also a deputy. At the same time they called upon Danton to come and explain to them the situation in Belgium. This almost amounted to a warrant for his arrest, similar letters having been sent to Philippe Égalité and Sillery. A rumour went round that Danton had also been arrested. On that very evening Marat had censured him at the Jacobins for what he called his lack of foresight. On April 1, at the Convention, Lasource roundly accused Danton of having been in collusion with Dumouriez in his monarchist *coup d'état*. Birotteau alleged that at the Committee of General Security Fabre d'Eglantine had proposed the restoration of royalty. Neither Lasource nor Birotteau was aware that at that very moment Danton had been in touch with the *émigré* Théodore Lameth, who has left an account of this in his memoirs. Danton put a bold face on the matter and countered their accusations by turning accuser himself. The friends of Dumouriez, he said, were Brissot, Gaudet, and Gensonné, who were in regular correspondence with him. The friends of royalty were those who had wanted to save the tyrant and those who uttered calumnies against Paris, the stronghold of the Revolution. The Mountain punctuated his violent attack with frenzied applause. Marat even suggested fresh accusations. "And what about their little supper parties?" he said; whereupon Danton rejoined: "They were not the only ones who had clandestine supper parties with Dumouriez when he was in Paris. . . ." "Lasource! Lasource was there!" cried Marat. "Yes," said Danton; "they alone are the accomplices of the conspiracy!" The manœuvre succeeded. The commission of inquiry which the Girondins had at first caused to be voted was never formed. What is more, Danton and Delacroix became members of the Committee of Public Safety, created on April 5 to take the place of the Committee of General Defence, but on a fresh basis. The new committee was to have only nine members, its meetings were to be held in secret, and its powers were to be increased.

A year later, the very Montagnards who had carried Danton in triumph because he had avenged them upon the Gironde repeated the accusations of Birotteau and Lasource, turning them against him. They too believed in his complicity with Dumouriez and had him cited before the Revolutionary Tribunal for royalism.

The Coalition had avenged its reverses of the previous year. Its armies were once more about to carry the war into French territory. And in face of this immense danger France was divided against herself. The Vendée was already in a blaze.

CHAPTER IX

The Vendée

THE clerical and royalist insurrection which broke out on March 10, 1793, in the department of the Vendée and the departments adjacent to it, was only the supreme manifestation, the most formidable episode, of the opposition and discontent which were seething among the mass of the populace throughout the whole of France. The ferment was, indeed, almost general, and everywhere its causes were mainly of an economic and social order. Political and religious causes played only a secondary part, as a corollary of the former. The abolition of the food-regulations by the decree of December 8, and the death of the King, were followed by a rapid rise in the prices of commodities and a recrudescence of destitution.

During February the assignat fell, on an average, fifty per cent in value. All the evidence concurs to establish the fact that the disproportion between wages and the cost of living had enormously increased.

On February 25 the deputy Chambon stated without contradiction that, in the departments of Corrèze, Haute-Vienne and Creuse black bread cost from seven to eight sous a pound, and added: "The indigent class in these unfortunate departments earns only nine or ten sous a day"; that is to say, their wages barely enabled them to buy a pound of bread a day! In the department of Yonne the price of wheat had tripled, and there too wages were barely sufficient to buy bread. "One proof," says M. Porée, "that food alone absorbed almost all the workman's earnings is that, if he was fed by his employer or customer, his wages were reduced by two-thirds. A locksmith who earned three livres ten sous without food received only one livre ten sous if his food was provided. The scanty wages which he brought home at night all went to buy bread for his wife and children."

The towns suffered even worse than the country districts. In Paris the food-shortage had become almost chronic. Disturbances broke out again after the King's trial, and those of February 24, 25, and 26 were particularly grave. They started with a riot of washerwomen, who complained that they could no longer buy soap, the price having risen from fourteen to twenty-two sous a pound. Grocers' shops were pillaged, and the revolutionary step

304

was taken of drawing up tariffs of fixed prices for commodities of prime necessity. A series of threatening petitions was received by the Convention, demanding that the assignat be made legal tender, that food-speculators be punished by death, and that maximum prices be fixed. On February 25, in the middle of the disturbances, Jacques Roux defended the pillaging of grocers' shops in the following terms: "I think," he said to the Commune, "that the grocers have merely made restitution to the people of the excessive sums which they had made them pay for a long time past."

At Lyons the situation was still more alarming. On January 26 four thousand silk-weavers requested the municipality to impose upon the manufacturers a tariff for the various processes. The manufacturers and the rich citizens organized to resist the operatives, who were supported by the municipality. Nivière-Chol, the Girondin mayor, resigned. He was re-elected on February 18, and on this occasion the central club, of which Chalier, president of the district tribunal, was the head, was sacked, the statue of Rousseau broken, and the tree of liberty burnt. The disorder was so serious that the Convention sent three commissaries, Basire, Rovère and Legendre, to Lyons, who tried in vain to hold the balance between the two parties, or rather classes, which were struggling with each other. The workmen, who were paying six sous a pound for bread, demanded a graduated tax upon capital, as well as a fixed tariff of wages, fixed prices for commodities, and the institution of a revolutionary army to impose these measures.

Without waiting for these requests to become law the local authorities, who favoured the cause of the people, and afterwards the commissaries of the Convention, proceeded to act under pressure of necessity. In spite of the law of December 8 the district directory of Chaumont continued to obtain supplies for its markets by commandeering. In the department of Aveyron, Bô and Chabot, the representatives on mission, imposed a war levy upon the rich to feed the needy. In the department of Lot, Saint-André revived the laws which had been abrogated and ordered statistical returns and commandeering of grain.

All the commissaries pointed out that the underlying cause of the disturbances and of the growing disaffection of the people against the existing Government was the rise in prices. "It is absolutely essential to enable the poor man to live if you want him to help you to complete the Revolution," wrote Saint-André to Barère on March 26. "In extraordinary circumstances everything must be disregarded save the great law of public safety." His letter is very interesting, for it emphasizes not only the economic reasons, but the political reasons, for the general discontent. The latter were not difficult to define. The violent struggles between the Girondins and the Montagnards had disseminated uncertainty, distrust, and discouragement. The landowners asked nothing better than to believe the Girondins, who had been repeating to them for several months past that the Montagnards had designs upon their property.

Fear of anarchy and of the agrarian law had drawn them towards the right. They almost regretted the monarchy, which they now began to regard as the surest guarantee of order. As for the artisans in the towns and the labourers in the country districts, the privations and destitution against which they were struggling made them ready to listen alternately to the incitements of the reactionaries and the appeals for a fresh revolution. Finally, the formation of the First Coalition, immediately followed by the defeats in Belgium and on the Rhine, revived the confidence and energy of the royalist party. Such was the economic and moral atmosphere in which was hatched the insurrection in the Vendée, for which the new levy of three hundred thousand men was the signal.

It must at once be said that the arbitrary character of the recruiting law laid it open to the most justifiable criticism. Article II, drawn up by Prieur of Marne, ran as follows: "In case voluntary enrollment should not produce the number of men fixed for each commune, the citizens shall be bound to complete it then and there, and for this purpose they shall adopt whatever method they shall consider the most fitting by a majority of votes." "Whatever methods may be adopted by the assembled citizens," said Article 13, "for completing their contingent, the required number shall be chosen from among unmarried men and widowers without children, between the ages of eighteen and forty inclusive." This meant that the choice of recruits would be complicated by politics and cabals. In the course of the debate the Montagnard Choudieu even proposed that the recruits should be chosen obligatorily by election. "I have proposed that they should be elected," he said, "because I thought that the assembled citizens would choose for preference the rich, whose families are in easy circumstances and have no need of their work; I observed, anyway, that as yet the rich have done little for the Revolution and that it is perhaps time for them to serve in person. It is, after all, an honour to serve one's country, and, since a later article grants the right of finding a substitute, I hold that it will be doubly beneficial to the poor citizen not to be chosen the first time, since with this bonus on enlistment paid by the rich he will be able to be more useful to his family, while serving his country." The Convention was indeed so unfaithful to the principles of the Declaration of the

Rights of Man as to refuse to impose personal service upon the rich, and here was a Montagnard praising the system of substitutes!

But this privilege granted to wealth could not fail to appear intolerable and unjust to a people whose sentiment of equality had made such progress since August 10. Besides, by leaving the choice of recruits to the arbitrary decision of a majority, the Convention was placing recruiting at the mercy of all the local passions which had been let loose. Even in the most patriotic departments there were crying abuses which aroused angry complaints and resistance. In the department of Sarthe, though it had raised fourteen companies in August 1792 instead of the six which it had been asked for, the young men protested against the exemption enjoyed by elected officials and married men. In many communes they tried to insist that the purchasers of national property—in other words, the profiteers of the Revolution—should for this very reason be singled out to go to the front before others. In nearly all the departments the abuses were very serious. Sometimes the aristocrats, being in the majority, marked out the republicans to leave. Sometimes the contrary was the case, according as there were coalitions of the rich or of the poor. It was no rare thing for the partisans of the refractory priests—as, for instance, in the department of Bas-Rhin—to single out the constitutional parish priests. It was only in communes where there was uniformity of opinion that enlistment was carried on by drawing lots, which recalled the old militia, but did not lend itself to the same abuses. In the towns and villages contributions were quite often levied upon the rich, and the money so obtained went to pay men to form the contingent. Struck by the drawbacks of the law, the department of Hérault, by an ordinance of April 19, 1793, desired to smooth them away by giving a special committee, formed by the local authorities, the right to choose the recruits by requisitioning them directly and in person. A contribution was levied upon the rich, which made it possible to compensate the citizens thus requisitioned. This method of recruiting had not been provided for by the law, but it had the great advantage of placing the levy under the control of the revolutionary authorities, and was therefore approved by the Convention, on May 13, 1793, after Barère had reported upon the subject, and held up as an example to others. Many departments adopted it—Doubs, Cher, Allier, Corrèze, and Haute-Vienne. When Paris had to raise twelve thousand volunteers to fight the troops of the Vendée, the same method was resorted to. Each of these volunteers— or rather pressed men—received a bonus of five hundred livres, from which they received the name of "five hundred livres heroes (*héros à cinq cent livres*)."

In the west, resistance to the recruiting law led to a terrible insurrection. On Sunday, March 10, the day fixed for drawing lots, and the following days, the peasants rose in revolt, from the Atlantic coast in the west to the towns of Cholet and Bressuire on the east. Armed with flails, spits, and a few guns and often led by their mayors, they entered the market towns with shouts of "We want peace! No drawing lots!" The National Guards were disarmed, the constitutional priests and municipal officials summarily executed, the official papers burnt, and the houses of patriots sacked. At Machecoul, the former capital of the region of Retz, the massacres, which were begun at the command of an ex-collector of the salt-tax named Souchu, lasted for more than a month, and had 545 victims. The president of the district assembly, Joubert, had his hands sawn off at the wrist before being stabbed to death with pitchforks and bayonets. Some patriots were even buried alive. On April 23 fifty bourgeois, bound two by two in a string, were all shot in a single day in a neighbouring meadow.

The Vendean peasant took a joy in killing the middle-class revolutionary, whom he had often met at the fair or market, the *monsieur* of whose indulgent contempt he was conscious, the unbeliever who attended the club inspired by Satan, the heretic who went to the constitutional mass. "Such was the popular fury," says the refractory priest Chevalier, "that it was enough to have been to the mass said by the intruding priest (*messe des intrus*) to be first imprisoned and then knocked on the head or shot, on the pretext that the prisons were full, as they had been on September 2."

These first bands were led by old soldiers, contrabandists, or salt-smugglers, ex-collectors of the salt-tax (*gabelous*) who turned against the Revolution on the abolition of their posts, or noblemen's servants. At first the leaders were men of the people: in Les Mauges the coachman Cathelineau, sacristan of his parish, and the gamekeeper Stofflet, an old soldier; in the Breton Marais the hairdresser Gaston, the attorney Souchu, the surgeon Joly. The nobles were far less pious than their farmers and appeared only later, sometimes after pressure had been brought to bear upon them: in the Marais the ferocious Charette, a former lieutenant in the navy; in Les Mauges the chivalrous Bonchamp, and in the same region d'Elbée, a Saxon who had adopted French nationality in 1757; in the Bocage, Royrand, a former lieutenant-colonel, Sapinaud, a former *garde-du-corps*, Baudry d'Asson, Du Retail; in Poitou, properly so called, Lescure and La Rochejacquelein—but these were the last to join the revolt; it was only the treason of Dumouriez, at the beginning of April, which decided them.

The refractory priests almost immediately came out of their hiding-places to kindle the zeal of the combatants. One of them, the Abbé Bernier, had a seat on the council of the Catholic and royal army. Another, the adventurer Guillot de Folleville, passed himself off as the Bishop of Agra *in partibus* and in this capacity presided at the Te Deums.

The rapid successes of the insurgents are not to be attributed merely to fanaticism and a thirst for martyrdom. They lived in a country not easily accessible, a wooded region intersected by hedges, favourable to ambushes, almost devoid of roads and highways, where there were few large centres of population, the inhabitants being scattered about in a host of isolated farms. The middle-class patriots living in the few towns were only a small minority.

The influence of the priests upon the insurrection cannot be denied, but it was only indirect. Barely a quarter of those holding cures at the time of the Civil Constitution of the clergy had taken the oath. A great number of parishes could not be provided with constitutional priests. A missionary order known as the Mulotins, whose headquarters were in the heart of the Bocage, at Saint-Laurent-sur-Sèvre, had organized a number of pilgrimages in 1791 and 1792, and miracles had taken place in several chapels. By this revolt the Vendean peasant wanted not only to avoid the military service which he loathed, but also to fight for his God and his King. The insurgents almost at once adopted as their badge a Sacred Heart cut out of cloth, which they wore on their short tunics. The peasant revolt assumed the appearance of a crusade.

From the outset the peasants advanced to the attack behind a living wall of prisoners, whom they drove before them. Skilled in dissimulation, and good shots, they fought for preference in open order, trying to rush the Blues and cut them off by their lines of sharpshooters. The nobles who commanded them had experience of war and knew how to seize strategic points and blow up bridges. They tried to reduce their rabble of followers to order; they organized parish and district councils, a system of accounts, and reserves. They obtained arms, cannon, and equipment in the towns which they surprised, and tried to form the nucleus of a permanent army by the aid of republican deserters, supplemented by their prisoners; but they never succeeded in co-ordinating their efforts otherwise than imperfectly. Charette was impatient of all discipline and unwilling to go outside his own district of the Marais; the other leaders were jealous of one another. In order to arrive at some agreement they raised Cathelineau, the saint of Anjou, to the rank of generalissimo, but he was never more than a nominal leader. The peasants were unwilling to go far from their parishes and leave their fields untilled. Besides, the commissariat was never more than rudimentary. When the peasant had consumed his victuals, he was obliged to leave the army. Thus the leaders had great difficulty in planning big operations of a sustained and methodical kind and were reduced to isolated exploits. It was this that saved the Republic.

On March 19, at the first news of the disturbances, the Convention passed a terrible decree inflicting the death penalty upon all rebels who should be taken with arms in their hands, and ordering the confiscation of their property. It was voted unanimously Lanjuinais even strengthened the original wording, which Marat, on the other hand, considered too severe. But the Girondins as a whole affected at first not to take the insurrection very seriously. They had already tried to conceal the seriousness of the defeats in Belgium. Brissot redoubled the campaign against anarchists in his newspaper and, in his number of March 19, represented the Vendeans as having been stirred up by the secret emissaries of the Montagnards, who were themselves agents of Pitt. The Gironde was throwing dust in the eyes of the revolutionaries and no longer seemed capable of sacrificing its grudges to the national interest.

The defence of the frontiers, which was in serious danger, absorbed almost all the troops of the line. It was at first only possible to detach one cavalry regiment for service in the Vendée, together with a little artillery, and the 35th legion of *gendarmerie*, composed of former Gardes Françaises and the victors of the Bastille. The greater part of the republican forces, which did not exceed 15,000 or 16,000 men, was formed of National Guards hastily raised in the neighbouring departments.

Fortunately the middle classes in the coast towns made a fine and successful resistance. Those of Les Sables d'Olonne twice beat off fierce attacks by the rebels, on March 23 and 29, and so did those of Pornic and Paimbœuf. Thus the Vendée was unable to communicate with England and the princes, who were at first unaware of the proportions assumed by the insurrection.

It was not till after the victories of Cathelineau and d'Elbée at Chemillé on April 11, of La Rochejacquelein at Les Aubrais on April 13, of the army of Anjou at Coron on April 19, after the capitulation of the republican general Quétineau at Thouars on May 5, with 4,000 muskets and 10 cannon, that the Executive Council at last decided to send regular troops to the west, first the legion of the north, commanded by Westermann, then special battalions formed by taking six men from each company in all the armies. Two armies were then organized: that of the coasts of Brest was stationed to the north of the Loire, under the command of Canclaux, and that of the coasts of La Rochelle, to the south, under the command of Biron.

During the early days there had been reason to fear that the conflagration might become general throughout the whole of France. When recruiting began, the royalists made a great effort. In most parts of the department of Ille-et-Vilaine large numbers of armed men mustered in force, about March 20, to shouts of "Long live King Louis XVII, the nobles and priests!" The situation was still more critical in Morbihan. La Roche-Bernard and Rochefort, the chief towns of two administrative districts, fell into the power of the insurgents, who committed atrocities there. Fortunately the commissaries of the Convention, sent down as delegates by the decree of March 9, were already at their posts when the revolt broke out. Sevestre and Billaud-Varenne acted with such energy that the peasants were crushed by the National Guards of the towns of Redon and Rochefort, and their leaders arrested. Thus the insurrection in Brittany was nipped in the bud, only to revive later at the time of the Chouannerie.[1]

In the department of Indre-et-Loire, Goupilleau and Tallien were forced to intern all the priests who were stirring up trouble, and all suspicious characters, and compel all the relatives of *émigrés* to report themselves at the chief town of their administrative district. In Vienne there were disorderly assemblages which had to be dispersed by force. In the department of Bas-Rhin, a fanatically Catholic region, there was a serious rising at Molsheim, which lasted for two days, March 25 and 26. But after the Vendée it was in Lozère and the neighbouring departments that royalism made its greatest effort. The same priests and nobles who had organized the camp of Jalès at the end of 1790 and 1791, the priors Claude Allier and Solier, and Marc Charrier, an ex-member of the Constituent Assembly, raised a troop of two thousand men at the end of May and kept the field for several days. Marvéjols and Mende fell into their hands for a while, and the middle-class patriots were pillaged and massacred. But reinforcements arrived from the army of the Pyrenees, and the republicans retook these towns almost immediately, capturing Charrier, who was sent to the scaffold.

The Vendean insurrection and the royalist riots which took place in

---

[1] Royalist insurrections went on sporadically till the time of the Consulate The nickname of Chouans given to the royalists is of uncertain origin. It may have arisen from their habit of using the cry of the owl (*chouette*) as a signal; or it may come from the soubriquet of Jean Chouan given to one of the royalist leaders. Cottereau.

connexion with it had the most serious effects upon the further development of the Revolution. The republicans were alarmed and large numbers of them left the Girondin party, which was loath to take vigorous measures, and went over to the Montagnards, who came out more and more strongly as the party of revolutionary resistance. The Montagnards themselves moved more towards the left. They had hitherto resisted the fixing of prices demanded by the Enragés, and even Marat had attacked Jacques Roux at the time of the food riots in Paris on February 25. But by this time the Montagnards had grasped the seriousness of the economic crisis. In order to keep in touch with the masses, they adopted the measures proposed by the Enragés, no doubt somewhat unwillingly, and obtained their passage: first, on April 11, that imposing the assignats as legal tender, and afterwards, on May 4, that fixing the maximum price for cereals.

But extraordinary or "revolutionary" measures now followed in quick succession, not only in the economic, but also in the political sphere. On March 20 vigilance committees were created to overawe and keep a watch on aristocrats and agents of the enemy, and these committees fed the Revolutionary Tribunal, which had been established ten days before. In order to enable the "representatives on mission" to crush all resistance, their powers were increased and they were made into proconsuls or dictators.

The counterblast to the Vendée was the Terror. But the Terror could be worked only by the Montagnards, who had created its machinery, and for their own benefit. And so the Vendée helped to dig the grave of the Gironde.

CHAPTER X

The Fall of the Gironde

THE defeats in Belgium and on the Rhine, the treason of Dumouriez, and the insurrection in the Vendée aggravated the struggle between the Gironde and the Mountain. The two parties vied with each other in accusations of treason. Lasource had cast it in the teeth of Danton during the tragic session of April 1. Danton and the Jacobins now took it up and turned it against their adversaries.

As early as April 5 the Jacobins sent word to their affiliated societies to send in a flood of petitions demanding the dismissal and recall of the members of the Convention who had betrayed their duty by attempting to save the tyrant. This idea of recalling the "appellants" was not a new one. It had already been formulated by the rioters of March 10, Varlet, Desfieux, and Fournier, otherwise known as the Enragés; but so far they had been repudiated by the Montagnards. Now, five days after Lasource's denunciation of Danton, the Jacobins lent the weight of their authority to this idea. It may easily be conjectured that Danton had acted as go-between in bringing about the necessary *rapprochement* between the Enragés and the Jacobins, and this *rapprochement* grew more marked as time went on. In order to purchase the support of the Enragés against the Gironde, the Jacobins and Montagnards rallied to the policy of fixing the maximum price for cereals.

The appeal issued by the Jacobins on April 5 was therefore an act which had grave consequences. Hitherto it had been the Girondins who had taken the initiative in proposing the exclusion of their opponents from the Convention; for instance, of Robespierre, Marat, the Duke of Orleans, and Danton. The Mountain now took the offensive in its turn; and it had behind it the leaders and agitators concerned in all the previous riots, to whom the starving crowds were accustomed to look for guidance.

Though the moral position of the Gironde had already been seriously impaired by the repeated reverses with which it had met in both its internal and its external policy, its parliamentary position still remained very strong. It is true that it no longer possessed the exclusive control of the Government. The composition of the Executive Council, which it had formed in its own image in its early days, had undergone an almost complete change. Roland had left the Ministry of the Interior just after the King's execution, and his successor, Garat, was a prudent man who was careful not to compromise himself. Gohier, who had been at the Ministry of Justice since March 20, was no more courageous than Garat. Beurnonville's successor at the Ministry for War, Colonel Bouchotte, was a second Pache, who staffed his offices with Enragés. Lastly, the new Minister of Marine, Dalbarade, who replaced Monge on April 10, was the nominee of Danton.

The Gironde could now count entirely only upon Lebrun and Clavière, who occupied the Ministries for Foreign Affairs and Finance. But the Executive Council no longer possessed the power to make decisions. It was in close subordination to the Committee of Public Safety, to which it had to report, and the Committee of Public Safety, formed on April 5, was no longer controlled by the Gironde. Out of the nine members of which it was composed at the outset, seven belonged to the centre and two, Danton and Delacroix, to the Mountain, and the latter had just recently joined the Jacobin party.

It was, therefore, the centre, those who prided themselves on their independence and refused to adopt the passions of either party, who held the Government in their hands. Their leaders were Barère and Cambon, who voted with the Mountain whenever it was a question of taking stern measures for the salvation of the Republic. But they still felt an insuperable distrust for the Paris Commune and for Danton, by whom it was often inspired. Almost every time a vote was taken on a personal matter or on one affecting Parisian affairs, they voted with the Gironde. And it so happened that the Gironde, though no longer controlling the Government, still had a majority in the Assembly. Before the treason of Dumouriez the Assembly still fairly often chose its presidents from the centre. From April 1 to May 31 there was a whole series of Girondin presidents: Lasource on April 18, Boyer-Fonfrède on May 2, Isnard on May 16; for the Jacobin circular of April 5 had had as its result to alarm the Plain and cause it to rally against the Mountain out of distrust. When the Gironde appealed to the departments to save the King, the Plain disowned it and voted with the Mountain against an appeal to the people. It was now the turn of the Mountain to appeal to the primary assemblies with a proposal to exclude the Girondins from the Convention. True to its principle, the Plain disowned it in its turn, as it had the

Gironde. The function of the Plain was to represent and defend the public interest against the factions.

Moreover, the Mountain was weakened by the departure of the eighty-three commissaries to raise the three hundred thousand new recruits. Almost all these commissaries had been chosen from its ranks—on purpose, as the Montagnards afterwards alleged, to keep some of their best speakers away from the Assembly. And it is a fact that on March 14 Brissot wrote in his newspaper: "In the National Convention the absence of the hottest heads (*les plus effervescentes*) enables us to debate matters in greater tranquillity and consequently with greater vigour." But the Gironde made a mistake in rejoicing over the departure of the Montagnard commissaries. It failed to see that the latter would get into touch with their former partisans in the departments, dispel their prejudices against Paris, and gradually win them over to their party.

The Gironde might have ignored the Jacobin circular of April 5. But not only was it impatient to clear itself of the accusation of complicity with Dumouriez; it also thought the moment propitious for crushing its rivals. It refused to regard the Montagnards as anything but covert agents of the Duke of Orleans. Now, Philippe Égalité had just been arrested as an accomplice of Dumouriez; and this gave it confidence.

On April 12 Gaudet read out the Jacobin circular of April 5 to the Convention and demanded that Marat, who had signed it in his capacity as president of the club, should be cited before the courts. After a violent debate an oral vote by roll-call was taken on the following day, by which Marat was cited before the tribunal by 226 votes to 93, with 47 abstentions. But the triumph was short-lived. The judges and jury of the Revolutionary Tribunal were all partisans of the Mountain. The Commune and a number of the Parisian sections got up demonstrations in favour of the "Friend of the People," and so did several provincial· clubs—for instance, those of Beaune and Auxerre. A huge crowd escorted him to the trial. Some questions were put to him for the sake of form and he was acquitted on April 24 in the most eulogistic terms. The crowd crowned him with flowers and carried him back to his seat in the Assembly on its shoulders, passing in procession through the assembled Convention. Marat was more popular and more formidable than ever. This impotent attempt at repression on the part of the Gironde had merely stimulated the desire for reprisals.

As early as April 15, two days after the appearance of Marat before the tribunal, thirty-five of the forty-eight Parisian sections, accompanied by the municipality and Pache, the mayor, brought down a threatening petition to the Convention directed against twenty-two of the most prominent Girondin leaders: Brissot, Guadet, Vergniaud, Gensonné, Grangeneuve, Buzot, Barbaroux, Salle, Birotteau, Petion, Lanjuinais, Valazé, Lehardy, Louvet, Gorsas, Fauchet, Lasource, Pontécoulant, etc. The petition was read out by young Rousselin, whose connexion with Danton was notorious, and Lasource did not fail to accuse Danton of having drawn up the list of twenty-two.

The Girondins replied to the address of the sections by proposing, with Lasource and Boyer-Fonfrède as their spokesmen, that the primary assemblies should be summoned to give their opinion on all the deputies without exception. But Vergniaud himself obtained the rejection of their motion as dangerous. It might have led to civil war throughout the whole country.

The Gironde made a great effort to recapture the majority even in Paris and once more to rouse the departments against the Mountain.

In a *Letter to the Parisians*, which appeared at the end of April, Petion attempted to rally all those who were on the side of order: "Your property is threatened, yet you close your eyes to this danger. War is being stirred up between the haves and the have-nots, yet you do nothing to avert it. A few schemers, a handful of factious persons, are laying down the law to you and dragging you into violent and ill-advised measures; yet you have not the courage to resist; you dare not appear in your sections to combat them. You see all rich and peaceable persons leaving Paris, you see Paris being reduced to impotence; yet you remain calm. . . . Parisians, shake off your lethargy at last, and send these poisonous insects back into their holes. . . ." Yet a year earlier, in a *Letter to Buzot*, Petion had himself exhorted rich and poor, the two sections of the third estate, to unite against the common enemy. But in Petion's eyes the enemy was no longer aristocracy, but anarchy.

His appeal came at a propitious moment. The rich were exasperated by the pecuniary sacrifices inflicted upon them in connexion with the recruiting. The revolutionary committees which had recently been established were beginning to get to work and subjecting them to strict supervision and incessant annoyances. They attended the assemblies of their sections and tried to gain control of public offices, to get their nominees on the revolutionary committees, and to rid themselves of the war contributions levied upon them by the sansculottes. During the week the labourers were detained at their work and could not attend political meetings. The rich managed to obtain a majority in several of the Paris sections (Butte des

Moulins, Mail, Champs-Elysées). At the Luxembourg and the Champs-Elysées there were demonstrations of "Muscadins" [1] against recruiting. Brissot's newspaper congratulated them upon their protest against "the inequitable ordinances of the municipality."

But there was a rally of the sansculottes, those in the different sections coming to one another's aid. And they were vigorously and skilfully supported by the Jacobins and the Commune. The latter gave orders for a number of arrests, while doing all it could to revive the glorious memories of August 10. One of the heroes of the attack on the Tuileries, Lazowski, a former factory-inspector and captain of the gunners of the faubourg Saint-Marceau, had just died, and on Sunday, April 28, the Commune gave him an imposing funeral, organized by the painter David, which provided an opportunity for passing all the Montagnard forces in review.

Robespierre, who was no visionary, but had a strong sense of reality and followed the slightest manifestations of public opinion with close attention, had realized from the very beginning that the Gironde could be defeated only by giving the sansculottes a direct interest in its overthrow. At the end of April he read out a declaration of rights, first at the Jacobins and afterwards at the Convention, which subordinated property to the interest of society and thus provided a theoretical justification for the policy of requisitioning beloved of the Enragés. He never ceased inciting the mass of the workers against the *"culottes dorées* (golden knee-breeches),"* as he called them, who were endeavouring to gain control of the sections. "You have aristocrats in the sections," he said at the Jacobins on May 8. "Turn them out! You have to make liberty secure; proclaim the rights of liberty and display your full energy. You have a vast populace of sansculottes with sound opinions (*purs*) and plenty of vigour. They cannot leave their work; make the rich pay them!" And he advised the sections to follow the precedent of the department of Hérault and raise a revolutionary army at the expense of the rich, to hold ill-disposed persons in check. In the same speech he further proposed the arrest of suspects, and in order to facilitate the accomplishment of their civic duties by the labouring class he further proposed that those in needy circumstances should be compensated for the time spent at the assemblies of their section. On the same day, May 8, Robespierre had proposed to the Convention that suspects should be held as hostages and that the poor who kept guard over them should be compensated.

The social policy expounded by Robespierre with such remarkable pre-

---

[1] "Exquisites," the nickname given to the *"embusqués"* of the day by the sansculottes. The name was applied to the young royalists.

cision was indeed a class policy. During the Constituent and Legislative Assemblies the sansculottes had placed their strength at the service of the revolutionary middle classes against the old regime for nothing, but the time for this idealistic fervour had gone by. The sansculottes had seen landowners growing rich by the purchase of national property or the sale of their commodities and goods at exorbitant prices, and had profited by the lesson. They were no longer ready to be exploited, and considered that the Revolution should feed those who had brought it about and were maintaining it.

Robespierre was merely echoing the voice of the people. The social policy which he developed at the Jacobins on May 8, the plan of paid organization of the labouring classes, had already been formulated a few days earlier by the democrats of Lyons, the friends of Chalier. On May 3 they had extorted from the departmental assembly of Rhône-et-Loire an ordinance commanding the formation of a revolutionary army of five thousand men, paid at the rate of twenty sous a day, by levying an extraordinary contribution of five millions on the rich. Chalier's idea was to enlist unemployed workmen in this army.

It is probable that Robespierre, who knew the Lyons revolutionary, was at once informed of this measure. But whereas in Paris the sansculottes gained the upper hand, the contrary was the case at Lyons, where the rich had the departmental assembly on their side, so that it was slow and unwilling in raising the revolutionary army, which never existed except upon paper. The Girondins of Lyons had no objection to an alliance with the former aristocrats and, thanks to their support, managed to gain control of most of the sections and revolutionary committees and neutralize the action of the Montagnard municipality, which it soon overthrew.

In Paris things happened quite differently, for the sansculottes, supported by the Commune and the departmental assembly, succeeded in maintaining themselves in control of the revolutionary committees—that is to say, the organs of surveillance and repression.

But it was not only at Lyons that the Girondins triumphed: they also gained control of the local authorities in a number of commercial towns, notably at Marseilles, Nantes, and Bordeaux.

At Marseilles, as at Lyons, the Girondins formed an alliance with the aristocrats. Having made themselves masters of the sections, they protested against the dismissal of Mouraille, the mayor, and Seytres, *procureur* to the Commune, which had been rashly ordered by Moïse Bayle and Boissel, the representatives on mission. Having next obtained control of the Hôtel de Ville, they expelled from Marseilles the simple-minded representatives on mission, who had been taken in by their manœuvre, and formed a revolutionary tribunal, which began to attack the Montagnards.

At Nantes and Bordeaux, on the other hand, the proximity of the Vendée prevented an alliance between the Girondins and the aristocrats. The commercial middle classes, who knew that they would be pillaged and massacred in the event of a victory of the Vendean peasants, remained faithful to the Republic. But they sent threatening addresses to the Convention aimed at the anarchists of the Mountain.

It is impossible to doubt that the Girondin resistance, or rather offensive, in the departments was the result of a plan hatched in Paris between the deputies of the party. On May 4 and 5 Vergniaud wrote vehement letters to the people of Bordeaux reproaching them with their indifference and calling them to his aid: "Since I am driven to it, I summon you to the tribune to defend us, if there is still time, to avenge liberty by exterminating tyrants. Men of the Gironde, arise! Strike terror to our Mariuses." The appeal was listened to. The men of Bordeaux immediately dispatched a delegation to Paris which read out at the bar of the Convention a violent philippic against anarchists, and Vergniaud persuaded the Convention to order that it should be posted up in public places. Barbaroux wrote letters to his friends in Marseilles similar to those which Vergniaud was writing to his fellow townsmen.

The resistance of the Girondins was proving an increasing hindrance to the action of the representatives on mission in the interior. It was already assuming the form of federalism—that is to say, of local particularism at odds with the central power. Garrau wrote from Agen on May 16: "One quite often hears it said, even in public, that since Paris desires to dominate, it is necessary to break away from it and form separate states. Hence the difficulty of procuring arms for the recruits leaving for the frontiers. Nobody is willing to part with them." The class struggle took precedence of patriotic needs. On May 23 Dartigoyte and Ichon, who were at Lectoure, complained of the ill will of the departmental authorities of Gers. On May 26 Levasseur and his colleagues denounced that of the departmental assembly of Moselle and its indulgence towards the enemies of the Revolution. The struggle betwen the two parties was paralysing the revolutionary defence and had to be stopped.

At the beginning of May the Gironde drew up a definite plan of campaign. It was to quash the authorities of Paris, summon armed forces from the departments to crush any possible resistance, and finally, in case of a reverse, retire to Bourges. The plan was an absurd one. To quash the authorities of Paris meant risking new elections, which might even hand

319

over the Hôtel de Ville to the Enragés, who were already complaining of the weakness and lack of energy of the Montagnards—witness the speech of Leclerc of Lyons at the Jacobins on May 16. It was madness to provoke a struggle with the Commune, for the latter had control of the only organized force—the National Guard and the revolutionary committees of the sections. To reckon upon help from the departments was a vain hope, for the levy of three hundred thousand men was already meeting with great resistance, and the middle classes displayed great reluctance to enlist. Nevertheless, the Girondin plan was carried into effect.

On May 17 the Commune accepted the resignation of Santerre, who notified them of his departure for the Vendée, and replaced him provisionally as commander of the National Guard by Boulanger, second in command of one of the most revolutionary sections, that of the Halle-au-Blé, which had been responsible for initiating the celebrated petition of April 15 against the twenty-two. On the same day Camille Desmoulins aroused the applause of the Jacobins by his *Histoire des Brissotins*, a stinging pamphlet in which, on the flimsiest grounds, he represented the Girondins as the hired agents of England and Prussia. At once, on the very next day, May 18, Guadet denounced to the Convention the Parisian authorities "those anarchical authorities, greedy alike for money and power," and proposed that they should be superseded within twenty-four hours, the municipality being replaced by the presidents of the sections. Finally, he proposed that the deputies' substitutes (*députés suppléants*) should meet at Bourges and take the place of the Convention, in case it was overpowered by force. But Barère intervened, in the name of the Committee of Public Safety. He considered the measures proposed by Guadet impolitic. Since the Commune was plotting against the Convention, an inquiry must be held, and Barère proposed to appoint a commission of twelve members for this purpose.

The commission of twelve consisted of none but Girondins, many of whom had been among the twenty-two denounced by the Commune as traitors: Boyer-Fonfrède, Rabaut Saint-Étienne, Kervélégan, Larivière, Boilleau, etc. The inquiry was opened at once. In the course of a meeting of delegates from the revolutionary committees at the Mairie, a municipal officer named Marino had advised the massacre of the twenty-two. His motion had been indignantly rejected by Pache. But the incident had been reported to the Convention by the Girondin section of La Fraternité. This gave the commission of twelve the opportunity of adopting severe measures. On May 24 it ordered all the revolutionary committees of the sections to submit their minute-books to it. This was the prelude to an examination of the most violent revolutionaries before the tribunal. On the same day the commission, on the report of Viger, passed a decree quashing by implication the irregular appointment of Santerre's successor. The most senior of the battalion commanders was to discharge the duties of commandant of the National Guard. The same decree strengthened the guard of the Convention, and fixed ten o'clock in the evening as closing-time for the assemblies of the sections.

The decree was passed without much resistance from the Mountain, whereupon the commission of twelve proceded to order the arrest of Hébert for an article in the *Père Duchesne* in which he had accused "the statesmen" of having organized the pillaging of grocery stores and bakers' shops in order to stir up disorder and obtain an opportunity for calumniating the Parisians. Varlet, the Apostle of Equality, who for several months past had never stopped stirring up the populace against the Gironde, was sent to join Hébert in prison on the same evening, and so was Marino. Two days later Dobsen, president of the section of the Cité and a judge on the Revolutionary Tribunal, was arrested in turn, together with the secretary of his section, for having refused to communicate his minute-books to the commission of twelve. A fresh decree was voted on May 26 suppressing the revolutionary committee of the section of L'Unité, forbidding the vigilance committees in future to assume the name "revolutionary," confining their functions to the surveillance of foreigners, and finally charging the Minister of the Interior to hold an inquiry into their operations.

These measures of repression precipitated the crisis which had been coming to a head ever since the treason of Dumouriez. The Commune and the Montagnard sections at once made common cause with Hébert, Varlet, Marino, and Dobsen. As early as May 25 the Commune demanded of the Convention the release of their officer. "Arbitrary arrest," they said, "is as good as a civic crown to men of worth." The reply made to the petitioners by Isnard, president of the Convention, was as violently declamatory as it was tactless: "Listen to the truths which I am about to tell you. . . . If ever the Convention were to be humiliated, if ever, by one of those insurrections which have followed one another incessantly since March 10, and of which the municipal authorities have never warned the Convention, it so happened that these constantly recurring insurrections were to do any injury to the national representative body, I declare to you, in the name of the whole of France, that Paris should be annihilated; men would soon be searching the banks of the Seine to see whether Paris had existed." This was a repetition of Brunswick's threats, applied to revolutionary Paris.

321

As soon as Isnard's answer became known, the agitation in Paris redoubled in violence. On May 26 the Club of Female Revolutionary Republicans, of which Claire Lacombe was president, held a street demonstration in favor of Hébert. Sixteen sections demanded that the Convention release him. In the evening at the Jacobins, Robespierre, who had hitherto viewed with repugnance the idea of infringing the parliamentary privilege of the national representative body and restoring it to unity by means of violence, now incited the people to revolt: "When the people is oppressed, when it has no resource left but itself, he would be a coward indeed who should not call upon it to rise. It is when all laws are violated, it is when despotism is at its height, it is when good faith and decency are being trampled underfoot, that the people ought to rise in insurrection. That moment has arrived." The Jacobins declared themselves to be in a state of insurrection against the corrupt deputies.

The intervention of Robespierre and the Jacobins was the decisive factor. On the following day, May 27, the Mountain recovered its energy and made a great effort in the Convention. Marat demanded the suppression of the commission of twelve "as hostile to liberty and as tending to provoke that insurrection of the people which is only too imminent, owing to the negligence with which you have allowed commodities to rise to an excessive price." The section of the Cité came to the Convention and demanded the liberation of their president, Dobsen, and the prosecution of the commission of twelve. Isnard replied in arrogant and sneering terms. Robespierre tried to answer him, but Isnard refused him a hearing, and a violent tumult broke out which lasted for several hours. Numerous deputations came to stimulate the ardour of the Mountain. In the middle of the night the Mountain, left alone with the Plain, voted, on the motion of Delacroix, that the commission of twelve be suppressed and the imprisoned patriots set at liberty. Hébert, Dobsen, and Varlet returned in triumph to the Commune and to their sections. The Gironde had now committed every possible blunder.

Yet it persisted in its course. On May 28 Lanjuinais protested against the decree abolishing the commission of twelve, alleging that it was illegally obtained, and Guadet supported him. Voting took place orally by roll-call and resulted in the re-establishment of the commission of twelve by 279 votes to 238. Danton's comment on the voting was as follows: "Having proved that we surpass our enemies in prudence, we will prove that we surpass them in audacity and revolutionary vigour."

That very day the section of the Cité, Dobsen's section, summoned a meeting of the other sections at the Évêché [2] for the following day, in order to concert the organization for an insurrection. The meeting at the Évêché, presided over by the engineer Dufourny, a friend of Danton's who had founded the Cordeliers Club, decided to nominate a secret insurrectionary committee composed first of six and afterwards of nine members, to whose decisions implicit obedience was promised. Among the nine were Dobsen and Varlet.

On May 30 the departmental assembly rallied to the movement by summoning a general assembly of the Parisian authorities for the following day at nine o'clock in the morning, in the hall of the Jacobins. Marat presented himself at the Évêché, and the insurrectionary committee resolved to sound the tocsin early on the following day.

The insurrection accordingly started on May 31, and, directed by the secret committee at the Évêché, developed according to the methods already tested on August 10. At six o'clock in the morning the delegates of the thirty-three Montagnard sections, led by Dobsen, presented themselves at the Hôtel de Ville, showed the full powers with which the members had invested them, and suppressed the Commune, the members of which retired into an adjoining room. Next the revolutionary delegates provisionally reinstated the Commune in its functions. The insurgent committee, which was now sitting at the Hôtel de Ville, dictated to the Commune, now reinstated by the people, what measures it was to take. It thus obained the nomination of Hanriot, commandant of the battalion of the Jardin des Plantes, as sole commander-in-chief of the National Guard of Paris. It was decided that the poorer National Guards who were under arms should receive pay at the rate of forty sous a day. The alarm-gun was fired towards noon. The assembly of the Parisian authorities, summoned to the Jacobins by the departmental assembly, resolved to co-operate with the Commune and the insurrectionary committee, the numbers of which were raised to twenty-one by the addition of delegates from the meeting at the Jacobins. The committee of twenty-one immediately placed all property under the protection of the citizens.

The Girondins had taken fright at the threat. Several of them did not dare to sleep at home on the night of the 30–1. They failed to attend the session of the Convention on the 30th, and their absence enabled the Mountain to obtain the majority. Isnard's term as president having expired, the Montagnard Mallarmé was elected president on May 30 by 189 votes, as against 111 cast in favour of Lanjuinais.

---

[2] The former palace of the Archbishops of Paris.

On May 31 the Convention assembled to the sound of the tocsin and of the drum beating to arms. This time the Girondins appeared in greater force than on the previous day. They protested against the closing of the city gates and against the tocsin and alarm-gun.

The Assembly was drifting helplessly when the bearers of petitions from the sections and the Commune appeared at the bar at about five o'clock in the afternoon. They demanded that the commissions of twenty-two and of twelve, besides the ministers Lebrun and Clavière, should be cited before the Revolutionary Tribunal, that a central revolutionary army should be raised, that the price of bread should be fixed at three sous a pound throughout the whole Republic by means of a levy on the rich, that nobles holding senior rank in the army should be dismissed, that armouries should be created for arming the sansculottes, the departments of State purged, suspects arrested, the right to vote provisionally reserved to sansculottes only, and a fund set apart for the relatives of those defending their country and for the relief of the aged and infirm.

This amounted to an extensive program of revolutionary defence and social measures. A fresh deputation next arrived, formed of delegates from the authorities of Paris and led by Lullier, and protested against the threats uttered by Isnard against Paris. The petitioners made their way into the hall and sat down beside the Montagnards. The Gironde protested against this intrusion, and Vergniaud left the hall with his friends, though they returned almost immediately. Robespierre ascended the tribune and supported the request for the suppression of the commission of twelve made by Barère, thanks to whom it had been established; but Robespierre opposed the motion, also proposed by Barère, for giving the Convention the right to requisition armed forces directly. When Vergniaud called upon him to conclude, Robespierre turned towards him and said: "Yes, I will conclude, but it will be against you! Against you, who, after the revolution of August 10, wanted to send those responsible for it to the scaffold; against you, who have never ceased to incite to the destruction of Paris; against you, who wanted to save the tyrant; against you, who conspired with Dumouriez; against you, who have relentlessly proceeded against those very patriots whose heads Dumouriez demanded. . . . Well, my conclusion is: the prosecution of all Dumouriez's accomplices and all those whose names have been mentioned by the petitioners. . . ." To this terrible apostrophe Vergniaud made no reply. The Convention suppressed the commission of twelve and, on the motion of Delacroix, approved the ordinance of the Commune granting two livres a day to workmen under arms. Outside the Tuileries the Montagnard sections fraternized with the

Girondin section of the Butte des Moulins, which had been falsely accused of assuming the white cockade.

Yet the rising of May 31 ended unsatisfactorily. That very evening at the Commune, Chaumette and Dobsen were accused by Varlet of weakness. Hébert alleged that the rising had been a failure and that it was the fault of the Évêché, which had acted too precipitately. Billaud-Varenne expressed his disappointment at the Jacobins: "The country is not saved; there were great measures of public safety to be adopted; it was today that the final blows at the faction should have been struck. I cannot imagine how patriots can have left their post without citing the ministers Lebrun and Clavière before the courts." Chabot next deplored Danton's lack of vigour.

On June 1 the National Guard remained under arms; the Commune and the insurrectionary committee received a visit from Marat and drew up a fresh address, which was carried to the Convention at nightfall by Hassenfratz. Its conclusion was a demand that proceedings should be taken against twenty-seven deputies. Legendre went still further and demanded the arraignment of the whole Convention. Cambon and Marat referred the petition to the Committee of Public Safety. Barère advised the deputies named in the proscription list "to have the courage to resign." Most of the Girondins had not appeared at the session. The leaders had met at the house of one of them, Meillan, where they endeavoured in vain to agree upon a plan of resistance.

While the Girondins were shilly-shallying, as was their wont, the insurrectionary committee continued to act. During the night of June 1–2 it ordered the arrest of Roland and Clavière. Roland managed to escape, but his wife was arrested in his stead. The insurrectionary committee, by agreement with the Commune, ordered Hanriot to "surround the Convention with an armed force sufficient to command respect, in order that the chiefs of the faction may be arrested during the day, in case the Convention refused to accede to the request of the citizens of Paris." Orders were given to suppress the Girondin newspapers and arrest their editors.

June 2 was a Sunday. Workmen thronged to obey Hanriot's orders, and soon eighty thousand armed men, with cannon heading their procession, surrounded the Tuileries. The session of the Convention opened with one piece of bad news after another. Fontenay-le-Peuple, the chief town of the department of the Vendée, had just fallen into the hands of the rebels, and so had Marvejols in Lozère, while Mende was threatened. At Lyons the royalist and Girondin sections had gained control of the Hôtel de

325

Ville after a fierce struggle, in which it was said that eight hundred republicans had perished. The Montagnard municipality and Chalier were prisoners. In a few words Saint-André pointed the moral of these grave events: "What we need are great revolutionary measures. In times of tranquillity sedition can be checked by the ordinary laws; when there is a great movement, when the audacity of the aristocracy is carried to extremes, we must have recourse to the laws of war; this measure is no doubt terrible, but it is necessary; it would be in vain for you to employ any others." Lanjuinais, courageous as ever, though poorly supported by the right, which was but thinly attended, denounced the revolt of the Commune and asked for its suppression. Legendre tried to throw him down from the tribune. A deputation from the insurrectionary committee came and demanded in threatening terms the immediate arrest of the twenty-two and the twelve. The demand was referred to the Committee of Public Safety.

The petitioners went out shaking their fists at the Assembly and shouting: "To arms!" Strict orders were forthwith given by Hanriot forbidding the National Guards to let any deputy go in or out. Levasseur of Sarthe justified the arrest of the Girondins. Next, Barère, no doubt by an understanding with Danton, proposed a compromise, in the name of the Committee of Public Safety. The twenty-two and the twelve were not to be arrested, but were called upon voluntarily to suspend the exercise of their functions. Isnard and Fauchet obeyed on the spot. But Lanjuinais and Barbaroux energetically refused to adopt this bastard solution: "Do not expect either resignation or suspension from me," said Lanjuinais. And Barbaroux echoed him with the words: "No, do not expect any resignation from me. I have sworn to die at my post and I will abide by my oath." Marat and Billaud-Varenne in turn rejected any compromise. "The Convention has no right to cause the suspension of any of its members," said Billaud. "If they are guilty, they must be sent before the tribunals."

The dispute was interrupted by several deputies, complaining that Hanriot had closed the doors. Barère declaimed against the tyranny of the insurrectionary committee, and was supported by Delacroix and Danton. Delacroix obtained the passage of a decree ordering the armed forces to retire. Danton obtained the passage of another, ordering the Committee of Public Safety to find out who was responsible for the orders given to the National Guard, and vigorously to avenge the outraged national majesty.

Next, at the prompting of Barère, the whole Convention started out, led by the president, Hérault de Séchelles, and attempted by a theatrical exit to force their way through the wall of steel with which they were surrounded. Hérault advanced towards Hanriot, who returned an ironical answer and gave the order: "Gunners, to your posts!" The Assembly walked round the palace, repulsed by bayonets on all sides, only to return crestfallen to its place and submit. On the motion of Couthon it gave up its members, but stipulated that they should be placed under arrest at their own homes under guard of a gendarme. Marat had the name of Dussault, "the old dotard," as he called him, struck off the list, together with those of Lanthenas, the "feeble-minded," and Ducos, "who erred in good faith."

Thus the struggle which had begun in the Legislative Assembly ended in the triumph of the Mountain. The Girondins were defeated because, having started a foreign war, they had failed to obtain victory and peace; because, having been the first to denounce the King and demand the Republic, they could not make up their minds to overthrow the former and proclaim the latter; because they hesitated at every decisive moment—on the eve of August 10 and on the eve of January 21; because their equivocal policy gave the impression that they were cherishing selfish aims—ulterior motives concerning ministerial portfolios or a regency, or a change of dynasty; because amid the terrible economic crisis which prevailed they were unable to propose any remedy and opposed in a narrow and bitter spirit all the claims of the class of the sansculottes, whose strength and rights they underestimated; because they opposed with blind obstinacy all the exceptional measures which the situation demanded; because, after voting against these, they tried to hamper their application; because, in short, they neglected the public safety and confined themselves to a narrow class policy benefiting the middle classes only.

June 2 was therefore more than a political revolution. The sansculottes overthrew not only a party, but, to a certain extent, a class of society. After the minority consisting of the nobility, which perished with the throne, it was the turn of the upper middle classes.

The revolution of August 10 had already been characterized by an obvious mistrust of parliamentarism. But the revolution of August 10 had spared the Assembly. This time, taught by experience, the sansculottes went a step further. They did not hesitate to mutilate the national representative body, though in this they were following the example set them by their opponents when they sent Marat before the Rvolutionary Tribunal. The class policy inaugurated in their turn by those responsible for June 2 could be adapted only with difficulty to the existing legal framework. A blow had been struck at the fiction of parliamentarism. The time for a dictatorship was at hand.

BOOK THREE
The Terror

CHAPTER I

The Federalist Revolt

THE revolution of June 2, like that of August 10, was due in the first place to revolutionary patriotism. The sansculottes of Paris, supported by those of the large towns, overthrew the Gironde for the same reasons as they had overthrown the monarchy: because they accused it of obstructing the defence of the Revolution. The revolution of August 10 had been a bloody one, but that of June 2 had not cost a single human life. The men of August 10 had not hesitated to seize control of all municipal institutions; those responsible for the events of June 2, on the other hand, after affirming their right to set up a fresh administration at the Hôtel de Ville, allowed the existing one to continue the exercise of its functions. Their insurrectionary committee had allowed itself to be swamped by new recruits chosen by the departmental and communal authorities. The legal Commune, reinstated by the committee, made it its business to moderate its course of action and remain in touch with the Government, which provided the necessary funds for paying the National Guards who had been under arms for three days. One historian has ventured to write, with a touch of exaggeration, that June 2 was not so much an insurrection as a *coup d'état*.

The situation was very different from that of the previous year. On August 10 the Government had been entirely re-formed at the same time as the Commune. And though this had not been enough to satisfy the revolutionary organizers, though antagonism had almost immediately broken out between the Legislative Assembly and the new Commune, the latter, by retaining possession of the Hôtel de Ville, had at least kept in its hands a means of bringing pressure to bear upon the legally constituted Government. On June 2 the insurrectionary committee disappeared with hardly a struggle. Most of its members allowed themselves to be absorbed in an organ purposely created for them, the vigilance committee of the department of Paris, which had in its hands the political control of the city and suburbs, under the guidance of the Committee of Public Safety, in whose pay it was. The insurgents of yesterday became the police of the morrow.

331

On August 10 the insurrection had attained without delay its main object, the imprisonment of the King in the Temple. On June 2, on the other hand, the insurgents only obtained a partial and precarious victory. The twenty-nine leaders of the Gironde, though in theory confined to their residences, each under guard of a gendarme, moved about the town freely, received visits, and gave supper parties. Twelve of them fled on the very first day, and eight more during the following days. Those who remained did not consider that all was lost. On June 5 Valazé in a haughty letter refused in advance the rumoured amnesty, and on the following day Vergniaud imperatively demanded a trial and threatened his accusers with the scaffold.

The Committee of Public Safety, which had failed to do anything but propose feeble compromises during the three days for which the insurrection had lasted, seemed crushed under the weight of accumulated responsibility which rested upon it. Having paid the expenses of the rising and provided the leaders of it with sinecures, the committee imagined that it would be able to evade carrying out their program, and actually dreamt of reinstating in the Convention the twenty-nine deputies under arrest. On June 5 it called upon Pache to hand over to it in the course of the day the documents upon which their indictment was based, "in default of which it will be forced to announce to the Convention that none exist." Needless to say, Pache turned a deaf ear to their request. The committee did not realize that the best way to prevent the Girondins from resorting to revolt was to recall them firmly to their patriotic duty and refuse to allow what was now a *fait accompli* to be called in question. It maintained the ministers Clavière and Lebrun in office for the time being, in spite of the fact that warrants had been issued for their arrest. Clavière was not replaced by Destournelles till June 13, and Lebrun by Deforgues till June 21. At the same time, as though desirous of giving pledges to the moderates, the committee demanded the resignation of the Minister for War, Bouchotte, beloved of the Montagnards, and in spite of Robespierre's opposition had him replaced by Beauharnais, a noble, who had, however, the good sense to refuse. In all these appointments the hand of Danton could be traced. Garat, the Minister of the Interior, another protégé of Danton's, tells us that the latter welcomed the idea, which he himself submitted to the committee, of negotiating with the defeated party with a view to avoiding civil war, and that in these negotiations an amnesty was in view.

On June 6, in a great report to the Convention, Barère proposed to do away with the revolutionary committees, which kept a watch on suspects and supervised the execution of the recruiting law—"instruments of anarchy and vengeance," as he called them—to appoint a fresh general staff for the Parisian Guard without delay, dismiss its commander, Hanriot, restore the liberty of the press, and send hostages chosen from among the members of the Convention into the departments represented by the deputies under arrest. "Danton," he says, "was the first to voice this opinion," and Danton did in fact support the measure on the following day, at the same time pronouncing an unqualified eulogy on the citizens of Bordeaux. This over-adroit policy could not but encourage the resistance of the Gironde and result in setting up in Paris itself a violent agitation which it would be difficult to calm. As early as June 6 seventy-five deputies of the right signed a protest against the violence done to the Convention, and several of them at once left Paris to assist the Girondin fugitives in rousing the departments. On June 15 the Assembly was forced to order a roll-call of its members and issue a threat to the absentees that their substitutes (*suppléants*) might be summoned. In Paris those responsible for the insurrection began saying that they were being cheated. Danton was sharply attacked at the Cordeliers on June 4 and at the Jacobins on June 7. Robespierre was convinced that it was waste of time to negotiate with the Girondins. Since civil war was inevitable, they ought, he thought, to wage it with the best chance of success, by interesting the sansculottes in the battle.

During the insurrection he had scrawled in his memorandum-book this remarkable note: "What we need is a single will (*une volonté une*). It must be either republican or royalist. If it is to be republican, we must have republican ministers, republican papers [i. e., newspapers], republican deputies, a republican government. The internal dangers come from the middle classes; in order to defeat the middle classes we must rally the people. Everything had been so disposed as to place the people under the yoke of the bourgeois and send the defenders of the Republic to the scaffold. They have triumphed at Marseilles, Bordeaux, and Lyons. They would have triumphed at Paris had it not been for the present insurrection. The present insurrection must go on until the measures necessary for saving the Republic have been taken. The people must ally itself with the Convention, and the Convention must make use of the people. The insurrection must gradually spread from place to place on the same plan; the sansculottes must be paid and remain in the towns. They must be supplied with arms, roused to anger, and enlightened, and republican enthusiasm must be inflamed by all possible means."

It was this program of action that Robespierre endeavoured to carry into effect, and impose piecemeal upon the Committee of Public Safety and the Convention.

On June 8 he vigorously combated the measures proposed by Barère two days previously and supported by Danton. He pointed out that counter-revolution already prevailed at Marseilles, Lyons, and Bordeaux and that its establishment had been anterior to the events in Paris. The dismissal of Hanriot and the reconstitution of his general staff would amount to a repudiation of the insurrection of June 2 and involve the risk of provoking a fresh one. The suppression of the revolutionary committees would give the aristocracy a chance of reprisals and disarm the republicans. His speech was at first greeted with violent murmuring, but ended amid applause. Saint-André gave it his unreserved support. "The question is," he said, "whether, on the pretext of liberty, liberty can itself be slain." Lejeune blamed the Committee of Public Safety for its weakness and blindness. Barère and Danton gave way, and themselves proposed the adjournment of the measures which they had proposed. "To desire that the Convention should undo June 2," says Michelet, "was to desire that it should humiliate itself, that it should admit having succumbed to fear and violence, and that it should annul all it had done that day."

When events justified Robespierre's apprehensions, and on June 13 news arrived of the revolt of the Norman departments, and when it became necessary to think about repressing it, Danton pronounced an impassioned panegyric on Paris and obtained the passage of a motion that Paris had saved the Republic. From that day onwards the right wing was silenced; but the delays and hesitations of the Committee of Public Safety had enabled the Girondin revolt to spread further. The revolt had been concerted and premeditated even before May 31. As early as May 24 the department of Jura had called upon the substitute deputies (*suppléants*) to meet at Bourges and form an assembly to take the place of the other. The department of Ain adopted this proposal on May 27. On May 15 Chasset, deputy for Lyons, wrote to his friend Dubost: "Our lives, and then our property, are at stake. So march, and rouse your friends." On May 25 the sections of Bordeaux held a general assembly and discussed the project of raising troops and leading them against Paris, etc.

The news of the insurrection in Paris only precipitated and extended a movement which had already begun. The Girondin leaders had the parts which they were to play already allotted to them. "Their flight," says their historian Claude Perroud, "was the result of a concerted plan which had been discussed among them; they have admitted this."

334

Buzot, who had taken refuge in his own department of Eure, prophesied that Marat would soon be dictator and that massacres would take place, and on June 7 he persuaded the department to raise a force of four thousand men. Calvados followed suit on June 9, by arresting Romme and Prieur (of Marne), the deputies charged with organizing the defence of the coasts against England. The Breton departments—Finistère, Ille-et-Vilaine, Côtes-du-Nord, Morbihan, and Mayenne—roused by Duchâtel, Meilhan, and Kervélégan, united themselves with Eure and Calvados in a general assembly for resistance to oppression. Caen became the capital of the Girondin west. Félix Wimpfen, who was in command of the army of the coasts of Cherbourg, went over to the insurrection, taking with him two regiments of cavalry. He was reinforced by three fine battalions raised in Brittany, composed, says Vaultier, a contemporary observer who fought side by side with them, "not of tousled, ragged Bretons, but entirely of young men of the best families of Rennes, Lorient, and Brest, all in uniform, dressed in fine cloth and perfectly equipped."

On June 7 Bordeaux expelled the representatives on mission Ichon and Dartigoyte; on June 9 it gave orders for the raising of a departmental force of twelve hundred men, summoned an assembly of representatives of all the insurgent departments at Bourges for July 16, and seized 350,000 piastres intended for expenditure on the navy and the colonies; on June 27 it further expelled Mathieu and Treilhard, the representatives on mission, sent from the Committee of Public Safety with proposals for an agreement; and finally, on June 30, it sent a letter, composed by Grangeneuve, to Custine, who was in command of the principal French army, calling upon him to rally to the good cause. But Custine's rejoinder was a patriotic sermon.

For a moment the insurrection spread throughout the whole of the south. Toulouse let the royalists out of prison and replaced them by partisans of Marat, besides raising a force of a thousand men. At Nîmes, whither Rabaut Saint-Étienne had betaken himself, the club was closed, the Maratists disarmed and imprisoned. Marseilles, which had been in open revolt even before May 31, kept back three thousand men intended for the army of Italy, and got into touch with the towns of the south.

On July 12 Toulon rose in revolt against Pierre Bayle and Beauvais, the representatives on mission, and imprisoned them in Fort Lamalgue, after forcing them to perform a public penance, taper in hand. Admirals Trogoff and Chaussegros rallied to the movement. By the middle of May Corsica, stirred up by Paoli, had elected an extraordinary council (*con-*

sulta), and the French were maintaining themselves only in Bastia and a few ports.

The revolt of the south was closely connected with that of Lyons, which itself had ramifications in the east and centre. Deaf to the conciliatory proposals brought from Paris by Robert Lindet, the Girondins of Lyons threw everybody suspected of Montagnard sympathies into prison. In order to strike terror to the hearts of the Jacobin workmen, who were numerous in certain parts of the city, they caused their leader Chalier to be condemned to death, and he was executed on July 16. The command of the troops at Lyons was shortly afterwards handed over to a returned *émigré*, the Comte de Précy.

By the middle of June about sixty departments were in more or less open rebellion. Fortunately the frontier departments had remained faithful to the Convention. The rising was widespread rather than deep. It was essentially the work of the departmental and district administrations, composed of rich property-owners. The communes, which were more popular in composition, showed themselves in general lukewarm or hostile. The raising of recruits ordered by the insurgent administrations met with the greatest difficulties. The labourers and artisans would not resign themselves to making sacrifices for the rich, who did nothing to better their lot. In spite of repeated appeals from the deputies Chambon and Lidon, the insurgents of Bordeaux could not get together more than four hundred men. When on July 7 Wimpfen reviewed the National Guard at Caen and asked for volunteers, only seventeen stepped out of the ranks.

But not only was the federalist revolt hampered by the popular indifference or hostility, but its very leaders, in spite of their sounding phrases, lacked faith in their cause and soon became divided among themselves.

Those of them who were sincere republicans could not fail to be uneasy about the foreign invasion and the Vendée, and this anxiety paralysed them. Those who were ambitious, seeing themselves rejected by the people, sought support from the Feuillants and even from the aristocrats. At Caen Félix Wimpfen, an avowed royalist, who already in September 1792, during the siege of Thionville, had entered into relations with the enemy, proposed to the Girondin deputies to call in the English. The deputies rejected his suggestion, but left him in possession of his command. As chief of his staff he had the Comte de Puisaye, who on the failure of the insurrection took refuge in the Vendée, together with the *procureur général syndic* of Calvados, young Bougon-Longrais, a friend of Charlotte Corday.

At Lyons, Précy sent the Chevalier d'Arthès to Switzerland to ask for assistance from the Bernese and Sardinians. On August 4 Joseph de Maistre, who was in charge of the King of Sardinia's spy system at Geneva, promised him that a diversion should be created in the Alps, and the promise was carried out. The Lyons royalists, however, kept their flag in the background and did not dare to proclaim Louis XVII, as those at Toulon had done.

The lack of forethought displayed by the Convention during the first few days was redeemed by its vigour and skill in organizing measures of repression. Warrants were issued for the arrest of the rebellious Girondin leaders, the members of the revolting departmental administrations were deprived of their office, the administrative centre of Eure was transferred from Evreux to Bernay, the department of Vaucluse was created with the object of separating the interests of Avignon and Marseilles, and the department of Loire carved out of that of Rhône-et-Loire in order to set up Saint-Étienne in opposition to Lyons.

The Convention drew a careful distinction between the leaders in these events and the minor actors, whom they had led astray. On June 26 Robert Lindet obtained the grant of three days' grace to the rebellious administrative bodies, in order to give them time to retract, a clever move which facilitated defections. The members of the administrative bodies of the department of Somme, who had been deprived of their offices on June 14, came and offered an explanation, and on June 17 the Committee of Public Safety sent them back unpunished. Saint-Just, who had been charged to report to the assembly on the deputies "placed under arrest," displayed striking moderation. "All those under arrest," he said on July 8, "are not guilty; the greater number of them were only led astray." He distinguished between three categories: the traitors, of whom there were nine (Barbaroux, Bergoeing, Birotteau, Buzot, Gorsas, Lanjuinais, Louvet, Petion, and Salle); the accomplices, of whom there were five (Gardien, Gensonné, Guadet, Mollevaut, and Vergniaud); and the misguided (*égarés*), whom he proposed to reinstate in the Convention, of whom there were fourteen. This moderation was calculated to conciliate waverers.

But, above all, the Mountain realized that it was necessary to rally the masses by making substantial concessions to them, according to Robespierre's plan, and obtained the passage of three great laws to this effect: (1) The law of June 3 on the procedure to be used in disposing of the property of the *émigrés*. This property was to be divided into small lots, poor purchasers being allowed ten years to complete their purchase. (2) The law of June 10 regulating the division of the property of the communes. It was to be divided up on a principle of equality, so much for

337

each inhabitant. This measure affected 8,000,000 *arpents* (acres), valued at 600,000,000 livres. (3) The law of July 17 which completed the ruin of the seigniorial regime by abolishing without compensation even those dues and payments based upon the production of the original titles. The last feudal parchments were to be destroyed, in order to prevent dispossessed property-owners from one day reviving their claims. Thus the fall of the Gironde would appear to the peasants as the final liberation of the soil from all burdens.

A decree of June 8 increased the salaries of officials and, in order to calm the middle classes, who were alarmed at the forced loan of 1,000,000,-000 livres, a decree was passed on June 23, on the motion of Robespierre, exempting all married people whose net income should be less than 10,000 livres, and unmarried persons with less than 6,000. This was a timely method of dividing and dissolving the Girondin party, which was largely composed of well-to-do people who would be won over if treated with consideration.

This moral offensive was completed and crowned by the rapid voting of a very liberal Constitution, which formed a telling rejoinder to the accusations of dictatorship brought by the Girondins. Whereas the Constitution drafted by Condorcet strengthened the Executive Council by causing it to be elected by the people and rendered independent of the Assembly, the Montagnard Constitution, drafted by Hérault de Séchelles, laid down the principle of the subordination of ministers to the national representative body. It abolished the indirect suffrage in two degrees which Condorcet had maintained for the election of deputies: in future their election was to take place, not on the very complicated system of the list vote (*scrutin de liste*), but by an absolute majority and direct and universal suffrage.

The administrative bodies alone were still to be elected by the electoral colleges, which were also to submit to the Assembly a list of eighty-three candidates, out of whom it was to choose the twenty-four ministers. Lastly, the Montagnard Constitution promised popular education, guaranteed the right to a livelihood, and made the declaration of war dependent upon a previous consultation of the country. It was submitted for popular ratification, and approved by 1,801,918 votes to 17,610. But there were more than 100,000 voters who only accepted it with federalist amendments, demanding that the twenty-two and the twelve—that is, the deputies under arrest—should be set at liberty, the laws passed since their arrest annulled, a fresh Assembly summoned, the representatives on mission recalled, the maximum price for corn abolished, etc. The plebiscite was everywhere marked by the collapse of the Girondin party, which was, however, only overthrown by the second Committee of Public Safety, nominated on July 10. On July 13 the Norman insurgents, who were marching to Paris, under the command of Puisaye, met a body of Parisian volunteers, who dispersed them at Brécourt, near Vernon, by a few cannon-shots. Robert Lindet was sent to Caen, and speedily pacified the region by reducing repression to a minimum.

At Bordeaux the resistance lasted longer. Ysabeau and Tallien, who had entered the city for the first time on August 19, were obliged to take refuge at La Réole, the Jacobin town. But the sansculotte sections of Bordeaux, stirred up by the representatives on mission, overthrew the Girondin municipality on September 18, and repression began.

For a moment there had been great danger in the south-east of a junction between the rebels of Marseilles and Nîmes and those of Lyons. Those from Nîmes advanced as far as Pont-Saint-Esprit; those from Marseilles, under the command of Villeneuve-Tourette, an ex-officer, crossed the Durance, seized Avignon, and got as far as Orange. But the department of Drôme remained faithful to the Mountain. From June 24 to 26 a congress was held at Valence of forty-two popular societies from the departments of Ardèche, Drôme, Gard, and Bouches-du-Rhône, and this congress, of which Claude Payan was the life and soul, organized the resistance. Carteaux had time to hurry to the spot with a detachment from the army of the Alps, in which Bonaparte was serving. He recaptured Pont-Saint-Esprit, separated the insurgents of Nîmes from those of Marseilles, and threw the latter back towards the south. He reached Avignon on July 27 and entered Marseilles on August 25, just in time to prevent the town from falling into the hands of the English, whom Villeneuve-Tourette had already summoned to his aid. But the English entered Toulon two days later, in reponse to an appeal from Admirals Trogoff and Chaussegros, who handed over to them the finest squadron in the French navy. In order to recapture Toulon a long siege was necessary, which lasted till the end of December.

Lyons was isolated. The departments of Jura and Ain, which might have sent assistance, had been speedily pacified by Bassal and Garnier (of Saintes), two deputies of the Convention, who had raised a little army of 2,500 men in Côte-d'Or and Doubs. But Lyons put up a stouter resistance than Bordeaux and refused to be intimidated by the bombardment started by Dubois-Crancé as early as August 22. Communications with the region of the Forez had remained open, and it was not completely invested till September 17, when Couthon, Maignet, and Châteauneuf-

Randon brought up the National Guards of Cantal, Aveyron, Puy-de-Dôme, and Haute-Loire. Lyons held out till October 9. Précy managed to escape to Switzerland with a handful of men. The repression was bound to be terrible.

The regions in which the revolt was dangerous were precisely those in which a large number of royalists had remained. There was no room for a third party between the Mountain, which was identified with the Republic, and royalism, which was the ally of the enemy. If the federalist revolt, which was the expression of the resentment of defeated politicians and class selfishness, had succeeded, it would certainly have led to a monarchist restoration.

The royalist insurrection in the Vendée had already forced the Convention to take a long step in the direction of the Terror—that is to say, the dictatorship of the central power and the suppression of liberties. The Girondin insurrection now prompted it to take a decisive step in the same direction. Till then the only suspects had been the royalists, but now a considerable section of the former revolutionary party fell into the category of allies of the enemy. Suspicion increased and it became more and more difficult to draw the line between good and bad citizens. How were true patriots, sincere friends of liberty, to be recognized if a Vergniaud and a Brissot, a Buzot and a Petion, who had been the first to shake the foundations of the throne and demand a republic, were now no better than traitors? The idea grew up that everybody who played any part in the Republic had to be subjected to incessant supervision, an inquisition into every movement of his life. The clubs, and shortly afterwards the administrative bodies, were purged, and each time this process was carried out, the ranks of the revolutionaries grew thinner. Since the Girondins had relied on the support of the property-owning classes, these now became suspect. Wealth was regarded as implying "aristocratic" views. The revolutionary party was soon to become no more than an ardent, jealous, energetic minority. After all, it is only minorities which require a dictatorship and violence. But the Jacobin minority was able to shelter its actions behind the great figure of the nation, whose defence and salvation it adopted as its mission.

CHAPTER II

Early Days of the Great Committee of Public Safety

(July 1793)

THE first Committee of Public Safety, dominated by Cambon, Barère, and Danton, had been formed on April 6, 1793, after the treason of Dumouriez, but succumbed on July 10, under the weight of its accumulated mistakes. It had humiliated the Republic by the vain attempts to negotiate secretly with the powers of the Coalition (the missions of Proli, Matthews, Desportes, etc.). It had succeeded neither in driving back the enemy on the frontiers, nor in preventing a formidable extension of the Vendean and federalist revolts. It had tolerated Custine's insolence and forgiven his reverses in Alsace, and, in spite of Bouchotte's opposition, it had appointed him to the command of the principal army, that of the north, which he left in a state of complete inaction. The committee had been either unable or unwilling to put down the shameless depredations of the army-contractors, who found protectors even among its own members. It had never seriously taken in hand either the financial problem or that of the cost of living. The only at all efficacious measure which was adopted under its auspices, having as its object the withdrawal of the assignats from circulation, was the decree of June 7, 1793, granting purchasers of national property who paid their instalments in advance a bonus of one-half of one per cent on each year's instalment. The same decree authorized the district collectors to sell the claims of the State against purchasers of national property The claims paid for by assignats were to be replaced by bonds carrying five per cent interest, and the hope was held out to the bondholders that they would one day be repaid in coin by the purchasers of such property, the right to whose instalments they had acquired. The system was ingenious, but it came too late, at a moment when confidence in the paper money and credit of the State was already seriously shaken. The measure caused the return of a certain number of assignats to the Treasury, but far too small a proportion of them to produce any effect upon the cost of living, which was rising daily by leaps and bounds. At the end of June the Enragés, who voiced the popular

341

discontent, got up a violent agitation on the occasion of the voting of the Constitution. Jacques Roux brought a threatening petition to the Assembly, and boats laden with soap were pillaged in the harbours of Paris. The Committee of Public Safety seemed no longer capable of securing order in the capital. Finally, at the beginning of July, an obscure royalist plot, in which General Arthur Dillon, the friend and protégé of Camille Desmoulins, was concerned, put the finishing touch to the suspicions resting upon Danton and Delacroix, who were rightly regarded as unreliable.

The new committee, elected on July 10 by an oral vote, consisted of nine members only: Jeanbon Saint-André, Barère, Gasparin, Couthon, Hérault, Thuriot, Prieur of Marne, Saint-Just, and Robert Lindet. The mandate given to these men was that of saving the State by those vigorous measures for which the public had looked in vain to their predecessors. They were full of good intentions of a general kind, but were far from being agreed upon a common program. Saint-André, Couthon, Hérault, and Prieur of Marne formed with Saint-Just the left wing of the committee. They were convinced that it was necessary to govern in close touch with the revolutionaries grouped in the clubs; to accede to their requests, feed and provide relief for the sansculottes in the towns who were struggling against distress, put down treason, introduce changes in the general staffs and administrative bodies—in short, to base themselves upon the lower classes in order to put an end to anarchy, restore unity of control and impose obedience upon all. They were ready to establish a class policy, for the rich, who had followed in the train of the Gironde, were falling away from the Revolution and even going over to royalism. But certain of their colleagues, Thuriot, Robert Lindet, and Gasparin, were alarmed at their boldness and afraid of making matters worse by throwing the whole of the middle classes into opposition by too vigorous a policy of repression, as well as of disorganizing the army by systematically attacking the generals of noble birth, with whom they believed it was impossible to dispense, on account of their competence. As for that fertile genius Barère, he passed from one shade of opinion to another according to circumstances.

The lack of agreement between the members of the committee was apparent from the first. On July 11 a series of vigorous measures was adopted, all of which were proposed by members of the left wing. Saint-André obtained the removal of Biron from his command in the Vendée. Couthon denounced the deputies Birotteau and Chasset, who were fomenting the insurrection at Lyons. He proposed to give orders for the arrest of all the deputies representing the department of Rhône and to proscribe

342

Birotteau, and the Convention passed a decree to this effect. On the following day the committee gave fresh pledges to the revolutionaries by ordering Custine to report himself in Paris at once and submit to an inquiry into the position of his army. But on the same day the committee, in the person of Bouchotte, met with a defeat. The Convention refused to appoint Dittmann, whom he had proposed to succeed Biron. On the motion of Cambon, it chose Beysser, who had soon to be removed from his command on account of his connexion with the federalists. What was more serious, at the same session Thuriot parted company with his colleagues on the committee and obtained the adjournment of a severe measure, passed on the motion of Chabot, making it incumbent upon the departmental administrative bodies to submit to the committees the letters which they had received from deputies of the right wing. "This decree," said Thuriot, "can only prove a cause of division, whereas we ought to rally men of all opinions round us." Unlike Couthon, Thuriot, faithful to his friend Danton's temporizing policy, did not want to go too deeply into the responsibilities incurred by the Girondin deputies.

These early days of the great committee gave but a small idea of what it was to become later; but it was urged on by irresistible necessities. "Revolutionaries are not born, but made," as Lazare Carnot said. In fact, these men had the dictatorship forced upon them. They neither desired nor foresaw it. The Terror, said Hippolyte Carnot, was a "dictatorship of distress," and the saying is profoundly true.

On July 13 Hérault de Séchelles, in the name of the committee, announced a piece of bad news: Condé, for lack of food and munitions, had probably been obliged to surrender; Valenciennes was gravely menaced and was about to meet with the same fate. The session was not yet at an end when news arrived of the assassination of Marat by Charlotte Corday.

This descendant of the great Corneille was royalist to the core. She read L'Ami du roi and the Petit Gautier. She was a royalist, but not a devout Catholic, and she did not attend the services of the Church. In her last moments she refused a priest. The Girondin revolt had seemed to her to be a step towards the restoration of the monarchy. Nurtured in the traditions of Roman history, she was indignant when she saw that at a review of the National Guard of Caen the inhabitants of the town refused to enlist in Wimpfen's army. She determined to give these cowards a lesson by striking a blow at the Montagnard who was regarded as most hostile to property, whom the Girondins had denounced for months past as an anarchist and a blood-thirsty oppressor. "I have killed one man," she said to her judges, "to save a hundred thousand."

Charlotte was quite convinced that she had dealt anarchy—that is to say, the Montagnard party—its death-blow. But she had given it new strength.

That very evening, at the Convention, Chabot represented the murder of the "Friend of the People" as the result of a royalist and Girondin plot which was to break out on the following day, the anniversary of July 14. He obtained the passage of a motion for the arrest of Depéret, whom Charlotte had visited before her crime. Couthon expressed his conviction that the royalists and Girondins were plotting for the dissolution of the Convention and the liberation of the young Dauphin, whom they intended to proclaim king. He proposed the arrest of the deputies for Calvados, and the trial before the Revolutionary Tribunal of the Girondin deputies who had already been arrested. Their lives were to pay for that of Marat. But once more the divisions in the Committee of Public Safety became evident. Thuriot, who on the previous day had extended his protection to the deputies who had written compromising letters, opposed the arrest of the deputies for Calvados and was supported by Delacroix. The Convention voted for the arrest of Fauchet only, but it was not long before it was drawn into further measures of repression.

Marat was very popular among the humbler classes, whose sufferings he had tended with a rough but sincere sympathy. His death by violence aroused the deepest emotion. The Jacobins, with Bentabole as their spokesman, proposed that this martyr of liberty should receive the honour of burial in the Panthéon. Robespierre had great difficulty in obtaining the rejection of the proposal, on the pretext that it was first necessary to avenge the victim. The Convention attended the funeral in a body on July 16. The Friend of the People was buried in the gardens of the Tuileries, in an artificial grotto adorned with poplars. His heart was suspended from the vaulted ceiling of the Cordeliers Club. For several weeks the Paris sections and most of the provincial towns held funeral celebrations in his honour, ending with appeals for vengeance. His bust was placed with those of Le Pelletier and Chalier on the walls of clubs and republican meeting-places.

Blood calls for blood. The execution of Chalier and the murder of Marat, occurring within three days of each other, provided a formidable argument for all those who were already calling for terrorist measures in order to repress counter-revolution, the ally of the enemy. It was necessary, they said, to avenge the victims, preserve the life of the patriot chiefs threatened by the daggers of the aristocrats, and put an end to weakness and consideration!

There was competition among the popular leaders, Leclerc, Jacques Roux, and Varlet, as to who was to take the place of Marat, who, while he was alive, had denounced their counter-revolutionary exaggerations. As early as July 16, Jacques Roux hastened to bring out a continuation of Marat's newspaper, to which he boldly gave the title, *Publiciste de la République française par l'ombre de Marat l'ami du peuple* (Publicist to the French Republic by the shade of Marat, Friend of the People). Young Leclerc was roused to emulation. On July 20 he started issuing the *Ami du peuple*, the title of which was borrowed from Marat's first newspaper.

The Enrages, who had hitherto possessed no press organ of their own, now owned two. Leclerc hastened to denounce the commercial aristocracy. In his eyes the high price of food was the result of a plot on the part of the rich. He denounced "the robbers of the public, enjoying the fruits of their plunder under the protection of the law," and expressed his surprise that the "patient and kindly people did not fall upon this handful of assassins" (July 23). He demanded that speculators in necessary commodities should be punished by death Jacques Roux soon imitated him, and, what was still more serious, Hébert in turn, in order to maintain the popularity of his *Père Duchesne*, which was now threatened with dangerous competition, vied with his rivals for the title which they had taken upon themselves of heirs of the Friend of the People. "If a successor to Marat is needed," he exclaimed at the Jacobins on July 20, "if a second victim is needed, here he is all ready and resigned; it is I!" While in no wise abating his personal hostility to the leaders of the Enragés, he borrowed their program piecemeal. In his No. 267 he proposed that suspects should everywhere be imprisoned in the churches; that, in order to feed the towns, the Republic should seize the harvest, paying compensation to the farmers; and that corn, wine, and all commodities should be divided among the departments in proportion to their population.

These incitements, which almost precipitated an insurrection of the Paris sections, fell upon favourable soil. By the end of that July the food shortage was becoming more acute. The insurgent departments of Brittany and Normandy had stopped sending supplies to the capital. Queues had begun again at the doors of the bakeries from early dawn, and there were disorders in the markets. The situation was so serious that the two Committees of Public Safety and General Security met during the night of July 20–1 to adopt emergency measures.

345

There was a danger that the Committee of Public Safety might be overpowered by the mob. Billaud-Varenne and Collot d'Herbois persuaded them to vote in a hurry the famous decree of July 27 on the repression of food-speculation.

Food-speculation (*accaparement*) was defined as the action of merchants in holding back from circulation goods or commodities of prime necessity, "without putting them up for sale daily and in public"; or the action, on the part of ordinary individuals, "of voluntarily causing or allowing commodities and goods of prime necessity to perish " All those holding supplies of these commodities were obliged to declare them at the town hall within a week. The municipalities were authorized to appoint commissaries for dealing with food-speculation (*commissaires aux accaparements*), whose salaries were to be paid out of the proceeds of the sales and confiscations. They were to check the returns and to see to it that the merchants put their commodities up for sale "in small lots and to all purchasers." In case of a refusal, they were to hold the sale themselves, handing over the proceeds to the merchants. Merchants failing to draw up a return, or making a false one, were to be punished by death, and so were functionaries who neglected to apply the law. Informers would be rewarded by a third of the amount confiscated. Finally, the sentences of the criminal tribunals on offences falling within the scope of this law were not to be subject to appeal.

Henceforward all commodities of prime necessity were under the control of the authorities. There was no more privacy for commerce. Cellars, granaries, and storehouses were to be inspected by the food commissaries, who had the right to call upon the owner to produce his invoices. A great step had been taken in the direction of the system of the Enragés.

The fact that such an important law could be proposed, debated, and passed without consulting the Committee of Public Safety or calling upon it to express an opinion is sufficient proof that it was far from having established its authority over the Assembly.

The committee came into collision with the covert opposition of the Assembly. On July 19 it had recalled a number of lukewarm or dubious representatives on mission: Courtois, who was suspected of speculating in army stores; Lesage-Senault and Duhem, who had come into conflict with the club at Lille; Goupilleau de Fontenay, who had shown himself hostile to the sansculotte generals sent to the army in the Vendée. On the following day Rühl, a moderate and a friend of Danton, denounced the commissaries of the Executive Council, who, if he was to be believed, were hampering the activity of the representatives on mission, besides being very expensive and quite useless. Baudot, another Dantonist, supported Rühl's motion, which looked very much like a rejoinder to the recall of the representatives on mission ordered by the Committee of Public Safety on the previous day. Billaud-Varenne defended Bouchotte's commissaries, and the motion was referred to the committee. But Rühl was not satisfied, and demanded that the committee should submit to the Convention a list of its agents abroad, with notes upon each of them. The motion was passed, with an amendment, proposed by Taillefer and Cambon, further ordering the committee to produce information about the commissaries of the Executive Council within twenty-four hours.

Hearing that Custine, who had been allowed to remain at large since he was recalled to Paris, had been greeted with sympathetic demonstrations by the habitués of the gambling-establishments in the Palais Royal, the committee had him arrested during the night of July 21–2, and on the same day dismissed his second in command, Lamorlière, who was temporarily in command of the army of the north. These two measures gave rise to a fresh debate in the Convention. This time Danton intervened in person. He pretended to applaud the arrest of Custine, but added: "I propose that the Minister for War and the Committee of Public Safety make a statement with regard to the charges brought against this general, so that the Convention may give its opinion on the matter." Devars wanted the committee to make its report then and there, but Drouet obtained the concession that no time limit should be fixed.

The removal of Lamorlière from his command and the arrest of Custine aroused sharp opposition in the heart of the committee itself from Gasparin, the only one of its nine members who was a soldier, and who as such guaranteed that the higher command of the armies was properly provided for. Gasparin did not appear at the session of the committee on July 23 and sent in his resignation on the following day, on grounds of health. When, a few days later, on July 27, Custine requested in the Convention that he might be informed of the reasons for his arrest, Thuriot, who shared Gasparin's point of view, proposed to refer his letter to the Military Committee and not to the Committee of Public Safety, and Robespierre had to ascend the tribune in order to prevent the matter from being withdrawn from the latter's competence.

Divided and weakened by the resignation of Gasparin and the open opposition of Thuriot, the Committee of Public Safety would shortly have come to an end had it not been strengthened by powerful support.

On July 24 it had to undergo a fresh attack. The republican troops carrying out operations against the Vendeans had been defeated at Vihiers

347

on July 18 and thrown back to the north of the Loire. A member of the previous committee, Bréard, took advantage of this reverse to request that on the following day the committee should make a statement on the situation in the Vendée and on the conduct of Bouchotte and his commissaries, who were throwing everything into confusion. Sergent added that the committee ought also to make a statement as to the removal of Biron from his command and the appointment of Rossignol, "a man said to be lacking in both ability and honesty." The Convention passed both these ominous motions. A letter was next read from the representatives on mission attached to the army of the north, Duhem and Lesage-Senault, announcing that they had just removed from his command and arrested the republican general Lavalette and his aide-de-camp Dufresse, who had been mainly responsible for the recall of Lamorlière. The representatives on mission, who had already been recalled by the committee, had signally revenged Lamorlière.

But this time the committee found a defender. Robespierre recalled the fact that at the time of Dumouriez's treason Lavalette had prevented Miaczynski from surrendering Lille to the Austrians. His enemy Lamorlière was regarded as a traitor by the republicans of the north, for, in disobedience to Bouchotte's orders, he had tried to remove all the artillery from Lille. Robespierre demanded that Lavalette and Dufresse be set at liberty and that the representatives on mission who had taken proceedings against them return immediately. He met with no opposition, and the matter was referred to the committee.

The struggle went on for another two days. On July 25 Cambon called upon Barère to make a statement about the Vendée which should reveal the whole truth. Dartigoyte made an attack on Bouchotte, whom Barère did not dare to defend. It was decided that the election of Bouchotte's successor should take place on the following day. The Assembly next elected Danton as its president and nominated Dartigoyte as secretary.

But once again Robespierre routed his adversaries. On the previous evening he had denounced the intrigue against Lavalette and Bouchotte at the Jacobins and pronounced a panegyric on the Committee of Public Safety, which, he said, must not be put in leading-strings, for "it must be supposed that it is made up of clever and politic men, it knows what use to make of them up to a certain point, and it might with advantage be referred to rather more often."

On the following day the clubs, no doubt at the instigation of Robespierre, appeared at the bar of the Convention. The Cordeliers demanded that Bouchotte should remain in office, "for it is he who has succeeded in democratizing (*sans-culottiser*) the army. Bouchotte has just frustrated the hideous counter-revolutionary plan devised by the perfidious Custine. His probity and patriotism are beyond doubt." Those who had been concerned in the revolution of August 10 joined in this eulogy of Bouchotte and blamed the Mountain "for maintaining what may be called an icy silence at the height of the storm which is beating upon the Republic." It was now Robespierre's turn to attack. Those who were asking for the dismissal of Bouchotte, he said, were "deceived by men who desired to see one of their creatures at the Ministry for War, in order to find another Beurnonville, who would not fail to find another Dumouriez." Now, it was Danton who had obtained the appointment of Beurnonville in the place of Pache. Danton did not breathe a word in reply, nor did anyone else. The Convention annulled without discussion the decree of the previous day by which it had decided to elect a successor to Bouchotte. The day had been won. Barère did not meet with a dissentient voice when he presented his report on the Vendée. The opposition had faded into thin air.

On that very evening the Committee of Public Safety invited Robespierre to join in its labours. According to Barère's account, it was on Couthon's initiative that this appeal was sent to Robespierre. A few days later he said that he had accepted it "against his inclination."

The advent of Robespierre to power opens up a new era. He brought to the committee not only his rare personal qualities, his coolness and courage, his acute insight, his formidable eloquence, his remarkable faculty of organization, and his entire disinterestedness, but more besides. Since the days of the Constituent Assembly, Robespierre had been the most popular of the revolutionaries among the artisans and humble classes, whose entire confidence he possessed. He was the unchallenged leader of the sansculottes, especially since the death of Marat. He did not enter the committee alone. He had behind him most of the militants, all those who formed the permanent nucleus of the clubs, all those who had irrevocably thrown in their lot with the Revolution, all those who had no alternative save to conquer or die.

The maintenance of Bouchotte in office meant that the democratization of the army general staffs was to continue. The entry of his protector Robespierre into the Government meant that in every part of the administration, whether civil or military, the sansculottes would be supported and their opponents silenced; that those in control of the Republic would no longer play a double game with the people, but would listen to their complaints, take pity upon their misery, and associate them with the effort to save the nation.

The policy which Robespierre was about to inaugurate was at once national and democratic. And as a preliminary test he was faced in Paris itself with a struggle against the extremists of the left, allied with the extremists of the right. He had to join battle with them in the midst of increasing scarcity, while news of disaster upon disaster was arriving from the frontiers. The fact that he did not despair, that he accepted power at such a moment, that he bore such a crushing burden without faltering, and that he succeeded in raising the Republic from the abyss, ought to be sufficient to establish his renown.

CHAPTER III

The Crisis of August 1793

WHEN Robespierre joined the Committee of Public Safety, on July 27, 1793, it was indeed high time. The position of the Republic appeared to be desperate. The armies were falling back along the whole of the north-eastern frontiers. On July 28 arrived the news of the capitulation of Mainz. The armies of the Rhine and Moselle promptly fell back upon the Lauter and the Sarre. Two days later Paris heard of the capitulation of Valenciennes. If the camp of Cæsar gave way, the road to Paris up the valley of the Oise would lie open to the strongest of the enemy armies. In the Alps, Kellermann, weakened by the loss of the forces which he had had to detach for service against the federalists of Rhône and the south, was with difficulty defending the roads through the Maurienne and the Tarentaise. The Spaniards were advancing in the Pyrenees. On July 28 the representatives on mission Expert and Projean sent warning from Perpignan that the inhabitants of Villefranche-de-Conflent had just called in the enemy. On July 27 the rebels in the Vendée had seized Les Ponts-de-Cé and were threatening Angers.

Even in the towns faithful to the Republic those who secretly cherished royalist sympathies were growing bolder. All those who were weary of war longed in their hearts for the victory of the enemy and the restoration of the monarchy to put an end to it all. From Cambrai, which was already threatened, Delbrel, Letourneur, and Levasseur, the representatives on mission, wrote on July 26: "The country population of these regions in general is so greedy for gold that every day the enemy is informed of a great deal of what is going on in our armies. We have whole villages devoted to the enemy's interest." Bassal, the representative on mission at Besançon, reported on July 31 that the news from Mainz was stimulating the audacity of the royalists, and expressed the fear that he would not be able to restrain the clericals. Shortly afterwards, in fact, a clericalist insurrection broke out in the mountains of Doubs.

The morale of the armies was going through a grave crisis. There had been murmurs of discontent from the troops of the line when Custine

351

was removed from the army of the north. The generals and officers of noble birth who had not emigrated found themselves surrounded by suspicion and exposed to incessant attacks. It was extremely difficult to replace them, and the command was constantly changing hands. The soldiers no longer trusted improvised leaders whom they did not know; and the leaders lacked confidence in themselves. Kept under close observation, they dared take no initiative; all they sought to do was to screen themselves. The best of them were thoroughly disheartened. On August 2 Generals Beauharnais and Sparre, of the army of the Rhine, sent in their resignation. While protesting their love for the Republic, they expressed their opinion that "in these times of revolution, when treason is becoming so frequent and the ex-nobles almost always seem to be the leaders in plots to destroy liberty (*liberticides*), it is the duty of those who, though stained with this hereditary taint, have liberty and equality graven upon their hearts, themselves to proclaim their own exclusion."

The disorder in the army of the Vendée was extreme, especially in the Parisian battalions formed of the "five-hundred-livre heroes." The untrained leaders by whom they were commanded thought more about carousing than fighting. The representatives on mission whose task it was to supervise them did not always agree. Some, like Goupilleau de Fontenay and Bourdon of Oise, upheld the old officers; others, such as Choudieu and Richard, trusted nobody but the new sansculotte leaders. All of them tried to throw the responsibility for the defeats on one another, and chaos prevailed.

The general situation was infinitely more critical than in the previous year, after the capture of Verdun, for the artisans in the towns, who had so far been the mainstay of the Revolution, were showing signs of nervous exhaustion and exasperation. At the end of July grave disorders arising from the shortage of food were reported from the towns in every part of the country: from Rouen, where Esnue La Vallée and Lecointre went in fear of a rising, from Amiens, where a tariff of food-prices was arbitrarily established and Chabot and André Dumont had to be sent to restore order, from Attichy in the department of Aisne and from the neighbourhood of Senlis, where tumultuous assemblies took place on a small scale, giving Collot d'Herbois and Isoré cause for serious anxiety, etc. The rivers having dried up, it was necessary at times to use hand-mills in order to prevent Paris from starving.

The Enragés felt that their hour had come, and fomented the general discontent. On July 29 Jacques Roux asked for a considerable force to be raised to aid in coping with the food problem. On August 6 he demanded that deputies in either of the three assemblies who had accepted the gold of tyrants should be guillotined. On August 8 he demanded the arrest of all bankers, who in virtue of their profession were, he said, the lackeys of kings, the hoarders of metallic currency, and the authors of famine. He also desired that "all the bad citizens who have acquired vast domains during the last four years, the self-seeking persons who have profited by the public misfortunes to enrich themselves, those deputies who, before their unexpected elevation to the Areopagus, had not a crown a day to spend and are now the owners of large properties, those deputies who carried on a butcher's trade in the fetid streets and now occupy panelled apartments [an allusion to Legendre], those deputies who, before travelling through Savoy and Belgium, took their meals at little inns and today keep open house, go regularly to the theatre, keep actresses, and support hired panegyrists [an allusion to Danton, Delacroix, Simond], should be made to disgorge." Jacques Roux hoped that the Feast of the Federation on August 10 would be the tomb of food-speculators and embezzlers.

On July 27 Théophile Leclerc in turn asked for the arrest of all suspicious persons "in order that the feast of August 10 may be celebrated with all possible solemnity." On July 31 he challenged those who accused him of bloodthirstiness in the following words: "I have been called a man of blood, I say, because I have openly admitted that a revolutionary ought, if necessary, to sacrifice a hundred thousand villains to the Revolution. Well, Frenchmen, I will lay bare my soul to you: I predict that you will be led to a point where you will no longer be able to hesitate between the death of our enemies and your own. . . . I state it as a fact that the maintenance of the nobles at the head of our armies has alone caused the death of a hundred and fifty thousand combatants." He renewed these appeals to violence in subsequent numbers of his paper and finally, on August 6, attacked the Convention: "People, have you reason to complain of your legislators? You asked them to fix the prices of all commodities of prime necessity; you were refused. You asked for the arrest of all suspicious persons; it has not been decreed. For the exclusion of nobles and priests from all civil and military posts; this has not been consented to. Nevertheless, the country ought to look for its salvation only to a revolutionary upheaval, which shall electrify its numerous inhabitants from end to end of it."

In the previous year, after the capture of Verdun, the Parisian revolutionaries had massacred the suspects in the prisons in order to strike terror to the allies of the enemy. A persistent rumour now went round that similar massacres were to begin again. Posters appeared advising

353

this, and on July 24 the *Journal de la Montagne* indignantly denounced their authors.

Simultaneously with the Enragés, the former Girondins who had stayed in Paris and the secret royalists also tried to take advantage of the food-shortage to start a great movement, first against the Commune and then against the Convention.

The architect Alexandre-Pierre Cauchois, a friend of Roland's, supported by his section—that of Beaurepaire, which was one of the most moderate in Paris—summoned delegates from thirty-nine out of the forty-eight Paris sections to the Évêché on July 31 and called for the records of the contracts granted to traders by the Commune, and for the opening of the municipal corn and flour storehouses. On the following day Cauchois, whom they had made their secretary, appeared with twenty-four commissaries from the Évêché before the directory of the departmental assembly at the Commune, used threatening language, announced that he represented the popular will, and demanded that the accounts be at once produced. Having been shown the door, he plastered the walls with threatening posters and continued for several weeks to hold meetings of his partisans at the Évêché. From his prison in the Abbaye, Carra, the Girondin deputy, closely and sympathetically followed the struggles of Cauchois and the sections against the Commune and promised himself that by their agency he would be avenged upon the Mountain.

In order to estimate the full gravity of the situation, we must not forget that at this date the Committee of Public Safety was anything but sure of a majority in the Convention and that its powers were limited. It did not yet control the other committees of the Assembly, which were in principle its equals. The only exclusive functions which it possessed were the supervision of ministers and the right of adopting provisional measures. It was not till July 28 that it obtained the right to issue warrants for arrests. Till then it was obliged to apply to the Committee of General Security for the right to make domiciliary visits, and that committee, largely composed of friends of Danton, was far from zealous in supporting it.

Again, the Committee of Public Safety had no armed force at its own special command to protect itself from mob violence. The line regiments and battalions of volunteers being away on the frontiers, all that was left in Paris was the National Guard, and this was under the direct authority of the Commune. If the Commune, the only effective power, were to fail the Government, the latter was bound to yield to the slightest riot. The Commune itself had the sections to reckon with, many of which were under the influence of covertly Girondin leaders or of the Enragés. The National Guards were not very trustworthy. They had displayed a great lack of energy in suppressing the soap riots. They, like the malcontents, were suffering from the food-shortage. The sole force behind the committee was a moral one, the force of opinion—a very weak force when shared among several persons. The anxious attention with which the Commune and the committee followed the slightest manifestations of public opinion by means of an army of "observers" suffices to show that they were haunted by the dread of a violent overthrow.

Fortunately, in Robespierre the committee had found a man capable of inspiring respect and an eloquent spokesman. Robespierre was the living link between the Commune and the Convention, between the Convention and the clubs, between Paris and France. It required all his unimpaired prestige to soften the clashes between the various elements of the revolutionary party and to impose a conciliatory solution of them. The efforts which he put forth during August 1793 were admirable.

In the first place, he rendered a signal service to the Revolution by ridding it of the demagogical agitation of the Enragés. If he combated them, it was not because he was afraid of their social policy. His own policy was summed up in the two words noted in his memorandum-book: "Food-supplies and popular laws." But the object of the Enragés was to sow distrust and foment violence and anarchy. They were in alliance with elements as dubious as those grouped under the standard of Roland's friend Cauchois.

Robespierre provoked the struggle, on August 5 at the Jacobins, in reply to Vincent, who was attacking the Convention in general, and Danton and Delacroix in particular. Vincent had proposed that the Jacobins should be invited to draw up lists of patriots for all vacant posts. Once the nomination to posts was in their power, they would have become the masters of the Government. Robespierre blazed up He complained that "new men, patriots of a day, should desire to ruin the people's oldest friends in its estimation." He defended Danton, whom, he said, they were calumniating: "Danton, whom they will never discredit till they have proved that they have more energy, genius, and love of country than he has." Then, turning from Vincent, he fell upon those whom he considered to be Vincent's instigators, Leclerc and Jacques Roux, "two men paid by the enemies of the people, two men denounced by Marat," two men who were now calling upon Marat's name for the purpose of discrediting true patriots.

On August 7 he returned to the charge, placing the Jacobins upon

355

their guard against exaggerated measures which would ruin the Republic. He denounced the plot of the Enragés to repeat the horrors of September. He delivered a lively panegyric on Pache, Hanriot, and the Commune, who were being attacked by Cauchois and the leaders of the sections. His speech made such an impression that the Jacobins elected him president that very day. On the following day he summoned to the bar of the Convention Marat's widow, Simone Évrard, who denounced "all the hypocritical pamphleteers who were dishonouring her husband's name" by propagating extravagant views under cover of it. "Now that he is dead, they are trying to perpetuate the parricidal calumny which represented him as an insensate apostle of disorder and anarchy." Robespierre had Simone Évrard's petition inserted in the *Bulletin*, and caused the conduct of Jacques Roux and Leclerc to be referred to the Committee of General Security for inquiry.

The fact that it was possible to celebrate the feast of August 10 without trouble or bloodshed was due to Robespierre.

As regards the delegates from the sections who were meeting at the Évêché, the Committee of Public Safety manœuvred skilfully. It received their deputation during the night of August 1–2 and gave them a courteous reply, but pointed out that, owing to the approach of the Federation of August 10, it would be better to postpone till the 12th or 15th the checking of supplies in the municipal storehouses which they demanded. The delegates allowed themselves to be deceived by this promise, and, once August 10 had gone by, the Commune, sure of the support of the committee, refused to open the storehouses. All it would consent to was to make changes in the staff of its food-control department. Pache accused Cauchois of calling for a statement of accounts only in order to reveal the true situation to the greedy speculators, "who would take advantage of it to raise prices; and to the counter-revolutionaries, who would take advantage of it to hold back the corn in neighbouring regions and prevent its arrival." Jacques Roux was repudiated by the section of Les Gravilliers, arrested, and kept in the cells at the Hôtel de Ville from August 22 to 27. At the same time, on the motion of Tallien, the Convention on August 25 ordered the assembly of delegates from the sections which had been sitting at the Évêché for three weeks to be dissolved, and they dispersed without resistance.

This result could not have been arrived at had not the Committee of Public Safety taken effective measures for provisioning Paris. It placed considerable sums at the disposal of the Commune: on July 24, 540,000 francs for the purchase of oxen and rice; on August 7, 2,000,000 for the purchase of grain and flour; on August 14, 3,000,000, etc. But money was not enough. It was necessary to overcome the ill will of the farmers. The committee sent energetic deputies as delegates from the Convention into the neighbouring departments to order a return of available supplies to be made, as at the moment of the capture of Verdun, to see that the corn still in the ear was threshed, to requisition labourers, etc. On July 26 Bonneval and Roux wrote from Eure-et-Loir that each canton would send a sack of corn to Paris for August 10, and this example was followed by many of the Fédérés, who arrived with carts loaded with food. Thus the food-supplies of the capital were replenished, and the Enragés were deprived of their principal argument against the Commune and the Convention.

On August 9 Barère had already obtained the passage of the famous decree organizing a "granary of abundance (*grenier d'abondance*)" in every district, supplied by the contributions in kind of those who were getting in their harvest and by a credit of a hundred million for the purchase of cereals. The bakers were placed under the close supervision of the communes, which were empowered to requisition their ovens. Those who stopped working were to be deprived of their civic rights and punished by a year's hard labour. It is true that the "granaries of abundance" hardly came into existence except on paper. Where was grain to be found to fill them, when the country was with difficulty living from hand to mouth? But the object of this decree, as of many others, was to calm apprehension and give the hungry masses a gleam of hope.

The Constitution was to be solemnly promulgated on August 10 before the delegates of the primary assemblies. If it was put in force immediately, if fresh elections were proceeded with before the revolts within the country were crushed, before the enemy was defeated, it would be a leap in the dark. The committee had no illusion as to the real strength of the Montagnard party. It knew that many of the electors had voted for the Constitution only with the covert intention of getting rid of the Montagnards as soon as it was put in force.

On July 26 Dubois-Crancé and Gauthier wrote from Grenoble advising the committee to declare ineligible for ten years "all those individuals who, either in the bosom of the Convention, among the administrative and judicial bodies, or in the sections," had taken part in the federalist revolt. "If you do not take this step before you disperse, in the next legislature you will see all the perfidious men who are now chafing at their restraints indulging, under the pretext of order, in every kind of measure destructive of liberty, and fabricating blood-thirsty

357

and vindictive laws against all those who have made and upheld the Revolution." The committee shared the views of these representatives on mission, but it went still further. It did not want an election at all. Perhaps it hesitated to violate by a decree of ineligibility the principles which it had proclaimed in the Constitution, thus providing the Girondins with an excellent pretext for accusing it of duplicity. When, on August 11, Chabot formally proposed to declare ineligible all those who had failed to appear at the primary assemblies without a reasonable motive for their absence, and all those who had refused to vote for the Constitution, the committee shelved his motion, which had been referred to it.

Lanthenas, a former friend of Roland's who had gone over to the Mountain, had proposed to celebrate the Federation of August 10 as "a fraternal jubilee, an epoch of general reconciliation among all republicans"—in other words, to extend a welcoming hand to the federalists and grant them a general amnesty. The idea was greeted with favour by the moderates in the Convention. Garat boasts in his memoirs that he won over Danton and Legendre to it. Barère seemed in favour of it, if we may believe a letter of the deputy Blad, dated August 5. But Hébert and Robespierre tried to prevent it. Hébert declared that the amnesty demanded by the "Endormeurs" (those advocating a policy of "forgive and forget") would have as its result the restoration of the monarchy.

The committee rallied to the opinion of Robespierre and Couthon, who were opposed to any compromise so long as federalism had not been crushed. On August 2 Couthon, supported by Robespierre, obtained a vote in favour of citing the Girondin Carra before the Revolutionary Tribunal for having in past days once proposed the restoration of the throne in favour of the Duke of York.

The committee may have feared that the partisans of the amnesty and of putting the Constitution in force would succeed in gaining the support of the Fédérés, who had arrived from all parts of France to take part in the Feast of the Federation on August 10. It did not hesitate to adopt strong measures. It posted secret agents along the roads, who searched the Fédérés, opened their letters, and arrested those who seemed to them suspect. When the deputy Thibault protested, on August 5, against these methods of intimidation, Couthon accused him of being an accomplice of the federalists, and Robespierre reduced him to silence. On August 7 the committee placed three hundred thousand livres at the disposal of Hanriot for keeping a discreet watch over the Fédérés, and fifty thousand livres at the disposal of Pache for compensating the poorer members of the vigilance committee of the sections.

These precautions were effective. Won over to the doctrines of the Jacobins, who placed their hall at the disposal of the Fédérés, made much of and flattered by the Montagnards in the sections and the Commune, the Fédérés laid aside their prejudices against Paris. Not only did they create no difficulties for the Committee of Public Safety, but on certain memorable occasions they were its stoutest supporters and on returning to their provinces became the missionaries of the Montagnard gospel. They were to be regarded as trustworthy enough to be associated with the work of government by a formal decree.

As early as August 6 their spokesman, Claude Royer, parish priest of Chalon-sur-Saône, declared in vigorous terms his opposition to putting the Constitution in force. "It is desired," he said, "by Feuillants, moderates, federalists, aristocrats, and counter-revolutionaries of every sort!" The moderates did not dare to ask for an amnesty; they did, however, venture to demand that the Constitution be put in force, no doubt because they thought they would be able to rely upon the support of the Hébertists. The idea of proceeding to fresh elections was fairly welcome to those who thought they would win a seat in the Assembly and take the place at the head of the Government of men whom they alleged to be worn out and whose control they endured with impatience. What they would have liked would have been to have the federalists simply declared ineligible before the elections.

Accordingly on August 11 Delacroix, with the object, he said, of confounding those who accused the Convention of desiring to establish itself permanently, proposed to prepare the way for summoning a fresh Assembly by immediately proceeding to a census of those eligible as voters and a delimitation of the electoral areas. This proposal was put forward without warning at a thinly attended session, in the absence of the members of the committee, and was carried without discussion. But that evening at the Jacobins Robespierre protested against this surprise vote. Seldom had he been more vehement. "Summoned against my inclination to the Committee of Public Safety," he said, "I have seen things which I should never have dared to suspect; I have seen, on the one hand, patriotic members making every effort to save their country, sometimes in vain, and, on the other hand, traitors conspiring in the very heart of the committee, with a boldness proportionate to their impunity. . . .[1] I

---

[1] In order to understand Robespierre's allusion, we must remember that, two days before, the Convention had referred to the committee for inquiry Montaut's denunciation of Reubell and Merlin of Thionville, whom he accused of having delivered up Mainz to the enemy. Robespierre and Couthon were convinced of the

have heard and read a proposal made to the Convention this morning and I confess that even now it is hard for me to credit it; I will not stagnate as a useless member of a committee or an Assembly which is on the point of disappearing. I shall be capable of sacrificing myself for the good of my country. . . . I declare that nothing can save the Republic if the proposal made this morning that the Convention be dissolved and its place taken by a Legislative Assembly is adopted. [Shouts of "No! No!" from the whole assembly.] The proposal which I am opposing will merely have as its result to replace the present members of the purified Convention by agents of Pitt and Coburg."

The indignation of Robespierre can be explained only by the fact that certain of his colleagues on the committee were also of Delacroix's opinion and were ready to accept the election of a new Convention. But the attitude of the Fédérés and Jacobins in calling upon the Assembly to remain at its post thwarted the manœuvre of the moderates. The decree passed on the motion of Delacroix remained a dead letter. In vain did Gossuin and Delacroix resume the perennial attack on Bouchotte on August 12; in vain did they propose that the absent members of the committee, Prieur of Marne and Saint-André, then on a mission to the armies, should be replaced by others; the support of the Fédérés overbore all opposition, and on the next day the powers of the committee were extended for a further period.

It was also on the proposal of the Fédérés that the great measure of the levy in mass was voted. The idea was first proposed on July 28 by Sébastien Lecroix, an agitator whose sphere of operations was the section of L'Unité. He said: "Let the hour when the tocsin was sounded against the palace of the tyrant, when his throne was shattered to fragments, be that when the tocsin shall be rung and the call to arms be sounded throughout the whole Republic; let the friends of the nation arm themselves and form new battalions, let those who have no arms transport munitions, let the women bring victuals or knead bread, let the signal for battle be given by the songs of the nation, and eight days of enthusiasm may do more for the country than eight years of fighting!" The idea met with a great success. First the sections and then the Commune adopted it. On August 5 it proposed that the immediate mobilization of all citizens between sixteen and twenty-five years of age should be decreed. Two days later the Fédérés began to move, but Robespierre

---

guilt of these two representatives on mission. They had to intervene and ask the committee for a report accusing them, but failed to obtain it. Thuriot, who had defended Reubell and Merlin from the tribune, protected them before the Committee.

knew how pitiful had been the result of the disorderly levies of peasants ordered in the departments bordering on the Vendée, and pointed out to them that the levy in mass was useless: "It is not men who are lacking, but generals, and patriotic generals." The Fédérés persisted. On August 12 their spokesman, Royer, declared in the Convention: "Now is the time to set a great example to the whole world and give a terrible lesson to the coalition of tyrants. Appeal to the people, let the people rise as one man, they alone can annihilate so many enemies!" This time Danton and Robespierre supported the measure. Danton pointed out that the recruiting of soldiers ought to be accompanied by a corresponding economic mobilization. He asked that the Fédérés should themselves be given the task of supervising an inventory of arms, food-supplies, and munitions in their cantons while the levy of men was proceeding. Robespierre proposed that they should further be instructed to suggest active, energetic, and trustworthy patriots to replace those members of the administrative bodies who were suspect. Since the Committee of Public Safety was in no hurry to vote the decree which they had demanded, the Fédérés again appeared at the bar on August 16, this time accompanied by the deputies of the forty-eight sections. The committee yielded, and on August 23 the Convention voted the famous decree, drafted by Barère in collaboration with Carnot: "From now until such time as its enemies have been driven out of the territory of the Republic, all Frenchmen are permanently requisitioned for the service of the armies The young men shall go and fight, the married men shall forge arms and transport food, the women shall make tents and clothes and serve in the hospitals, the old men shall have themselves carried into public places to rouse the courage of the warriors and preach hatred of kings and the unity of the Republic. Public buildings shall be turned into barracks, open spaces into armouries, cellar floors shall be washed to extract salt-petre," etc. All the young men from eighteen to twenty-five years of age who were unmarried, or widowers with no children, were to form the first class of the levy. They were to meet without delay at the chief town of their district, where they were to be formed into battalions under a banner bearing the words: "The French people uprisen against tyrants! (*Le peuple français debout contre les tyrans!*)"

It was the first time in modern history that the entire resources of a nation at war, men, food, and goods, were placed under the control of the Government. The Republic, to quote Barère's expression, now formed one great besieged city, a vast camp.

The progress of events had given a singularly wider scope to the part played by the Committee of Public Safety. It could no longer confine itself to the task of supervision originally assigned to it. It now governed, and even took part in administration over the heads of the ministers, who were now mere clerks; so much so that it felt the need itself of increasing its strength by appealing to the technical experts which it lacked. Since Gasparin's resignation it no longer counted among its members a single professional soldier. When the levy in mass was voted in principle, it hastily recalled Carnot, a captain in the engineers, from the army of the north, where he had been sent on mission, and invited him to undertake the control of the military operations; it offered the control of army factories to another engineer, a friend of Carnot, Prieur of Côte d'Or. Carnot and Prieur of Côte d'Or were appointed members of the committee on August 14.

Danton would have liked to give legal sanction to the situation existing *de facto* by turning the Committee of Public Safety into a provisional government. He proposed this on August 1 and asked that a secret fund of fifty millions be placed at the disposal of the committee. But Robespierre pointed out that the working of the Government would not be improved by destroying the activity of the ministers; on the contrary, it would be disorganized. On the following day Hérault de Séchelles pointed out that Danton's motion was useless and dangerous. "If by increasing our numbers we are made to descend to administrative details, we shall be ruined." The committee consented to the secret fund of fifty millions only on condition that it should merely have the right to sign orders upon it, the fund remaining in the Treasury. It is obvious that, while treating Danton with consideration, the committee supposed him to be actuated by ulterior motives. Was it not Danton's friends, and at times Danton himself, who had caused it the greatest difficulties during this terrible crisis of August 1793?

The committee had thwarted the intrigues of the moderates only thanks to the support of the Commune and the Jacobins. It had drawn nearer and nearer to the most ardently revolutionary elements. Would it always manage to control them? It still had many obstacles to surmount before it achieved a stable equilibrium.

CHAPTER IV

The Hébertist Bid for Power and the Inauguration of the Terror

SUPPORTED by the boards of the Ministry for War and the agents sent by Bouchotte to the armies to keep a watch on the generals (and sometimes on the representatives on mission), and relying upon the group of political refugees who would be handed over to their former masters in the event of a premature peace, Hébert was above all for war to the bitter end or till a complete victory had been gained. He could not imagine any peace policy that was not at the same time a policy of monarchist restoration. Cloots, who desired to push back the frontiers of France as far as the Rhine, seconded him with all his might, and his paper, *Le Batave*, swelled the chorus of the *Père Duchesne*.

Hérault de Séchelles, who with Barère directed the diplomatic business of the Committee of Public Safety, shared the views of his friend Cloots. On August 18 he sent a secret agent, Catus, to Mühlhausen to make preparations for the union with France of this little industrial republic allied to the Swiss cantons. He took a special interest in Savoy, which it had been his task to organize after the annexation, and from which he brought back a mistress, the dark-haired Adèle de Bellegarde. Savoy was once more invaded, this time by the Piedmontese. On August 25 Hérault proposed to send two representatives on missions there, Dumas and Simond, to drive back the enemy and remove the misgivings of the inhabitants as to the good faith of France. But the moderates in the Convention, all those who had applauded Danton's attempts to come to terms with the "tyrants," looked askance at the proposal. Duhem, who had just been recalled from his mission in the north, opposed it, casting doubts upon the purity of the Savoyards' revolutionary principles, and he was supported by Gossuin. In vain did Simond, a native of Savoy, remind them that his fellow-countrymen had formed six battalions of volunteers, who were fighting well. In vain did Tallien exclaim that France would be dishonoured if she abandoned the Savoyards, who had united themselves to her. The Assembly remained indifferent. Prieur of Marne and Barère had to intervene before the Convention would consent to send help to the department of Mont-Blanc.

After this debate the Hébertists had no doubt that there was a strong party of pacifists—that is to say, secret royalists—in the Convention, and ascribed to their influence the delays in the trial of Custine, the exoneration of Reubell and Merlin of Thionville, who had capitulated at Mainz, the persecutions suffered in the Vendée by Rossignol, who had been temporarily deprived of his command by Bourdon of Oise and Goupilleau de Fontenay, and the vexations to which certain of Bouchotte's agents were subjected by some of the representatives on mission.

It is true that Robespierre undertook the defence of Rossignol and on August 23 pronounced a eulogy on the services rendered by the commissaries of the Executive Council who had been sent to the armies, but the Hébertists believed themselves strong enough to take the offensive against their opponents. The Père Duchesne no longer confined himself to attacking Danton and his friends, "the traitors who sit with the Mountain," as he called them. He wanted to restore the power of the ministers and make them and their agents independent of the Assembly, the representatives on mission, and the committees. "Montagnards," he wrote in No. 275 of his paper, "so long as the committees usurp all powers, we shall never have a government, or we shall have a detestable one. The reason why kings did so much harm on earth was that there was nothing to oppose their will; nor is there anything to oppose that of your committees. . . . We shall never have any liberty, our Constitution will be nothing but a delusion, so long as the ministers are mere messenger-boys (*galopins*) at the orders of the lowest sweepers of the Convention." Hébert boldly demanded that the part of the Constitution providing for the election of the ministers should at once be put in force. His defeat of August 20, when the Convention had appointed Paré, Danton's former clerk, to the Ministry of the Interior, was still rankling. He would have his revenge, he thought, when the people chose their ministers! Robespierre had all the difficulty in the world in preventing the Jacobins from following Hébert and supporting his proposal that a fresh Executive Council should be chosen by popular vote!

The Hébertists continued their campaign. They complained that nobles were allowed to keep their posts, that in certain regions patriots were persecuted—witness the Mauger affair at Nancy—that the Committee of General Security was extending its protection to aristocrats, that it was causing delays in the trial of the Girondins and Marie Antoinette; they pointed out the predominance of royalism in the Paris theatres, where plays such as *Pamela*, in which were to be heard praises of the nobility and the English Government, were being acted amidst

364

applause, or *Adèle de Sacy,* in which were to be seen a queen and her son basely detained in prison and afterwards set free and reinstated in their rights and honours. The committee forbade the performance of these two suspicious pieces.

As a result of the drought, which had stopped the working of the mills, the food-shortage had reappeared at the end of August and there were angry murmurings. Hébert attacked not only the food-speculators, but the whole of the trading classes in ·an article of which his rivals the Enragés might have been jealous: "The country! Bosh! [Hébert's expression is more gross.] The traders have no country. As long as they thought the Revolution would serve their interests, they supported it; they lent their aid to the sansculottes in destroying the nobles and the old courts of law, but only in order to replace them by aristocrats. And so, since there are no longer any active citizens, since the luckless sansculotte enjoys the same rights as the rich tax-collector, all these *j— f—* have turned their coats and are striving tooth and nail to destroy the Republic. They have bought up all food-supplies in order to sell them again for their weight in gold, or else bring famine upon us" (No. 279).

To make things worse, bad news was coming in from the provinces. The royalists and moderates were doing their best to obstruct the levy in mass: at the end of August there were disorderly assemblages in Seine-et-Marne, unrest at Rennes, a revolt in the district of Saint-Pol (August 27), plots at Rouen, a mutiny of the 5th Dragoons at Laon (August 28), disorderly assemblages of unwilling recruits and deserters in Haute-Garonne and Ariège (August 30), etc.

The Hébertists were not content with lecturing the Convention and the Government. They were preparing for a fresh insurrection. The time had come, they thought, for them in turn to seize the power.

On August 28 Hébert proposed at the Jacobins to draw up an address to the Convention in favour of purging the army general staffs, depriving nobles of their commands, and other measures of public safety. The forty-eight sections and the popular societies of Paris were to be associated with the petition. He was loudly applauded. Boy, a Fédéré, broke out into threats against the Convention. He was called to order, but applauded by the public in the galleries. Royer, the former spokesman of the Fédérés, supported the petition, the principle of which was accepted.

On the following day Billaud-Varenne, on his return from the army of the north, reported the confusion which had followed the loss of the camp of Famars. He criticized before the Convention the inaction of the Government and proposed to set up a commission whose duty it should be to watch over the execution of the laws and send the guilty to the scaffold. In vain did Robespierre try to parry the blow which Billaud had just aimed at the Committee of Public Safety. The proposed commission would necessarily be the rival of the committee, which it would paralyse, and it would be a source of disorders and conflicts. "It is to be feared," he said, "that this commission will be more concerned with personal enmities than with honest supervision, and so become a regular committee of denunciation. It is not for the first time that I perceive the existence of a perfidious scheme for paralysing the Committee of Public Safety under the guise of assisting it in its labours!" The Assembly was indifferent, and there were even murmurs to be heard. Danton came to the assistance of Robespierre, who had defended him at the Jacobins three days before. "The Committee of Public Safety is already harassing the Executive Council. If you create a commission, it will harass the committee; perhaps instead of a fresh activity you will only create a fresh inquisition." But having said so much, Danton, true to his usual tactics, proposed a compromise. They would do better, he said, to add three new members to the committee. His motion was referred to the committee, which was in no hurry to submit a list of the three members whom it was desired to add to it, for it could not have avoided including Billaud-Varenne. As for the latter, he made no sign.

But the Hébertists were gaining control of the Jacobins, and Danton began to shout with them, in order to regain the popularity which was slipping from him. On August 30 he proclaimed before the club that the Convention, in concert with the people, would make a third revolution if necessary, "in order at last to complete the regeneration from which it expects to obtain happiness, but which has been delayed till now by the monsters who have betrayed it." Next Royer appealed to the example of Marat. Why was his advice not listened to? "Those who are now speaking are no longer listened to. Must one be dead before one is in the right? Let Terror (*la Terreur*) become the order of the day! It is the only way to alarm the people and force them to save themselves!" Royer was given the task of drafting a fresh version of the petition initiated by Hébert—making the fourth.

Robespierre made desperate efforts to ward off the threatened insurrection. But events were playing into the hands of the Hébertists. On September 2 Soulès, a commissary of the Executive Council, returned from the south with the news that the English had entered Toulon on August 26. Billaud-Varenne at once ascended the tribune and attacked the Committee of Public Safety for keeping the news a secret. On that very evening at the Jacobins the Hébertists obtained the affiliation to the club of the Society of Female Revolutionary Republicans, in spite of the connexion between the president, Claire Lacombe, and Théophile Leclerc. Hébert further obtained the passage of a resolution that the club should meet on the following morning at nine o'clock and join the sections and popular societies in their demonstration before the Convention.

Robespierre obtained a delay of two more days, and the Jacobins did not appear at the Convention either on September 3 or 4. But on the 4th the entry of the English into Toulon was officially announced. In the morning the Hébertists marshalled their troops. The locksmiths and building operatives assembled in the rue du Temple and the rue Sainte-Avoye and went to the Commune to demand an increase of wages. Their spokesman questioned Pache. "Is there food in Paris?" he said. "If there is, bring it out; if there is not, tell us the reason why. The people has risen, the sansculottes who made the Revolution offer you their arms, their time, and their lives!" Chaumette hurried to the Convention to calm the demonstrators, or else to free himself from responsibility. He brought back the decree by which it had just pledged itself to establish fixed prices for all commodities and goods of primary necessity within a week—in other words, a general maximum. The effect produced was nil. "It is not promises we need, it is bread, and that at once," shouted the crowd, which had now increased. Then Chaumette got up on a table. "I too have been poor," he said, "and so I know what poverty means! We have here an open war of the rich against the poor; they want to crush us. Well, we must forestall them, we must crush them ourselves, we have the power in our hands!" And Chaumette called upon the Commune to demand of the Convention the immediate organization of a revolutionary army "with the object of going into the districts where the corn has been commandeered, securing the quotas, facilitating their delivery, stopping the manœuvres of the selfish rich, and handing them over to the vengeance of the law." Hébert called upon the labourers to stop work on the following day and go in a body to the Assembly with the people: "Let them surround it as they did on August 10, September 2, and May 31, and not leave their posts till the national representatives have adopted such means as will save us. Let the revolutionary army set out the moment the decree has been passed; but, above all, let the guillotine follow every section, every column of the army!" Most of the sections remained in session till very late at night, and one of them, that of the Sansculottes, declared itself in a state of insurrection against the rich.

367

If the repetition of August 10 and May 31 which was being prepared was to succeed, it was necessary that the Jacobins should be won over, as they had been on the eve of those great days. In vain did Robespierre, seconded by Renaudin, put the club on its guard against a plot which would fill the aristocracy with joy. In vain did he denounce "a plot for starving Paris and plunging it in blood." In vain did he undertake the obligation, in the name of the Committee of Public Safety, of providing for the necessities of the people and putting down food-speculators. His appeal for calm was not listened to. Royer threw the blame on the committee, some of whose members were perverse. Barère had "followed a tortuous course during the Revolution." In vain did Robespierre defend Barère, who might be weak, but was active and useful. Royer continued his attacks and cried shame upon the Jacobins for their timidity. "What have you done during the last week?" he said. "Nothing. Show yourselves as you were during the days of trial when you saved liberty. Change your tactics, I implore you; act, and stop talking!" He was frantically applauded, and Robespierre kept silence. It was impossible to check the movement. On the following day, September 5, a long procession, headed by Pache and Chaumette, started out from the Hôtel de Ville for the Convention. The demonstrators carried placards on which could be read: "War on tyrants! War on aristocrats! War on food-speculators!"

The Assembly was prepared for this visit and, following a report from Merlin of Douai, had just voted without discussion that the Revolutionary Tribunal should be divided into four sections, sitting concurrently. Pache, as spokesman of the Commune and sections, explained that the people were weary of the food-shortage, which had as its causes the selfishness of property-owners and the manœuvres of food-speculators. Chaumette read the petition demanding the formation of the revolutionary army, which had already been decreed after June 2, but had been postponed owing to the intrigues and panic of the guilty. The guillotine was to accompany the army. Robespierre, as president of the Convention, replied that the people could rely upon the solicitude of the Convention. "Let all good citizens rally round it!" he concluded, as though it were threatened.

Billaud-Varenne carried the demands of the petitioners a step further. He demanded the arrest of suspects and revived his former motion for the creation of a commission for supervising the execution of the laws. "If revolutions are protracted, it is because none but half-measures are ever taken!" It was in vain that Saint-André announced, in order to gain time, that the Committee would consider the proposed measures. He was abruptly interrupted by Billaud-Varenne: "A nice thing it would be for us to amuse ourselves with arguing. We must act!" In vain did Basire try to come to the aid of the committee by putting it on its guard against the leaders of the sections, who might well be mere agents of disorder controlled by the aristocracy, as at Lyons, Marseilles, and Toulon. He was interrupted by murmuring, and Danton, anxious to re-gain his popularity, sprang to the tribune. They must take advantage, he said, of the sublime impulse of the people, whose desires were dictated by the national genius. They must immediately pass the decree estab-lishing the revolutionary army, without waiting for the report of the committee. In order to frustrate the schemes of the aristocrats alluded to by Basire, he proposed to pay an allowance of forty sous a meeting to the sansculottes attending the assemblies of the sections, which were to be reduced to two a week. He further proposed to allot a credit of a hundred millions for the manufacture of arms, and to speed up the procedure of the Revolutionary Tribunal. All these measures were passed.

The indefatigable Billaud-Varenne returned to the charge about the arrest of suspects and obtained the passage of a measure to the effect that in future the members of the revolutionary committee, whose busi-ness it was to keep a watch on them, should receive a salary. He also obtained a vote in favour of citing the ex-ministers Clavière and Lebrun before the Revolutionary Tribunal; and the long and tumultuous ses-sion at last ended with the election of Billaud as president of the As-sembly in place of Robespierre, whose term had expired.

On the following day the Committee of Public Safety accepted the situation and asked the Convention to supplement it by three new mem-bers: Billaud-Varenne, Collot d'Herbois, and Granet. Gaston complained that the committee was not conducting the siege of Lyons with suf-ficient vigour. Danton blamed it for being too stingy with the money: "Fit a handle to the big wheel, and so give a great impulse to the polit-ical machine. For this purpose use the great means which love of country suggests; otherwise you are not worthy of the functions entrusted to you." Gaston, roused to enthusiasm, proposed that Danton, that brain worthy to inspire a revolution, should also be added to the committee, and the Convention decided accordingly. But Billaud-Varenne and Collot were the only ones who accepted their nomination. Danton and Granet refused. Danton's refusal, which he ascribed to his desire to prove his disinterestedness to his accusers, was a serious matter; for Danton, to quote the words of Jaurès, then "occupied a position analogous to that of a powerful deputy nowadays who, though eligible for the ministry, has refused office. Even if he had not desired it, he would have become a centre of opposition. Even when he appeared to support the Committee of Public Safety, his assistance aroused suspicion." But it is possible that Danton refused from another motive. He had played as important a part as Billaud in the momentous resolutions passed on September 5. Why, then, had not the Committee of Public Safety proposed his name to the Convention as it had done that of Billaud? Danton must have said to himself that the committee did not want his assistance.

Henceforward Hébertism was represented in the Government by Collot d'Herbois and Billaud-Varenne. This had certain advantages. The committee was now in touch with the Cordeliers and the little clubs which came under its influence. It was less afraid of being swamped and submerged by the populace, which it was now to endeavour to control and direct.

The first article of the Hébertist program, from which all the others were deduced, was war to the bitter end. On September 6 the Englishman Matthews, whom Danton had employed in his secret negotiations with Grenville, was arrested on his return from London. The semi-official journalist Ducher, a protégé of Barère's, started a campaign against pacifists in the *Moniteur,* and on September 24 the committee resolved to maintain no regular ambassadors except to the two "free" nations, the Americans and the Swiss, and to send only secret agents to the countries of the other powers. In order to display its resolution to cut off all communication, even of an unofficial nature, with the enemy, it further decided not to negotiate with any foreign agent or minister who had not "a positive character with regard to the French Republic" (that is, who was not regularly accredited to the French Republic).

In adopting the Hébertist program of war to the bitter end the committee was also forced to adopt the means of carrying it out. Till then the Terror had been intermittent. Suspects were arrested at random and released almost immediately. Henceforward the Terror became permanent. Merlin of Douai provided it with a code in his Law of the Suspect, of which he obtained the passage on September 17.

Hitherto there had been no definition of suspects. This law made good the deficiency. "The following persons shall be reputed to be suspects: (1) those who, by their conduct or connexions, their conversation or writings, have shown themselves partisans of tyranny or federalism, and enemies of liberty; (2) those who cannot give satisfaction, as prescribed by the decree of March 21, with regard to their means of subsistence and the discharge of their civic duties; (3) those who have been refused certificates of civicism; (4) public functionaries suspended or dismissed from their functions by the National Convention or its commissaries and not reinstated . . . (5) such ex-nobles, together with the husbands, wives, fathers, mothers, sons, daughters, brothers, sisters, and agents of *émigrés* as have not consistently manifested their attachment to the Revolution; (6) those who emigrated during the period between July 1, 1789 and the publication of the decree of March 30, 1792, even if they have returned to France within the period prescribed by this decree or before." These provisions, elastic as they were, suspended a terrible threat over the heads not only of real suspects, but of all those capable of giving trouble to the Government, and, what was more, of the indifferent and timid, since it included even those citizens whose only fault was that they had failed to fulfil their duties as electors. It included officials within its scope, since the discharge of the disloyal or lukewarm would instantly be followed by their imprisonment.

The revolutionary committees were likely to be kept busy. But the Committee of General Security, which directed their activity from above, was suspect to the Jacobins, who taxed it with indulgence towards contractors, pretty women soliciting favours, aristocrats, and foreign bankers. On September 13, after a sharp debate, the Convention passed a decree that a fresh Committee of General Security should be nominated, and that in future the Committee of Public Safety should draw up the list of proposed members. It was further decided that all the other committees should be renewed in the same fashion by the Committee of Public Safety. This measure was decisive. Henceforward the Committee of Public Safety was invested with a pre-eminence, a right of watching over and supervising all the other committees, which had hitherto been its equals. It now possessed the reality of power, since it could make up the other committees as it pleased, purge them, and dominate them.

And so the Hébertist bid for power did not have as its sole results to make terror the order of the day, organize surveillance and repression on a permanent footing by the Law of the Suspect, bring about the fixing of prices ("Law of the Maximum") demanded by the sansculottes, and organize the revolutionary army for extorting food from the farmers; it had also given a strong impetus to the revolutionary Government.

The Committee of Public Safety, which before this time had had to face the mistrust, jealousy, and covert or open opposition of part of the Convention, found its powers considerably strengthened. On September 11 Barère obtained the re-establishment of the right of ministers to send agents to the departments and armies. Further, on September 13 a decree was passed making it the business of the popular societies to draw the committee's attention to all agents who were untrustworthy or suspected of unsound political principles, "especially those employed in selling goods or supplies to the armies, so that such agents may no longer usurp the allowances and posts due only to true republicans." By this means the clubs became part of the machinery of government. It may be said that the dictatorship of the committee was beginning, but it would be making a serious mistake to suppose that this dictatorship was established without fresh jars. The "moderantist" opposition checked by Hébertism had had to fall back, but it had not been defeated.

CHAPTER V

Hondschoote and Wattignies

IN spite of all the eloquence of Robespierre, who defended it, the great Committee of Public Safety would not have succeeded in maintaining itself against the dangerous attacks of the "fight-to-a-finish" party of the left and the defeatists of the right had it not rapidly gained some victories over the enemy.

Few as its numbers were—first nine and afterwards twelve members —it did not hesitate to send some of its members to the theatre of war to obtain information at all critical moments. Immediately after the capture of Valenciennes it commissioned Saint-André and Prieur of Marne, accompanied by Lebas, of the Committee of General Security, to inspect the north-eastern front as rapidly as possible and concert with the generals the urgent measures to be taken. The generals of the armies of the Moselle and Rhine joined them in a conference at Bitche on August 8 and 9 and consented to send immediate reinforcements of 11,000 men to the army of the north, to be followed by a fresh force of 20,000 men, whose place was to be taken by contingents withdrawn from the garrisons in the interior. The representatives on mission next visited the army of the north, stopping at Charleville on their way to reorganize the arms-factory, and inspecting the fortress of Péronne, which they found in a lamentable condition. On their return to Paris, on August 23, they explained to the committee that it was necessary to change tactics, render the armies more mobile, operate rapidly and in masses, dismiss the general staffs, and keep a strict watch upon the contractors. Civilians though they were, they outlined at a stroke the program which Carnot was to carry out.

Carnot and Prieur of Côte d'Or, who joined the committee on August 14, would both have passed their lives as men of science and distinguished engineers had it not been for the Revolution. Carnot, who was known by his celebrated *Essay on Machines* (1783), hated fuss and worked in silence. Having been entrusted with missions to the armies ever since the days of the Legislative Assembly, he had visited the frontiers and knew both the commanding officers and the soldiers. A great worker, possessing uncommon resolution and power of concentrated thought, he took over the military board which Saint-Just had already created before his arrival. He expanded this board and supplemented it by specialists, paying but little attention to their opinions and asking nothing of them but good service. Among them were Clarke, who was entrusted with the map and topographical department, Montalembert, whose special department was the artillery, and Le Michaud d'Arçon, who was particularly proficient in the attack and defence of fortresses. Carnot corresponded in person with the generals. Plans of campaign and appointments to commands were discussed by the committee. Civilians like Saint-Just, Saint-André, Prieur of Marne, and Robespierre made it their business to acquaint themselves with and discuss the reasons for the measures proposed by the specialist Carnot and gave their consent to them only on mature consideration. Carnot gave his full confidence to Bouchotte, who deserved it, for he "possessed great merits as an administrator, untiring activity, and constant and reasoned application" (A. Chuquet). Nor did he lack initiative. He was the first to use the system of relays for the rapid transport of troops by wagon, the first to use the telegraph for military communications. He was honest, put down extravagance, and often made a happy choice of his subordinates. At any rate it is rather difficult to draw a distinction between Bouchotte's and Carnot's share in the common achievement, but the latter had the good quality of defending his collaborators against the furious attacks which were constantly being made on them.

As for Prieur of Côte d'Or, he had charge from the outset of the whole department concerned with *matériel*—that is, war manufactures, artillery, muskets, side-arms, and munitions, besides hospitals and ambulances.

There was a deficiency of everything: raw materials, factories, engineers, foremen, and labourers. The arsenals were empty, having purposely been left idle by Louis XVI's last ministers. On July 15 the number of men under arms was 479,000, and 500,000 were to be raised by the compulsory levy. There were neither guns nor equipment for them; there were not even enough for the troops at the front. English cruisers were blockading the coasts. It was necessary to obtain from the soil of France what had hitherto been purchased abroad: saltpetre from India, copper from Spain, England, and Russia, steel from Sweden, Germany, and England. Fortunately the members of the committee loved science not only for its immediate and utilitarian services, but for its own grandeur and beauty. Carnot and Prieur of Marne next turned to men of science and called the leading chemists and engineers of the day to their aid:

Monge, Berthollet, Fourcroy, Chaptal, Périer, Hassenfratz, Vandermonde, etc. They not only asked their advice, but associated them closely with their work by entrusting them with missions and responsibilities. Vandermonde was given control of the manufacture of side-arms; Hassenfratz was appointed commissary of arms-factories on the 27th Brumaire (November 18); Chaptal, a protégé of Robespierre's, joined the powder and saltpetre department; Fourcroy, a pupil of Lavoisier, discovered a process of extracting copper from bell-metal, and bells became the copper-mines of France; Monge drew up a clear summary of the *Art of Manufacturing Cannon*, which served as a guide to metallurgists, etc. The committee placed the Château of Petit-Meudon at the disposal of the scientists, with the adjacent park as an experimental station. Experiments were carried on there in great secrecy with gunpowder composed of fulminates, hollow bullets, incendiary bullets, the semaphore invented by Chappe, and the first military balloons. Monge organized a great factory for guns and cannon in Paris, and other factories were created in the departments.

But it took months before the works so amazingly improvised could be set going, and it was not till the end of 1793 that the various manufactories began to yield results. The first six guns to leave the Paris factory were presented to the Convention on November 3. In the mean time it was necessary to press on and obtain victories at all costs, in order to restore the shaken morale of the troops and their leaders.

The committee was convinced that victory was impossible unless the whole army was animated by a republican spirit. It did not confine itself to circulating patriotic newspapers among the soldiers, but set to work to obliterate every trace of the old regime left in the troops of the line. It ordered that on August 15 at latest they should lay aside their old uniforms for good and assume the blue uniform of the volunteers. The new army, composed mainly of young soldiers, was lacking in cohesion, and sometimes seized with panic. What it lacked in endurance and coolness was to be made up for by mass offensives. The generals received the order to attack.

Kilmaine, an Irishman who had been in command of the army of the north since the removal of Lamorlière, was lacking in confidence. On August 7 he had abandoned the camp of Cæsar and fallen back upon Arras, leaving the road to Paris open, which produced a deep sensation. Pache's son-in-law, Xavier Audouin, admitted at the Jacobins that, if the enemy liked, they could reach the capital in four days. Parties of Austrian cavalry were overrunning the departments of Aisne and Somme and got as far as Noyon. Fersen and Mercy-Argenteau urged Coburg to send all his cavalry straight against Paris, in order to deliver the Queen, who had been transferred to the Conciergerie on August 1. But Coburg no longer had the whole forces of the Coalition at his disposal. In obedience to the orders of Pitt, who had ordered him to capture Dunkirk as a bridgehead on the continent, the Duke of York had started for the coast on August 10 with thirty-seven thousand men, English, Hanoverians, and Dutch. This separation between York and Coburg, which was due to a selfish policy, was the salvation of the Republic.

The Committee of Public Safety deprived Kilmaine of his command and replaced him by Houchard, an old soldier of fortune covered with wounds, who was regarded as trustworthy because he was of plebeian stock and owed his advancement to the Revolution. Carnot obtained the appointment of Houchard and encouraged and guided him. When, on August 17, he heard that the English were marching on Dunkirk, he sent Jourdan in pursuit of them. Jourdan tried to intercept them at Linselles on the next day, but York eluded him, crossed the Yser unexpectedly on August 21, captured eleven French cannon at Ostcapelle, and on August 23 summoned Dunkirk to surrender. But Carion, commandant of Bergues, had already given orders to open the sluices and flood the country surrounding the fortress, so that it could not be completely blockaded. It received reinforcements, brought up by Jourdan, and was bravely defended by Souham and Hoche. Houchard had received orders on August 25 to take advantage of the absence of Coburg, who was occupied with the siege of Le Quesnoy, and York, who was engaged in the siege of Dunkirk, and cut their communications by falling on the Dutch troops guarding the Lys. He did not obey his instructions to the letter, but scattered his forces instead of concentrating them, and, having seized Tourcoing on August 28, instead of turning in the direction of Ypres and Nieuport to cut the communications of the English with Belgium, he took the shortest route to go to the relief of Dunkirk—that is, through Cassel. He thus came in contact with Freytag's corps of observation, which had been stationed about the approaches to the Grande Moere in order to protect York against an attack from the south. After a brush with the enemy on September 6 at Ostcapelle and Rexpoëde, Freytag fell back on Hondschoote during the night of September 6–7. For two days desultory and confused fighting went on round the village, which was taken and retaken. On September 8, at ten o'clock in the morning, Houchard thought the battle was lost, and had it not been for Delbrel, the representative on mission, he would have given orders to retreat. The attack was resumed.

The representatives on mission, Delbrel and Levasseur (of Sarthe) rode at the general's side at the head of the attacking columns, Levasseur having a horse killed under him. At one o'clock in the afternoon Freytag retreated towards Furnes. Houchard ought to have followed him up vigorously, for he had a fresh division at his disposal which had not yet taken part in the battle—the Hédouville division. But he lost this opportunity of destroying the Hessian and Hanoverian army as it fell back in disorder, neither taking Furnes, nor cutting off the retreat of the English army besieging Dunkirk. York hurriedly escaped by the road along the dunes, leaving part of his heavy artillery behind him.

The victory was incomplete, but it was the first won by the republican troops for a long time. It wiped out the memory of Aldenhoven, Neerwinden, Raismes and Famars, and the "Carmagnoles" recovered their pride and faith in the Revolution.

Unfortunately Houchard went on making mistakes. He did not arrive in time to relieve Le Quesnoy, which capitulated on September 12. Delbrel saved Bouchain and Cambrai by bringing up food and reinforcements on his own authority. Houchard was disheartened, and, instead of collecting all his forces and falling upon Coburg, who was still separated from York, he fell back upon Arras and led his troops back to the camp of Gavrelle, disobeying the orders which he had received to take the offensive. The representatives on mission denounced him to the Government, and on September 20 the committee removed him from his command. When his papers were searched, letters were discovered from the enemy generals in which the exchange of prisoners was discussed, together with matters of no importance. The letters were couched in polite terms, which offered sufficient foundation for accusing him of dealings with the enemy and treason. Poor Houchard was sent before the Revolutionary Tribunal.

The committee did not rest content with dismissing the general staff of the army of the north. A few days later the blow fell on the generals in command of the armies of the Rhine and Moselle—on the former, Landremont, for writing on September 12 that he would find it hard to defend the Weissenburg lines and that if they were broken, Strasbourg would be unable to hold out for more than three days; and on the latter, Schauenbourg, for allowing himself to be defeated on September 14 at Pirmasens, leaving twenty cannon and two thousand prisoners in the hands of the enemy. These repeated dismissals and the entire renewal of the general staffs of the three principal armies brought down a fierce attack on the committee in the Convention, which lasted for two days,

September 24 and 25. Thuriot had already sent in his resignation on September 20, rather than accept the dismissal of Houchard. Round him had collected a group of the representatives on mission who had been recalled—Duhem, Briez, Bourdon of Oise and Goupilleau de Fontenay, Duroy and the ex-members of the Committee of General Security who had been removed from their posts on September 14. The opposition nearly won the day, and the Convention added one of them, Briez, to the Committee of Public Safety. But Barère, Billaud, Saint-André, and Prieur of Marne put up a good defence, till Robespierre ascended the tribune. He addressed himself over the heads of the Convention to the whole country. He pointed out the vastness of the task which the committee bore on its shoulders: "Eleven armies to be directed, the burden of the whole of Europe to be supported, traitors to be unmasked on all sides, emissaries hired by the gold of foreign powers to be frustrated, dishonest administrative bodies to be watched and prosecuted, obstacles and hindrances to the execution of the wisest measures to be removed everywhere, all tyrants to be combated, all conspirators to be overawed." He next took the offensive: "Those who are denouncing us are themselves being denounced to the committee; accusers today, they will become the accused of tomorrow." He unmasked them pitilessly: "The first [Duhem] came out as the partisan of Custine and Lamorlière, he persecuted patriots in an important fortress [Lille], and he has again dared recently to propose to abandon a territory united to the Republic [Savoy]. . . . The second [Briez] has not yet made reparation for the shame with which he covered himself by coming back from a fortress of which the defence had been entrusted to him, having handed it over to the Austrians [Valenciennes]. No doubt if such men as these succeed in proving that the committee is not composed of good citizens, liberty is lost, for it will hardly be to them that enlightened opinion will give its confidence or hand over the reins of government."

This virulent extempore speech of Robespierre's, full of such contempt for his accusers, completely routed them. Briez was so crushed that he refused nomination to the Committee of Public Safety, and the committee obtained a unanimous vote of confidence and the approval of all its actions.

The consequences of this great parliamentary battle were considerable. It was now admitted that the representatives on mission, who formerly corresponded direct with the Convention, must be subordinated to the committee and that the latter, which had already chosen the members of the other committees since September 14, was in future to have the power to recall the representatives without risking its own existence. For a time at least the opposition had been overawed. On October 10 Danton, who had kept silence during this great debate, asked for leave to retire to Arcis-sur-Aube on grounds of health.

The last obstacles accumulated by the moderates to hamper revolutionary measures had now been removed. The revolutionary army, for which powers had been given by the decree of September 5, was now organized. The proceedings against the Girondin leaders, which had been so often adjourned, were now really to begin. On October 3 Amar made his report in arraignment of them. But, most important of all, the fixing of prices, provided for by the decree of September 4, was at last put into execution by the great law of September 29. Economic terrorism went hand in hand with political terrorism.

The consequences of the parliamentary victory of September 25 made themselves felt in the military sphere also. The committee now had a free hand in democratizing the general staffs. It took advantage of the liberty which it had won to appoint quite young generals to the command of the three principal armies, one after the other, common soldiers who had risen from the ranks, all three of whom were to justify the expectations which had been formed of them: Jourdan to the army of the north on September 24, Pichegru to the army of the Rhine on September 28, and lastly Hoche to the army of the Moselle on October 22. The choice was much bolder than that of Houchard had been. The latter was an old professional soldier who had taken part in all the campaigns of the old regime since the Seven Years' War. The others were all young men who had received no professional training, self-taught men, who had not yet risen to the rank of non-commissioned officers by 1789 (Jourdan was born in 1762, Pichegru in 1761, Hoche in 1768). The committee reaped the reward of its daring. These young generals, who owed everything to the Revolution, espoused its cause completely and staked their whole existence on victory. They were of an age at which the passions are strong, when a man rushes forward without a look backward. But for them Carnot's offensive tactics would have been impracticable. Their dash was not impaired by the theories of the schools; they owed everything to practice and experience. By their audacity and powers of rapid adaptation they disconcerted the rigid and hidebound generals of the Coalition. A new war called for new men, a national war needed leaders whose every fibre bound them to the nation.

The incomplete victory of Hondschoote was shortly followed by another victory, that of Wattignies, the work of Jourdan and Carnot.

After the capture of Le Quesnoy, Coburg, according to his habit, hesitated as to what course to adopt. He lost a fortnight regrouping his forces between the Sambre and the Scheldt, a fortunate respite of which Carnot took advantage to provide covering forces for Péronne and Guise. At last, on September 28, Coburg decided to march on Maubeuge with the Hanoverians and Dutch, whom he had summoned to join him. He easily threw the Desjardins division into disorder, crossed the Sambre on the following day at Hautmont, cut the communications between Maubeuge and Avesnes, and invested Maubeuge, where the representatives on mission, Hentz, Drouet, and Bar, had shut themselves up with a strong garrison of 22,000 men.

With admirable rapidity Carnot, who had joined Jourdan's army, concentrated 45,000 men at Guise between October 6 and 10; 4,000 reached Guise from Sedan in three days, after a march of sixty-five miles, and 8,000 from Arras, having covered the same distance in the same time. By October 11 the concentration was complete. General Merenvue, who was in command of the artillery, was deprived of his command for not bringing up the munitions fast enough. Jourdan and Carnot at once marched on Maubeuge. They ordered the attack for October 15—an enveloping attack on both wings—while the French centre was to open a cannonade against the enemy. The imperial troops stood firm for the first night. During the night Carnot transferred 7,000 men from his left to his right wing and at dawn began the attack on the village of Wattignies with his reinforced right wing, placing himself in person at Jourdan's side at the head of the attacking columns. Wattignies was taken and retaken, finally remaining in the hands of the French. On the evening of the 16th Coburg gave orders to retreat, after losing 2,200 men, and Maubeuge was saved. The commandant of the fortress, Chancel, who had not made a single sortie during the battle, was deprived of his command.

It is true that the victory was not decisive, for Coburg was not followed up and was able to summon the English to his aid from Furnes and establish himself undisturbed on the left bank of the Sambre to cover Brussels. But Wattignies was the second victory won by the sans-culottes in a pitched battle since their defeats in the spring. Maubeuge was the second fortress they had delivered. Their confidence in themselves increased, and, Carnot having now proved himself, his reputation was established. Events had justified the bold policy of the Committee of Public Safety. It could no longer be taxed with disorganizing the army by punishing the old generals and replacing them by callow and inexperienced young men.

To its success at Wattignies the committee could add the recovery of Lyons from the rebels. It had urged on the siege with all its might, for it was in a hurry to employ against Toulon the army engaged in the siege. It had grown impatient at Dubois-Crancé's delay in starting the bombardment. Dubois-Crancé was of noble birth, and the committee, imagining him to be a traitor, recalled him on October 6, together with his colleague Gauthier, for having stated in their last letter that they would not be strong enough to prevent a sortie on the part of Précy, whereas the reports previously sent in by Sandoz, the adjutant-general, tended to show that if the "Muscadins" attempted a sortie, they could succeed only by using balloons. Three days after the order for his recall, on October 9, the republican troops made a victorious entry into Lyons, but Précy escaped with a thousand men. The committee was convinced that this escape, foretold by Dubois-Crancé, was further proof that the latter was in league with the rebels.

Good news was now pouring into Paris. On October 17, the day after Wattignies, the Vendeans met with a serious defeat at Cholet and crossed to the right bank of the Loire at Saint-Florent. The Piedmontese had already been driven out of Maurienne and the valley of the Arve at the end of September, and the Spaniards had had to evacuate Roussillon and the Basque country.

The committee was able to indulge in a retrospect, and measure the work accomplished in two months. On October 23 it addressed a proclamation to the armies in which a triumphant note was already audible. "The cowardly satellites of tyranny have fled before you," it ran. ". . . They have abandoned Dunkirk and their artillery, they have hastened to escape from total ruin by placing the Sambre between themselves and your victorious columns. At Lyons a blow has been struck at federalism. The republican army has entered Bordeaux to deal it the final blow. The Piedmontese and Spaniards have been driven out of our territory. The defenders of the Republic have just destroyed the rebels of the Vendée."

No doubt all difficulties were not yet surmounted. There were still some alarming shadows in the picture. Toulon was still holding out. Wurmser was threatening Alsace. The Vendeans, who had crossed to the north of the Loire to effect a junction with the English reinforcements, were not yet crushed. Coburg had still to be reckoned with on the Sambre, and the Scheldt was not yet secure.

But on the whole by the end of October 1793 the committee was not unjustified in looking forward to the future with confidence. It had demanded a dictatorship at the great session of September 25 in order to save the country. The country was not yet saved, but it was already on the way towards recovery. The invalid had regained his morale.

CHAPTER VI

The Establishment of the Revolutionary Government

SINCE September 20, the date of Thuriot's resignation, the committee had got rid of the last Dantonist included in its ranks and had become more homogeneous. Since October 3, the date of Amar's report against the Girondins, the Convention had docked itself of 136 of its members (41 cited before the Revolutionary Tribunal, 19 who had fled and been proclaimed outlaws, and 76 others who, having signed protests against June 2, had been placed under arrest, and saved from the scaffold by Robespierre). This was a serious loss, which was bound to have as its immediate consequence a proportionate weakening of the opposition, which had never ceased to combat the committee since its inception. The committee could now breathe freely, and sent away half its members as delegates on various missions (Prieur of Marne and Saint-André to reorganize the fleet at Brest and Lorient, Couthon to Lyons, Saint-Just to Strasbourg, and, after the return of Robert Lindet, who had been in Normandy, Collot d'Herbois to Lyons). But though the committee had increased its authority in Paris itself, there was still much work to be done in order to extend and establish it throughout the whole of France.

The establishment of the revolutionary Government—that is to say, the co-ordination of emergency measures under the sole direction of the committee—was carried out in two stages, and for reasons of two different kinds: firstly, in September and October 1793, for reasons mainly political; and afterwards, in November and December 1793, for reasons mainly economic. During the former of these periods, what was chiefly necessary was to secure the levy in mass, by urging on the activities of the local authorities and repressing the last traces of federalist resistance. During the latter, the object was to make possible the application of the general maximum voted on September 29, but only put in force in the middle of October.

The Montagnard Constitution, enclosed in a cedar coffer standing before the president of the Convention's desk, had been postponed till the coming of peace. The old Constitution, that of 1791, remained in force, except for those parts which had been modified by new laws. It was a constitution with decentralizing tendencies, very ill suited to a state of war. The administrative and judicial authorities had everywhere had their origin in election. The revolutionary authorities themselves—for instance, the committees whose business it was to keep watch on suspects —had at the outset had the same origin. In times of foreign and civil war, elected authorities are not to be trusted. And, as a matter of fact, even after election had been abolished, revolutionary committees composed of secret aristocrats existed at the very height of the Terror.

In order to avert this danger the Convention had adopted as its general practice the employment of representatives on mission, armed with unlimited powers. These proconsuls, who were as powerful as Richelieu's intendants, had not hesitated to crush recalcitrant authorities. Since they could not be everywhere at the same time, they sought the aid of the Fédérés of August 10 in carrying out the first levy of men, and delegated part of their powers to them.

For example, Maure, who was operating in the department of Yonne, entrusted to his delegates, by an ordinance of September 17, the right of drawing up the list of the young men requisitioned, preparing a return of corn and commandeering it, making an inventory of guns and causing them to be deposited at the chief town of each district, besides procuring information about suspicious persons. These powers were already singularly extensive and reduced the regularly elected authorities to functions of an almost entirely consultative nature.

But let us take the case of Laplanche, who was entrusted with the levy in mass in the department of Cher. He went much further than Maure. By an ordinance of September 27 he not only gave his delegates the necessary powers to requisition men, arms, and food-stuffs, but authorized them to carry out domiciliary visits, disarm ill-disposed persons and suspects, seize the "superfluous provisions" which they might find in such persons' houses, and distribute them to the poor. He further authorized them to arrest suspects, levy revolutionary contributions upon them, and with the proceeds relieve the unfortunate. He set up over the heads of the delegates of the cantons district commissaries with even more extensive powers. They were to have powers "to remove weak, neglectful, or corrupt administrators, whether civil or military," and fill their places provisionally, without having recourse to election. Laplanche's commissaries really used the powers which he had conferred upon them. They ordered the dismissal even of priests who had taken the oath to the Constitution, ordered transfers of officials, levied contributions on the rich (249,000 livres in the district of Vierzon, 313,000 in that of Sancerre, etc.), relieving the poor with the proceeds—especially those who had sons in the army—and presenting sums to the hospitals and popular societies. One of them, Labouvrie, stripped the churches of their sacred vessels. He did not yet dare to forbid worship, but he preached against Catholicism, closed parish churches, and, as early as the beginning of October, taught that the cult of Liberty and Equality was all that was needed.

The other representatives on mission sometimes used the strong methods of Laplanche and sometimes the prudent methods of Maure.

Fouché was one of those who believed that the Revolution could be saved only by an energetic class policy applied for the benefit of the sansculottes. By an ordinance of September 19 he established in the chief town of every district in the department of Nièvre a committee of surveillance and philanthropy, authorized to levy upon the rich a contribution proportionate to the numbers of the indigent. On September 26 he issued orders to the bakers at Moulins that they were in future to make only one kind of bread, known as "bread of Equality," to be sold at a uniform price of three sous a pound, made possible by allotting a sum to compensate the bakers and recovering it from the rich. The usual price had previously been ten sous a pound. Having abolished poverty, he prohibited begging and idleness, by an ordinance of the 24th Brumaire, saying that "all beggars or idle persons shall be imprisoned." Farmers who refused to submit to the requisitioning were pilloried in the public square with a placard bearing the words: "Starver of the people, traitor to the country!" If the offence was repeated, they were put in prison till the peace, and their goods sequestrated, with the exception of what was strictly necessary for them and their families (October 2). Fouché also ordered that metallic currency should be compulsorily exchanged for assignats. If manufacturers closed their workshops, he threatened that the shops should be seized and worked at the owner's expense for the benefit of the Government. "Men blush to be rich here," he wrote on October 13. Like Laplanche, a former vicar-general, Fouché, an ex-Oratorian, made himself conspicuous by his anti-clerical measures. He requisitioned church plate and sent it to Paris, and secularized the cemeteries by his famous ordinance commanding that over their gates should be placed the naturalist inscription, "Death is an eternal sleep." When the revolutionary calendar was instituted by the decree of October 5, he organized the civic celebrations of *décadi* (the tenth day) in the place of the mass, and raised a small revolutionary army to put his ordinances into execution.

Dubouchet in Seine-et-Marne, Le Carpentier in Manche, Baudot in Haute-Garonne, Taillefer in Lot, Roux-Fazillac in Charente, Lequinio and Laignelot in Charente-Inférieure, André Dumont in Somme, did more or less the same as Laplanche and Fouché. But other representatives on mission, such as Maure, confined themselves to the purely administrative work of the levy in mass and even repudiated their colleagues' innovations. Lastly, there were departments which had not yet been visited by the representatives on mission and where the application of the revolutionary laws on food-speculation, requisitioning, suspects, etc., had had to be left to the old elected authorities. The result was an amazing diversity in the administrative system. In some places terrorism and the rule of the clubs prevailed, with the support of the sansculottes. In others there was no apparent change: the rich were unmolested, nobody was imprisoned, the existing authorities were undisturbed, and the priests enjoyed complete tranquillity.

The Committee of Public Safety tried to direct and regulate the activity of the representatives on mission, not always with success, for their operations took place at a distance from Paris, and owing to the slowness of communications they had no time to wait for instructions from headquarters. Only rarely did they submit to Paris the difficulties which presented themselves; they dealt with them on the spot according to their own inspiration, whether good or bad.

At first the committee applauded the class policy of Laplanche, Fouché, and their like, and on August 29 congratulated Fouché upon levying contributions on the rich: "This means of public safety is also a measure of personal security against the just indignation of the people, which can no longer endure the excess of its misery." Robert Lindet shared the views of his colleagues who had remained in Paris, and wrote to them from Caen on August 29 that it would be dangerous to arm the poor if the rich were not first made to see reason.

The committee also approved of the imprisonment and dismissal of officials (see its letters to Le Carpentier on September 7 and Carrier on September 8). But it soon became uneasy at the anti-clerical, or, rather, antichristian policy of some of the proconsuls. "It seemed to us," it wrote to André Dumont on the 6th Brumaire, "that during your recent operations you have made too violent an attack on the objects of Catholic worship. . . . We must take good care not to furnish the hypocritical counter-revolutionaries, who are trying to stir up civil war, with any pretext that may appear to justify their calumnies. We must not give them occasion to say that we are violating the liberty of worship and making war on religion itself." Robespierre had already taken alarm at the decree of October 5 instituting the new calendar, and made an entry in his memorandum-book as follows: "Indefinite adjournment of the decree on the calendar"—which shows that he intended to oppose the execution of the law which was to serve as a pretext for dechristianization. How could a class policy favouring the sansculottes be carried out if their convictions were to be outraged?

While approving the vigorous measures of the proconsuls, the committee soon saw their dangers. It congratulated Maure upon putting down the arbitrary actions of his delegates, the Fédérés of August 10, and the revolutionary committees (14th Brumaire). It called upon Laurent, who was on mission in the department of Nord, to dissolve the revolutionary force which he had raised, saying in a letter of 2nd Frimaire that "counter-revolutionary tactics may take possession of this organ of terrorism and suddenly re-establish the system of departmental forces which was at one time a threat to liberty. Purge the National Guard; it will render the same services and will not give rise to the same alarms." Two days later it wrote to Maure to dissolve his revolutionary army as soon as he left the department of Yonne.

When the levy in mass had been completed and the committee had recalled the representatives on mission who had organized it, it took good care to insert in the decree a provision stating that the powers of the representatives' delegates were immediately to cease (13th Brumaire). A decree of 19th Brumaire charged the committee to demand an account of the use made of their powers by these delegates.

The representatives on mission having been recalled and their delegates done away with, the old elected authorities once more resumed the duty of executing the laws. The committee was bound to consider how to establish harmony between the various authorities—those which had their basis in election and those born of the revolutionary dictatorship. It was necessary to define their respective spheres and subordinate them all to the central power—in other words, to substitute an ordered and permanent centralization for the chaotic and intermittent centralization which had developed at random under pressure of necessity. It was all the more necessary since the economic situation demanded it.

The law of September 29 on the "general maximum" fixed the price of all commodities already subject to the law on food-speculation of July 27. With the exception of cereals, flour and forage, tobacco, salt and soap, the price fixed for which was uniform for the whole of France, other commodities and goods of prime necessity were to have their prices fixed by the district authorities at a rate a third higher than the average price in 1790, so that what cost three livres in 1790 could not exceed four livres in 1793. Those failing to conform to the law, whether buyers or sellers, would be subject to a fine, for which they would be jointly responsible, amounting to a sum equal to twice the value of the object fraudulently sold, and payable to the informer. They would also be entered on the list of suspects. It would have been fruitless to fix the prices of commodities without at the same time fixing the daily wage of the labourers. The law fixed a maximum wage at a rate half as much again as that of 1790, so that a workman earning twenty sous in 1790 would now earn thirty. The fixed rate of wages was to be established by the municipalities, whereas the tariff of commodities fell within the sphere of the district authorities. Workmen who should refuse to work at the official wage were to be impressed by the municipalities and punished by three days' imprisonment.

The committee cherished no illusions as to the difficulties of applying such a law, which forced owners to sell at a loss, without compensation, goods which they had previously been selling at three or four times the price. Even the previous law of May 4, on the maximum price of cereals only, had had as its immediate result to empty the markets. How were the towns and armies to be provisioned if the victualling of them was left dependent upon local elected authorities, secretly hostile to the revolutionary laws? To put in force the general maximum would necessarily involve a recrudescence of compulsion—that is to say, of terrorism—and at the same time a decisive movement towards devising a stricter, more organized, and more absolute centralization.

Two days before the tariff of maximum prices was posted in Paris, on October 10, Saint-Just, in a bitter, gloomy speech, consisting entirely of trenchant maxims, expounded to the Assembly a plan for a new organization of the Republic, a sort of provisional constitution, which seemed to him necessary in order to surmount the terrible obstacles which he foresaw. "The laws are revolutionary, but those who execute them are not. . . . The Republic will not be founded until the will of the sovereign shall repress the monarchical minority, and reign over it by right of conquest. You need no longer deal gently with the enemies of the new order of things, and liberty must at all costs prevail. You have to punish not only traitors, but even the indifferent; you have to punish all those who remain passive within the Republic and do nothing for it. . . . Those who cannot be governed by justice must be governed by iron; tyrants

388

must be oppressed!" Saint-Just justified this program of desperate terrorism by drawing a terrible picture of the civil and military bureaucracy and likewise of the economic and moral state of the country. He pointed to those in charge of the hospital organization, who were supplying the rebels of the Vendée with flour, the officials charged with executing the law on food-speculation, who were themselves speculating in food, the purchasers of national property, who were buying it cheap with depreciated paper-money, the rich growing richer owing to the fall in the value of the assignat and the rise in the cost of living. "Patriotism is merely a form of lip-service; everybody sacrifices others, while making no sacrifice of his own interest." He foresaw that the law of the general maximum would set up fresh speculation. He could see but one remedy: to provide the Government with the vigour which it lacked. In every grade responsibility must go hand in hand with execution: "The sword must everywhere be set up beside the abuse." They must rely upon the poor and the common soldiers, whose sufferings they would relieve. "If a soldier is unfortunate, he is unhappier than other men, for why should he fight if he has nothing to defend but a government which abandons him?" The representatives on mission with the armies ought to be the fathers and friends of the soldiers; they should sleep with them in their tents and share their life. For the purpose of seeing that the orders of the committee were carried out, they should place under its supervision not only the Executive Council, as before, but the generals and all constituted authorities. It should be proclaimed that the Government was revolutionary until the peace; that is to say, that the Constitution voted in June would be set aside for good, the dictatorship legalized, and the elective principle temporarily subordinated to the principle of authority. The committee was to have powers to supervise—that is to say, quash—the constituted elective bodies. In order to obtain the rapid execution of the revolutionary laws the committee would no longer correspond directly with the departmental administrations, but with those of the districts, which would become the mainspring of the new organization.

In order to ensure the application of the maximum a fresh return was to be made of all the cereals in the Republic, which would enable them to exercise the right to commandeer on the strength of correct information. The country was to be divided into zones for purposes of provisioning and Paris was to be provisioned for a year from its own special area. Resistance would be crushed by the central revolutionary army, detachments of which would be quartered on the recalcitrant communes at the

389

expense of the rich. Saint-Just further foreshadowed the creation of a special tribunal, a sort of *Chambre ardente*,[1] which should force contractors and all those who had handled public funds since 1789 to make restitution.

All the measures which he proposed were voted without discussion. The fears which he had voiced with regard to the efficacy of the maximum were at once realized. In Paris and every town in France, as soon as the tariff was posted, the shops were immediately invaded by an eager crowd and emptied of their wares. Tradesmen, having nothing left to sell, began to close their shops. In Paris Chaumette threatened them with confiscation, and the Commune, at his instigation, requested the Convention "to concentrate its attention on raw materials and factories, in order to place them under requisition by fixing penalties for those holding or manufacturing goods who allow them to lie idle; or even to place them at the disposal of the Republic, which has no lack of labour to turn them all to a useful purpose." Expropriation was thus to lead to collectivism, the Republic itself exploiting the whole product of agriculture and industry. But neither the Convention nor the committee was prepared to go as far as that and bring about a social revolution in order to ensure the application of the maximum, which they had had forced on them against their will.

The Commune acted with the utmost dispatch. It controlled the distribution of the forthcoming commodities by commandeering and by the institution of cards for bread, meat, sugar, and soap—that is to say, by rationing. It put down the increasing number of liquor frauds by establishing commissaries to act as tasters (*commissaires dégustateurs*). It empowered the commissaries for food-speculation to make domiciliary visits, even in private houses. It endeavoured to obtain the observance of the fixed tariffs by police measures and by threatening delinquents with the Law of the Suspect. Most of the towns imitated or even forestalled the example of Paris.

But though the distribution of the existing supplies of goods was effected as well as could be managed, revictualling became more and more difficult, for it was no longer to the interest of merchants to renew their stocks. In order to revive the exchange of goods, the stopping of

---

[1] The name first given to the court instituted in 1535 by Francis I for the trial of heretics, and later to the special commissions appointed by Louis XIV—e. g., for the trial of Fouquet—and by Louis XV for reducing the debt. These latter were specially aimed at speculators.

which would have checked production and promptly led to a shortage of everything, they had to take a further step in the direction of centralization. On October 22 the committee had a commission of three members set up, known as the Commission of Supplies (*Commission des subsistances*) and armed with the widest powers. By its right of seizure (*préhension*) it was empowered to take possession of all commodities at the maximum price. It was to distribute these commodities among the districts and have supreme control over the whole of agricultural and industrial production, transport, manufactures, mines, coal, wood, imports, and exports; and it had power to call in armed force. It was to prepare a revision of the maximum, the settling of which would no longer be left to the arbitrary decision of the local authorities, but made subject to fixed principles, laid down by Barère on the 11th Brumaire. Prices were to be fixed at the source: "(1) At the storehouses of raw materials; (2) at the factory; (3) at the wholesale merchant's; (4) at the retail merchant's"; and, lastly, allowances for transport would be granted according to the distance. In order to prepare the way for this graduated and uniform tariff, which should secure the profit of the manufacturer, the merchant, and the retailer, in order to revive trade, the Commission of Supplies embarked upon an immense inquiry, entrusted to a special board, the *bureau du maximum*. The inquiry lasted for several months, so that the new tariffs of maximum prices could not be ready till the spring of 1794. Meanwhile the country had to live from hand to mouth—that is, by requisitioning and rationing.

Robert Lindet was recalled from his mission in Calvados on November 2 to assume control of the Commission of Supplies. He tells us that he opposed the use of the revolutionary army for purposes of requisitioning, and it was merely sent to garrison the towns of the Île-de-France. As it remained inactive, the special revolutionary tribunal which was to have accompanied its movements was never set up.

Rather than use military force in requisitioning and fixing prices the committee preferred to strengthen administrative centralization. On the 28th Brumaire Billaud-Varenne went to the Convention and repeated Saint-Just's criticisms of the ill will of the subordinate authorities, who allowed decrees favouring the lower classes to become a dead letter—for instance, that granting relief to the relatives of volunteers, and those relating to supplies. He proposed to force all authorities to give an account of their acts every ten days, to publish the laws in a special bulletin, to render the purse and person of all officials liable to penalties, and, lastly, to authorize the representatives on mission and the committee to replace without election all defaulting or suspect authorities. On the 9th Frimaire he further proposed forbidding the representatives on mission to delegate their powers, so that there should no longer be any intermediary between the committee and the districts, besides dissolving all departmental armed forces and suppressing all departmental vigilance committees tainted with federalism. His project was definitively voted on the 14th Frimaire, with an amendment which still further strengthened it. On the 3rd Frimaire Danton made the point that the execution of the laws ought no longer to be entrusted to elected authorities. "I propose," he said, "that each department shall have a national procurator (*procureur national*), that, in order to destroy the influence of family fortune and wealth, it shall be the Committee of Public Safety which appoints these supervisors, these agents of the whole people, who will no longer be local men as they are at present, but representatives of the Republic." After some hesitation the committee accepted the establishment of these national agents, appointed by the Government and not elected, who already foreshadowed Napoleon's prefects. When Fayau and Merlin of Thionville defended the elective principle, Couthon replied: "At the present moment we must be careful not only to have no dangerous public functionaries, but also to avoid dubious ones."

By this law of the 14th Frimaire, which, with a few alterations, was to be the provisional Constitution of the Republic for the duration of the war, the whole administration of France centred on Paris, as it had done before 1789. The elected authorities which still survived were under the supervision of the national agent appointed by the committee and armed with the right of requisitioning, as well as of denouncing officials. The latter knew that at the slightest shortcoming they would be dismissed and consequently added to the list of suspects. No elections would be held to replace them, as had been the case even during the period of the levy in mass, but the representatives on mission or the national agents would confine themselves to consulting the popular society before drawing up the list of substitutes. A decree of the 5th Brumaire suspended the election of municipal bodies. For all practical purposes the sovereignty of the people, the electoral power, became concentrated in the clubs— that is to say, in the party in power. The clubs themselves underwent a process of purging. The revolutionary Government became the dictatorship of a party exercised for the benefit of a class, the class of consumers, artisans, small property-owners, and the poor, led by men of the middle classes who had irrevocably thrown in their lot with the Revolution, and in particular by those members of this class who were enriching themselves by the manufacture of army supplies.

The dictatorship of a party or a class is as a rule only established by force, and in time of war this is necessarily so. Revolutionary government had as its inevitable accompaniment the Terror.

CHAPTER VII

Revolutionary Justice

THERE is hardly an instance of a country engaged in a foreign war complicated by civil war in which the government has not adopted a summary and expeditious system of justice for putting down communications with the enemy, plots, and revolts.

The Constituent Assembly had created a High Court, elected by the electoral colleges of the departments, for trying crimes involving the security of the State. This new judicial body had acquitted or avoided bringing to trial those sent to it by the Legislative Assembly, thus disappointing the expectations of the revolutionaries. After the insurrection of August 10 the victorious Commune demanded the establishment of an extraordinary criminal tribunal, a sort of court martial, of which the judges and jury were elected by the sections of the capital. This tribunal, which was set up on August 17, pronounced a few death sentences, the effect of which was mitigated by its acquittals. It did not prevent the September massacres. The Girondins, to whom it was suspect on account of its Montagnard origins, abolished it on November 29, 1792, the High Court having already disappeared since September 25, so that the Revolution no longer possessed any court for trying political offences. Those accused of plotting against the security of the State, such as Sainte-Foy and Dufresne Saint-Léon, agents of the civil list, Madame de Rohan-Rochefort, who was accused of being in communication with Bertrand de Moleville, who had emigrated, Dietrich, ex-mayor of Strasbourg and an accomplice in the rebellion of Lafayette, and many others, were brought before the ordinary criminal tribunals, which invariably acquitted them. The Girondins controlled the Government, the victorious armies of France were in occupation of Belgium, so the Revolution thought it was safe to adopt a generous policy.

But at the beginning of March arrived news of the defeat at Aldenhoven, the loss of Liége, and then of the insurrection in the Vendée. Fresh troops were raised in a hurry, as had been done immediately after the capture of Longwy. As early as March 8 representatives of the Paris sections presented a request "that a tribunal should at once be established, from which there should be no appeal, to put a stop to the audacity of the ringleaders (*les grands coupables*) and of all enemies of the common weal." The commissaries just appointed by the Convention for raising the levy of three hundred thousand men in the departments declared that they would not leave for their posts until the decree establishing the revolutionary tribunal had been passed. After sitting day and night amid an uproar, the Assembly resolved to set up an extraordinary criminal tribunal, of which the judges and jury should be nominated by the Convention itself and not, as previously, by the people. "The tribunal shall have cognizance of all counter-revolutionary enterprises, of all crimes against the liberty, equality, unity, and indivisibility of the Republic and the internal and external security of the State, and of all plots aiming at the restoration of the monarchy or the establishment of any authority infringing the liberty, equality, and sovereignty of the people, whether the culprits be officials, civil or military, or ordinary citizens." It was to judge without appeal on points either of fact or of law. The property of those sentenced to death should be confiscated to the Republic, with the reservation that provision was to be made for the subsistence of their needy relatives. Since they were in a hurry to set the new tribunal to work, it was decided that temporary judges and jury should be appointed, drawn at first from Paris and the neighbouring departments, and by March 13 they were nominated by the Assembly.

But the Girondins, who had had the establishment of this tribunal forced upon them, soon took their revenge by the election of the commission of six, which was alone to have the right to cite accused persons before the political tribunal. The commission was composed of five Girondins and only one Montagnard (Prieur of Marne) and instituted no proceedings, so that the tribunal was paralysed.

But on April 2 news arrived of the treason of Dumouriez. The judges and jury of the tribunal at once went to the Convention and complained of the inaction to which they were reduced. "The people knows the conspirators and desires their punishment!" On the motion of Albitte the commission of six was suppressed. Three days later Charlier proposed that the public prosecutor should be authorized to cite directly before the Revolutionary Tribunal, with no preliminary decree from the Convention, all those accused of plotting. Danton raised the point that, since that class of criminal was so numerous, the Convention would simply not have time to examine the records of all the cases and would waste precious time in voting for their trial. "If despotism were to triumph," he added, "you would soon see a provost's court [1] (*tribunal prévôtal*) in every department, for beheading all patriots, even those who had not made an active display of patriotism." And, sure enough, provosts' courts were seen at work in 1815. Danton did, however, obtain a stipulation that no general, minister, or deputy should be cited before the tribunal without a previous decree of the Convention. These proposals were voted, in spite of Barbaroux, who protested against handing over the dictatorship in judicial matters to a single man, the public prosecutor.

The Revolutionary Tribunal held its first session on the very next day, April 6, and tried a returned *émigré*, who had been found at Bourg-la-Reine with two passports and a white cockade in his possession. The *émigré* was sentenced to death, amid the tears of the judge and jury. These were no cruel lawgivers; in performing a duty which was painful to them, they firmly believed that they were saving the Revolution and France.

The Girondins were imprudent enough to send Marat before the tribunal, on a charge of inciting to pillage, murder, and the dissolution of the Convention. Marat's trial ended in a triumphant acquittal on April 24. On April 23 the tribunal acquitted a whole series of generals: d'Harambure, who was accused of communicating royalist proclamations to the municipality of Neubreisach; d'Esparbès, who had become governor of Santo Domingo in succession to Blanchelande, previously condemned to death for having imprisoned patriots and fomented the revolt of the aristocrats; next, in May, Miranda, Stengel, and Lanoue, who had been implicated in the disasters in Belgium. Two generals only were condemned to death as accomplices of Dumouriez: Miaczynski and Lescuyer, against whom the charges were overwhelming. The sessions now went on quietly, observing all the forms of law, and both accusers and defenders were allowed to express themselves freely.

In spite of the federalist insurrection the tribunal did not act precipitately. Between June 4 and 18 it devoted long sittings to the trial of the Breton conspiracy, and though it sentenced twelve of La Rouarie's accomplices to death, it also acquitted thirteen persons. The twelve who were condemned to death cried: "Long live the King!" and embraced one another on the scaffold. The philosophical police-agent Dutard wrote in his account of this execution: "I must tell you that these executions produce the greatest effects politically, the most important of which is that

---

[1] The *prévôt royal* under the *ancien régime* had as one of his functions that of presiding over a tribunal. As his title implies, his function was to represent the royal power, and he was accordingly regarded as an emblem of tyranny.

they calm the resentment of the people at the ills which it is enduring. In them its vengeance is satisfied. The wife who has lost her husband, the father who has lost his son, the tradesman whose business has gone, the workman who pays such high prices for everything that his wages are reduced to practically nothing, perhaps consent to reconcile themselves to the ills which they endure only when they see men whom they believe to be their enemies more unfortunate than themselves."

Montané, the president of the tribunal, attempted to save Charlotte Corday. The third question put to the jury was worded as follows: "Did she commit [the murder] with premeditation and with criminal and counter-revolutionary intentions?" Montané struck out of the draft the words "premeditation" and "counter-revolutionary," in the hope that the crime might be regarded as an act of madness or an ordinary murder. During the trial preceding this—that of the murderers of Léonard Bourdon, the member of the Convention who had been molested and struck during his mission to Orleans—Montané had already, on sending the sentence to be printed, struck out of the text the usual formula: "The property of condemned persons is confiscated to the Republic," so that no confiscation could take place; though, according to the account of Prieur of Marne, there were several millionaires among those sentenced. Montané's two alterations were at once discovered and he would have been sent to the scaffold had not Fouquier-Tinville purposely allowed him to remain forgotten in prison.

The trial of Custine occupied almost all the second half of August. "General Moustache" fought his case inch by inch, replied to every witness, and called a number of generals on active service as witnesses, to whom the court refused a hearing. The public was obviously favourable to him, and the jury wavered. The Jacobins became agitated. "It must not be," said Robespierre at the club on August 25, "that a tribunal established to help on the Revolution should hold it back by its criminal delays; it ought to be as active as crime, it ought to be always equal to the offence." Custine was sentenced two days later and died bravely on August 28. He was guilty of nothing but insubordination to the orders of Bouchotte, incautious language, and defective organization in the field. He was the scapegoat for the capitulation of Mainz and Valenciennes.

It was the events of September 5 that brought about the triumph of Hébertism. A fresh period in the history of the tribunal began, its members being now increased as a result of the report of Merlin of Douai and divided into four sections, two of which sat concurrently. The list of new judges and jurymen was proposed by the Committee of Public

Safety and the Committee of General Security jointly. Both were drawn from the middle classes or the liberal professions. Among them were to be seen ex-priests, such as Lefetz or Royer; painters and engravers, Châtelet, Topino-Lebrun, Sambat, Prieur, and Girard; a banker, Victor Aigoin; doctors and surgeons, Souberbielle, Bécu, and Martin; representatives of trade and industry, Duplay and Billon; goldsmiths and jewellers, Klipsis, Girard, and Compagne; tailors, Aubry, Grimont, and Presselin; locksmiths, such as Didier; shoemakers, such as Servière; printers, such as Nicolas; a hatter, Baron; a grocer, Lohier; a vinegar-manufacturer, Gravier, etc. There were no sansculottes properly so-called, unless we include among them bureaucrats such as Clémence, who was employed in printing assignats. Among them were two genuine marquises, Antonelle and Leroy de Montflabert, who assumed the name of "Dix-Aôut" (Tenth of August). All or nearly all of them had had some education.

The instrument of repression had now been perfected and adjusted; it had next to be made to give better results. Counter-revolution was not only attacking the existing Government by revolts, plots, treason, and espionage, but by the perhaps even more formidable weapon of famine, and frauds connected with supplies and contracts. On September 29, the very day upon which the Convention voted the great decree on the general maximum, it also decided that dishonest contractors should be treated as conspirators and thus rendered liable to trial before the Revolutionary Tribunal. This terrible decree was passed in response to the complaints of young recruits, who had laid on the table of the Assembly a pair of shoes with soles made of wood and cardboard. The commission for the control of contracts (*Commission des marchés*) displayed great activity, large numbers of tradesmen being cited before the tribunal for fraud, illicitly raising prices, violation of the law of the maximum, and food-speculation.

With the month of October began the great political trials: that of the Queen, which lasted from October 14 to 16, and then that of the Girondins, which required a week, from October 24 to 30.

The condemnation of the Queen, "the Austrian woman (*l'Autrichienne*)," as she was called, was a foregone conclusion. She died bravely, while a vast crowd shouted: "Long live the Republic!"

The twenty-one Girondins attempted to defend themselves. Only one of them, Boileau, showed a lack of fortitude; he announced that his eyes were opened, that he was repentant and a sincere Montagnard; but this did not save him. The others stood their ground. Vergniaud, Brissot, and Gensonné made speeches in reply to the witnesses, who were their enemies.

The Jacobins grew angry and demanded from the Convention a law which should rid the tribunal "of formalities which stifle the conscience and hinder conviction," a law which "should give the jury the power to state that they had sufficient information." Osselin proposed a wording which Robespierre considered too vague. "I propose," said Robespierre, "to decree that after three days' discussion the president of the tribunal shall ask the jury if their conscience is sufficiently enlightened. If they answer in the negative, the trial shall go on till they declare that they are in a position to pronounce sentence." The decree was voted and at once carried to the Revolutionary Tribunal, which was sitting. The jury were consulted and at first replied that their consciences were not sufficiently enlightened. It was the sixth day of the trial. But that very evening they declared that their minds were made up. The twenty-one Girondins, condemned to death by a unanimous verdict, greeted the sentence with cries and vehement protests. Valazé stabbed himself as they left the court. The tribunal ordered that his dead body should be taken on a cart to the place of execution. A huge crowd collected to witness the death of the Girondins, shouting: "Down with the traitors!"

The law for speeding up trials was bound to have as its inevitable result an increase in the number of convictions. Between August 6 and October 1 twenty-nine death sentences, nine sentences of deportation, and twenty-four acquittals were pronounced, not to mention a hundred and thirty cases in which it was found that there were no grounds for proceedings. During the three following months, up to January 1, 1794, out of 395 accused persons, 194 were acquitted, 24 punished by deportation, imprisonment, or hard labour, and 177 condemned to death, 51 in October, 58 in November, and 68 in December.

Political trials followed one after the other. Philippe Égalité, who had given so many pledges to the Revolution, was convicted as an accomplice of the Girondins and Dumouriez, because his eldest son, afterwards Louis Philippe, had followed the general in his treason. By hounding him to his death the Montagnards hoped to clear themselves of the accusation of Orleanism so often brought against them by their opponents. Next it was Madame Roland's turn to suffer in the place of her husband, who had disappeared, though in any case she was compromised by her correspondence with Barbaroux and Duprat. On hearing of her death her husband committed suicide, less perhaps from grief than in order to prevent the confiscation of his property, for he had a daughter. Next it was the turn of Bailly, the ex-mayor of Paris, to expiate on the scene of his "crime," amid the insults of the spectators, the massacre of republicans on the Champ de Mars. Next came the Girondin Pierre Manuel, the Feuillants Barnave and Duport-Dutertre, then Generals Brunet, Houchard, Lamorlière, and Biron. The last proclaimed his royalist sentiments from the scaffold, thus providing a certain justification for the sentence which he had received. These famous condemnations should not make us forget the obscure persons condemned as a result of the various laws on emigration, food-speculation, dealings with the enemy, or seditious language, who were far more numerous.

The Revolutionary Tribunal was established at a time when the news of the insurrection in the Vendée had not yet reached Paris, and was originally intended to be the only one for the whole of France. After that time other parts of France also rose in revolt, and the Paris tribunal could no longer cope with the task of repression. In the regions rent by civil war, military methods were resorted to. The law of March 19, 1793, aimed at the Vendeans, created military commissions of five members, who sentenced to death rebels captured arms in hand, after merely verifying their identity. As for rebels arrested without arms, the law provided that they should be cited before the ordinary criminal courts, which tried them by revolutionary methods—that is to say, without appeal on points of fact or law.

The severity of repressive measures in the provinces was in direct proportion to the danger of the revolt. The rising in Normandy, which was settled after the bloodless engagement at Vernon, only led to a few dismissals and arrests. There was not a single death sentence in Calvados during the whole of the Terror. The Convention was content with a single symbolic action. On the motion of Delacroix and Thuriot, it decreed on July 17 "that the house owned by Buzot at Évreux should be razed, and that on its ruins should be raised a signpost with the following inscription: 'Here was the abode of the villain Buzot, who, though a representative of the people, conspired to bring about the ruin of the Republic.'"

The revolt at Lyons, which took place later, was infinitely more serious. The rebels had imprisoned or executed a number of Montagnards. Here the reprisals were severe, and assumed not only a political but a social character. On October 12, after hearing Barère's report, the Convention passed the following motion: "The city of Lyons shall be destroyed. Every house inhabited by the rich shall be demolished. Nothing shall remain but the poor man's house, the habitations of slain or proscribed patriots, buildings specially employed in industry, and public buildings devoted to charity and public instruction."

As long as Couthon and Maignet were in residence at Lyons, now known as Ville-Affranchie, the repression was not excessive. Couthon had himself carried to the Place Bellecour and struck a few houses with a mallet, which were then slowly pulled down. But at the beginning of November Collot d'Herbois and Fouché arrived, with a detachment of the revolutionary army under the command of Ronsin. Collot organized a great expiatory celebration on the Place des Terreaux in honour of the memory of Chalier, and mass executions began. The old commission of popular justice set up by Couthon was suppressed as being too indulgent, and replaced by a revolutionary commission under the presidency of Parrein. The shooting of prisoners, singly and in batches, supplemented the work of the guillotine, which was considered too slow. On the 14th Frimaire (December 4), sixty young men, who had been sentenced to death, were exposed to cannon-fire on the plain of Les Brotteaux, bound together in couples between two parallel trenches dug to receive their bodies. The cannon-fire killed only a third of them, and the rest had to be finished off by musket-fire. On the following day two hundred and eight prisoners sentenced to death were shot on the same spot, on the 18th Frimaire sixty-seven, on the 23rd thirty-two. These executions did not stop till the 22nd Pluviôse (February 10). Parrein's commission pronounced the death sentence on 1,667 prisoners. These butcheries were all the more abominable since they were not excused by the excitement which follows a struggle. The siege had been over for two months when they started. Nor were they of any use as a warning to others, for Collot himself wrote to the committee on the 17th Brumaire: "Even the executions do not produce all the effect that might be expected. The duration of the siege and the daily risks run by everybody have produced a sort of indifference towards life, if not an entire contempt for death. Yesterday a spectator returning from an execution said: 'It is not so very bad. Now, what can I possibly do to be guillotined? Insult the representatives?' " A man with a cool head would have concluded that the death penalty ought to be used sparingly. Collot, who had been an actor, drew the opposite conclusion—that the guillotine must be supplemented by other methods. He even proposed to Robespierre, though without success, to scatter through the whole of France the sixty thousand workmen of Lyons, who, according to him, would never be republicans.

The civil war in the west was a horrible one, and repressive measures in these regions were particularly severe. Military commissions were set up in the chief towns—Angers, Rennes, Laval, Tours, Nantes, etc—to try the Vendeans who were captured bearing arms. The one at Angers condemned sixty-nine rebels to be shot at Doué on the 3rd Nivôse, sixty-four on the following day, two hundred and three on the 6th, a hundred at Angers on the 23rd, etc. At Angers those condemned to death were led to the place of execution, La Haie-aux-Bonshommes, now known as the Champ des Martyrs, accompanied by bands and the authorities in full dress, and with soldiers lining the route.

The repression carried out by Carrier at Nantes surpassed even the fusillades of Lyons in its horror. Carrier, an Auvergnat of violent temperament and addicted to drink, arrived the day after the defeat of the "Mayençais"[2] at Torfou and the capture of Noirmoutier, which had been handed over to Charette by its inhabitants. He believed himself to be surrounded by traitors, and perhaps even feared for his life. In order to ensure the execution of his orders, as well as to protect himself, he surrounded himself with a red guard, known as the Compagnie Marat, the forty members of which each received fifteen livres a day. At the same time he organized a secret police under the leadership of two arrant ruffians, Fouquet and Lambertye, who were afterwards condemned to death for their malversations. Prisoners from the Vendée poured into Nantes by hundreds and thousands. Typhus and cholera broke out in the prisons into which they were packed, and the epidemic threatened to spread to the inhabitants of Nantes whose duty it was to mount guard over them. In order to expedite the clearing of the prisons Carrier then organized the "Noyades." Lighters or rafts were got ready, in which scuttle-holes had previously been pierced; Carrier's guard crowded them first with priests and afterwards with Vendeans, floated their human cargoes into the middle of the Loire, opened the scuttle-holes, and sank them. On the 27th and 29th Frimaire Carrier signed with his own hand two orders, by the first of which twenty-four "brigands"—two of whom were aged thirteen and two fourteen—and by the second of which twenty-seven "brigands" of both sexes were put to death without trial or formalities of any sort. One would have to be either very prejudiced or very ignorant to deny his personal responsibility. But what is absolutely true is that at the moment these horrors created no sensation among the famine-stricken inhabitants of Nantes. Carrier spared the middle-class population and confined himself to sending up to the Revolutionary Tribunal in Paris one hundred and thirty-two food-speculators and federalists, who were acquitted after Thermidor. Signs of public reprobation began to appear only at the end of his mission, when the mass executions threat-

---

[2] The garrison of Mainz, which had capitulated to the Austrians, and, being considered too untrustworthy to fight on the north-eastern frontier, was transferred to the Vendée.

ened the health of the city. At the lowest computation the Noyades accounted for two thousand victims. A military commission, the Bignon commission, had four thousand Vendeans shot who had escaped from the battles of Le Mans and Savenay. They were buried in the quarries of Miseri beneath a thin layer of earth, and the stench of the charnel-house was wafted down to the city, which it terrified. It was then that a tardy reaction towards pity took place.

At the period of which we are now writing, the end of 1793, the blood-thirsty side of the Terror was confined to the regions laid waste by civil war, and behind the front of the armies. Central France—containing the great majority of the departments—saw nothing of the Terror but dismissal and arrests, sometimes the fixing of prices and measures of dechristianization. The guillotine was but rarely used in these peaceful regions. If by chance a few death sentences were pronounced, it was against returned émigrés or priests, food-speculators or coiners, who were tried by the ordinary tribunals.

The Terror was so inevitable in the circumstances of the time that the royalists would have instituted it against the republicans had they been the stronger, as, indeed, they subsequently did in the year III and in 1815. The correspondence of the émigrés leaves no room for doubt on this point. "I believe it to be necessary to punish the Parisians by terrorism," wrote Montmorin, the Prime Minister and the Queen's confidant to the Comte de La Marck as early as July 13, 1792. "No more gentleness, no more half-measures," wrote the Duc de Castries in his memorandum of April 1793. "The brigands who have ravaged France, the factions who have disturbed Europe, the monsters who have assassinated the King, must disappear from the face of the earth." The Comte de Flachslanden added: "I am of the opinion that resistance will continue until the Convention has been massacred." This was the general opinion among the émigrés. "Their language is horrible," said Lombard, secretary to the King of Prussia, who accompanied them on the campaign in the Argonne. "If we were prepared to abandon their fellow-citizens to their vengeance, France would soon be no more than one monstrous cemetery" (July 23, 1792). As a general rule the revolutionaries slew lest they too might be slain. Even in France itself, in parts where there were not very many of them—in the Vendée, at Marseilles, Lyons, or Toulon—they had been executed without mercy. They were in a state of legitimate defence. But not only were they defending their ideas, their persons, and their property; they were at the same time defending their country. Joseph de Maistre pronounced a judgment against which there can be no appeal: "What did the royalists want when they called for a counter-revolution, to be effected abruptly and by force? They were asking for the conquest of France, and therefore its division, the annihilation of its influence, and the annihilation of its king." And in 1793 Joseph de Maistre was controlling the secret police of his master the King of Sardinia.

CHAPTER VIII

The Foreign Plot

THE Committee of Public Safety was as much afraid of the Revolution's secret enemies as it was of its open enemies. It felt itself to be surrounded by spies. D'Antraigues, a former member of the Constituent Assembly, who played the part of a sort of minister of police to Louis XVIII, the title now assumed by the Count of Provence, maintained agents in Paris, who regularly sent information to him in Verona in letters written in sympathetic ink. Assuming the mask of demagogues, these agents even made their way into the offices of the public departments. In order to frustrate spies Robespierre made the following entry in his memorandum-book: "Have two plans, one of which is to be revealed by the clerks."

It was suspected at an early stage that foreign gold had helped not only to find out the military secrets of France, but also to stir up disorder and create difficulties of all kinds for the Government. On July 11, 1793, in a great report voicing the opinions of the first Committee of Public Safety, which had just been overthrown, Cambon stated to the Convention that the economic and financial crisis had also been aggravated, if not provoked, by the manœuvres of the enemy. "Since I have seen Pitt," he said, "drawing five millions sterling for secret expenditure, I am no longer surprised that disorder has been fomented with this money throughout the whole of the Republic. They have succeeded in bringing about the fall of our exchange by means of a fund of a hundred and twenty millions in assignats. And with five millions sterling Pitt has acquired five hundred millions in assignats, with which he is carrying on a terrible war against us. Certain officials in the departmental administrations are seconding him. 'How is the Republic to be destroyed?' they have said. 'By discrediting the assignats.'"

Cambon was indulging in a mere hypothesis. But at the end of July a portfolio lost by an English spy on the ramparts at Lille was brought to the Committee of Public Safety. The documents contained in it made it absolutely certain that since January the spy had distributed considerable sums to his agents scattered throughout the whole of France.

405

He had made a monthly allowance of twenty-five hundred livres to a Frenchman named Duplain. He had distributed money at Lille, Nantes, Dunkirk, Rouen, Arras, Saint-Omer, Boulogne, Thouars, Tours, and Caen, the very places in which disorders had broken out. He had given instructions to his correspondents to prepare fuses impregnated with phosphorus in order to set fire to arsenals and forage stores; and considerable damage had actually been caused by fire at Douai, Valenciennes, the sail-yards at the port of Lorient, the cartridge-factory at Bayonne, and the artillery park at Chemillé. "Cause the exchange to rise to two hundred livres to the pound sterling," he wrote to the same correspondent. "See that Hunter is well paid, and assure him in my lord's name that all his losses will be made good to him, besides double commission. . . . The assignats must be discredited as much as possible, and such as do not bear the king's effigy refused. Bring about an increase in the price of all commodities. Give orders to your merchants to buy up and keep out of the market all objects of prime necessity. If you can persuade Cott . . . to buy up tallow and candles at any price, make the public pay as much as five livres a pound for them."

After reading out these documents at the great session of August 1, Barère wound up with the conclusion that all English subjects who had come to reside in France since July 14, 1789 must be expelled. Cambon considered this measure too indulgent, for it applied to English subjects only. He proposed, as a measure of general security, to arrest provisionally all suspicious foreigners without distinction. "Do you suppose," he said, "that the Austrians in France are not as much agents of Pitt as the English? It will be enough for us to leave the Americans and Swiss unmolested." Couthon reminded the Assembly that the English Government had declared those of its nationals who should invest their funds in France to be traitors to their country. "I propose that as a measure of reciprocity you should decree: (1) that all Frenchmen depositing funds with London banks shall be mulcted in a fine equal to the sum in question, half of which shall be payable to the informer; (2) that those who have deposited money in London before the publication of this decree shall be forced to declare it within a month, under pain of the same fine, and shall further be regarded as suspects and placed under arrest." All these proposals were voted.

Hitherto the Revolution had repeatedly acted in a friendly spirit towards enemy subjects resident in France. Many of them had even obtained posts in the public departments; there were actually some in the revolutionary committees, and some with seats in the Convention, such as Anacharsis Cloots or Dentzel or Thomas Paine. Nothing was easier for the spies than to represent themselves as foreign patriots persecuted for their opinions. These martyrs of liberty received a cordial welcome and found powerful protectors not only in the clubs, but even in the committees of the Convention, even in the Government.

The English banker Walter Boyd, banker to Pitt and the Foreign Office, and his partner, Ker, had opened a branch of their London house in Paris. He succeeded in winning the good graces of the deputies Delaunay of Angers and Chabot, who protected him when he was in danger. In return for a payment of two hundred thousand livres Chabot, a member of the Committee of General Security, managed to have the seals which had been placed on Boyd's bank during the night of September 7–8 removed, and a month later, when Boyd was threatened with arrest, Chabot obtained a passport for him, by means of which he succeeded in escaping and returning to England.

When Danton was arrested, a letter from the Foreign Office to the banker Perregaux of Neuchâtel, a Prussian subject settled in Paris, was found among his papers, requesting him to pay over considerable sums—three, twelve, and one thousand livres respectively—to various persons alluded to by the initials C. D., W. T., and De M. as a reward for "the essential services which they have rendered us in fanning the flames and stirring up the Jacobins to a paroxysm of fury." This letter can only have been among Danton's papers because Perregaux had handed it over to him as interesting him directly. There is every ground to suppose that Perregaux was in frequent communication with the English Government.

The Belgian banker Berchtold Proli, an Austrian subject, said to be a natural son of the Chancellor Kaunitz, had received from the Austrian Government the mission of bribing the Belgians of the Vonckist party. Having settled in Paris, he founded a newspaper, *Le Cosmopolite*, for the defence of Austrian policy. On the declaration of war the newspaper no longer served any purpose and ceased to appear. Proli became friendly with journalists such as Camille Desmoulins. Living in great style in his apartment in the Palais Royal, he succeeded in gaining the confidence of Hérault de Séchelles, a voluptuary like himself. Even after joining the Committee of Public Safety, Hérault employed him as his secretary. The minister Lebrun and Danton entrusted him with secret diplomatic missions and he became an intimate friend of Desfieux, the leading member of of the Correspondence Committee of the Jacobins, of which he had, moreover, been treasurer. Through Desfieux, a very suspicious character, he got to know all the secrets of the club. Desfieux was almost illiterate and

Proli used to write his speeches for him. Proli was on friendly terms with a number of Montagnard deputies, such as Bentabole, Jeanbon Saint-André, and Jay de Saint-Foy. Desfieux was under the protection of Collot d'Herbois, though he had been implicated by one of the documents in the iron safe, and was regarded as being a paid tout for Mme de Saint-Amaranthe's gambling-den.

Another Belgian banker, Walckiers, an Austrian subject who, like Proli, had played a dubious part in the Revolution in his country, came and settled in Paris after the treason of Dumouriez. As he was very rich, he was suspected of scattering money among journalists and members of the clubs to forward the interests of Austria.

Guzman, a Spanish grandee who had become an outcast from his class and was also engaged in banking and intrigue, had obtained a following in the section of the Piques by his liberality. He managed to get a place on the insurrectionary committee which prepared the revolution of May 31, but he was already so suspect that he was turned out of it. Later, Saint-Just taxed Danton with having had dinners with Guzman costing a hundred écus a head.

Two Moravian Jews, Siegmund Gotlob and Emmanuel Dobruska, who had been contractors to the Emperor Joseph II in his war against the Turks and had consequently been raised to the rank of nobles, under the name of Schönfeld, had arrived in France just on the eve of the declaration of war. They presented themselves at the club at Strasbourg in the character of persecuted patriots, changed their name to Frey (i.e., free), and managed by well-timed liberality to secure the protection of Charles Laveaux, a member of the club and editor of the *Courrier de Strasbourg*, who was at that time engaged in opposition to the Feuillant Dietrich, mayor of the city. They accompanied Laveaux and the Fédérés of Bas-Rhin to Paris on the eve of August 10, and it was not long before they made useful friends in Paris among influential deputies such as Louis of Bas-Rhin, Bentabole, Simond, Richard, Gaston, Piorry, and Chabot. They submitted schemes to Lebrun, Minister for Foreign Affairs, and frequently received letters of exchange from abroad. They acquired an interest in the privateers of the Republic. They lent money, bought national property, and kept open house in a fine mansion which they had taken, formerly the property of an *émigré*. In order to escape the repressive measures affecting aliens, they tried to become naturalized Frenchmen by adopting an old man. They became members of the Jacobins on the proposal of Chabot, who went surety for them. They were denounced as spies at an early stage, but for a long time escaped all inquiry. Even after Chabot had been turned out of the Committee of General Security, they were not molested. Chabot was present at the domiciliary visit carried out at their house on September 26. A few days later, on October 6, he married their young sister, who had a marriage portion of two hundred thousand livres, and came to live in their mansion. He had the impudence to announce this marriage at the Jacobins, giving it as a proof that he was now settling down and giving up his dissolute life. But he was shouted down, and the report went round that the marriage portion of two hundred thousand livres which Leopoldine Frey brought to Chabot had been provided by Chabot himself, who had devised this means of concealing the proceeds of his depredations.

All these strangers of doubtful reputation, many of whom were agents of the enemy, played a considerable part in the political movement, and it was not long before this aroused the misgivings of the Committee of Public Safety. Even those who had for a time espoused the cause of Lafayette or Dumouriez, like Proli and his inseparable Desfieux, now flaunted a patriotism of the reddest shade and urged the most extreme measures. They formed a considerable proportion of the Hébertist party. The "Père Duchesne" was an intimate friend of Kock, the Dutch banker, who gave good dinners at his house at Passy. Anacharsis Cloots, "the orator of the human race," who had a seat in the Convention, was the moving force of a great newspaper, Le Batave, the organ of the foreign exiles, which carried on a campaign similar to that of the Père Duchesne. Now, Cloots, true to the Girondin methods of propaganda, never ceased preaching the necessity of stirring up revolution in the neighbouring countries. In a manifesto which he read out on October 5 from the tribune of the Jacobins, he demanded for France her natural frontiers—that is to say, the Rhine frontier. His friend Hérault de Séchelles, once a Girondin like himself, who, with Barère, controlled the foreign policy of the Committee of Public Safety, sent secret agents into Switzerland, whose propaganda caused some alarm. But Robespierre and the other members of the committee, whose great concern at that time was to obtain for France provisions and raw materials for her army factories, realized the danger of Hérault's imprudent policy, which might have closed the Swiss market to them. They repudiated the project of annexing Mühlhausen and recalled the secret agents dispatched beyond the Jura. At the same time they recalled Genêt, the French minister in the United States, who had caused misgivings in Washington by his political intrigues, and on October 11 even gave orders for his arrest. In a great speech before the Convention on the 27th Brumaire, Robespierre endeavoured to reassure neutrals—Americans, Danes, and Turks as well as Swiss—with regard to the intentions of revolutionary France. The latter, he said, cherished no dreams of subjugating the whole world. She only desired to defend her liberty and the independence of small nations. It was the Coalition powers alone who were animated by a spirit of conquest! Such a speech, which was greeted by applause from the Convention, must have seemed alarming to the foreign exiles and their Hébertist protectors, who saw salvation only in a fight to the finish, leading up to a universal republic.

But the foreign exiles caused yet further anxiety to the Committee of Public Safety. When, on September 5, the Convention stopped the permanent sittings of the sections and limited their meetings to two in every *décade*,[1] the Hébertists evaded the law by creating popular societies in every section, which met every evening. The ingenious Proli, with the help of his friends Desfieux, the Bordeaux Jew Pereira, and the dramatist Dubuisson, had devised a means of federating these popular societies in a central committee of which he had the control. This powerful organization, in direct contact with the sansculottes of the sections, was a rival power not only to the Jacobins, but to the Commune and even the Convention. From these federated popular societies, which claimed to represent the whole people, might spring an insurrection of the sections like those which had taken place at Lyons, Marseilles, and Toulon, a repetition of May 31 in the opposite sense, which would once more purge the Convention and hand over France to anarchy, ending in defeat and the restoration of the monarchy. Proli, Pereira, and their friends did not conceal the contempt which they felt for the Convention or their distrust of the deputies in general. But towards the middle of Brumaire the central committee of the popular societies sent a petition round from section to section requesting the Convention to abolish the salaries of priests and do away with the public worship sanctioned by the Constitution.

Since the institution of the revolutionary calendar, a number of civic celebrations had taken place in the towns on the tenth day (*décadi*), which became the revolutionary Sunday: for instance at Havre on October 21 (30th of the first month), or at Clermont, Oise, on the 10th Brumaire. But though the decadal festivals came into competition with the religious ceremonies, they had not superseded them. Tollet, the bishop of the department of Nièvre, had even taken part in the first civic ceremonies organized by Fouché. A few priests had already renounced their

---

[1] The week of ten days established by the revolutionary calendar.

orders and married, and a few churches had been closed, but the constitutional clergy as a whole remained in being. Cambon had already induced the Convention to admit that the priests were no longer state officials and that their salaries were not of the nature of a stipend, but only an allowance. On the same day the bishops' stipends had been reduced to six thousand livres, and those of their vicars-general to twelve hundred livres (September 18, 1793). Since September 5 unmarried priests were excluded from the vigilance committees, and since the 7th Brumaire ecclesiastics could no longer be appointed as teachers in the state schools.

Lastly, on the 13th Brumaire the sums standing to the credit of the Church funds, and the proceeds of pious foundations, were confiscated, so that the upkeep of worship became a charge upon the generosity of the faithful. Certain of the representatives on mission had secularized the cemeteries, encouraged the marriage of priests, and presided over civic celebrations; but they had not closed the churches. The priests married by Fouché in the department of Nièvre had not ceased to say mass. Laignelot and Lequinio transformed the church at Rochefort into a temple of Truth, but they did not interfere with the priests in the exercise of their functions. In the department of Somme, André Dumont insulted the priests and forced them to hold their services on the tenth days (*décadi*), but he did not abolish the services.

Worship went on in spite of everything. The petition of the central committee of the popular societies, by depriving it of its last resources, threatened its very existence. Those responsible for the petition did not conceal their intention of dealing the death blow to "sacerdotal despotism" by abolishing the salaries of priests. On the evening of the 16th Brumaire, accompanied by the deputies Cloots and Léonard Bourdon and the Jew Pereira, they paid a visit to Gobel, Bishop of Paris, roused him from his sleep, and represented to him that he ought to sacrifice himself to the public weal by ceasing to exercise his functions and persuading his clergy to close the churches. Gobel consulted his episcopal council, which pronounced in favour of submission by fourteen votes to three; and on the following day, the 17th Brumaire, he paid a visit first to the departmental assembly of Paris and then to the Convention and announced that he and his vicars-general renounced the exercise of their functions as ministers of the Catholic religion. He deposited his cross and ring on the table and next assumed the red cap amidst applause. He was immediately imitated by a number of deputies who were bishops or parish priests, and their example was followed throughout the whole of France. Three days later, on the 20th Brumaire, the Paris Commune celebrated a great

411

civic festival in the Cathedral of Notre-Dame, converted into a temple of Reason, in which figured an actress dressed in the tricolour and symbolizing Liberty. The Convention was invited by the Commune, and attended in a body. Dechristianization had been let loose. The plundered churches were closed by thousands and became republican temples.

The Committee of Public Safety was already struggling against the food-shortage; it was trying to obtain the application of laws as difficult to put into execution as the maximum and the law on requisitioning; and it had the maintenance of public order at heart. It was therefore alarmed at such a serious and sudden movement, which might revive civil war, and did as a matter of fact provoke a number of riots—a movement of which the irresponsible authors, foreigners and enemy aliens like Proli and Cloots, were already suspect in its eyes.

On the very evening of the 17th Brumaire, Robespierre sharply censured Cloots, on his appearance at the Committee of Public Safety after the abdication of Gobel, in the following words: "But you told us recently that it was necessary to enter the Netherlands, restore their independence, and treat the inhabitants like brothers. . . . Why, then, do you try to estrange the Belgians from us by offending prejudices to which you know them to be strongly attached?" "Oh," replied Cloots, "the harm is already done. We have been taxed with impiety a thousand times." "Yes," replied Robespierre, "but there were no facts to go upon!" Cloots turned pale, could think of no answer, and went out. Two days later he obtained his nomination as president of the Jacobins.

Robespierre was convinced that the religious revolution, which could benefit nobody but the Coalition, had been the result of an intrigue on the part of their agents, like all the extreme and impolitic measures forced upon the Convention by demagogues, such as the creation of the revolutionary army and the maximum. In his first great speech of the 27th Brumaire he traced at great length the hand of Pitt in the internal disorders of France since 1789 and plainly insinuated that those who were overthrowing the altars might very well be counter-revolutionaries disguised as demagogues.

Though the Convention as a whole was disinterestedly patriotic, there were none the less in its ranks some who gambled on the Bourse, and some rogues. On September 14 it had already been necessary to expel from the Committee of General Security the deputies Chabot, Julien of Toulouse, Basire, and Osselin, whom rumour accused of protecting contractors, aristocrats, and bankers of dubious character. The house of Julien of Toulouse was searched on September 18 and the results confirmed these suspicions. Chabot was so frightened that he burnt a number of papers in his fireplace.

The Committee had their eye on the contractors and those who protected them. As early as July 20 Dornier, who drew up the reports of the Transport Committee (*Comité de charrois*) and the Committee of Public Safety, had exposed the scandal of the contracts granted by the ex-minister Servan to d'Espagnac, a transport contractor, who had managed to obtain payments in cash amounting to 5,443,504 livres a month for a service on which he could have spent only 1,502,050 livres in assignats which had depreciated fifty per cent! In spite of the protection which he enjoyed from Delacroix, Chabot, and Julien of Toulouse, d'Espagnac was arrested. On July 29 Villetard presented a crushing report attacking Servan, who was in turn dismissed and arrested. The former contracts were cancelled and transport was placed under government control. Shortly afterwards, in September, the affair of the deputy Robert came to light. This former journalist and friend of Danton had some barrels of rum in his cellar, which formed his stock-in-trade. On the pretext that rum was not a brandy, he had not declared this liquor, as the law on food-speculation obliged him to do. He came into conflict with the section of Marat, which denounced him to the Convention. After violent debates, which covered him with moral reprobation, he was able to escape the penalties of the law only by presenting the rum to his section. Next there was the affair of the deputy Perrin of Aube, who had obtained contracts amounting to more than five millions for supplying the army with cloth, while at the same time accepting a position as member of the Contracts Committee (*Comité des marchés*), so that he was himself the inspector of what he supplied. Perrin was denounced by Charlier and Cambon on September 23; he confessed, was cited before the Revolutionary Tribunal, and condemned to twelve years in irons.

Of all these scandals the most serious was that of the India Company (Compagnie des Indes), which broke out at the very moment when foreigners were starting the movement for dechristianization. Owing to the position of the persons implicated in it, and the sensation which it aroused, its importance went beyond that of a mere piece of rascality. It had considerable political significance, for it was at the root of the divisions within the Mountain and gave substance and reality to the foreign plot suspected by the Committee of Public Safety. It accentuated the struggle between the parties by conjuring up the spectre of the betrayal of their country for gold.

During the great dangers of July and August 1793, while famine was threatening and the exchange falling heavily, the financial deputies with whom we are already acquainted had conceived the idea, partly in order to win popularity at small cost and partly to enrich themselves, of denouncing those financial companies whose shares stood at a higher figure on the Bourse than the public securities. Delaunay of Angers, supported by Delacroix, denounced the fraudulant devices invented by these companies for escaping taxation. Fabre d'Eglantine accused them of exporting French money to enemy countries and depreciating the assignats by exchanging them for safer securities, which they sent out of the country. Julien of Toulouse went further. He accused the India Company of having advanced money to the late "tyrant." Seals were placed on the India Company's offices and papers. Fabre uttered threats against the fire- and life-insurance companies, the water companies, and the Caisse d'Escompte, and a decree voted on August 24 gave powers for the abolition of limited companies. Seals were placed on the premises of the Caisse d'Escompte.

While Delaunay and his accomplices, Chabot, Basire, Julien of Toulouse, and Fabre d'Eglantine, were alarming these companies, they were at the same time carrying out bear operations in their shares by means of a fund placed at their disposal by d'Espagnac.

They were not sufficiently versed in financial affairs to write the speeches which they delivered from the tribune themselves. Delaunay, Chabot, Basire, and Julien of Toulouse were only the agents of an adventurer skilled in affairs, the famous Baron de Batz.

This younger son of a Gascon family, who seems to have procured a false pedigree in order to enter the army before 1789, had become very rich by fortunate speculations. He possessed the greater part of the shares in the Paris Water Company (Compagnie des Eaux de Paris) and in the life-insurance company founded by the Périer brothers a few years before the Revolution. He lived in great style and had the most fashionable actresses as his mistresses. While he was a deputy to the Constituent Assembly, his knowledge of finance caused him to be nominated as a member of the Liquidation Committee, of which he became the president. He delayed the liquidation of the pensions granted under the *ancien régime* as long as possible, for he was a royalist. He was suspected of countenancing secret advances of funds to the Court. When war was declared, he emigrated and served for a while in the army of the princes as aide-de-camp to the Prince of Nassau-Siegen, but returned to France just after June 20 to offer his services to the King. On the day after his return Louis XVI entered in his account-book: "Return and perfect conduct of M. de Batz, to whom I owe 512,000 livres." It is a curious thing, which gives food for thought, that Batz, royalist though he was, possessed the entire confidence of Clavière, the Girondin minister, who protected him on various occasions. During the events of August 10 he crossed to England, but returned to France at the beginning of January 1793, and, with the aid of the Marquis de La Guiche, attempted to save the King on the very day of his execution. With incredible audacity, just as the carriage drove by which was carrying Louis XVI to the scaffold, he crossed the boulevard shouting: "Long live the King!" but he eluded all pursuit. Lullier, *procureur général syndic* to the department of Paris, was entirely devoted to him: He had also acquired protectors in the police and the Commune. In May 1793 Clavière, who was still Minister of Public Taxation (*contributions publiques*), gave him a certificate of civism. At that time his confidant and secretary was Benoist, a former agent of Danton's, and a fellow-citizen and intimate friend of Delaunay of Angers. This Benoist had been entrusted by Dumouriez with secret missions to the Duke of Brunswick in Germany just before the declaration of war, and afterwards by Danton with missions to London immediately after August 10, and to Brunswick immediately after Valmy. He served as intermediary between Batz and the financial deputies and was the mainspring of the blackmail levied on the financial companies and of the operations on the Bourse to which this blackmail gave rise. Towards the middle of August Batz gave a dinner to his friends and accomplices at his house at Charonne. Chabot, Basire, Delaunay, Julien of Toulouse, and Benoist were present, besides Laharpe the writer, Duroy the banker, and a few ladies: the ex-Marquise de Janson, who was trying to save the Queen, Mme de Beaufort, who was Julien's mistress, the actress Grandmaison, the Baron's mistress, and a lady from Beaucaire, the mistress of Laharpe. It is probable that the conversation was not exclusively concerned with business. The Baron was the confidential agent of the princes and tried to interest his accomplices in the Convention in saving the Queen and the Girondins. Chabot afterwards revealed that he had offered a million to anybody who would help him to bring about the Queen's escape and that he was seconded by the Marquise de Janson. The plot was almost discovered at that very moment. On September 9 Zingrelet, the locksmith, in a declaration to the police commissary of the section of the Luxembourg, disclosed the fact that, happening to be at the house of the Marquis de La Guiche on the previous day, where he had gone to see one of the servants who was a friend of his, he had heard La Guiche say to Batz: "Batz, my friend, if the federation of the departments is not maintained, France is ruined; the Mountain and the sansculottes will massacre us all." Thereupon Batz said: "I will sacrifice my last sou for it. We must at all costs save Guadet, Brissot, Vergniaud, and all our friends. Many of the departments are determined to support us; my plan will lead to the disappearance of the Mountain and the sansculotte rogues." The woman Fontanges, he added, had said: "If Batz carries through our plans, we shall have saved France." On the strength of this denunciation Batz's house at Charonne was searched for the sake of form, but of course nothing was found. All Batz had to do was to change his residence. Only insignificant persons were arrested. As for the Baron, he continued to frequent assiduously the society of those deputies who were his accomplices. Chabot himself tells us that he received a visit from him on the 19th Brumaire.

Let us bear in mind that these financial affairs had an undercurrent of royalist intrigue. After rigging the market in connexion with the India Company for two months, Delaunay proposed on October 8 a decree regulating its liquidation. The decree was so worded that it enabled the company to evade paying the tax on a quarter of its dividends, besides the fines which it had incurred for its previous frauds. It further authorized the company to carry out its own liquidation, under the sole supervision of commissaries appointed by the Minister of Public Taxation. Fabre d'Eglantine, who had so far fought the company vigorously, was astonished at the tender handling of the company in Delaunay's report and obtained the passage of an amendment stipulating that the liquidation should be carried out by the agents of the State and not by the company itself. The text of the decree as passed was sent to the commission for the revision of its drafting. Twenty-one days later Fabre d'Eglantine and Delaunay handed to Louis, deputy for Bas-Rhin and secretary to the Assembly, a definitive text, which appeared in the *Bulletin*, without its being noticed by anybody at the time that it had undergone two serious modifications, both of them to the advantage of the company. In direct contradiction to Fabre d'Eglantine's amendment the liquidation was to be carried out by the company. Moreover, it would only have to pay the fines which it had incurred for fraudulant operations in which it could not prove its good faith.

Why had Fabre made this sudden change of front? Fabre had a very bad reputation. In 1789 he had obtained a safe-conduct from the King in order to escape his creditors. At the moment of the invasion in 1792, when he was Danton's secretary at the Ministry of Justice, he had obtained from Servan, the Minister for War, a contract for shoes, the carrying out of which had given rise to serious remonstrances from the next minister, Pache. He kept mistresses and carriages and frequented the society of bankers of every nationality. The only explanation he was able to give later, at his trial, of his signature to the false decree can hardly be taken seriously; it was that he had signed it without reading it!

It is established by Chabot's admissions and the documents relating to the case that Delaunay and his associates, Chabot, Basire, and Julien of Toulouse, had extorted from the India Company a sum of five hundred thousand livres, as the price of the decree which empowered it to carry out its own liquidation, while cheating the Treasury of considerable fines and taxes which the company ought to have paid. Fabre d'Eglantine had not been one of the gang at the outset. He had not been present at the dinner in August at the Baron de Batz's house at Charonne. Chabot tells us that he was speculating on his own account, and Proli adds that he used to take the advice of a banker named Levrat, whose family came from Lyons. If he at first opposed the decree proposed by Delaunay, it was no doubt with the intention of forcing him to come to terms with him. If he finally gave his signature, it was because Delaunay consented to give him a share in the five hundred thousand livres.

Fabre was a clever man with more than one card up his sleeve. He saw that Hébert and the Jacobins were fiercely denouncing the swindling financiers in the Convention. Even his friend Danton had been attacked. He reflected that the Hébertist mar-plots were vulnerable, for they numbered certain suspicious aliens among their ranks. Backed up by Dufourny and Lullier, his friends on the departmental administration of Paris, he boldly took the offensive against this Hébertist vanguard of aliens. At the end of September Dufourny issued a warrant for the arrest of Proli and his intimate friend Desfieux, who were not released until October 12, thanks to the intervention of Collot d'Herbois and Hérault de Séchelles. In order to disarm suspicion, Fabre backed up the Committee of Public Safety with all his might in its struggles with the aliens. While Chabot and Delaunay of Angers attempted to prevent the sequestration of their property, he went even further than Robespierre, who considered the measure indispensable and who in the end obtained its passage, on October 10. How could Fabre be suspected of being in league with the bankers after the part he had played in causing the seals to be placed on their offices and papers? At the very time when he was making terms with Delaunay for withdrawing his opposition to the decree for the liquidation of the India Company, he thought of a bold manœuvre, intended

417

to secure him the confidence of those in power, which at first met with complete success. Towards October 12 he asked to be given a hearing by ten members of the two governing committees whom he had specially chosen—Robespierre, Saint-Just, Lebas, Panis, Vadier, Amar, David, Moyse Bayle, and Guffroy—and denounced to them a great plot against the Republic hatched by the extreme war-party among the revolutionaries, who, taking them all round, he said, were no more nor less than agents of the enemy. He mentioned the names of Proli and his friends, Desfieux, Pereira, and Dubuisson, who, if he was to be believed, were finding out the Government's secrets, who were the inseparable associates of the most dangerous bankers, such as Walckiers, Simon, and De Monts, all of them natives of Brussels and agents of the Emperor—or, again, such as Grenus of Geneva and Greffülhe. He mentioned Proli and Desfieux as dictating the policy of newspapers "which appear to be patriotic, but to practised eyes are anything but that—as, for instance, *Le Batave.*" He next attacked the protectors of these foreign agents whom he had denounced: Julien of Toulouse, Chabot, and lastly Hérault de Séchelles. The two former were mere instruments in the hands of Desfieux and Proli, who had inveigled Chabot to the houses of the Brussels banker Simon and his female associates. They had married Chabot "to the sister of one Junius Frey, which is not his real name, for he is really the Baron Schönfeld, an Austrian, with relatives at present holding commands in the Prussian army." What was the marriage portion of two hundred thousand livres, of which Chabot made no secret, but the price of his corruption?

According to Fabre, Hérault de Séchelles was likewise a mere instrument in the hands of Proli, who knew through him all that went on in the Committee of Public Safety. Hérault de Séchelles employed a number of suspicious persons on secret missions abroad, such as Pereira, Dubuisson, Coindre, Lafaye. Fabre insinuated that he, too, might well be involved in the foreign plot. A curious and significant detail, which escaped the notice of the members of the Committee, was that Fabre, who denounced Chabot and Julien of Toulouse so harshly, said nothing about their friend and accomplice Delaunay of Angers. The latter had just allotted him his share of the five hundred thousand livres from the India Company.

The members of the committee were entirely disposed to listen to Fabre d'Eglantine's confidences. "There are factions within the Republic," Saint-Just had said in his great speech of October 10, in which he had proposed the sequestration of the property of English subjects. "The faction of its foreign enemies, the faction of the robbers who serve it only in order to drain its breasts, but are dragging it to its ruin through exhaustion. There are also certain men impatient to obtain employment, to attract attention, and to profit by the war." At the same session, in reply to Chabot, who had declared against sequestration, Robespierre added: "From the very beginning of the Revolution it must have been noticed that there are two quite distinct factions existing in France: the Anglo-Prussian faction and the Austrian faction, both united against the Republic, but divided from each other by their separate interests. You have already struck a serious blow at the Anglo-Prussian faction; but the other is not dead, you have to crush it." The Anglo-Prussian faction was that of Brissot, who had had a passing impulse in favour of placing the Duke of York or the Duke of Brunswick on the throne of France. The Austrian faction, which had to be crushed in its turn, was that of Proli, Guzman, Simon, Frey, and their like, who were protected by Chabot. Robespierre now defined his idea more clearly. "I distrust without distinction all those foreigners," he said, "whose face is covered with a mask of patriotism and who endeavour to appear more republican and energetic than we are. They are the agents of alien powers; for I am well aware that our enemies cannot have failed to say: 'Our emissaries must affect the most ardent and exaggerated patriotism,' in order that they may the more easily insinuate themselves into our committees and assemblies. It is they who are sowing discord, who beset the most esteemed citizens and even the most incorruptible legislators; they use the poison of moderantism and the arts of exaggeration in order to suggest ideas more or less favourable to their secret views. . . . ."

Fabre d'Eglantine knew that he would be speaking to willing ears in revealing the foreign plot to Saint-Just, Robespierre, and eight of their colleagues on the Committee of General Security. They were so convinced that he was speaking the truth that they hastened, on that very day or the following ones, to arrest several Hébertist agitators or agents of Hérault de Séchelles, the very exaggeration of whose patriotism made them appear suspect. Among them were Louis Comte, a former agent of the Committee of Public Safety, who had denounced Danton as suspected of being in league with the federalists and royalists of Calvados; Maillard, the famous "Tape-Dur," who since August 10 had been the director of an extraordinary secret-police force and whose vigilance Fabre d'Eglantine no doubt dreaded; the agitator Rutledge, of English origin, who had played an important part in the Cordeliers Club and knew the past record of Fabre d'Eglantine, whom he had formerly denounced as a friend of Necker and Delessart; and the Dutch banker Van den Yver, who had been Madame Dubarry's banker and a friend of Anacharsis Cloots. All of these were arrested on October 11 and 12 as a result of Fabre's denunciations.

Robespierre entered in his note-book: "Hesse, to Orleans, to be dismissed." And, though he had given such pledges to the Revolution that he was known as General Marat, the former German prince Charles of Hesse was removed from his command on October 13.

From this time onwards the foreign plot was in the forefront of the Government's thoughts. Robespierre had already but little confidence in Hérault de Séchelles, who had been by turns a Feuillant, a Girondin, and a Hébertist. He knew the elegant scepticism of this ex-aristocrat, formerly a very rich libertine, who now lowered himself to howl with the demagogues. Hérault had not only committed the imprudence of admitting a man like Proli to his intimacy, having him live in his house and making him his secretary; he had brought back from his mission in Savoy the dark-haired Adèle de Bellegarde, wife of a colonel serving in the army of the King of Sardinia, and supported Anacharsis Cloots's favourite policy of war to the bitter end. Robespierre and his colleagues on the Committee of Public Safety were convinced that his zeal was suspect. Robespierre made the following entry in his note-book: "Infamous violation of the secrets of the committee either by the clerks or by other persons. . . . Above all, drive out any traitors who may be seated in our midst." Hérault de Séchelles was kept away from the deliberations of the Government by an ordinance signed by Carnot, who sent him on a mission to the department of Haut-Rhin. On arriving at Belfort, on the 14th Brumaire, Hérault desired to get into touch with his colleagues Saint-Just and Lebas, who had just been sent on an extraordinary mission to Strasbourg. Lebas wrote to Robespierre on the 15th Brumaire: "Hérault has just intimated to us that he has been sent into the department of Haut-Rhin. He proposes to correspond with us. Our surprise is extreme. . . ." Saint-Just added a note to the same letter, saying: "Confidence has no longer any value when one shares it with corrupt men." Hérault was never to resume his seat on the Committee of Public Safety. Fabre d'Eglantine's denunciation had ruined him in the eyes of his colleagues.

Less fortunate than Fabre d'Eglantine, his accomplices in falsifying the degree on the liquidation of the India Company—Basire, Chabot, and Julien of Toulouse—were attacked almost every day at the Jacobins or in the press—especially Chabot, whom his marriage with an Austrian lady made conspicuous. The former Capuchin now passed his whole time in an agony of terror. On October 14 (the 23rd of the first month) the Committee of General Security subjected him to a long examination arising out of a denunciation brought against him by one Rocin, who had been employed by d'Espagnac in his affairs and now accused Chabot of having abetted, to the detriment of Rocin, the swindles of this contractor, who was now under arrest. He was also questioned about the burning of his papers, the release of the royalists Dillon and Castellane, for which he had given orders when he was still sitting on the Committee of General Security, his dealings with stock-brokers, and the increase of his fortune. Chabot saw himself on the verge of the abyss. Realizing that the Government was hopelessly hostile to him, he made efforts to create himself a party in the Convention by denouncing the dictatorial and inquisitorial tendencies of the two Committees of Public Safety and General Security, and at first met with some success.

On the 17th Brumaire, the very day of Gobel's abdication, Amar had gone to the Convention on behalf of the Committee of General Security to ask for the arrest of the deputy Lecointe-Puyraveau, whom, on the strength of a letter addressed to him, but intercepted by the section of the Halle-au-Blé, he suspected of being in league with the Vendeans. Chabot's friend Basire undertook the defence of the accused deputy by cleverly stressing the point that, if they sent a deputy before the Revolutionary Tribunal on the strength of such a slender proof, not a single member of the Convention would be able to feel safe in future; and the Assembly refused to pass the decree proposed by Amar.

Two days later Dubarran, speaking in the name of the Committee of General Security, came and asked for proceedings to be taken against the deputy Osselin, against whom there were overwhelming charges. Though he had drafted the law against the *émigrés*, Osselin had failed to apply it to an *émigrée*, the Marquise de Charry, whom he had made his mistress. He had personally acted as surety for her while he was still a member of the Committee of General Security; he had found a refuge for her, first in the house of Danton and afterwards with his brother, a married priest living in the neighbourhood of Versailles. The facts were so patent and Osselin's reputation so bad—he was a notoriously shady speculator—that this time the motion for citing him before the tribunal was passed.

But on the following day Chabot, Basire, Thuriot—all those who had been friends of Osselin's and felt themselves to be as guilty as he was—recovered their courage. Philippeaux, seconded by Romme, proposed that the Assembly should oblige all its members to make a statement of the amount of their fortunes since the Revolution.

Basire objected to the proposal as "eminently calculated to favour the projects of the aristocrats and cause divisions among patriots." "Patriots," he said, "ought not to be harassed and worried by judicial proceedings. . . . There is not a single Muscadin who does not rejoice to see those who started the Revolution, those who were the first to lay the foundations of liberty, mounting the scaffold." He inveighed against "the system of terrorism" with which patriots were being threatened. On the intervention of Thuriot, Philippeaux's motion was rejected.

Emboldened by this first success, which rid the financial deputies of an indiscreet inquiry into their fortune, Chabot wanted to go further. He reverted to the proceedings against Osselin, which had been voted on the previous day, and proposed that it should be made impossible to send any deputy before the Revolutionary Tribunal without a previous hearing by the Assembly. In terms of greater vehemence and precision than Basire, he in turn arraigned the tyranny which the committees exercised over the deputies. "Death would have no terrors for me," he said. "If my head is necessary to the salvation of the Republic, let it fall! But the important point in my eyes is that liberty should triumph, that terror should not crush all the departments; the important point in my eyes is that the Convention should debate, and not merely pass a decree on the strength of a report; the important point in my eyes is that there should not always be unanimity with regard to every decree. For if there is no right wing, I will form one by myself alone, if I lose my head for it, in order that there may be an opposition, and that it may not be said that we pass decrees on trust and without discussion." Thuriot did not confine himself to supporting Chabot. Without mentioning names, he attacked Hébert and his partisans, those who preached "maxims which tend to annihilate genius and everything connected with commerce and industry," the men "who want to immerse themselves in the blood of their fellow men." After a somewhat sharp debate Chabot's motion was carried.

By this means the swindlers in the Convention hoped to escape the vigilance of the committees, which would no longer dare to have any of them arrested if it were necessary every time to face a public debate, representing both sides of the question, before an Assembly which was already showing its distrust of them.

But they had reckoned without the Jacobins, who on the following day, with Dufourny, Montaut, Renaudin, and Hébert himself as their spokesmen, protested vehemently against a vote which would secure the impunity of swindlers and inflame the audacity of counter-revolutionaries. Chabot, Basire, and Thuriot were the object of violent attacks, and Hébert obtained a decision that they should form the subject of a commission of inquiry nominated by the Jacobins.

When, on the 21st and 22nd Brumaire, Dubarran and Barère proposed to the Convention that Osselin should not be given a hearing and that the decree voted on the 20th Brumaire should be annulled, they met with no opposition. Thuriot, Chabot, and Basire made an abject retractation, and on the following day, the 23rd Brumaire, Thuriot was expelled from the Jacobins.

Chabot, livid with terror, feared, as he himself admits, that his house might be searched. He was greatly embarrassed by a packet of assignats for a hundred thousand livres which Benoist had handed him as his share of the five hundred thousand livres paid over by the India Company. He would have to explain where they came from! Then Chabot came to a desperate resolution. In order to shield himself he imitated Fabre d'Eglantine, only he did it clumsily. He hurried off and denounced his accomplices, first to Robespierre and then to the Committee of General Security. He told them that the Baron de Batz and his agent Benoist had bribed Delaunay and Julien of Toulouse to blackmail the India Company, which had handed him, Chabot, a hundred thousand livres to bribe Fabre d'Eglantine, though he had done nothing of the sort; that the Baron de Batz was also paying the Hébertists to denounce the deputies whom he was endeavouring to corrupt. He insinuated that Hébert, Dufourny, and Lullier, his own accusers, were agents of Batz. Batz, according to Chabot, was not only trying to enrich himself, but wanted to overthrow the Republic by bringing about the disgrace of the deputies whom he had first corrupted. His conspiracy had two branches: one concerned with corruption, represented by Delaunay, Benoist, and Julien of Toulouse; the other concerned with defamation, represented by the Hébertists. Batz had already tried to save the Queen and the Girondins. Chabot had only pretended to welcome his proposals in order to discover his plans and afterwards denounce them. He had risked his reputation to save the Republic! Basire in turn confirmed Chabot's story of the blackmailing of the India Company by Delaunay and Julien of Toulouse at the instigation of the Baron de Batz. He brought Danton's name into the affair several times, by repeating that Delaunay reckoned upon his assistance. But Basire refrained from denouncing the Hébertists. Chabot had accused Hébert of having had Marie Antoinette transferred to the Temple at the

423

request of the former Duchesse de Rochechouart, and represented all the measures demanded and obtained by the Hébertists—for instance, the maximum—as a means of disgusting the people with the Revolution and driving it to revolt. Basire confined himself to the question of the operations on the Bourse.

The members of the committee were convinced that there was a considerable subtratum of truth in the accounts given by Basire and Chabot. But, on the other hand, they had no doubt that these two informers, whom they had already been watching, were as guilty as their colleagues Delaunay and Julien of Toulouse; so they gave orders for the arrest of all four of them. In the warrant for their arrest were included Batz's bankers, Benoist, Simon, Duroy, and Boyd, and the notorious Proli, with whom they coupled his friend Dubuisson. Delaunay was locked up in the Luxembourg at the same time as Chabot and Basire. Julien managed to elude their pursuit and found a refuge on the very premises of the Committee of General Security, in the apartment of a clerk of the committee—which throws a curious light on the way in which the revolutionary Government was served by its closest agents. Boyd had already fled and Batz managed as usual to throw the police off his track, by escaping to the south of France. Simon was at Dunkirk, whence he sailed for Hamburg. Instead of him they arrested the famous Saint-Simon, the future theorist of socialism, who was speculating in national property with his friend Count Redern, a Prussian subject. Proli was lying hidden in the neighbourhood of Paris, where he was not discovered till later.

It is remarkable that, contrary to the hopes of Chabot and Basire, the two committees did not molest either Hébert, Dufourny, Lullier, or the friend and instigator of the two last-mentioned, Fabre d'Eglantine. On the contrary, they were convinced that, though Fabre had signed the false decree as well as Delaunay, he was completely innocent. And their conviction was based, not so much on an examination of the documents, which they only examined carelessly, as on Fabre's denunciation a month previously of Chabot, Hérault de Séchelles, and the bankers and agents of foreign powers. In their credulity they believed that this agent of justice had been a prophet. In Chabot's and Basire's revelations they saw only the confirmation of their suspicions. And in their simplicity they entrusted to Fabre the task of examining into this affair, in which he was directly implicated, with the help of Amar. As for Danton, whom Basire in particular had implicated, they did not want to molest him. On the contrary, they begged Basire to omit all reference to him in the fair copy of his denunciation.

They were less concerned with the financial side of the affair—which they passed over carelessly—than with its political and patriotic side. They really believed in the genuineness of the foreign plot. Billaud-Varenne, in his speech to the Convention on the 28th Brumaire, warned it against "the dubious enthusiasm," "the astutely exaggerated zeal," of those who were disseminating calumny and suspicion and accepting money from Pitt to set at variance and slander patriots.

Not for a moment did Hébert and his friends dream of defending Proli, Desfieux, Dubuisson, and their like, whom the infamous Chabot had denounced as agents of Pitt. Hébert was trembling for himself. Collot d'Herbois was absent on mission at Lyons and was no longer there to defend his friends and protect them against Chabot's attacks. Cloots, who had remained silent when they arrested his friend the banker Van den Yver, continued to say nothing. Nobody ventured to doubt the genuineness of the plot. On the 1st Frimaire, Hébert abjectly thanked Robespierre at the Jacobins for protecting him against denunciations. He went further and retracted his previous attacks upon Danton, masking his retreat by an imperative demand that the accomplices of Brissot who were still alive, and with them Madame Élisabeth, should be handed over to Fouquier-Tinville. Momoro followed him, giving the lie to the statement that the Cordeliers had had any idea of getting up an agitation or insurrection at the prompting of Dubuisson or Proli. And, like Hébert, Momoro wound up on a note of bold denunciation of the priests: "So long as a single one of these men, formerly such liars, is left who has not yet solemnly abjured his impostures, we are still bound to tremble, if a single priest is left, for now, changing their tactics, they are trying, with a view to maintaining themselves, to induce the people to pay for their farces. They must be punished, and then all the harm will cease." Hébert and Momoro gave Robespierre an excellent opening. He contemptuously brushed aside their policy of violence: "Is it true that our most dangerous enemies are the impure remnants of the race of our tyrants? . . . Who is going to believe that the punishment of the contemptible sister of Capet would impress our enemies more than that of Capet himself and his contemptible consort?" So let there be no more useless guillotinings! Such was Robespierre's answer to Hébert, and he added immediately afterwards, as a rejoinder to Momoro, that there must be no anti-religious exaggeration! "You say that you fear the priests?" he said. "The priests are still more afraid of the progress of enlightenment. You are afraid of the priests! While they are hastening to abdicate their titles in order to exchange them for those of municipal and administrative officials and even of presidents

425

of popular societies. Only take their patriotism on trust on the strength of their sudden abjuration and they will be quite satisfied with you. . . . I can see but one way of reviving fanaticism, and that is to affect to believe in its power. Fanaticism is a savage and capricious beast; it fled before the approach of reason; but pursue it with loud shouts and it will come back again." Thus boldly did Robespierre speak out to the dechristianizing party, whose calculated demagogy he saw through quite clearly. He did not want a new fanaticism to be set up under the pretext of crushing fanaticism. He repudiated the theatrical pretences of the anti-clericals. He laid stress upon the grave dangers of the religious revolution. He asserted that the Convention would see to it that liberty of worship was respected. He pointed out that dechristianization was a move cunningly devised by the "cowardly emissaries of foreign tyrants," who desired to set France ablaze and cause her to be detested by all peoples. He mentioned the names of those whom he believed to be guilty—Proli, Dubuisson, Pereira, and Desfieux—and disposed of them in an impassioned philippic. He had them turned out of the club, and Cloots, who was presiding, uttered not a word in their defence.

The effect of his speech was enormous. For the last ten days the dechristianizing movement had met with no obstacles to its progress. From this day onward the press underwent a change of front. The Convention again found strength to resist the agitation of demagogues, and shortly afterwards, on the 18th Frimaire, it explicitly confirmed liberty of worship.

The Hébertists gave up the struggle. Just before this they had been accusing Basire and Chabot. Now, when Basire and Chabot rose up and accused them in turn, they trembled and took refuge under the ægis of Robespierre, who gave them his protection, while humiliating and discrediting their policy.

Chabot's denunciation, coming on top of that of Fabre d'Eglantine, acquired a vast importance for this very reason. It was now to dominate the duel between the parties and aggravate party hatred by patriotic anxiety. The Foreign Plot had become a concrete reality. It was the canker which was to consume the Mountain.

CHAPTER IX

The Indulgents

BEFORE Chabot's and Basire's great denunciation the opposition to the revolutionary Government had been merely sporadic and intermittent. It had not become an organized system. It had criticized the application of revolutionary measures, not their actual principle. It was a covert and indirect opposition, an affair of stratagems and ambushes.

Jacques Roux alone, towards the middle of September, had risked an open and direct protest. "A government does not make itself loved and cherished," he wrote in his No. 265, "by dominating men by terrorism. . . . It is not by embroiling and overthrowing everything, by spreading fire and bloodshed and turning France into one vast bastille, that our Revolution will conquer the world. . . . To impute a man's birth to him as a crime is a revival of fanaticism. There are more innocent people than guilty in prison. . . ." Jacques Roux wrote this from the prison of Sainte-Pélagie, where he had been confined. But what influence could be exerted by this belated wisdom on the part of a man who had urged on all the excesses which only filled him with horror since he had been their victim? The similar protests formulated by Leclerc met with equally little response, and their newspapers ceased to exist.

The opposition of the Indulgents was far more dangerous. Its leaders were orators of genius, most of whom had taken part in public affairs either on the committees or on missions. They were bound to gather round them all those to whom the Terror caused misgivings—and the name of these was Legion.

What they needed was a leader. From the very first, Chabot had thought of Danton. On leaving the Committee of General Security on the 26th Brumaire, he went to see Courtois and informed him of what was happening. Courtois hastened to warn Danton. Realizing that the inquiry into the India Company affair might implicate him, the weary tribune hastened to return to Paris, where he arrived by the evening of the 30th Brumaire. He returned full of hatred for the Hébertists, to whose furious attacks he had been exposed, and most uneasy as to the attitude of the

427

Committee of Public Safety, which had heard Louis Comte's denunciation of him. For a long time past he had condemned the policy of the committee. He had disapproved of the trial of Custine, the dismissal of generals of noble birth, and the trial of the Queen, "which," he said to Duplain, "destroyed all hope of coming to terms with the foreign powers"; for he could see no salvation save in a speedy peace, at whatsoever price it might have to be purchased. He had shed tears when he found himself powerless to save the Girondins. Garat tells us that, on his return from Arcis, Danton confided to him his plan of action, which he justly calls a conspiracy, for his plan aimed at nothing less than the ruin of the revolutionary Government and a complete change of regime. The idea was, in fact, to sow discord in the committees, to win over Robespierre and Barère, and then, having divided and circumvented the committees, to have them replaced by fresh ones, if necessary by insurrection, and, once in possession, to steer resolutely towards the right, in order to make peace, open the prisons, revise the Constitution, restore the influence of the rich, bring about the return of the *émigrés,* and liquidate the Revolution by coming to terms with all its enemies.

Now, things happened exactly as Garat says. Danton carried on the policy already laid down in outline by Basire, Chabot, Thuriot, Fabre d'Eglantine, etc., but with more prudence and skill. In order to gain over and ensnare Robespierre, Danton hastened, as early as the 2nd Frimaire, to condemn the use of violence against Catholicism, and skilfully threw out the idea that it was time to put an end to the Terror: "I propose that the blood of men should be spared!" On the 6th Frimaire he asked that the conspiracy denounced by Chabot and Basire should be reported upon promptly, and expressed himself in such terms as to include in the conspiracy all those who had demanded terrorist laws. In defending Chabot and Basire he was defending not only himself, but at the same time all the financial deputies—Guffroy, Courtois, Reubell, Merlin of Thionville, Thuriot, Boursaut, Fréron, Barras, Tallien, Bentabole, Rovère, and many others. Plucking up their courage, they at once raised their voices against Bouchotte, the favourite of the Hébertists. On the 11th Frimaire Danton was bold enough to oppose such a popular measure as the compulsory exchange of metallic currency for assignats, a measure advocated by the Cordeliers and Cambon and already put in force by many of the representatives on mission. "Now that federalism has been crushed," he said, "revolutionary measures ought to be the necessary outcome of your existing laws. . . . From now onwards every man who becomes an ultra-revolutionary will produce results as dangerous as an out-and-out counter-revolutionary could do. . . . Let us recall those of our commissaries who, no doubt with good intentions, have adopted the measures reported to us, and in future let no representatives issue any ordinances save in harmony with our revolutionary decrees. . . . Let us remember that though things may be overthrown by the pike, it is only with the instruments of reason and genius that the structure of society can be erected and consolidated." The rich were not forced to exchange their gold for republican paper-money. On the contrary, the ordinances of representatives on mission were quashed, and property-owners breathed again.

The wave of reaction was already so strong that the vacillating Chaumette deserted the Hébertist cause and allowed himself to be carried away by it. At the very time when Danton was successfully opposing the conversion of metallic currency into assignats, he was denouncing to the Commune the revolutionary committees of the sections, who, according to his account, were indulging in arbitrary acts of every kind, and appeared to arrest aristocrats only "in order to obtain a loop-hole for attacking the best-authenticated patriots." He wanted to summon the members of these committees to the Hôtel de Ville to give an account of their actions and receive instructions. But Billaud-Varenne took alarm at his moderantist language, pronounced a eulogy on the Law of the Suspect, which, by frustrating treason, had brought about the victories on the frontiers, and taxed Chaumette with courting popularity "by leaving the odium of rigorous measures to the Convention." Chaumette's ordinance was annulled (14th Frimaire), and Chaumette's name struck off the books of the Cordeliers (27th Frimaire).

The Indulgents made a great effort to gain control of the Jacobins. Danton, who had ceased to attend the meetings regularly in former days, now appeared at them assiduously. On the 13th Frimaire he vehemently opposed the proposal that the church at Havre should be placed at the disposal of the club in that town for holding its meetings. "I ask you to beware of those persons who want to carry the people beyond the limits of the Revolution and are proposing ultra-revolutionary measures." An ex-priest, Coupé of Oise, rejoined sharply that the churches were the property of the people and that it could "dispose of its property at will in order to hold meetings on such premises as seemed most convenient to it." Danton wanted to reply, but was interrupted by violent murmuring. He was forced not only to protest that he had no intention of "paralysing the energy of the Revolution," but to make an apology for his private as well as his political life: "Am I not the same man who was at your side in moments of crisis? Am I not he whom you have often embraced as your friend and who is bound to die with you?" It was in vain that he placed himself under the protection of Marat's name; the public in the galleries shouted him down, and the members of the club "shook their heads and smiled with pity," according to Camille Desmoulins's account, "as at the speech of a man condemned by the suffrage of all." Weary of the struggle, he was forced so far to humiliate himself as to ask for a commission of inquiry to examine into the charges brought against him. He would have been lost had it not been for Robespierre, who obtained a vote against the commission of inquiry, while carefully pointing out that he had not always been of Danton's opinion and that there had even been occasions on which he had had to censure him for certain things—for instance, at the time of Dumouriez and Brissot. Robespierre wished to avoid divisions between the revolutionaries. "The patriots' cause is one," he said, "like that of tyranny; they are all united by the same interest!" His intervention is all the more to be praised in that he shared the opinion of Coupé of Oise with regard to the actual fact which had given rise to the debate, so much so that on the next day he and Billaud signed the ordinance granting the Jacobins of Havre the use of the Capuchin church.

So far the Indulgents had had only one newspaper, the *Rougyff* or the *Frank en vedette*, owned by the deputy Guffroy, who made laborious efforts to imitate the gutter style of the *Père Duchesne*. Camille Desmoulins once more took up his pen and on the 15th Frimaire launched the *Vieux Cordelier*. He also had to provide for his own defence. Camille was compromised by the bad company he had kept—with d'Espagnac, to whose brother he had rendered services when, in the days of the Constituent Assembly, he was in trouble over the business of the scandalous exchange of the countship of Sancerre; with Dithurbide, the lessee of a gambling-den, whose interests he had maintained against Brissot; with the royalist journalist Richer de Sérizy, his boon companion; with General Arthur Dillon, who had been arrested for plotting; and with many others—so that he had long been suspect to the Jacobins. This "old Cordelier" was merely a Cordelier who had grown older. His tactics were simple. He had borrowed them straight from Chabot and Basire. His opponents were agents of Pitt. "O Pitt, I do homage to your genius!" Such were the first words of his newspaper. All those attacked by the Hébertists were victims of Pitt. Chabot had said: "There are among the Montagnards both corrupters and corrupt." Desmoulins corrected him: there were neither corrupters nor corrupt; they were all above suspicion. They were innocent victims of Hébertists paid by Pitt to defame the national representative body. Desmoulins demanded entire liberty for the press.

It was all very well for him to say that he would make only a moderate use of it; he was offering the royalists a means of making themselves heard during the life-and-death crisis through which the country was passing. His number was eagerly read by all the more or less open aristocrats in Paris.

The Indulgents pushed their attack vigorously. On the 15th Frimaire Merlin of Thionville demanded that Basire and Chabot should be removed from the close confinement in which they were being kept. His request was not acceded to, but two days later Thuriot desired that means should be sought of releasing the patriots kept in prison in virtue of the Law of the Suspect. Next, on the 19th Frimaire, Simon, an intimate friend of Chabot and the Freys, proposed at the Jacobins that the societies should have the right to demand the release of imprisoned patriots. If his proposal had been accepted, there would have been no more need for the revolutionary committees. The members of the clubs would have become sacrosanct. Their cards of membership in the Jacobins would shelter them from all inquiry. Robespierre exposed the trap: "They want to check you in your rapid advance, as if you had reached the end of your labours. . . . Are you, then, ignorant that treason is rife in your armies? Are you ignorant that, with the exception of a few trusty generals, the only good element you possess are the soldiers? Aristocracy is more dangerous than ever at home, for it has never been more perfidious. It used to give battle openly, but now it is in your midst, it is in your bosom, and, disguised under a veil of patriotism, it secretly stabs you with dagger blows against which you are not on your guard." The Indulgents realized that Robespierre would not be so easy to circumvent as they had thought.

They redoubled their blows against the Hébertists. In his No. 2. Desmoulins indulged in a violent attack on Cloots, as responsible for the dechristianizing policy devised by Pitt. "Cloots is a Prussian; he is a first cousin of Proli, the object of so many denunciations. He has worked on the *Gazette universelle* [a royalist paper], in which he waged war on patriots. . . . It was Guadet and Vergniaud who stood sponsor for him and had him naturalized as a French citizen by a decree of the Legislative Assembly. . . . For the last five years he has never failed to date his letters from Paris, and it is not his fault if the Kings of Denmark and Sweden preserve their neutrality and are not indignant that Paris should proudly proclaim herself the metropolis of Stockholm and Copenhagen."

On the following day it was Hébert's turn to be baited at the Jacobins. Bentabole, a boon companion of Chabot and Frey, taxed him with displaying too much heat in his denunciations. "I ask him," he said, "whether he is in the secret of the conspiracies; I ask him why, in speaking of a deputy, he said that he would no more abandon Chabot the monk than he would Roland the cuckold? Why does he appear to condemn Chabot, and regard him as guilty before his trial? Why has he attacked Laveaux for having spoken in favour of a supreme being? As for me, enemy though I am of all superstitious practices, I declare that I shall always believe in a supreme being." This was the first time that anybody had dared to defend Chabot at the Jacobins. Hébert piteously denied that he had preached atheism: "I declare that I preach to the inhabitants of country districts that they ought to read the Gospel." This incident shows to what lengths the Indulgents now carried their audacity.

They already thought themselves strong enough suddenly to provoke a change in the composition of the Committee of Public Safety, whose powers expired on the following day, the 22nd Frimaire. This sudden attack had been carefully led up to by repeated attacks on Bouchotte and his agents. On the 16th Frimaire Philippeaux, a conceited simpleton, whom the committee had hurt by ignoring his denunciations of Rossignol and Ronsin, addressed an open letter of extreme violence to the Committee. "If," he said, "the men whom you are protecting were not guilty, [the commission of inquiry which I have demanded] would have established their innocence. If they were guilty, you have become their accomplices by securing their impunity, and the blood of twenty thousand patriots slaughtered in consequence of this false measure cries out against you for vengeance."

On the 22nd Frimaire Bourdon of Oise proposed that a new committee should be formed: "Though the majority possess the entire confidence of the Convention and the people, there are some members of it whom one would be very glad not to see there any longer." Merlin of Thionville proposed that a third of the committee should be changed every month. In spite of Cambacérès the majority decided that the election should take place on the following day.

That same evening Fabre d'Eglantine had Coupé of Oise turned out of the Jacobins, for the sole reason that he had censured the marriage of priests, but in reality because he had not dared to stand out against Danton during the preceding days. One of the Indulgents taxed Cloots with his connexion with the family of Van den Yver, Dutch bankers compromised by their relations with Madame Dubarry. Robespierre disposed of Cloots in a terrible arraignment, of which both the substance and the language were borrowed from the *Vieux Cordelier* of two days before. Cloots was so crushed that he could find no answer and was struck off the books.

If the committee had been renewed, there is no doubt that the Indulgents would have kept Robespierre and confined themselves to getting rid of the members connected with the Hébertists—that is, Hérault, Collot, Billaud, and Saint-André, all of whom, together with Cloots, Proli, and Desfieux, had regularly frequented the society of Hébert. But on the 23rd Frimaire the renewal was adjourned on the intervention of a friend of Saint-André's, Jay de Sainte-Foy, who pointed out that it would be impolitic to change the committee at the very moment when the aristocrats were putting forth their last efforts, and the foreign powers were placing the Convention "between the Scylla of an exaggerated patriotism and the Charybdis of moderantism."

This respite enabled Robespierre to recover himself. If he had not yet seen whither the manœuvre of the Indulgents was leading, No. 3 of the *Vieux Cordelier* opened his eyes. This time Desmoulins did not confine himself to attacking the Hébertists, but aimed over their heads at the whole of the existing Government, attacking it as with a battering-ram. He opened by drawing an astute parallel between the monarchy and the Republic, in which, under the pretext of recalling the crimes of the Roman Cæsars, he lashed those of the Republic. This device was not a new one. It was the method of the Encyclopædists, a method of covert allusion and perfidious irony. The writer's true thought was concealed under the very negation of it. He did not, he said, want to please the royalists; and, shielding himself behind Tacitus, he traced before their eyes a terrible picture of the Republic. He soon put aside Tacitus, indeed, and alluded by name to the ultra-revolutionaries, who were, he said, as guilty as the freedmen of the Cæsars. Montaut, for instance, who was demanding from the Convention the lives of five hundred persons, who wanted the army of the Rhine to shoot down the army of Mainz, who proposed to put half the population of France into bastilles and place barrels of powder under them. Finally Desmoulins made a direct attack on the whole body of revolutionary institutions: "With the fortunate exception of the 1,200,000 soldiers in our armies, there is nobody at this day in France who does not make laws; for the commissaries of the Convention make laws, the departmental, district, and municipal authorities, the sections, and the revolutionary committees make laws, and, God forgive me, I believe the fraternal societies make them too." He also fell foul of the committees of the Convention for their stupidity and conceit. Their patriotic ignorance had done more harm than the counter-revolutionary cleverness of a Lafayette and a Dumouriez.

This audacious third number created a great sensation. It was a condemnation of the existing system by one of those who had created it, a damaging attack on the Terror by the man who had incited the people to tear down the street lamps. What joy for the aristocrats, and how sad for sincere revolutionaries! The campaign was launched just at the moment when Chabot, Basire, and Delaunay were being interrogated on the subject of their crimes. People were sure to think that the Terror which the Indulgents wanted to abolish was the Terror which they dreaded for themselves; that the scaffold which they desired to overthrow was the scaffold which awaited them.

So sharp was the attack that those in power were at first staggered by it. On February 27 Fabre boldly denounced before the Convention Vincent, Bouchotte's under-secretary and one of the leading men in the Cordeliers; Ronsin, the commander of the revolutionary army, who had already been accused by Philippeaux; and Maillard, the leader of the Tape-Durs, whom Fabre had already had imprisoned in Brumaire, but who had had to be released for lack of proofs. He brought a vague charge against Vincent, on no definite grounds, of having hired agents to obstruct the operations of the representatives on mission and of having distributed among his friends orders postponing their enlistment. In his attack on Ronsin he referred to a notice dealing with the repression of the rebels at Lyons, "a horrible placard which one cannot read without a shudder." Without more ado the Convention ordered the arrest of the three persons whom he had denounced, though all of them occupied important positions. If Vadier had not defended Héron, his agent on the Committee of General Security, he would have met with the same fate. Three other agents of the Executive Council were also placed under arrest without any further formalities—an unusual proceeding. The Convention was striking at the most highly placed agents of the revolutionary Government with no inquiry and without even asking the advice of the responsible committees which had chosen them.

That evening the Hébertists only ventured to raise a feeble protest at the Jacobins. Raisson raised his voice in favour of Ronsin, but was talked down by Laveaux, Dufourny, and Fabre, who exulted over their fallen foes. On the 29th Frimaire Bourdon of Oise exclaimed in delight that "the counter-revolutionary faction in the offices of the Ministry for

War would soon be crushed." But he had reckoned without Collot and Robespierre.

Collot had already been struck at through Proli and Desfieux, whom he had at first defended, and since the arrest of his agent, Ronsin, he saw that he himself was threatened directly. A deputation from Lyons had left for Paris with the object of denouncing the horrors of the mass shootings of prisoners which he had ordered. He, too, hastened to Paris to forestall the denunciation. In order to strike people's imaginations he brought Chalier's head with him, and went to the Commune with a great procession to offer them this relic. On the 1st Nivôse all the most ardent patriots in Paris accompanied him in procession from the Place de la Bastille to the Convention. One of them proposed that the remains of the martyr Chalier, which were displayed to the Convention, should be honoured with burial in the Panthéon. Couthon supported his proposal and went even further. He proposed to remove from the Panthéon General Dampierre, the friend of Danton, who had been killed at Valenciennes and was, according to him, no more nor less than a traitor. Danton, at whom this direct hit was aimed, protested, undertook the defence of Dampierre, and had Couthon's proposals referred to the committee.

Collot next rose to vindicate himself. He appealed to the decree of the Assembly and the orders of the committee. He admitted the mass shootings of prisoners, but minimized them. He pronounced a eulogy on the two military commissions which had condemned the rebels. The Dantonists did not dare to answer him, and his acts were approved. But Fabre d'Eglantine made a bitter attack on Mazuel, a lieutenant of Ronsin's, and obtained a decree that he should be arrested.

On the same evening Collot cried shame upon the Jacobins for their weakness: "Two months ago, when I left you, you were all thirsting for vengeance upon the infamous conspirators of the city of Lyons. . . . If I had arrived in Paris three days later, perhaps I should have been cited before the courts!" He made common cause with Ronsin, on whom he pronounced an enthusiastic panegyric, and drew a picture of the joy of the aristocrats when they heard of his arrest. "Your colleagues, your friends, your brothers, will be under the threat of assassination!" He wound up with an attack on the Indulgents. Courage is infectious. The Hébertists, who had been giving way and retreating for the last month, now imitated Collot and assumed a bold front, denouncing in their turn Momoro, Goupilleau, Nicolas, Desmoulins, who had for long past narrowly escaped the guillotine, Hébert, Bourdon of Oise, who had been

435

Marat's enemy, Philippeaux and his odious pamphlet, and Fabre d'Eglantine, who was on friendly terms with all the aristocrats. The Jacobins made common cause with Ronsin and Vincent and demanded that they should be set at liberty.

But if Collot had succeeded in redressing the situation, it was because he had the support of the committee. Robespierre's views had undergone development. Not that he approved Collot's actions at Lyons; far from it. He had not answered any of the urgent letters which Collot had written to him while on mission. But though Robespierre had followed the campaign of the Indulgents with sympathy at first, because he would have been glad to eliminate the agents of disorder and violence, he became distrustful when he saw them indulging their resentment and personal revenge, paving the way for reaction in No. 3, of the *Vieux Cordelier*, attacking trusty henchmen like Héron and Bouchotte, who possessed his confidence, and his colleague Saint-André, whose character and talent he esteemed.

Next, on the 29th Frimaire, the affair into which Amar was examining as a result of Chabot's denunciation took a step forward. Amar and Jagot examined the original of the falsified decree for the liquidation of the India Company. They ascertained that it bore the signature of Fabre d'Eglantine and that he had accepted a wording absolutely contrary to his amendment. Their astonishment was so great that on the 6th Nivôse they resolved to exclude Fabre from the inquiry. Robespierre now began to wonder whether he had not been duped by Fabre, a clever rogue, guiltier than those whom he was denouncing in order to throw dust into people's eyes.

Robespierre considered nothing but the interest of the Revolution. Was this the moment to let suspects out of prison in order to reincarcerate the soundest patriots? Was it the moment to relax or destroy the revolutionary laws, when the Vendeans had crossed to the north bank of the Loire and were inflicting defeat after defeat upon the republican troops sent in pursuit of them; when Wurmser had forced the Weissenburg lines and was encamped before the gates of Strasbourg; when the English and Spanish were still in possession of the chief French port on the Mediterranean? Was this the moment to disorganize the revolutionary Government, when the Commission of Supplies had barely started its work, and the great law of the 14th Frimaire was just beginning to be put in force?

Speaking at the Jacobins on the 3rd Nivôse, Robespierre took up a position transcending all party. The hall was unusually crowded, some persons offering as much as twenty-five livres to obtain a place in the galleries. The Indulgents wanted to obtain the annulment of the resolution by which the club had defended Ronsin and Vincent, but met with a preliminary check. Collot in tragic tones announced the death of Chalier's friend Gaillard, a patriot of Lyons, who had committed suicide in despair. That, he said, was what moderantism led to! Levasseur of Sarthe delivered an arraignment of Philippeaux, who came from the same part of the country, referring to him as a garrulous liar. Philippeaux replied in the same tone. He reaffirmed all his accusations against the sansculotte generals commanding in the Vendée, accused them of embezzling the public funds, of thinking of nothing but high living, and of being fools, cowards, and traitors. An uproar arose in the hall. Danton intervened, with an affectation of impartiality, and demanded silence on behalf of Philippeaux. "Perhaps nobody is to blame in all this but the events," he said; "in any case, I request that all those who have anything to say on this matter should be listened to." Robespierre, after censuring Philippeaux for his ill-advised attacks on the Committee of Public Safety, refused to see anything in the dispute but a matter of personal spite. He urged Philippeaux to sacrifice his vanity. Unlike Danton, who asked for an inquiry, no doubt in order to prolong the incident, Robespierre endeavoured to cut it short by an appeal for union. Turning to the Hébertists, as he had done to Philippeaux, he asked them to wait calmly for the verdict of the committees on Ronsin, Vincent, and Maillard. "Did not Marat appear calmly before the Revolutionary Tribunal? Did he not return in triumph? Has not Chabot, who has rendered the greatest services to the common weal, been arrested?"

But Philippeaux refused the olive-branch offered him by Robespierre and made a more direct attack upon the committee, and Danton repeated his proposal for a commission of inquiry. "I ask Philippeaux," said Couthon, "whether, on his soul and conscience, he believes that there is treason going on in the war in the Vendée?" "Yes," replied Philippeaux. "Then," rejoined Couthon, "I, too, ask for the nomination of a commission." The link between the Indulgents and the committee was now severed.

The Hébertist Momoro seized the occasion to offer the committee the assistance of his friends, but on certain conditions only. "Let patriotism be upheld," he said, "let patriots cease to be oppressed, and all republicans, rallying round the Committees of Public Safety and General Security, the Convention, and the Mountain, will defend the Republic to the last drop of their blood!" Robespierre, who possessed every sort of courage, promptly took up the covert challenge which he detected as underlying these advances: "Do they wish to persuade us that the Convention is oppressing patriots? Have they forgotten that the Brissotins are no more, that the Mountain is there and will always see that justice is done to republicans?" He added that the Convention would do its duty to the end, without fear of insurrections. This was a warning to the Hébertists that if they were thinking of resorting to intimidation, they were making a mistake.

Thus Robespierre took up a central position between Philippeaux and Momoro, a very strong position, which soon won him the greatest popularity among the populace, who realized that the safety of the Revolution lay in union among the revolutionaries. Now, on the very day after the great session of the 3rd Nivôse at the Jacobins, news reached Paris of the recapture of Toulon by Dugommier's republican troops. The committee's position was thus strengthened, and Robespierre took advantage of this on the 5th Nivôse to deliver before the Convention a vigorous apology for the revolutionary Government, a timely rejoinder to the *Vieux Cordelier*. From the fundamental distinction between constitutional and revolutionary government, the state of war and the state of peace, he deduced with much logic a justification of the Terror. Taking his stand upon the public interest as upon a rock, he fulminated against the extremists on both sides, alluding to "moderantism, which is to moderation what impotence is to chastity, and excess, which bears as much resemblance to energy as dropsy does to health. . . . Democratic barons are the brothers of the marquises at Coblenz, and red caps (*bonnets rouges*) are sometimes nearer to red heels (*talons rouges;* that is, aristocrats) than might be supposed." On the following day Barère denounced the *Vieux Cordelier,* and Billaud-Varenne obtained the annulment of a decree, voted a few days previously on Robespierre's motion, for organizing a Committee of Justice, to be entrusted with the mission of going through those in the prisons and releasing those who had been wrongfully arrested.

Since the Vendeans had been crushed at Le Mans and Savenay, and Hoche had routed the Austro-Prussians at Geisberg and recaptured Landau, the committee had consolidated its position and grown bolder. The Indulgents were losing ground every day.

On the 15th Nivôse the discovery of the draft of the original decree on the liquidation of the India Company, among the papers sealed up in Delaunay's house, provided definite proof of Fabre d'Eglantine's guilt. On the 19th Nivôse Robespierre denounced the scoundrel who had deceived him, and four days later Fabre was arrested. When, on the following day, Danton committed the supreme imprudence of intervening in his friend's favour, he brought down upon himself Billaud-Varenne's terrible rejoinder: "Woe to those who sat by his side and may still be his dupes!"

Not only had the Indulgents failed in their attempt to check the Terror, but they were themselves threatened. They risked being implicated in the trial of the swindlers whom they had defended. They had discredited clemency by claiming it for unworthy persons.

CHAPTER X

From the Citra-revolutionaries to the Ultra-revolutionaries

THE Indulgents had in their favour the secret sympathy of the majority of deputies, whom the revolution of June 2 had converted, in appearance only, to the doctrines of the Mountain—that is, the doctrines of Public Safety. If it had not been for the brilliant services that it had rendered, the committee would more than once have been overthrown. It maintained itself only by proving itself to be necessary. But it could act, it could set the vast machine of revolutionary government in motion, only by the aid of the confidence and support of the sansculotte agitators, who now not only harangued the clubs, but filled the offices of the new bureaucracy. These new men, the product of the war, for the most part young, and fresh from the schools in which the heroes of Greece and Rome had been held up to them as examples, were defending in the Revolution not only an ideal, but a career. They staffed the offices of the Ministry for War, and, as commissaries of the Executive Council or the Committee of Public Safety, kept a watch on the generals and even the representatives on mission; they were strongly represented on the revolutionary committees and the tribunals engaged in the work of repression, and by their means the orders of Paris were executed and Paris was kept well-informed. The whole system of government depended upon their loyalty and goodwill.

The campaign of the Indulgents directly affected them, by threatening not only their persons but their employment. Many of them were included in the formidable category of alien agents or ultra-revolutionaries. The representatives on mission whom they kept under observation or alarmed, frequently had them arrested. Thus the internecine struggles of the revolutionaries were not confined to the lists of the Jacobins in Paris or the Convention, but spread to the whole of France. Breaking out as they did just at the moment when the great law of the 14th Frimaire was being put into execution, when the purging of administrative bodies and clubs was proceeding everywhere and the Commission of Supplies was in course of being organized, there was great danger that the new regime

440

might be paralysed even before it had assumed its normal form. We can conceive no just idea of the gravity of the crisis unless we leave the capital and examine the country at large.

The clash was apparent everywhere. In Alsace Saint-Just and Lebas, who had been entrusted with an extraordinary mission after the capture of the Weissenburg lines, held no communication with the representatives on mission to the armies of the Rhine and Moselle, J.-B. Lacoste and Baudot, who consequently took offence. Saint-Just ordered the arrest of the leader of the foreign exiles, Euloge Schneider, formerly vicar-general to the constitutional bishop Brendel, and now a public prosecutor. Schneider had just got married and had made a sensational entry into Strasbourg with his young bride at his side, in a carriage escorted by horsemen with drawn sabres. Saint-Just had him pilloried for some hours on the platform of the guillotine, previous to sending him before the Revolutionary Tribunal. "This punishment," wrote Lebas to Robespierre on the 24th Frimaire, "which he has brought upon himself by his insolent conduct, was also dictated by the necessity for putting down foreigners. Let us put no trust in cosmopolitan charlatans and rely on none but ourselves." At the same time Saint-Just suppressed the "Propagande," a sort of travelling club which the representatives on mission to the army of the Rhine had organized to spread republicanism in the country districts.

Lacoste and Baudot protested loudly. They wrote to the Convention on the 28th and 29th Frimaire that the degrading punishment suffered by Schneider had caused consternation among patriots and had made the aristocrats more dangerous and insolent than ever. They praised the orators of the Propagande, "all of whom are imbued with the red-hot zeal of the Père Duchesne," and at the same time asked to be recalled.

There was a clash in Lorraine, where, after ordering Marat Mauger, leader of the local Hébertists, to be arrested for speculation and sending him before the Revolutionary Tribunal, Balthazar Faure purged the club at Nancy by arresting the leading revolutionaries. But J.-B. Lacoste and Baudot accused their colleague of having become the idol of the aristocrats, hurried to Nancy, purged the club in the opposite sense, and dismissed Faure's partisans, who were sent to prison in place of the released patriots. On the 3rd Pluviôse Faure asked for an inquiry.

There was a clash at Sedan, where, during Nivôse, Perrin (of Vosges) ordered Vassan, the leader of the club and mayor of the town, to be arrested as an "ultra" (i.e., ultra-revolutionary). His colleagues Massieu and Élie Lacoste protested and took Vassan's side.

There was a clash at Lille, where Hentz and Florent Guiot, who had taken the place of Isoré and Châles, ordered the arrest of Lavalette and Dufresse, whom their predecessors had placed at the head of their departmental army; they released at the same time a great many suspects. Châles, who had stayed at Lille to nurse a wound received while fighting the enemy, protested, and accused them of protecting aristocrats.

There was a clash in the department of Haute-Saône, where the younger Robespierre released hundreds of suspects arrested for federalism and "fanaticism." His colleague Bernard of Saintes, who was bitterly hostile to religion and was filling the prisons, entered upon a violent struggle against him.

There was a clash in the department of Loire, where the fiery Javogues drew up an arraignment of Couthon and the Committee of Public Safety. He denounced the decree on freedom of worship, and the institution òf national agents, pointed to the persecution of patriots, and, in a letter of the 16th Pluviôse to Collot, stated his conclusion as follows: "There is counter-revolution in the Committee of Public Safety, which has sent the infamous Gouly to stir up counter-revolution in Ain." Couthon protested from the tribune on the 20th Pluviôse. Javogues was recalled and censured, and Fouché ordered the arrest of his agent Lapallu, who was sent before the Revolutionary Tribunal.

Gouly, who had already been denounced by Javogues, was next accused of protecting aristocrats by Albitte, who replaced him in the department of Ain. In a letter of the 11th Pluviôse Albitte accused Gouly of having imprisoned the best patriots, released priests, nobles, and nuns, and failed to put the revolutionary laws into execution.

But this same Albitte, who was taxing Gouly with moderantism in the department of Ain, had himself been denounced by Barras and Fréron a few weeks previously, in a letter of October 20, for his weakness in dealing with the rebels at Marseilles. He had failed to levy contributions on the rich, they said, and was surrounded by none but *"messieurs."*

Barras and Fréron, since they were friends of Danton, were regarded as Indulgents. After the capture of Toulon these Indulgents were responsible for blood-thirsty reprisals. A letter from them dated the 16th Nivôse runs as follows: "During the first few days after we entered the town, the patriots imprisoned on the vessel *Le Thémistocle* (that is, interned during the siege) told us who were the guiltiest of the rebels and we ordered them to be shot on the spot. . . . But we have set up a commission of worthy Parisian sansculottes as commissaries of the executive power. . . . It has been working two days and is going on well. . . . Eight hundred traitors of Toulon have already been punished by death." They applied the same methods at Marseilles as at Toulon, ordering the disarming of all the inhabitants without exception, and organizing a revolutionary commission entirely composed of Parisians, like the one at Toulon, which sentenced a hundred and twenty persons to death in ten days. They wanted to pull down the finest buildings and deprive the city of its glorious name, calling it "Sans Nom" (Nameless). The patriots of Marseilles protested, demanded the restoration of their arms, recalled the fact that they had contributed towards the victory of Carteaux, and wanted to organize at Marseilles a congress of all the clubs in the south. Barras and Fréron dispersed the congress, closed the headquarters of the sections, and arrested and sent before the Revolutionary Tribunal the two patriots Maillet, the president, and Giraud, public prosecutor to the criminal tribunal. The patriots of Marseilles rejoined by accusing Barras and Fréron, with some probability, of enriching themselves by despoiling the merchants whom they imprisoned, only to release them in return for hard cash. The younger Robespierre and Ricord, their colleagues on mission, had already denounced them to the Committee of Public Safety. At Marseilles the committee lived up to its name, recalling Barras and Fréron on the 4th Pluviôse. The latter posed as victims of the ultras, and.on their return to Paris went to swell the ranks of the Indulgents. But it is evident that this was not so much a case of a political as of a personal quarrel and a struggle between the influence of the local authorities and that of the delegates of the central power. The words "ultra" and "citra" often served to cover very different types.

At Lyons, as at Marseilles, the quarrel between the ultras and citras was the form taken by the revolt of the local patriots, who were friends of Chalier and of the functionaries sent down from Paris. On the 14th Pluviôse at the Jacobins Marino accused the former of having sown the seeds of discord between the detachment of the revolutionary army brought there by Collot d'Herbois and the troops of the line who formed the garrison of the city. The troops of the line complained that Ronsin's soldiers were better paid than they were. "For three days and three nights," said Marino, "the cannon have been mounted for action, the houses lit up, and our brethren ready to massacre one another." After the arrest of Ronsin, Fouché, who had at first had a hand in the mass shootings, changed his attitude. On the 18th Pluviôse he ordered the executions to be stopped and on the 24th forbade any fresh arrests. This amounted to an amnesty for the past. At the same time he calmed the misgivings of the aristocrats through the agency of Mollet, an ex-Oratorian like himself. The bloodthirsty Fouché was now attacking Chalier's friends as ultras, but at the same time these so-called ultras were in conflict with Marino, Tolède and their like—that is to say, with partisans of Ronsin and Hébert whom Fouché continued to employ and protect.

At Bordeaux, where Tallien and Ysabeau began to denounce the ultras at an early date, the important matter was to close the mouths of certain inconvenient agents of surveillance who were interfering with the personal calculations of the representatives on mission. The military commission which they had set up, with a disreputable person named Lacombe as its president, at first displayed great severity, and Saige, an ex-mayor, who had a fortune of ten millions, and Birotteau, a member of the Convention, were sent to the scaffold. But the representatives and their commission soon grew more humane. The four brothers Raba, who were rich merchants, had been released on payment of a fine of 500,000 livres, the banker Peixoto had been mulcted in 1,200,000 livres, the merchant Lafond and the broker Lajard in 300,000 livres each, etc. The release of these prisoners did not escape the vigilance of the agents of the Executive Council, who denounced the luxury of the representatives on mission to the authorities in Paris, pointing out that Tallien was cohabiting with the beautiful Teresa Cabarrus, daughter of the director of the Spanish Bank of Saint Charles, a "modern Dubarry" whom he had released from prison and who flaunted at the civic festivals with the red cap of liberty on her head. Ysabeau and Tallien denounced their denouncers as agents of Pitt, schemers in embroidered and gold-laced uniforms who issued in swarms from the offices of the Ministry for War. As regards Teresa Cabarrus, they added frankly in a letter of the 2nd Nivôse: "It is supposed that Tallien was to marry a foreign lady. This alleged marriage is a falsehood, as you will learn by consulting General Brune, who was more closely connected with the *citoyenne* in question than Tallien. He ought to be acquainted with the respectability of a house which he visited every day." On the 12th Pluviôse, in order to silence those who had denounced them, they ordered the arrest of the members of the vigilance committee of Bordeaux, who, according to them, were guilty of arbitrary actions. "We proceed against schemers, false patriots, and ultra-revolutionaries as courageously as we have proceeded against all the enemies of liberty," they wrote on the 17th Pluviôse. Henceforward moderantism was the order of the day at Bordeaux, as at Lyons.

In the department of Gard, Boisset, the representative on mission, turned all ardent patriots out of office, dismissed their leader, Courbis, mayor of Nîmes, the Marat of the south, and released hundreds of suspects; though this did not prevent him from closing churches and condemning the decree of the 18th Frimaire on freedom of worship, which goes to prove that the destruction of Catholicism was not exclusively characteristic of what is known as Hébertism.

At Avignon the revolutionary Agricole Moureau, a judge on the tribunal, was sent before the Revolutionary Tribunal by Rovère and Poultier, whose speculations in national property he had exposed. The patriot Taboureau at Orléans, the patriot Lherbon at Soissons, the brothers Gerboin at Amboise, Mogue, commissary of the Executive Council at Blois, and many others were thrown into prison as ultras.

There is nothing surprising in the fact that, at the height of the Terror, aristocrats, and even secret royalists, succeeded in gaining control of the organs of the revolutionary Government. At a time when the masses were illiterate and education a luxury and when social distinctions were still very strong, the cultivated minority was bound to exert a considerable influence. The rich had still their following of dependents and their prestige. It was easy for them to adopt the political colour prevailing at the moment by means of a few patriotic donations. In Pluviôse the club at Besançon had as its president the brother of an *émigré*, the ex-Count Viennot-Vaublanc, who made a parade of Maratist opinions, and this was not an isolated exception.

In the department of Creuse, Vernerey, the representative on mission, succeeded in snatching from the Revolutionary Tribunal and the scaffold Gravelois, a good republican and mayor of a rural commune in the district of La Souterraine, whom the aristocrat judges of the tribunal of Guéret had represented as a dangerous anarchist.

We must bear these facts in mind if we are to realize the profound disturbance which the struggle between the ultras and the citras aroused in the whole of France. Conflicts sprang up on every side which threatened the very existence of the revolutionary system of government. Instead of acting as arbiters the representatives on mission very often threw themselves into the fray and bandied mutual accusations of the gravest malpractices. Denunciations, dismissals, arrests, and the purging of public bodies succeeded one another rapidly in a conflicting sense. And all the while the administration and government had to be carried on, plots put down, the towns and armies fed, and Europe conquered. The committees groped their way forward amid a fog of intrigue. It is a miracle that they were not more often deceived and that they succeeded in avoiding the fresh traps which were constantly being laid for them. If they had been divided against themselves, they would have been ruined, and the Republic with them.

The committees did not intend that sincere patriots, who were merely guilty of disinterested enthusiasm, should be persecuted under the pretext of attacking the real ultras. They were afraid of getting out of touch with the republican masses. In the blows that threatened the agents of the Executive Council they divined indirect manœuvres against themselves. The citras seemed even more dangerous to them than the ultras.

They had Châles recalled by a decree of the 27th Nivôse, but a month later they tried to get rid of his accuser, Florent Guiot, by sending him to Finistère (30th Pluviôse). They took the side of the patriots of Marseilles by recalling Barras and Fréron, on the 4th Pluviôse. Carrier was denounced by their agent, young Jullien, for his ostentatious luxury, his despotism toward the local authorities—in fact for his crimes—and recalled on the 18th Pluviôse, in spite of Carnot's opposition. Balthazar Faure was recalled on the 5th Pluviôse, and the patriots of the north-east were released and reinstated in their posts. Boisset was in turn recalled on the 3rd Ventôse, and his victim Courbis reinstated in his office as mayor of Nîmes, etc.

The Committees protected patriots, but they did not intend to allow clumsy and indefinite reprisals against former federalists who had rallied to the Mountain. During their mission in Normandy two Indulgents, Delacroix and Legendre, had sent the municipal officers of Conches before the Revolutionary Tribunal as federalists. Robert Lindet wrote to Fouquier-Tinville that he would appear as a witness at their trial. He requested the tribunal to adjourn the case, and on the 15th Nivôse it was declared to be adjourned. On the same evening, at a joint session of the two committees, Lindet announced that he would send in his resignation if the trial was proceeded with, and the majority sided with him. On the 24th Pluviôse, Voulland obtained the passage of a decree withdrawing the federalist administrators of the departments round Lyons from the jurisdiction of Fouché and Collot d'Herbois's extraordinary commission. The trial of the 132 inhabitants of Nantes sent up to Fouquier by Carrier was adjourned, etc.

Concerned though they were to put an end to reprisals, the committees had, for all that, no intention of moderating the Terror. On the contrary, they believed it to be more necessary than ever, for they still felt themselves surrounded by plots and treachery. "No peace, no truce with the despots, no pardon, no amnesty for conspirators and traitors—such is the cry of the nation!" wrote Couthon, in a letter of the 4th Pluviôse.

While Hébert and his friends were walking warily as regards the committee, and the Père Duchesne was expressing his wrath in gentler accents, the Indulgents, on the other hand, were redoubling their attacks. On the 12th Nivôse Bourdon of Oise denounced Bouchotte's assistant Daubigni. On the 18th Nivôse, on the pretext that the ministers were squandering public money on subsidizing the Hébertist press, he obtained a decree from the Convention depriving them of the right of sanctioning any expenditure without previously receiving the express authorization of one of the committees—a most serious measure, which threatened to paralyse the public services in time of war. The Committee of Public Safety did not hesitate to violate the decree, ordering the commissaries of the Treasury to make payments, as hitherto, on the sole warrant of the ministers.

Westermann had been removed from his command by the committee for having distributed thirty thousand muskets among the inhabitants of the Vendée, with which they had renewed the civil war. A panegyric on the general, who opportunely appeared at the bar of the Convention, was pronounced·by Lecointre, who persuaded the Convention to make a formal exception to the decree for the imprisonment of dismissed functionaries, thanks to which Westermann was left in entire possession of his liberty. On the same evening Robespierre fulminated at the Jacobins against "the new Brissotins, more dangerous, more perfidious, and more despicable than the last."

Again, on the 3rd Pluviôse, Bourdon of Oise expressed his indignation at the fact that, on the previous day, when the Convention had gone in a body to the Place de la Révolution to celebrate the anniversary of the death of the tyrant, four condemned prisoners had been executed in its presence: "This is a deliberate plan hatched by malignant persons to make people say that the national representative body is composed of cannibals." He obtained a decree that the Committee of General Security was to give an explanation of this incident, as if it had been premeditated.

Not a day passed on which the committees were not heckled. On the 5th Pluviôse Danton seized the occasion of the arrest of Camille Desmoulins's father-in-law to obtain a resolution that the committee were to present an exhaustive report on the release of prisoners which had taken place; on the 9th, Rühl obtained the passage of a decree calling upon the Committee of Public Safety to inquire into the conduct of Bouchotte in connexion with the detention of a Frenchman at Mainz as a hostage; on the 10th, on the strength of a complaint from a captain in the mercantile marine, who had failed to obtain the promotion in the navy which the Convention had promised him as a reward for his services, the Minister of Marine, Dalbarade, was examined at the bar of the Convention, and it took the united

447

intervention of Barère, Saint-André, and Couthon to save him from the Revolutionary Tribunal.

There could be no better sign of how precarious the situation of the Government still remained than these continual attacks, which were often successful.

The committees were forced by the very pressure of events to move in the direction of the ultras and the clubs. On the 23rd Nivôse the Committee of General Security ordered the release of Mazuel, a victim of Fabre d'Eglantine, and on the following day Fabre was sent to prison in his place. On the 14th Pluviôse Ronsin and Vincent were at last set free, after a report by Voulland, in spite of the keen opposition of Bourdon of Oise, Philippeaux, Legendre, Dornier, Loiseau, Clauzel, Charlier, and Lecointre. Danton had been in favour of the release, while loudly proclaiming that he would also support that of Fabre d'Eglantine as soon as the report of his affair was heard. It was a sort of bargain, a two-sided mutual amnesty, which he was indirectly proposing to the committees; but they turned a deaf ear. If Danton desired conciliation, oblivion for the past. and an understanding, why did he not demand it from his own partisans first? Why did they never cease attacking the Government and its agents?

On the 17th Pluviôse Robespierre informed them of the Government's view of the matter. "What we have to avoid," he said, "is not so much an excess of energy as an excess of weakness. Perhaps zealous fervour is not the greatest stumbling-block which we have to avoid, but rather weariness in well-doing and fear of our own courage." Revolutionary government would be maintained until the peace. And Robespierre threatened "the cabal" which had attempted "to sow division between the representatives sent into the departments and the Committee of Public Safety" and "to subject them to annoyance on their return."

The Terror was to last for the duration of the war; so Robespierre had said But the Indulgents considered that the time had come to make peace. As early as the 29th Frimaire, Bourdon of Oise declared that it would not be long before the English made a peace offer to France. Danton was soon to have in his hands the letters written to him by Miles, an agent of Pitt, sent through the agency of Noël, the French minister in Venice, proposing to open a conference in Switzerland with a view to the cessation of hostilities. Other indirect overtures had been made by Holland and Spain to the French agents Caillard and Grouvelle. Even Austria had sounded Bacher, the French agent in Basel. There is no doubt that if Danton had been in power, he would eagerly have welcomed these preliminary advances. In No. 7. of the *Vieux Cordelier*, which did not appear till after his death, Desmoulins made a forcible pronouncement in favour of a peace policy.

But in two high-sounding speeches made by Barère on the 3rd and 13th Pluviôse the Committee of Public Safety poured scorn upon the secret overtures of the tyrants, which seemed to them to conceal a trap and to have no object save that of encouraging all the open or secret enemies of the revolutionary Government in France and arresting the progress of her armies. "Who dares to speak of peace?" he said. "It is those who hope to postpone counter-revolution for a few months, a few years, by giving foreigners and tyrants time to recover themselves, time to suck the people dry, to renew their supplies of provisions and withdraw their armies. . . . The monarchies require peace, the Republic requires martial energy; slaves need peace, republicans need the ferment of liberty." War was necessary not only to liberate the territory already invaded, but to consolidate the Republic at home. No peace before a brilliant victory, and, above all, victory over the English. Robespierre brought up the crimes of the English Government for discussion at the Jacobins, not so much to create a diversion from party struggles as to bring it home to the public that peace with Pitt was impossible.

But in order to carry on the war, which would prolong the sufferings of the sansculottes, the committee was obliged to carry out an increasingly bold social policy, which would still more estrange it from the Indulgents, the habitual protectors of the property-owning classes. The Indulgents had paralysed the law on food-speculation in its very essence by refusing to vote the amendments necessary for its execution. On the 2nd Nivôse they had succeeded in striking at its weakest point by obtaining a decree—on the occasion of the trial of Gaudon, the wine-merchant, whom they had saved from the scaffold—to the effect that the only penalty provided in it, death, should no longer be pronounced by the judges. It can hardly be doubted that they hoped that the law of the maximum, which, owing to its hasty drafting, was constantly being sent back for amendment, would before long be abrogated in practice, like the law on food-speculation. But the committee would not withdraw from its position. It urged on the Commission of Supplies, and on the 3rd Ventôse Barère was able to lay before the Convention the scheme of a general maximum which was to regulate prices for the whole of France and make good the defects of the original law. The sansculottes would feel that they were being defended.

The campaign was about to open. The committees resolved to strike a great blow which would crush their opponents and rouse the enthusiasm of the masses. On the 8th Ventôse Saint-Just, as their spokesman, deliv-

449

ered a sensational speech containing the program of a fresh revolution.

Hitherto the Terror had been regarded even by its most fervent authors as a transitory expedient which would disappear with the peace. Saint-Just represented it in a totally new light, as the necessary condition for the establishment of a democratic republic. He laid it down as a principle that the Republic could not be assured of survival unless it was provided with such civil institutions as should purify the morals of citizens and render them naturally virtuous. "A State in which such institutions are lacking," he said, "is but an illusory republic. And since everybody interprets liberty as meaning the independence of his passions and his avarice, the spirit of conquest and selfishness is established between one citizen and another, and the individual idea of his own liberty formed by every man according to his interest leads to the slavery of all." Until these civil institutions of which he was shortly to outline the plan had been successfully created and had extirpated selfishness from the hearts of citizens, Saint-Just declared, the Terror must be maintained. "What constitutes a republic is the destruction of that which is opposed to it." After an impassioned apology for the executions ordered by the Revolutionary Tribunal, which were but a feeble rejoinder to the barbarities of monarchical governments, this man, whom Michelet calls the "archangel of death," held the threat of the guillotine *in terrorem* over all those who spoke of indulgence, and indicated the chief of them by barely veiled allusions. "There is one who carries in his heart the design of forcing retrograde action upon us and oppressing us." Every eye must have been fixed on Danton, especially when Saint-Just went on: "There is one who has waxed fat on despoiling the people and, glutted with their spoils, insults them and advances in triumph, drawn onwards by the crime for which he thinks to excite our compassion, for we can no longer keep silence upon the impunity of those who are most guilty, who desire to destroy the scaffold because they are afraid of ascending it." The Assembly waited breathlessly for the end of the arraignment. Was he going to ask it to hand over to Fouquier-Tinville the heads of those whom he had previously marked down? But Saint-Just suddenly changed his course. He demanded not heads, but a revolution in property: "The force of events is perhaps leading us towards unforeseen results. Wealth is in the hands of a fairly large number of enemies of the Revolution; the people, the workers, are placed by their necessities in dependence upon their enemies. Do you imagine that an empire can exist if the structure of society favours those who are opposed to the very form of its government? Those who make revolutions by halves are only digging their own graves. The Revolution

450

is leading us to recognize the principle that he who has shown himself the enemy of his country cannot own property in it. A few strokes of genius are still necessary to save us. . . . The property of patriots is sacred, but the property of conspirators exists for the needy. The needy are the powers of the earth. They have the right to speak with authority to the governments which neglect them."

And Saint-Just obtained the passage of a decree by the terms of which the property of persons recognized to be enemies of the Republic should be confiscated. In his mind this was no theoretical decree, but a definite measure which was going to be carried into effect; for on the 13th Ventôse he obtained the passage of a fresh decree, ordering every commune to draw up a list of needy patriots, and all vigilance committees to submit to the Committee of General Security a list of all those imprisoned on a political charge since May 1, 1789, with notes on each. On the strength of this extensive inquisition the two committees were to give judgment without appeal on the confiscation of the property of enemies of the Revolution, while at the same time the Committee of Public Safety was to draw up a list of the needy patriots to whom the confiscated property was to be distributed.

After the property of the clergy and the *émigrés* the Revolution was taking possession of all that still belonged to its enemies. It had put up for sale the property belonging to the first two categories, and the sales had benefited nobody but those possessing the means of purchasing them. It was now about to distribute the property of the newly-created category among the revolutionary proletariate for nothing.

Neither the Hébertists nor the Enragés had ever dreamed of such a radical measure, such a vast transference of property from one political class to another. There were perhaps three hundred thousand persons detained on suspicion in the new bastilles—three hundred thousand families threatened with expropriation. The Terror was assuming an unforeseen and impressive character. It was no longer a question of temporarily holding down a hostile party by force; but of dispossessing it for good, annihilating its means of subsistence, and, by means of the property of which it had been despoiled, promoting to social life the class of the perpetually disinherited. Moreover, as Saint-Just had repeated after Robespierre, the intention also was to prolong the revolutionary dictatorship as long as necessary in order to found the Republic *de facto* by this enormous fresh expropriation, while establishing it in the minds of men by means of civil institutions. The Terror was no longer ashamed of itself. It was becoming

451

a system of government, the blood-red crucible in which the accumulated ruins of everything pertaining to the old order were to be fused into the future democracy.

It seemed as if this time the committee, which had been groping its way the last two months between the citras and the ultras, had definitely made up its mind. It took its stand resolutely on the side of the ultras, and went even further than they did. Saint-Just's whole effort had been directed against the Indulgents. His conclusions were a formidable attempt to extract a social program from the confused aspirations of Hébertism.

The strange and amazing thing to him was that he was neither understood nor followed by the very party which he wanted to satisfy.

CHAPTER XI

The Fall of the Factions

THE committee expected its social program to meet with resistance from the right, but not from the left. It looked as if Danton intended to shake off his torpor. On the 4th Ventôse, when Élie Lacoste, as spokesman for the Committee of General Security, proposed to hand over to Fouquier-Tinville the judges of the military tribunal of the department of Ardennes, who were suspected of aristocratic leanings, he protested against the measure and obtained its adjournment. "We pass decrees," he said, "before acquainting ourselves with the facts, on trust and on the strength of mere reports. I declare that I cannot grasp what has been said, that I cannot exercise my functions as member of a political jury. It is time that the Convention once more took its fitting place, and gave judgment only after fully acquainting itself with the facts. The nation must not be ruined because we have been cowardly, weak, or dumb. This is only the preamble to my political views. I shall make them known in due time." But it was a preamble big with menace.

When Saint-Just obtained the passage of the decree expropriating suspects, Danton tried to parry the blow by proposing that the revolutionary committees should first be purged by the Committee of General Security, by expelling "the false patriots in red caps." His proposal was referred to the committees, who shelved it.

If the Hébertists had had the slightest political sense, they would have rallied round the committees, who were making repeated advances to them—so much so, that Collot d'Herbois pronounced a eulogy on Carrier at the Jacobins on the 3rd Ventôse. But most of them were not so much desirous of carrying out a social program as impatient to satisfy their ambitions and grudges. They had, strictly speaking, no social policy. In this respect Hébert was extremely lacking in resources. According to him, all their ills arose from the food-speculators, and his only remedy was the guillotine. His latest numbers were full of savage attacks on the trading classes. "I will no more spare the greengrocer who sells carrots than the biggest merchant," he said in his No. 345, "for, *f—*, I see a league of all those who sell against all those who buy, and I find as much bad faith among the hawkers' stalls as in the big shops." It was a serious imprudence to attack retailers like this, and they did not forget his threats! Jacques Roux had had an occasional inkling of the social question. Hébert could not see beyond the problem of food-supplies, which he hoped to solve by childish but violent means.

Ronsin and Vincent, those proud souls and indomitable characters, desired vengeance upon Fabre d'Eglantine and Philippeaux, who had denounced them. They had no confidence in either the Convention or its committees. Robespierre, who had prevented Desmoulins from being struck off the books at the Jacobins, was in their eyes a hypocritical and danger-ous moderate. They could not forget how their friend Brichet had been struck off the books of the Jacobins; Robespierre had had him expelled on the 19th Pluviôse because he had proposed to exclude from the Con-vention the "frogs of the Marsh"[1] and send the seventy-five Girondins who were in prison before the Revolutionary Tribunal. Like Momoro, they had been indignant at the refusal of the Jacobins to welcome Vincent among them (23rd and 26th Pluviôse). Momoro had seen in the rejection of Vincent's candidature proof of a plot, which he denounced to the Cordeliers. On the 24th Pluviôse he indulged in an outburst against "the worn-out men, the broken reeds," who called the Cordeliers extremists because they were patriots, which they themselves were no longer willing to be.

From this moment the Cordeliers once more went over to the opposi-tion. On the 4th Ventôse Hébert denounced to them the new faction of the Endormeurs—that is, the Robespierrists. "Camille has been represented to us as a child, Philippeaux as a madman, Fabre d'Eglantine as an honest man. Citizens, beware of the Endormeurs [those who are lulling you into security]. . . . We are told that the Brissotins have been annihilated, yet there are still sixty-one guilty persons left to punish." The Cordeliers resolved to revive Marat's newspaper. To invoke Marat, whose heart was preserved at the club as a relic, was not only to shelter themselves behind a great popular name, but to proclaim a definite policy. The Marat whom they glorified was the Marat of the September massacres, the Marat who had advised the people to choose a dictator.

Hébert and his friends thought they would be able to exploit for their own purposes the extreme destitution which again made itself felt in the

---

[1] i.e., the deputies of the Plain, or Marsh, occupying an intermediate position be-tween the parties of the left and the right, and in the habit of hopping in either direction when scared.

capital as the winter advanced. Again there was fighting in the markets and at the door of the bakeries. "The aspect of Paris is beginning to be terrible," wrote Latour la Montagne, a secret agent, on the 4th Ventôse. "One meets nothing in the markets and streets but a vast crowd of citizens running, jostling one another, shouting, shedding tears, and offering on every side a picture of despair; the sight of all these movements might make one think that Paris was already a prey to the horrors of famine." "The evil is extreme," noted Siret, another secret agent, on the next day. "The whole faubourg Saint-Antoine poured out on the Vincennes road and pillaged everything that was being brought into Paris. Some paid, others made off without paying. The peasants, in distress, vowed that they would never bring anything to Paris again. It is most urgent that an end should be put to this brigandage, which will end very shortly in starving the capital." The commissaries for food-speculation redoubled their domiciliary visits, seized the rare supplies of food that appeared in the streets, and shared them. One day Ducroquet, commissary for the section of Marat, seized thirty-six eggs at the house of a citizen with seven persons to feed, and distributed the thirty-six eggs among thirty-six different persons.

On the 4th Ventôse the Cordeliers proposed that the revolutionary army should be increased in order to punish food-speculators. On the 5th the Commune and sections presented a petition for the severe and unrestricted application of the law on food-speculation. For lack of goods the workmen in the army-supply factories were idle. The workmen in the forges and arms-factories went on strike and demanded an increase of wages. The agitation took a threatening turn. On the 10th Ventôse, at the meeting of the section of the Marchés, Bot the bootmaker, a member of the revolutionary committee, declared that if the food-shortage continued, they would have to go round the prisons, massacre the prisoners, and roast and eat them. There were widespread rumours of another September 2. Anonymous posters advised that the Convention should be dissolved for its incapacity and replaced by a dictator who should succeed in restoring plenty.

The Cordeliers believed that it would be easy for them to carry out another successful insurrection, which should place them in power. On the 14th Ventôse Carrier gave the signal: "Insurrection, a holy insurrection; that ought to be your rejoinder to the scoundrels!" Hébert once more uttered a lengthy denunciation of the Endormeurs on the committees, the ambitious persons who were protecting Chabot and Fabre and the seventy-five Girondins. Encouraged by Boulanger, second in command of the National Guard of Paris, who shouted: "Père Duchesne, have no fear;

455

we, we shall be the Pères Duchesne who strike the blow"; and urged on by Momoro and Vincent, who cried shame upon his weakness, he ventured to mention names: Amar, a nobleman, ex-treasurer to the king of France, who had paid two hundred thousand livres for his patent of nobility; the ministers Paré and Deforgues; Carnot, who wanted to get rid of Bouchotte and replace him by his "idiotic and malevolent" brother. He did not, however, dare to mention Robespierre by name, but he made a pointed allusion to him, and his conclusion was the same as Carrier's: "Yes, an insurrection, and the Cordeliers will not be the last to give the signal which shall be a death blow to the oppressors!" The Cordeliers draped the Declaration of the Rights of Man in black, to symbolize the oppression of which they said they were the victims.

But their appeal fell on deaf ears. The masses had no confidence in the efficacy of the guillotine in restoring plenty, and the commissaries of food-speculation were frankly unpopular on account of their vexatious proceedings. Momoro did indeed carry with him the section of Marat, which tried to rouse the Commune on the 15th Ventôse. But the Commune remained cold and hostile. Lubin, its president, lectured the petitioners and pronounced a eulogy on the committees. Chaumette advocated calm, and Hanriot repudiated the agitators. The vigilance committee of the department of Paris, though composed of ardent revolutionaries, who had taken part in the overthrow of the Girondins on June 2, issued a quantity of posters putting the populace on its guard.

The sudden aggression of the Hébertists surprised the Committee of Public Safety, but did not take it unawares. It decided to set the machinery of justice in motion at once, but, foreseeing that the citras would try to turn to their own profit the proceedings taken against the ultras, it openly announced from the outset that it would mercilessly combat both factions.

In a report which he made to the Convention on the 16th Ventôse, Barère pointed out that the food-shortage was the work of the very persons who were complaining of it, and proposed that legal proceedings should be instituted. The public prosecutor, he said, should at once open an inquiry as to those responsible for composing and distributing incendiary posters and for the distrust which had been aroused in the dealers and farmers who supplied Paris with food. "Let conspirators of every kind tremble! The faction of the Indulgents and the peace party (*Pacifiques*) ought to be watched just as much as that of the alleged Insurgents!" And he announced that Amar was at last about to lay before the Assembly his report on Chabot and his accomplices.

If the committee had not had those who were preaching insurrection

456

arrested on the spot, this was because Collot d'Herbois had taken upon himself to attempt a supreme effort at conciliation. The man responsible for the mass shootings at Lyons could not abandon the man responsible for the Noyades at Nantes without exposing himself. That very evening, at the Jacobins, he proposed to send a deputation to the Cordeliers, as in the time of Jacques Roux, to "induce them to execute justice on the schemers who had led them astray." The schemers, whose names Collot had scorned to mention, were present at the meeting. They had been preaching insurrection only two days before, but all they could do now was to abase themselves by an abject retractation. "Nothing was said about making insurrections," said Carrier, "except in case circumstances made it necessary. May I lose my head if any motion was proposed against the committee!"

On the 17th Ventôse a delegation from the Jacobins, headed by Collot, visited the Cordeliers. Momoro, Hébert, and Ronsin in turn made a public apology. The crape draperies covering the framed copy of the Rights of Man were torn down and handed over to the Jacobins as a sign of fraternity. The two clubs swore an "indissoluble union." It looked as if Collot had won the day.

But all the Cordeliers had not approved of their leaders' retractation. On the 19th Ventôse Vincent made a declamatory oration against "crom-wellistes," against skilful orators and their great speeches—that is to say, against Collot. There were stormy explanations at the club. Certain sections, dominated by Vincent's friends, continued the agitation—that of Brutus, for instance, which on the 21st Ventôse made a declaration to the Convention that it would stand its ground until all secret royalists, federalists, moderates, and indulgents were exterminated. On the same day the section of Finistère, composed of journeymen, demanded through their spokesman, Boulland, a decree for "deparalysing" the revolutionary army and trying food-speculators summarily.

On the 21st Ventôse the committees learnt from various quarters, and in particular from Haindel, an officer in the Germanic legion, that the Hébertists were really preparing for the insurrection which they had repudiated. They were to make their way into the prisons, slaughter aristocrats, then seize the Pont-Neuf and the Arsenal, assassinate Hanriot and his staff, and finally, after setting fire to the premises of the committees of the Convention, complete their operations by appointing a "grand judge"—that is to say, a sort of dictator—who should preside over executions and distribute the money found at the Mint and the Treasury among the people. Haindel named those who had tried to win him over to the plot, a student of surgery named Armand, a doctor named Beysser, etc. A general without a command, Laumur, confided to Westermann, in calling upon him for assistance, that men were being secretly brought to Paris from the revolutionary army and that the grand judge whom it was proposed to appoint was Pache.

Armed with these data, the committees decided to act without delay, so as to nip the plot in the bud. Billaud-Varenne, who had returned from his mission to Port-Malo, Couthon and Robespierre, who were just recovering from illnesses, were present, on the 22nd Ventôse, at a joint session, which approved the conclusions of the report in which Saint-Just was to pronounce an indictment against the two factions who were playing into the hands of the enemy. On the same evening Fouquier-Tinville was summoned before the committee, and on the following day, during the night of the 23rd–24th Ventôse, the chief Hébertist leaders were arrested amid general apathy. Most of the sections came and congratulated the Convention during the following days, and the Commune itself joined in their congratulations, though rather tardily.

The trial of the Hébertists, which lasted from the 1st to the 4th Germinal, was first and foremost a political trial. The charge first brought against them—that they were responsible for the famine—soon faded into insignificance before the fresh and infinitely more serious accusation of having planned an insurrection. In order to give colour to the former charge Hébert was linked with his friend Ducroquet, a commissary of food-speculation, and Antoine Descombes, an agent of the Commission of Supplies. In order to prove the charge of being in league with the enemy —for there could be no plot without Pitt and Coburg—Anacharsis Cloots, Proli, and Kock were included in the accusation, together with Desfieux, Pereira, and Dubuisson, secret agents of the Ministry for Foreign Affairs. The rest—Ronsin, Mazuel, Vincent, Leclerc, and Bourgeois, heads of departments of the Ministry for War, Momoro, etc.—were the leaders who were preparing the insurrection.

All of them were condemned to death except the police spy Laboureau, who was acquitted. The execution took place amidst an immense crowd, which shouted insults at the defeated factions. They died bravely, with the exception of Hébert, who showed signs of weakness.

The committees had resigned themselves to attacking the ultras only in self-defence. They forbade Fouquier to proceed against Hanriot, Boulanger, and Pache, who were implicated by certain of the depositions, and Carrier was not included in the indictment. They dreaded a reaction which might be turned to the profit of the Indulgents, whom they regarded as their most dangerous opponents. "The greatest danger," said Robespierre at the Jacobins on the 25th Ventôse, "would be a *rapprochement* between patriots and the cause of the conspirators." The decree of the 23rd Ventôse, arraigning the Hébertists before the Revolutionary Tribunal, contained double-edged provisions, artfully worded by Saint-Just; for example, the one declaring those who had given shelter to *émigrés* to be traitors to their country, and the one including in the same category those who might try to throw open the prisons. The former might apply to Danton, who had received in his house an *émigrée*, the Marquise de Charry. The latter might include all those who were calling for clemency.

At last, on the 26th Ventôse, Amar presented his report containing the indictment of the fraudulent speculators—that is to say, Chabot, Basire, Delaunay, Fabre, etc. His pettifogging report, which confined itself almost entirely to the financial side of the affair, satisfied neither Billaud nor Robespierre, who both regretted that he had not turned his attention to the political aims of this conspiracy of corruption. At the moment when the Hébertists were about to answer before Fouquier for the crime of having desired to degrade and dissolve the Convention, Billaud and Robespierre turned the same accusation against the swindlers and the Indulgents.

Unless we are to suppose that Danton had suddenly become deaf and blind, he must have been aware of what was going on. On the 4th and 8th Ventôse he had expressed, in threatening language, his intention of calling the committee to account. Suddenly he held his peace. Is it to be supposed that he looked favourably upon the insurrection of the Cordeliers and tried to join forces with Ronsin to overthrow the Government? There are a number of signs which so corroborate one another as to make it possible to believe that the secret understanding which the committees alleged to exist between the two branches of the conspiracy was not a fiction. General Laumur was an intimate friend of Westermann, in whom he confided. There were witnesses who afterwards deposed that Westermann had mentioned Danton as the grand judge. Ever since Danton had spoken in favour of the release of Ronsin and Vincent, a month before, the Hébertists had kept on good terms with him. Some of them were known to be followers of Danton's, and Carrier had praised him to Westermann.

However this may be, it was not until after the proceedings against the Hébertists that the Indulgents seemed to be alive to the situation. The plot had proved abortive, and danger was drawing near. Camille Desmoulins once more took up his pen. In Nos. 5 and 6 of the *Vieux Cordelier* he had been profuse in his retractations, but he now composed his No. 7

in quite a different spirit. He cried shame upon the Convention for its servility to the committees, indulged in an enthusiastic defence of British institutions, at the very moment when Robespierre was vilifying them, and recalled how an English jury had just acquitted the citizen Bennett, who had expressed a wish for the victory of France; whereas in France men were sent to the scaffold for merely using defeatist language. Finally he wound up with a violent attack upon Barère, who had refused to listen to the peace proposals of the powers. Passages in the manuscript found among his papers went still further. He accused the Committee of Public Safety of having chosen none but incompetent generals and having systematically dismissed and sent to the guillotine all those of any ability: Dillon, Custine, Dubayet, Harville, and Lamorlière. Once more he called upon all those who were weary of the Terror and the war to join in the struggle. His No. 7 amounted to an indictment of the committees, which he had recently been handling gently. But the committees were on the watch. Desenne, Desmoulins's printer, had his premises searched and was arrested on the 24th Ventôse. The committees were forewarned and forearmed.

On the 28th and 30th Ventôse the Indulgents did indeed attempt to resume their everlasting attack on Bouchotte and the agents of the committee. They even succeeded for a moment in obtaining a decree ordering the arrest of Héron, one of the chief agents of the Committee of General Security. But Couthon, Moyse Bayle, and Robespierre opposed the attack in turn. Couthon declared that "the moderates, who are at odds with their consciences, and consequently dread vigorous and revolutionary measures . . . desire the death of the Government" by depriving it of its best agents. Robespierre declared in a threatening tone that the committees would not suffer the sword of tyranny to touch a single patriot. He denounced those who desired to ruin the most ardent·revolutionaries by confounding them with Hébertism. "Only yesterday," he said, "a member burst into the Committee of Public Safety and with a fury which it is impossible to describe demanded three heads." Robespierre had no need to mention the name of this blood-thirsty Indulgent, but Héron was saved.

Was it as a consequence of this alarm that Billaud asked his colleagues on the committees to arrest Danton, who was, he said, the rallying-point of all counter-recolutionaries? It was only the resistance of Robespierre, who was averse from abandoning his old brothers in arms, that delayed this inevitable step for a few days. In order to prove to the mass of patriots that the trial of the Hébertists would not be to the advantage of reaction, it was absolutely necessary to carry out the threat which had for so long been hanging over the advocates of clemency.

It looks as if the latter, who had taken the alarm since the passage of the decree for the arraignment of Basire, Chabot, and Fabre, had staked their last hopes on Robespierre. Danton met him two or three times at the houses of Laignelot and Humbert. According to Courtois, Danton wept, and protested against the slanders which were being repeated with regard to his mission in Belgium and the increase of his fortune. "Believe me, Robespierre, shake off intrigue, and join the patriots," are the words attributed to him by Daubigni. But Robespierre, it appears, remained unmoved.

Westermann is said to have advised Danton to take the initiative, saying: "They will kill you." "They would not dare to attack me," replied Danton. Thereupon Westermann became pressing and proposed a *coup de main* against the committees. Danton refused: "Better a hundred times to be guillotined than to be a guillotiner!" Was this due to over-confidence, or weariness, or a conviction that after the failure of the Hébertist insurrection any other attempt at insurrection was doomed to the same failure? The intrepid Danton, though forewarned, stayed at home and waited inactive.

Billaud finally succeeded in overcoming Robespierre's last hesitations. The two committees held a joint session on the evening of the 10th Germinal and, after listening to an indictment drafted by Saint-Just and afterwards corrected by Robespierre, ordered the arrest of Danton, Delacroix, Philippeaux, and Camille Desmoulins, as the accomplices of Chabot, Fabre d'Eglantine, and the other swindlers whom they had defended. All the members present signed it except Rühl and Lindet.

The committees had risked a decisive move in which they were not sure of success. Since the execution of the Hébertists the citras had made great progress. Legendre was president of the Jacobins, and Tallien of the Convention.

At the opening of the session of the 11th Germinal Delmas demanded that the committees should be summoned to attend it. The Assembly gave the order, and Legendre, prompted by a letter received that very morning from Delacroix, at once pronounced an enthusiastic eulogy upon Danton: "I hold Danton to be as true a patriot (*aussi pur*) as myself." Murmurs were heard, whereupon Clauzel shouted: "President, uphold the liberty of opinion," to which Tallien replied theatrically: "Yes, I will uphold the liberty of opinion; yes, every man shall say freely what he thinks; we will

461

all remain here to save liberty!" Enthusiastic applause greeted these threatening words, and Legendre concluded with a proposal that the arrested deputies should be summoned to the bar of the Assembly and given a hearing before their accusers were allowed to speak. Fayau took offence at this motion, as creating a privilege. Neither the Girondins nor Chabot nor Fabre nor anybody else had been given a hearing before they were sent before the Revolutionary Tribunal. Why should there be two different standards? The Assembly hesitated, in a ferment of emotion. According to Courtois, he himself, Jean Debry, and Delmas, pointing at the members of the committees, vociferated: "Down with the dictators, down with the tyrants!"

But Robespierre ascended the tribune and made a speech thrilling with passion, of which the profound sincerity touched and subjugated the Assembly: ". . . They are trying to make you afraid of abuses of power— of that national power which you have exercised and which is not vested in a few men only. They are afraid that the accused persons may be oppressed; that is to say, they do not trust the national justice, they do not trust the men who have won the confidence of the National Convention, they do not trust the Convention which gave them this confidence, or public opinion, which sanctioned it. I say that he who trembles at this moment is guilty, for innocence is never afraid of the public vigilance. . . . They have tried to inspire terror in me, too; they have tried to persuade me that the danger which is approaching Danton might reach me too; he has been represented to me as a man to whom I ought to cling, as a shield who might defend me, as a rampart which, if once overthrown, would leave me exposed to the shafts of my enemies. People have written to me, Danton's friends have sent me letters and besieged me with their speeches. They have thought that the memory of a former connexion, my old-time faith in virtues which prove to be false, would induce me to slacken my zeal and my passion for liberty. . . . What do I care for danger? My life belongs to the country; my heart knows no fear; and if I were to die, it would be without reproach or ignominy." An ovation greeted these words, and Legendre made an abject retractation: "Robespierre knows me very little if he believes me to be capable of sacrificing an individual to liberty."

Amid a deep silence Saint-Just read out his indictment, which described in detail the suspicious past of the accused, their intrigues with Mirabeau, their secret dealings with the Court, their connexions with Dumouriez, the way in which they had been compromised with the Girondins, their equivocal behaviour at all the great crises—August 10 and May 31—their efforts to save the royal family, their insidious campaign in favour of clemency and peace, their covert opposition to all revolutionary measures, their complicity with swindlers, their association with dubious foreigners, and their perfidious attacks on the Government. Subsequent research has confirmed Saint-Just's judgment on almost all these points. The Convention approved his report unanimously.

But the final scene was to be played out before the Revolutionary Tribunal. The trial, like that of the Hébertists, lasted for four days, from the 13th to the 16th Germinal, but it was far more eventful. The process by which the fourteen defendants had been brought together at the same trial was not due to chance. There was no lack of good reasons for connecting Delacroix, Danton, and Desmoulins with Chabot, Basire, Delaunay, and Fabre. Hérault de Séchelles might have found a place in the same batch as the Hébertists, for he had been the friend and patron of Proli and Cloots, but he had been mentioned in the denunciations made by Basire and Chabot, and by linking him with Fabre, who had first denounced him, the committees had desired to draw attention by a striking example to the close and secret connexion between the ultras and the citras, and their joint complicity in the work of destroying the revolutionary Government. As for Philippeaux, he was expiating the accusations of treason which he had brought against the committee, and the exaggerated praises of Desmoulins. These leading personages were supplemented by a job lot of minor figures, mostly foreign agents. The presence of the Freys side by side with their brother-in-law, Chabot, was quite natural. The contractor d'Espagnac, the protégé of Chabot and Julien of Toulouse, and even of Danton, was not out of place at the trial of these fraudulant speculators. The adventurer Guzman, whom Danton had admitted to his intimacy, was there to act as a foil to him. And lastly Westermann, who had been involved in all the intrigues of Dumouriez and Danton, who was reputed to be guilty of pillage and robbery and had been denounced by Marat, was quite in keeping with the rest of the collection.

The financial side of the affair was gone into on the first day. Cambon appeared as witness for the prosecution, and Hermann, the president of the tribunal, read out some damning letters from d'Espagnac. The defendants hotly denied the charges and threw the blame on Julien of Toulouse, who had escaped prosecution by flight.

The second day was almost entirely taken up with the examination of Danton. The tribune had recovered all his arrogance. Not content with defending himself by lying boldly, he attacked his accusers, mocked them, threatened them, and carried things off with a bold front. "Vile impostors, come forth, and I will tear off the mask which protects you from being prosecuted in the public interest." His outbursts could be heard from the street, and an awed crowd gathered round. The judges and jury were uneasy. The Committee of Public Safety was ill at ease and gave Hanriot orders to arrest the president and the public prosecutor, who seemed to them guilty of weakness. Was not Fouquier a distant relation of Desmoulins, to whom he owed his appointment? But the committee changed its mind and finally cancelled the order, which had already been communicated to Hanriot. On the other hand, several members of the Committee of General Security went into court to lend the support of their presence to any judges or members of the jury who might be weakening.

The third day was devoted to the examination of the rest of the accused, who imitated Danton's tactics by demanding that the members of the Convention whom they had cited as witnesses should be given a hearing, and by provoking violent scenes. Fouquier, hard pressed, and badly supported by Herman, wrote a distracted letter to the Convention consulting it about summoning the witnesses demanded by the accused. By the time the committees received his letter, they already had in their hands a denunciation by which a prisoner in the Luxembourg, Laflotte, an ex-minister of the Republic in Florence, warned them that on the previous day two prisoners confined in the same room as himself, General Arthur Dillon and Simon, a member of the Convention, had tried to persuade him to join in a plot to deliver Danton and his friends. Dillon had communicated by letter with the wife of Desmoulins, who had provided a thousand écus for forming a crowd round the court. Dillon, Simon, and their associates were to gain possession of the keys of the Luxembourg and then go to the Committee of General Security and massacre the members. We now know that General Sahuguet, a cousin of d'Espagnac, who was on leave in the Limousin, had received a note from Dillon and d'Espagnac summoning him to return to Paris with all possible haste to aid in their deliverance. Barras informs us that several friends of Danton's, among them General Brune, had promised him to attend the court in force and carry him off. But they failed to answer the summons.

Armed with Fouquier's letter and Laflotte's denunciation, the committees sent Saint-Just to the Convention as their spokesman to describe the ferment among the accused and obtain the passage of a decree which should give the tribunal powers to exclude from the trial any prisoner who should resist or insult the national tribunals. The decree was passed unanimously, without discussion, and taken down to the court that same evening by Vadier in person.

On the following day, the 16th Germinal, Fouquier gave orders for the decree passed on the previous day and Laflotte's denunciation to be read out to the prisoners. The last of them—that is to say, the more insignificant ones—were questioned, and then Fouquier had the question put to the jury whether they considered themselves to be in possession of sufficient information. Danton and Delacroix protested vehemently: "We are going to be judged unheard! Let there be no deliberation! We have lived long enough and are ready to fall asleep on the bosom of glory! Let us be led to the scaffold!" They next cast aspersions upon the judges. The tribunal applied the decree and pronounced them to be excluded from the trial. All of them were condemned to death except Lullier, who stabbed himself in prison a few days later. If we may believe the depositions made at the trial of Fouquier by Renaudin and Topino-Lebrun, members of the jury, and by Paris the clerk, Herman and Fouquier entered the room in which the jury were deliberating and communicated to them a secret document which finally convinced those who were still hesitating.

The condemnation of the Indulgents and fraudulent speculators caused no apparent emotion among the people. They were led to execution amid complete indifference. How could Frenchmen of any shade of opinion take any interest in adventurers who, while serving and betraying the different parties in turn, had only worked for their own personal profit? Even the Thermidorian Convention was to refuse to rehabilitate Danton, Delacroix, Fabre d'Eglantine, Chabot, Basire, and Delaunay.

CHAPTER XII

The Reorganization of the Revolutionary Government

THE factions having been overthrown one after the other, the committees were rid of all inconvenient opposition for a few months. The Convention, which had been so importunate before, now acquiesced in all their proposals. The most important decrees were passed almost without discussion. The deputies kept silence and no longer took the initiative. The sessions were so lacking in interest that, in order to fill them, a secretary read out a lengthy précis of the correspondence. It was now that the dictatorship of the Government really began.

The administrative bodies of Paris were purged and filled with safe men, Payan, Moine, and Lubin taking the place of Chaumette, Hébert, and Réal, Pache being later replaced by Lescot-Fleuriot. The new authorities were docile, but, being composed of officials, they no longer represented the people. The popular societies of the sections, which had increased in number during the summer of 1793, were suspected of including a number of aristocrats masquerading in the cap of liberty, and disappeared during Floréal under pressure from the Jacobins, who withdrew their affiliation. Apart from the sections, which were open twice in every ten days, there was only one free platform left—that of the Jacobins. But it was closely watched, and nearly always occupied by officials of the Revolutionary Tribunal or the public departments. The new terrorist bureaucracy was all-pervading, and this became such a crying scandal that Dubois-Crancé proposed to exclude its members from the clubs. But when his letter was read at the Jacobins on the 13th Germinal, it created a fine disturbance and he was immediately denounced to the Committee of Public Safety as an Indulgent and a "disorganizer." The committees, and especially Saint-Just, were aware of the evil, but they could not shake themselves free of it. If the officials were driven out of the clubs, who would be left? The basis of the Government became narrower and proportionately more concentrated.

The press, which had still been so full of life and passion before Germinal, lost all independence. Nothing was left but official or semi-official journals, the latter more or less subsidized. So many journalists had lost their lives in consequence of their opinions that those who were left had learnt the value of prudence. As for the theatres, in future they played none but duly approved patriotic pieces.

The committees, then, governed with no apparent obstacle. But they had no illusions on the matter. They knew what was hidden beneath the rising tide of silence. "The Revolution has become paralysed," wrote Saint-Just in his *Institutions*. "All principles have become enfeebled; nothing is left but intriguers wearing the red cap of liberty. The methods of terrorism have deadened the sense of crime, as strong drinks deaden the palate."

What use would those forming the Government make of the unlimited power which they had bought so dearly? They first tried to precipitate matters. The revolutionary army of Ronsin, nicknamed "Cromwell," had alarmed them; so on the 7th Germinal they abolished it. Three ministers had been implicated in the doings of the factions: Bouchotte in those of the ultras, Deforgues and Paré in those of the citras. Carnot obtained the suppression of ministers, who were replaced by twelve executive commissions, each formed of two or three members and modelled on the type of the two already existing commissions, those for supplies and for arms and powder. The committee had opposed this measure on several occasions when it had been demanded by the Dantonists. Now that the latter were before the tribunal, the committee adopted it as its own, and nobody was found to point out the inconsistency.

The representatives on mission in the departments had often followed very divergent and even contradictory policies. On the 30th Germinal the committee simultaneously recalled twenty-one of them. It would have liked to carry on the administration solely by means of the national agents, whom it controlled. Saint-Just, who had a passion for uniformity, wrote in his *Institutions:* "We ought to inquire into the system of collective authorities, such as municipalities, administrative bodies, vigilance committees, etc., and see whether the secret of founding the Revolution on a solid basis is not to be found in assigning the functions of these bodies to a single official in each of them." But the time was not yet ripe for Bonaparte, with his prefects and mayors; and Saint-Just kept the idea which he had at the back of his mind to himself.

The committee desired at least to deprive the representatives on mission of the chief of their revolutionary powers—that of establishing special tribunals. The decree of the 27th Germinal, voted as a result of Saint-Just's report, ordered that those accused of conspiracy should in future be tried in Paris only, before the Revolutionary Tribunal. The decree of the 19th Floréal, proposed by Couthon, expressly abolished the revolutionary tribunals and commissions created by the representatives on mission. The committee, however, reserved the power of maintaining certain of them in exceptional cases; for instance, that organized by Joseph Lebon at Cambrai, behind the front of the army of the north, the commission sitting at Noirmoutier, etc.

The Committee did not mean to abate the Terror, but to concentrate it under its own immediate supervision. It was indignant and uttered threats when, after the arrest of Hébert, the rumour went round Paris that the busts of Marat and Chalier were about to disappear. In order to calm the misgivings of the terrorists it redoubled its attacks upon their persecutors. It recalled Fouché, in order to punish him for having included the friends of Chalier in the repressive measures for putting down Hébertism (7th Germinal), and it ordered the reopening of the club at Lyons which had been closed by Fouché. A decree drawn up by Robespierre suspended all proceedings against the patriots of Lyons who had been persecuted during the siege. When Fouché returned to Paris to vindicate himself before the Jacobins, Robespierre put them on their guard against his explanations (19th Germinal).

It was the same everywhere—for instance, at Sedan, Lons-le-Saunier, Lille, etc. The patriots were protected, while the repressive measures aimed at the enemies of the existing system were intensified. The decree of the 27th Germinal removed all former nobles and the subjects of enemy powers who had not obtained express permission to reside in Paris to a distance from the capital, as well as from all fortified towns in the war area and from ports. In order to punish the counter-revolutionaries of Vaucluse, the committee organized on the 21st Floréal the terrible commission of Orange, which tried cases without a jury and in forty-two sessions condemned to death 332 prisoners out of 591. It approved Maignet's action in burning down the counter-revolutionary village of Bédoin, where the tree of liberty had been cut down and no republican witness could be found.

The committee had made Terror the order of the day, but accompanied by its corrective, "Virtue." It took severe measures against corrupt revolutionaries. In Vaucluse Maignet discovered an immense "black band," the members of which, under cover of their official positions, were proceeding to pillage the national property. He knew that his predecessors, Rovère and Poultier, had extended their protection to these robbers masquerading in the cap of liberty. He did not hesitate to strike at their leader, Jourdan Coupe-Tête, in whose favour Tallien tried in vain to touch the hearts of the Jacobins on the 16th Floréal, and Jourdan was sent to the scaffold. Ysabeau, who was continuing Tallien's corrupt practices at Bordeaux, was recalled on the 25th Floréal. Bernard of Saintes, who had been involved in shady transactions at Montbéliard and Dijon, met with the same fate on the 15th Germinal. This was a warning to the tainted remnant of Danton's faction. The committee honoured virtue not only with its lips, but in its heart.

By this means it hoped to conciliate public opinion. It did not want its agents to strike terror to the masses. "It is necessary," said Saint-Just on the 26th Germinal, "that you should restore confidence in civil life. It is necessary that you should make it understood that revolutionary government does not signify war or a state of conquest, but the transition from evil to good, from corruption to probity." Harmless citizens were to be protected against the abuse of power and even against excess of zeal. The representatives on mission in the west had prolonged the insurrection of the Chouans by their "infernal columns," which burnt the property of the insurgents and of peaceable citizens indiscriminately; the committee therefore recalled them. Rossignol, who remained untouched so long as he was attacked by the Indulgents, was removed from his post on the 8th Floréal. Turreau, who had carried out the policy of devastation, and all his lieutenants, were recalled from the army of the west on the 24th Floréal, and on the 4th Prairial a new ordinance put an end to this system of extermination and replaced it by a system of declarations and returns of the inhabitants and crops.

In the department of Haut-Rhin, Foussedoire was trying to force the Alsatians to exchange their metallic currency for assignats. He asked for permission to establish a revolutionary tribunal and levy contributions on the rich; in reply to this he was recalled on the 12th Prairial. Foussedoire had not realized that terrorist methods were now to be reserved for conspirators only and were to be abolished for all who were not conspiring.

The proceedings of the Hébertists had aggravated the food-shortage. The committee now repudiated and abolished them and made it its business to restore confidence to the trading class. The decree of the 12th Germinal suppressed the commissaries of food-speculation, who were as much hated as the old tax-collectors had been, and mitigated the provisions and penalties of the law on food-speculation. Wholesale merchants alone were still forced to declare their supplies and post their prices. The division of the country into supply areas (*zones d'approvisionnement*) was abolished on the 6th Prairial except for corn and forage. The Commission of Supplies encouraged the export of luxury goods, consulted the trading classes about its measures, protected them against denunciations, entrusted them with missions abroad, and endeavoured to establish credits to pay for what they purchased. It is true that the committee kept the food-regulations and fixed prices in force. It controlled all foreign trade through its agencies and the mercantile marine, which it had commandeered. But it made legislation more elastic and inaugurated a policy of stimulating production. It encouraged manufacturers by subsidies and premiums, and traders by advancing them money. The food-shortage became less acute.

It was labour which now caused the greatest anxiety. The calling up of the first levy had decreased the available supply of workers, at the very moment when the increase in the number of factories and workshops engaged on work for the army had created a tenfold demand. The workmen had profited by this to obtain an increase of wages, which was in general greater than that of the cost of living. The establishment of the maximum wage certainly displeased the working-class as a whole, and particularly the many workers in the war factories, who were subject to strict discipline and could not evade the law as easily as the independent workers. It was too great a temptation to them to make the official wage correspond with that of the free workers. In Paris ordinary manual labourers, messengers, coachmen, and water-carriers earned from twenty to twenty-four livres a day, whereas specialized workers of the first grade in the arms-factories earned barely sixteen, those of the second grade eight livres five sous, and those of the lowest grade three livres. Thus it is not surprising that the workmen engaged in the numerous war factories in Paris lived in what may be called a permanent state of agitation. The committee, which urgently needed their services, raised their wages and allowed them to nominate commissaries to discuss them with its own agents, but it never succeeded in satisfying them, for the discrepancy between what they demanded and what was allowed by law was too great. The committee felt that if it yielded as regards the maximum wage, it would also be forced to give way as regards the maximum prices for commodities, so that the whole economic and financial structure which it had painfully built up would collapse. It therefore adopted an attitude of resistance towards the labouring class. If it occasionally yielded, it did so with a bad grace, and the new Commune followed its example. Payan, in the name of the Commune, lectured the free workmen who were forming unions (as may be seen in the Proceedings of the Commune for the 2nd, 13th, and 16th Floréal, etc.). It was necessary to stop the works undertaken by the departmental authorities of Paris, because the journeymen, whom they had intended to pay only forty-eight sous, demanded three livres fifteen sous, and the carpenters from eight to ten livres (9th Messidor).[1]

It seems, indeed, that the movement among the workers was general throughout the whole country. Refusals to work were so frequent that on the 15th Floréal Barère had to obtain the passage of a decree by the terms of which all those engaged in the handling, transport, and sale of goods of prime necessity might be requisitioned, and to threaten with the Revolutionary Tribunal those of them who, by their laziness, should form a criminal conspiracy against the food-supplies of the people.

"The system of the maximum," as M. G. Lefebvre has rightly observed, "was calculated to develop a spirit of class solidarity in the proletariate. It opposed the property-owning to the wage-earning classes." It did more than this. It tended to ruin small tradespeople and artisans, by reducing them to the position of wage-earners. Bakers, for instance, who received the official supply of flour became mere municipal employees. Saint-Just, who wanted to give the property of suspects to the poor, realized that the social problem was dominated by the financial problem. He would have liked to withdraw the assignats from circulation, for they were the weak spot in the Republic, giving rise to the high cost of living, speculation, the fixed prices which were starving the towns, and the requisitions which were provoking disorder among property-owners. But how could the assignats be dispensed with when they were, so to speak, the sole resource of the Treasury? By Floréal expenditure had risen to 283,419,073 livres, as opposed to receipts of 44,255,048 livres; in Messidor to 265,000,-000 as opposed to 39,000,000. The quantity of assignats in circulation was rising steadily. On the 26th Floréal it amounted to 5,534,160,385 livres, and in spite of the fixed values which supported the forced circulation, in spite of the closing of the Bourse, in spite of the ordinance of the 21st Pluviôse fixing the exchanges at a uniform rate, the republican currency was slowly becoming depreciated. Cambon made efforts to economize on the debt. In the previous year he had created the great book (*Grand Livre*) of the public debt for the purpose of converting the permanent debt of the old regime by exchanging it for fresh securities and thus republicanizing it; and now, by the law of the 23rd Floréal, he converted the terminable annuities, consolidated them, and reduced them by deductions, at the risk of provoking loud protests from the holders, who had already been seriously hit by the depreciation of the assignats, which they

---

[1] See National Archives, F. 10451.

were receiving in payment of their arrears. Cambon, thought Robespierre, was increasing the number of the Republic's enemies.

With the peasants crushed by requisitions and transport services, the workmen worn out by chronic underfeeding and fiercely bent upon winning a rate of wages refused them by law, the traders half ruined by the fixed prices, and the property-owners robbed by the assignats, a profound discontent was seething beneath the apparent calm. The only people to profit by the new regime were the growing crowd of agents of the new bureaucracy and those engaged in war manufactures.

The Government was under no illusion and nerved itself for a supreme effort. In spite of everything it intended to found the Republic in which it had put its faith, and loved all the more in proportion to its uncertainty about the future. It remembered that the monarchy had been shaken by the rising of the poor and needy under pressure of famine.

The application of the laws of Ventôse distributing the fortune of suspects among the poor sanculottes called for an extensive inquiry, which would take several months. On the 22nd Floréal, Barère announced that the revolutionary committees had already sent in their decision with regard to forty thousand prisoners. But there were three hundred thousand cases to be examined. Barère flattered himself that a return of the needy element in the population would be ready in less than six weeks. But it never was ready, although the committee created an Indigence Board (*bureau des indigents*) for the purpose. In spite of his optimism Barère drew attention to the unwillingness to carry out the law displayed by certain communes. A rumour had been set on foot that the committee was going to deport to the Vendée the needy persons mentioned in these returns. On the 22nd Floréal, pending the completion of the inquiry, the committee instituted the Book of National Benevolence (*Livre de la bienfaisance nationale*), in which were entered the infirm and disabled poor, who were to receive graduated relief and allowances in case of illness. An ordinance of the committee, dated the 5th Prairial, allotted relief to the infirm and disabled beggars of the city of Paris at the rate of from fifteen to twenty-five sous a day. But in the rest of the country there was great delay in opening the Book of Benevolence, and the 9th Thermidor arrived before the law had been carried into effect. In the eyes of the Government these partial measures were a mere prelude. "There ought to be neither rich nor poor," wrote Saint-Just. ". . . Opulence is an infamy." His project consisted in making the State the heir of those dying without direct relatives, abolishing the right of leaving property by will, and forcing all citizens to render a yearly account of how they used their fortune. In order to with-

472

draw the assignats from circulation he also wanted a special tax to be imposed "upon all those who have controlled affairs and been in the pay of the public treasury." Such plans remained mere dreams and were at variance not only with the individualist spirit of the time, but also with the necessities created by the war. How could the committee carry out a class policy consistently when, since Germinal, it had made it its aim to reassure all interests? The illiterate and needy masses over whom it brooded with such solicitude were a burden rather than a support to it. They looked on dully at events which were beyond their comprehension. Fundamentally, the whole policy of the Government was based upon the Terror, which nothing but the war could induce the country to tolerate. But the Terror was destroying the respect of the public for the existing system of government.

The committee concentrated its chief efforts upon the younger generation. On the 13th Prairial Barère declared that it was necessary to revolutionize the young as they had revolutionized the armies. Drawing his inspiration from the fortunate experiment of the school of arms, which, during Ventôse, by suitable courses of instruction in the manufacture of powder, saltpetre, cannon, etc., had trained in a month young men drawn from the whole of France, afterwards distributing them as foremen among the various workshops, it founded the School of Mars (*école de Mars*), for the purpose of giving training, both military and civic, to three thousand young men, half of them chosen from among the sons of small farmers or artisans and half from those of volunteers wounded on active service, in the ratio of six to every district. The School of Mars was to be carried on under canvas on the plain of Les Sablons.

There was also a project for creating a training-school for teachers (*école normale*) on the same model, for training professors and teachers inspired with the new revolutionary faith; but this was not carried into effect till after Thermidor. Meanwhile a sincere effort was made to apply the law of the 5th Nivôse, which rendered attendance at the primary schools obligatory and made the salaries of the teachers a charge on the State. But it was hard to staff the schools, and they were slow in opening. By the end of 1794 there were only a hundred and eighty districts in which there were a fair number of them. Saint-Just wanted to endow the schools out of the national property. He laid down the principle that before belonging to its parents the child belongs to the State, and drew up a project for a system of education on the Spartan plan.

The regions which offered the greatest resistance to the Revolution were those in which the population was ignorant of French: Alsace, the

473

Basque country, Corsica, the countship of Nice, Brittany, and Flanders. Barère instituted teachers of French for these regions, who were chosen by the clubs and were not only to teach the language of liberty, but at the same time to preach *civisme*. In this matter also the decree was only carried out to a limited extent, owing to the lack of suitable teachers. Grégoire desired that local dialects should be extirpated in the same way as foreign languages, for "unity of language is an integral part of the Revolution." On the 16th Prairial he composed a fine address to Frenchmen in the name of the Convention: "You detest political federalism; then abjure that of language."

By acting in this way they were working for the future, whereas the present called for all their attention. The religious question had not been solved. Freedom of worship prevailed in theory, but had been suppressed as a matter of fact in many regions. Many of the representatives on mission considered all priests suspect, interned them when they did not abandon their functions, and sometimes even ordered the church towers to be pulled down. Others had been more tolerant, and allowed public worship to continue. Attempts were made everywhere to supersede Sunday by the festival of the tenth day (*décadi*), but they were not always successful. The population of regions which had remained very religious regretted their priests and gave the patriotic festivals a cold reception. Even in the national workshops it was difficult to make the men work on Sundays. If the closing of the churches had taken place all at once, it would undoubtedly have provoked a great popular insurrection, for during the weeks preceding the decree of the 18th Frimaire, tardily though it was promulgated, there were a number of risings of devout Catholics; at Coulommiers and Amiens, for instance, and in the departments of Lozère, Haute-Loire, Loire, Corrèze, Hérault, Cher, Nièvre, Meuse, Ardennes, etc. The ferment lasted the whole winter and had not died down by spring. If it did not assume large proportions, this was due to the very lack of any coherent plan in the behaviour of the representatives on mission. The persecution was at no time general, so that it did not occur to the faithful to band themselves together. When their priests were taken from them, many parishes celebrated "blind" masses, as they were called, at which the sacristan or the schoolmaster officiated. Even in Paris worship never entirely ceased.

The committee, which had at first been unwilling to see anything but a foreign manœuvre in the dechristianizing movement, had no idea of reversing its policy now that the movement was almost complete. But it wanted to purify and perfect it and make it acceptable to the masses

474

by giving it a positive content. The tenth-day festivals had grown up at random. The objects of their celebration were liberty, country, and reason. The important thing was to give them a uniform organization and a common doctrine. The men of that age, even those who had emancipated themselves from the Christian dogmas completely, even atheists like Silvain Maréchal, did not believe that the State could dispense with a creed and a form of worship. They held that the State, like the Church in former days, had the cure of souls. It would be failing in its prime duty if it took no interest in men's consciences. It was necessary to connect the political morality taught at the civic ceremonies with a philosophic moral-ity, the fount of private virtue. It was the general conviction that faith in God was the foundation of society.

On the 25th Germinal, after Chaumette's execution, the Convention decreed that the remains of the author of the profession of faith of the Savoyard Vicar [2] should be transferred to the Panthéon. Robespierre had been charged to submit to the Convention the desired decree concerning the tenth-day celebrations, and did so on the 18th Floréal, prefacing it with a touching speech which aroused the enthusiasm of the Assembly and the country. In it he affirmed that the Revolution was now in possession of a philosophic and moral doctrine and would no longer have anything to fear from an aggressive revival of the old dogmatic religions. He pre-dicted the approaching end of all priesthoods, and the reconciliation of all Frenchmen in the pure, simple worship of the Supreme Being and Nature; for, in his eyes, God and Nature were one. In the future every tenth day would be set apart for the glorification of a civic or social virtue, and the Republic would furthermore celebrate the four great anniversaries of July 14, August 10, January 21, and May 31.

Robespierre was elected president of the Convention on the 16th Prairial by a unanimous vote, which exceeded all recent majorities (485), and presided, with a bunch of flowers and an ear of wheat in his hand, over the magnificent festival in honour of the Supreme Being and Nature which took place on the 20th Prairial (normally Whitsunday) amid a vast concourse of people. Similar festivals were celebrated throughout the whole of France on the same day, with equal success. The republican temples everywhere inscribed above their doors: "The French people recognizes the Supreme Being and the immortality of the soul." It seemed as though the committee had achieved its object of rallying all French-men in a general sentiment of pacification and fraternity. Men of all

---

[2] Jean-Jacques Rousseau.

parties sent enthusiastic congratulations to Robespierre. Boissy d'Anglas publicly compared him to "Orpheus teaching mankind the principles of civilization and morality." Laharpe, the fashionable man of letters, did homage to him in a private letter. Nor were atheists, such as Lequinio and Maréchal, the last to applaud. On the other hand, a number of Catholics declared their satisfaction, since in default of their priests God had been restored to them. They saw in the early and abundant harvest a sign that Providence was protecting the Republic. The last services celebrated by the priests disappeared without disturbance and were replaced by civic masses. Priests over sixty years of age or infirm, who had hitherto been left at liberty, were now interned by the decree of the 22nd Floréal. The impression produced abroad was extraordinary. "It was really believed," says Mallet du Pan, "that Robespierre was going to heal the breach caused by the Revolution." People were all the readier to believe this since the French armies were everywhere victorious. They had not heard the sarcasms and threats uttered by a few deputies against the president of the Convention during the festival of the Supreme Being. They could not see that hatred and envy lurked beneath the brilliant adornment of wreaths, flowers, hymns, addresses, and speeches, and that the interests which were still menaced by the Terror and could find no use for Virtue were only awaiting an opportunity to take their revenge.

CHAPTER XIII

Fleurus

REVOLUTIONARY France would not have accepted the Terror had it not been convinced that it would never achieve victory unless it consented to the suspension of its liberties. It resigned itself to the dictatorship of the Convention, and afterwards to that of the committees, in the hope that its sacrifices would not be in vain; and it was not mistaken.

In the spring of 1794 it might well be proud of the army which was now ready for service. This army was homogeneous. All distinctions between troops of the line and volunteers had disappeared, even as regards uniform. Brigading had started and was proceeding rapidly. The demibrigade, consisting of two battalions of volunteers and one line battalion, was a serviceable unit consisting of three thousand men, provided with light artillery, and more mobile than the former regiments. The general staffs had been purged and confidence was now established between officers and men. The commanding officers, many of whom had risen from the ranks, set an example in enduring privations. They slept under canvas and lived like the sansculottes. The friction formerly existing between the generals and the representatives on mission had disappeared. The representatives were now carefully selected and suceeded in making themselves obeyed without acting harshly. They interested themselves in the well-being of the troops and inspired them with their own civic ardour, even placing themselves at the head of the attacking columns. Discipline had been restored everywhere by exemplary punishments, and the women who had crowded into the camps and devoured their provisions had been sent away. A close watch was kept over the contractors; private enterprise was replaced by govenment control, and the inspectors-general of transport, who operated in pairs, were putting an end to embezzlement. The purified army, inspired by an ardent patriotism, had become a pliant and docile instrument in the hands of Carnot. Its effective strength had been doubled by the first levy, the recruits of which had been trained during the winter and drafted into the old battalions in the spring. Eight hundred thousand men were ready for service, trained, incorporated in their units, disciplined, and full of contempt for the mercenaries of the Coalition. There was no further risk that they would be checked in their successes, like Hoche after Kaiserslautern, by lack of arms and munitions. The war factories, organized scientifically, though in feverish haste, were beginning to yield their full output. The Parisian factory alone turned out 2,699 new guns between the 21st and 30th Ventôse, and repaired 1,497. The seven other factories in the provinces produced about the same quantity. Thanks to the saltpetre manufacture started under the Revolution, the huge powder-factory of Grenelle, the largest in Europe, produced from six to eight thousand pounds of powder a day during Prairial, and twenty thousand by Messidor.

The committee felt that victory was at hand. Its diplomacy was not inactive, but only aimed at definite and attainable objects. It was first placed at the service of the country's economic needs. France was threatened with total blockade. She could only provide for the subsistence of her armies and procure supplies for her industries by keeping open communications with the rest of the world. She therefore devoted her energies to cultivating the friendship of the Swiss, the Scandinavian countries, the Hanse towns, the Americans, the Barbary States, the Genoese, and the Turks. Perregaux, Schweitzer, and Humbert, the agents of the committee, were constantly travelling through Switzerland, buying up horses, cattle, forage, stuffs, iron, copper, etc. Through Switzerland the produce of Swabia and even of Austria found its way to Belfort. The English, whose fleet commanded the Mediterranean and who had just taken possession of Corsica, endeavoured to prevent the Genoese from sending supplies to the Mediterranean ports of France and the army of the Alps. The committee kept Genoa neutral by threatening it with the French army, advancing along the Apennines. In order to attract the traders of the Hanse towns, the Americans, and the Scandinavians to the Atlantic ports of France the committee returned those of their ships which had been put under an embargo or declared lawful prize, paid more than the maximum price for the wheat it imported from them, and facilitated the export of French goods to them, such as wine, brandy, silk, coffee, etc. It sent a strong mission to the United States to buy wheat, which was paid for out of the credits which France still maintained in that country since the War of Independence. Washington, whose misgivings had been removed by the recall of Genêt, was now requested to recall his ambassador in Paris, Morris, of whose hostility the committee was aware. He complied with the request and appointed Monroe, who did not arrive till just after the 9th Thermidor.

Neutral vessels approaching the coasts of France were molested by English cruisers. The committee therefore encouraged Bernstorff, the Danish minister, to form a league of neutrals with Sweden and the United States in order to uphold the freedom of the seas. Bernstorff signed a convention with Sweden. But Grouvelle, the French agent at Copenhagen, committed the imprudence of entrusting to the ordinary post his dispatches for Paris, which were not in cipher, and they were seized by the English cruisers. Pitt was thus informed of the negotiations, which were already far advanced, and managed to avert the danger by resorting to threats. He was seconded, moreover, by the American Hamilton, the friend of Washington, who feared that his country might be compromised by dealing with the Jacobins.

England, together with her allies, Spain and Holland, possessed an enormous naval superiority. But even after the catastrophe at Toulon the committee did not despair. Vigorously pressed on by Saint-André and Prieur of Marne, who took up their quarters at Brest, the construction of new ships was carried on with enthusiasm, the gaps due to the emigration of officers of noble birth were filled up with officers from the mercantile marine, the pay of the sailors and workmen was increased to induce them to work night and day, the bad discipline which had wrought havoc was severely repressed, and cordage, tar, wood, and copper were commandeered throughout the whole of France. By spring the fleet concentrated at Brest was fit not only to protect the coasts against a landing of reinforcements, which would set the Vendée ablaze, but also to escort convoys and even to resume the offensive. Meanwhile French privateers inflicted considerable losses upon enemy trade.

The progress of the French army and navy struck neutral or enemy observers with wonder and astonishment. The American agent William Jackson described them in detail to his friend Pinckney in a long report of April 1794. After describing the "splendours" of revolutionary France he already expresses the fear that, intoxicated by the victories which he predicts, she may allow herself to be drawn into a policy of conquest. About the same time, on March 9, 1794, the clear-sighted Mercy-Argenteau addressed a prophetic warning to his master the Emperor. He already saw that the Coalition could find salvation only if it used the same means as were succeeding so well for the French, and advised an appeal to the German nation.

On January 20, 1794 the Emperor communicated to the Diet a proposal for a general armament of the German people. But his proposal met with no success. However passive they might be, the peoples of central

Europe felt in a confused way that the cause of the kings was not their own. In spite of a rigid censorship the catchwords of Jacobinism had found a response. In Hungary a democratic priest named Martinovicz, affiliated with Weishaupt's Illuminati, and an ex-officer, Lazcovich, who hated the German yoke, founded a secret society recruited from the middle classes, and even from the nobility, which applauded the French victories. Recruiting for the army became harder every day, and the loans met with no greater success, for the middle classes tightened their purse-strings. In Prussia, where the industrial system was a recent creation of Frederick the Great, the war led to acute unemployment, and there was unrest among the Silesian weavers, rioting taking place at Breslau in April 1794. In some places the peasants refused to pay their seigniorial dues. This agitation prompted Frederick William to reject the Austrian proposal for recruiting the masses. The Belgians were lukewarm, and the rich abbeys responded with no enthusiasm to appeals for subsidies. It was only in Great Britain that the war against France was of a national character, and even there—especially in Scotland—there was still stubborn opposition, which Pitt could crush only by emergency legislation and severe repression.

The Coalition, whose whole strength was based upon mercenary armies, had never been very united; it was now on the eve of falling to pieces.

However much Frederick William might hate the sansculottes, he none the less listened to those of his counsellors who represented to him that the real enemy was Austria, not France. He demanded that his allies should pay him back what he was spending for military purposes, and threatened to withdraw his troops if they did not do so on the spot. Thugut refused. "Physically speaking, we haven't a penny," he wrote to Mercy on April 1, 1794. But in order to prevent the defection of Prussia, Pitt pledged himself to pay the large sums demanded. Holland followed the example of Prussia and, backed up by England, demanded of Austria a rectification of frontier in the Netherlands. Spain was obstructive. Her admirals and generals had had violent disputes with their English colleagues at Toulon. Godoy refused to grant Pitt the proposed commercial treaty; Aranda advised making peace and was exiled from court on a charge of conspiracy. English money was the only cement which could keep the tottering Coalition together.

The cracks were still further widened by an unexpected blow. On March 24 Kosciuszko entered Poland with a little band equipped in Saxony, and called his fellow-countrymen to arms. He obtained a surprise victory over the Russians at Raslovice on April 4, and drove them out of

Warsaw on the 19th and Vilna on the 23rd. But the Polish people failed to rise. Kosciuszko, who had not dared to abolish serfdom and who spared the interests of the nobles because they alone had responded to his appeal, did not succeed in collecting more than seventeen thousand men, who were, moreover, badly armed. His hazardous coup did not make it necessary for the Prussians or Austrians to withdraw a single soldier from the French front, and in a few weeks the Polish bands were dispersed. But this unexpected apparition of the Polish question between the two allies at Berlin and Vienna aggravated their latent disagreements.

The discords within the Coalition reacted upon their plan of campaign and their operations. There was constant bickering among the generals, none of whom would obey any orders but those of his own court, as is shown by a dispatch from Trautmannsdorf to Kaunitz, dated May 19, 1794. The English, who were finding the money for the Prussian army, wanted to make use of it to protect the Netherlands and Holland. The Emperor opposed this, out of distrust of the intentions of the Court of Berlin, which desired to prevent too great a dismemberment of French territory and so to deprive Austria of the fruits of her victory. "If we were to summon the Prussian army to the Meuse," wrote Thugut to Stahremberg on May 1st, "and establish a close connexion with it, based upon joint operations, it is evident that the King would still be in a position to check progress which he might consider too rapid, and bring us to a stop at the very moment when a fortunate turn of events might offer us some hope of achieving our great object, the weakening of France." The Prussian army was therefore to remain in the Palatinate, opposite the Sarre, and Coburg would content himself with Blankenstein's little corps, which was defending Treves and securing his communications with the Netherlands.

Coburg, however, received orders to march on Paris with his whole force. He already held Condé, Valenciennes, Le Quesnoy, and the Forest of Mormal—that is to say, the approaches to the gap of the Oise. His front was driven like a wedge into French territory between the Sambre and the Scheldt, between the two republican armies of the north and of the Ardennes, so that he was able to manœuvre on inside lines. But he had not entire control of his forces; he had to reckon with the Duke of York and the Prince of Orange, who were acting in connexion with him. Besides, the sansculottes possessed a constantly increasing superiority in numbers. As early as the end of May he demanded reinforcements. Pitt refused them, advising the Austrians to make use of the Prussians, whom they had not wanted. Instead of reinforcements, which never arrived,

Coburg received the young Emperor, who came to encourage his troops by his presence. As early as the middle of May, Mack, the head of Coburg's general staff, advised Francis II to make peace. After the first reverses, we learn from a letter from Waldeck to Thugut of June 14, the English, Dutch, and Hanoverians wanted to leave the main army and hasten to the support of the coast towns which were threatened. The situation was decidedly favourable to the revolutionary troops.

Carnot's instructions were that the decisive blows were to be struck at Coburg. Jourdan had come to a stop after his victory at Wattignies, as Hoche had done after the capture of Worms. Carnot, weary of ordering him in vain to attack Flanders, deprived him of his command on the 20th Nivôse, as he was to do to Hoche two months later, as a punishment for failing to carry out the offensive against Treves. But whereas Hoche, who was reputed to be a Hébertist, was sent to prison, Jourdan was again sent for on the 20th Ventôse and given the command of the army of the Moselle. On the 17th Pluviôse Pichegru, who was more pliant but less straight-forward, was placed at the head of the army of the north, with the army of the Ardennes subordinate to him. Thus he had control of the two arms of the vice which was to crush Coburg between the Lys and the Scheldt. Carnot increased his effective forces, and by Germinal he had at his disposal more than 250,000 men, commanded by such lieutenants as Marceau, Kléber, Vandamme, Souham, and Macdonald. In order to stimulate their ardour Saint-Just and Lebas were sent to the army, which they inspired with their own enthusiasm. On the 11th Pluviôse Carnot reminded all the generals of his instructions. "The great blows are to be struck by the army of the north. The armies of the Rhine and Moselle are to co-ordinate their movements with it. General rule: to act in mass formation and take the offensive. Join action with the bayonet on every occasion. Give battle on a large scale and pursue the enemy till he is utterly destroyed." For other reasons besides strategic ones he was anxious for an offensive. The food-shortage in the country was acute. On the 11th Germinal he wrote to the representatives on mission with the army of the north: "I ought not to hide from you that we are lost if you do not very soon enter the enemy's territory in order to obtain supplies and goods of every kind, for France cannot long hold out against the strained conditions in which she is existing at present. . . . We must live at the enemy's expense or perish. The defensive spells dishonour and ruin." Carnot never ceased urging Pichegru to forestall the attack of the imperial troops; but Pichegru wasted a month in inspections and did not attack till the 9th Germinal, in the direction of Le Cateau, and was driven back with a loss.

Coburg laid siege to Landrecies. All the diversions attempted with the object of raising the siege were a failure, and Landrecies capitulated on the 11th Floréal after a bombardment of four days. The imperial troops had gained a fresh bridge-head on the Sambre.

Without losing any time Saint-Just and Lebas organized an entrenched camp at Guise, to bar the way to Paris. Cambrai, which was being hard pressed, contained many royalists, and Carnot suspected treachery. A month earlier Vandamme had sent Carnot two letters promising him 240,000 livres as the price of his aid. Saint-Just and Lebas sent their colleague Joseph Lebon into Cambrai as their delegate, to set the guillotine to work against the enemies within its walls. Carnot next ordered Jourdan to march to the relief of the army of the Ardennes with all the forces he could withdraw from the army of the Moselle, which was to remain on the defensive behind the Sarre while awaiting reinforcements from the west. At the same time Carnot recommended to Pichegru a vigorous offensive on both wings, against Courtrai and Ypres on the one hand, and Charleroi on the other. The republicans entered Courtrai on the 7th Floréal and Furnes on the 10th, and defeated the imperial troops before Tourcoing on the 29th, capturing sixty cannon and two thousand prisoners. Five times the army of the Ardennes, rallied by Saint-Just, crossed and recrossed the Sambre in a furious struggle. Charleroi was besieged and relieved in turns. But now Jourdan came up. He drove the imperial troops out of Dinant on the 10th Prairial, and three days later effected a junction with the army of the Ardennes. The republicans crossed the Sambre for the sixth time, and Charleroi capitulated on the 7th Messidor. Coburg, who hurried to its relief with his main army, tried on the following day to drive the republicans out of the fortified positions which they had prepared on a front of thirty kilometres, forming an arc of a circle cut, as it were, by the Sambre. His five attacking columns were thrown back on the left by Kléber, on the right by Marceau and Lefebvre, and in the centre by Championnet, and afterwards cut down between the redoubts by the sabres of Hautpoul's cavalry. The French lay down to sleep on the battlefield of Fleurus and maintained possession of Charleroi.

On the 29th Prairial the army of the north had taken Ypres, with eighty cannon and 5,800 prisoners, and on the 15th Messidor entered Ostend. The two victorious armies of Pichegru and Jourdan started on their converging march upon Brussels, which they entered on the 20th Messidor, Antwerp and Liége falling on the 6th Thermidor.

Not a week went by now without one of Barère's Carmagnoles announcing to the Convention some fresh success from all the frontiers: on the 5th Floréal Badelanne recaptured the St. Bernard pass from the Piedmontese, on the 9th Floréal the army of the Alps took Saorgio, on the 15th Prairial the army of the western Pyrenees drove the Spaniards out of the camp of Les Aldudes, on the 1st Prairial Mont Cenis was captured, on the 9th Prairial Collioure, Saint-Elne, and Port Vendres were re-captured by the army of the eastern Pyrenees, etc.

On the 25th Prairial Saint-André and Prieur announced that the great convoy of wheat expected from America had arrived at Brest. In order to protect it on the voyage the French fleet under Villaret-Joyeuse had fought a sharp action with the English fleet under Howe on the 9th Prairial, during which the *Vengeur du peuple* had gone down amid shouts of *"Vive la République!"* The English had met with such losses that they did not follow up the French and were forced to return to their ports.

It is true that at the beginning of Prairial the two armies of the Rhine and the Moselle had suffered a severe shock, Möllendorf and his Prussians having driven the French out of Kaiserslautern. But Hentz and Goujon were sent up hurriedly with instructions to win a victory or die in the attempt. On the 14th and 15th Messidor the two French armies resumed the offensive simultaneously under the command of Moreaux. On the 25th Messidor the Prussians, sheltered behind their entrenchments, were driven out of Trippstadt by furious charges, and the French re-entered Pirmasens and Kaiserslautern.

By the end of Messidor the war was once more carried into the enemy's territory beyond the Alps and Pyrenees. Augereau invaded the Ampurdan while Müller marched on Fuentarrabia, which he entered on the 14th Thermidor. The army of Italy was reinforced, and prepared to invade Piedmont.

The character of the war had changed. It was no longer, as in 1792, a question of stirring up revolution among the peoples and turning them into the allies of the Republic. "We have to live at the expense of the enemy; we are not entering his territory to take him our money," wrote Carnot to the representatives on mission on the 8th Prairial. There was an end of propagandism. J.-B. Lacoste and Baudot organized a systematic exploitation of the Palatinate. "Evacuation agencies" dispatched to France 2,000 sacks of cereals. 4,000 oxen, a million pints of wine, 120,000 rations of hay, 600,000 rations of straw, etc. Eighty thousand men lived on the inhabitants for two months, not to speak of the war contributions levied on them: three millions on the Duchy of Zweibrücken (Deux-Ponts), two millions on Bliescastel, four millions on the *grand bailliage* of Neustadt, all, needless to say, in metallic currency. The same rules were

484

applied to Belgium. "We must strip the country," wrote Carnot on the 15th Messidor, "and make it impossible for it to provide the enemy with the means of returning. . . . Remember that the infamous Dumouriez caused us to lose a thousand millions of our money there." Jourdan, who was in command of the army of the Sambre-et-Meuse, as the army of the Ardennes had been rechristened, received orders on the 26th Messidor to levy a contribution of fifty millions in metallic currency on Brussels. Tournai was to pay ten millions, and so on.

Yet the committee was inspired by no spirit of conquest. It wanted the war to pay its own expenses, but it had no idea of annexing the occupied territories. "We are marching," said Billaud-Varenne on the 1st Floréal, "not to conquest, but to victory; not that we may be carried away by the intoxication of triumph, but that we may cease our blows the very moment that the death of an enemy soldier becomes useless to liberty." The committee did not want the Republic to be ruined by militarism. When Milhaud and Soubrany proposed to conquer Catalonia and annex it to France, Couthon replied on the 7th Prairial: "It seems to us more in conformity with our interests and principles to try to turn Catalonia into a little independent republic, which, under the protection of France, will serve as a barrier at the point where the Pyrenees end. This arrangement would no doubt be flattering to the Catalonians, and they will adopt it even more readily than union with France. . . . In the mountains you must extend our boundaries as far as possible, consequently establishing yourselves for good in the whole of the Cerdagne, the valley of Aran— in short, all that lies on this side of the mountains. . . . But if Catalonia became a French department it would be as difficult to keep as what was formerly Roussillon is today." The committee, which was waging war upon foreign languages in the provinces conquered by the former monarchy, had no anxiety to annex populations which their language as well as their customs would make it hard to assimilate. It wanted France to remain one and indivisible.

"In Belgium," explained Carnot on the 2nd Thermidor to the representatives on mission with the armies of the north and of the Sambre and Meuse, "we want to keep only as much as will secure our own frontier— that is to say, on the left the whole of West Flanders and Dutch Flanders, on the right the country between the Sambre and Meuse, and in the centre only what lies on this side of the Scheldt and the Haisne—so that Antwerp and Namur may be the two supporting points, the frontier bending inwards in a circle, well covered by rivers, and so that the enemy will be unable to enter without finding himself surrounded in the very act."

It can be seen upon what bases the committee would have negotiated peace had it still been in power when peace was concluded. England would no doubt have vetoed the handing over of Antwerp to France. But Austria, which was not anxious to keep Belgium, could easily have been given compensation in Germany for the slight cessions demanded by Carnot. If the frontier of Alsace and Lorraine had been kept unchanged, Austria would have been able to sign the continental peace at the same time as Prussia and Spain, which were showing an increasing unwillingness to continue the war in the interest of England.

The 9th Thermidor was not only fatal to the internal consolidation of democracy; it also prolonged the struggle abroad and launched France upon a policy of conquest which was to make her hated by the nations, and ultimately led to her exhaustion.

The Committee of Public Safety had achieved victory by the Terror. But if the Terror proved itself to be an efficacious instrument when put to the test, it was because those who wielded it had remained united in a common consciousness of the national needs. On the day when by some unhappy chance their union ceased, or personal passions triumphed in their hearts over the public weal, the Terror would be dishonoured and become no more than a common weapon, which might in case of need be seized by unworthy hands and used to stab the best citizens.

CHAPTER XIV

Thermidor

THE revolutionary Government was a hydra with two heads, for the two Committees of Public Safety and General Security which constituted it possessed in principle equal powers and were bound to hold joint sessions to give their decision on questions of major importance. But the balance had gradually been overset in favour of the Committee of Public Safety. Billaud-Varenne and Robespierre did not hesitate to censure Amar in public for the inadequacy of the report on Chabot which he had drawn up for the Committee of General Security, and even obtained a decree from the Convention that his report should not be printed till it had been revised and corrected. Amar was bound to cherish a feeling of keen resentment at being treated like a schoolboy, especially since he could not be ignorant of the criticisms which, though not publicly expressed, were made by his censors among themselves on the strange way in which he had handled the grave affair entrusted to his care.[1] The suspicion of which Amar was the object recoiled upon the committee which had chosen him as its organ. From this time onwards it was the members of the Committee of Public Safety who took charge of the more important reports, even when they were concerned with matters more properly lying within the sphere of the Committee of General Security. It was Saint-Just who fulminated against the Hébertist and Dantonist conspiracies. It was also Saint-Just who introduced the report on the great law of the 27th Germinal on "the repression of conspirators, the removal of nobles, and general police measures," and this law sanctioned fresh encroachments on the part of the Committee of Public Safety. So far it had been confined to administration, but now, by Article 1 of this law, it obtained the same rights of tracing the accomplices of conspirators and citing them before the Revolutionary Tribunal as the Committee of General Security. They were further charged, by Article 5, "to take measures for the inspection of the authorities and public agents whose duty it is to co-operate with the

---

[1] For this subject see my book *L'Affaire de la Compagnie des Indes.*

administration," and by Article 19 they were obliged "to demand a strict account from all agents, to take proceedings against those who may abet plots or use the power entrusted to them in a way subversive of liberty." By these provisions the Committee of General Security lost the right of maintaining discipline among the numerous army of officials. The Committee of Public Safety at once organized a board of administrative surveillance and disciplinary control and entrusted the dictatorship of it to Saint-Just, whose place when on mission was taken sometimes by Couthon, sometimes by Robespierre. Amar and his friends on the Committee of General Security complained bitterly of the "triumvirate" which had ousted them. They maintained—though this was not in accordance with the facts—that the disciplinary measures of the triumvirate thwarted their own; and this was how the friction began.

If the Committee of Public Safety had remained united, it might have ignored the ill humour of that of General Security. But the eleven members of which it was composed had personalities too strong, too imbued with the consciousness of the services they had rendered, to tolerate with patience the pre-eminence of one of their number who appeared to eclipse the rest. Whether by his own seeking or not, Robespierre had become the real head of the Government in the eyes of all revolutionary France. His popularity, which had always been considerable, had increased out of all proportion since the fall of the factions which he had attacked to their face. But Robespierre, whose whole character was instinct with an impassioned sincerity, did not always spare the self-esteem of his colleagues in the Government. Severe to himself, he was equally so to others. Reservations and criticisms were more frequent upon his lips than compliments. Since he had been so cruelly deceived in his friends, he now refused to make any until he was sure of his ground; he rarely gave his confidence and maintained towards most people a cold and distant reserve which might have been mistaken for calculation or ambition. He felt himself to be misunderstood, and suffered from it. By a weakness which shows plainly that his character was not an overbearing one, he often vindicated himself and replied to the secret criticism which he suspected, and, by so speaking of himself, laid himself open to the accusation of ambition, which was a torture to him.

Since this facile but terrible accusation of ambition had been formulated by the Girondins and repeated by the Hébertists, it had never ceased to be current among those who had cause, or imagined themselves to have cause, to complain of this influential man, whose power they still further exaggerated. In this heavily charged atmosphere the tide of suspicion kept rising. The stern Carnot wrote in his report of the 12th Germinal: "Woe to a republic in which the merit of a single man, or even his virtue, should have become necessary!" And the straightforward Billaud-Varenne echoed him as follows on the 1st Floréal: "Every people jealous of its liberty ought to be on its guard against the very virtues of the men occupying eminent posts." Carnot had not labored the point; but Billaud, as though the danger which he pointed out were near at hand, expatiated at length on the tyrants of ancient Greece. "That knave Pericles," he said, "concealed beneath a show of popular sympathies the chains which he forged for the Athenians; for a long time he made men believe that he never ascended the tribune without saying to himself: 'Remember that you are about to speak to free men'; yet this same Pericles, having succeeded in seizing absolute power, became the most blood-thirsty despot." More than one of his audience realized that Billaud was aiming at Robespierre.

To all appearance the Convention had been silenced, but intrigue was rife. The proconsuls who had been recalled for their exactions were uneasy at the decree making virtue and honesty the order of the day. They had as allies all those of their colleagues who had been concerned in the Hébertist and Dantonist plots and who feared that they too might be sent before Fouquier-Tinville. Opposition was gradually taking shape beneath the surface, with fear as its motive force and binding medium. If Robespierre had been nothing but an ambitious man, it was a fine opportunity for him to create himself devoted adherents among these tremblers who courted his protection. Fréron, Barras, Tallien, Fouché, who were to be his most formidable opponents, paid him visits and wrote him imploring letters. By removing their misgivings he might have brought them to his feet and attached them to his fortunes; but he contemptuously repelled them. What is more, he made no attempt to conceal the fact that he was working for their punishment. Their crimes had been a stain on the Terror and had made the Republic hideous in men's eyes. And Robespierre, who desired with all his soul to found a real democracy, was convinced that nothing but great examples would rally public opinion, which was in a state of perplexity. The wretches who had abused the unlimited powers entrusted to them for the public salvation ought not to be raised above the justice of the Revolution, which had the right to be terrible only so long as its operation was general and impartial, meting out equal justice to all the guilty, the most powerful and the humblest alike.

The proconsuls who had been recalled asked that their operations should be approved, whereupon the Convention referred them to the two committees. Not only did Robespierre refuse to grant this approval to those most deeply involved, but he maintained that four or five of them must be sent before the Revolutionary Tribunal.

If we are to believe the explanations offered after Thermidor by the surviving members of the committees, the latter seem at first to have consented to the arrest of Alquier, but immediately afterwards changed their minds and decided, in principle, that they would consent to the arrest of no more deputies. Barras, on the other hand, maintains, in an autograph page of his memoirs, that Robespierre refused to sign a list of thirty-two deputies to be arrested, and that this list had been drawn up in the Committee of General Security. At the time, Robespierre stated, at the Jacobins, that he had been ill-naturedly credited with drawing up proscription lists in which he had really had no hand. We may no doubt conclude from this contradictory evidence that the disagreement arose out of particular cases. Nobody was arrested, because there was no agreement as to the names of the persons to be arrested.

But it is certain that the members of the Convention who were threatened imagined, rightly or wrongly, that Robespierre was their most dangerous opponent. He received a number of anonymous letters threatening him with death. Legendre and Bourdon of Oise stated, after the trial of the Dantonists, that they had both been asked to stab Robespierre before the assembled Convention. These plans of assassination were not a mere manœuvre having as its object to intimidate him. Barras and Merlin of Thionville now never went out unarmed. They and the bolder spirits met at the Café Corazza or at Doyen's restaurant on the Champs-Élysées, where they were joined by Courtois. The excitable Tallien carried a dagger concealed about his person.

On the 3rd Prairial an order of the Committee of Public Safety, drafted by Robespierre, ordered the arrest of Teresa Cabarrus. On the same day one Admiral, formerly employed at the royal lottery, who had taken part in the defence of the Tuileries on August 10 in the battalion of the Filles Saint Thomas, lay in wait for hours for Robespierre to leave the committee. Failing to find Robespierre, whom he had intended to kill, he fired his pistols at Collot d'Herbois that same evening, but missed him and hit a locksmith, Geffroy, who had rushed to the assistance of the representative. The sensation caused by this attempted assassination had not yet died down when the report went around that during the evening of the 4th Prairial a girl, aged twenty, Cécile Renault, had presented herself at Duplay's house (where Robespierre had his lodging), and urgently requested to see Robespierre. When she was arrested, a knife and penknife were found in her possession, and she replied that she would shed all her blood if they could have a king, and that she had been to Robespierre's house only "to see what a tyrant was like."

While thousands of addresses poured in congratulating Collot and Robespierre upon having escaped the blows of Pitt, Tallien, Fouché, and their friends were adroitly influencing the press and public opinion.

In his report upon the attempted assassination Barère quoted a phrase from a letter written by an Englishman which had been intercepted. "We are very much afraid of Robespierre's influence," this ran. "The more concentrated the French republican Government becomes, says the minister [Pitt], the stronger it will be, and the harder it will be to overthrow." When this appeared in the *Moniteur* and the *Bulletin* of the Convention, this phrase was stated to have been written by an agent of the committee. Barère had to insert a correction on the following day. "One member of the committee," he said, "was isolated; we appeared to centralize the Government in the person of a single member, whereas it rests upon all the members of the committee. The most dangerous errors might arise from this; it might be concluded that the Convention no longer exists, no longer counts, that the armies are now only fighting for a single man, to whom we ought to do greater justice. This man is a true patriot (*pur*)." This correction unfortunately drew attention to the predominant position occupied by Robespierre and lent itself to comments of every kind, especially as Barère next proceeded to read out extracts from English newspapers, in which the French soldiers were called the soldiers of Robespierre. Tallien must have been quite pleased with Barère.

Intrigue went on at the Jacobins just as it did at the Convention. On the 6th Prairial Rousselin, a former agent of Danton, who afterwards became secretary to Barras, made the insidious proposal that in order to protect the lives of the members of the Committee of Public Safety they should be surrounded by a personal guard, and that civic honours should be rendered to the courageous Geffroy during the festival in honour of the Supreme Being which was announced to take place. Robespierre scented a trap, expressed his indignation at the attempt to draw down envy and calumny upon him by heaping him with superfluous honours and isolating him in order to diminish the esteem in which he was held; and he had Rousselin's name struck off the books of the Jacobins.

Rousselin had been a mere instrument in the hands of others. The day before the meeting at the Jacobins, on the 5th Prairial, Lecointre, a deputy deeply implicated with Bourdon of Oise by his attacks on the committee, and by trade a merchant, under accusation of speculating in coal and soda, drafted an indictment of Robespierre, which he persuaded eight

491

of his colleagues to sign. He did not publish it till just after Thermidor, but passed it round secretly from hand to hand. These nine bravoes entered into an engagement to assassinate Robespierre "in the open Senate." The Dantonist Baudot tells us that Thirion, one of those who had signed it, showed him the document and tried without success to induce him to take part in the plot.

It seems probable to me that Robespierre was aware of Lecointre's and Tallien's schemes at the time and suspected them of having instigated the attempts at assassination. On the 7th Prairial he replied in a fiery impromptu speech from the tribune of the Convention to the accusations which were being whispered against him. "Do you want to know," he said, "who it is that are ambitious? Find out who it is that protect swindlers, encourage counter-revolutionaries, excuse attempted assassinations, despise virtue, and corrupt political morality." And he proceeded to brand "this motley gang of factionists and schemers." "So long as this corrupt (*impure*) race exists, the Republic will be unfortunate and in a precarious position. It is for you to deliver it from them by an imposing display of energy and unfaltering harmony. . . . Those who are seeking to divide us, those who are obstructing the working of the Government, those who slander it daily by their speeches and perfidious insinuations, those who seek to form a dangerous coalition against it, formed of every baneful passion and irritable vanity, of every interest opposed to the public interest, are our enemies and the enemies of the country. They are the agents of the foreigner." His appeals were in vain. The Committee of General Security had already entered into an alliance with Lecointre, Tallien, Fouché, and their associates, who were at once informed of everything that was discussed in the counsels of the Government. Fouche succeeded in having himself appointed president of the Jacobins on the 13th Prairial.

It was not long before Robespierre provided his adversaries with a most dangerous weapon by taking part in drafting and obtaining the passage of the law of the 22nd Prairial on the Revolutionary Tribunal. It is true that this law had been on the stocks for the last two months—ever since the decree of the 27th Germinal, confirmed on the 19th Floréal, had suppressed the revolutionary tribunals in the departments and concentrated all persons accused of political offences in Paris—and its chief provisions had already appeared in the ordinance establishing the commission at Orange. But the Committee of General Security, which had already had the report on the two decrees of the 27th Germinal and the 19th Floréal taken out of its hands, might legitimately take offence at not having been even consulted about the new decree, which was submitted to the Convention

492

by Couthon. Robespierre and Couthon no doubt had weighty reasons for preventing the Committee of General Security, which was directly responsible for the supervision of the Revolutionary Tribunal, from taking part in the discussion of such a vital question. Their great idea, which found expression in the decrees of the 8th and 13th Ventôse, was to use the Terror as a means of depriving the aristocrats of their property, which was then to be distributed among the poor. Saint-Just had introduced an article into the decree of the 27th Germinal ordering that "popular commissions" should be established by the 15th Floréal, whose business it would be to go through the prisoners awaiting trial and draw up a list of those whose property was to be confiscated after they had been deported or sentenced to death by the Revolutionary Tribunal. But the two committees were in no hurry to set up these commissions, upon which the new social revolution was to depend. The decree of the 23rd Ventôse had provided for six commissions. The first two, which were to deal with the prisons in Paris, were not created till the 25th Floréal, by an ordinance drafted by Billaud-Varenne. In their reply to Lecointre, after Thermidor, the members of the former committees were to take credit for having delayed the formation of the popular commissions as long as possible. They explained that those of the 25th Floréal had been set up only under pressure from Saint-Just, and gloried in having paralysed their working and systematically refused their signatures to their decisions. Gracchus Vilate, an instrument of Barère's, said justly enough that one of the deep-lying causes of the opposition to the triumvirate was its social program. It seemed clear to him, he said, that if the triumvirate wanted to proscribe certain deputies, it was because it regarded them "as obstacles to the agrarian policy and the prolongation of terrorism, which was its instrument." Are we to suppose that Couthon and Robespierre, angered by the dilatoriness of the Committee of General Security in applying the laws of Ventôse, and imputing it to them as a crime, resolved to force the situation and bring it face to face with the irrevocable by preventing it from taking part in the preliminary examination of the law of the 22nd Prairial? Robespierre was afterwards to blame this committee for recruiting its agents among persons of a most suspicious character, and, on the 26th Messidor, Dumas added the definite charge that four aristocrats from his department, whose names he mentioned, had found employment under it. About the same time it was discovered that a person who had emigrated five times occupied a post as clerk at the Revolutionary Tribunal, where he had found employment through the agency of Naulin, his uncle, who was one of its judges.

Couthon therefore introduced the new law in the name of the Committee of Public Safety only. Accused persons were no longer allowed to employ counsel for their defence, for to allow this was to provide a platform from which royalism and the enemy could obtain a hearing and to favour the rich at the expense of the poor. "The natural defenders and necessary friends of accused patriots are the patriot juries; conspirators ought not to find any." The preliminary examination of accused persons was abolished. In the absence of written proofs or the evidence of witnesses the juries might henceforward be content with moral proofs. The definition of enemies of the Revolution was extended to include "those who may seek to mislead opinion and hinder the instruction of the people, to deprave morals and corrupt the public conscience. . . ." At any rate, the Revolutionary Tribunal was reconstituted and its staff increased. Couthon did not conceal the fact that the law which he proposed was not so much a measure of justice as a law of extermination. "The time within which enemies of the country are punished ought not to exceed the time necessary for recognizing them as such; the point is not so much to punish them as to annihilate them."

When Couthon had finished reading his report, which was listened to in dead silence, Ruamps exclaimed: "This decree is important, I propose that it should be printed and adjourned. If it were to be adopted without adjournment, I would blow out my brains." Lecointre proposed an indefinite adjournment; but Barère protested, while consenting to an adjournment for not more than three days. Robespierre was less conciliatory and demanded an immediate debate. "For two months past," he said, "the Convention has been threatened with the assassin's knife, and the moment in which liberty appears to be obtaining a brilliant triumph is that chosen by the enemies of the country for conspiring with increased audacity." Robespierre had still ringing in his ears the threats of death uttered against him two days before by Lecointre, Thirion, and Bourdon of Oise in the midst of his triumph at the festival of the Supreme Being. He stressed the point that an adjournment would make people think that dissension had arisen between the Convention and its committee. "Citizens," he said, "they want to divide you, they want to frighten you!" and he adroitly reminded them that he had defended the seventy-five Girondins against the Hébertists. "We are exposing ourselves to personal assassination in order to hunt down public assassins. We are quite prepared to die; only let the Convention and the country be saved!" There was a burst of applause, and the law was passed then and there, with scarcely an objection.

But on the following day Bourdon of Oise asked for an explanation of the article giving the public prosecutor and the committees the right to cite deputies directly before the Revolutionary Tribunal. "The Convention did not understand that the power of the committees was to be extended to include the members of the Convention without a previous decree." There were shouts of "No! No!" from all quarters, and Bourdon went on: "I expected this fortunate interruption. It proclaims that liberty is imperishable." Bernard of Saintes supported Bourdon, and Merlin of Douai obtained the adoption of a wording maintaining the right of the Convention. The deputies who had been menaced breathed again. The only part of the obnoxious law which had remained in their minds was what concerned them personally.

Had Robespierre and Couthon, despairing of obtaining the consent of the Convention to the indictment of the corrupt proconsuls whom they wanted to punish, deliberately inserted in their draft the ambiguous provision which Bourdon of Oise had caused to be deleted? On the following day, at the second reading, they protested indignantly against the insidious calculations which had been imputed to them. In arrogant language they demanded the suppression of the amendment upholding the privilege of the Assembly as an insult to themselves. They accused Bourdon of evil intentions, and a violent scene arose. "Let the members of the two committees understand," cried Bourdon, "that though they are patriots, so are we, as much as they are!" Robespierre denounced certain schemers who were endeavouring to stir up the representatives who had been recalled from their missions and to win over a section of the Mountain in order to form a party of their own. Bourdon interrupted him: "I request that these allegations should be supported by proofs. It has just been stated in so many words that I am a scoundrel!" Robespierre rejoined: "I did not name Bourdon; woe to him whom the cap fits! But if he insists upon recognizing himself in the portrait which duty has forced me to draw, it is not in my power to prevent him." Then, turning toward Tallien, though again mentioning no names, he recalled that two days previously a deputy on his way out of the Convention had struck certain clerks of the Committee of Public Safety and called them traitors. "If the patriots thus attacked had defended themselves, you can well imagine that this affair would undoubtedly have taken an angry turn; you would have been told on the next day that representatives of the people had been insulted by persons employed by the Committee of Public Safety." Robespierre saw in this incident proof of an intrigue against the committee. "Who was it," he asked, "that told those to whom I am referring that the Committee of Public Safety intended to attack them? Who told them that there were proofs in existence against them? Has the committee so much as threatened them? . . . If you knew all, citizens, you would know that we might more justly be accused of weakness!" Tallien tried to deny the imputation, but was browbeaten by Robespierre and Billaud-Varenne. Robespierre met him with the words: "Three hundred witnesses have heard him. Citizens, you can judge what those who back up crime by lying are capable of. It is easy to say which is the assassin and which the victim." And Billaud added: "Tallien's impudence exceeds all bounds. He lies to the Assembly with incredible audacity." Couthon and Robespierre obtained the vote which they were asking for, but such a session left indelible traces in men's memories.

There can be no doubt that Robespierre's adversaries now made a great effort behind the scenes to overthrow him. At this very time a former police spy, Roch Marcandier, who had been literary secretary to Camille Desmoulins, drew up an address to the forty-eight Paris sections calling upon them to revolt against Robespierre's dictatorship. "If that crafty demagogue no longer existed, if he had paid for his ambitious manœuvres with his head, the nation would be free and everyone could publish his ideas. Paris would never have seen in her bosom that host of assassinations vulgarly known by a misnomer as verdicts of the Revolutionary Tribunal." Marcandier was denounced by Legendre and arrested on the 25th Prairial, when some pamphlets were found at his house, ready to be printed, in which Robespierre was compared to Sulla. On the very day of the arrest Robespierre had been warned by a letter from Cellier, a messenger at the national audit department (*Comptabilité nationale*), that Lecointre was circulating a document containing an indictment of him.

The fact is significant in itself that no member of the Committee of General Security had spoken during the debate on the law of the 22nd Prairial. Five days had not gone by before the committee avenged itself for the contempt poured upon it by Robespierre by aiming an underhand attack at him, through the agency of Vadier, which was to add still further complications to an already strained situation. Vadier, a sceptical old libertine, whose heart knew but one faith, atheism, had never forgiven Robespierre for the decree establishing the official cult of the Supreme Being. On the 27th Prairial he denounced to the Convention a fresh conspiracy, hatched by fanatics grouped around an aged visionary, Catherine Théot, the "Mother of God," who, in her narrow quarters in the rue Contrescarpe, announced to the poor and needy the approaching termination of their misery by the arrival of the Messiah, who would regenerate all things upon earth. On the flimsiest evidence Vadier implicated in the conspiracy Quesvremont-Lamothe, a physician to the Duke of Orleans, a certain Marquise de Chastenois, and Dom Gerle, an ex-member of the Constituent Assembly, who was Catherine's spiritual director. His object was not only to pour ridicule upon the idea of religion and hinder the pacification which Robespierre had thought to achieve by his decree on the national festivals, but to make the charge recoil upon Robespierre himself. The preliminary examination was to show that Dom Gerle had obtained a certificate of civism from Robespierre, and that Catherine Théot numbered among her congregation the sister-in-law of Duplay, the carpenter with whose family Robespierre lodged. The police agents, who had kept a watch upon Catherine's meetings, attributed to her the assertion that Robespierre was the Messiah whose advent as a regenerator she foretold. When all this was revealed before the Revolutionary Tribunal, it was calculated that the pontiff of the Supreme Being would be overwhelmed with derision. We can understand why Vadier recommended Lecointre to have a little patience.

But Robespierre was not the man to fall into the trap of a Vadier. He had the matter referred to the Committee of Public Safety, demanded the documents bearing on the case from Fouquier-Tinville, and on the 8th Messidor extorted from his colleagues an order for adjournment, though not without difficulty. The suspicious Billaud-Varenne pointed out that by so doing they were violating an express decree of the Convention. The scene degenerated into an altercation, the noise of which could be heard outside the building. The committee decided that in future it would hold its sessions on the storey above, so as to be beyond the reach of indiscreet listeners. There were further scenes on both the preceding and the following days. Robespierre failed to obtain the dismissal of Fouquier-Tinville, whose close connexion with Lecointre was known to him.

At the beginning of Floréal, Carnot had already had a sharp argument with Saint-Just about the arrest of an agent of the powder and salt-petre commission proposed by the former. Saint-Just, who was braving danger at the front, could not endure that Carnot should act as dictator in matters concerning the war. They lost their tempers, and threats were exchanged. Saint-Just taxed Carnot with protecting aristocrats—which was the fact. Carnot defied him, and shouted at him and Robespierre: "You are ridiculous dictators!" A more serious incident took place between the two just after Fleurus. Saint-Just, on his return from the army, censured Carnot for not consulting him before ordering Pichegru to withdraw fifteen thousand infantry and fifteen hundred cavalry from Jourdan's army—a senseless measure, he said, which would have lost them the battle of Fleurus had it been carried out. Levasseur (of Sarthe), who was present at the dispute, tells us that it was very violent and degenerated in a general mêlée. Robespierre was again called a dictator by Billaud, and also by Collot. Collot's intervention is no doubt explained by the fact' that he felt a community of interests with Fouché, with whom he had "improvised the thunderbolt" which descended upon the rebels of Lyons on the plains of Les Brotteaux. It was impossible to take proceedings against Fouché without implicating Collot. At the session of the 9th Thermidor Billaud censured Robespierre for having ordered the arrest of "the best revolutionary committee in Paris, that of the section of L'Indivisibilité." In my opinion there can be no doubt that this arrest gave rise to an acrimonious discussion in the committee at the beginning of Messidor, when Robespierre tried to obtain its confirmaton (7th Messidor). As a matter of fact the members of this revolutionary committee had been denounced on definite charges made by the president of their section himself, who accused them of swindling. Robespierre was bound to think that those of his colleagues who defended these swindlers were in league with his enemies.

Robespierre did not appear again at the Committee after the 15th Messidor. From this date to the 9th Thermidor he signed only five documents, which were brought to him at his house. He had been insulted and stigmatized as a dictator by his colleagues while under the constant threat of the assassin's dagger. On the 12th Messidor again, Payan, the national agent, submitted to the Committee of General Security the interrogatory of an aristocrat named Rouvière, who had obtained admission to the Duplays' house, armed with a knife, a penknife, and razors.[2] Robespierre's heart was filled with bitterness. At every moment perfidious journalists were distorting his words or heaping upon him exaggerated eulogies, which were more dangerous than criticism. Thus, in reporting a speech which he had made at the Jacobins on the 3rd Messidor, the editor of the *Journal de la Montagne* added the following comment: "Every word of this orator is as good as a phrase, every phrase as good as a speech, so much sense and energy are to be found in all he says."

Robespierre took refuge at the Jacobins, his last rampart against his enemies. As early as the 13th Messidor he warned the club that he had lost all authority over the Government. "In London," he said, "I am denounced to the French army as a dictator, and the same calumnies are repeated in Paris. You would shudder if I told you in what quarter. It

---

[2] National Archives, F. 73822.

is said in London that in France imaginary assassinations are invented in order to surround me with a military guard. Here I am told, with reference to Cécile Renault, that there was certainly a love-affair at the bottom of the matter, and that I am presumed to have had her lover guillotined. . . . If I were forced to give up part of the functions entrusted to me, I should still be left with that of representative of the people, and I would wage war to the death on tyrants and conspirators." Had he reckoned that his colleagues on the committee would take advantage of his absence to propose that his place in the Convention should be filled by another? Was he reserving his strength for the debate which would take place on that day? Did he want to force Vadier, Amar, Billaud, Collot, and their friends to come out into the open and attack him? If this was so, he made a false calculation, for they acted as if they had heard nothing, and their protégés, such as Fouché and Tallien, had time to bring influence to bear upon the waverers in the Convention, and alarm them by spreading a report that Robespierre wanted their heads and was alone responsible for the blood which streamed in floods from the guillotine.

This period was marked by the height of the Terror. From the 23rd Prairial to the 8th Thermidor, the Revolutionary Tribunal pronounced 1,285 death sentences and only 278 acquittals, whereas during the forty-five preceding days it had condemned 577 as opposed to 182 acquittals. In spite of everything, the prisons filled faster than they were emptied. On the 23rd Prairial there were 7,321 persons in the Paris prisons. On the 10th Thermidor there were 7,800. Batch after batch was sent to the guillotine in rapid succession. Accused persons who had never seen each other were "amalgamated" in the same batch. The spies in the prisons, on the alert to catch the slightest word, made up lists of alleged conspirators at random. Heads fell like slates from a roof; thirty-one ex-judges of Paris and Toulouse who had once protested against the abolition of the parlements; thirty-five inhabitants of Verdun who had given too good a reception to the Prussians in 1792; Lavoisier and twenty-eight farmers-general, those "blood-suckers of the people"; Admiral, Cécile Renault, and fifty-two others who were all led to execution in red shirts as parricides; the conspirators of Bicêtre, in two batches, of thirty-seven and thirty-six respectively; seventeen inhabitants of Caussade who had worn mourning for Louis XVI; 156 persons implicated in the conspiracy at the prison of the Luxembourg. Fouquier-Tinville wanted to have the latter all tried at once, on a huge platform set up in the court-room, but the committee forced him to divide them into three batches.

The public conscience revolted against this orgy of murder. The time was long past when the crowd thronged to executions as to a show. Now the shops closed along the route of the sinister carts as they jolted over the cobble-stones. The position of the guillotine had to be changed, and it was removed to the gate of Le Trône. Public sentiment, the general disgust at this bloodshed, was no doubt the trump-card in the hand of Robespierre's enemies. They had taken advantage of the respite with which he had provided them and were secretly undermining the revolutionary Government. One of the Paris sections, that of the Mountain, resolved on the 1st Messidor to open a register in which those who had accepted the Constitution of 1793 should sign their names; and it soon numbered two thousand signatures. It was an adroit manœuvre, which aimed at proposing that the Terror should be stopped and the Constitution put in force. On the 11th Messidor the section apologized for its action before the Convention, explaining that it had been deceived by schemers.

The new Indulgents naturally made the most of the victories which now followed one upon the other. In order to celebrate them fraternal feasts were organized in the streets, to which rich and poor brought their own food, and "thee-and-thoued" each other with the familiarity of a levelling age. The rapid success of these fraternizations aroused the misgivings of the Commune and the Government. "Far from us," said Payan on the 27th Messidor, "be all these meetings with the partisans of despotism! Far from us be this system by which they want to persuade us that no more enemies exist within the Republic!" On the following day Barère denounced this fresh trap laid by the aristocrats. These so-called "fraternal" meals were, according to him, merely "a premature amnesty." As they touched glasses with the sansculottes, the aristocrats would cry: "Our armies are victorious everywhere; it only remains to make peace, to live on friendly terms, and to put an end to this revolutionary Government, which is terrible."

But how was the revolutionary Government to be maintained and the pressure of the Indulgents and corrupt persons, backed up by public opinion, resisted if the committees remained divided and Robespierre continued his opposition at the Jacobins? Reports of the quarrels within the Government had spread even to the provinces and alarmed the representatives on mission, as is proved by letters from Richard on the 27th Prairial, Gillet on the 23rd Messidor, Bô on the 3rd Thermidor, etc. When Ingrand passed through Paris, he was pressed by Ruamps to join in the plot against Robespierre, but indignantly refused, and predicted that in overthrowing Robespierre they would at the same time overthrow the revolutionary Government and the Republic. The members composing the Committee of Public Safety felt the same as Ingrand. At the end of Messidor, no doubt under the influence of Barère, they made an effort to effect a *rapprochement* with Robespierre. Barère repeatedly asserted the necessity of maintaining the Terror. On the 9th Messidor he threatened the corrupt element in the following words: "The representatives of the people, alive to the interests of the people and to their own security, will manage to profit by victory abroad to annihilate all impious coalitions or parricidal plots at home, which are due to a few men who mistake their personal weariness for that of the people, and their uneasy consciences for the public conscience." On the 16th Messidor, after obtaining the passage of a decree ordering that the enemy garrisons of Condé, Valenciennes, Le Quesnoy, and Landrecies should be put to the sword if they did not surrender within twenty-four hours after being called upon to do so, Barère uttered an enthusiastic apology for the Terror, and gave warning against premature clemency. "Compromise with them [the enemies at home] today," he said, "and they will attack you tomorrow and massacre you without pity. No, no, let our enemies perish! I have said it before: it is only the dead who never come back."

Robespierre was under no misapprehension with regard to Barère's intentions. He, too, thought that the Terror ought to go on until the property of the counter-revolutionaries had been finally distributed among the poor and until the civil institutions for which Saint-Just was drawing up a scheme had been established and secured. On the 23rd Messidor he had Dubois-Crancé struck off the books of the Jacobins, and had Fouché called upon to clear himself from the charges against him. Fouché failed to appear and was in turn struck off the books on the 26th Messidor. The committees not only refused to take the part of the members who had been expelled, but displayed a certain hostility to them. Dubois-Crancé was recalled from his mission in Brittany on the 26th Messidor. As for Fouché, on the 25th Messidor he obtained a vote from the Convention ordering the committees to prepare a report upon his mission with the least possible delay; but he waited in vain for the report.

On the 4th and 5th Thermidor the two committees held a joint plenary session, and by way of a striking manifestation of their firm determination to prolong the Terror and carry out its full social consequences they at last created the four popular commissions which had remained in abeyance, but were indispensable if the laws of Ventôse on sorting out the suspects and distributing their property were to be put into force. The ordinance, drafted by Barère, is dated the 4th Thermidor.

501

According to Lecointre, it was their intention, by giving this pledge, to effect a reconciliation with the triumvirate, and, as a matter of fact, Robespierre did attend the session on the following day, when mutual explanations were exchanged. Saint-Just pointed out that none but agents of the enemy could represent Robespierre as a dictator, for neither the army, the finances, nor the administration depended upon him; and David supported Saint-Just. Billaud-Varenne said to Robespierre: "We are your friends, we have always followed the same course as you." Saint-Just was charged by the joint committees to submit to the Convention a report on the political situation, with instructions to defend the revolutionary Government. He was, however, recommended by Billaud and Collot not to mention the Supreme Being.

On the same evening Barère, delighted at having restored harmony, announced to the Convention that none but ill-disposed persons could have persuaded them that there was any division or misunderstanding in the Government or any wavering in revolutionary principles. He related that during the last few days powder intended for the armies had been held up and the bellows at certain forges injured; that an attempt had been made to break open the prison of Bicêtre, and numerous acts of sabotage had taken place; and he wound up with the threatening words: "But the measures adopted by the two committees yesterday for hurrying on the trial of the enemies of the people who are under arrest throughout the whole of the Republic are going to be put in force, and will restore to the nation the security which incessant attempts are being made to wrest from it, that imposing calm which is the outward sign of the strength of the consolidated Republic!"

On the following day Couthon took up his cue at the Jacobins and sang the praises of "the ardent and energetic men, prepared to make the greatest sacrifices for the country," of whom the committees were composed. "Though there may have been personal divisions, none have ever existed with regard to principles." And Couthon ascribed the origin of the clouds which he desired to dispel to the entourage of the Government. He expressed the hope that the Convention would soon crush "the five or six little human figures whose hands are filled with the wealth of the Republic, and hideous with the blood of slaughtered innocents." He complained, however, that some companies of the Paris cannoneers had been sent to the army of the north, and showed some misgivings with regard to the School of Mars; but Lebas reassured him.

We are forced to believe, however, that everybody in the two camps had not laid down his arms and that the lead given by Barère and Couthon

502

was badly followed up. Sijas, the head of one of the departments of the Ministry for War, continued at the Jacobins to denounce Pille, a commisary for army transport, who, he said, was employing aristocrats, reinstating generals who had been suspended, stripping Paris of its artillery, and acting in a mysterious fashion. Pille was a nominee of Carnot's, and the words of Sijas met with some response. On the 6th Thermidor at the entrance of the Convention there had been shouts of "We must have another May 31!" On the following day Barère praised Robespierre for condemning this seditious language at the Jacobins. But this did not prevent the Jacobins from presenting a petition to the Convention on the same day denouncing Pille and the alleged Indulgents who desired to assassinate patriots. They asked that justice should be meted out to traitors and swindlers, and to one Magenthies who, in order to cast ridicule upon the decree on the Supreme Being, had asked that anyone who should defile the divine name by an oath should be put to death. Was it necessary, in order to satisfy the Jacobins, that the Committees should dismiss Pille and send to the scaffold the corrupt deputies whose heads Couthon and Robespierre had never ceased to demand for the last two months? But at this same session of the 7th Thermidor Dubois-Crancé had vindicated himself and called upon Robespierre to acknowledge his mistake. The Convention decided that the committees should present their report on his case within three days. Robespierre would thus be forced to come forth from the Jacobins and make an explanation before the Assembly.

Had Robespierre, at the plenary session of the 5th Thermidor, given his adherence to the program of reconciliation put forward by Barère, and, it would seem, accepted by Saint-Just and Couthon? It is permissible to doubt it. All his grievances had not yet been satisfied. He wanted to wrest the control of the war from Carnot, who had failed to execute the decree of the 7th Prairial forbidding any prisoners to be made among the English and Hanoverians and who was surrounded by a council of experts composed of aristocrats. Like Sijas, he saw in the removal of a section of the Parisian cannoneers a dark manœuvre aimed against the Commune and his own nominee, Hanriot. He had not forgiven either the Committee of General Security or Billaud and Collot for the protection which they always extended to such men as Fouché and Tallien. During the last few days shouts of "Great arrest of Robespierre" had been heard in the streets, and the committee had remained inactive. Robespierre had just learnt, from a report of Faro, the commissioner of police, that on the 5th Thermidor Amar and Voulland had paid a visit to the Girondin deputies in prison and made all sorts of advances to them: "Is your correspondence intercepted? Are you refused all the comforts of life—coffee, syrup, chocolate, or fruit? Do they fail to give you the treatment due to your position?" On hearing that the deputies were receiving the same treatment as the rest of the prisoners, Amar shed tears. "It is an abominable crime!" he said. "Tell us, my dear colleagues, who they are that have degraded the representatives of the nation. They shall be punished. The committee shall mete out justice to them." It is true that, after giving orders that the deputies should be allowed privileged treatment, Amar and Voulland changed their minds and subsequently maintained the application of the ordinary law in their case; but Robespierre suspected that an agreement was being arrived at between the Plain, which had so far supported him, and his opponents in the Mountain. And it was this, as much as Dubois-Crancé's challenge, which caused him to break silence.

Accordingly, on the 8th Thermidor, without previously consulting either Saint-Just or Couthon, who would no doubt have dissuaded him, he endeavoured to obtain the fulfilment of his whole program direct from the Convention. After protesting, in a long but impressive speech, against the calumnies representing him as a dictator animated with evil intentions towards the Assembly, he threw the blame for the excessive use of the guillotine upon his opponents, the terrorists who had turned Indulgents. "Is it we," he said, "who have thrown patriots into dungeons and carried the Terror into every walk of life? It is those monsters whom we have accused!" He affirmed that the revolutionary Government was necessary, but that the only persons whom it ought to strike down without hesitation or pity were conspirators. His slanderers, however, who, he said, called themselves Indulgents, but were nothing but swindlers, were ruining the revolutionary Government in men's eyes by tormenting peaceable persons in order to have the right to protect aristocrats. "The Revolutionary Tribunal was being rendered odious in order to bring about its destruction." He next made a bold attack on the Committee of General Security and its employees, "a horde of scoundrels protected by Amar and Jagot." He blamed Vadier for the affair of Catherine Théot, and proposed not only that the suspect committee should be renewed, but also that in future it should be subordinate to the Committee of Public Safety. Nor was this all; the Committee of Public Safety was also to be purged. It had not enforced the decree on the English prisoners; it had sown discord among the generals and protected the military aristocracy. This was a hit at Carnot. Nor was Barère spared, in spite of the advances he had made during the past few days: "You are told a great deal about our victories, with an academic levity which would lead one to suppose that they had

504

cost our heroes neither blood nor labour; described with less pomp, they would appear grander." The diplomatic sphere—which was Barère's department—had been absolutely neglected. The agents employed abroad were traitors. Robespierre next blamed Cambon for his financial system, at once mean, extravagant, vexatious, and extortionate. The decree on annuities, he said, had justly aroused a great deal of discontent. He wound up with a challenge to the horde of swindlers who had managed to impose their domination.

The impression produced was so profound that Lecointre himself, one of the swindlers, proposed that the speech should be printed, and the proposal was carried with the support of Barère, in spite of a protest from Bourdon of Oise. On Couthon's motion it was next voted that it should be sent to all the communes. Was Robespierre on the eve of a triumph? His adversaries recovered themselves. Vadier tried to give an explanation about Catherine Théot. Next Cambon lent passion to the debate by a fiery speech. "Before I am dishonoured," he said, "I will speak to France!" He accused Robespierre of paralysing the Convention. His vehemence infused courage into Billaud-Varenne, who requested that Robespierre's speech should be examined by the committees before being sent to the communes. "If it is true that we do not enjoy liberty of opinion," he said, "I had rather my dead body should serve as a throne to an ambitious man than that I should become the accomplice of his misdeeds by my silence." He had gone straight to the point. Panis called upon Robespierre and Couthon to name the deputies whom they were accusing. Robespierre refused to reply, and this was his ruin. All those who had anything to reproach themselves with felt themselves threatened. Bentabole and Chalier demanded that the decree ordering his speech to be printed should be annulled. Barère felt the wind veering and trimmed his sails accordingly. He censured Robespierre for failing to attend the sessions of the committee, but for which he would not have written his speech. The Convention annulled the decree for sending the speech to the communes. Robespierre no longer commanded a majority. He had cast away his shield.

It is true that on the same evening he was greeted with prolonged applause at the Jacobins, where he repeated his speech. His opponents, Billaud and Collot, who attempted to reply, were shouted down and forced to leave the club amid shouts of "The conspirators to the guillotine!" But the Jacobins merely passed a resolution to hold a debate on the "conspiracy." Robespierre did not desire another May 31. In spite of his reverse on the previous day, he thought it possible to regain his majority. He did not mean the struggle to go beyond the parliamentary lists. He had not foreseen that henceforward it would be impossible for him to speak in the Assembly.

The members of the committees were drifting in a state of perplexity. During the night of their return from the Jacobins, Billaud and Collot had a violent scene with Saint-Just; but the only result of their discussion, which lasted till dawn, was a proclamation drawn up by Barère, warning the public against the ascendancy of certain men and the ambition of certain military leaders, whose names were not mentioned.

The decisive step was taken by the corrupt proconsuls whom Robespierre had been threatening for the last two months and who knew they would be lost if he were to triumph. Tallien had received a frantic letter from his mistress, who was about to be cited before the Revolutionary Tribunal. He and Fouché made repeated efforts to win over the Plain. They were at first rejected by Palasne Champeaux, Boissy d'Anglas, and Durand Maillane, who were suspicious of the repentance of these terrorists; but they bound themselves by such pledges that their third attempt was successful. The Plain abandoned Robespierre, on condition that the rapacious Montagnards should help them to put down the Terror. Before the opening of the session all arrangements had been made to stifle the voices of Robespierre and his friends, with the complicity of the president of the Assembly, Collot d'Herbois.

At the opening of the session Saint-Just attempted to read the clever speech which he had composed with the object of throwing all the blame on Billaud, Collot, and Carnot; but he was at once interrupted violently by Tallien, who accused him of isolating himself from the committee by speaking personally in his own name. "I demand," he said, amid a triple round of applause, "that the veil be completely torn down." Billaud next recalled the previous evening's session at the Jacobins and alarmed the Assembly by suggesting that there was to be another May 31, which would end in its massacre. He accused Robespierre of protecting Hébertists, Dantonists, nobles, and swindlers, of persecuting patriots, of being sole author of the decree of the 22nd Prairial—in a word, of being a tyrant. "Death to the tyrants!" repeated the chorus. Robespierre attempted to reply. Collot refused him a hearing, in favour of Tallien. The latter brandished a dagger at the new Cromwell, declaimed against the men of the stamp of Verres by whom he was surrounded, and demanded the arrest of his creatures. Thereupon the arrest of Hanriot, Boulanger, Dufresse, and Dumas was voted. Barère obtained the abolition of the post of commander-in-chief of the National Guard. A fresh attempt to reply on the part of Robespierre was stifled by the president's bell, rung by Thuriot, who had succeeded Collot as president. Louchet and Loseau proposed the arrest of the "dominator." The younger Robespierre asked to share the fate of his brother. Couthon and Saint-Just were put under arrest, together with the two Robespierres. Lebas demanded the honour of sharing in their proscription, which was granted. "The Republic is lost," said Robespierre, as he walked towards the bar of the Assembly. "The brigands are triumphing."

It was five o'clock in the evening. But all problems were not solved. The Commune and Hanriot rose in revolt by a spontaneous impulse, closed the city gates, sounded the call to arms and afterward the tocsin, and summoned the sections, calling upon them to send their cannoneers to the square before the Town Hall and to take the oath to defend their liberty and country. At half past five, with more courage than reflexion, Hanriot and a handful of gendarmes made an attempt to release the arrested deputies. He kicked in the doors of the premises of the Committee of General Security, where they were locked up, but was at once surrounded and pinioned in his turn before the eyes of those whom he had intended to deliver. This incident had disastrous results. Robespierre and his friends believed that, having lost its leader, the insurrection had no chance of success. Henceforward they placed all their trust in the Revolutionary Tribunal, and by the time they left, each for a different prison, they were resigned to their fate.

But the movement hourly gained in strength. The gunners of the sections were massed in the Place de Grève with their artillery. The civil and revolutionary committees of the working-class sections of the east and south and the artisan sections of the centre were sworn in. The Jacobins met and got into touch with the Commune. Towards eight o'clock in the evening the energetic Coffinhal, with part of the artillery, marched on the Convention, released Hanriot, and carried with him even the guard of the Assembly. He might easily have wound up the day by seizing the members of the committees, who fled in dismay. "Citizens," shouted Collot, who was presiding, "now is the instant to die at our posts!" But Coffinhal did not complete his victory. He confined himself to bringing back Hanriot in triumph to the Hôtel de Ville.

The Convention breathed again. It hastened to entrust Barras with the mission of obtaining it an armed force, and Barras, with the aid of six other deputies, gave the signal which rallied the moderate sections. Summoned by his emissaries, the merchants of the section of the Lombards, the bankers of that of Le Pelletier, the speculators of the Palais Royal, and the rich middle-classes from the sections of the west hurried to the aid of the Convention. With them came the last remnants of Hébertism and

Dantonism, enrolled by the two Bourdons, Tallien, Rovère and Fréron. But it took time to collect these scattered and motley troops. Meanwhile Barère obtained the passage of a decree proscribing the rebellious Commune, together with all those who had eluded the warrants issued by the committees for their arrest. He reckoned that this terrible measure would strike terror to the half-hearted and paralyse the insurrection, and he was not mistaken.

Since Coffinhal's high-handed action the insurrection had been marking time. The Commune obviously intended to entrust the control of it to the proscribed deputies. But though they were released one after the other by the police commissioners, they were in no hurry to act. The elder Robespierre at first refused to go to the Hôtel de Ville. Couthon wanted to stay in prison and did not leave till after midnight. The younger Robespierre alone presented himself as soon as he could at the meeting of the Commune, to which he made a speech. When the decree of proscription became known, the elder Robespierre followed his brother's example and joined the other deputies on the Executive Committee created by the Commune. Lebas sent a letter to the commandant of the camp at Les Sablons. Robespierre signed an appeal to the section of Les Piques. Municipal officers were sent to the sections to keep them on the side of the Commune. It was at last resolved to arrest the chief members of the Convention. But the night was far advanced. Weary of waiting in vain, the artillery and National Guards—who were, moreover, canvassed by Barras's agents —had gradually withdrawn. The Place de Grève was half empty. They had to think of defence rather than attack. In order to prevent defections the Commune toward midnight had the front of the Hôtel de Ville illuminated.

Barras hesitated to march against them, but towards two o'clock in the morning he made up his mind. A traitor had just revealed to him the password given by Hanriot. The troops of the Convention moved off in two columns. The column of the left, led by Léonard Bourdon and swelled by the battalion of the section of Les Gravilliers, gained an entry by surprise by using the password and shouting: "Long live Robespierre!" and penetrated as far as the room in which the Executive Committee was sitting. Robespierre and Couthon were in the middle of writing a proclamation to the armies. The younger Robespierre threw himself out of the window, where he was picked up with a broken thigh. Lebas shot himself with a pistol. The elder Robespierre attempted to do the same, but broke his lower jaw. The survivors, twenty-two in number, were sent to execution on the following day, with no further formality than the verification of their identity. On the 11th Thermidor seventy members of the Commune were guillotined in the same summary fashion.

It looked as if, even in the working-class quarters, the populace of Paris had been comparatively lukewarm in its support of the Commune. The artisans complained of the cost of living. The workmen in the factories had been in a ferment for several days past. On the 5th Thermidor the Commune had proclaimed a maximum daily wage, which had caused general discontent among the wage-earners. On the very morning of the 9th Thermidor the masons and stone-cutters of the section of L'Unité had talked of stopping work, and this same section, which had formerly been Hébertist, actually took the side of the Convention. Towards four o'clock in the afternoon an assembly of workmen had taken place on the Place de Grève to demand a modification of the maximum. It was in vain that, about eight o'clock in the evening, the Commune threw the responsibility for the new tariff on Barère, "who has belonged to every faction in turn and has had a daily wage fixed for the workmen in order to make them starve to death." It failed to dispel all prejudices, and when the municipal officials were led to execution, shouts were raised as they passed by of "Down with the maximum," mingled with obscenities.

What tragic irony! Robespierre and his party went to their death largely for having tried to use the Terror as the instrument of a fresh upheaval affecting property. With them the levelling Republic, without rich or poor, which they had dreamt of establishing by the laws of Ventôse, received its death blow. The heedless sanculottes were soon to regret the maximum which they had execrated, and in vain to rise in insurrection in order to obtain its re-establishment.

For the moment the only party which grasped the importance of the victory of the rapacious terrorists by the aid of the Plain was that enlightened section of the lower middle classes and artisans whom Robespierre had initiated into public affairs and which staffed a number of clubs and revolutionary administrative bodies. Among them the sorrow was heartfelt, and it can be detected even in the admissions of the Thermidorians. Thibaudeau, afterwards a prefect under the Empire, tells us that the authorities in his department (Vienne) first stopped the circulation of his address on the 9th Thermidor. On the 21st Thermidor Laignelot wrote to the committee from Laval that the malevolent genius of the tyrant still lived on. "It is stunned, but not annihilated. In the popular societies all the leaders were in favour of Robespierre." At Nevers those arriving from Paris who announced the fall of Robespierre were put in prison on the spot. When the news of the arrest of Robespierre reached Arras and Nîmes, the clubs proposed to arm and hurry to his aid. A number of patriots committed suicide in despair (the engraver Mauclair in Paris, Bourdon, a judge, at Nîmes, etc.).

But the Thermidorians had now the mechanism of the Terror at their command. They released their partisans from the prisons and crowded them with Robespierrists. Hostages of the reaction which they had let loose, they were to be drawn further than they had intended. There were many who towards the end of their days repented of the part they had played on the 9th Thermidor. In the person of Robespierre they had slain the democratic Republic for a century.

Born of the war and its sufferings, cast in the mould of terrorism in opposition to its own basic principle, the Republic, owing to the force of circumstances, was fundamentally no more than an accident, in spite of its prodigious achievement. Resting on an increasingly narrow basis, it was misunderstood by the very persons whom it desired to associate with its existence. It had required all the fervent mysticism of its creators, and their superhuman energy, to make it last until victory was secured abroad. Twenty centuries of monarchy and slavery are not wiped out in a few months. The strictest laws are powerless to change human nature and the social order at a single stroke. Robespierre, Couthon, and Saint-Just, who desired to prolong the dictatorship in order to lay the foundation of civil institutions and overthrow the rule of wealth, were well aware of this. They could have succeeded only if the full dictatorship had been in their hands alone. But Robespierre's uncompromising character, which made him break with his colleagues in the Government at the very moment when they were making concessions to him, was enough to bring about the collapse of a structure existing in a legal vacuum. A memorable example of the limitations of the human will in its struggle against the resistance of material things.

Index

INDEX

i

Iron industry, prerevolutionary, 11.
Iron safe, 257.
Isnard, 138, 264, 314, 321, 322, 323, 326.
Isoré, 352, 442.
Italy, 291.

J

Jackson, 479.
Jacobins, 77, 116, 117, 121, 124, 131, 153,
157, 232, 233, 247, 250, 298, 302, 313,
322, 325, 333, 336, 344, 348, 355, 366,
397, 399, 407, 409, 412, 415, 422, 457,
461, 466, 498, 506.
Jagot, 436, 504.
Jalès, 74.
Jallet, 42.
Jancourt, 133, 150.
Jaurès, 57.
Jardin des Plantes, 323.
Javogues, 442.
Jeanbon, 342.
Jefferson, 61.
Jemappes, 277.
Jewish persecutions, 51.
Jews, 60.
Joly, 308.
Joseph, 11, 408.
Joubert, 308.
Jourdan, 376, 379, 482, 483, 497.
Julien, 167, 181, 412, 414, 420, 423, 424,
446, 463.
Justice, organization of, 90.
Justice, revolutionary, 394.

K

Kaunitz, 128, 147, 280, 407, 481.
Kellermann, 220, 276, 280, 351.
Ker, 407.
Kerangal, 53.
Kersaint, 175, 231, 269, 293.
Kervélégan, 320, 335.
Kilmaine, 375.
Kléber, 482, 483.
Klipsis, 398.
Klopstock, 217, 291.
Knights of the dagger, 125.
Kock, 279, 409, 458.
Körner, 291.
Kosciuszko, 217, 480.

L

Laborde, 68.
Laboureau, 458.
Labouvrie, 385.
Laclos, 36, 220.
Lacombe, 322, 367, 444.
Lacoste, 146, 151, 152, 441, 453, 484.
Lacretelle, 78.
Lacroix, 252.
Lafaye, 418.
Lafayette, 6, 23, 24, 26, 28, 45, 48, 52,
55, 58, 61, 63, 66, 70, 76, 79, 115, 119,
123, 124, 129, 131, 133, 138, 148, 149,
150, 152, 153, 154, 158, 159, 160, 168,
219, 257, 282, 394.
Laflotte, 464.
Lafond, 444.
Laharpe, 415, 476.
Laignelot, 386, 411, 461, 509.
Lajard, 152, 270, 444.
Lally-Tollendal, 59, 60, 66.
La Marck, 70.
Lamarque, 302.
Lamballe, 181, 238.
Lambesc, 47.
Lambinet, 149.
Lameth, 6, 17, 26, 61, 63, 68, 71, 80, 119,
125, 126, 129, 131, 133, 139, 141, 145,
147, 149, 152, 160, 175, 184, 246, 257,
262, 303.
Lamethists, 79, 125.
Lamoignon, 25, 28, 58.
Lamorlière, 347, 348, 375, 378, 400, 460.
Lamothe, 16.
Landremont, 290, 377.
Lange, 207.
Langeron, 33.
Lanjuinais, 41, 68, 186, 229, 231, 247,
261, 310, 316, 322, 323, 326, 337.
Lanoue, 396.
Lansdowne, 262.
Lanthenas, 118, 327, 358.
Lapallu, 442.
Laplanche, 384, 386.
Laporte, 146, 168, 180, 246, 247, 254.
Larivière, 151, 186, 244, 320.
Lasource, 138, 149, 156, 186, 229, 237,
264, 278, 284, 291, 303, 313, 316.
Latouche, 123.
Latour-Manbourg, 59, 160.
Laumur, 458, 459.

THE END